BUDDHIST PHILOSOPHY

BUDDHIST PHILOSOPHY

Essential Readings

Edited by
William Edelglass
Jay L. Garfield

OXFORD
UNIVERSITY PRESS
2009

OXFORD
UNIVERSITY PRESS

Oxford University Press, Inc., publishes works that further
Oxford University's objective of excellence
in research, scholarship, and education.

Oxford New York
Auckland Cape Town Dar es Salaam Hong Kong Karachi
Kuala Lumpur Madrid Melbourne Mexico City Nairobi
New Delhi Shanghai Taipei Toronto

With offices in
Argentina Austria Brazil Chile Czech Republic France Greece
Guatemala Hungary Italy Japan Poland Portugal Singapore
South Korea Switzerland Thailand Turkey Ukraine Vietnam

Published by Oxford University Press, Inc.
198 Madison Avenue, New York, New York 10016
www.oup.com

Library of Congress Cataloging-in-Publication Data

Buddhist philosophy : essential readings / edited by William Edelglass
and Jay L. Garfield.
p. cm.
Includes translations of texts from various languages.
ISBN: 978-0-19-532817-2 (pbk.); 978-0-19-532816-5 (cloth)
1. Philosophy, Buddhist. 2. Buddhism—Doctrines. I. Edelglass, William.
II. Garfield, Jay L., 1955–
B162.B847 2009
181.'043—dc22 2008018648

Printed in the United States of America
on acid-free paper

True vision is the vision that consists of knowledge, nothing else; this is why a scholar should focus on seeking knowledge of reality. ... Wisdom is the ambrosia that brings satisfaction, the lamp whose light cannot be obscured, the steps on the palace of liberation, and the fire that burns the fuel of the defilements.

—Bhāviveka[1]

1. Bhāviveka, *The Heart of the Middle Way*, III.1, III.6, trans. Malcolm David Eckel.

Dedicated with gratitude to our teachers and students, from whom we have learned so much.

Acknowledgments

We gratefully acknowledge the careful editorial work on this volume by Claudine Davidshofer, Kris Miranda, and Jason Stigliano, philosophy students at Colby College. We would also like to acknowledge Colby College for its generous support of Claudine's work as a summer research assistant and the Colby Department of Philosophy for funding Kris and Jason's editorial assistance. For assembling the index with his characteristic skill and care, we gratefully acknowledge Peter Blair of Marlboro College. Finally, we would like to express our gratitude to Peter Ohlin and his editorial team at Oxford for their support of this project.

Contents

Contributors

Dan Arnold is Assistant Professor of Philosophy of Religion at the University of Chicago Divinity School. His first book—*Buddhists, Brahmins, and Belief: Epistemology in South Asian Philosophy of Religion* (Columbia University Press, 2005)—won an American Academy of Religion Award for Excellence in the Study of Religion.

James Blumenthal is Associate Professor of Buddhist Philosophy in the Philosophy Department at Oregon State University. He is the author of *The Ornament of the Middle Way: A Study of the Madhyamaka Thought of Śāntarakṣita* (2004) and editor of *Incompatible Visions: South Asian Religions in History and Culture* (2006).

José Ignacio Cabezón is XIVth Dalai Lama Professor of Tibetan Buddhism and Cultural Studies at the University of California, Santa Barbara. Cabezón is author, editor, or translator of eleven books and over thirty articles. His most recent book, *Freedom from Extremes* (with Geshe Lobsang Dargyay), is a translation of a sixteenth-century Tibetan polemical work on the doctrine of emptiness.

Bret W. Davis is Assistant Professor of Philosophy at Loyola University Maryland. In addition to earning a Ph.D. in Western philosophy, he also spent over a decade in Japan working on Buddhist and Japanese philosophy. He is author of *Heidegger and the Will* and coeditor of *Japanese Philosophy in the World* (in Japanese).

James Duerlinger is Professor of Philosophy at the University of Iowa. He is the author of the *Indian Buddhist Theories of Persons* (2003), *Plato's Sophist* (2004), and numerous articles on topics in Buddhist philosophy, ancient Greek philosophy, and the philosophy of religion.

Malcolm David Eckel is Assistant Dean and Director of the Core Curriculum at Boston University. His scholarly interests focus on Buddhist philosophy in India and Tibet, particularly the tradition known as "Svatantrika-Madhyamika." He is the author of *Buddhism* (Oxford, 2002), *To See the Buddha: A Philosopher's Quest for the Meaning of Emptiness* (Princeton, 1994), *Jñānagarbha's Commentary on the Distinction between the Two Truths* (SUNY, 1987), and numerous articles on the Indian and Tibetan tradition.

William Edelglass is Assistant Professor of Philosophy at Marlboro College. Previously he taught at the Institute of Buddhist Dialectics, Dharamsala, India. His research focuses on Buddhist philosophy, environmental philosophy, and twentieth-century continental philosophy.

Alan Fox received his Ph.D. in religion from Temple University in 1988, and joined the Philosophy Department at the University of Delaware in 1990. He has published on Daoism and Chinese Buddhism, and has won numerous teaching awards.

Jay L. Garfield is Doris Silbert Professor in the Humanities and Professor of Philosophy at Smith College, Professor in the Graduate Faculty of Philosophy at the University of Massachusetts, Professor of Philosophy at Melbourne University, and Adjunct Professor of Philosophy at the Central Institute of Higher Tibetan Studies. His most recent books are his translation of Tsong Khapa's commentary on Nagarjuna's *Mūlamadhyamakakārikā* (Ocean of reasoning) and *Empty Words: Buddhist Philosophy and Cross-cultural Interpretation*.

Brendan S. Gillon has taught at the University of Alberta and the University of Toronto, in their departments of philosophy, and now teaches in McGill University's department of linguistics. His many publications are primarily concerned with natural language semantics, Sanskrit linguistics, and the history of logic and metaphysics in early classical India.

Charles Goodman is Assistant Professor in the Philosophy Department at Binghamton University. He is the author of several articles about Buddhist philosophy, and a forthcoming book, *Consequences of Compassion: An Interpretation and Defense of Buddhist Ethics*.

Peter N. Gregory is the Jill Ker Conway Professor of Religion and East Asian Studies at Smith College and the president of the Kuroda Institute for the

Study of Buddhism and Human Values. His research has focused on medieval Chinese Buddhism, especially the Chan and Huayan traditions during the Tang and Song dynasties, on which he has written or edited seven books.

PETER HARVEY is Professor of Buddhist Studies at the University of Sunderland, UK. He is author of *An Introduction to Buddhism: Teachings, History and Practices* (Cambridge University Press, 1990), *The Selfless Mind: Personality, Consciousness and Nirvāṇa in Early Buddhism* (Richmond, UK: Curzon Press, 1995), and *An Introduction to Buddhist Ethics: Foundations, Values and Issues* (Cambridge University Press, 2000).

RICHARD HAYES earned his doctorate in Sanskrit and Indian Studies at the University of Toronto. He has taught in the departments of philosophy and religious studies at the University of Toronto and McGill University. He is currently Associate Professor in the Department of Philosophy at the University of New Mexico.

STEVEN HEINE is Professor of Religion and History as well as Director of the Institute for Asian Studies at Florida International University. He specializes in East Asian and comparative religions, Japanese Buddhism and intellectual history, and Buddhist studies. He has published twenty books and dozens of articles.

C. W. HUNTINGTON, JR., is Associate Professor of Religious Studies at Hartwick College in Oneonta, New York. He is the author of *The Emptiness of Emptiness: An Introduction to Early Indian Mādhyamika* (1989) and a number of articles on early Indian Madhyamaka.

HANS-RUDOLF KANTOR is Associate Professor at Huafan University's Graduate Institute of East Asian Humanities, Taipei. His fields of specialization are Chinese Buddhism, Chinese philosophy, comparative philosophy, and Chinese Intellectual History. He has published numerous articles on these topics and is also the author of *Die Verknüpfung von Heilslehre und Ontologie in der chinesischen Tiantai* (1999).

MATTHEW T. KAPSTEIN is Director of Tibetan Studies at the Ecole Pratique des Hautes Etudes, Paris, and Numata Visiting Professor of Buddhist Studies at the University of Chicago Divinity School. His publications include *The Tibetan Assimilation of Buddhism, Reason's Traces: Identity and Interpretation in Indian and Tibetan Buddhist Thought,* and *The Tibetans.*

GEREON KOPF received his Ph.D. from Temple University and is presently Associate Professor for Asian religions at Luther College. His publications include *Beyond Personal Identity* and numerous articles on Dōgen and

Nishida Kitarō. He is presently co-authoring the *Historical Dictionary of Zen Buddhism* for Sacrecrow Press and co-editing *Merleau-Ponty and Buddhism* for Lexington Books.

LEONARD W. J. VAN DER KUIJP is Professor of Tibetan and Himalayan Studies, and Chair of the Department of Sanskrit and Indian Studies and the Committee on Higher Degrees in Inner Asian and Altaic Studies, Harvard University. His research focuses on Indo-Tibetan intellectual history and Tibetan-Mongol relations during the thirteenth and fourteenth centuries.

DAN LUSTHAUS has taught Buddhism and Asian thought at the University of California-Los Angeles, University of Illinois Champaign-Urbana, and Bates College, and is currently Research Associate at Harvard University. His writings include *Buddhist Phenomenology: A Philosophical Investigation of Yogācāra Buddhism and the* Ch'eng wei-shih lun and *A Comprehensive Commentary on the Heart Sutra (Prajñāpāramitā-hṛdaya-sūtra) by K'uei-chi,* in collaboration with Heng-Ching shih, as well as numerous essays and articles.

MICHEL MOHR is Assistant Professor in the Department of Religion at the University of Hawai'i. He has published widely on language and ritual in the Zen traditions and is currently working on an English version of his two-volume, *Traité sur l'Inépuisable Lampe du Zen: Tōrei (1721–1792) et sa vision de l'éveil (Treatise on the Inexhaustible Lamp of Zen: Tōrei and his vision of awakening).*

JIN Y. PARK is Associate Professor of Philosophy and Religion at American University. Park's research focuses on Zen Buddhism, Buddhist-Continental comparative philosophy, and modern Korean Buddhism. Her publications include *Buddhisms and Deconstructions* (2006), *Buddhism and Postmodernity: Zen, Huayan, and the Possibility of Buddhist-Postmodern Ethics* (2008), and *Makers of Modern Korean Buddhism* (forthcoming).

GRAHAM PARKES is Professor and Head of the Department of Philosophy at University College Cork, in Ireland. He is the author, editor, and translator of numerous texts on German, French, Chinese, and Japanese philosophy. He is currently working on a book titled *Returning to Earth: Toward a More Global Philosophy of Nature.*

NOA RONKIN received her DPhil from Oxford University and is the author of *Early Buddhist Metaphysics: The Making of a Philosophical Tradition* (RoutledgeCurzon, 2005). Her research interests are concerned with a range of issues in comparative Indian philosophy, and with philosophical and psychological interpretations of Theravada Buddhism. She is currently the Associate Director of the Stanford Center on Ethics.

GARETH SPARHAM teaches Tibetan Language at the University of Michigan. His many publications include *The Ocean of Eloquence: Tsong Kha Pa's Commentary on the Yogācāra Doctrine of Mind, The Tibetan Dhammapada, The Fulfillment of All Hopes: Guru Devotion in Tibetan Buddhism,* and *Tantric Ethics: An Explanation of the Precepts for Buddhist Vajrayāna Practice.* His most recent works, *Abhisamayālaṃkāra with Vṛtti and Ālokā* and *Golden Garland of Eloquence,* are part of a series of translations of Indian and Tibetan Prajñāpāramitā texts.

KARMA LEKSHE TSOMO is Associate Professor of Theology and Religious Studies at the University of San Diego. She studied Buddhism in Dharamsala, India, for fifteen years and received a doctorate in comparative philosophy from the University of Hawai'i, with research on death and identity in China and Tibet. She is the author of *Into the Jaws of Yama, Lord of Death: Buddhism, Bioethics, and Death* and editor of a series of books on women in Buddhism.

BROOK ZIPORYN is Associate Professor in the Departments of Philosophy and Religion at Northwestern University. His publications include *Evil and/or/as the Good: Omnicentrism, Intersubjectivity and Value Paradox in Tiantai Buddhist Thought* (Harvard, 2000) and *Being and Ambiguity: Philosophical Experiments with Tiantai Buddhism* (Open Court Press, 2004).

BUDDHIST PHILOSOPHY

Introduction

From the standpoint of every Buddhist tradition, the central event in the history of Buddhism was the historical Buddha, Siddhartha Gautama, achieving awakening at Bodh Gaya, India. According to these traditions, his awakening under the bodhi tree consisted in his attainment of profound insight into the nature of reality, which in turn enabled the solution of the central problem toward which Buddhism is oriented—the universality and pervasiveness of suffering. The Buddha argued that this suffering is caused most immediately by attraction and aversion, and that the root cause of attraction and aversion is confusion regarding the fundamental nature of reality. As a consequence, the Buddha taught that his liberating insight into the nature of reality is the antidote to the confusion, and hence to the attraction and aversion it causes, and therefore, in the end, to suffering itself. This is the core content of the four noble truths expounded in his first discourse at Sarnath, the *Dhammacakkappavattana-sutta* (*Discourse that Sets in Motion the Wheel of Doctrine*) and is the foundation of all Buddhist philosophy.

The Buddhist world, however, is vast, and generated numerous schools of thought and philosophical systems elaborating these fundamental insights, with a substantial and internally diverse philosophical canon comparable to that of Western philosophy. Though there are important core views that characterize a philosophical approach as Buddhist, there is considerable variety in detail.

While Buddhist philosophy as a whole is aimed at soteriological concerns, involving the goal of attaining release from suffering, or the insight into the nature of reality that enables it, Buddhist philosophical concerns are principally metaphysical, epistemological, ethical, and hermeneutical. Metaphysics is foundational simply because the root of samsara—of the world of suffering—is confusion regarding the nature of reality, and liberation from suffering requires insight into that nature. Thus, it is not surprising that much Buddhist philosophy is concerned with an analysis of the fundamental nature of reality. But in order to attain liberation, one must come to *know* this nature, in a direct and immediate way, and cease to be deceived by merely apparent reality. Epistemology is hence a central concern of the tradition. The path to liberation sketched by the Buddha is a path of ethical perfection as well, as he held that morality is central to developing a real appreciation of the nature of reality and that a great deal of the suffering we encounter is caused by immorality. Buddhist ethics is hence a rich tradition. Finally, the plethora of schools of Buddhist thought, and the large body of literature consisting of conflicting arguments and positions attributed to the Buddha, demands a hermeneutical strategy for explaining and resolving doctrinal conflict, and for ordering commentarial literature. Hermeneutics thus became a highly developed discipline in Buddhist traditions.

Central to any Buddhist view of reality is the insight that all phenomena are impermanent, without essence (or selfless), and interdependent. The confusion the Buddha aimed to extirpate is the view that phenomena are enduring, independent, and have essential cores. Impermanence is understood in a Buddhist framework in two senses, usually referred to as "gross" and "subtle" impermanence. The gross impermanence of phenomena consists simply in the fact that nothing has been here forever, and nothing lasts forever. All phenomena arise at some point, when the proper constellation of causes and conditions is present, age constantly during their existence, changing in various ways as they age, and eventually pass out of existence. At a more subtle level, on this view, all phenomena are merely momentary. Since to be identical is to share all properties, and later stages of any object fail to share all properties, nothing retains its identity from one moment to the next. Everything arises, exists, and ceases at each and every moment. On this view, the observable phenomena that we take to be enduring, including ourselves, are causal continua of momentary phenomena to which we conventionally ascribe an identity that is nowhere to be found in the things themselves.

Selflessness and interdependence are closely connected to impermanence. In the West, we are accustomed to thinking of selves as personal, and as attached to human beings, and perhaps also to animals. Buddhist philosophers refer to the self so conceived as "the self of the person," connoting the self attributed by subjects of experience to themselves. But the more general idea of self at work in Buddhist philosophy is broader than this, further encompassing what is referred to in Buddhist traditions as "the self of phenomena." The idea is this: Just as when we ascribe a self to ourselves as subjects, we ascribe to ourselves a permanent, independent, enduring entity that is the ultimate referent of the term "I" and the possessor of our body and mind and the subject of our experience, so when we experience the objects around us as relatively permanent, independent, and substantial we thereby, at least implicitly, ascribe to them a substantial core that endures through superficial changes, that is the possessor of their parts, and that is the ultimate referent of a demonstrative "that," or of a noun phrase denoting the object in question. The idea of a self, then, is the idea of this enduring, independent core, common to the attribution of the self to persons or subjects and to external phenomena or objects.

Buddhists argue that there is no such self, in the case of either persons or external phenomena. Persons, as well as the objects of their experience, in virtue of being merely continua of causally connected episodes, lack a substantial core. Moreover, since all phenomena, including persons, exist only as causally connected continua, and since the causes and conditions of any episode in any continuum are themselves dependent on indefinitely many causes and conditions, both within and external to the conventionally identified continuum of a person or an object, all things exist only in thoroughgoing interdependence on countless other things. In short, things arise in dependence on innumerable causes and conditions; endure in dependence on innumerable causes and conditions; and cease in dependence on innumerable causes and conditions.

A great deal of Buddhist thought is devoted to adumbrating this framework of dependent origination. While this introduction cannot go into great detail, it is important in reading any Buddhist philosophy to keep in mind that dependent origination does not only involve causal interdependence. It is often characterized as tridimensional. The first dimension is the causal dimension emphasized so far. But second, there is synchronic interdependence between any whole and the parts in which it consists. Any complex depends for its existence and character on its parts; its parts, in turn, depend on the wholes that they comprise. I rely on my stomach, lungs, brain, and bone for my existence, but none of these could exist or function were it not part of a whole organism. Finally, in virtue of the lack of any intrinsic identity in spatiotemporally extensive entities, everything that we identify as a thing, once again including ourselves, depends for that identity—and so, for the only existence it has as an enduring or distinct entity—on conceptual designation. The only thing that makes a table a table is a convention that collects four legs and a top into a single entity as a referent for the word "table."

All of this grounds the idea whose articulation is so central to Buddhist philosophy in the Māhāyana schools that dominate later Indian and all Tibetan and East Asian Buddhist philosophy—the emptiness of all things. It is easy to misunderstand the claim that everything is empty. In order to avoid the most basic and tempting misunderstanding, namely, that this is a doctrine of universal nihilism, it is important to remember that to be empty is always to be empty of *something*. In a Buddhist context, reality is not empty of *existence,* but is empty of *inherent existence,* or of *essence* (*svabhāva*). On this view, conventional phenomena exist, but they do not exist with essences. Nothing is independent of causes and conditions, part-whole relations, or conceptual imputation; nothing is permanent; nothing has any characteristic on its own that makes it the thing that it is. Things, according to proponents of these systems, are empty of *all of that.* Having said this, there is considerable dispute within the tradition regarding the relevant notion of essence, and regarding just what it is to be empty in the relevant sense.

Recognizing the emptiness of all phenomena conceptually is, according to most Buddhist philosophers, not all that difficult: good philosophical analysis will suffice. But coming to perceive and to recognize phenomena as empty, most would argue, is a difficult achievement. It requires extirpating deep-seated impulses to reify ourselves and others, to regard ourselves and others as permanent, as consisting of a substantial core over which properties are laid, and to regard ourselves and others as essentially independent and only accidentally interacting agents and objects. These are the delusions, Siddhartha Gautama argued, that trap us in suffering.

The fact that everything exists in a causally interdependent, conventional way but is at the same time ultimately empty grounds the doctrine of the two truths. The first truth is the conventional, or concealing (*saṃvṛti, vyāvahāra*) truth or reality (*satya*); the second is the ultimate (*paramārtha*) truth or reality. Conventional truth is the realm of persons, objects, dogs, cats, trees, tables, and hard currency. Conventionally, objects exist, endure, and have a whole range of fascinating properties. But ultimately, they are empty. They exist only as impermanent, conventional designations, as we can see when we pursue careful philosophical analysis. The conventional truth is what appears to uncritical consciousness, and is regarded as deceptive, in that conventional phenomena appear to ordinary folks as though they exist inherently, even though they do not. The ultimate truth is what appears on careful analysis, or to those who have cultivated their cognitive powers to the point where they apprehend things spontaneously as empty. When things appear in this way, they appear nondeceptively.

Much of Buddhist thought is dedicated to understanding the complex relation between the two truths, and there is much diversity of opinion on this question. It is important, however, to note that they are presented as two *truths,* not as truth and falsehood, or as appearance and reality. Working out how this can be the case is no easy matter. Part of the agenda is set for the Mahāyāna schools by the famous declaration in the *Heart of Wisdom Sūtra* that "form is empty; emptiness is form; emptiness is not different from form; form is not different from emptiness." In some deep sense, on this view, the two truths are one. To be conventionally real is to be empty of inherent existence; to be empty of inherent existence is what it is to be conventionally real.

Buddhist debates concerning the nature of reality and truth naturally lead to concern with questions of how knowledge is attained. For the most part, Buddhist philosophers have argued that perception and inference are the only valid sources of knowledge; first-person verification is systematically valorized over the authority of scriptures or teachers. Ultimately, though, because most Buddhist philosophers believe that words can only denote nonexistent universals, and the particulars that actually exist are inexpressible, they argue that since inference is always verbal and conceptual, and therefore engaged with the nonexistent, even inference is to be abandoned by the awakened mind.

The Buddha, however, employed language to teach the Dharma, and Buddhist philosophers have devoted much attention to considering how linguistic meaning is achieved and how language should be employed on the Buddhist path. For some, the answer to the question of how to use language has resulted in systematic treatises that proceed via linguistic argument, inference, and conceptual thought. For others, the only way to point to the linguistically inexpressible truth has been through employing enigmatic silence or the provocative, and noninferential, use of language found in the kōan.

While Buddhists understand insight into the nature of reality to be necessary for liberation, it is generally not regarded as sufficient. Insight is an antidote to ignorance, but liberation also requires the overcoming of attachment and aversion, which is achieved through the cultivation of moral discipline and mindfulness. For this reason Buddhists have devoted much thought to the question of which acts, intentions, consequences, virtues, and states of mind lead to this kind of mental transformation and thereby the alleviation of suffering. In moral thought, there is more agreement than in other areas of Buddhist philosophy, yet there is still a great diversity of approaches to moral questions in Buddhist traditions. These include elements that resemble virtue ethics, deontology, and utilitarianism, but Buddhist ethics is best approached on its own terms rather than as a species of one of the Western traditions. It is best characterized as a kind of moral pluralism, as a sustained effort to solve a fundamental existential problem using a variety of means. Its scope is sometimes broader than that of Western ethical theory, inasmuch as such cognitive states as ontological confusion are regarded as moral, and not simply as epistemic failings; and sometimes narrower, taking vows as grounding fundamental moral concerns, as opposed to general sets of obligations. Many important debates in contemporary Buddhist moral thought concern the relation between Buddhist ethics and questions of social, political, and economic justice. These are addressed in the final chapters of this volume.

Texts purporting to express the words of the Buddha and historical commentaries provide a multiplicity of conflicting accounts of the doctrines that are supposedly basic to a Buddhist worldview. In response to these competing accounts, Buddhist thinkers developed hermeneutical methodologies to distinguish between those texts that offer a merely provisional account intended for a particular audience at a particular time, and those texts that articulate a definitive account of the nature of reality. To justify a particular text as definitive required a discussion of fundamental philosophical questions of metaphysics and ontology, epistemology, language, hermeneutics, philosophy of the person, and ethics. For more than two thousand years, then, Buddhists have been arguing about these methodological questions with each other and also with non-Buddhist philosophers, resulting in an extensive set of texts on the philosophy of language and hermeneutic theory.

Our purpose in this volume is to present some of these Buddhist philosophical debates as they appear in historically influential and philosophically significant texts. While no anthology of Buddhist philosophy could possibly be complete, either historically or topically, we have selected texts that illustrate the varied and rich philosophies of Buddhist traditions that represent diverse responses to core philosophical questions. We have ordered our selections of Buddhist primary texts into five parts: (1) Metaphysics and Ontology; (2) Philosophy of Language and Hermeneutics; (3) Epistemology; (4) Philosophy of Mind and the Person; and (5) Ethics. Each part begins with a brief introduction that situates the questions and debates that will follow. Each selection, in turn, is preceded by an introductory essay, contributed by an eminent scholar of Buddhist philosophy. These introductions provide commentary on the selected texts, situating them historically and clarifying their philosophical contributions. The aim of these introductions is to make the selected texts accessible to students of Buddhist intellectual traditions who lack extensive training in Buddhist thought and to enable those trained primarily in Western philosophy to approach and to teach these texts as philosophical works that can fruitfully engage with Western philosophical texts and concerns. A bibliography of suggested readings follows each selection for those interested in pursuing further explorations of the issues it addresses.

The texts selected here raise numerous perplexing questions. Indeed, the very project of "Buddhist philosophy" itself raises questions concerning the nature of philosophy and how one ought to pursue crosscultural interpretation. For the editors, engaging these questions over the years has been an enduring source of intellectual excitement and philosophical insight. With this volume we hope to make that excitement and insight accessible to a new generation of students of the vast and rich traditions of Buddhist philosophy.

PART I

METAPHYSICS AND ONTOLOGY

Buddhist metaphysics revolves around four fundamental concepts—impermanence (*anitya*), selflessness (*anātman*), interdependence (*pratitya-samutpāda*), and emptiness (*śunyatā*)—and the elaboration of the idea that reality comprises two truths—a conventional and an ultimate truth. The development of Buddhist philosophy from the time of the historical Buddha, Siddhartha Gautama, to the present consists in the articulation of these ideas, their interrelationships, and their implications in progressively greater detail and with increasing sophistication, as well as the proliferation of alternative understandings of these ideas represented by distinct schools of thought. Much of the fecundity of Buddhist philosophy is due to the extended debates between these schools, as well as dialogue with non-Buddhist philosophical schools in India and East Asia, in which the metaphysical theses to which each school was committed were amended and made more precise.

As a consequence of this multiplicity of views, and as a consequence of the development of Buddhist philosophy over time, it is almost always impossible to answer the question "What do Buddhists think about X?" univocally. Nonetheless, the disparate traditions are united by a common problematic that emerges from the need to articulate a coherent conception of an impermanent, selfless, empty reality within the rubric of the two truths. The texts collected in this section trace several strands in the development of these ideas from the earliest stratum of Buddhist metaphysical literature—the Pali suttas—to twentieth-century Buddhist philosophy in Japan.

The *Kaccāyanagota-sūtra* is one of the discourses of the Buddha collected in the Pali canon, systematized soon after his death. It represents the earliest stratum of Buddhist philosophy. Here the Buddha diagnoses the roots of suffering in ignorance embodied in opposing metaphysical errors: the error of reification that consists in taking things that exist only conventionally to exist ultimately, and the error of nihilism, which consists in denying even the conventional existence of things in virtue of their ultimate emptiness. He characterizes the middle path in metaphysics at which Buddhism aims as a denial of each extreme, and hence as an acceptance of the world as conventionally real, but as ultimately unreal, urging that this metaphysical view is the necessary condition of the cessation of the attachment and aversion that in turn underlie suffering.

The Pali view of the nature of the relation between conventional and ultimate truth was a kind of mereological reductionism: apparent wholes are conventional truths; the fundamental psychophysical entities in which they ultimately consist are the ultimate truths. This view is articulated in the Pali Abhidhamma, or supplement to the Dhamma (doctrine) and the selection from the Abhidhamma presented here is a fine example of the kind of reductive metaphysical analysis that idea generated.

Nāgārjuna (c. second century C.E.) continues the exploration of the relation between the two truths, arguing for the thesis that dependent origination and emptiness are identical, and so that the conventional and ultimate truths are identical, and that understanding this is the foundation of all Buddhist doctrine. This idea is encapsulated in Nāgārjuna's thesis that emptiness itself is empty, and so dependently originated and only conventionally existent. This view is articulated most explicitly and extensively in his magnum opus, *Mūlamadhyamakakārikā* (Fundamental verses on the Middle Way), which is the foundational text for the Madhyamaka tradition, and is the subject of extensive commentarial literature in India, Tibet, and China. In chapter XXIV of the *Mūlamadhyamakakārikā*, presented here, Nāgārjuna explores the relationship between dependent origination and emptiness.

Vasubandhu is one of the founders of the Yogācāra school, an idealist, phenomenological school that arose about five hundred years after Madhyamaka. Philosophers of this school take conventional truth to be a cognitive projection, and all conventional phenomena to be mere aspects of consciousness. Their dependent origination consists in the fact that they depend for their existence on mental episodes, and their ultimate truth is the fact that they are empty of any external existence or dual relation to subjectivity. This school is noteworthy for its articulation of the doctrine of three natures—an imagined (*parikalpita*), an other-dependent (*paratantra*), and a consummate (*parinișpanna*). In the text included here, *Trisvabhāvanirdeśa* (Discourse on the Three Natures), Vasubandhu expounds this doctrine and its relation to the two truths and to interdependence.

Yogācāra and Madhyamaka represented alternative metaphysical schemes in Indian Buddhism. The former was idealist, denying the reality of the external world, and accepting the ultimate reality of mind as the foundation of illusion and as the substratum for awakening; the second took external reality more for granted, but at the same time argued that mind is every bit as empty as any external object. Śāntarakṣita (725–788), who was also one of the principal figures involved in the propagation of Buddhism in Tibet, attempted a synthesis of these two positions, conceived squarely in the framework of the two truths, and grounded in the epistemology and logic developed by Dignāga and Dharmakīrti. In *Madhyamakālaṃkāra* (Ornament of the Middle Way), Śāntarakṣita argues that Yogācāra presents a correct account of the conventional truth, and Madhyamaka a correct account of the ultimate truth. The selection presented here demonstrates his unique approach to arguing for the emptiness of phenomena, his signature "neither one nor many argument."

When Buddhism entered Tibet, the Indian scholastic tradition quickly took root and flowered in a massive outpouring of sophisticated Buddhist scholarship, in many ways continuous with Indian Buddhist philosophy, but also innovative. One of the many issues that preoccupied Tibetan metaphysicians was a debate regarding the nature of the emptiness of emptiness. Some argued that emptiness is *intrinsically* empty—that is, that like all conventional phenomena, it is empty of anything that makes it what it is, namely, emptiness. Others argued that the fact that emptiness, unlike conventional phenomena, is an ultimate truth entails that while it is *extrinsically* empty—that is, empty of everything other than its emptiness—it is not *intrinsically* empty, or empty of that which makes it emptiness. The Tibetan philosopher Mipam Namgyel (1846–1912) attempts to resolve this dispute in the selection from his *Lion's Roar Affirming Extrinsic Emptiness.*

The Chinese Huayan Buddhist tradition reframed Indian concerns about the identity of and difference between the two truths in terms of a complex hierarchy of philosophical perspectives articulated through a rich set of metaphors, and developed an account of interdependence as interpenetration both among conventional phenomena and between the conventional and the ultimate. The selection from the work of the Chinese philosopher Dushun (c. 600 C.E.) takes the statement in the *Heart Sūtra* that "form is empty; emptiness is form; form is not different from emptiness; emptiness is not different from form" as a framework for developing this perspective.

The Japanese monk-scholar Dōgen (1200–1253) takes the perspectivalism of Huayan as a rubric for understanding convention, emptiness, interdependence, and the relation between these one step further. Whereas Huayan philosophers took it for granted that perspectives are always the perspectives of sentient beings, and that conventional reality arises from the conventions of the sentient, Dōgen takes seriously the idea that even the nonsentient can be understood as having perspectives, that a full understanding of the interdependent, empty, and conventional nature of reality requires taking those perspectives into account, and that the world as a whole, sentient and nonsentient, can be taken as a text whose content is emptiness. This view is articulated in "Mountains and Waters as Sūtras," one of the chapters of his major work *Shobogenzo*, presented here.

Nishitani Keiji (1900–1990) continues in the twentieth century the Zen tradition brought to Japan by Dōgen in the thirteenth, but with an eye firmly on its Indian roots. Nishitani draws on a phenomenological reading of Indian Yogācāra thought and a Madhyamaka understanding of the identity of the two truths. He advances with great philosophical rigor the view, originating in Indian Buddhism, but articulated with such force by Dōgen, that awakened understanding must be a direct, nonconceptual, and nondual cognitive relation to reality.

1

Theravāda Metaphysics and Ontology

Kaccānagotta (*Saṃyutta-nikāya*) and *Abhidhammatthasaṅgaha*

Noa Ronkin

The Sutta-piṭaka

Although early Buddhism cannot be reduced to a systematic philosophy, what lies at its heart, according to its own understanding of the matter, is Dharma (Pali Dhamma). In Indian thought, Dharma is the truth about the world: the underlying nature of things, the way things are in reality. One might say, therefore, that at the heart of Buddhism lies a metaphysical Truth. Yet in the *Sutta-piṭaka*—the collection of the Buddha's discourses in the Triple Basket collection of Pali texts regarded as canonical by the Theravāda school of Buddhism—the Dhamma is presented in a way that notably refrains from metaphysical underpinnings. The Dhamma is understood to be a path of practice in conduct, meditation, and understanding leading to the cessation of the fundamental suffering (*dukkha*) that underlies the human condition as lived in the round of rebirth (*saṃsāra*). The texts repeatedly state that the Buddha taught only what is conducive to achieving that goal of cessation, or nirvana (Pali *nibbāna*), and there are strong suggestions, as captured by the renowned undetermined questions, that purely theoretical speculations, especially those to do with certain metaphysical concerns about the ultimate nature of the world and one's destiny, are both pointless and potentially misleading in the quest for nirvana.[1]

1. For the ten undetermined questions see, for instance, *Majjhima-nikāya* I 426; *Aṅguttara-nikāya* V 193; *Dīgha-nikāya* I 187; *Saṃyutta-nikāya* IV 395. See also Gethin

Nevertheless, while it is true that the Buddha suspends all views regarding certain metaphysical questions, he is not an antimetaphysician: nothing in the texts suggests that metaphysical questions are completely meaningless, or that the Buddha denies the soundness of metaphysics per se. Instead, Buddhism teaches that to understand suffering, its rise, its cessation, and the path leading to its cessation is to see reality as it truly is. Reality, as seen through the lens of Buddhist epistemology, is not a container of persons and substances, but rather an assemblage of interlocking physical and mental processes that spring up and pass away subject to multifarious causes and conditions and that are always mediated by the cognitive apparatus embodied in the operation of the five aggregates (*khandhas*). Indeed, the main doctrinal teachings found in the *suttas,* including the postulate of impermanence (*anicca*), the principle of dependent origination (*paṭiccasamuppāda*), and the teaching of not-self (*anattā*), are all metaphysical views concerning how processes work rather than what things are. Thus while the Dhamma is silent on ontological matters, it is grounded in what may be identified as process metaphysics: A framework of thought that hinges on the ideas that sentient experience is dependently originated and that whatever is dependently originated is conditioned (*saṇkhata*), impermanent, subject to change, and lacking independent selfhood. Construing sentient experience as a dynamic flow of physical and mental occurrences and rejecting the notion of a metaphysical self as an enduring substratum underlying experience, the Buddha's process metaphysics contrasts with substance metaphysics.[2]

Process metaphysics has deliberately chosen to reverse the primacy of substance: it insists on seeing processes as basic in the order of being, or at least in the order of understanding. Underlying process metaphysics is the supposition that encountered phenomena are best represented and understood in terms of occurrences—processes and events—rather than in terms of "things," and with reference to modes of change rather than to fixed

---

1998: 66–68. All references to the Pali texts are to volume number and page of the Pali Text Society editions.

2. Western metaphysics has been dominated by a substance-attribute ontology, which has a marked bias in favor of "objects." While Plato's view of reason and his doctrine of the realm of Forms illustrate the predominance of the notion of substance, substance metaphysics reached its highest perfection in Aristotle's writings and has thereafter dominated much of traditional philosophy from the ancient Stoics through the Scholastics of the Middle Ages and up to the distinguished authors of modern philosophy. Notwithstanding this dominance and its decisive ramifications for much of Western history of ideas, since as early as the period of the pre-Socratics another standpoint that goes against the mainstream current of Western metaphysics has been present. This variant line of thought, designated by modern scholarship as "process metaphysics" or "process philosophy," focuses on the ontological category of occurrences—mainly events and processes—rather than on that of material objects, and is concerned with the notion of becoming rather than of being. See Rescher 1996.

stabilities. The guiding idea is that processes are basic and things derivative, for it takes some mental process to construct "things" from the indistinct mass of sense experience and because change is the pervasive and predominant feature of the real. The result is that *how* eventualities transpire is seen as no less significant than *what* sorts of things there are.[3]

The following selection from the *Saṃyutta-nikāya* shows that rather than deny metaphysics, the Dhamma urges one to understand *how* things are. It instructs one to avoid wrong views (*diṭṭhi*), particularly the two extremes of existence and non-existence that are oftentimes referred to as eternalism and annihilationism.[4] Instead, one should contemplate through meditative practice the middle way between these two extremes, and the middle way is articulated in terms of dependent origination and not-self.[5]

The *Saṃyutta-nikāya* was likely compiled as a repository for *suttas* disclosing the Buddha's metaphysical insight into the nature of reality, thus serving the needs of the doctrinal specialists in the monastic order and of those monks and nuns who had already fulfilled the preliminary stages of meditative training and were intent on developing direct realization of the ultimate truth. This supposition is supported by the text's nonsubstantialist perspective and its thematic arrangement of the doctrinal formulas that form classifications of the Buddha's discourses and culminate in the Abhidhamma—such as the twelvefold chain of dependent origination, the five aggregates, the six sense bases, the eight factors of the path, and the Four Noble Truths.[6]

Translation: *Kaccānagotta* (*Saṃyutta-nikāya* II 17–18)

At Sāvatthi. Then the Venerable Kaccānagotta approached the Blessed One, paid homage to him, sat down to one side, and said to him: "Venerable sir,

3. For a detailed explanation of the early Buddhist interest in "how" experience and the self are, rather than in "what" they are, see Hamilton 2000, particularly chap. 5.

4. In the *Brahmajāla-sutta* that opens the *Dīgha-nikāya,* the Buddha lists sixty-two types of wrong view and refutes them all, particularly targeting eternalism and annihilationism. See *Dīgha-nikāya* I 12.

5. Gethin (1992: 155) says in this context: "The point that is being made is that reality is at heart something dynamic, something fluid: however one looks at it, reality is a process.... True process, true change, cannot be explained either in terms of eternalism (a thing exists unchanging) or annihilationism (a thing exists for a time and then ceases to exist). The process of change as described by dependent arising is thus a middle between these two extremes, encapsulating the paradox of identity and difference involved in the very notion of change."

6. See Bhikkhu Bodhi, introduction to *The Connected Discourses of the Buddha* 2000: 31–33. The following translation originally appeared in Bhikkhu Bodhi 2000. We gratefully acknowledge permission to republish this work.

it is said, 'right view, right view.' In what way, venerable sir, is there right view?"

"This world, Kaccāna, for the most part depends upon a duality—upon the notion of existence and the notion of nonexistence. But for one who sees the origin of the world as it really is with correct wisdom, there is no notion of nonexistence in regard to the world. And for one who sees the cessation of the world as it really is with correct wisdom, there is no notion of existence in regard to the world.

"This world, Kaccāna, is for the most part shackled by engagement, clinging, and adherence. But this one [with right view] does not become engaged and cling through that engagement and clinging, mental standpoint, adherence, underlying tendency; he does not take a stand about 'my self.' He has no perplexity or doubt that what arises is only suffering arising, what ceases is only suffering ceasing. His knowledge about this is independent of others. It is in this way, Kaccāna, that there is right view.

"'All exists': Kaccāna, this is one extreme. 'All does not exist': this is the second extreme. Without veering towards either of these extremes, the Tathāgata teaches the Dhamma by the middle: 'With ignorance as condition, volitional formations [come to be]; with volitional formations as condition, consciousness [comes to be] . . . name-and-form . . . the six sense-bases . . . contact . . . feeling . . . craving . . . clinging . . . existence . . . birth . . . aging-and-death [come to be]. Such is the origin of this whole mass of suffering. But with the remainderless fading away and cessation of ignorance comes cessation of volitional formations; with the cessation of volitional formations, cessation of consciousness . . . ' Such is the cessation of this whole mass of suffering."

The Abhidhamma

The first conscious attempt to ground the Buddha's scattered teachings in a comprehensive philosophical system was introduced with the advance of the Abhidhamma (Sanskrit Abhidharma) tradition—a doctrinal movement in Buddhist thought that arose during the first centuries after the Buddha's death (fourth century B.C.E. onward) together with the spread of the Sangha across the Indian subcontinent. Having its own distinctive theoretical and practical interests, the Abhidhamma resulted in an independent branch of inquiry and literary genre documented in the third basket of the Pali canon, the *Abhidhamma-piṭaka,* its commentaries, and its various explicatory Abhidhamma manuals. This selection is taken from one such manual, the *Abhidhammatthasaṅgaha,* a compendium of the Theravādin Abhidhamma system that has long been the most commonly used introductory manual for the study of Abhidhamma in Sri Lanka and Southeast Asia. The text is traditionally attributed to Anuruddha and was likely composed in the late sixth or early seventh century. To properly appreciate the implications of this text for Buddhist metaphysics, however, one needs to understand something of the development of the Buddhist concept of *dhamma*.

In the Sutta literature, both the singular and plural forms *Dhamma/dhammas* ordinarily refer to the contents of the Buddha's discourses, to the fundamental principles he taught.[7] In addition to signifying the basic elements of the Buddha's teaching, though, the plural term *dhammas* also denotes the objects that appear in one's consciousness while practicing insight meditation. These are particularly mental objects of the sixth sense faculty, namely, *manas* (a most ambiguous term in the Sutta literature that is normally translated as "mind"), alongside the objects of the five ordinary physical senses.[8] By *dhammas*, then, the Buddha and his immediate followers understood the physical and mental processes that make up one's experiential world, and the nature of this experience was analyzed in such terms as the five aggregates, the twelve sense spheres, and the eighteen elements (*khandha, āyatana, dhātu*). The Abhidhamma, though, developed yet another mode of analysis that in its view was the most comprehensive and exhaustive, namely, the analysis of experience in terms of *dhammas*.

Within the specific context of meditation, the Abhidhamma significantly changed its conception of the plurality of *dhammas*. The Abhidhamma treatises draw subtle distinctions within the scope of the mental and systematize the term *manas* so that it acquires a host of different technical meanings. *Dhammas* are here reckoned a pluralistic representation of encountered phenomena; not merely mental objects, but all knowable sensory phenomena of whatever nature, namely, the phenomenal world in its entirety as we experience it through the senses. This broad rendering includes the narrower sense of *dhammas* as objects of *manas* when the latter signifies mental cognition qua an aspect of discriminative consciousness, or rather mental cognitive awareness (*manoviññāṇa*, often translated literally as "mind-consciousness"), now deemed the central cognitive operation within the process of sensory perception.[9] *Dhammas* as the objects of mental cognitive awareness may now be rendered as apperceptions in the sense of rapid mental events by means of which the mind unites and assimilates a particular perception, especially one newly presented, to a larger set or mass of ideas already possessed, thus

7. That in this sense the singular and plural forms *dhamma/dhammas* are interchangeable (like "teaching" and "teachings" in English) is illustrated by recurring passages that refer to the Buddha's ninefold teaching (*navaṅgabuddhasāsana*), i.e., the nine divisions of the Buddhist texts according to their form or style, although such passages must belong to a later period in which these distinct nine divisions were acknowledged. See, for instance, *Majjhima-nikāya* I 133; *Dīgha-nikāya* II 100; *Aṅguttara-nikāya* II 103, 178, and III 88; and *Vinaya* III 8. It is customary to apply the uppercase Dhamma to the Buddhist teaching and the lowercase *dhamma*/s to the individual doctrinal principles that make up the teaching.

8. E.g., *Majjhima-nikāya* III 62; *Saṃyutta-nikāya* I 113 and 115–16, II 140 (here all the senses are referred to as *dhātu*), IV 114 and 163; *Aṅguttara-nikāya* I 11.

9. E.g., *Vibhaṅga* 10, 14–15, 54, 60–2 and 71; *Dhātukathā* 7–8, 34, 41, 63, and 67; *Kathāvatthu* 12, 19–20, and 67.

comprehending and conceptualizing it. Insofar as these dhammic apperceptions interact with the five sensory modalities of cognitive awareness that arise in dependence on their corresponding material phenomena, then they are fleeting "flashes" of psychophysical events as presented in consciousness.

Thus, in the canonical Abhidhamma literature, a *dhamma* acquires the technical sense of an object of a specific mental capability called mental cognitive awareness and, in this sense, an instance of one of the fundamental, short-lived physical and mental events that interact to produce the world as we experience it. The Abhidhamma provides a systematic account of the constitution of sentient experience by offering a method of describing any possible *dhamma* instance, both in its exclusiveness and in relation to its causal origins and conditioning factors. The overarching inquiry subsuming both the analysis of *dhammas* and their synthesis into a unified structure is called the "*dhamma* theory."[10]

The *dhammas* fall into four broad categories—consciousness (*citta*), mentalities (*cetasika*), materiality (*rūpa*), and nirvana—each of which is analyzed in great detail.[11] Consciousness is divided into eighty-nine basic types of consciousness moments, assemblages of consciousness and associated mentalities that are organized by various guidelines, the most fundamental of which reveals a fourfold hierarchy according to four spheres. At the bottom of this fourfold psychological hierarchy are the fifty-four types of sensuous-sphere consciousness (*kāmāvacara*): a broad category typical of the normal state of mind of human beings, but also of hell beings, animals, and various kinds of divine being known as the lower gods (*devas*), all of whom are reborn in the existential plane of the five senses. Next there are the fifteen types of consciousness pertaining to the sphere of pure form (*rūpāvacara*), followed by the twelve types of consciousness of the formless sphere (*arūpāvacara*), and culminating in the eight kinds of supra-mundane or transcendent (*lokuttara*) consciousness that have *nibbāna* as their object.

The following selection from the *Abhidhammatthasaṅgaha* includes only the analysis of the sense-sphere consciousness, beginning with unwholesome consciousnesses at the bottom, followed by consciousnesses that concern the mechanics of bare awareness of the objects of the five senses, and then by wholesome sense-sphere consciousnesses. In technical Abhidhamma terms, our basic experience of the physical world is encompassed by a limited number of classes of sense-sphere consciousness that are the results of twelve unwholesome and eight wholesome classes of sense-sphere consciousnesses.

10. Thus none of the various other renditions of the word *dhamma* as "state," "phenomenon," "principle," "teaching," etc., conveys its precise meaning as the most basic technical term of the Abhidhamma.

11. Theravādin Abhidhamma describes eighty-two *dhammas* or possible types of occurrence encompassed in these four broad categories, but the term *dhamma* also signifies any particular categorial token. Thus, according to the Theravādin typology, there are eighty-two possible types of occurrence in the encountered world, not eighty-two occurrences.

Like the Nikāya worldview, then, the canonical Abhidhamma is accommodated within the category of antisubstantialist metaphysics, and the focus of its analysis of sentient experience is epistemological rather than ontological: it is concerned with the conditions of the psychophysical occurrences that arise in consciousness, and in this sense form one's "world," not with what exists per se in a mind-independent world. Yet the *dhamma* theory and its analysis of consciousness showcase the Abhidhamma's shift from the implicit, process metaphysics operative in the Buddha's teaching to an intricate event metaphysics. This system of thought now dissects the physical and mental processes that make up sentient experience into their constitutive consciousness moments, replacing the idea of a psychophysical process by the notion of a *dhamma* qua a mental event as analytical primitive and the basis of a complex theory of consciousness.

As part of its doctrinal development, the Abhidhamma was later subject to a gradual process of systematization and conceptual assimilation, accompanied by a growing tendency to reify the *dhammas* and an increasing interest in establishing their true nature. Thus, in the commentarial tradition, the concept of "particular nature" (*sabhāva*) plays a major role. Often understood as "essence," *sabhāva* is regarded as that which gave an impetus to the Abhidhamma's growing concern with ontology. The selection here includes an abridged version of the *Abhidhammatthasaṅgaha*'s commentary, the *Abhidhammatthavibhāvinī*, that exemplifies the spirit of the postcanonical commentarial tradition and its use of the concept of *sabhāva*. The text is ascribed to Sumaṅgala and is dated to the twelfth century.[12]

Translation: *Summary of the Topics of Abhidhamma*

(*Abhidhammatthasaṅgaha*) by Anuruddha and Exposition of the Topics of the Abhidhamma (*Abhidhammatthavibhāvinī*) by Sumaṅgala being a commentary to Anuruddha's *Summary of the Topics of Abhidhamma*.

Homage to him, the Blessed One, the Worthy One, the Perfectly Awakened One.

Prologue

1. Having paid respect to the incomparable Perfectly Awakened One, along with the Good Dhamma and the Supreme Community, I shall utter the Summary of the Topics of Abhidhamma.

12. The following translation originally appeared in Wijeratne and Gethin 2002. We gratefully acknowledge permission to republish this work.

Chapter 1: Consciousness

2. The topics of Abhidhamma spoken of therein in full are from the ultimate standpoint four: consciousness, mentalities, materiality, and *nibbāna*.

Commentary

Consciousness (*citta*) is that which is conscious; the meaning is that it knows (*vijānāti*) an object. [...]

Or else consciousness is the means by which the associated *dhammas* are conscious. Alternatively, consciousness is the mere act of being conscious (*cintana*). For it is its mere occurrence in accordance with conditions that is called "a *dhamma* with its own particular nature" (*sabhāva-dhamma*). In consideration of this, it is the definition of the particular natures of ultimate *dhammas* that is taken as absolute; the explanation by way of agent (*kattar*) and instrument (*karaṇa*) should be seen as a relative manner of speaking. For a *dhamma*'s being treated as an agent, by attributing the status of "self" to the particular function of a *dhamma,* and also its being [treated] in consequence as an instrument, by attributing the state of agent to a group of conascent *dhammas*, are both taken as a relative manner of speaking. The explanation in these terms should be understood as for the purpose of indicating the nonexistence of an agent, etc. apart from the particular nature of a *dhamma*. The meaning of the word *citta* is also elaborated as that which causes variegation and so on. [...]

That which exists in the mind by occurring in dependence upon it is *mentality* (*cetasika*). For it is unable to take an object without consciousness; in the absence of consciousness there is no arising of any mentality at all. But consciousness does occur with an object in the absence of certain mentalities; so mentality is said to occur in dependence upon consciousness. [...]

That which is afflicted (*ruppati*) is *materiality* (*rupā*); that which "comes to or is brought to change (*vikāra*) as a result of such opposing conditions as cold and heat" is what is meant. [...]

That which is deliverance (*nikkhanta*) from craving, considered as "entanglement" (*vāna*) because it stitches and weaves together existence and nonexistence, or that by means of which the fires of greed, etc., are extinguished (*nibbāti*) is nibbāna.

3. Therein, to take consciousness first, it is fourfold: that which belongs to the sense sphere, that which belongs to the form sphere, that which belongs to the formless sphere, that which is transcendent.

4. Therein what belongs to the sense sphere? [Consciousness] accompanied by happiness, associated with view, and without prompting[13] is one kind; the same with prompting is one kind; consciousness accompanied by happiness, dissociated from view, and without prompting is one kind; the same with prompting is one kind; consciousness accompanied by equanimity, associated with view, and without prompting is one kind; the same with prompting is one kind; consciousness accompanied by equanimity, dissociated from view, and without prompting is one kind; the same with prompting is one kind. All these eight are called the consciousnesses accompanied by greed.

Commentary

Among these four kinds of consciousness, sense-sphere consciousness is also fourfold by division into wholesome, unwholesome, resultant, and *kiriya*.[14] Later he will use the term "beautiful" for the fifty-nine or ninety-one types of consciousness that are neither demeritorious nor without motivations in the phrase *apart from the bad and unmotivated they are called beautiful;* so that he can do this, he explains the demeritorious and motivationless first of all. Among these, because consciousnesses accompanied by greed arise from the start in the consciousness processes of one who has taken rebirth, these are explained first; next, because of their similarity in having two motivations, he explains those accompanied by unhappiness, and then those with one motivation. Dividing it into eight by the classification of feeling, wrong-view and volition, he explains the root of greed with the words beginning accompanied by happiness.

Herein, "happy mind" (*sumano*) means a pleasant mind or someone who has that, that is, the consciousness [itself] or the person with that consciousness. The state of that [consciousness or person], because it gives rise to

13. Prompting (*saṅkhāra*) is a mental coefficient of and the requisite for an instance of consciousness, what constitutes its potentiality. For example, according to Buddhaghosa, when one, unhesitatingly and unurged by others, performs such merit as giving, then one's consciousness is unprompted (*asaṅkhārika*). But when one performs merit hesitatingly, out of incomplete generosity, or because one was urged to do so by others, then one's consciousness is prompted (*sasaṅkhārika*). See *Visuddhimagga* XIV 84.

14. Gethin explains in his introduction to the translation of the text (p. xx): "The term *kiriya* means literally something like 'action' and is used in the Abhidhamma to qualify those mental events or states of consciousness that neither produce kammic results (*vipāka*) nor themselves constitute such results: *kiriya* states are neither kamma—whether wholesome or unwholesome—nor its result. As such, *kiriya* is used to characterize two broad types of consciousness: first certain basic consciousnesses that occur for all beings as part of the process of being conscious; secondly and more significantly the consciousness of the arahat, which, since it is free of the motivations of greed, hatred and delusion, does not produce results to be experienced in future births."

the name and idea of this, is happiness (*somanassa*). It is a term for pleasant mental feeling. Accompanied by this, joined by virtue of arising as one and so forth, or "in that state of arising as one," is being *accompanied by happiness.*

View (*diṭṭhi*) is "seeing wrongly." For since a general word can have a particular referent according to context and so forth, here, view is stated as just "wrong seeing." [...]

Prompting is what prepares and equips the consciousness in the form of furnishing it with energy, or consciousness is prepared and equipped by it in the said fashion. It is that exertion of oneself or others which precedes by way of giving assistance to a consciousness that is slowing down in a particular action. In this case the prompting designates the consciousness's particular state of energy when it has arisen because of the preceding occurrence in the consciousness-flow of oneself or of others. When that is not there, it is unprompted; just this is *without prompting* (*asaṅkhārika*). Along with prompting is *with prompting* (*sasaṅkhārika*). Thus it is said:

The particular quality [which is] produced by the preceding exertion and which produces the consciousness is prompting; it is by virtue of this that there is here the condition of [being] without prompting, and so on.

Or else with prompting and without prompting are stated entirely with reference to the presence or absence of prompting, not on account of its presence or absence in the [preceding] associated activity [of consciousness]: a consciousness that occurs by virtue of the actual existence of prompting, even when that prompting occurs in a different flow [of consciousness], has prompting and so is *with prompting.* [...]

Perceiving, experiencing, or feeling appropriately or fittingly by staying in the manner of being in the middle is *equanimity* (*upekkhā*). Alternatively, equanimity is perception (*ikkhā*) or experience that possesses (*upeta*), is joined to and not obstructed by pleasure and pain; for when pleasure and pain are not obstructions, it occurs adjoining them. *Accompanied by equanimity:* this is in the way stated. [...]

The respective arising of these eight [types of consciousness] should be understood as follows. When one joyfully enjoys the objects of the senses in association with such wrong views as "there is no danger, etc., in sense objects" or when, with a mind that is naturally sharp, without effort, one considers as intrinsically worthy (*maṅgala*) things that are seen, then the first unwholesome consciousness arises. When one does so with a mind that is sluggish and with effort, then the second arises. When wrong views are not present and one joyfully takes full pleasure in sexual intercourse or strongly desires another's wealth or takes another's goods with a mind that is naturally sharp, without effort, then the third consciousness arises. When one does so with a mind that is sluggish and with effort, then the fourth arises. When, either because of something wanting in the sense-objects or because of the absence of the other causes of happiness, they are without happiness in the four cases, then the remaining four accompanied by equanimity arise.

5. Consciousness accompanied by unhappiness, associated with aversion, and without prompting is one kind; the same with prompting is one kind; these two together are called the consciousnesses associated with aversion.

6. Consciousness accompanied by equanimity, associated with doubt is one kind; consciousness accompanied by equanimity, associated with restlessness is one kind; these two together are called the very deluded consciousnesses.

7. And so in this way twelve unwholesome consciousnesses have been given in full.

8. Those rooted in greed [can be] eightfold, those rooted in hatred twofold, and those rooted in delusion twofold—in this way the unwholesome can be twelve.

9. Eye-consciousness accompanied by equanimity, and similarly ear-consciousness, nose-consciousness, and tongue-consciousness; body-consciousness accompanied by pain, receiving consciousness accompanied by equanimity, and investigating consciousness accompanied by equanimity: these seven consciousnesses are called unwholesome-resultant consciousnesses.

10. Eye-consciousness accompanied by equanimity [...as above], and investigating consciousness accompanied by happiness: these eight consciousnesses are called wholesome-resultant unmotivated consciousnesses.

11. Five-door-adverting consciousness accompanied by equanimity; mind-door-adverting consciousness accompanied by equanimity; smile-producing consciousness accompanied by happiness: these three are called unmotivated *kiriya* consciousnesses.

12. In this way eighteen unmotivated consciousnesses have been given in full.

13. The unwholesome results are seven, the meritorious results eight, the *kiriya* consciousnesses three: hence the unmotivated are eighteen.

14. Apart from the bad and the unmotivated, consciousnesses are called beautiful; there are fifty-nine or ninety-one of them.

Commentary

In this way thirty types of consciousness as twelve unwholesome and eighteen without motivations have been indicated; next, in order to establish the designation "beautiful" for those apart from these, the words beginning *Apart from the bad and the unmotivated* are said. Apart from the [consciousnesses which are] bad because of leading to the suffering of the realms of misfortune, etc., produced by oneself, and apart from the [consciousnesses that are] without motivations because of non-association with motivations, the twenty-four sense-sphere and the thirty-five higher and transcendent [consciousnesses] come to *fifty-nine* consciousnesses; alternatively, when the eight types of transcendent consciousness have each been increased fivefold by distinction of the associated *jhāna* factors, they come to *ninety-one;* leading to beautiful qualities and being associated with the wholesome motivations of lack of greed etc., they are *called* or said to be *beautiful.*

15. Consciousness accompanied by happiness, associated with knowledge, and without prompting is one kind; the same with prompting is one kind. Consciousness accompanied by happiness, dissociated from knowledge, and without prompting is one kind; the same with prompting is one kind. Consciousness accompanied by equanimity, associated with knowledge, and without prompting is one kind; the same with prompting is one kind. Consciousness accompanied by equanimity, dissociated from knowledge, and without prompting is one kind; the same with prompting is one kind. All these eight are called wholesome consciousnesses belonging to the sense-sphere.

16. Consciousness accompanied by happiness [...as above]. All these eight are called sense-sphere resultant consciousnesses with motivations.

17. Consciousness accompanied by happiness [...as above]. All these eight are called sense-sphere *kiriya* consciousnesses with motivations.

18. And so in this way twenty-four sense-sphere wholesome, resultant, and *kiriya* consciousnesses which have motivations have been given in full.

19. By division of feeling, knowledge, and prompting, the sense-sphere meritorious, resultant and *kiriya* [consciousnesses] with motivations are reckoned as twenty-four.

20. In the sense sphere there are twenty-three results, twenty meritorious and demeritorious, and eleven *kiriya;* all together there are fifty-four.

Commentary

Now to indicate all the types of consciousness belonging to the sense sphere being grouped together, the words beginning *In the sense sphere twenty-three* are said. In the sense sphere there are seven unwholesome resultants, sixteen wholesome resultants with and without motivations, thus there are *twenty-three* resultant [consciousnesses]; there are twelve unwholesome and eight wholesome [consciousnesses] making *twenty meritorious and demeritorious* [consciousnesses]; three without motivations and eight with motivations make *eleven kiriya* [consciousnesses]; *all together* by internal division of wholesome, unwholesome, resultant and *kiriya* [consciousness], there are just *fifty-four* [consciousnesses], although they are innumerable by division of time, place and individual consciousness continuity; this is the meaning.

Bibliography and Suggested Reading

Bodhi, Bhikkhu, trans. (2000) *The Connected Discourses of the Buddha: A New Translation of the Saṃyutta Nikāya, Vol. 1.* Oxford: The Pali Text Society in association with Wisdom Publications.

Cousins, L. S. (1981) "The *Paṭṭhāna* and the Development of the Theravādin Abhidhamma." *Journal of the Pali Text Society* 9: 22–46.

Cousins, L. S. (1995) "Abhidhamma." In J. R. Hinnells, ed., *A New Dictionary of Religions.* Oxford: Blackwell.

Gethin, Rupert. (1998) *The Foundations of Buddhism.* Oxford: Oxford University Press.

Gethin, Rupert. (1992) *The Buddhist Path to Awakening: A Study of Bodhipakkhiyā Dhammā.* Leiden: Brill.

Gombrich, Richard F. (1996) *How Buddhism Began: The Conditioned Genesis of the Early Teachings.* London: Athlone Press.

Hamilton, Sue. (2000) *Early Buddhism: A New Approach.* Richmond, Surrey, England: Curzon Press.

Karunadasa, Y. (1996) *The Dhamma Theory: Philosophical Cornerstone of the Abhidhamma.* Kandy: Buddhist Publication Society.

Rescher, Nicholas. (1996) *Process Metaphysics: An Introduction to Process Philosophy.* Albany: State University of New York Press.

Ronkin, Noa. (2005) *Early Buddhist Metaphysics: The Making of a Philosophical Tradition.* Critical Studies in Buddhism Series and the Oxford Centre for Buddhist Studies Monograph Series. London: Routledge-Curzon.

Steward, Helen. (1997) *The Ontology of Mind: Events, Processes and States.* Oxford: Clarendon Press.

Wijeratne, R.P. and Rupert Gethin, trans. (2002) *The Summary of the Topics of Abhidhamma, Exposition of the Topics of Abhidhamma.* Oxford: The Pali Text Society.

2

Nāgārjuna's *Mūlamadhyamakakārikā* (*Fundamental Verses of the Middle Way*)

Chapter 24: Examination of the Four Noble Truths

Jay L. Garfield

Nāgārjuna (c. second century C.E.) is the founder of the Madhyamaka or Middle Way School of Buddhist philosophy and, with the exception of the historical Buddha himself, is the most influential philosopher in the Mahāyāna tradition. He probably lived in the lower Krishna River valley in the present state of Andhra Pradesh in India.[1] In his treatises on metaphysics and epistemology *Mūlamadhyamakakārikā* (Fundamental verses on the Middle Way), *Yuktiśaṣṭika* (Sixty verses of reasoning), *Śūnyatāsaptati* (Seventy verses on emptiness), *Vidalyasūtra* (Devastating discourse), and *Vigrahavyāvartanī* (Reply to objections), he develops the argument that all phenomena are empty of essence, but exist conventionally, interdependently, and impermanently.

That all phenomena are dependently originated is the heart of Buddhist ontological theory. In the Mahāyāna tradition, this dependency is spelled out in three ways: all phenomena are dependent for their existence on complex networks of causes and conditions; a dollar bill, for instance, is dependent on the printing press that printed it, the miners who extracted the ore out of which the metal for the press was smelted, the trees that were pulped for the paper, the United States Treasury, and so on. All wholes are dependent on their parts, and parts on the wholes they help to make up. The dollar bill depends for its existence on the particles of paper and ink that constitute it but also, for its existence as a dollar bill, on the entire economic system in

1. See Walser 2005 for biographical speculation.

which it figures. Finally, all phenomena are dependent for their identities on conceptual imputation. The dollar bill is only a dollar bill, as opposed to a bookmark, because the United States Treasury so designates it. To exist, according to Buddhist metaphysics, simply is to exist dependently in these senses, and hence to be merely conventionally existent.

To exist dependently is, importantly, to be empty of essence. For a Mādhyamika, like Nāgārjuna, this emptiness of essence is the final mode of existence of any phenomenon, its ultimate truth. For to have an essence is to exist independently, to have one's identity and to exist not in virtue of extrinsic relations, but simply in virtue of intrinsic properties. Because all phenomena are interdependent, all are empty in this sense. Just as the conventional truth about phenomena is made up by their interdependence, their ultimate truth is their emptiness. These are the two truths that Nāgārjuna adumbrates throughout his corpus.

It follows immediately that the emptiness of all phenomena that Nāgārjuna defends is not *nonexistence:* to be empty of essence is not to be empty of existence. Instead, to exist is to be empty. It also follows that emptiness is not a deeper truth hidden behind a veil of illusion. The emptiness of any phenomenon is dependent on the existence of that phenomenon, and on its dependence, which is that in which its essencelessness consists. Emptiness is itself dependent, and hence empty. This doctrine of the emptiness of emptiness, and of the identity of interdependence, or conventional truth, and emptiness, or ultimate truth, is Nāgārjuna's deepest philosophical achievement. The two truths are different from one another in that the ultimate is the object of enlightened knowledge and is liberating, while the conventional is apprehended by ordinary people through mundane cognitive processes. Nonetheless, they are in a deep sense identical. To be empty of essence is simply to exist only conventionally. The conditions of conventional existence are interdependence and impermanence, which, as we have seen, for Nāgārjuna, entail essencelessness.

This understanding of the two truths is, in turn, deeply connected to Nāgārjuna's doctrine of the emptiness of emptiness. This doctrine allows him to defend his account of the emptiness of all phenomena from the charge of nihilism—of denying that anything at all actually exists—frequently leveled, both in ancient India and in modern Western commentaries, against Madhyamaka.[2]

It might appear that the distinction between conventional and ultimate reality is tantamount to the distinction between appearance and reality, and that Nāgārjuna holds that the conventional truth is merely illusion, in virtue of being empty, while the ultimate truth—emptiness—is what is real. But Nāgārjuna argues that emptiness is also empty, that it is essenceless, and exists only conventionally as well. The conventional truth is hence no less real than the ultimate, the ultimate no more real than the conventional.

2. See Wood 1994 for a contemporary nihilistic reading.

Nāgārjuna hence strives to develop a middle path between a realism that takes real phenomena to be ultimately existent in virtue of being actual, and a nihilism that takes all phenomena to be nonexistent in virtue of being empty. Instead, he argues that reality and emptiness are coextensive, and that the only coherent mode of existence is conventional existence.

Nāgārjuna's principal treatise, *Mūlamadhyamakakārikā,* a chapter of which we present here, is the subject of numerous Indian and Tibetan commentaries, which differ among themselves regarding interpretative details. The principal Indian commentaries are composed by Buddhapālita (third century), Bhāvaviveka (fifth century), and Candrakīrti (sixth century). Among Tibetan commentaries, the most extensive is that by Tsongkhapa (fourteenth to fifteenth centuries), *Ocean of Reasoning*. Tsongkhapa follows Candrakīrti closely, but also attends to Buddhapālita, Bhāvaviveka, Avalokitavrata, and other Indian and Tibetan literature relevant to Nāgārjuna's text.

The interpretative disagreement that finds Buddhapālita and Candrakīrti on one side and Bhāvaviveka on the other is thematized in Tibetan doxographic literature as the distinction between *thal gyur pa* (translated into Sanskrit by Western commentators as *prāsaṅgika*), or reductio-wielders, and *rang rgyud pa* (translated into Sanskrit by Western commentators as *svātantrika*), or defenders of one's own position.

The principal disagreement between these two readings of Nāgārjuna's method concerns his dialectical method. Buddhapālita and Candrakīrti read him as relying exclusively on reductio arguments, refuting his opponents' positions on their own terms, but without developing any independent arguments for any ontological position of his own, in virtue of his eschewal of the project of providing an account of the fundamental nature of reality, on the grounds that there is no such nature. Bhāvaviveka and his followers, such as Avalokitavrata and Śāntarakṣita, argue on the other hand that Nāgārjuna does, at least implicitly, advance independent arguments for a substantive thesis regarding the nature of ultimate reality, namely, its emptiness.[3]

Nāgārjuna is a master dialectician, who often responds to an opponent who levels a reductio argument against Nāgārjuna that not only is he himself not committed to the absurd conclusion the opponent foists on him, but that the opponent himself is committed to that very conclusion, thus turning a reductio aimed at his own position into one aimed at his opponent. Chapter 24 of *Mūlamadhyamakakārikā* presents a particularly dramatic instance of this rhetorical strategy. This chapter appears late in the text, and represents the climax of an extended analysis of reality in terms of emptiness. Though its nominal topic is the status of the four noble truths, the doctrinal foundation of all of Buddhism, in fact it is about emptiness itself and the relationship between the two truths.

In this chapter, Nāgārjuna imagines an opponent charging him with nihilism and with contradicting all of Buddhist doctrine in virtue of arguing that

3. For more detail on this debate, see McClintock and Dreyfus 2002.

all things are empty. In reply, Nāgārjuna argues that one can only understand Buddhist doctrine and reality in terms of emptiness, and that it is the opponent who denies emptiness who is in fact a nihilist and a heretic.

The chapter divides roughly into six major sections. Verses 1–6 represent the opponent's attack, and level the charges of heresy and nihilism. The opponent argues that Nāgārjuna, in asserting that all things are empty, denies the reality of suffering, its causes, its cessation, and the path, and hence of all that is important to Buddhism, and all that is real. Verses 7–15 castigate the opponent for misunderstanding Nāgārjuna's view. Nāgārjuna asserts the doctrine of the two truths and indicates that by understanding their relation to one another the nihilist reading of emptiness can be avoided, but that a failure to do so entails nihilism. In a memorable metaphor, he charges the opponent with adopting the very nihilist position with which he charges Nāgārjuna.

Verses 16–19, the heart of the chapter, argue that emptiness and dependent arising (ultimate and conventional truth) are identical, and that all conventional existents are empty. Pay special attention to 18, in which Nāgārjuna equates emptiness and dependent arising and asserts that each is conventionally existent, as is the relation between them. Verses 20–35 demonstrate that Buddhist doctrine can only be understood in the context of emptiness. Nāgārjuna goes through each of the four truths, the three Buddhist refuge objects (Buddha, Dharma, and Sangha) and the goal of the attainment of Buddhahood, showing that each presupposes emptiness for its cogency. Verses 36–39 demonstrate that emptiness is the only coherent ontology on general consideration, and verse 40 reconnects the entire analysis to the four noble truths.[4]

Translation

1. If all this is empty,
   There would be neither arising nor ceasing,
   And for you, it follows that
   The Four Noble Truths do not exist.
2. If the Four Noble Truths did not exist,
   Then understanding, abandonment,

4. There are several English translations of the entire *Mūlamadhyamakakārikā:* Streng 1967; Inada 1970, Kalupahana 1986, Garfield 1995, Batchelor 2000. A partial translation of Candrakīrti's commentary, *Prasannapadā,* is available in English (Sprung 1979), and a complete translation of Tsongkhapa's commentary (*Ocean of Reasoning*) is available (Tsongkhapa 2006). The following translation originally appeared in Garfield, 1995. We gratefully acknowledge permission to republish this work.

Meditation and realization
Would not be tenable.

3. If these things did not exist,
The four fruits would not exist.
Without the four fruits, there would be no attainers of the fruits,
Nor would there be practitioners of the path.

4. If so, without the eight kinds of person,
There would be no sangha.
If the Four Noble Truths do not exist,
There can be no exalted Dharma.

5. If there is no Dharma and sangha,
How can there be a buddha?
If emptiness is conceived in this way,
The existence of the three jewels is undermined.

6. Hence you undermine the existence of the fruits;
As well as the profane;
The Dharma itself;
And all mundane conventions.

7. Here we say that you do not understand
Emptiness, or the purpose of emptiness,
Or the meaning of emptiness.
As a consequence you are harmed by it.

8. The Buddha's teaching of the Dharma
Is based on two truths:
A truth of worldly convention
And an ultimate truth.

9. Those who do not understand
The distinction between these two truths
Do not understand
The Buddha's profound teaching.

10. Without depending on the conventional truth
The meaning of the ultimate cannot be taught.
Without understanding the meaning of the ultimate,
Nirvana is not achieved.

11. By a misperception of emptiness
A person of little intelligence is destroyed.
Like a snake incorrectly seized
Or like a spell incorrectly cast.

12. Knowing that the Dharma is
Deep and difficult for simpletons to understand,
The Buddha's mind despaired of
Being able to teach it.

13. Since the absurd consequences you adduce
Are not relevant to emptiness,
Your rejection of emptiness
Is not relevant to me.

14. For him to whom emptiness makes sense,
Everything makes sense.
For him to whom emptiness does not make sense,
Nothing becomes sense.

15. When you foist on us
All of your errors,
You are like a man who has mounted his horse
And has forgotten that very horse.

16. If you regard all things
As existing in virtue of their essence,
Then you will regard all things
As being without causes and conditions.

17. Effects and causes;
And agent, instrument, and action;
And arising and ceasing;
And the effects will be undermined.

18. That which is dependent origination
Is explained to be emptiness.
That, being a dependent designation,
Is itself the middle way.

19. There does not exist anything
That is not dependently arisen.
Therefore there does not exist anything
That is not empty.

20. If all this were nonempty, as in your view,
Then there would be no arising and ceasing.
It would follow that the Four Noble Truths
Would not exist.

21. If it is not dependently arisen,
How could suffering come to be?
Suffering has been taught to be impermanent,
And so cannot exist through its essence.

22. If something exists through its essence,
How could it ever be arisen?
It follows that for one who denies emptiness
There could be no sources of suffering.

23. If suffering existed essentially,
Its cessation would not exist.

So if one takes it to exist essentially,
One denies cessation.

24. If the path had an essence,
Practice would not be tenable.
If this path is to be practiced,
It cannot have an essence.

25. If suffering, arising and
Ceasing are nonexistent,
By what path could one seek
To obtain the cessation of suffering?

26. If it is not understood
Through its essence,
How could it come to be understood?
Doesn't essence endure?

27. In the same way, the complete understanding of
The activities of relinquishing, realizing,
Meditating and the four fruits
Would not make sense.

28. For an essentialist,
How could it be possible
To attain those fruits
That are already essentially unattained?

29. Without the fruits, there would be no
Attainers of the fruits or practitioners.
If the eight kinds of person did not exist,
There would be no sangha.

30. If the Noble Truths did not exist
The noble Dharma would not exist.
If there were neither Dharma nor sangha,
How could a buddha come to exist?

31. For you, it would follow absurdly that a Buddha
Would be independent of enlightenment.
And for you, it would follow absurdly that
Enlightenment would be independent of a buddha.

32. For you, one who is
Essentially unenlightened,
Even by practicing the path to enlightenment
Could not achieve enlightenment.

33. Nobody could ever perform
Virtuous or non-virtuous actions.
If all this were nonempty, what could one do?
What can one with an essence do?

34. For you, even without virtuous or non-virtuous causes
There would be an effect.
According to you there is no effect
Arisen from virtuous or non-virtuous causes.

35. If for you, an effect arose
From virtuous or non-virtuous causes,
Then, having arisen from virtuous or non-virtuous causes,
How could that effect be nonempty?

36. Those who deny emptiness,
Which is dependent origination,
Undermine all of
The mundane conventions.

37. To deny emptiness is to assert that
No action would be possible;
That there can be action without effort;
And that there can be an agent without action.

38. If there were essence, all beings
Would be birthless, deathless,
And eternally enduring.
They would be void of a variety of states.

39. If they were nonempty,
Then there would be neither achievement of that which has not been achieved;
Nor the act of ending suffering;
Nor the abandonment of all of the afflictions.

40. Whoever sees dependent arising
Also sees suffering
And its arising
And its cessation, as well as the path.

Bibliography and Suggested Reading

Batchelor, Stephen. (2000) *Verses from the Center.* New York: Riverhead.

Garfield, Jay. (1995) *Fundamental Wisdom of the Middle Way: Nāgārjuna's Mūlamadhyamakakārikā.* New York: Oxford University Press.

Inada, Kenneth. (1970) *Nāgārjuna: A Translation of his Mūlamadhyamakakārikā* with an Introductory Essay. Tokyo: The Hokuseido Press.

Kalupahana, David. (1986) *Mūlamadhyamakakārikā of Nāgārjuna: The Philosophy of the Middle Way.* Albany: State University of New York Press.

McClintock, S., and G. Dreyfus, eds. (2002) *The Svātantrika-Prāsaṅgika Distinction: What Difference Does a Difference Make?* Boston: Wisdom.

Sprung, Mervyn. (1979) *Lucid Exposition of the Middle Way: The Essential Chapters from the Prasannapadā of Candrakīrti*. London: Routledge and Kegan Paul.

Streng, Frederick. (1967) *Emptiness: A Study in Religious Meaning*. Nashville: Abdingdon Press.

Tsongkhapa. (2006) *Ocean of Reasoning: A Great Commentary on Nāgārjuna's Mūlamadhyamakakārikā*. Translated by Ngawang Samten and Jay Garfield. New York: Oxford University Press.

Walser, Joseph. (2005) *Nāgārjuna in Context: Mahāyāna Buddhism and Early Indian Culture*. New York: Columbia University Press.

Wood, Thomas E. (1994) *Nāgārjunian Disputations: A Philosophical Journey through an Indian Looking-Glass*. Honolulu: University of Hawai'i Press.

3

Vasubandhu's *Trisvabhāvanirdeśa* (*Treatise on the Three Natures*)

Jay L. Garfield

The *Trisvabhāvanirdeśa* (*Rang bzhin gsum nges par bstan pa*) is one of Vasubandhu's short treatises (the others being the *Treatise in Twenty Stanzas* [*Viṃsatikā*] and the *Treatise in Thirty Stanzas* [*Triṃśikākirikā*]) expounding his Cittamātra, or mind-only philosophy. Vasubandhu and his older brother Asaṅga are regarded as the founders and principal exponents of this Buddhist idealist school, which developed in the fourth or fifth century C.E. as the major philosophical rival within the Mahāyāna Buddhist tradition to the older Madhyamaka tradition. The latter school, founded by Nāgārjuna, urges the emptiness—the lack of essence or substantial, independent reality—of all things, including both external phenomena and mind. Vasubandhu, however, reinterprets the emptiness of the object as being its lack of *external* reality, and its purely mind-dependent, or ideal, status. At the same time, however, he argues that the foundational mind is nonempty since it truly exists as the substratum of the apparent reality represented in our experience. The position is hence a kind of idealism akin to, but different in important ways from, the idealisms defended by such Western philosophers as Berkeley, Kant, and Schopenhauer.

The text introduces the fundamental doctrine of Buddhist idealism, and clarifies in remarkably short compass its relations to the other principal doctrines of that school—that all external appearances are merely ideal and originate from potentials for experience carried in the mind. The central topic of the text is the exposition of how this view entails the cittamātra theory of the three natures—the view that every object of experience is characterized by three distinct but interdependent natures. Vasubandhu's idealism is distinctive in its insistence that a coherent idealism requires the positing of these three natures—the *parikalpita* or imagined nature, the *paratantra* or dependent nature, and the *parinispanna* or consummate nature—and in its subtle analysis of the complex relations between the natures themselves, involving the thesis of their surface diversity but deep unity.

The translation into English of the terms denoting the three natures is no straightforward matter. Each denotes a *nature* (Tib.: *rang bzhin,* Skt.: *svabhāva*). But each of the three qualifiers added to this term to denote one of the three natures creates a subtly ambiguous compound, and plays on this ambiguity form part of the structure of Vasubandhu's ingenious verse treatise. On the one hand, each characterizes the nature itself—part of what it is to be a phenomenon. On the other hand, each characterizes the relation of the subject to the phenomenon, or the character of the subjectivity that constitutes the representation of the phenomenon. The text is hence simultaneously an essay in ontology and in phenomenology. As far as Vasubandhu is concerned, what it is to be a *phenomenon* is to be an *object* of a mind, and this treatise is an exploration of what it is to be an object so conceived. So questions about subjectivity and questions concerning the ontology of the object are closely intertwined.

"Imagined" translates the Tibetan *kun brtags* or Sanskrit *parikalpita.* These terms connote *construction* by the mind more than they do nonexistence—hallucination rather than fiction. But this simile can be misleading. To be imagined in this sense is not to be hallucinatory as opposed to being real—it is to be constructed as an object by the operation of the mind. "Other-dependent" translates *gzhan gyi dbang* or *paratantra.* Something that is other-dependent in this sense exists only in and through dependence on another thing. In this case, the emphasis will be that phenomena exist in dependence on the mind and its processes.

I use "consummate" to translate *yongs su grub pa* or *parinispanna.* This is the most difficult of these three terms to translate. Others have used "perfect," "perfected," "thoroughly established," "thoroughly existent," "completed," and "ultimate."[1] Each of these choices has merit, and the variety of options illustrates the range of associations the term has in Tibetan or Sanskrit. When affixed to "nature," it connotes on the objective side the nature an object has when it is thoroughly understood. On the subjective side, it connotes the nature apparent to one who is fully accomplished intellectually and meditatively. It represents the highest and most complete understanding of a phenomenon.

There is a grammatical feature of the Sanskrit terms that deserves mention as well. *Parikalpita* and *parinispanna* are each past participles, whereas

1. Kochumuttom (1982), Thurman (1984), Wood (1991), John Powers (*Introduction to Tibetan Buddhism* [Ithaca, NY: Snow Lion Publications, 1995]), Anacker (1984), Nagao, G. (1991), and Cabezon (1992), respectively.

paratantra is nominal. *Paratantra-svabhāva,* the dependent nature, hence has a special place in the trio as a kind of basis of the other two. The central doctrine of Buddhist ontology is that all phenomena are dependently arisen. The dependent nature captures this fact. It hence has a claim to a *kind* of primacy or ultimate status. Imagination, though, is something that is *done.* The imagined nature that we ordinarily experience is a superimposition on the dependent nature. When we imagine things, we take them to be objects distinct from, or dually related to, our own subjectivity; to exist independently, and externally. Consummating our understanding is also something that is *done.* When we achieve consummate knowledge, we stop imagining, and experience the dependent nature as it is, empty of the duality, independence, and externality we once imagined it to have. The consummate nature of things is the fact that they are not as they are imagined to be.

Things appear to us as independently existent. But the objects of our experience, as we experience them, exist only in dependence on our minds. Without our subjectivity, there can be no objects. But given their actual mind-dependent status, of which we can be aware through careful philosophical reflection or through extensive meditative accomplishment, we can say that these *apparent things,* such as independently existent elephants and coffee cups, are always nonexistent. States of mind exist in their place, *experiences of elephants and coffee cups,* masquerading as independent phenomena. *That* nonexistence—the nonexistence of the apparent reality—is the consummate nature that all such phenomena have.

Vasubandhu also distinguishes the mind in its role as transcendental subject from its role as object, as it appears to itself. In the first aspect, to which Vasubandhu refers as the "foundation consciousness" (Tib.: *kun gzhi,* Skt.: *ālaya-vijñāna*), the mind functions as the condition of the appearance of phenomena, and hence as the ground of the possibility of the imagined and other-dependent natures. But in its second aspect—the "emerged consciousness" (Tib.: *'jug pa'i shes pa,* Skt.: *pavṛtti-vijñāna*)—the mind exists as the object of introspection, and is conditioned both by external phenomena that appear in perception and by its own phenomena. Hence it constantly evolves, and emerges in new states as a consequence of experience. The seven aspects of the mind to which Vasubandhu alludes in verse 6 are the five sensory consciousnesses, the introspective consciousness apprehending the self as object, and the reflective consciousness of the transcendental subject of experience.

Vasubandhu also thematizes subject/object duality in this text, arguing that although ordinary subjectivity presents its objects as distinct from itself, this is illusory, and the consummate nature is in fact nondual. His account is subtle and is always pitched in both a metaphysical and a phenomenological voice. He asks of each of the natures in what sense it implicates such a duality as part of the structure of the object of experience and in what sense it is in fact nondual. But he also asks these questions regarding the nature of the corresponding object of subjectivity itself. So in each case he asks whether, or in what sense, in a subject considering things *as other-dependent,* and so on...there is such a duality, as well as asking whether, or in what sense, each nature implicates such a duality in the structure of the object.

Consider, for example, a teacup from the standpoint of its other-dependent nature: From this standpoint, the cup as I experience it, the only cup I see, exists as an entity dependent on the mind. The cup so-considered certainly exists: It exists as a mental phenomenon—as a representation. On the other hand, we can ask what the objective character[2] of that representation is. Then the answer is simple, and takes us back to the imagined nature: The cup considered *objectively* is the real, independent cup of naïve understanding, which, when we understand it from the standpoint of the dependent nature, does not exist at all, just in virtue of the fact that from this standpoint it is dependent. So, from the perspective of the dependent nature, the cup—the dependent mental phenomenon we mistake for a real cup—like the refraction pattern we mistake for water in a mirage—exists. But that real cup that is the *content* of that mental episode does not.

Now we come to the consummate nature of our cup. The cup we have been considering all along, whether from the standpoint of the imagined or the dependent nature, is, in an important and common sense, dual in nature. In its imagined nature, it is an independent object of mind, and so is distinct from the subject which apprehends it. But in its dependent nature, as an episode of mind, it is still, as a mere episode or mental act, distinct from the mind, which is its agent or subject. In the consummate nature, this duality vanishes. For the consummate nature of the cup is the very fact of its illusory status—that it is nothing other than an aspect of mind. Hence the apparent, dual, cup is, in its consummate nature (or, equivalently—from the point of view of one of consummate attainment) utterly nonexistent. *But that nonduality really exists.* That *is* the final nature of the cup.[3] And in this sense, the consummate nature embraces both existence and nonexistence: the nonexistence of the cup as dual is its true existence as nondually related to the mind apprehending it. This consideration of duality and nonduality as the mediators of existence and nonexistence in the consummate is a distinctive feature of *Trisvabhāvanirdeśa.*

All of this is central to Vasubandhu's creative union of ontology and phenomenology. Vasubandhu's characterization of the status of the objects of experience is at the same time self-consciously a characterization of the character of subjectivity itself. Not only does Vasubandhu argue that we can only make sense of objects if we ascribe to them these triune natures,

2. In the scholastic or Cartesian sense—the character of the mental object itself.

3. Note how this account of the ultimate nature of a phenomenon contrasts with that given by Mādhyamika philosophers such as Nāgārjuna or Candrakīrti, according to whom not even the emptiness of the cup can be said to exist in this sense. It is at this crucial point in ontology that Cittamātra and Madhyamaka are utterly discontinuous.

but he also argues that a complete account of experience—especially of the experience of a sophisticated and accomplished philosopher or meditator—requires an account of three distinct aspects of subjectivity, which are related to one another as are the three natures themselves. Our experience involves a superimposition of illusory externality and independence on states of consciousness; deep reflection allows us to understand and to eliminate this illusion.

This phenomenology is crucial to the soteriological purport of the system. For this is not speculative philosophy for its own sake but a philosophical system designed to guide a practitioner to buddhahood in order that he or she can work to alleviate the suffering of all sentient beings. And buddhahood requires a clear understanding of the nature of one's own mind, of the objects of one's own experience, and of the nature of dependent origination that makes up their reality, as well as the unreality of our misleading experience of them, which is the source of all suffering.

Trisvabhāvanirdeśa is unique in Vasubandhu's corpus in its exposition of idealism as involving the doctrine of the three natures, in its detailed analysis of the natures themselves, and in its exploration of their relations to one another. In *Viṃsatikā-kārikā,* Vasubandhu clearly defends idealism against a series of objections but does not explicitly articulate the roles of the three natures in his idealistic theory or expound its structure. In *Triṃśikākirikā,* Vasubandhu explores the relation between the three natures and the three naturelessnesses (naturelessness with respect to characteristic [*laksaḥa-nisvabhāvatā, mtshan nyid ngo bo nyid med*], naturelessness with respect to production [*utpatti-nisvabhāvatā, skye ba ngo bo nyid med*], and ultimate naturelessness [*paramārtha-nisvabhāvatā, don dam pa'i ngo bo nyid med]*) adumbrated in the *Saṃdhinirmocana-sūtra* but does not explore their relation to idealism, *per se,* or their relations to one another. It is only in the *Trisvabhāvanirdeśa* that he explicitly analyses idealism as implicating the three natures, and explains in detail how they are interconnected.

Sthiramati, in his commentary on *Triṃśikākirikā (Triṃśikākirikā-bhāsya)* argues that the three natures and the three naturelessnesses are equivalent. His understanding of the three natures as equivalent to the three naturelessnesses of the *Saṃdhinirmocana-sūtra* is adopted uncritically by such Tibetan doxographers as Tsongkhapa[4] and Khedrupjey (mKhas grub rJe).[5] The adoption of this commentarial tradition, which emphasizes the homogeneity of the *Saṃdhinirmocana-sūtra* with Vasubandhu's and Asaṇga's thought, along with the exposition of the three natures as presented in *Triṃśikākirikā* and *Viṃsatikā,* reinforces the elision of this more mature and explicit articulation of Vasubandhu's theory from subsequent developments of Yogācāra. The emphasis of the dominant Madhyamaka school on naturelessness as a fundamental metaphysical tenet and its need to see Yogācāra

4. See *Legs bshad snyings po,* translated in Thurman 1984.
5. See *sTong thun chen mo,* translated in Cabezon (1992).

as the penultimate step to its own standpoint lends further impetus to this tendency to assimilate these two doctrines. Of all of the Mādhyamikas, only Candrakīrti really takes the *trisvabhāva* doctrine itself seriously as a target for critique (*dBu ma la jugs pa, Madhyamakāvatāra*).[6]

The thirty-eight verses of the text divide neatly into six sections. In the first six verses, Vasubandhu introduces the three natures and provides a preliminary characterization of each. He emphasizes that the other-dependent is experienced in ordinary consciousness through imagination, and that the consummate nature is the fact that that imaginary nature is nonexistent. In verses 7–9 he sketches two schemata for thinking about the character of mind from the standpoint of three nature theory. On the one hand there is the foundation consciousness, which is the repository of the seeds of experience and action, and on the other hand there are the constantly evolving introspectible sensory consciousnesses that we experience through the ripening of these potentials.

Verses 10–21 develop a dialectically complex and elegant discussion of how to view the polar pairs of existence/nonexistence, duality/unity, and affliction/nonaffliction in relation to each of the three natures, culminating in a discussion of the senses in which the natures are identical to one another and the senses in which they are different. For each nature, there is a sense in which it is real and a sense in which it is unreal; a sense in which it issues in subject-object duality and a sense in which awareness of it deconstructs that duality. The imagined and the other-dependent are essentially involved in affliction; the consummate is free from all affliction.

Verses 22–25 present the natures hierarchically from the standpoint of pedagogy and soteriology. The imagined nature is easiest to understand and most familiar to us, and so is presented first. Understanding the imagined nature leads one to understand the dependent, and to separate the dependent from the imagined, leading to an understanding of the consummate.

Vasubandhu presents the famous simile of the hallucinatory elephant conjured by the stage magician in verses 26–34. This is probably the most famous and often-cited moment in this text. In a vivid and simple image, Vasubandhu presents a way of understanding the three natures, their relation to one another, to idealism, and of the phenomenology they suggest to Buddhist soteriology. We are asked to imagine a magic show in which a magician, using some simple props and a mantra, induces the audience to see a nonexistent elephant. The elephant, which is seen, and is the intentional object of the perceptual and cognitive states of the crowd, is the imagined nature—it exists as illusion, gives rise to affective and conative states, to other cognitive states, and so on, but is not real outside of the minds that perceive it, and does not exist as it appears. The percept, as opposed to the elephant, is a real cognitive state that is in fact empty of the elephant. That is the dependent nature, mistaken for an elephant, but really only a cognitive

6. Translated in Huntington and Wangchen 1992 (see esp. pp. 162–168).

process. The fact that there is no elephant at all is the consummate nature of the elephant. All subject-object duality in the experience is illusory, and is tied up with the imagined. The foundation consciousness is compared to the mantra. It is the source of the illusion. Reality, the dependent nature stripped of all superimposition, is compared to the props used by the magician. They are not seen at all in the experience of the elephant, only once the mantra has stopped working or, less metaphorically, when the foundation consciousness is purged of all seeds of delusion.

The concluding four verses are devoted to the soteriological implications of the text. Understanding the nature of our phenomenology and of the nature of reality enables the cessation of the suffering that arises from attachment to and aversion from illusory objects, and leads to liberation.[7]

Translation

1. The imagined, the other-dependent and
   The consummate:
   These are the three natures
   Which should be deeply understood.
2. Arising through dependence on conditions and
   Existing through being imagined,
   It is therefore called other-dependent
   And is said to be merely imaginary.
3. The eternal non-existence
   Of what appears in the way it appears,
   Since it is never otherwise,
   Is known as the nature of the consummate.
4. If anything appears, it is imagined.
   The way it appears is as duality.
   What is the consequence of its non-existence?
   The fact of non-duality!
5. What is the imagination of the non-existent?
   Since what is imagined absolutely never
   Exists in the way it is imagined,
   It is mind that constructs that illusion.

7. This translation is from the Tibetan text. The principal version used is that in the sDe dge edition of the Tibetan canon (Si 12a–14a). The Peking edition was used for comparison, and is in complete concordance. Anacker 1984 and Wood 1991 each reprint the original Sanskrit text. This translation originally appeared in Jay L. Garfield, *Empty Words: Buddhist Philosophy and Cross-Cultural Interpretation* (New York: Oxford University Press, 2002), pp. 130–135. We gratefully acknowledge permission to republish this work.

6. Because it is a cause and an effect,
   The mind has two aspects.
   As the foundation consciousness it creates thought;
   Known as the emerged consciousness it has seven aspects.
7. The first, because it collects the seeds
   Of suffering is called "mind."
   The second, because of the constant emergence
   Of the various aspects of things is so called.
8. One should think of the illusory non-existent
   As threefold:
   Completely ripened, grasped as other,
   And as appearance.
9. The first, because it itself ripens,
   Is the root consciousness.
   The others are emergent consciousness,
   Having emerged from the conceptualization of seer and seen.
10. Existence and non-existence, duality and unity;
    Freedom from affliction and afflicted;
    Through characteristics, and through distinctions,
    These natures are known to be profound.
11. Since it appears as existent
    Though it is non-existent,
    The imagined nature
    Is said to have the characteristics of existence and non-existence.
12. Since it exists as an illusory entity
    And is non-existent in the way it appears
    The other-dependent nature
    Is said to have the characteristics of existence and non-existence.
13. Since it is the non-existence of duality
    And exists as non-duality
    The consummate nature
    Is said to have the characteristics of existence and non-existence.
14. Moreover, since as imagined there are two aspects,
    But existence and non-existence are unitary,
    The nature imagined by the ignorant
    Is said to be both dual and unitary.
15. Since as an object of thought it is dual,
    But as a mere appearance it is unitary,
    The other-dependent nature
    Is said to be both dual and unitary.
16. Since it is the essence of dual entities
    And is a unitary non-duality,

The consummate nature
Is said to be both dual and unitary.

17. The imagined and the other-dependent
Are said to be characterized by misery (due to ignorant craving).
The consummate is free of
The characteristic of desire.

18. Since the former has the nature of a false duality
And the latter is the non-existence of that nature,
The imagined and the consummate
Are said not to be different in characteristic.

19. Since the former has the nature of non-duality,
And the latter has the nature of non-existent duality,
The consummate and the imagined
Are said not to be different in characteristic.

20. Since the former is deceptive in the way it appears,
And the latter has the nature of its not being that way,
The other-dependent and the consummate
Are said not to be different in characteristic.

21. Since the former has the nature of a non-existent duality,
And the latter is its non-existence in the way it appears,
The other-dependent and the consummate
Are said not to be different in characteristic.

22. But conventionally,
The natures are explained in order and
Based on that one enters them
In a particular order, it is said.

23. The imagined is entirely conventional.
The other-dependent is attached to convention.
The consummate, cutting convention,
Is said to be of a different nature.

24. Having first entered into the non-existence of duality
Which is the dependent, one understands
The non-existent duality
Which is the imagined.

25. Then one enters the consummate.
Its nature is the non-existence of duality.
Therefore it is explained
To be both existent and non-existent.

26. These three natures
Have the characteristics of being non-cognizable and non-dual.
One is completely non-existent; the second is therefore non-existent.
The third has the nature of that non-existence.

27. Like an elephant that appears
Through the power of a magician's mantra—
Only the percept appears,
The elephant is completely non-existent.

28. The imagined nature is the elephant;
The other-dependent nature is the visual percept;
The non-existence of the elephant therein
Is explained to be the consummate.

29. Through the root consciousness
The nonexistent duality appears.
But since the duality is completely non-existent,
There is only a percept.

30. The root consciousness is like the mantra.
Reality can be compared to the wood.
Imagination is like the perception of the elephant.
Duality can be seen as the elephant.

31. When one understands how things are,
Perfect knowledge, abandonment,
And accomplishment—
These three characteristics are simultaneously achieved.

32. Knowledge is non-perception;
Abandonment is non-appearance;
Attainment is accomplished through non-dual perception.
That is direct manifestation.

33. Through the non-perception of the elephant,
The vanishing of its percept occurs;
And so does the perception of the piece of wood.
This is how it is in the magic show.

34. In the same way through the non-perception of duality
There is the vanishing of duality.
When it vanishes completely,
Non-dual awareness arises.

35. Through perceiving correctly,
Through seeing the non-referentiality of mental states,
Through following the three wisdoms,
One will effortlessly attain liberation.

36. Through the perception of mind-only
One achieves the non-perception of objects;
Through the non-perception of objects
There is also the non-perception of mind.

37. Through the non-duality of perception,
Arises the perception of the fundamental nature of reality.

Through the perception of the fundamental nature of reality
Arises the perception of the radiant.

38. Through the perception of the radiant,
And through achieving the three supreme Buddha-bodies,
And through possessing Bodhi:
Having achieved this, the sage will benefit him/herself and others.

Bibliography and Suggested Reading

Anacker, Stefan. (1984) *Seven Works of Vasubandhu, the Buddhist Psychological Doctor.* New Delhi: Motilal Banarsidass.

Cabezón, José. (1992) *A Dose of Emptiness: An Annotated Translation of the Stong thun chen mo of Mkhas grub dge legs dpal bzang.* Albany: State University of New York Press.

Huntington, C. W., with Geshe Ngawang Wangchen. (1989) *The Emptiness of Emptiness: An Introduction to Early Indian Mādhyamika.* Honolulu: University of Hawai'i Press.

Kochumuttom, Thomas. (1982) *The Buddhist Doctrine of Experience: A New Translation and Interpretation of the Works of Vasubandhu the Yogācārin.* New Delhi: Motilal Banarsidass.

Nagao, Gadjin. (1991) *Mādhyamika and Yogācāra: A Study of Mahāyāna Philosophies.* Albany: State University of New York Press.

Thurman, Robert. (1984) *Tsong Khapa's Speech of Gold in the Essence of True Eloquence.* Princeton: Princeton University Press.

Williams, Paul. (1989) *Mahāyāna Buddhism: The Doctrinal Foundations.* London: Routledge.

Wood, Thomas. (1991) *Mind Only: A Philosophical and Doctrinal Analysis of Vijñanavāda.* Honolulu: University of Hawai'i Press.

4

Śāntarakṣita's "Neither-One-Nor-Many" Argument from *Madhyamakālaṃkāra* (*The Ornament of the Middle Way*)

A Classical Buddhist Argument on the Ontological Status of Phenomena

James Blumenthal

The central tenet of the Madhyamaka School of Mahāyāna Buddhist thought is that all phenomena are empty of any essential unchanging nature. The term "emptiness" is said to properly describe the ontological character of all things. One of the classical arguments used by philosophers of the Madhyamaka School to demonstrate this emptiness, this lack of any essence, any intrinsic nature, any enduring fixed identity, or any absolute mode of being in persons or phenomena whatsoever is the "neither-one-nor-many" argument. Though it has been utilized in slightly varying forms by a number of great Madhyamaka thinkers, including Śrigupta, and Atiśa, the quintessential exposition of the neither-one-nor-many argument is found in *The Ornament of the Middle Way* (*Madhyamakālaṃkāra*), a text by the late period Indian Buddhist philosopher Śāntarakṣita (725–788).

The argument (stanza 1) posits that there can be no ultimate nature or essence in things because nothing has a fundamentally unitary or manifold nature. In other words, since anything that has a nature must have either an ultimately unitary or manifold nature—the two being inclusive of all possible alternatives for things with a nature—and since nothing has a unitary or manifold nature, therefore, phenomena must not have any nature at all. Following this broad-based statement of his argument, Śāntarakṣita proceeds to apply this reasoning to all instances in which his philosophical rivals, both Buddhist and non-Buddhist, have claimed that some things, such as persons or phenomena, do have a unitary, inherent nature (stanzas 2–60). Śāntarakṣita then turns (stanza 61) to the question of whether or not entities asserted by his opponents to have a nature can possess a manifold nature. There he argues that since the existence of a manifold nature would depend on the aggregation of true singularities, and there are no true singularities, there must also be no true manifold nature in any entity either. Because singular and manifold natures are inclusive of all possibilities for entities that have a nature, one must conclude that no entity whatsoever has any inherent nature.

A Brief Analysis of the Application of the Argument

Śāntarakṣita first applies the neither-one-nor-many argument to the non-Buddhist Sāṃkhya system (stanza 2), which asserts the existence of *Prakṛti,* a Fundamental Nature or creator God that is claimed to be the singular, permanent, uncaused, and unobstructed absolute cause of all that exists. Śāntarakṣita argues that if there is a singular, permanent, unobstructed cause of phenomena, then all phenomenal effects should exist at all times. There should be no periodic arising and ceasing of objects, since the cause of their existence would always be present and never change. If the cause of their existence never ceases, it would be illogical for the effects, the existent phenomena of the world, to ever cease, to be impermanent, or to only occasionally arise since the unchanging, unobstructed cause of such effects would always be present. But we know from direct experience that phenomena arise and cease over time. Thus, the existence of such an inherently singular and unchanging absolute cause of the phenomenal world is contradicted by our direct experience.

Śāntarakṣita then uses the neither-one-nor-many argument to critique the Vaibhāśika assertion of three types of truly singular phenomena: uncompounded objects of wisdom known by the knowledge that arises in the meditative equipoise of a yogi, uncompounded space, and uncompounded infinitesimally small partless particles (stanzas 3–15). With regard to the first example, the object of wisdom of the meditative equipoise of a yogi could not be permanent and singular and also related to successive moments of consciousness, as Vaibhāśikas claim, because successive moments of consciousness are changing and distinct. If the object of wisdom were enduring and related to multiple distinct moments of consciousness, then it could not be truly or inherently single since there would be part related to moment number 1 of consciousness, part related to moment number 2 of consciousness, and so on.[1]

1. Such objects of knowledge could even fall into the logical fallacy of being cognized out of temporal order if they are truly singular, since what is cognized in moment number 2 of consciousness would be the same as what is cognized in moment number 1 of consciousness and moment number 3 of consciousness. This is the case because if such an object of wisdom is inherently singular, it cannot have a relationship with different moments in time since that would entail the object having parts relating to distinct moments, thus undermining its true singularity.

Śāntarakṣita again uses a related line of reasoning to refute the existence of inherently singular and infinitesimally small partless particles that are asserted by the Vaibhāśika school to be the building blocks of gross phenomena (stanzas 11–15). Śāntarakṣita's examination begins by questioning precisely how inherently singular particles can combine with one another. The three exhaustive alternatives for ways of combining, according to Śāntarakṣita, are that the first particle has others joining it from various directions, surrounding it and touching, or surrounding it and not touching. Each of these alternatives requires that the central particle have others around it in various directions in order for them to combine into gross objects. Thus, there must be a particle above, one below, one to the east, one to the west, and so on. If they combine from various directions in this way, then the central particle must have a part facing above, a part facing below, a part facing to the east, and so on. And if that were the case, it could not be truly singular, due to the presence of parts. The only way truly singular partless particles could combine is to occupy the exact same inherently singular point in space—they must be directionally partless—and that would undermine the possibility of gross, spatially expansive objects such as books, chairs, land, and water, and so on. Therefore, there must be no inherently existent partless particles, and thus, partless particles must not be the building blocks of the gross phenomenal world.

Śāntarakṣita then (stanzas 16–21) introduces his analysis of the relationship between subjects, or consciousness, and objects by examining the topic of self-cognizing cognition (*svasaṃvedana, rang rig*).[2] This analysis of the Sautrāntika manner of accepting self-cognizing cognition begins by defining this self-cognizing or reflexively aware quality as the very nature of consciousness (stanza 16). Śāntarakṣita then critiques the Sautrāntika view of consciousness as self-cognizing, partless, and inherently singular *and* also distinct from external objects. Śāntarakṣita finds both assertions—the inherently unitary quality of the mind, and the externality of objects of consciousness—to be problematic. He argues that, if a consciousness that is self-cognizing is also truly singular, then the knower (i.e. the consciousness), the act of knowing, and the known (i.e. the object of consciousness) must all truly be one. Even the known, the objects of consciousness that are said to be distinct from it, must be indistinct from consciousness, since consciousness is partless and they have a relationship with consciousness. That which is truly singular cannot be related with something from which it is distinct, because then it would be manifold, having parts related to that which is distinct from it. Maintaining such a position would therefore be illogical.

2. The term has also been translated as "reflexive awareness," "reflexive consciousness," "self-awareness," and "self-knowing consciousness," among many others. Each of these terms captures nuances of the meaning of this difficult technical term, and depending on context and specific usage, one may be more appropriate than the other.

It holds something explicitly explained to be three (knower, knowing, and known), and determined to necessarily be manifold on analysis, to be one. And it demands a relationship of identity between that which is distinct from consciousness and consciousness itself. Śāntarakṣita, thus, is criticizing both the inherent singularity and the tenability of external objects in one sweeping argument.

Śāntarakṣita goes on (stanzas 22–34) to investigate and criticize the assertions of three different interpretations or subschools of Sautrāntika, which assert the true existence of aspects or representations (*akāra, rnam pa*),[3] described by his commentators as the Non-Pluralists, the Half-Eggists, and the Proponents of an Equal Number of Consciousnesses and Objects. The Sautrāntika Non-Pluralists claim that there is an inherently singular consciousness that cognizes a multiplicity of objects. Śāntarakṣita argues that this notion is absurd, since the unitary consciousness would have to have multiple parts related to the cognition of multiple real representations or images of objects like colors, shapes, and so on.[4]

The next opponent, the Sautrāntika Half-Eggists (24–30), are said to claim that they avoid the faults of the Non-Pluralists by asserting that though multiple representations or aspects of objects seem to appear simultaneously with consciousness, we are mistaken in that assumption because they in fact appear one by one in rapid succession. Thus, the singular consciousness actually only cognizes one representation or image at a time. For example, when we see a painting, we do not see all the colors at once, but rather see the blue image, then green, then red, and so on, but in such rapid succession that we think that we see a painting all at once. In response, Śāntarakṣ ita turns our attention from the visual consciousness to the aural consciousness and asks why aural cognitions do not seem to arise simultaneously as visual images do. He uses the example of two Sanskrit words: *latā* and *tāla*. If their aspects or aural representation appeared as rapidly as visual images are claimed to, then the two words would be indistinguishable since the syllables would be heard simultaneously.

Śāntarakṣita identifies an additional fallacy in stanzas 26 and 27. The opponent claims that consciousness is momentary like the representations it perceives, but also, inconsistently, that consciousness endures for some time. The assumption of duration is necessary in order to explain how

3. In order to clarify what is meant by *aspect, representation* or *image,* we can use the example of a red mug. One aspect of the mug would be its redness; another might be its shape, or its size. Each of these three subschools of Sautrāntika asserts that such images or aspects truly exist.

4. Moreover, Śāntarakṣita argues that external objects with multiple true aspects could not be established as actually existent by an inherently singular consciousness since being related to the multiple aspects or images of the objects by virtue of cognizing it would undermine the tenability of that consciousness being truly singular. Thus, Śāntarakṣita rejects both their assertion of the true singularity of consciousness and their assertion of the existence of external objects.

consciousness pieces together, however erroneously, the distinct consecutive images or representations, and comes to the incorrect conclusion that they are perceived simultaneously. A momentary singular conceptual consciousness could not piece together such successive images.

The system of Sautrāntika Proponents of an Equal Number of Consciousnesses and Representations, who attempt to avoid these problems by claiming that as many truly singular minds arise as there are images or representations in their objects of perception, is the next view addressed by Śāntarakṣita (stanzas 31–34). The basic criticism leveled here is quite similar to the critique of partless particles. In order for there to be as many truly singular consciousnesses as there are representations of objects, the representations must be truly singular as well. If we take the example of a painting with multiple representations of various colors, the question arises as to where the truly singular representations are. If the patch of blue is taken to be truly singular, and so analogous to a representation that corresponds to a truly singular consciousness, then the patch of blue must not have parts, such as a part bordered by a red patch and another part bordered by a green patch. If it did, then by analogy, a consciousness apprehending such a representation would also have parts and would not be truly unitary.

Śāntarakṣita then continues his analysis of subjects, or consciousness, and their relation to objects of consciousness by briefly examining seven classical non-Buddhist Indian philosophical schools: Vaiśeṣika, Naiyāyika, Jain, Mīmāṃsaka, Lokāyata, Sāṃkhya, and Vedānta (stanzas 35–40).[5] Faults are found with each of the first six because each asserts, in varying ways, a truly singular consciousness that perceives objects that are manifold. Such an assertion is incoherent: if the objects of perception have parts, then the consciousness cognizing them also must have parts, since it is related to all the parts of its objects. A unitary consciousness is incompatible with a manifold object. Vedāntas argue that they avoid this difficulty because they deny the existence of external objects. Śāntarakṣita, however, still finds their claim of a conventional multiplicity of objects in the world that appear to consciousness contradicts their assertion of a nondual unitary consciousness.

The final third of the neither-one-nor-many argument addresses the claims of several subschools of Yogācāra/Cittamātra thought. The subschools are divided into Proponents of True Representations and Proponents of False Representations. The Proponents of True Representations are further divided into three subschools, corresponding to the three Sautrāntika subschools: the Non-Pluralists, the Half-Eggists, and the Proponents of an Equal Number of Consciousnesses and Objects. The primary difference between these schools and their Sautrāntika corollaries is that while Sautrāntikas assert that objects are external to consciousness, the Yogācārins claim that they are not truly distinct from the consciousness perceiving them. Śāntarakṣita begins (stanza 46) with a

5. Śāntarakṣita treats each of these systems in much greater detail in his encyclopedic doxographical work *Tattvasaṃgraha.*

general critique of Yogācāra tenets before addressing specific subschools in the following stanzas. He raises the question of how consciousness could be truly singular if, as Yogācārins claim, it exists in a nondual relationship with a multiplicity of objects and aspects of those objects. Either the consciousness does not have a truly unitary nature, due to its relationship with multiple aspects of objects, or those aspects are all identical, which contradicts direct perception.

Many of his criticisms of the three subschools of Yogācāra Proponents of True Representations are quite similar to those he leveled against the Sautrāntika Proponents of True Representations. In both cases, they hold that representations, like colors and shapes, do truly exist. According to Śāntarakṣita, if the Yogācāras hold these representations to truly exist, even if not separately from consciousness, the same kind of reasoning that refutes the Sautrāntikas would also apply to the Yogācāra Proponents of True Representations.

The refutation of Yogācāra Proponents of False Representations (stanzas 52–60) consists of eight reductio ad absurdum arguments. Śāntarakṣita begins by presenting their position (stanza 52) before moving into his eight reductios. According to Śāntarakṣita, the Proponents of False Representations claim to avoid the faults of their Yogācāra counterparts, who accept truly existent representations, because they say the singular consciousness does not actually apprehend a multiplicity of representations, since such representations are actually false.

An assortment of criticisms of this view arises in the eight reductios. In the first, Śāntarakṣita questions how one could have a clear experience of the representations of an object if those representations do not actually exist. Moreover, the second reductio relies on the claim that if representations of objects are false, and thus the red representation of a red mug does not exist, one could not correctly perceive that mug itself, which is absurd. It would not even be correct to call our perceived information "knowledge," since it would merely correspond to things that do not exist. Furthermore, consciousness could not perceive representations at all if they were nonexistent, since nonexistent phenomena could not cause one to perceive. For these reasons, among others, Śāntarakṣita finds the views and positions of the Yogācāra Proponents of False Representations to be irreparably incoherent.

Since thorough analysis of his Buddhist and non-Buddhist opponents has revealed that no singular or unitary nature actually exists, and since a manifold nature would depend upon the aggregation of unitary natures, Śāntarakṣita concludes that there is no inherent nature in anything at all, since single and manifold natures are inclusive of all possibilities of inherent natures in phenomena.[6]

6. The subject headings in square brackets have been inserted to help facilitate an easier reading of the text. They are not part of Śāntarakṣita's original. This translation is a revised version of selections from Blumenthal 2004, which includes complete translations and a detailed study of Śāntarakṣita's *Ornament of the Middle Way* and Gyaltsab's *Remembering "The Ornament of the Middle Way."* I thank Snow Lion Publications for permission to reprint portions of this book.

Translation

[Statement of the Neither-One-Nor-Many Argument]

(1) These entities, as asserted by our own [Buddhist schools] and other [non-Buddhist schools], have no inherent nature at all because in reality they have neither a singular nor manifold nature, like a reflected image.

[Application of the Argument: Analysis of Objects]

Refutation of Unitary Objects Asserted by Non-Buddhists

(2) Permanent [causal] entities are not themselves singular because they contribute to [the production of] successive effects. If each successive effect is distinct, then [the argument in favor of] permanent [causal] entities [that are truly singular] degenerates.

[Application of the Argument: Analysis of Objects]

Refutation of Unitary Objects Asserted by Buddhists

(3) Even those uncompounded objects known by the knowledge which arises in the meditation [of an *ārya*], according to the [Vaibhāśika] system, are not unitary because they are related to successive moments of knowledge.

(4) If the nature of the object known by a previous consciousness continues to exist subsequently, then the previous cognition would still exist in the latter and, similarly, the latter would exist in the former.

(5) If the nature of the [latter object] does not arise in the earlier time and the [earlier object] does not arise at the latter time, then uncompounded phenomena like consciousness must be objects known to arise only for a moment.

(6) If the previous [uncompounded object] arises from the power of [the causes and conditions of the uncompounded object of] an earlier moment, then it would not actually be uncompounded, like minds and mental states.

(7) If you accept that these momentary objects arise independently because there is no dependence on others, then they must either exist permanently or not exist at all.

(8) What is the purpose of investigating objects that have no meaningful ability to act? What is the purpose of lustful people inquiring whether a eunuch is attractive or not?[7]

[Application of the Argument: Analysis of Objects]

Refutation of Unitary Persons

(9) It is clearly understood that a person [of the type asserted by Vātsīputrīyans] has neither a single nor a manifold nature, since such a person cannot be explained as momentary or nonmomentary.

[Application of the Argument: Analysis of Objects]

Refutation of Unitary Pervasive Space

(10) How can pervasive entities [such as space] be unitary given that they are related with various directions?[8]

[Application of the Argument: Analysis of Objects]

Refutation of Unitary Gross Objects

(10 [cont.]) Gross objects are also not unitary since [some parts of] such entities can be visible [while other parts] are not visible.

[Application of the Argument: Analysis of Objects]

Refutation of Unitary Partless Particles

(11) What is the nature of the central [partless] particle which faces singly towards [another] particle yet abides [with other partless particles in various directions], either around and joining with it, or around it with space between [the particles], or around it without space between them?

7. Śāntarakṣita borrowed this stanza that summarizes his point from Dharmakīrti's *Pramāṇavārttika* 1:211.

8. Uncompounded space here is defined as a lack of obstructive contact. It is not the type of space one finds in a hole or an empty glass, but the abstract concept of space that can either be occupied by material objects or not. The Vaibhāśika assertion is that space, so defined, is truly singular and permanent, unaffected by the movements of objects within space. Śāntarakṣita argues that it does not make sense to describe pervasive uncompounded space as unitary since it has relations with other entities in various directions. If that is the case, then there are parts, and uncompounded space is not inherently singular. Nothing with parts is inherently singular or unitary.

(12) If it were asserted that the [central] particle also faces entirely toward another such [unitary, partless] particle, then if that were so, wouldn't it be the case that [gross objects such as] earth and water and the like would not be spatially expansive?

(13) If you accept [partless particles with sides] which face other such particles [in different directions], then if that is the case, how could even the most minute particles be singular and partless?

(14) Particles have thus been established to have no inherent nature. Therefore, it is evident that eyes and other gross substantial entities, etc., which are asserted [to be real] by many of our own [Buddhist] schools and other [non-Buddhist] schools, are directly known to have no inherent nature.

(15) The nature of these [entities] is said to be comprised of those [particles]. The qualities of these [entities], their actions, and even their universals (*sāmānya, spyi*) and particularities are said to be made up of those [particles and therefore must not inherently exist].

[Application of the Argument: Analysis of Subjects in Relation to Objects]

The Mind, its Objects, and Its Means of Perception: Self-cognizing Cognition (*svasaṃ vedana, rang rig*), as Asserted by Buddhists

(16) Consciousness is produced in the utterly opposite way from that which is of an inanimate nature. That which is not the nature of being inanimate is the self-knowledge of this [consciousness].

(17) Self-cognizing cognition is not an entity that exists [with its object] as agent and action because it would be incorrect for consciousness, which is of a single, partless nature, to be three (i.e., knower, knowing, and known).

(18) Therefore, since this is the nature of consciousness, it is capable of self-consciousness (*bdag shes*). How, though, could that cognize the nature of objects from which it is distinct?

(19) Since its nature does not exist in external objects, given that you assert that objects of consciousness and consciousness are different, how could consciousness know objects other than consciousness?

[Application of the Argument: Analysis of Subjects: Refutations of Inherently Singular Consciousness]

Critique of an Epistemology Asserting Valid Cognition of True Representations (*Satyākarā*) That Are External to Consciousness

Statement of the Sautrāntika Reasoning

(20) According to some, consciousness knows representations (*akāra, rnam pa*) directly, in spite of the fact that the two (i.e., consciousness and representations)[9] are actually distinct. Since the representations appear just like a mirror reflection, they claim it is suitable to consider the experience by mere imputation [to be accurate].

Refutation of the Vaibhāśika Proponents of No Representations

(21) However, there cannot be externally cognized representations for those who do not assert a consciousness that reflects representations of objects.

Refutation of Three Subschools of Sautrāntika Proponents of True Representations

(22) Since they are not distinct from the unitary consciousness, there cannot be a multiplicity of representations. Therefore knowledge of the object could not be established by the force of the representation.

(23) Consciousness cannot be unitary since it is not separate from representations. If that were not the case, how would you explain the two (i.e., consciousness and a multiplicity of representations) to be unitary?

(24) [Colors such as] white and the like arise in succession to the consciousness, yet because they arise quite rapidly, the foolish conceive of them as arising simultaneously.

(25) When the mind which hears the sounds of such words as *latā* [and *tāla*][10] arise very rapidly, why does it not hear [the two syllables] as if they were arising simultaneously [thus rendering the two words indistinguishable]?

9. The Sanskrit term *akāra* (Tib. *rnam pa*) can be aptly translated as "representation," "image" or "aspect." The sense of aspect is that one aspect of a field may be the green color of the grass. Another aspect may be its shape. These are also images or representations to an eye consciousness. I use each of these terms as translations for *akāra* depending on the context.

10. *Tāla* is not included in the verse stanza to keep meter, but we know of its intention to be there from Śāntarakṣita's *Auto-Commentary on The Ornament of the Middle Way.*

(26) Even if we were to consider only conceptual minds, [the representations] would still not be known in succession. Since they do not remain for a long time, all minds are similar [to representations/aspects] in the rapidity with which they arise.

(27) Therefore, all objects appear to be apprehended simultaneously as distinct representations, not successively.

(28) Even with regard to [the example of] a burning torch, the arising of the mistaken instantaneous appearance of a wheel of fire [due to rapidly twirling the torch] would not be [a result of] joining the boundaries between [memories of distinct] perceptions because it appears very clearly.

(29) This joining of boundaries is done by the memory [of the mental consciousness], not by the seeing [of an eye consciousness], because an [eye consciousness] cannot apprehend past objects.

(30) Since the object of that [memory] has perished, it is not clear. Therefore the appearance of the wheel of fire is not clear.[11]

(31) If one were to claim that when someone sees the base of the representations of a painting, as many minds will arise simultaneously as there are representations in that [painting,] then,

(32) If that were the case, even when cognition is of a single representation type such as the color white, etc., since there is a distinct beginning, middle, and end to that, there will be a variety of objects of observation [within that cognition of a single representation].

(33) I honestly do not feel that [a representation] such as the color white, etc, which is like the nature of a particle that is a partless singularity, has ever appeared to any consciousness.

(34) [According to our opponent,] the sources of the five [sense] consciousnesses are representations of objects made of accumulated [partless parts]. Minds (*citta, sems*) and mental states (*caitta, sems byung*) are objects established in the sixth [source of perception].

11. Stanzas 28–30 argue that if our cognitions of gross objects are primarily pieced together with memories of images, then contrary to the Half-Eggist's assertions, our cognitions of such objects could not be clear since memories are by definition not clear. Śāntarakṣita's example is the appearance of a wheel of fire that arises when rapidly twirling a burning torch. It seems to be a clear appearance, but could not be since it is formed by the joining of memories, which are not clear, by definition.

[Application of the Argument: Analysis of Subjects and Its Relation to Objects]

The Mind, Its Objects, and Its Means of Perception as Asserted by Non-Buddhists

Five Refutations of Views Maintaining a Unitary Consciousness as Asserted by Non-Buddhist Schools

(35) Even according to the scriptures of non-Buddhists [such as the Vaiśeṣ ikas and Sāṃkhyas[12]], the appearance [of gross objects] as singular to consciousness would not occur because its objects are substances which have qualities (*guṇa, yon tan*), etc.

(36) [According to the views of the Jains and Mīmāṃsakas,] all entities are [manifold] like the nature of a gem emitting [colorful] rays. It would be irrational for the mind that apprehends those entities to appear in the nature of singularity.

(37) Even for proponents of the [Lokāyata] system which accepts the establishment of all sense faculties and objects as compounds of [the four elements such as] earth and the like, it is still impossible [for consciousness] to engage with unitary entities.

(38) Even according to the position [of the Sāṃkhyas,] who claim that [the five subtle elements such as] sound, etc. are [the nature of the three qualities such as] excellence and the like, a consciousness of the appearance of a unitary object is illogical because objects appear in the nature of the three [qualities].

(39) Regarding the tri-fold nature of entities, if the appearance of that [type of entity] is incompatible with a consciousness that is of a truly unitary nature, then how could one claim that [consciousness] apprehends that object?

(40) [Since] they do not even assert the existence of external objects, [Vedāntas ask] why the suitability of maintaining a consciousness that is permanent and to which arises various appearances, either simultaneously or successively, is so difficult to accept.

Refutation of the Sautrāntika Proponents of False Representations

(41) Cognitions of [uncompounded phenomena such as] space, and the like, illuminate a variety of appearances because of the appearance of many [conceptual representations of] letters for the appearance of the mere word (i.e., s-p-a-c-e).

12. Śāntarakṣita's *Auto-Commentary* indicates his opponents in this stanza by mentioning Kaṇāda, the founder of the Vaiśeṣika school and Kapila, a famous Sāṃkhya philosopher.

(42) Although there are some who assert consciousness to which manifold [representations] do not appear, still it is not suitable to establish their existence from the perspective of the ultimate because it has already been seen that there is a logical fallacy in asserting the existence of such, with these characteristics.

(43) Therefore it is established from all perspectives that consciousness occurs with the appearance of manifold representations, and thus like the [many] distinct representations, cannot logically be of a single nature.

[Application of the Argument: Analysis of Subjects]

Refutation of Various Proponents of Yogācāra/Cittamātra: Proponents of True Representations

(44) However, [according to the Yogācāra,] representations are manifest due to the ripening of latent potentialities of a beginningless personal continuum. Although they appear, since it is the result of a mistake, they are like the nature of an illusion.

(45) Although their [view is virtuous], we should think about whether such things [as the representations known by consciousness] according to [the Yogācāra proponents] actually exist or if they are something contentedly accepted only when left unanalyzed.

(46) Since contradictions would ensue with regard to those unitary [representations] *even if* the actual consciousness were manifold, [consciousness and representations] are undoubtedly distinct.

(47) If representations are not distinct [from the singular consciousness], then it would be difficult to respond to the following logical consequence with regard to moving and rest, etc.; due to the movement of one, all would move.

(48) Even according to the system of those maintaining external objects, if representations are not separate [from each other], then they would all also certainly be engaged as a single phenomena and not other than that.

(49) If you accept an equal number of consciousnesses and representations, then it would be difficult to overcome the same type of analysis as is made regarding particles.

(50) If one [consciousness experiences] a variety [of representations], wouldn't that be like the system of the [Jain] Sky Clad (Digambara)? A variety

[of representations] are not the nature of singularity just as manifold precious gems and the like [are not the nature of singularity].

(51) If the variety [of representations] exists in a single nature, how could they appear in a variegated nature and how could parts such as those which are obstructed and those which are unobstructed, etc. be distinguished?

Refutation of Yogācāra/Cittamātra: Proponents of False Representations

(52) Some say that [consciousness] does not naturally possess representations of these [objects]. In reality, representations do not exist but appear to consciousness by virtue of a mistake.

(53) If [representations] do not exist, there will likewise be no [consciousness] clearly experiencing them. That [clear, non-dual consciousness] is not like a consciousness [asserted by the Sautrāntikas] which is distinct from entities.

(54) Likewise, the [representation of this entity] will not be known as that [representation] to anyone [because] entities are representationless. In the same way bliss is not experienced in non-bliss and color is not seen in whiteness.

(55) With regard to representations, "object of knowledge" (*shes pa'i don*) is not actually the correct term because [the representation] is distinct from the knowledge itself (*shes pa'i bdag*), like flowers growing in the sky and the like.

(56) [Consciousness] is incapable of experiencing [representations] even when they are examined because non-existent things have no functional abilities, like the horn of a horse. To claim that a non-existent [representation] has the ability to generate a conscious self-appearance is irrational.

(57) What reason is there that would account for a relationship between those [representations] that are definitely experienced, and consciousness? It is not one of identity and not a relationship of one arising from the other.

(58) If there is not cause [for representations], how is it suitable that they arise only on occasion? If they have a cause, how could they not have an other-dependent [nature] (*paratantra-*[*svabhāva*], *gzhan gi dbang* [*gi ngo bo*])?

(59) If [representations] do not exist, then consciousness [with representations] also would not exist due to the non-existence of the representations. Being like a clear, round crystal, consciousness would not really experience [objects].

(60) If this is only known due to a mistake, then why does it rely upon mistakes? If it arises due to the power of a mistake, it is still other-dependent.

[Wrapping Up the Neither-One-Nor-Many Argument]

Demonstrating That Phenomena Lack a Manifold Nature

(61) We have found with analysis that no entity whatsoever has an [inherently] single nature. Those that have no single nature must also not have a manifold nature.

[Establishing the Pervasion of the Argument]

Entities Have No Nature at All

(62) The existence of an entity belonging to a class other than that which has a single or manifold [nature] does not make sense because the two are exhaustive of all possible alternatives.

(63) Therefore, these entities are characterized only by conventionality. If someone accepts them as ultimate, what can I do for that person?

Bibliography and Suggested Reading

Blumenthal, James. (2004) *The Ornament of the Middle Way: A Study of the Madhyamaka Thought of Śāntarakṣita.* Ithaca, N.Y.: Snow Lion.

Blumenthal, James. (2008) "Śāntarakṣita." In Edward N. Zalta, ed., The Stanford Encyclopedia of Philosophy. http://plato.stanford.edu. Stanford: Stanford Metaphysics Research Lab, Center for the Study of Language and Information.

Doctor, Thomas H. (2004) *Speech of Delight: Mipham's Commentary on Santaraksita's "Ornament of the Middle Way."* Ithaca: Snow Lion Publications.

McClintock, Sara L. (2003) "The Role of the 'Given' in the Classification of Śāntarakṣita and Kamalaśīla as Svātantrika-Mādhyamikas." In Georges Dreyfus and Sara McClintock, eds., *The Svātantrika-Prāsaṅgika Distinction: What Difference Does a Difference Make?* Boston: Wisdom, pp. 125–171,

Padmakara Translation Group. (2005) *The Adornment of the Middle Way: Shantarakshita's Madhyamakalankara with Commentary by Jamgon Mipham.* Boston: Shambhala Publications.

Tillemans, Tom J. F. (1982) "The 'Neither One Nor Many' Argument for *śūnyatā* and Its Tibetan Interpretations: Background Information and Source Materials." *Études de Lettres* (University of Lausanne) 3: 103–128.

Tillemans, Tom J. F. (1983) "The 'Neither One Nor Many" Argument for Śūnyatā and Its Tibetan Interpretations." In E. Steinkellner and H. Tauscher, eds., *Contributions on Tibetan and Buddhist Religion and Philosophy.* Vienna: Arbeitskreis für Tibetische und Buddhistische Studien, 305–320.

Tillemans, Tom J. F. (1984) "Two Tibetan Texts on the 'Neither One Nor Many' Argument for *Śūnyatā.*" *Journal of Indian Philosophy* 12: 357–388.

5

Mipam Namgyel

The Lion's Roar Affirming Extrinsic Emptiness

Matthew T. Kapstein

Fourteenth-century Tibet witnessed a remarkable upsurge of interest in philosophical speculations concerning the nature of mind, and its relationship to ultimate reality and to the Buddhist goal of enlightenment. A major inspiration was found in the scriptures belonging to the so-called third turn of the doctrinal wheel, among the teachings attributed to the Buddha. In contrast with the "first wheel," which included those scriptures emphasizing the impermanence and unsatisfactoriness of mundane phenomena, and the "second wheel," which focused on their emptiness, the "third wheel" was thought to consist of the Buddha's discourses concerning "Buddha-nature," or the "nucleus of the tathāgata" (*tathāgatagarbha*), the potential for awakening with which all beings are imbued. The same texts also often introduced concepts relating to the idealist trends in Buddhist philosophy, such as the theory that phenomena have their basis in the "consciousness of the ground-of-all" (*ālayavijñāna*) and the notion that consciousness, in turn, is essentially luminous in its nature. Tibetan thinkers became especially interested in investigating these and similar topics in part owing to the spread of systems of meditation and yoga that made use of similar concepts in connection with spiritual discipline and ritual. The presence of these ideas in an important group of Indian treatises attributed to the future Buddha Maitreya, especially the *Sublime Continuum of the Greater Vehicle* (*Mahāyānottaratantraśāstra*) and related works, led a growing number of scholars to argue that the highest teachings of the Buddha were in fact to be found therein, rather than in the Perfection of Wisdom *sūtras* of the "second wheel" and the Madhyamaka philosophy associated with them, wherein emptiness is the central idea. The debates to which this divergence of perspectives gave rise became some of the most hotly contested areas of Tibetan Buddhist thought, and among the richest in terms of the great range of interpretations that emerged.[1]

The themes that aroused the most intensive controversies were those that appeared to suggest Buddhist concessions to the substantialist metaphysics of the Indian Brahmanical schools, with their belief in a permanent self or soul (*ātman*) characterized in some contexts as having the attributes of being, consciousness, and bliss. Buddhist thinkers were thus at pains to distinguish, almost from their first appearance, the teachings of the "ground-of-all" and Buddha-nature from various substantialist and therefore unacceptable "doctrines of self" (*ātmavāda*).[2] D. S. Ruegg has argued that interpretation of the contested new doctrines exhibited two broad tendencies. On the one hand, he shows, there were thinkers who sought to maintain that the doctrines in question were not intended literally but were to be regarded as part of a teaching strategy tailored to the needs of those not yet ready to apprehend the radical concept of universal emptiness that was the genuine purport of the Buddha's message. But on the other, there were those who insisted that the teachings of Buddha-nature and the like had indeed been seriously intended, though liable to be misunderstood unless they were apprehended in their proper relationship with other Buddhist discourses on the ultimate truth and not confounded with the non-Buddhist teachings of the substantial self. For the latter thinkers, the Buddha was believed to have affirmed that there is a literal sense in which all sentient beings may be said to be imbued with the potency for attaining enlightenment.[3]

In Tibet, the most radical stance with respect to these matters was articulated by the teacher and adept Dölpopa Sherab Gyeltsen (Dol po pa Shes rab rgyal mtshan) (1292–1361/2) of the Jonangpa order of Tibetan Buddhism, a school specializing in the esoteric doctrines of the *Tantra of the Wheel of Time* (*Kālacakratantra*). Dölpopa's key notion was "extrinsic emptiness" (*gzhan stong*), by which he intended to define the ultimate truth (*paramārthasatya*) in its relation to the superficial, apparent phenomena making up ostensible, or relative, truth (*saṃvṛtisatya*). According to Dölpopa, in short, the Buddhist absolute is not a void, but a plenitude.[4] Insisting that this was the true

1. The issues briefly surveyed in this paragraph are most recently studied in depth, with full reference to the earlier relevant scholarship, in Mathes 2007. In this volume, pertinent aspects of Buddhist idealist philosophies are introduced in chapters 3 and 18.

2. On the Indian Buddhist critique of Brahmanical theories of the self, refer to chapters 23, 25, 26, 27, and 28 below.

3. On the reception and interpretation of the theory of Buddha-nature, see, especially, Ruegg 1989.

4. Dölpopa's life and teachings are best approached through the excellent study by Stearns 1999.

understanding of the Buddha's message, adherents of extrinsic emptiness sometimes referred to it as the Great Middle Way (*dbu ma chen po*).[5]

Dölpopa's teaching ignited a firestorm of controversy that has endured among Tibetan Buddhists down to this day. His views were rejected by many philosophers, including the great Tsongkhapa (1357–1419), founder of the Gelukpa (dGe lugs pa) order, which has dominated Tibetan Buddhism in recent centuries and to which the Dalai Lamas belong. According to the most vociferous of the critics, Dölpopa's concept of extrinsic emptiness was little more than a form of Brahmanical ontology in Buddhist guise.[6] Nevertheless, there were important defenders of Dölpopa's position, including his Jonangpa successor Tāranātha (1575–1634),[7] as well as others who believed that Dölpopa's views, although expressed in too extreme a fashion, were derived from a genuine insight without which the cardinal teaching of emptiness risked being misunderstood as suggesting a type of nihilism. The problem for the latter thinkers was how to retrieve what was deemed valuable in Dölpopa's approach, without committing oneself to the substantialism for which he had been harshly criticized.

Among the settings in which the revival of the philosophy of extrinsic emptiness was particularly forceful was far eastern Tibet (Khams) during the nineteenth century. Here, as had been the case in earlier times, a spiritual culture in which the practical disciplines of tantra and yoga were especially prominent seems to have motivated renewed speculation in this area. One of those whose views became particularly influential was the famed polymath Mipam Namgyel (Mi pham rNam rgyal, 1846–1912) of the Nyingmapa order, whose works inspired the reformation of Buddhist education in colleges throughout eastern Tibet. His interpretations of extrinsic emptiness, however, are subtle and difficult, and have come to be contested even among his successors.[8]

The text partially translated here, *The Lion's Roar Affirming Extrinsic Emptiness,* is Mipam's best known "defense" of Dölpopa's teaching, and the work most often mentioned by those who consider Mipam to have been a true proponent of the extrinsic emptiness philosophy. Others, however, hold

5. Though this expression is sometimes taken as a buzzword for the extrinsic emptiness teaching, it was not exclusively used in this fashion. Others who believed, too, that they held the key to comprehending the Madhyamaka philosophy also used it from time to time.

6. The Gelukpa critique of Dölpopa's system is introduced in Ruegg 1963. Cabezón and Dargyay 2007 provide a leading Sakyapa's critical response to both Dölpopa and Tsongkhapa.

7. Kapstein 2001a introduces aspects of Tāranātha's thought in relation to Dölpopa.

8. For pertinent studies of Mipam's philosophical contributions, refer to Williams 1998, Pettit 1999, and Karma Phuntsho 2005. For a translation of his major contribution to Madhyamaka thought, see Doctor 2004.

that it is no more than Mipam's discussion of the best argument that can be mounted in favor of a position that he considers to be not tenable in the final analysis. A close reading of the argument convinces me that the latter point of view is probably correct, and that *The Lion's Roar* is in fact a remarkably tame attempt to clarify the contribution that extrinsic emptiness makes in a context in which the highest insights of Madhyamaka thought are characterized in terms of freedom from the proliferation of dichotomous categories (*mtha' gnyis spros bral*), including such oppositions as those of the extrinsic or intrinsic emptiness of the absolute.[9]

As Mipam's argument is quite subtle, the reader may find a concise restatement useful at the outset. Presupposed here is a distinction between two categories of philosophical reasoning that Mipam always takes pains to carefully distinguish.[10] There is "reasoning that investigates conventions" (*tha snyad dpyod pa'i tshad ma*), based primarily on the logical system of the Indian master Dharmakīrti, for which truth abides in the coherence of the system itself and, above all, in its pragmatic efficacy.[11] Second, there is "reasoning that investigates the ultimate" (*don dam dpyod pa'i tshad ma*), for which truth consists in, as Mipam expresses it, the "accord between reality and appearance" (*gnas snang mthun pa*). Because this accord is never realized in cognitive operations involving consciousness bifurcated as apprehended object and apprehending subject, truth—such as it is for such consciousness—can be only the coherence established by reasoning investigating conventions. For this reason, there is an important sense in which the ultimate cannot be in the scope of thought, and even such notions as "freedom from the proliferation of dichotomous categories" and "accord between reality and appearance" must be themselves understood as elements of conventional reasoning, which generates conceptual models in order to think an absolute that it can never attain. Indeed, because thinking cannot escape its inherent basis in binary processing, even our modeling of the absolute interprets its realization in terms of an object of insight, namely emptiness, and a subject, gnosis (*jñāna*), whereby emptiness is realized. Mipam's technical vocabulary systematically differentiates, therefore, between two quite different types of subject-object distinction: the phenomenal apprehended object and apprehending subject (*gzung-'dzin*) of ordinary mundane consciousness, and the notional object and subject (*yul yul can*) posited as a model in order to speak of what is in fact the nondual realization of emptiness.

9. "Intrinsic emptiness" (*rang stong*) is the term used primarily by adherents of extrinsic emptiness to characterize those interpretations of Madhyamaka according to which the absolute is itself inherently empty. The Gelukpa followers of Tsongkhapa, whose approach is sometimes described in this way, strongly object, however, to the designation "intrinsic emptiness," considering it to be little more than a caricature of Tsongkhapa's teaching. See chapter 11 below.

10. For a concise introduction to Mipam's philosophical method, refer to Kapstein 1988.

11. See Dunne 2004.

With this in mind, it will be seen that Mipam in a sense defuses the explosive challenge of Dölpopa's teaching by insisting that, if extrinsic emptiness is to be affirmed at all, it must be as an aspect of the reasoning that investigates conventions and *not* the absolute. Once this is clear, the path is open for demonstrating why our conventions for discussing the ultimate require something like extrinsic emptiness discourse. Thus, while we must speak of the ultimate as free from the dichotomy of subject and object, we are nevertheless constrained, if we are to speak of its realization, to speak of emptiness and the gnosis that realizes it; for even the characterization "nondual" requires the attribution, by a subject, of a property, "nonduality," to the absolute taken as an object. This much is required by the rules of grammar. Talk of the ultimate, unlike the ultimate itself, requires talk of its properties, even if these be restricted to negative properties. It follows, then, that a discourse of the absolute cannot refrain from being a discourse that affirms some things of the absolute and denies others, and that, because the absolute cannot be empty with respect to that which is affirmed of it, it is only "extrinsically empty" with respect to what is denied. This, in a nutshell, is Mipam's argument. In effect, he holds that it is in the elaboration of a conventional metalanguage with reference to talk of the absolute that the philosophy of extrinsic emptiness finds its footing, for on this level the rules of assertion and negation, and all that flows from their orderly application, must be permitted to hold.

To the extent that Mipam's discussion hinges on an implied imperative, whereby reason forges a path from the attribution of properties to things to assumptions regarding the being of those things and the properties concerned, it will be seen that he is entertaining puzzles that are in some respects similar to those that have troubled Western philosophers in relation to Anselm's controversial ontological argument for the existence of god. Moreover, while Mipam's conception of ultimate truth as an accord between reality and appearance recalls the Western scholastic definition of truth as "adequation of intellect and being" (*adequatio intellectus et rei*), it is noteworthy that for Mipam this defines truth not as we have it, but as we might realize it to be. Although space does not permit full consideration of these matters here, suffice it to suggest that Mipam's arguments turn on questions of abiding philosophical interest, above and beyond the peculiar Tibetan Buddhist guise in which they appear in his work.

The Tibetan text of *The Lion's Roar* was edited by Mipam's leading disciple and literary executor, Jamyang Lodrö Gyamtso ('Jam dbyangs blo gros rgya mtsho, 1871–1926), the regent of Zhechen Monastery in Khams. As made clear in the colophon, Mipam's core arguments were preserved in short notes, to which Jamyang Lodrö Gyamtso added verses and introductory and concluding matter.[12] For this translation, I have abridged the

12. *Ghzan stong khas len seng gei nga ro.* The edition of the text I have followed is the Ser-lo dgon-pa xylographic print, which faithfully reproduces the original Sde-dge edition.

work by retaining just the key elements of the argument, which appear to be derived from the original record of Mipam's own words. A full translation, differing in some respects from the interpretation offered here, may be found in Pettit 1999.

Translation

The proponents of extrinsic emptiness establish the textual traditions of the Great Middle Way, of profound and definitive meaning, with reference to the single essential intention disclosed in the transmitted precepts of the Conqueror that belong to the final irreversible wheel of definitive significance, which teaches the indestructible, eternal path; as well as in Maitreya's teaching of the *Supreme Continuum of the Greater Vehicle,* noble Asaṅga and his brother Vasubandhu's profoundly meaningful discourses, and lord Nāgārjuna's *Collection of Eulogies* and other transmissions of the definitive significance of the *sūtras;* and in such tantras as the glorious *Wheel of Time,* together with the elucidations of their intention such as the *Trio of Commentaries by Bodhisattvas.*[13] Though the essential intention of these works is exceedingly profound and extensive, nowadays everyone, whether or not he knows how to uphold the burden of textual explanation, just says whatever comes to his lips, and this is very much in error. So, if I speak of this in brief, then, in order to establish definitively the philosophical system of extrinsic emptiness, first, in accordance with the texts of lord Nāgārjuna, you must establish all principles to be without substantial nature.[14] If that is not known, then one cannot establish the manner in which ostensible truth is intrinsically empty, while ultimate truth is empty extrinsically. Therefore, at the outset, the significance of the freedom from elaboration that each must intuit for oneself must be established.[15]

Following this, concerning the significance of that ultimate truth that is free from elaborations, when it is realized by a subject—nonconceptual gnosis—then one may speak of the "ultimate" with reference to both object and subject, which have come into accord with respect to the abiding nature of

13. The authors and works mentioned make up the essential canon of extrinsic emptiness thought. The *Trio of Commentaries* refers to the major Indian commentaries on the important esoteric works *Cakrasaṃvaratantra, Hevajratantra,* and *Kālacakratantra.*

14. On Nāgārjuna's philosophy, refer to chapter 2.

15. "Freedom from elaboration" (Skt. *niṣprapañca,* Tib. *spros bral*) is Mipam's preferred way of speaking of the end of Madhyamaka teaching. The "elaborations" referred to are the dichotomous categories of being and nonbeing, production and annihilation, permanence and impermanence, etc. For a discussion of the canonical Buddhist notion that enlightenment "must be intuited by each oneself" (Skt. *pratyātmavedanīya,* Tib. *so so rang gis rig par bya ba*), in relation to Mipam's thinking, see Williams 1998 and my response, Kapstein 2000.

reality and its appearance. The object and subject for which abiding reality and appearance are not in accord are what are called "ostensible."

When these matters are investigated through the conventional means of knowledge, one employs such distinctions as those of deceptive and undeceptive, or errant and inerrant. That which is established to be undeceptive and inerrant is the ultimate, while the ostensible is the opposite. Both the well-known exposition of the two truths with reference to emptiness and appearance, and their presentation in terms of the accord or disaccord of abiding reality and appearance that has just been set forth, have been originally taught in the *sūtras* and great treatises, and so are not approaches that were newly contrived by the proponents of extrinsic emptiness. [. . .]

The two truths must be understood to be affirmed as different, that is, their unicity is denied; and so this can never be understood in terms of the way of establishing the two truths according to which appearance and emptiness are [conceived as being] different oppositions of a single essence.[16] That being so, those errant appearances in which abiding reality and appearance do not accord appear in error, but in point of fact are not proven [to be as they appear]. It is for this reason that they are called "ostensible." But the other [i.e. the ultimate] is proven in accordance with what appears in inerrant vision, and so is not falsified by [any] epistemic criteria. For this reason it is called "ultimately existent" and "veridically proven." This need not be taken to say that it is veridically proven that appearance is different from emptiness. For, from the first, having established the expanse of reality to be the coalescence of appearance and emptiness, or emptiness that is endowed with what is supreme among all forms,[17] it is in that way that abiding reality, ultimate truth, is affirmed.

Therefore, it is that sort of ultimate that is not empty intrinsically. As a conventional example, a rope of variegated color may be likened to ultimate truth, and a snake [mistakenly seen in place of the rope] to ostensible truth. One must then distinguish between proving them to be one conventionally, and not proving them to be one; for it is not possibly the case that both are errors or that both are true.

16. The concept of "different oppositions of a single essence" (*ngo bo gcig la ldog pa tha dad*) is regularly invoked in Gelukpa philosophy to explain how, for instance, a pot may be regarded at once as a "physical object used to carry water" and "veridically empty." However, Mipam insists here, in the context of reasoning that investigates conventions, that the two truths be regarded as mutually exclusive, so that this principle cannot apply: the same thing cannot be unequivocally *both* absolute and relative in the same way that emptiness and appearance may be properties attributed to a common locus.

17. Emptiness "endowed with what is supreme among all forms" (Skt. *sarvākāravaropeta*, Tib. *rnam kun mchog ldan*) is the idiom used in the *Tantra of the Wheel of Time* to express the coalescence of appearance and emptiness, a concept that may be traced to the affirmation, in the Perfection of Wisdom *sūtras*, that "form is emptiness, emptiness form."

Thus, the ultimate is not intrinsically empty, for, with respect to the ultimate, the inerrant subject and object both exist; and there can be no epistemically valid falsification whereby what exists might be shown to be otherwise; and, because the arguments that establish emptiness have been previously set forth, that point [i.e. that "all principles are without substantial nature"] has already been established. Moreover, with respect to that which is proven by the correct epistemic criteria for the analysis of conventional truth, no one in the world, not even the gods, can rightfully dispute it.

Therefore, because the ultimate is intrinsically veridical and undeceiving, it is never empty of those principles [i.e., its being veridical and undeceiving]; for, if it were empty [of them], there would have to be some criterion establishing [it to be] untruth and error, and that is not possible. For, if it were, the peace that is nirvāṇa would have to be an unreliable goal, and that affirmation—except for demons, extremists, and disputants who lack standards—is not put forth by those who have respect for this teaching.

Although the ultimate abiding reality is primordially such, those errant appearances wherein [the ultimate] is not so realized, which are subject to epistemic criteria that prove [those errant appearances] to be untruth and error, are what, in this context, are called "ostensible," the significance of which accords with that of terms meaning "obscured." Thus, the ultimate is empty of that ostensible [appearance], while those subjects and objects that constitute errant appearances, and are termed "ostensible," are intrinsically empty—for instance, as the rope is empty of the snake.

This must be emphatically affirmed. According to other philosophical systems that proclaim the refutation of extrinsic emptiness, truthlessness is what is to be proven by the analysis of the ultimate, and cannot be affirmed to be an object of negation. So, too, absence of elaboration is what is to be proven by the arguments of culminating analysis, but it is not their object of negation. Therefore, if there be no affirmation of truthlessness and the absence of elaboration, it would then be the case that you could not establish anything at all according to the philosophical system of your tradition. Accordingly, if the ultimate, like the ostensible, were intrinsically empty, one could not establish the ultimate to be inerrant and the proven abiding reality, and the ostensible to be errant and unproven in its essence. For "empty" in this context involves the analysis of some ground of emptiness that is empty with respect to some principle.[18]

If the ultimate were empty intrinsically, there would be no difference between the negation of errant appearances and the non-negation of inerrant appearances by means of the epistemic criteria for the analysis of truth or falsehood. It would be like holding it to be much the same whether both the rope and the snake exist, or both do not.

18. For instance, a common object such as a pot may be taken as a "ground of emptiness" (*stong gzhi*) that is shown to lack veridical being (*bden grub*).

Emptiness is conclusively exemplified by the emptiness of the ostensible. Because that [ostensible appearance] is not established to be veridically proven, the grasping of it as veridical is errant cognition, whereby one is deceived and so meanders through saṃsāra. Therefore, because that sort of errant subject and object are both in this context the ostensible, if emptiness were not conclusively exemplified through their being empty, then it would follow that even the absence of veridical being would not conclusively exemplify emptiness, and that by negating apprehending-as-veridical meditation on emptiness would not be conclusively exemplified.[19]

Similarly, it is owing to the negation of the elaborated object and subject that the emptiness which is the absence of the phenomenal subject-object dichotomy is fully realized in this system. Because all the elaborations of the dualistic appearances of the phenomenal subject-object dichotomy are subsumed in the errant object and subject, and established to be the ostensible in this context, and because the ultimate is empty with respect to that, then, if emptiness is not thereby conclusively exemplified, it would follow that non-elaboration would not exemplify emptiness, and the intellect that meditatively cultivates non-elaboration would not conclusively exemplify the meditative cultivation of emptiness.

But, you may ask, is not that ultimate both non-veridical and unelaborated?

[In response we ask:] Where is there anything that is not both non-veridical and unelaborated, even if ultimate? Take, for example, the relative in this context [which, given the preceding arguments, must be also non-veridical and unelaborated, though it appears otherwise in error].

But, if the ultimate is non-veridical and empty, then why do you [proponents of extrinsic emptiness] say that it is veridically established and not empty intrinsically?

[Response:] In this context, the point is that "veridically established" and "not empty" refer to establishment and existence from the perspective of the epistemic criteria of conventional analysis. So you are merely contesting what you have not understood at all![20]

Then aren't you affirming it to be veridically established though at the same time not veridically established, and to be emptiness though also non-empty?

19. Our disposition to apprehend as veridical, to reify the objects of perception and cognition, is, for Tibetan Buddhist thought, the key manifestation of the ignorance that is at the root of mundane existence. It is therefore the task of meditation on emptiness to uproot this cardinal error.

20. Mipam's argument here turns on the crucial distinction between the two types of reasoning. In effect, Mipam holds that the opponent commits a category error by confounding the conclusion of ultimate analysis, for which not even the ultimate possesses "veridical being," with the conventional analysis that he holds to be the proper context for the affirmation of extrinsic emptiness.

[Response:] How's that? For just as you hold that, as the counterpart to establishing appearance as ostensible and emptiness as ultimate, it would be inappropriate, when analyzing the ultimate, to negate non-veridicality and non-elaboration, just so we similarly affirm that, in a system holding error to be the ostensible and the inerrant to be the ultimate, it would be inappropriate to negate the ultimate-as-inerrant together with the veridical establishment of its inerrancy. For that reason, the great promulgator Asaṅga has said:

> Where something is not, there is an emptiness of that. Beyond that, what remains exists.

Accordingly, in all cases, when propounding a textual tradition of refutation and proof, although one must refute what is not established by reason, one must not refute points that are established by reason. This must be affirmed, or else, if everything is refuted in common, then because the epistemic criteria which establish the difference between authentic and inauthentic doctrinal expressions and [their] expressed meanings are overturned, it becomes impossible for any certainty to arise.[21]

But, one may wonder, do you not affirm the expanse of reality that transcends refutation and proof, and that is an object of individual intuitive awareness?

[In response,] one should ask why [the opponent] asks that.

[He may say:] It is because, having established your textual tradition as one-sidedly affirming the negation of the object of negation and the proof of what is to be proven, you abide on that stage whereupon the objective is not to affirm that all may be negated [so that refutation and proof are transcended in the understanding of emptiness].

[To this we respond by saying that,] because the expanse of reality that is an object of individual intuition is beyond refutation and proof, ultimately we do affirm something like this [i.e., your affirmation that all may be negated]. Such an ultimate being proven, then, in this context, which concerns the conventional proof that that is indeed what is proven to be the ultimate, this is treated as subject to proof and refutation, so that there is no contradiction between these two [approaches]. For, if there were not this affirmation that the ultimate is conventionally proven to be intrinsically not empty, it would follow that there also is not an ultimate that is free from refutation and proof. For that reason, just as conventionally, if the affirmation of absence of substantial essence be opposed, it follows that the presence of substantial essence is proven, so too, if the ultimate's being intrinsically empty is not proven, then it follows that that ultimate [which had been supposed to be intrinsically empty] is not the ultimate, but is ostensible.

21. In short, conventional reasoning must resist the temptations of unrestrained skepticism.

If you think, "in that way, your saying that 'by the ultimate's being established to be intrinsically devoid of all veridicality and elaboration, emptiness is not exemplified and the ultimate is thus not empty intrinsically,' is mere verbiage, a conventional quibble that leads to the unredeemable view that becomes fixated on emptiness as an entity, to the non-equivalence of mundane being and peace, the ultimate alone becoming eternal and constant, and to other such faults," then you've not understood even the first thing about this great philosophical system. Just as emptiness is affirmed [by you] to be non-veridical and unelaborated, how is there veridicality and elaboration in it? The mere affirmation that the ultimate is established as the ultimate, by indicating it not to be relative, engages the conventions of empty and non-empty, and that, in this context, is what is to be proven. Therefore, if by affirming that conventionally it follows that one harbors a view objectifying emptiness as an entity, then it will similarly follow that by affirming non-veridicality [one harbors] the unredeemable view that is fixated upon the mark of emptiness's being a nonentity, and by affirming nonelaboration [one harbors] the unredeemable view that objectifies emptiness as an ineffable entity.

In sum, in this context the ground for the designations of ultimate and relative is grasped as, respectively, the inerrant and errant object and subject. The inerrant ultimate is affirmed to exist as the object of the inerrant intellect, as veridical, and as empty with respect to relative error. Conventionally, it is held to be intrinsically not empty, and to exist in the vision of those who are sublime. [. . .]

Bibliography and Suggested Reading

Cabezón, Jose Ignacio, and Geshe Lobsang Dargyay. (2007) *Freedom from Extremes: Gorampa's "Distinguishing the Views" and the Polemics of Emptiness.* Boston: Wisdom.

Doctor, Thomas, trans. (2004) *Speech of Delight: Mipham's Commentary on Śāntarakṣita's "Ornament of the Middle Way."* Ithaca: Snow Lion Publications.

Dunne, John. (2004). *Foundations of Dharmakīrti's Philosophy.* Boston: Wisdom.

Kapstein, Matthew T. (1988) "Mi-pham's Theory of Interpretation." In Donald Lopez, ed., *Buddhist Hermeneutics* (Honolulu: University of Hawai'i Press, 1988), 149–174. Reprinted (with some revision) in chap. 13 in Kapstein 2001b.

Kapstein, Matthew T. "We Are All Gzhan stong pas." *Journal of Buddhist Ethics* 7 (2000): 105–125; www.buddhistethics.org/.

Kapstein, Matthew T. (2001a) "From Kun-mkhyen Dol-po-pa to 'Ba'-mda' Dge-legs: Three Jo-nang-pa Masters on the Interpretation of the *Prajñāpāramitā.*" Chap. 12 in Kapstein 2001b.

Kapstein, Matthew T. (2001b) *Reason's Traces: Identity and Interpretation in Indian and Tibetan Buddhist Thought*. Boston: Wisdom.

Karma Phuntsho. (2005) *Mipham's Dialectics and the Debates on Emptiness*. London: Routledge.

Mathes, Klaus-Dieter. (2007) *A Direct Path to the Buddha Within: Gö Lotsāwa's Mahāmudrā Interpretation of the Ratnagotravibhāga*. Boston: Wisdom.

Pettit, John. (1999) *Mipham's Beacon of Certainty: Illuminating the View of Dzogchen, the Great Perfection*. Boston: Wisdom.

Ruegg, David Seyfort. (1963) "The Jo naṅ pas: A School of Buddhist Ontologists according to the Grub mtha' śel gyi me loṅ." *Journal of the American Oriental Society* 83: 73–91.

Ruegg, David Seyfort. (1989) *Buddha-nature, Mind and the Problem of Gradualism in a Comparative Perspective: On the Transmission and Reception of Buddhism in India and Tibet*. London: School of Oriental and African Studies.

Stearns, Cyrus. (1999) *Buddha from Dolpo*. Albany: State University of New York Press.

Williams, Paul. (1998) *The Reflexive Nature of Awareness: A Tibetan Madhyamaka Defence*. Richmond, England: Curzon Press.

6

Dushun's *Huayan Fajie Guan Men* (*Meditative Approaches to the Huayan Dharmadhātu*)

Alan Fox

The Huayan tradition in China takes its basic inspiration from the apocryphal Mahāyāna text known as the *Huayan Jing* ("Avataṃsaka" or "Flower Garland" sūtra). One of the most basic models in the Huayan tradition, both historically and philosophically, is the idea of the Fourfold Dharmadhātu, which highlights the perspectivalism for which Huayan is famous. This model is suggested in an early work attributed to Dushun (c. 600 C.E.), a miracle worker and healer who was retrospectively designated First Patriarch of the Huayan tradition in China. Here we present a translation of Dushun's seminal text *Huayan Fajie Guan Men* (*Meditative Approaches to the Huayan Dharmadhātu*).

Dharmadhātu (Ch. *fajie*) can be translated as "Realm of Dharmas," where the word "dharmas" refers to all the myriad factors of experience, and thus can be used to describe "the world." Dharmadhātu is the manifold of data that is apprehended and cognized by human consciousness, though such a polarity needn't require making an ontological distinction between the data that is cognized and the consciousness that cognizes. The Huayan authors, especially the early ones, are influenced substantially by the *Heart Sūtra*'s classic pronouncements about the identity of form and emptiness, and also by the apocryphal *Awakening of Mahāyāna Faith* (*Dasheng Qixin Lun*). The four Dharmadhātus do not refer to four different worlds or levels of reality, but rather to four different perspectives on a single phenomenological manifold. The first of these is what might be called the ordinary perspective, and the others are accessed through meditation.

The first perspective, or Dharmadhātu, is called "phenomenal," or *shi*. This refers to our tacit, common-sense view of things as causally autonomous and discrete. The second Dharmadhātu is "principle," or *li*. This refers to the deeper commonality shared by a range of concrete particulars. Though in general Buddhism is antiessentialist, still the language of essentialism often creeps into the discussion. In this sense, "principle" is described as "essence," even though, as it turns out in this analysis, the essence of things is their lack of essence. In this text, the principle that all phenomena have in common is that they are all *śūnya*, or empty of self-being (Skt. *svabhāva*, Ch. *zixing*). The third Dharmadhātu refers to the "nonobstruction of *li* and *shi*" (*lishi wuai*), the realization that the emptiness or generality of things does not in any way interfere with their particular presence in the field of experience. Finally, the most profound perspective is represented by the fourth Dharmadhātu of "nonobstruction of *shi* and *shi*" (*shishi wuai*).

This is the Huayan way of understanding *pratītyasamutpāda* or "codependent origination." *Pratītyasamutpāda*, especially in the Mahāyāna understanding, refers to the fact that all dharmas are simultaneously the cause and the effect of all other dharmas. Therefore, *pratītyasamutpāda* is a synonym for *śūnyatā*, because to be caused by everything else is to be empty of self-causation. The *Qixin Lun* illustrates this way of looking at *pratītyasamutpāda* using the example of water and waves, and the Huayan patriarch Fazang offers a number of famous metaphors for this notion of intercausality, such as the "jeweled net of Indra," the Golden Lion, and the room of mirrors. For instance, in his *Commentary on the Huayan Fajie Guanmen*, Zongmi describes Fazang's metaphor of the room of mirrors in the following way: "If one uses the metaphor of the mirror and the lamp, it is as if one places a mirror at each of the four sides and the four corners, altogether consisting of eight mirrors. Moreover, mirrors are also placed above and below, to make ten mirrors in all. In the middle is placed a single lamp. Each of the ten mirrors mutually enters the others, just as, when a single mirror is encompassed by the other nine mirrors, it already accommodates the nine within itself." This somewhat psychedelic vision of the world as composed of events/objects, all of which are interpenetrating and being interpenetrated by other events/objects, is putatively the Buddha's description of his experience while under the Bodhi tree, still deeply meditating, as elaborated on at great length in the *Huayan Jing*'s descriptions of worlds within worlds within worlds.

The meditations that are referred to in the text translated here, however, only involve three levels. This is because the first Dharmadhātu refers to our tacit, naïve acceptance of the autonomy of entities. Since the text is concerned only with meditations that call into question the validity of this tacit view, the first level of meditation actually refers to contemplation of the second Dharmadhātu.

One important distinction made by the *Commentary on Meditative Approaches to the Huayan Dharmadhātu* and elaborated on by the commentators is between two different ways of understanding "emptiness" (Skt. *śūnyatā*, Ch. *kong*). In Chinese and Sanskrit, as well as in English, the terms for emptiness are equivocal. In common usage, emptiness means absence or nonexistence. Zongmi calls this "nihilistic" emptiness and says that "nihilistic emptiness means vacuity, openness, absence, or extinction." This text usually distinguishes between nihilistic emptiness on the one hand and "true" emptiness on the other, which is called *śūnyatā*, or lack of self-being (Skt. *svabhāva*, Ch. *zixing*). In the Dharmadhātu model, emptiness corresponds to principle and form to phenomena, which links the Dharmadhātu model to the famous axiom in the *Heart Sūtra* that "form is identical to emptiness, emptiness is identical to form."

In relating emptiness to principle and form to phenomena, Dushun is drawing on what seems to be a conventional Chinese analytic device, *tiyong*, or "substance and function." This model was used already during the early Han, but was most dramatically employed by the neo-Confucian Zhuxi.[1] It serves to distinguish between descriptions of what something essentially is and descriptions of what it does, and seems to anticipate the distinction between universal and specific qualities. This use of Chinese categories to illustrate the Buddhist idea of emptiness is one reason the Huayan tradition is seen as a uniquely Chinese form of Buddhism.

Translation

In outline, there are three levels, compiled by the monk Dushun of Jongzhong South Mountain. The first level [of meditation] is "True Emptiness." The second level is "nonobstruction of Principle and Phenomena." The third level is "universal pervasion and complete accommodation."

The First Level: Meditation on True Emptiness

The First Level is the Dharma of the meditation on true emptiness, within which there are four topics and ten approaches. The first topic is the meditation on the convergence of various forms back into emptiness, the second topic is the meditation that clarifies the identity of emptiness and form, the third is the meditation on the nonobstruction of emptiness and form, and the fourth is the meditation on the total elimination of all fixation.

In the first of these topics, there are four approaches.

The First Approach: form is not identical to emptiness because it is identical to emptiness. Why do we say this? Form is not identical to nihilistic emptiness. Therefore it is not identical to emptiness. Because the collective essence of form is truly empty, this is why the text says "...because it is

1. For more discussion on this, see Chan 1989.

identical to emptiness." Consequently form is identical to true emptiness and not nihilistic emptiness. Therefore it is said that because form is truly empty, it is not nihilistically empty.

The Second Approach: form is not identical to emptiness because it is identical to emptiness. How can this be? The characteristics "blue" and "yellow" are not in themselves the principle "true emptiness." Therefore it was said that form is not identical to emptiness. However, blue and yellow are without individual essence, so it is not the case that they are not empty. That is why it was said that form is identical to emptiness. Because the emptiness of blue and yellow, which refers to their lack of individual essence, is not itself blue or yellow, it was said that they are not identical to emptiness.

The Third Approach: form is not identical to emptiness because it is identical to emptiness. How is this so? Because within emptiness there is no form, it is not identical to emptiness. The manifold of forms is without individual essence, however, and therefore it is empty. Consequently it is precisely because the formal manifold is itself empty that there can be no form within emptiness. It is therefore because form is empty that form is not the principle of true emptiness....

The Fourth Approach: form is identical to emptiness. How is this so? There can be no formal dharma[2] which is other than truly empty, because formal dharmas necessarily have no self-nature. Therefore form is precisely empty. All other dharmas should be considered to be just as empty as form.

The Second Topic: The meditation that illuminates the identity of emptiness and form, in which there are also four approaches.

The First Approach: emptiness is not identical to form because it is identical to form. How is this so? Because nihilistic emptiness is not identical to form, therefore it is said that it is not form. But there can be no True Emptiness apart from form, and so it is said that emptiness is identical to form. True Emptiness is identical to form, so it must be the case that nihilistic emptiness is not identical to form.

The Second Approach: emptiness is not identical to form because emptiness is identical to form. How can this be? Because the principle of "emptiness" is not "blue" or "yellow," it is said that emptiness is not identical to form. But emptiness is not totally other than blue and yellow, and so it is said that emptiness is identical to form. Because emptiness is not totally other than blue or yellow, it is not identical to blue or yellow. Therefore it is said that emptiness is identical to form and also not identical to form.

The Third Approach: emptiness is not identical to form because it is identical to form. How can this be? Because emptiness is that which supports, not that which is supported. Therefore it is not identical to form. However, there must be a support for there to be that which is supported. Therefore

2. The term "formal dharma" is taken to refer to form, or *rūpa*, as one of the five *skandhas*, or "aggregates of personality."

emptiness is identical to form. It is precisely because emptiness is the support of form that it is not the same as form; it is also because it is the support that it is identical to form. Thus it is both different from and the same as form....

The Fourth Approach: emptiness is identical to form. How so? Because whatever is truly empty cannot be other than form, because of the principle that dharmas are without selfhood. Therefore true emptiness is not nihilistic emptiness. Therefore emptiness is identical to form. Just as emptiness and form are like this, all dharmas should be similarly considered.

The Third Topic: Meditation on the nonobstruction of emptiness and form.

This means that form is entirely non-other than emptiness, because emptiness is entirely the exhaustion of form. Thus it is when form is exhausted that emptiness manifests. It is also the case the emptiness is entirely nondifferent from form, because form is entirely the exhaustion of emptiness. Thus it is that emptiness is identical to form, and yet emptiness is not [thereby] concealed. Therefore when a bodhisattva observes form, he cannot but see emptiness, and meditation on emptiness is nothing other than the seeing of form. They do not hinder or obstruct each other, and can be regarded as varieties of the same teaching....

The Fourth Topic: Meditation on the total elimination of all fixation.

This means that the true emptiness which is contemplated cannot be said to be identical to form, nor can it be said that emptiness is not identical to form, nor that form is identical to emptiness, nor that form is nonidentical to emptiness. All dharmas are inexpressible. Even their inexpressibility is also inexpressible. Furthermore, these words themselves are inconceivable. True emptiness is totally transcendent, and completely inaccessible to conceptual fixation. It is not linguistic....

The Second Level: Meditation on the Nonobstruction of Principle and Phenomenon

The First Approach: Principle encompasses phenomena. This means that the nature of the encompassing principle is not partial or limited, even though the phenomena that are encompassed are particular and distinct. The principle completely encompasses each and every phenomenon. Encompassing is not merely partial. How can this be? Because the true principle cannot be divided up. Therefore, each and every speck of dust contains the infinite true principle without the slightest imperfection.

The Second Approach: Phenomena encompass principle. This means that the phenomena that encompass are necessarily discrete, and the principle that is encompassed is necessarily non-discrete. These discrete phenomena are completely identical with the nondiscrete principle, not merely partially identical. How is this so? Because phenomena are without individual essence, as is principle. Therefore a single speck of dust encompasses the entire Dharmadhātu, and yet is not impaired. All dharmas are like that speck of dust, and should be similarly considered. This complete encompassing approach overcomes passionate obsession and transcends all particular points of view. No worldly metaphors can do it justice. It is as though the entire ocean were within a single wave, without the reduction of the ocean. It is as though a small wave were to completely encompass the whole ocean without the enlargement of the wave. Simultaneously, the ocean completely encompasses every wave, and yet the ocean is not differentiated. And each wave all at once completely encompasses the whole ocean, and yet there is not only one wave. Furthermore, while the whole ocean completely encompasses a single wave, this doesn't prevent it from entirely encompassing all other waves as well. While a single wave completely encompasses the whole ocean, all other waves also each completely encompass the whole ocean without mutually obstructing each other. . . .

The Third Approach: Phenomena are established in dependence on principle. This means that phenomena have no individual essence, and so there must be an actual principle in order for them to be established. Because all phenomena arise conditionally, therefore all are without intrinsic nature. It is due to the principle of absence of nature that phenomena are established. Just as water is a necessary cause for the production of waves, it is in dependence on the *tathāgatagarbha*[3] that dharmas can be said to exist.

The Fourth Approach: Phenomena can reveal principle. This means that because phenomena appropriate principle, phenomena are vacuous and principle is real. Because phenomena are vacuous, the entire principle is manifested within all phenomena perfectly clearly. This is just as the vacuousness of the characteristics of the wave causes the essence of the water to be evident. Thus should one understand this principle of the middle way.

The Fifth Approach: Phenomena are subsumed by principle. This means that since phenomena appropriate principle, the characteristics of phenomena are all thus exhausted. Only the ubiquity of the one true principle is evident because, apart from true principle, there cannot be even the merest fragment of a phenomenon. Therefore, this is just like the way water subsumes the waves so that there is no wave that is not exhausted. Thus is the water preserved by the exhaustive loss of identity of the waves.

The Sixth Approach: Phenomena can conceal principle. This means that true principle, when it accords with conditions, establishes phenomenal dharmas, but since these phenomenal dharmas are contrasted with principle, accordingly this causes phenomena to become apparent and principle to become nonapparent. This is the same as the water that establishes the waves. When the water moves, the waves are apparent, and when the water

3. *Tathāgatagarbha,* or "womb of Buddhahood," is a way of referring to soteriological potential. In Mahāyāna Buddhism, it is understood as the germ of Buddhahood that is "owned" by all sentient beings.

is calm, the waves are hidden. A *sūtra* says "The Dharmakaya circulating through the five paths is designated 'sentient beings.'" Therefore when sentient beings are evident, Dharmakaya is not evident.

The Seventh Approach: True principle is the same as phenomena. This means that whatsoever is true principle cannot be external to phenomena. Because of the principle that dharmas are without selfhood, phenomena must depend on principle, and so they are vacuous and without individual essence. The fact that this principle completely makes up all phenomena is regarded as the true principle. This is the same as the water's identity with the waves, in that there is no movement that is not wet. Therefore, the very water itself is the waves.

The Eighth Approach: Phenomenal dharmas are identical to principle. This means that conditionally arisen phenomenal dharmas must be without intrinsic nature. It is precisely because they are without intrinsic nature that they are all entirely authentic. Therefore it is said that sentient beings are already "thus," and need not await extinction to achieve this identity. This is the same as the superficial movements of the waves—they are entirely identical to the water. They have no distinct characteristics of their own.

The Ninth Approach: True principle is not a phenomenon. This means that the principle that is identical with phenomena is not itself a phenomenon, because the true and the false are different, because the substantial is not vacuous, and because that which is depended on is not the same as that which depends on it. This is the same as the way the water, which is identical to the waves, is not itself a wave, because movement is different from wetness.

The Tenth Approach: Phenomenal dharmas are not a principle. This means that the phenomena that are totally inclusive of principle are never themselves a principle, because characteristics (*lakṣaṇa*) and nature are different from each other, and because that which depends on is different from that which is depended on. Therefore phenomena are entirely principle, and yet their characteristics remain evident. This is the same as the waves, which though composed entirely of water, are not themselves water, because the meaning of movement is different from the meaning of wetness....

The Third Level: Meditation on Total Pervasion and Accommodation

Phenomena, like principle, are permeable, pervasive, and all-embracing without obstruction, combining and blending in complete freedom. The discussion consists of ten approaches.

The First Approach: Principle is similar to phenomena. This means that since phenomenal dharmas are vacuous, their characteristics cannot but be ultimately void. Since the nature of principle is truly real, its essence cannot but be evident. Thus phenomena are not distinct from other phenomena—it is entirely principle that makes up phenomena.

Therefore although bodhisattvas may often look at phenomena, they are observing principle. But they speak of phenomena as though they were not the same as principle.

The Second Approach: Phenomena are similar to principle. This means that phenomenal dharmas are none other than principle. Therefore, phenomena accord with principle and so are completely pervasive. Accordingly, while a single speck of dust encompasses the entire Dharmadhātu, and Dharmadhātu entirely encompasses all dharmas, this single minute speck of dust is also, like the nature of principle, entirely present within all dharmas. Like this single, minute speck of dust, all phenomenal dharmas are also thus.

The Third Approach: Each phenomenon accommodates principle and other phenomena. This means that the myriad phenomenal dharmas are not identical with principle, and that therefore even though the original individuality of a phenomenon is preserved, it is still able to broadly accommodate, just like a single minute speck of dust that is not large is able to accommodate and include the infinite Dharmadhātu. Since all dharmas in the countless Buddha worlds are never apart from the Dharmadhātu, therefore they are all together evident within a single speck of dust. Like a single speck of dust, all dharmas are also thus. Thus principle and phenomena interfuse and interpenetrate and therefore are not identical and not different. This can be summed up in four statements.

The first is that the individual is within the individual. The second is that the individual is within the multitude. The third is that the multitude is within the individual, and the fourth is that the multitude is present within the multitude. Each has its own reasoning. Consider this.

The Fourth Approach: The nonobstruction of the universal and the specific. This means that the nonidentity of all phenomenal dharmas with principle is equivalent to their nondifference. Thus, although a particular phenomenal dharma does not depart from its own single location, it entirely encompasses every single speck of dust in all of the ten directions. Because nondifference is equivalent to nonidentity, therefore each individual phenomenon entirely encompasses the ten directions without moving. At a single position, it is both far and near, both encompassing and abiding in, without hindrance and without obstruction.

The Fifth Approach: The nonobstruction of the broad and the narrow. This means that the nonidentity of phenomena and principle is equivalent to their nondifference. Without any impairment of a single speck of dust, each is capable of broadly accommodating all the Buddha Lands and oceans in the ten directions. Because of this equivalence of nondifference and nonidentity, each phenomenon can broadly accommodate the whole Dharmadhātu in all ten directions without a single minute speck of dust thereby becoming large. Thus the tiniest phenomenon is both broad and narrow, both large and small, without hindrance and without obstruction.

The Sixth Approach: The nonobstruction of pervasion and accommodation. This means that when all specks of dust are viewed from the perspective of a single speck of dust, their total pervasion is equivalent to their broad accommodation. Therefore when each speck of dust is encompassed by all the others, it also conversely contains them all. All dharmas are entirely present within the individual itself. Moreover, because their broad accommodation is equivalent to their total encompassing, this single speck of dust is encompassed by all the distinct dharmas contained within it. Therefore when this speck of dust itself encompasses the others, the others already are encompassing it, which is able to accommodate and enter, simultaneously encompassing and containing without obstruction.

The Seventh Approach: The nonobstruction of including and entering. This means that, when viewing a single dharma from the perspective of all dharmas, this single dharma's entrance into all the others is equivalent to it including all the others. Therefore, when the multitude entirely enters into the individual, that individual conversely resides within the multitude that is within itself, simultaneously and without obstruction. Consider this. Moreover, because including others is equivalent to entering others, when an individual dharma entirely resides within the multitude it is also the case that the multitude is always present within the individual simultaneously and without obstruction.

The Eighth Approach: The nonobstruction of interpenetration. This means that when the multitude is seen from the perspective of a single dharma, there is inclusion and entrance. In general, there are four aspects to this: (1) the individual includes the multitude just as the individual enters the multitude; (2) the multitude includes the individual and the multitude enters into the individual; (3) the individual includes the individual and the individual enters into the individual; and (4) the multitude includes the multitude while the multitude enters the multitude. There is simultaneous merging without obstruction.

The Ninth Approach: Mutual presence without obstruction. This means that, when viewing the individual from the perspective of the multitude, again there is entering and including, and again we have four statements: (1) the multitude includes the individual and enters the individual; (2) the multitude includes the multitude and enters into the individual; (3) the multitude includes the individual and enters into the multitude; and (4) the multitude includes the multitude and enters into the multitude, simultaneously interpenetrating without obstruction.

The Tenth Approach: Universal interfusion without obstruction. This means that the multitude and the individual are all universally simultaneous. When they are viewed from each other's perspective, each of the previous two sets of four statements universally interfuses without obstruction.

Bibliography and Suggested Reading

Chan, Wing-tsit. (1989) *Chu Hsi: New Studies*. Honolulu: University of Hawai'i Press.

Chang, Garma. (1971) *Buddhist Teaching of Totality: the Philosophy of Hwa Yen Buddhism*. University Park: Pennsylvania State University Press.

Cleary, Thomas. (1983) *Entry into the Inconceivable: An Introduction to Hua-yen Buddhism*. Honolulu: University of Hawai'i Press.

Cleary, Thomas, trans. (1984) *Flower Ornament Scripture*. Boston, Shambhala Publications.

Cook, Francis. (1977) *Hua-yen Buddhism: The Jewel Net of Indra*. University Park: Pennsylvania State University Press.

Gimello, Robert and Peter Gregory, eds. (1983) *Studies in Ch'an and Hua-yen*. Honolulu: Kuroda Institute.

Gregory, Peter. (1995) *Inquiry into the Origins of Humanity: An Annotated Translation of Tsung-mi's "Yuan jen lun" with a Modern Commentary*. Honolulu: Kuroda Institute.

7

Dōgen's "Mountains and Waters as *Sūtras*" (*Sansui-kyō*)

Graham Parkes

This poetic and profound chapter of Dōgen's (1200–53) *Shōbōgenzō* was first delivered as a lecture in the year 1240.[1] The title—*Sansui* (literally: "mountains waters") means "landscape" and *Kyō* refers to the scriptures of the Buddha's oral teachings—expresses a central idea in Japanese Buddhist philosophy: that the natural world can be experienced and understood both as a spiritual sermon and sacred scripture, as a spoken and written expression of the Buddhist teachings. Some background may render this more understandable.

After Buddhism spread from India to China, some Chinese thinkers began to ask—perhaps under the influence of Daoist ideas—whether the Mahāyāna extension of the promise of Buddhahood to "all sentient beings" went far enough. A long-running debate ensued in the eighth century, in which thinkers in the Tian-tai school argued that Mahāyāna universalism undermined the distinction between sentient and nonsentient beings, and that Buddha-nature is to be ascribed not only to plants, trees, and the earth, but even to particles of dust.[2] In Japan, the first Buddhist thinker to elaborate the idea of the awakened nature of all phenomena and make it central to his thought was the founder of Shingon esoteric Buddhism, Kūkai (744–835).

1. Although the title is always translated as "The Mountains and Waters Sūtra," I don't believe that Dōgen was presuming to write a sacred text. I have inserted "as" in order to bring out the main meaning of the essay (as explained at the beginning of the introduction).
2. For an illuminating account of this debate, see LaFleur 1989.

Kūkai developed a highly sophisticated but very down-to-earth philosophy that emphasized the possibility of "attaining enlightenment in this very body" (*sokushin jōbutsu*). He also argued that the Dharmakāya, which had been regarded as eternal, absolute reality, is nothing other than the "reality embodiment" of the cosmic Buddha Dainichi Nyorai (Skt. Mahāvairocana). Natural bodies thereby become central to Japanese Buddhist practice and thought. Kūkai elaborated this idea into the teaching of *hosshin seppō:* "the Dharmakāya expounds the Dharma," or "the Buddha's reality embodiment expounds the true teachings."[3] Although this exposition does not take place for our benefit (there are other, more directly beneficent Buddhas who see to that), we can become able to "overhear" this expounding through practice in listening with the "third ear."

Just as the natural world can be heard as Dainichi's expounding the Dharma, it can also be *read* as a sacred scripture, in which all phenomena are the letters or written characters. In an essay on the *Mahāvairocana Sūtra,* Kūkai writes that the ultimate text of that *sūtra* is the entire universe: "the vast and boundless text that exists spontaneously and permanently, namely, the mandala of the Dharma of all the Buddhas."[4] More graphically, he writes in one of his poems:

> Being painted by brushes of mountains, by ink of oceans,
> Heaven and earth are the bindings of a *sūtra* revealing the truth.[5]

Again, it takes practice to be able to read this *sūtra,* and the emphasis in this case would be on opening the "third eye" through mandala meditation and other forms of visualization.

Dōgen's philosophy has roots in common with Kūkai's thought, especially with respect to his understanding of the natural world. Corresponding to Kūkai's identification of the Dharmakāya qua Dainichi with the physical universe is Dōgen's understanding of natural landscape as "the body of the Buddha." In an early chapter of the *Shōbōgenzō,* "Voices of the Valleys, Forms of the Mountains" (Keisei-sanshiki), he quotes a verse by the eleventh-century Chinese poet Su Dongpo:

> The voices of the river-valley are the Wide and Long Tongue,
> The forms of the mountain are nothing other than his Pure Body.[6]

Perhaps in order to avoid the absolutist connotations of the traditional idea of the Dharmakāya, Dōgen substitutes for Kūkai's *hosshin seppō* the notion of *mujō-seppō,* which emphasizes that even insentient beings (*mujō*) expound

3. For a fine explication of this idea, see Kasulis 1995.
4. Kūkai, cited in Abe 1999: 275.
5. Kūkai, cited in Hakeda 1972: 91.
6. Dōgen 1994: 1:86. One of the Buddha's distinguishing features is his wide and long tongue.

the true teachings: "The insentient preach the Dharma. In this preaching the Buddhas are present and the patriarchs are present."[7] Dōgen encourages, like Kūkai, practice that effects an opening up of normal, everyday awareness so that such preaching may become audible. "When we each get rid of our husk, we are not restricted by former views and understanding, and things which for vast kalpas have been unclear suddenly appear before us."[8]

Kūkai's notion that the ultimate *sūtra* is the universe itself appears again in Dōgen, who counters an overemphasis on study of literal scriptures in certain schools of Buddhism by maintaining that *sūtras* are more than ancient texts and scrolls containing written characters. In the chapter "The Buddhist Sūtras" (*Bukkyō*) he writes:

> What has been called "the *sūtras*" is the whole Universe in the ten directions itself; there is no time or place that is not the *sūtras*. They use...the words and letters of the heavens above and the human world; they use the words and letters of the world of animals and the world of angry demons; they use the words and letters of the hundred weeds and the ten thousand trees.[9]

The words and letters of plants and animals differ from those employed by humans, and thus constitute "natural language" in the literal sense. This, then, is the main theme of "Mountains and Waters as Sūtras": insofar as we can dissolve our unexamined prejudices and conventional modes of experience, we can come to appreciate the natural world as "the actualization of the ancient Buddha Way" (sec. 1), and to hear and read it as a sermon and sacred scripture expounding the Buddhist teachings. One prejudice to be overcome is that only we humans walk, and that beings such as mountains stand still. But what is our actual experience of walking in the mountains? Well, when one walks the mountains appear to move, and when one stops they appear to stop moving—unless of course one turns one's head, in which case they begin to move again. What is immediately given to one's perception when one walks are mountains in motion: but because we (think we) know that mountains don't really move, we have formed the habit of mentally construing them as standing still. (The geologists tell us that mountains do indeed move, but too slowly for the human eye to perceive.)

Dōgen says that viewing the world from the usual anthropocentric standpoint is like "looking through a bamboo tube at the corner of the sky" (sec. 6). For a fuller experience, he recommends entertaining the perspectives of other beings, such as mountains, drops of water, celestial beings, hungry ghosts, dragons, and fish. "'In the mountains' means the blossoming of the entire world. People outside the mountains do not realize or

7. Dōgen, "Insentient Beings Expound the Dharma, " in Dōgen 1994: 3:114.
8. Dōgen, "Voices of the Valleys, Forms of the Mountains," in Dōgen 1994: 1:85.
9. Dōgen, "The Buddhist *Sūtras*," in Dōgen 1994: 3:102.

understand the mountains' walking" (sec. 4). Here he is contrasting the view ("outside the mountains") that regards mountains as objects standing over against a subject, or as representations in a human consciousness, with one that breaks out of the anthropocentric perspective by driving to the heart of the mountain itself. *San chū* ("in the mountains": literally, "mountain center") here refers to experience from the heart, or center, of the mountain itself, thus from a broader—because at least bicentric—perspective.[10] (And so forth, through other beings, to a polycentric perspectivism.)

A brief look at what Dōgen says about water will afford a better sense of his "perspectivism." One reason he focuses on water (as did the classical Daoist thinkers who influenced him) is because it is susceptible to multiple transformations: "When water solidifies, it is harder than a diamond. [. . .] When water melts, it is gentler than milk" (sec. 11). It can also appear, mysteriously, as dew, and scald unpleasantly as vapor when boiled. After invoking the idea of the "four views of water" from the Indian Buddhist tradition, Dōgen asks: "Are there many ways to see one thing, or is it a mistake to see many forms as one thing?" (sec. 12). The answer: Yes, there are many ways to see, for example, water, and there is no reason to regard any one way as privileged because fully adequate; and yes, it is a mistake to see many forms as one thing, if this view leads to an idea of some essential being of water apart from its myriad manifestations ("there is no original water"). But this does not prevent particular bodies of water from being quite different from, say, bits of earth, since each particular phenomenon, occupying a unique position in the complex web of interrelations that is the world, "abides in its own dharma-position" (sec. 13).

Because Dōgen subscribes to the Kegon (Huayan) Buddhist idea of nonobstruction, when he writes "there is a world in water" (sec. 20), he is talking not only about water but about each and every phenomenon—as a jewel in Indra's Net—in which the entire relational network is reflected. (Not unlike Blake's seeing "the universe in a grain of sand.")

There is no space here to articulate the ecological implications of this gem of an essay, but one thing is clear: insofar as natural phenomena are not only a locus of enlightenment but also sources of wisdom and companions on the Buddha Way, if we wantonly destroy them for our own benefit, we actually thereby diminish our own opportunities for fulfillment.[11] After all, "Such mountains and waters of themselves become wise persons and sages" (sec. 22).[12]

10. One is reminded here, appropriately, of Aldo Leopold's beautiful essay "Thinking Like a Mountain."

11. For a discussion of this issue, see Parkes 2003.

12. The following translation is abridged from "Mountains and Waters Sūtra," translated by Arnold Kotler and Kazuaki Tanahashi, in Tanahashi 1985: 97–107. We gratefully acknowledge permission to republish this work.

Translation

1 Mountains and waters right now are the actualization of the ancient buddha way. Each, abiding in its dharma-position, realizes completeness.[13] Because mountains and waters have been active since before the Empty Eon, they are alive at this moment. Because they have been the self since before form arose they are emancipation realization.

2 Because mountains are high and broad, the way of riding the clouds is always reached in the mountains; the inconceivable power of soaring in the wind comes freely from the mountains.

3 Priest Daokai of Mt. Furong said to the assembly, "The green mountains are always walking; a stone woman gives birth to a child at night."[14] Mountains do not lack the qualities of mountains. Therefore they always abide in ease and always walk.[15] You should examine in detail this quality of the mountains walking. Mountains' walking is just like human walking. Accordingly, do not doubt mountains' walking even though it does not look the same as human walking. The buddha ancestors' words point to walking. This is fundamental understanding. You should penetrate these words.

4 Because green mountains walk, they are permanent. Although they walk more swiftly than the wind, someone in the mountains does not realize or understand it. "In the mountains" means the blossoming of the entire world. People outside the mountains do not realize or understand the mountains' walking. Those without eyes to see mountains cannot realize, understand, see, or hear this as it is. If you doubt mountains' walking, you do not know your own walking; it is not that you do not walk, but that you do not know or understand your own walking. Since you do not know your walking, you should fully know the green mountains' walking. Green mountains are neither sentient nor insentient. You are neither sentient nor insentient. At this moment, you cannot doubt the green mountains' walking.

5 You should study the green mountains, using numerous worlds as your standard. You should clearly examine the green mountains' walking and

13. I have changed the translation of *hō-i* as "phenomenal expression" to the more literal "dharma-position," since the term refers to the way every phenomenon arises and perishes at a particular point in the vast and dynamic network of interrelations that, for Dōgen, makes up the world.

14. A quotation from a thirteenth-century Chan Buddhist text *Jiatai pudenglu* (Jiatai record of the universal lamps), chap. 3.

15. "Walking" in this chapter refers to Buddhist practice, but also more generally to the movement, or impermanence (arising and perishing), that characterizes all phenomena.

your own walking. You should also examine walking backward and backward walking and investigate the fact that walking forward and backward has never stopped since the very moment before form arose, since the time of the King of the Empty Eon.

If walking stops, buddha ancestors do not appear. If walking ends, the buddha-dharma cannot reach the present. Walking forward does not cease; walking backward does not cease.[16] Walking forward does not obstruct walking backward. Walking backward does not obstruct walking forward. This is called the mountains' flow and the flowing mountains.

6 Green mountains master walking and eastern mountains master traveling on water. Accordingly, these activities are a mountain's practice. Keeping its own form, without changing body and mind, a mountain always practices in every place. Don't slander by saying that a green mountain cannot walk and an eastern mountain cannot travel on water. When your understanding is shallow, you doubt the phrase "Green mountains are walking." When your learning is immature, you are shocked by the words "flowing mountains." Without fully understanding even the words "flowing water," you drown in small views and narrow understanding.

Yet the characteristics of mountains manifest their form and life-force. There is walking, there is flowing, and there is a moment when a mountain gives birth to a mountain child. Because mountains are buddha ancestors, buddha ancestors appear in this way. Even if you see mountains as grass, trees, earth, rocks, or walls, do not take this seriously or worry about it; it is not complete realization. Even if there is a moment when you view mountains as the seven treasures shining, this is not the true source. Even if you understand mountains as the realm where all Buddhas practice, this understanding is not something to be attached to. Even if you have the highest understanding of mountains as all Buddhas' inconceivable qualities, the truth is not only this. These are conditioned views. This is not the understanding of the buddha ancestors, but just looking through a bamboo tube at the corner of the sky.

Turning an object and turning the mind is rejected by the great sage. Explaining the mind and explaining true nature is not agreeable to buddha ancestors. Seeing into mind and seeing into true nature is the activity of people outside the way.[17] Set words and phrases are not the words of liberation. There is something free from all of these understandings: "Green mountains are always walking," and "Eastern mountains travel on water." You should study this in detail. [...]

16. "Walking backward" is an allusion to the "step back" that is required in Zen practice to reach our "original nature."

17. Dōgen rejects these pairs of activities as inadequate because they mistakenly regard mind and nature as separate.

11 Water is neither strong nor weak, neither wet nor dry, neither moving nor still, neither cold nor hot, neither existent nor nonexistent, neither deluded nor enlightened. When water solidifies, it is harder than a diamond. Who can crack it? When water melts, it is gentler than milk. Who can destroy it? Do not doubt that these are the characteristics water manifests. You should reflect on the moment when you see the water of the ten directions as the water of the ten directions. This is not just studying the moment when human and heavenly beings see water; this is studying the moment when water sees water. This is a complete understanding. You should go forward and backward and leap beyond the vital path where other fathoms other.[18]

12 All beings do not see mountains and waters in the same way.[19] Some beings see water as a jeweled ornament, but they do not regard jeweled ornaments as water. What in the human realm corresponds to their water? We only see their jeweled ornaments as water. Some beings see water as wondrous blossoms, but they do not use blossoms as water. Hungry ghosts see water as raging fire or pus and blood. Dragons see water as a palace or a pavilion. Some beings see water as the seven treasures or a wish-granting jewel. Some beings see water as a forest or a wall. Some see it as the Dharma nature of pure liberation, the true human body, or as the form of body and essence of mind. Human beings see water as water. Water is seen as dead or alive depending on causes and conditions.

Thus the views of all beings are not the same. You should question this matter now. Are there many ways to see one thing, or is it a mistake to see many forms as one thing? You should pursue this beyond the limit of pursuit. Accordingly, endeavors in practice-realization of the way are not limited to one or two kinds. The ultimate realm has one thousand kinds and ten thousand ways.

When we think about the meaning of this, it seems that there is water for various beings but there is no original water—there is no water common to all types of beings. But water for these various kinds of beings does not depend on mind or body, does not arise from actions, does not depend on self or other. Water's freedom depends only on water. Therefore, water is not just earth, water, fire, wind, space, or consciousness. Water is not blue, yellow, red, white, or black. Water is not forms, sounds, smells, tastes,

18. This is a recommendation to entertain the perspective of the other (phenomenon that one wants to understand) and from there as many other perspectives as are appropriate for the context.

19. Dōgen is alluding here to the "four views of water" in the Mahāyāna tradition. The glossary for the Tanahashi translation cites the following passage from the commentary on Asaṅga's *Treatise on Emerging Mahāyāna* by Asvabhā (450–530): "It is like water, whose nature remains the same. But as celestial beings, human beings, hungry ghosts, and fish do not carry the same effect (from past causations), they each see water differently. Celestial beings see it as jewels, people in the world see it as water, hungry ghosts see it as pus and blood, and fish see it as a palace" (Tanahashi 1985: 285).

touchables, or mind-objects. But water as earth, water, fire, wind, and space realizes itself.

For this reason, it is difficult to say who is creating this land and palace right now or how such things are being created. To say that the world is resting on the wheel of space or on the wheel of wind is not the truth of the self or the truth of others. Such a statement is based only on a small view. People speak this way because they think that it must be impossible to exist without having a place on which to rest.

13 Buddha said, "All things are ultimately liberated. There is nowhere that they abide." You should know that even though all things are liberated and not tied to anything, they abide in their own dharma-position. However, when most human beings see water they only see that it flows unceasingly. This is a limited human view; there are actually many kinds of flowing. Water flows on the earth, in the sky, upward, and downward. It can flow around a single curve or into bottomless abysses. When it rises it becomes clouds. When it descends it forms abysses. [...]

16 Now when dragons and fish see water as a palace, it is just like human beings seeing a palace. They do not think it flows. If an outsider tells them "What you see as a palace is running water," the dragons and fish will be astonished, just as we are when we hear the words "Mountains flow." Nevertheless, there may be some dragons and fish who understand that the columns and pillars of palaces and pavilions are flowing water. You should reflect and consider the meaning of this. If you do not learn to be free from your superficial views, you will not be free from the body and mind of an ordinary person. Then you will not understand the land of buddha ancestors, or even the land or the palace of ordinary people.

Now human beings well know as water what is in the ocean and what is in the river, but they do not know what dragons and fish see as water and use as water. Do not foolishly suppose that what we see as water is used as water by all other beings. Do not foolishly suppose that what we see as water is used as water by all other beings. You who study with Buddhas should not be limited to human views when you are studying water. You should study how you view the water used by buddha ancestors. You should study whether there is water or no water in the house of buddha ancestors.

17 Mountains have been the abode of great sages from the limitless past to the limitless present. Wise people and sages all have mountains as their inner chamber, as their body and mind. Because of wise people and sages, mountains appear. You may think that in mountains many wise people and great sages are assembled. But after entering the mountains, not a single person meets another. There is just the activity of the mountains. There is no trace of anyone having entered the mountains.

When you see mountains from the ordinary world, and when you meet mountains while in mountains, the mountains' head and eye are viewed quite differently. Your idea or view of mountains not flowing is not the same as the view of dragons and fish. Human and heavenly beings have attained a position concerning their own worlds which other beings either doubt or do not doubt. You should not just remain bewildered and skeptical when you hear the words "Mountains flow"; but together with buddha ancestors you should study these words. When you take one view you see mountains flowing, and when you take another view, mountains are not flowing. One time mountains are flowing, another time they are not flowing. If you do not fully understand this, you do not understand the true Dharma wheel of the Tathāgata.

An ancient buddha said, "If you do not wish to incur the cause for Unceasing Hell, do not slander the true Dharma wheel of the Tathāgata." You should carve these words on your skin, flesh, bones, and marrow; on your body, mind, and environs; on emptiness and on form. They are already carved on trees and rocks, on fields and villages. [...]

20 It is not only that there is water in the world, but there is a world in water. It is not just in water. There is also a world of sentient beings in clouds. There is a world of sentient beings in the air. There is a world of sentient beings in fire. There is a world of sentient beings on earth. There is a world of sentient beings in the phenomenal world. There is a world of sentient beings in a blade of grass. There is a world of sentient beings in one staff. Wherever there is a world of sentient beings, there is a world of buddha ancestors. You should thoroughly examine the meaning of this.

21 Therefore water is the true dragon's palace. It is not flowing downward. To consider water as only flowing is to slander water with the word "flowing." This would be the same as insisting that water does not flow. Water is only the true thusness of water. Water is water's complete virtue; it is not flowing. When you investigate the flowing of a handful of water and the not-flowing of it, full mastery of all things is immediately present.

22 There are mountains hidden in treasures. There are mountains hidden in swamps. There are mountains hidden in the sky. There are mountains hidden in mountains. There are mountains hidden in hiddenness. This is complete understanding. An ancient buddha said, "Mountains are mountains, waters are waters." These words do not mean mountains are mountains; they mean mountains are mountains. Therefore investigate mountains thoroughly. When you investigate mountains thoroughly, this is the work of the mountains. Such mountains and waters of themselves become wise persons and sages.

Bibliography and Suggested Reading

Abe, Ryūichi. (1999) *The Weaving of Mantra: Kūkai and the Construction of Esoteric Buddhist Discourse.* New York: Columbia University Press.

Dōgen. (1994) "Voices of the Valleys, Forms of the Mountains." In *Master Dogen's Shobogenzo,* translated by Gudo Wafu Nishijima and Chodo Cross. 4 vols. Woking, Surrey, England: Windbell.

Dōgen. (2001) "Mountains and Waters Sūtra." Translated by Carl Bielefeldt. Soto Zen Text Project, www.stanford.edu/group/scbs/sztp3/translations/shobogenzo/translations/sansuikyo/sansuikyo.html.

Hakeda, Yoshito S. (1972) *Kūkai: Major Works.* New York: Columbia University Press.

Kasulis, Thomas P. (1995) "Reality as Embodiment: An Analysis of Kūkai's *Sokushinjōbutsu* and *Hosshin Seppō.*" In Jane Marie Law, ed., *Religious Reflections on the Human Body.* Bloomington: Indiana University Press, 166–185.

Kim, Hee-Jin. (2004) *Dōgen: Mystical Realist.* Boston: Wisdom.

Kim, Hee-Jin. (2006) *Dōgen on Meditation and Thinking: A Reflection on His View of Zen.* Albany: State University of New York Press.

LaFleur, William R., ed. (1985) *Dōgen Studies.* Honolulu: University of Hawai'i Press.

LaFleur, William R. (1989) "Saigyō and the Buddhist Value of Nature." In J. Baird Callicott and Roger T. Ames, eds., *Nature in Asian Traditions of Thought: Essays in Environmental Philosophy.* Albany: State University of New York Press, 183–209.

Parkes, Graham. (2003) "Mountain Brushes, Ink of Oceans: Nature as Sacred in Japanese Buddhism." In H. Eisenhofer-Salim, ed., *Wandel zwischen den Welten.* Frankfurt: Peter Lang, 557–574.

Tanahashi, Kazuaki. (1985) *Moon in a Dewdrop: Writings of Zen Master Dogen.* New York: North Point Press.

8

Nishitani Keiji's "The Standpoint of Zen: Directly Pointing to the Mind"

Bret W. Davis

Nishitani Keiji (1900–1990) is arguably the most famous and most significant modern "philosopher of Zen." There are of course many renowned modern Zen masters, and a number of famous modern Japanese philosophers—beginning with Nishida Kitarō, the founder of the Kyoto School, of which Nishitani is the central figure of the second generation. Yet Nishitani stands out for being a first-rate philosopher who also thoroughly practiced and reflected on Zen Buddhism.

Nishitani never simply conflated the critical and speculative thinking of philosophy with the experiential practice of Zen; rather, he saw philosophy's rational pursuit of wisdom and Zen's embodied "investigation into the self" as mutually supportive endeavors in a life of "sitting [in meditation], then thinking; thinking, then sitting." Although he was by profession a philosopher, he was one who recognized the limits of merely intellectual inquiry in fully addressing the existential plight of human beings, especially in an age of nihilism. Both his philosophical studies and his personal journey led him to take up the practice of Zen together with the study of Buddhist thought.

Although Nishitani always preferred to consider himself first and foremost a philosopher, rejecting for example the label of "natural theologian of Zen," he did come to philosophize explicitly from and about what he called "the standpoint of Zen." Even so, in the preface to his magnum opus, *What Is Religion?* (translated as *Religion and Nothingness,* 1982), he says that "this does not mean that a position is being taken from the start on the doctrines of Buddhism as a particular religion or on the doctrines of one of its sects." While he tends to adopt the central terms of his philosophy from Buddhism, and from Zen in particular, this is said to be done only "insofar as they illuminate reality and the essence and actuality of human being."[1] Nevertheless, near the end of *What Is Religion?* Nishitani does claim: "If I have frequently had occasion to deal with the standpoints of Buddhism, and particularly Zen Buddhism, the fundamental reason is that [the original form of reality and the original countenance of human being] seem to me to appear there most plainly and unmistakably."[2]

In the preface to the sequel volume to his magnum opus, *The Standpoint of Zen,* Nishitani explains the role of philosophy for him as that of a two-way mediator between Zen and the everyday world. He writes of "proceeding on a path from the pre-philosophical to philosophy, and then further from philosophy to the post-philosophical. Yet at the same time this implies the reverse direction, in other words, a return path from the standpoint of the 'practice' of Zen, through the standpoint of philosophy, and back to the place of the pre-philosophical."[3]

When Nishitani speaks of "philosophy" here, he is clearly referring in part to the Western academic discipline that was introduced into Japan beginning in the latter half of the nineteenth century, in several areas of which he himself was a leading expert. (Nishitani wrote extensively on German Idealism and existentialism, as well as on Meister Eckhart and Christian mysticism.) But he is presumably also referring to the philosophies of Mahāyāna Buddhism, with which he also became intimately familiar. Whereas in *What Is Religion?* he often alludes to Madhyamaka, Tiantai, and especially Huayan thought, in the passages excerpted here from the opening chapter of *The Standpoint of Zen* he seeks to clarify the relation of Vijñaptimātratā ("consciousness-only," also known as Cittamātra or "mind-only") philosophy to Zen, as well as comparing and contrasting these along the way with aspects of Western thought.

While drawing deeply on consciousness-only or mind-only philosophy for its understanding of the "mind" that is to be "directly pointed to" in order to "see into one's own true nature and become a Buddha," ultimately Zen emphasizes the necessity of "slicing right through the field of the eighth consciousness" (Hakuin). That is to say, in order to enable a direct nondual engagement in the world, one must cut off the very root of the ego-subject's karmic consciousness, a consciousness that allows the world to be experienced only through dualistic lenses crafted by habitual volitional impulses. Nishitani claims that the nondualistic standpoint of Zen, attained by way of uprooting this source of dualistic consciousness, can ultimately be understood no more in terms of "idealism" than in terms of "materialism."

1. Nishitani 1986–95: 10:v; Nishitani 1982: xlix.
2. Nishitani 1986–95:10:288; Nishitani 1982: 261.
3. Nishitani 1986–95:11: 8.

In the first half of "The Standpoint of Zen," which is not reproduced here, Nishitani explains Zen in terms of what Daitō Kokushi called an "investigation into the self" (*koji-kyūmei*). Nishitani compares and contrasts this investigation with Socrates' quest to "know thyself," as well as comparing and contrasting Descartes's method of doubt with the "great doubt" involved in Zen practice. In the second half of "The Standpoint of Zen," from which the following selections are taken, he proceeds to examine the "direct pointing to the mind" that is the ultimate aim of this radical path of self-investigation.[4]

Translation

...Zen is the standpoint which exhaustively investigates the self itself. It is also spoken of as the way which sees through to the original face of the self....Zen is [ultimately then] the standpoint of "directly pointing to the human mind, seeing into one's own true nature and becoming a Buddha."...How is the "human mind" conceived in this expression? The term *mind* is one which is constantly used throughout Buddhism, not only in Zen. What does this term refer to? Generally speaking, how we conceive the mind is thought to radically influence how we view the human being. The same holds true for how we view "the self": the way we view the mind may give rise to various ways of thinking when we investigate the self. The divergence in the Eastern and Western views of the human being may be said to be based on the difference in how the mind is thought of, and in turn how the self is viewed.

Ordinarily we think of ourselves as having a mind, or that there is a mind within us. When the mind is thought of as the unity of various faculties such as sensation, the appetites, cognition and the like, then the self becomes that which possesses these faculties. And since all things in the world, including human beings, are known only via the self's sensations and intellect, the self is the vantage point from which all things come to be seen. In this sense, the self takes on the appearance of always being located at the center of everything. The mental faculties of the self are like beams of light emitted in all

4. The text presented here consists of selections from the second half of Nishitani's "Zen no tachiba" (The standpoint of Zen); the subtitle has been added by the editor. The original text was first published in *Kōza Zen*, vol. 1 (Tokyo: Chikuma Shobō, 1967) before being placed at the beginning of a book by the same title, *The Standpoint of Zen*, which is now available as vol. 11 of Nishitani 1986–95. The translation, which has been reprinted here with only a few modifications by the editor, was done by John C. Maraldo and published in *The Eastern Buddhist* 17/1 (1984): 1–26 (with the exception of the first two sentences, the selections reprinted here are from pp. 12–26). The translator informs us that he was able to consult directly with Nishitani, and that "revisions have been made by the author in collaboration with the translator." We gratefully acknowledge permission to republish this work.

directions from this center. Entailed by this notion of self is a mode of being: it is itself the center of the world. The self sees and grasps the self placing itself in the center, opposite all other things. This is the self's self-centered mode of being and way of seeing. That is, thinking of the self as having a mind, and thinking of this mind as the unity of various faculties, both reflect the self's self-centered mode of being.

On the other hand, a completely opposite way of viewing matters is also possible, and in fact has existed since ancient times. In contrast to viewing the mind from the vantage point of one's "self," the mind is seen from the vantage point of the "world."... From this viewpoint, that which is seen as the faculties the self "possesses" within it, each "faculty" or "power" *sui generis,* can also be seen as something which extends throughout the world and has universality.... Assuming a different way of viewing things, then, the mind or faculties within us can be seen as something extending to all other living beings, with the world as its field. From this perspective, the "minds" which exist within all individual living things or human beings are individuations of the great "mind" extending throughout the world....

The way of seeing which sees the mind from the field of the world forms the basis of diverse myths in both East and West, and has found its way into various religions and philosophies. It constitutes from the beginning a strong undercurrent in the history of Western philosophy, where concepts like World-soul and World-mind have often appeared. Suffice it here to cite as examples the names of Anaxagoras, Plotinus and Schelling. Viewed from such a perspective, the "mind" assumes rather the central position in the universe or world and forms the vantage point from which all things are to be seen. The minds of individual living beings, as well as of individual humans, are as it were beams of light emitted from that center. We cannot go into details here, but a way of seeing along these lines has deeply permeated the *Geistesgeschichte* of the world. Looking at the human being as a microcosm over against the macrocosm, for example, derives from such a way of seeing. In a word, it can be called a cosmocentric way of viewing the mind....

The two ways of viewing the mind, cosmocentric and self-centric, have been inseparably preserved throughout Buddhism, in marked contrast to the West.... In Buddhism, the mind that discriminates between subject and object, and between the mind itself and other things, has been considered from a holistic standpoint as part of cosmic, universal mind. As representative of this standpoint we can cite the theory of *vijñaptimātratā,* consciousness-only.[5] In rough outline, the theory of consciousness-only is a system which places in the center of Buddhist doctrine the "mind," ontologically

5. *The doctrine of vijñaptimātratā* ("consciousness-only") is generally synonymous with *cittamātra* ("mind-only"). The school that developed this philosophy is most often referred to as Yogācāra.

speaking, or "consciousness" (*vijñāna*) epistemologically speaking, or in general "mind-consciousness."...

As is commonly known, consciousness-only theory distinguishes eight consciousnesses. The first five are sensations such as seeing, hearing and the like; the sixth, *mano-vijñāna* or thought-consciousness, unifying the first five, gives rise via judgment to cognitive knowledge. It seems almost comparable to the *sensus communis* and judgmental intellect combined of the medieval scholastic theory of mind in the West. In the seventh, *manas* or self-consciousness, the unifying function of the sixth becomes consciousness for-itself; here, along with self-attachment (*ātma-grāha*), arises the notion of ego-self, and one lapses into a self-centered way of being.... [Thus] far this theory for the most part runs parallel to the structure of "consciousness" as it has been conceived in the West since ancient times. However, a fundamental difference from the Western way of viewing consciousness and mind appears when the Eastern doctrine posits, as the ground of all, an eighth root consciousness, called the *ālaya* or store consciousness.

The *ālaya*-consciousness most aptly manifests the character of mind previously said to be universal on the world-plane. Constituting the basis of our minds, it is at the same time of the nature of what may be called a cosmic consciousness, or rather a cosmic unconscious. This unconscious is of course not to be understood merely in a psychological sense, but also as having ontological significance such as is implied in the concept of "life." Just as the "life" of living things is thought on the one hand to be the root potentiality out of which faculties such as sensations, emotions, impulses, appetites and finally intelligence are generated, and taken on the other hand as pervading our flesh and giving it life, the *ālaya*-consciousness is understood to include the aspect we call universal "life" of the world-plane.... Such an *ālaya*-consciousness lies latent at the base of the human mind and of the minds of all living things. And the activity of the human mind, acting from within the sphere of the *ālaya*-consciousness, sets in motion the consciousnesses up to the seventh one like a seed stretching out, and gives rise to our seeing, hearing, perceiving and knowing, our egoistic notions and ego-attachment. All these are the synthetic acts of the seven consciousnesses, whose influence in turn reaches the very depths of the mind and leaves traces in the *ālaya*-consciousness. These traces are deposited as new seeds in the *ālaya*-consciousness and thus become the potentialities for new activity in our mind-consciousness....

Our egoistic mode of being, our being ego-selves, signifies the mode of being of a mind-consciousness which divides subject and object, self and external world, or which, in terms of *vijñaptimātratā* or consciousness-only theory, divides consciousness (*vijñāna*) and its surrounding world of objects (*visaya*), and is in this sense the discriminating mind. It is the mind which grasps itself as if it were isolated from the world. Nevertheless, one of the fundamental teachings of consciousness-only theory consists in bringing to light the inauthenticity of this discriminating mind. The standpoint of discrimination is that of placing the ego-self in the center, regarding the things of the so-called external world, and becoming attached to them. But attachment to things is only the other side of attachment to self. It is a two-fold process: in the course of being attached to itself, the ego-self is attached to things, and in the course of being attached to things, it is attached to itself. While dividing self and things, it is tied to things and hence can neither truly become one with things nor truly become one's self. This mode of being is an essential, intrinsic aspect of the human mind; but regarded from the field of the *ālaya*-consciousness which forms the basis of this discriminative mind, the standpoint of the latter proves to have no foundation in truth whatsoever, to be "imaginary in nature" (*parikalpita svabhāva*).

Discriminative knowledge is essentially falsehood (*abhūta parikalpa*). Yet at the same time, considering the essential connection between the seventh consciousness which is the seat of the discriminating mind, and the eighth or *ālaya*-consciousness, we can see how difficult it is to shake off this falsity. For the *ālaya*-consciousness which becomes the ground for pointing out the falsity of discrimination is at the same time the hidden root of discrimination; the two are as inseparable as roots from the earth. Therefore, in order to free oneself from the discriminating mind and negate its falsity, one must break through the eighth as well as the seventh consciousness. To crack the rigid frame of the ego-self, the force binding the frame together must also be torn loose from its roots up. This great latent force, determining the apparently free discriminative activity of the ego-self from within its hidden depths, imparts to it the character of necessity called karma. The connection between the seventh and eighth consciousnesses can in this sense also be designated the "karma-consciousness" of *The Awakening of Faith in the Mahāyāna*. Breaking through the frame of the ego-self is only accomplished by cutting the roots of this karma-consciousness which reach to its depths. This is the meaning of Zen master Hakuin's saying, "Slice right through the field of the eighth consciousness."

To cut through the mind of self-attachment that arises in the form of the ego-self is at the same time to go beyond the world (or the so-called "three worlds" of desire, form, and formlessness). This is the "great death" of Zen, which cuts through the roots of life and death for the first time. In consciousness-only theory, it is said that in extinguishing *vijñāna* or consciousness, the *visaya* or world of objects over against it is finally extinguished. What comes to be manifest here is the non-discriminating or fundamental knowledge which in usual Buddhist parlance is called *prajñā*. Its standpoint is that which has transcended the world to the "other shore," which has gone beyond all possible beings in their very beingness, i.e., insofar as they are thought to *be*, and in this sense is called absolute emptiness (*śūnyatā*). This of course does not mean void or empty in a privative sense, emptiness as opposed to fullness. Rather it is the standpoint of the oneness of mind and things. Here all things cease to be the world of objects over against the discriminative mind, and manifest their true form in the field of absolute emptiness. All things manifesting their true form is nothing other than nondiscriminating knowledge. This then is the standpoint of the great wisdom of the oneness of things and mind, the wisdom that is *prajñā*. It is here that the realization of self as no-self, the awareness of one's own true self, occurs. All things are brought to light as being originally without self-nature, "self"-less, as being no-self-nature. All things are "no-self-nature as emptiness." And this at the same time means that each and every thing becomes manifest in its true reality. Consciousness-only theory calls this field of self-realization or awareness "*parinispanna svabhāva*"—perfected, real nature.

Earlier I cited the Zen saying, "Directly pointing to the human mind, seeing into one's own true nature and becoming a Buddha." From the example of consciousness-only theory just given we may surmise the kind of background against which "the human mind" is understood. Based in its depths on the universal mind coextensive with the whole world which it has in common with all other animals, the human mind sinks roots as far as the *ālaya*-consciousness that may be said to underlie the "three worlds" in their entirety. And where this underlying basis is overcome, there the field of absolute emptiness is lying in wait. This overall background is borne deep in the mind of even a single human being and forms his or her self-nature.... But within one's own mind to which one returns is stored the source of the mind of all living things, that is to say, the place of *prajñā*-emptiness which is oneness with things as they really are. The investigation of one's own mind, when it is radically pursued, takes on the meaning of seeing through to the core of sentient beings, the world, and Buddha....

Our Zen slogan—"Directly pointing to the human mind, seeing into one's own true nature and becoming a Buddha"—can be said to gather the doctrine of "mind" with its epistemological, ontological and cosmological character as found, for example, in consciousness-only theory, directly into the standpoint of existence and to turn it into the real content of existential self-investigation....

In the tenth century, during the Period of the Five Dynasties in China, Hōgen Bun'eki (Fayan Wenyi), who had founded a particular style of Zen known as the Hōgen School, wrote a verse on "perfected real nature." Since we have touched upon the consciousness-only theory, let us cite this verse as an example of how this doctrine was assimilated into Zen and given existential import.

> With reason exhausted, feelings and deliberations are forgotten.
> How can there be a likeness [to anything]!
> Right here this frosty night's moon
> Sinks serenely into the river valley ahead.
> Ripened fruit hangs heavy with monkeys,
> The mountains deepen as if to lead astray.
> Raising my head, there's still some light—
> Originally to the west of my abode.

"Perfected real nature" means that by way of the investigation of self the Buddha-nature of the self comes to be manifest out of the self like an unearthed jewel. At the point where the discriminating mind (the "feelings and deliberations" of our verse) has scrutinized reason exhaustively and reached the extremity of reason, it forgets itself, and forgets reason as well. Our original self-nature, Hakuin's "self-nature as no-nature," shines forth as something beyond comparison. "My mind is like the autumn moon," writes the Chinese poet Hanshan (Cold Mountain); but, he continues, it really withstands all comparison—this moon shining purely in the deep, blue pool of water. In Hōgen's verse, the moon setting in the river valley on a frosty night, the monkeys coming to pick the fruit, etc., all only depict features of Hōgen's daily mountain life. All this, however, is no other than "perfected real nature" as the Zen state. It is, as it is, the mind of Hōgen, a man of Zen. We must not understand the features expressed in this verse as a description of a landscape. The Zen master Kassan Zenne (Jiashan Shanhui, named after the mountain of his abode), was once asked, "How are things around Kassan?" He replied, "Monkeys holding their young in their arms retreat behind the blue ridge, birds holding flowers in their beaks plummet before the blue cliff." Tradition has it that Hōgen said of this phrase, "For thirty years I mistook this to be a picture of the world around Kassan." Whatever Hōgen might have really meant at the time he said this, the features of Hōgen's mountain life in the verse above as well are not just a description of the world around a quiet, secluded place in the mountains.

At the conclusion of his *Faust* Goethe has the Chorus Mysticus sing, "*Alles Vergängliche ist nur ein Gleichnis*"—all changing things are only the likeness [of eternal things]. The expression "likeness" in the second line of Hōgen's verse is indeed the equivalent of this *Gleichnis*. But for Goethe the features of mountain life too would belong to the world of changing things, would be only a likeness of eternal things. Yet Hōgen's self-nature is something wholly beyond likening. It transcends the distinction between impermanence and eternity; it goes beyond the relativity of impermanent vs. eternal. If we are to speak of the impermanent, then the features of this mountain life are impermanent through and through, are not even a likeness, metaphor, or symbol of eternal things. They are, as they are, the real aspects of mountain life. Or, if we are to speak of the eternal, they are eternal through and through, for which we cannot even find a likeness in the impermanent. They are, as they are, emptiness, and absolute emptiness, as such, is the suchness of mountain life—is ultimately Hōgen's own mind. In comparison, even Goethe can be said to have lapsed into reason, into *logos*. Hōgen's state here reveals the existentialized version of the "perfected real nature" of consciousness-only theory.

The problem of mind came to be a central issue throughout the history of Buddhism.... What we said above of Hōgen and consciousness-only theory was nothing more than simply one example of this—except that the occasion of Hōgen's attaining satori for the first time bears a special relation to consciousness-only theory. The story is as follows. On a pilgrimage seeking the Way with two companion monks, Hōgen stopped to rest at the temple of a Zen priest named Jizō (Dicang) one rainy day. When the rain cleared and they were about to set off again, Jizō, who had come to see them off, remarked, "It is said you usually expound the doctrine that the three worlds are mind only." Then, pointing to a rock in the garden, he asked, "Is that rock inside your mind or outside it?" "Inside my mind, of course," was the answer Hōgen gave, typical of consciousness-only theory. Jizō immediately retorted, "By what karmic fate I do not know, but a man is wandering around with a lump of stone in his mind. He must feel quite heavy." At a loss for a word to counter, Hōgen at length took off his sandals again and stayed on together with his companions, advancing various views to settle the issue. After a month or so of this, the monk Jizō at last said, "According to the Buddha Dharma, all things come into view [as they are]." It is said that Hōgen was greatly enlightened upon hearing this.

"All things come into view [as they are]" means that the Buddha Dharma manifests itself precisely therein, that every single thing is manifest entirely as it is, as clearly and distinctly as what one sees in one's own hand. This is the basic principle of "three worlds—mind only," but as it is treated from the standpoint of Zen. In the way of self-investigation called "directly pointing to the human mind," this signifies that "I" directly see "myself" in the appearance of every single thing just as it is, as though two mirrors were mutually reflecting one another. In contrast, when Hōgen first answered "in my mind," his "three worlds—mind only" was, to use the modern idiom, an idealistic position. It was a standpoint of seeing the rock as a mental entity. Yet the opposite of this mentalism of "mind only," i.e., a materialism of "things only," would fare no better. So long as the materialist is unable to see in one manifest rock the reality of the self that absolutely cannot be objectified, the shadow of the self that sees the rock will be projected, so to speak, upon the rock's hidden side. Materialism cannot escape the situation that the problem of the mind lies concealed in the appearance of every material thing. Or we can put it this way: if idealism's "in the mind" loads the rock into the front of the mind, materialism's "outside the mind" sticks the mind onto the back of the rock. From the standpoint of Zen, both mind and things are seen from a perspective that completely transcends these two opposed ways of seeing.

Bibliography and Suggested Reading

Davis, Bret W. (2004) "The Step Back through Nihilism: The Radical Orientation of Nishitani Keiji's Philosophy of Zen." *Synthesis Philosophica* 37: 139–159.

Davis, Bret W. (2006) "The Kyoto School." In Edward N. Zalta, ed., *The Stanford Encyclopedia of Philosophy*. http://plato.stanford.edu/archives/spr2006/entries/kyoto-school/.

Heisig, James W. (2001) *Philosophers of Nothingness: An Essay on the Kyoto School.* Honolulu: University of Hawai'i Press.

"In Memoriam Nishitani Keiji 1900–1990." (1992) Special issue, *The Eastern Buddhist,* new ser., 25/1.

Nishitani Keiji. (1982) *Religion and Nothingness.* Translated by Jan Van Bragt. Berkeley: University of California Press.

Nishitani Keiji. (1986–95) Nishitani Keiji Chosakushū [Collected works of Nishitani Keiji]. Tokyo: Sōbunsha.

Nishitani Keiji. (1990) *The Self-Overcoming of Nihilism.* Translated by Graham Parkes with Setsuko Aihara. Albany: State University of New York Press.

Nishitani Keiji. (1991) *Nishida Kitarō*. Translated by Yamamoto Seisaku and James W. Heisig. Berkeley: University of California Press.

Nishitani Keiji. (2006) *On Buddhism.* Translated by Seisaku Yamamoto and Robert E. Carter. Albany: State University of New York Press.

"Religion and the Contemporary World in Light of Nishitani Keiji's Thought." (1997), *Zen Buddhism Today* 14.

Unno, Taitetsu, ed. (1989) *The Religious Philosophy of Nishitani Keiji.* Berkeley: Asian Humanities Press.

PART II

PHILOSOPHY OF LANGUAGE AND HERMENEUTICS

Buddhism, despite its protestations that the truth it aims to articulate is inexpressible, beyond the domain of words and language, expresses this view, and indeed all of its views, through language. It also comprises a vast corpus of texts that are often not mutually consistent—though each claims a lineage extending back to the Buddha himself—and are articulated in the context of a scholastic tradition of commentary, subcommentary, and compendium. Hence, Buddhist philosophy naturally turns its attention to the nature of language and meaning and to theories of interpretation. This part collects a range of Buddhist philosophical investigation into these matters.

One important question to ask about language and texts concerns their epistemic authority. Dignāga (early sixth century C.E.), in the selection from his *Pramāṇasamuccaya,* argues that texts by themselves are never authoritative, as all epistemic authority rests either in perception or inference. He also argues that language is never directly referential, but is at best an inferential instrument. Inasmuch as words denote universals (which do not exist), and particulars (which alone do exist) cannot be expressed, linguistic meaning cannot be direct. Instead, when we use or hear language, we create or exploit signs that can guide action, but never symbols that denote what we might naïvely think they mean.

While Dignāga's text is principally concerned with the philosophy of language and logic, Jñānagarbha's (eighth-century) *Verses on the Distinction between the Two Truths*, composed near the end of the golden age of Buddhist philosophy in India, presents an example of Buddhist hermeneutical practice. Jñānagarbha addresses in very small scope a number of his predecessors who are often taken to be at odds with one another, including both Mādhyamikas and Yogācārins of various stripes. His text on the two truths, while most directly a philosophical analysis of the truths themselves and of their relations to one another, attempts a creative synthesis of the views of his illustrious predecessors. According to Jñānagarbha's account, on correct interpretation, his Buddhist predecessors' views are mutually consistent, thus managing to salvage nearly every position defended in the tradition despite their prima facie tensions.

This conciliatory hermeneutic strategy proved to be influential. In Tibet, particularly in the Gelukpa tradition, Nāgārjuna's Madhyamaka metaphysics and Dharmakīrti's logically inflected epistemology were both received with great enthusiasm, despite their apparently opposed views regarding the nature of language and of argument. Nāgārjuna appears to argue quite explicitly, for instance, that Mādhyamikas have no views and assert no philosophical theses. Dharmakīrti, on the other hand, argues that philosophy proceeds through arguments that establish positions and defend views. Tsongkhapa, the founder of the Gelukpa school, resolves this tension by arguing that careful interpretation of Nāgārjuna's claims is required, and that when properly interpreted it is clear that he does not eschew all views or theses, but only *false* ones. Here we present an articulation and defense of this hermeneutical strategy by Tsongkhapa's student Khedrupjey (1385–1438) from his encyclopedia of philosophy, the *Great Digest* (*Stong thun chen mo*).

An alternative approach to resolving hermeneutical inconsistencies, one practiced in India (most influentially by Śāntarakṣita in *Madhyamakālaṃkāra*) and in Tibet (most notably by Tsongkhapa in *Lam rim chen mo*), but with special vigor in China, is the construction of doxographic hierarchies. In these hierarchies, apparently conflicting views can be represented neither as the same, nor as genuine competitors at the same level, but rather as sequential steps, with more sophisticated views replacing inferior positions as one progresses from ignorance to awakening. One of the most impressive Chinese practitioners of the doxographic art is Zongmi (active in the eighth and ninth centuries). In the section of his *Inquiry into the Origin of the Human Condition* we present, he ranks philosophical positions, demonstrating how each raises difficulties that can only be resolved by the next, and how taken together, the various apparently divergent positions lead one on a path to the highest view.

The difficulty that language poses for Buddhism, in virtue of the Buddhist acknowledgment that language is inadequate for the expression of ultimate truth and yet is necessary to indicate that truth, is explored by Dōgen (1200–1253) in the selections from *Shōbōgenzō* presented in this part: *Kattō* and *Osakusendaba*. Here Dōgen reflects on the use of articulate silence to explain the ultimate, but also the intimate relation between silence and speech: only speech can make silence articulate; only silence articulates the real meaning of meaningful speech; and much of significance occurs extralinguistically.

One of the best known but most enigmatic uses of language in the Buddhist philosophical landscape is the kōan, which is central to Rinzai Zen practice. *Kōan* practice reminds us of Dignāga's thesis that language can never be directly meaningful, but useful only as a tool to guide us, not to referents, but to cognitive action. It also reminds us of Dōgen's insistence that what Buddhist philosophy aims to express is ultimately inexpressible, at least via language. Tōrei Enji (1721–1792) addresses the use of kōan and the way language functions in kōan practice in the chapter of *Treatise of the Inexhaustible Lamp of Zen* we present here.

9

Sensation, Inference, and Language

Dignāga's *Pramāṇasamuccaya*

Richard Hayes

Dignāga probably flourished in the early decades of the sixth century C.E. Numerous works on various aspects of Buddhist theory are attributed to him. All the excerpts here are taken from a work called *Pramāṇasamuccaya* (PS; Collection of writings on sources of knowledge). This work is made up of six chapters. The first is on sensation, the second, third, and fourth on inference and argumentation, the fifth on the nature of language, and the sixth on various fallacies and mistakes in reasoning or presentation of an argument.

Dignāga wrote at a time when Buddhists were disputing with one another about which *sūtras* most accurately reported the Buddha's teachings. Rather than entering into that dispute, he argued that all knowledge comes from exactly two sources, namely, the senses and reasoning. He further argued that there is no overlap between these two sources; each has its own distinct subject matter. The immediate knowledge of the senses provides knowledge of particular sense data. These sense data, being unique, cannot be expressed in language, for language deals only in generalities. Once these sense data are associated with other sense data, either of the present time or of the past, one is no longer in the realm of sensation. Rather, one is in the realm of concepts. Only concepts can be named; indeed, they are the sole referents of all verbal expressions. Dignāga followed the standard Buddhist view that each sense faculty has only one kind of datum that it can operate on. So, for example, the eye can sense the color red, and the tongue can sense a sweet taste, and the hands can sense pressure and temperature, but there is no sense faculty that can sense a cherry as a whole. The idea of cherry is superimposed on the data of the senses. A sweet taste can be sensed, but a cherry can only be conceived. Long before Dignāga, Buddhists had developed the notion that only sense data are primitively real, while concepts are derivative realities. Since most of the turmoil that sentient beings experience comes from the concepts they impose on primitively real objects of experience, a common Buddhist strategy for reducing turmoil is to eliminate as much conceptualization as possible and just to experience what is presented to the senses without adding narratives and commentary. Dignāga's project is based on these standard Buddhist theories and practices.

In saying all that he said about particulars and concepts, Dignāga differed from most non-Buddhist Indian thinkers who had preceded him. The standard non-Buddhist view was that a particular object such as a cow could be seen, smelled, touched and tasted, and it could be experienced as a cow because one also directly sensed the universal cowhood that inhered in the particular animal. Universals, in other words, were said to be no less primitively real than particular sense data, and whole objects were said to be just as primitively real as the sensible parts of which they were composed. Much of what Dignāga wrote, therefore, was aimed at showing the untenability of the views that various non-Buddhists held. He denied the reality of wholes as something that exist over and above their parts and thus took an antiholistic stance. He denied that universals are sense objects and thus took a nominalist (or, perhaps more accurately, conceptualist) stance.

In the excerpts that follow, only his own views are given; the detailed refutations he offered of other positions have been left out for lack of space. The principal argument against universals as external objects apprehended by the senses is found in various passages in the fifth chapter of the PS. The gist of the argument is as follows. Universals were described in classical Indian tradition as entities that are simple and indivisible and yet can occur in a plurality of individuals. Being simple, they are unconditioned and thus never come into being or cease to exist. On this view, cowhood occurs as a feature of all and only those individuals that we perceive as cows, and it would exist even if there were no cows, although in the absence of individuals in which to inhere it would remain unknown to us. In rejecting this view, Dignāga argued that if a universal is apprehensible through the external sense faculties, then it must be located in space, in which case we can ask where a universal is located. If it is located wholly in any one individual, then it cannot be said that it resides in a plurality of individuals. If it resides partially in each individual, then it is not undivided. Nothing can be both simple and resident in a plurality of distinct individuals, so the universal as commonly defined is an impossibility. If it is impossible for a universal to be an external sensible object, the only existence it can have is as a concept.

Dignāga's most influential doctrines were those pertaining to the nature and limits of language. There are two doctrines in particular that were defended by nearly all Buddhists in India and Tibet who lived after his time. First, he argued that verbal testimony is not a separate source of knowledge but is a species of inference. Second, he argued that words have no referents but are meaningful only insofar as they rule out or preclude the use of other words in accordance with essentially arbitrary social conventions devised by human beings. These doctrines require some explanation.

Most non-Buddhist philosophers held the view that sense experience and inference both yield fallible cognitions and that the only way to arrive at infallible knowledge is to appeal to statements that are unlike those composed by ordinary human beings. Some who believed in nonhuman statements claimed that they were eternal and so had never been composed, while others claimed that they were composed by God, who is both omniscient and free from all inclinations to be deceptive. Whatever its origin or lack thereof, this special body of infallible knowledge, called the Veda, was said to be the source of knowledge about things that could not be observed or arrived at through reason; examples of such extraempirical and extrarational things were the consequences of rituals, why Sanskrit nouns are assigned their genders, a variety of ethical principles, and why people belong to their castes. In response to this view of the legitimacy of scripture, Dignāga argued that all language is human, that a statement expressed in language is nothing but a complex inferential sign, and that, like all other inferential signs, a statement is reliable only to the extent that it meets the three criteria of a good inferential sign (which are laid out in the excerpt below from chapter 2). Any sign, whether a word or an object, is informative of something beyond itself only if has been observed with the signified and has never been observed in the absence of the signified. So smoke is a sign of fire because it meets these criteria, and the word "fire" is a sign of fire only because it meets the same criteria. A sign, according to Dignāga, never directly indicates the detailed nature of what is signified by it. Rather, it informs the observer of the sign only that the signified thing is not absent. So when a person sees smoke arising in the distance, he can know only that fire is not absent in the vicinity of the smoke; he cannot know anything about the actual nature of the fire. Similarly, when someone says "Fire!" all the hearer of the statement can know is that some notion of fire is not absent from the speaker's thoughts. Objects and words, then, both serve as signs of the nonabsence of the thing signified, but little more.

Of course, in practical life when one observes a series of objects, one can arrive at more refined inferences than would be possible through the observation of just one object. Similarly, if one hears someone say "There is a large fire on the balcony of the high-rise apartment building across the street," she can have a more refined picture of the speaker's thoughts than she could have if the speaker had only said "Fire!" A series of words put together in a grammatically well-formed sentence rules out much more than a single word rules out. The principle, however, remains the same: signs do not directly indicate states of affairs but only rule out some states of affairs, namely, those that are incompatible with the sign. The Sanskrit word for the act of ruling out or preclusion is *apoha*. Dignāga's claim, then, is that any item of language, whether it be a word or a sentence or a long composition, indicates only *apoha* (an exclusion of what is incompatible or a complex intersection of exclusions of what is incompatible).

In general, inference is something that one does better as one has more experience of the world. A newborn child might see smoke but never guess that fire is behind it. Inference is highly dependent not only on memories of previous experiences but also on having noticed the circumstances under which some experiences have not taken place. The same that can be said of inference in general is also true, of course, of the special type of inferential process that involves human language. Getting meaning out of a series of articulate sounds requires a thorough knowledge of the social conventions governing the use of sounds. These conventions are not fixed; they vary from one region to another and from one time to another. There is, therefore, a fluidity to language, as a result of which whatever one gleans through words and sentences is always provisional and fallible. This is true whether the sentence was composed by a fool, a Buddha, or a god. Therefore, even if one has the guidance of the words of the Buddha, these words are useful in proportion to one's recollections of her experiences of the world.[1]

Translation

Chapter 1: On Sensation (*Pratyakṣa*)

The sources of knowledge, sensation and inference are exactly two in number, since *there are two kinds of knowable object*. There is no other knowable object than a particular, which has a particular characteristic, and a universal, which has a general characteristic. We shall show that sensation has a particular as its content, and inference has a universal as its content. What about the cognition of a thing such as color that is apprehended through an aspect such as impermanence, or that is apprehended more than once? That apprehension does exist, but *there is not a further source of knowledge with respect to combining it*. For after apprehending the color through the

1. The PS is written in verse with the author's own prose commentary. The excerpts here are taken from the prose commentary of the first, second, and fifth chapters. The passages in verse are indicated by italics. The chapter and verse numbers are indicated in square brackets following a passage. So "PS 1.2" indicates the commentary to the second verse of chapter 1. The translation of PS1 here was made for this volume. The excerpts from PS 2 and PS 5 are revised versions of translations that appeared in Hayes 1988.

particular characteristic, which is inexpressible, and the general characteristic, which is the fact of being a color, one joins them in the mind with impermanence, thinking "the color is impermanent." Therefore, there is no further source of knowledge. [PS 1.2]

Nor is a further source of knowledge needed *for recognizing something again and again.* Why? *Because that would lead to an infinite regress.* If every cognition, *like memory,* is believed to be a source of new knowledge, then a source of knowledge would have no final grounding. Memory, desire, and anger are not further sources of knowledge with respect to previously known objects; recognition is the same.

Sensation is devoid of conceptualization. That cognition that has no conceptualization is known as sensation. Now what is this thing called conceptualization? It is *association with names, universals, and so forth.* In the case of proper names, a thing is qualified by a name, such as "Ḍittha."[2] In the case of words for universals, a thing is qualified by a universal, such as "cow." In the case of adjectives, a thing is qualified by a quality such as "white." In the case of verbal nouns, a thing is qualified by an action, such as "a cook." In the case of possessive nouns a thing is qualified by a substance, such as "oarsman."[3] Some say that "cook" and "oarsman" are things qualified by relationships. Others believe that a thing is qualified by nothing more than a vacuous expression. In any case, that cognition in which there is no conceptualization is sensation. [PS 1.3]

Chapter 2: On Inference (*Anumāna*)

The inferential process is of two kinds: that which is for one's own sake, and that which is for the sake of other people.[4] Of these two, *inference for oneself consists in discerning an object through a sign that has three characteristics.* Inference for oneself is discerning an inferable object through a sign that has the three characteristics explained below. *As was the case above [with sensation], this refers [not only to the cognitive process] but also to the resulting cognition.* The resulting cognition is explained in this case in the same way as it was explained in the case of sensation, that is, with reference to a cognition's

2. This is a stock example of a name that is a pure sound that has no underlying meaning.

3. The formation of new words in Sanskrit has been described in detail by the grammatical tradition. There exist many suffixes that form new nouns out of more primitive nouns. What Dignāga is talking about here are possessive nouns. If one adds a suffix to the word for staff or oar, one gets a new word meaning a staff-holder or an oarsman.

4. Dignāga set a trend, especially among Buddhist philosophers, of making a careful distinction between the reasoning that a person does for his own edification and the presentation of evidence designed to persuade others. The latter task requires some rhetorical devices and observation of the interlocutor's prior beliefs, while reasoning is more purely logical in nature.

having two aspects.[5] Now if both [sensation and inference] are characterized as cognitions, what is the difference between them? *Their fields of operation and essential natures are dissimilar.* Sensation and inference have distinct fields of operation, and their essential natures are also distinct in accordance with their having different cognitive images. [PS 2.1]

How can verbal testimony be classed as inference? Words such as "heaven" do not express any object at all.[6] *The statements of credible persons are inference insofar as they have the common character of not being false.* Because when one hears the statements of credible people, the resultant cognition is not false, and because this makes them similar to inference, we say that verbal testimony is a kind of inference. Furthermore, it is claimed that the name-giving was previously seen firsthand. This view denies that there can be an inference with respect to such things as the hypothesis of primordial substance [because primordial substance, by definition, cannot be experienced firsthand]. The phrase "through a sign that has three characteristics" must be explained. The successful sign is *present in the inferable object and what is similar to it and absent in their absence.* The inferable object is a property-bearer qualified by a property. After observing the sign there, either through sensation or through inference, one confirms that it is also present in a general way, either wholly or partially, in what is of the same class. Why is that? Because the restriction is that the sign occur in *only* what is similar, there is no restriction that it *only* occur. But in that case it could be argued that nothing is accomplished by saying "it is absent in their absence." This statement is made in order to emphasize that the sign, being absent in the absence of objects like the subject, is not present in what is other than or incompatible with the inferable object. Here then is the sign with three characteristics from which we discern the sign-bearer. [PS 2.5]

Chapter 5: On Linguistic Signs as Indicating Exclusions (*Apoha*)

We have discussed the two means of acquiring knowledge. But some claim that verbal communication is an additional means of acquiring knowledge.

5. In the discussion of sensation, in a passage not included in the translation here, Dignāga observes that many verbal nouns refer both to a process and to what results from the process. Using an English example of the same phenomenon, we can say that "sensation" can refer both to the act of sensing and to the thing that is sensed. Similarly, "inference" can refer both to the act of inferring and to the piece of knowledge that results from that process.

6. This question presumably reflects a Buddhist point of view. A Buddhist might reject the Veda altogether, because the Veda refers to objects, such as heaven, that cannot be known in any way other than by reading about them in scriptures. Inference is said to be a source of knowledge, but the Veda, according to the hypothetical questioner, is not knowledge at all. So, he asks, how can that which is not a source of knowledge be a species of that which is a source of knowledge?

Verbal communication is no different from inference as a means of acquiring knowledge. For it names its object in a way similar to the property of having been produced, that is, by precluding what is incompatible. Like the property of having been produced, a linguistic sign reveals part of the object to which it is applied, namely, the part with which it is necessarily related, and it reveals this part by excluding what is incompatible.[7] Therefore it is no different from inference. [PS 5.1]

There are those who argue as follows. A general term expresses every one of its own particulars. But a particularizing expression is applied to what is so expressed in order to limit it. To those who hold such a view, we reply *a general term does not express particulars, because they are unlimited in number.* For, since the particulars are unlimited in number, it is not the case that each one can be associated with the expression; an expression that is not associated with an object cannot express that object, and so there is cognition of nothing but the expression's form.

Moreover, [a general term cannot express particulars] *because it is errant* [with respect to any given particular].[8] Since the verbal symbol "real" applies to qualities and so forth in the same way that it applies to substances, it does not explicitly express [either substance or quality], but rather its errancy gives rise to uncertainty [as to whether, in a given case, the verbal symbol is expressing a quality or whether it is expressing a substance].

Some think that a verbal symbol expresses either just a universal or just the [universal's] relation to particular instantiations. [They maintain this view] on the grounds of ease [of determining the expression's relation to either of these two expressible objects] and on the grounds of [the expression's] inerrancy. But neither of these two alternatives is acceptable. *Nor [does a general term express] the relation of the universal itself, because it is heard without a difference with words referring to particulars.* If it were the case [that a general term expressed a universal or a relation], [the word "real"] would not be used attributively with words like "substance" that refer to particulars in expressions such as "real substance," "real quality," "real action," and so on. But in fact we do observe such expressions. Neither reality nor relation is a substance or a quality, but rather both are properties of a substance or of a quality. As has been said [by Bhartṛhari]: "Two words, one expressing a quality and the other the locus of the quality, as a rule have different case-markings; it is established that two words expressing [the same] substance are in grammatical agreement." [PS 5.2]

7. The stock example of an inference used by Dignāga is "Sound is impermanent, because it is produced." Here one observes the fact of being produced and then reasons that since being produced is incompatible with being permanent, sound cannot be permanent. This inferential knowledge contains no information about sound except its lack of permanence. Similarly, a linguistic sign transmits no information about a topic except that certain things cannot be said to be true of that topic.

8. A sign is said to be errant when it occurs both in the presence and the absence of what it putatively signifies. An errant sign is inconclusive.

But on this matter it is said that a relation is expressible through properties of its relata. One expresses it thus by making it an [intentional] object, but an object is connected with other things. A relation is that which relates. Like desire and so forth, it relates one thing to another. Therefore, since a relation is expressible through the properties of its relata, there is no word expressing it through its own intrinsic properties. Therefore, it cannot be what is expressed by a general term. [PS 5.3]

Some say it is just the instantiation of the universal that is expressed by a general term. They hold this view on the grounds that (1) it is possible for a term expressing a particular to be modified by a qualifier, (2) it is easy to determine the relationship between the term and its meaning, and (3) the expression is inerrant from the object to which it refers. To this view we reply *a general term does not express an instantiation, because a word that expresses an instantiation is grammatically subordinate.* And if this theory is true, the word "real" does not express a substance directly, but rather it expresses a substance to which the word's form and the universal are subordinate. Because it does not encompass such species of reality as the jug and so forth, there is no genus-species relation, in which case the word "real" and "jug" are not coreferential. If the designation of one word is not encompassed by another word, there is no coreferentiality. For example, since the word "white" expresses a substance only insofar as that substance is qualified by the quality white that is expressible by the word, the word "white" does not encompass such properties as sweet flavor, although such properties may also be in the substance that has the property white. Therefore sweet flavor is not a species of white color. The same principle applies also in the case under consideration.

Furthermore, a general term cannot express only an instantiation of a universal *because it is applied figuratively* to the instantiation. The word "real" literally expresses either its own word-form or a universal; in being applied to one of those two things, it applies to an instantiation metonymically. Any object to which an expression is applied metonymically is not the thing literally expressed by that expression. [PS 5.4]

A word's meaning cannot be anything other than preclusion. Why? A substratum must be either identical with or different from its component parts. Considering the first of these alternatives, it cannot be identical, because *a unified complex entity does not exist, since it would then follow that the components are identical to each other.* If the complex entity were a unity, then the two objects blue and lotus would not be different from it. Therefore, since they do not differ from the unity, they would not be different from one another. Moreover, a unified complex entity does not exist, *because it would then follow that the complex entity would be many.* Since the complex entity is not different from the several components making it up, its plurality would follow from the thesis of identity. Therefore, it does not exist. But even if the existence of a complex entity is accepted, the two objects blue and lotus cannot have a single substratum, because even when both words are applied to a single object, *they do not give up their individual meanings.* The meaning of each of the individual words "blue" and "lotus" is its own universal, and this remains true when they are in a compound expression. Therefore how can they be in grammatical agreement? [PS 5.17]

Bibliography and Suggested Reading

Hattori, Masaaki. (1968) *Dignāga, On Perception: Being the Pratyakṣaparic-cheda of Dignāga's Pramāṇasamuccaya.* Cambridge: Harvard University Press.

Hayes, Richard P. (1988) *Dignāga on the Interpretation of Signs.* Dordrecht: Kluwer Academic.

Matilal, Bimal Krishna. (1998) *The Character of Logic in India.* Edited by Jonardon Ganeri and Heeraman Tiwari. Albany: State University of New York Press.

Potter, Karl H., ed. (2003) *Encyclopedia of Indian Philosophies.* Volume Vol. 9. *Buddhist Philosophy from 350 to 600* A.D. Delhi: Motilal Banarsidass.

10

Jñānagarbha's *Verses on the Distinction between the Two Truths*

Malcolm David Eckel

Among the encyclopedic texts that dominate the landscape in the later history of Indian Buddhist philosophy, Jñānagarbha's *Verses on the Distinction between the Two Truths* can seem slight, almost to the point of insignificance. But the importance of the text is not measured simply by its size. In just a few condensed and difficult verses, it gives a compelling account of the relationship between the two dominant schools of Mahāyāna philosophy (Madhyamaka and Yogācāra) and sets the stage intellectually for the introduction of Buddhist philosophy to Tibet.

Writing in the eighth century, between the time of Dharmakīrti (whose influence is evident throughout the text) and Śāntarakṣita (who provided the text with a subcommentary), Jñānagarbha marks a transition between the polemical spirit of the sixth century, when philosophers like Bhāviveka drew sharp lines between the different Mahāyāna traditions, and the more syncretic or accommodating spirit of the ninth century, when philosophers like Śāntarakṣita and Kamalaśīla attempted to bring the insights of Madhyamaka, Yogācāra, and Buddhist logic together into a single, unified vision of Mahāyāna Buddhist thought.

Jñānagarbha's verses present many difficulties for a casual or novice reader. The verses were meant to be memorized, and they provide only a cryptic outline of key ideas. In practice they would have been supplemented by commentaries, both oral and written, and would have been used by readers (or listeners) who were already familiar with the basic issues and ideas. The biggest challenge for a modern reader is to fill in the intellectual background so that it is possible not only to understand Jñānagarbha's references to other schools, but to see how he used them as foils to develop his own distinctive approach to Mahāyāna thought.

The most important concept in Jñānagarbha's intellectual background is stated clearly in the title: it is the "distinction between two truths." This distinction is given its classic formulation in the founding text of the Madhyamaka tradition, Nāgārjuna's "Root Verses on the Middle Way" (*Mūlamadhyamakakārikā*):

> The Buddha's teaching is based on two truths: ordinary relative truth and ultimate truth. Those who know the distinction between the two truths know the profound reality in the Buddha's teaching. It is impossible to teach the ultimate without basing oneself on the conventional, and it is impossible to attain nirvana without understanding the ultimate (vv. 24.8–10).

Jñānagarbha echoes Nāgārjuna's words in verses 2 and 3, and he mentions the concept of a "basis" (*āśraya*) in verses 23 and 24. The word "basis" can have several different meanings, but here it functions primarily in a verbal sense. The "basis" of a word is the object to which it refers. Nāgārjuna's point is that you cannot talk about the ultimate without using words in a conventional way.

Jñānagarbha expands Nāgārjuna's distinction between relative (*saṃvṛti*) and ultimate (*paramārtha*) truths in verses 8 and 12 by distinguishing between correct and incorrect relative truth. He explains that this distinction is based on the ability to produce "effective action" (*artha-kriyā*). By this he means that correct relative truth is capable of producing significant, pragmatic effect (just as a fire can be used to cook rice), while incorrect relative truth is not. The concept of "effective action" comes from Dharmakīrti and is one important sign of Dharmakīrti's influence on Jñānagarbha's thought. The category of "incorrect relative truth" might have been expanded to include various kinds of perceptual illusion, as it is in other Madhyamaka works. Instead, Jñānagarbha focuses on the things that are imagined by philosophers, especially the idea that anything has any real identity (*svabhāva*). This point is a reminder that Jñānagarbha's verses are directed at the errors of other philosophers, especially those who do not share his view of reality.

Jñānagarbha's definition of relative truth has other important features. In verse 3, he explains that relative truth "corresponds to appearances." The Tibetan translation of this formula (*ji ltar snang ba*) stresses the aspect of "appearance." The Sanskrit original simply means "according to vision" (*yathādarśana*). As Jñānagarbha develops his account of relative truth, it is clear that the word "vision" (*darśana*) refers to "perception" (*pratyakṣa*), the means of valid knowledge (*pramāṇa*) that Buddhist logicians such as Dharmakīrti treated as the means of access to ultimate truth. By equating perception with relative truth, Jñānagarbha sets himself apart in a striking way from the Buddhist logicians. Dharmakīrti thinks that perception is ultimate; Jñānagarbha thinks that it is merely relative.

Altogether, Jñānagarbha mentions three characteristics of correct relative truth: it "arises dependently" (verse 8), is capable of "effective action" (verse 12), and "should not be analyzed" (verse 21). Other Madhyamaka writers from Jñānagarbha's own time group these three characteristics together into a single formula. Jñānagarbha discusses them in three separate verses. A thoughtful reader might want to consider why Jñānagarbha gives each of these concepts separate treatment. This question is especially important when Jñānagarbha gets to the elusive concept of "no-analysis" (*avicāra*) in verse 21. What does it mean to say that relative truth "should not be analyzed"? What kind of analysis does Jñānagarbha have in mind? Are there any other examples of a concept like this in the history of philosophy? Could it be taken, for example, as a Buddhist response to the Socratic idea that "the unexamined life is not worth living"? Is it similar to the Zen idea that a person who sits should "just sit"?

The answers to some of these questions come more clearly into focus when Jñānagarbha develops his definition of ultimate truth. His first move in this direction comes at the end of his definition of relative truth in verse 3, where he says simply that "the other must be something else." The ultimate is defined initially as something other than the relative. In what respect it is "other" becomes clear in verse 4, when Jñānagarbha says that "reason" (*nyāya*) is ultimate. Someone who is familiar with Dharmakīrti's epistemology will recognize that this assertion is very strange. Jñānagarbha has just said that perception is relative; in this verse he says that "reason" is ultimate. These two claims turn Dharmakīrti's understanding of the two truths upside down. For Dharmakīrti, perception is ultimate, and inference is relative. As surprising as it may seem, Jñānagarbha believes that reason, rather than perception, is the way to gain access to ultimate truth.[1]

Jñānagarbha's position not only seems to contradict Dharmakīrti; it also seems to violate a fundamental Buddhist claim that the Dharma is "inaccessible to logical reasoning."[2] Jñānagarbha responds to the second of these two problems by distinguishing between two kinds of ultimate: the ultimate that can be expressed in words and concepts and the ultimate that cannot. In his subcommentary, Śāntarakṣita explains that verses 5–7 have to do with the second kind of ultimate. Verse 5 says that the ultimate "does not correspond to appearances." In other words, it cannot be known by perception. Verse 6 responds to a Yogācāra objection by saying that the ultimate cannot

1. Dan Arnold has argued that this is a characteristic Madhyamaka response to the "foundationalist" epistemology of the Buddhist logicians. He also has compared this argument to Kant's view that it is possible to understand the conditions of truth simply through the exercise of reason. See Arnold 2005: 121–131.

2. Candrakīrti quotes a *sūtra* that describes the Dharma as "inaccessible to logical reasoning" (*atarkāvacāra*). For this passage and its parallels in other scriptural sources, see *Mūlamadhyamakakārikās (Mādhyamikasūtras) de Nāgārjuna avec la Prasannapadā Commentaire de Candrakīrti,* Bibliotheca Buddhica 4 (St. Petersburg, 1903–1913; reprint ed. Osnabrück: Biblio Verlag, 1970): 498–499.

even consist of perception itself (lit. "self-cognition"); and verse 7 says that not even a Buddha sees the ultimate. In effect, Jñānagarbha says that the ultimate can be understood in two different ways. From a relative point of view, it consists of rational cognition, but from an ultimate point of view, when it is analyzed by reason, it is not an object of cognition and it is not even cognition itself.

After defining correct relative truth in verse 8, Jñānagarbha returns to the two kinds of ultimate in verse 9, where he refers to the first kind of ultimate as the "negation of arising." This is the ultimate that results from a process of rational investigation and can be expressed in words and concepts. In verses 9 and 10, Jñānagarbha turns the process of analysis on this ultimate and finds that it is nothing but a reflection of relative truth: "It is reality-as-object (*tattvārtha*), but it is not reality." Of course, this negation does not need to be the end of the process. It also is possible to examine this negation and find that it, too, is a reflection of relative truth. The argument only ends, if it ends at all, in verse 11 with a reference to the famous scriptural account of Vimalakīrti's silence. When Mañjuśrī asks Vimalakīrti to explain the "entrance into the doctrine of nonduality," Vimalakīrti says nothing at all.[3] It is tempting to call Vimalakīrti's silence an expression of the ultimate ultimate (or the ultimate viewed from the ultimate point of view). But what does it mean to say that silence "expresses" the ultimate? What kind of truth is Vimalakīrti attempting to convey by his silence? (And what kind of truth is Jñānagarbha conveying by referring to the story of Vimalakīrti's silence?) Is it a particular state of affairs? Is it a particular mode of awareness? Is it a way of responding to all states of affairs or modes of awareness? If it is a "way," what kind of way is it?

Jñānagarbha's analysis of the two kinds of ultimate does not stop here. In verses 16–21, he again examines the rational ultimate and finds it lacking: "From the point of view of reason, the meaning of the words 'ultimately do not arise' does not arise." Verse 17 draws out the implications of this point in a new way, when it says that "the relative and the ultimate are identical, because there is no difference between them." Another way of making this point is to say that the ultimate ultimately is only relative. This verse directly contradicts verse 4, where Jñānagarbha said that "reason is ultimate, not relative." By contradicting himself, Jñānagarbha forces us to consider two questions. First, what is the status of the contradiction? Is the contradiction real, or is it only apparent? Second, whether it is real or apparent, what does the contradiction tell us about the structure of the argument as a whole?

The first question is easy to answer, even though the implications of the answer are complex. The two truths are not simply truths; they are different perspectives on truth. From the relative perspective, the two truths are different; from the ultimate perspective, there is no difference between them.

3. Étienne Lamotte, trans., *The Teaching of Vimalakīrti*, English trans. by Sara Boin (London: Pali Text Society, 1976), chapter 8.

By tacking back and forth between these two perspectives, Jñānagarbha not only tells us about the two truths; he gives his argument a distinctive structure. The text begins with a clear distinction: the relative is one thing, and the ultimate is another. Then the text makes the distinction go away. Finally, by eliminating the distinction between the ultimate and the relative, it returns us to the realm of relative truth, where distinctions again come into play. When Jñānagarbha says, in verses 17 and 20, that reason (along with the Buddha's teaching) "corresponds to appearances," he is saying not only that there is no difference between the relative and the ultimate; he is also saying that the ultimate, as a form of relative truth, can serve as the basis for valid distinctions. This sequence of claims gives the argument a three-part structure: it begins with distinctions, leads to the denial of distinctions, then leads back to the distinctions from which it began. It is no accident that Jñānagarbha introduces the concept of "no analysis" in verse 21. More than any other, this is the concept that marks his return to relative truth and the realm of distinctions.[4]

Whether this three-part structure makes Jñānagarbha's argument a form of dialectic or simply an example of paradox makes a fine point for discussion. Regardless of what we call it, this three-part structure is surprisingly common in Mahāyāna literature. It characterizes the work of Bhāviveka (sixth century), a Mādhyamika who clearly influenced Jñānagarbha's thought.[5] It also is present in Zen. Dogen's "Genjōkoan" ("To study the Buddha way is to study the self. To study the self is to forget the self. To forget the self is to be actualized by myriad things.") follows a similar circular pattern. A reader might ask whether this pattern is present in Mahāyāna Buddhism more generally. If so, what implications does it have for understanding Buddhist epistemology and ethics in a broader sense?

Within the larger structure of the argument, there are several points where Jñānagarbha engages specific opponents. It is useful to identify these opponents to understand their role in the text. In verse 1, Jñānagarbha says that the text is directed at "great heroes" who misunderstood the two truths. The subcommentator explains that these "great heroes" are "Dharmapāla and so forth." Dharmapāla was a well-known sixth-century Yogācāra commentator. If we look carefully, we can see traces of earlier disputes about the relationship between the two truths of the Madhyamaka and the three natures of the Yogācāra. In verse 6, for example, a Yogācāra opponent objects that it is only "imagined nature" (*parikalpita-svabhāva*) that does not appear (or is not seen). Implicitly the objector is affirming that absolute nature

4. On the significance of "no analysis" in Madhyamaka tradition more generally, see Malcolm David Eckel, "The Satisfaction of No Analysis: On Tsong kha pa's Approach to Svātantrika Madhyamaka," in Georges B. J. Dreyfus and Sara L. McClintock, ed., *The Svātantrika-Prāsaṅgika Distinction* (Boston: Wisdom Press, 2003)

5. On the significance of this three-part pattern in the work of Bhāviveka, see Eckel 1994.

(*parinișpanna-svabhāva*) *is* seen. Jñānagarbha responds by saying that that there ultimately is no cognition (or seeing) at all. The dispute reappears in verse 24, where Jñānagarbha denies that imagined nature has any real "basis" (*āśraya*). When Jñānagarbha says in verse 37 that "whatever is empty of imagined nature and arises dependently corresponds to appearances," he is saying that "dependent nature" (*paratantra-svabhāva*) is relative rather than ultimate. This point gestures in the direction of a Yogācāra-Madhyamaka synthesis that appeared in the next generation of Madhyamaka scholars, in the work of Śāntarakṣita and Kamalaśīla.

One of the most puzzling arguments in the text appears in verse 25, where Jñānagarbha says that "some who are known for bad arguments say that, if things do not arise in a real sense, they do not arise in a relative sense." It is possible that this verse is a reference to the Mādhyamika scholar Candrakīrti (seventh century) who was sharply critical of other Mādhyamikas who asserted the reality of relative truth. Candrakīrti's views were the source of the Prāsaṅgika-Madhyamaka tradition and had great influence in Tibet. If this verse does refer to Candrakīrti, it is a rare attempt on the part of an Indian scholar to respond to Candrakīrti's criticism. The verse is obscure, however, and it is by no means certain that Candrakīrti is the opponent.

Finally, it is worth noting that verse 14 marks a shift in Madhyamaka thinking away from the ontological concerns that characterized early Madhyamaka works toward the epistemological concerns that dominated the later stages of Buddhist thought in India. Nāgārjuna begins the "Root Verses on the Middle Way" by arguing that nothing can arise from itself, from something else, from both, or from no cause at all. All Mādhyamika authors develop similar arguments to show that nothing can have any identity (*svabhāva*) in its own right. Here Jñānagarbha develops an argument about the arising of *cognitions* rather than the arising of *things,* showing how the epistemological turn in Buddhist thought, associated particularly with Dignāga and Dharmakīrti, influenced the development of even the most basic Madhyamaka arguments about the nature of reality.[6]

Translation

1. The two truths have already been distinguished, but I will distinguish them again, because great heroes have misunderstood, to say nothing of others.

2. Those who know the distinction between the two truths do not misunderstand the Sage's teaching. They acquire all prerequisites and achieve their goal.

6. The translation that follows is based on the Tibetan translation of the Sanskrit original, as transcribed in Eckel 1987. This text contains a translation of Jñānagarbha's commentary on the verses, along with selections from Śāntarakṣita's subcommentary and extensive notes.

3. The Sage taught two truths: the relative and the ultimate. The relative corresponds to appearances; the other must be something else.

4. Because it cannot be contradicted, reason is ultimate, not relative. Why? The relative can be contradicted, even though appearances can be true.

5. The ultimate cannot be something that corresponds to appearances; it does not appear at all to someone who is omniscient.

6. Someone may say that it is only imagined nature that does not appear. But self-cognition is impossible, because it leads to a denial of causal efficacy.

7. The Omniscient One knows what exists and what does not; if he does not see something, one should closely analyze what kind of thing it is.

8. The thing itself (*vastu-mātra*), which is empty of anything that is imagined and arises dependently, is correct relative [truth]. Anything that is imagined is incorrect.

9. The negation of arising is consistent with reality (*tattva*), so we think [that it is reality]. But if there is nothing to negate, then in reality there clearly can be no negation.

10. If there is nothing to negate, the negation must be imagined, and it must be relative. It is reality-as-object (*tattvārtha*), but it is not reality.

11. In reality, [reality-as-object] is nondual, because it is free from conceptual diversity. This is why the bodhisattva [Vimalakīrti] was silent when Mañjuśrī asked him about reality.

12. Correct and incorrect relative [truth] may be similar in appearance, but they are distinguished by their ability or inability to produce effective action (*artha-kriyā*).

13. If you think that things correspond to appearances rather than to reason, we agree, but it is a different story if you think that they correspond to reason.

14. Many do not produce one, many do not produce many, one does not produce many, and one does not produce one.

15. We think that relative [truth] is [a cognition] by which or in which reality is concealed; all of it is true, but it is not true ultimately.

16. From the point of view of reason, the meaning of the words "ultimately do not arise" does not arise. Other statements should be interpreted in the same way.

17. We think that the relative and the ultimate are identical, because there is no difference between them. Reason also corresponds to appearances.

18. The parts of an inference are constructed on the basis of something that appears in the minds of both parties to an argument.

19. When this happens, there is an inference; otherwise, there is not. If logicians use such inferences, who will refute them?

20. If someone says that, from the point of view of reason, there is no arising even in a relative sense, this is true. This is why the [Buddha's] teaching corresponds to appearances.

21. Since [relative truth] corresponds to appearances, it should not be analyzed. Something is contradicted if, when analyzed, it becomes something else.

22. If someone asks why one thing appears to be caused by another, it is just that one thing appears to be caused by another. What more is there to say?

23. [Relative truth] has an imaginary basis; no [real basis] appears anywhere. Even something like a tree does not depend on a basis.[7]

24. Imagined nature is not based on anything. If it were, who could deny that it is dependent?

25. Some who are known for bad arguments say that if things do not arise in a real sense, they do not arise in a relative sense, like the son of a barren woman.

26. If relative [truth] is impossible, what harm can this argument cause? Something should be accepted only when it has been analyzed by reason.

27. If [this opponent] says that we contradict perception, why shouldn't this be true of his position as well? If a point is contradicted by a means of valid knowledge, one cannot be confident of its validity.

7. The commentary explains that the word "basis" (*gzhi, āśraya*) refers to the parts into which a complex object can be analyzed. The word "tree," for example, can be analyzed into "branches and so forth." The "branches and so forth" are the "basis" for the use of the word "tree."

28. We do not deny the appearance of form. It is wrong to deny anything that is experienced.

29. But we do deny arising and so forth, which do not appear, but which others imagine to be real.

30. It is right to use [reason] to deny just what is imagined. To deny something that is not imagined is only to contradict oneself.

31. [The Buddha] teaches karma and results just as they appear to him as he sees them. For this reason, all [karma] corresponds to appearances.

32. [The Buddha], whose very nature is compassion, sees that concepts cause bondage, and he explains bondage and liberation through [teachings] such as mind-only.

33. Concepts are a reification of mind and mental phenomena in the three realms. [The Buddha] sees that they cause bondage and teaches accordingly.

34. We think that even nonexistent things can be effective in a way that corresponds to appearances, but [Buddhas] do not see existent things as effective at all.

35. Others [imagine] that conventional terms refer to things, but this is impossible. This is said from the point of view of reason, because nothing can appear and nothing [can arise].

36. If things arise from causes, in what sense are they annihilated? If they cease when [their causes] cease, explain how they can be permanent?

37. The Omniscient One sees that whatever is empty of imagined nature and arises dependently corresponds to appearances.

38. This is not contradicted in the least by those who think that because it is impossible to know the contents of someone else's mind, omniscience is only imagined.

39. When [a Buddha] takes no notice of a subject, object, or self, signs do not arise, and when his concentration is firm, he does not get up.

40. The place where he is located is the basis of every inconceivable virtue. It is incomparable, worthy of worship, a guide, and quite inconceivable.

41. It is the Dharma Body of the Buddhas, in the sense that it is the body of all *dharmas*, the basis of every inconceivable virtue, and rational in nature.

42. Do not be one-sided. Consider whether there are any faults in this distinction between the two truths.

43. It is hard to be born as a human being; a pure mind is very weak; the wilderness of rebirth is hard to cross; life itself is very fleeting.

44. A good teacher is hard to find. So do not be resentful, even if, for lack of merit, you have no conviction.

45. It will come from gradual practice. But if you are angry, the opportunity will be far away.

46. May the merit that I have gained by distinguishing the two truths cause the whole world to develop the seed of understanding.

Bibliography and Suggested Reading

Arnold, Dan. (2005) *Buddhists, Brahmins, and Belief: Epistemology in South Asian Philosophy of Religion.* New York: Columbia University Press.

Dreyfus, Georges B. J., and Sara L. McClintock, eds. (2003) *The Svātantrika-Prāsaṅgika Distinction: What Difference Does a Difference Make?* Boston: Wisdom.

Eckel, Malcolm David. (1987) *Jñānagarbha's Commentary on the Distinction between the Two Truths.* Albany: State University of New York Press.

Eckel, Malcolm David. (1994) *To See the Buddha: A Philosopher's Quest for the Meaning of Emptiness.* San Francisco: HarperCollins. Reprint, Princeton: Princeton University Press.

11

Language and the Ultimate: Do Mādhyamikas Make Philosophical Claims?

A Selection from Khedrupjey's *Stong thun chen mo* (*Great Digest*)

José Ignacio Cabezón

Madhyamaka (or Middle-Way) philosophy—one among the four major schools of Indian Buddhist philosophy, according to the Tibetan tradition—became one of the most influential philosophical views in the history of Buddhism. But Madhyamaka, the "theory of emptiness," is not a uniform and homogeneous tradition. Over the centuries, different interpretations of Madhyamaka arose, and both Indian and Tibetan scholars debated the Madhyamaka's most fundamental tenets.

Such differences of opinion never led to a split in the Indian Madhyamaka—that is, to different Madhyamaka subschools. However, Tibetans, with their penchant for classification, sought to bring order to Indian Madhyamaka by grouping together certain figures and texts into a fixed doxographical scheme (Cabezón 1990). For example, they created subcategories of the Madhyamaka such as Svātantrika (Advocates of Autonomous Reasoning) and Prāsaṅgika (Advocates of Reductio Arguments) based, inter alia, on the preference of certain Indian figures for formal syllogistic reasoning and for argumentation using reductio ad absurdum, respectively. After the thirteenth century in Tibet, it was the latter of these two schools, the Prāsaṅgika, that came to be accepted as the perfect expression of the Buddha's thought, that is, as the truth.

Whatever differences may have existed between Indian Mādhyamikas, there is nonetheless a certain core around which a Mādhyamika identity as a whole can be structured. Mādhyamikas generally agree, for example, on the following points.

1. Things are empty (*śūnya*): they lack essences or inherent existence. Neither persons nor phenomena exist independently, from their own side, but exist in a web of interdependent relationships.
2. Ordinary beings constantly err. Instead of seeing things as empty of inherent existence, they see them (to use a term *not* found in the texts) as "full," which is to say as being more real than they are. This misperception (or, more accurately, mis*con*ception) of the world—this tendency to reify phenomena—is the chief cause of suffering.
3. Since the basic problem is one of attributing an excess of reality to a world that lacks it, the corrective, according to the Madhyamaka, necessarily involves negating something. It involves mentally "subtracting out" or "emptying out" the excess reality we involuntarily attribute to things so as to bring the mind to an understanding of the way things are.
4. Because negation is a conceptual operation, language and conceptual analysis play a substantial role in this process of correcting our misconceptions about the world.

While such views are held in common by most Indian and Tibetan Mādhyamikas, there existed (and exists) a great deal of controversy among Middle-Way philosophers concerning the *implications* of these core tenets. At least in Tibet, controversies have raged over each of the following issues:

1. There has been debate over what precisely is denied or negated when one says that things are "empty." How "strong" is that negation? Or put another way, how *much* is being negated? Does the Madhyamaka negate existence in general, or only a certain kind of existence (true or inherent existence)? Does the negation imply or affirm anything positive in its wake? Is the ultimate truth *just* a negation, or does it have a positive dimension?
2. There has also been debate about the role that language and conceptual thought play in bringing one to an understanding of the ultimate truth. No Mādhyamika would deny that language and logic have *some* role to play in understanding reality, but some Mādhyamikas claim that a very specific form of conceptual thought known as *inference* (*anumāna, rjes dpag*)—knowledge born from syllogistic reasoning—is a sine qua non to understanding the ultimate. Others, taking a more pragmatic approach, claim that inference is *not* indispensable—that whatever words and arguments work work. Some believe that language and reasoning bring us to the understanding of reality *itself,* whereas others claim that, although helpful initially, conceptual thought and language, operating through a process of dichotomy, are incapable of yielding knowledge of the real ultimate truth, which must be nondual.
3. Related to this debate about the expressibility and conceivability of reality, there is a controversy concerning the question of the status of philosophical claims and beliefs in Madhyamaka thought. Even the

ineffabilists—those who maintain that language can*not* depict the ultimate—have to admit that Mādhyamikas have written (and reasoned) a great deal. What then is the status of all of these doctrinal claims in Madhyamaka philosophy? Do Mādhyamikas believe them or not? For example, when Mādhyamikas put forward an argument to an opponent, do they accept the various claims they are making, or is their use of logic a mere show put on for the sake of others?

These questions were all hotly debated in Tibet.

Among the more interesting debates is the one that involves language and the nature of philosophical claims. If the ultimate is ineffable and inconceivable, what then is the point of Madhyamaka philosophy? Of what use are the voluminous writings of Mādhyamika philosophers? Some Tibetans believed that Mādhyamikas were unlike other philosophers insofar as, having freed themselves of false conceptual constructions, they put forward no philosophical claims and held no philosophical views of their own. Beliefs, after all, privilege one position over another, and since Mādhyamikas have purged their minds of dichotomous conceptualization, they should have no beliefs, and hence no preference for one philosophical view over another. For the Tibetans who held this view, the Madhyamaka was at most a bitter pill offered to the conceptually infirm, but one that Mādhyamikas themselves had no need of swallowing. In opposition to this were those who believed that the Madhyamaka was a philosophical system in its own right—indeed the "highest" or most perfect philosophical expression of the Buddha's thought. Khedrupjey (mKhas grub rje), and others committed to this view, claim that Mādhyamikas hold and defend philosophical positions just like any other philosophers.

Our selection is from the *Great Digest* (*sTong thun chen mo*) of the fifteenth-century Tibetan scholar Khedrupjey,[1] a disciple of Tsongkhapa,[2] founder of the Gelukpa (dGe lugs pa) school of Tibetan Buddhism. Khedrupjey succeeded his teacher (and Tsongkhapa's elder student) Gyaltsapjey[3] on the throne of Ganden (dGa' ldan) Monastery, making him the third throne holder of Tsongkhapa's seat. As we shall see from what follows, Khedrupjey was an avid polemicist—in fact, he was Tsong kha pa's first great defender. He was also one of the greatest philosophical minds in the history of Tibet.

Tsongkhapa was an epistemological optimist. He believed in the power of language and logic. Arguing that the ultimate truth could be expressed in words, he claimed that it was conceptually accessible—that it was the object of inference. While an inferential understanding of emptiness was not, according to Tsongkhapa, sufficient to gain liberation—the conceptual

1. Mkhas grub Dge legs dpal bzang, 1385–1438. On the life of Khedrupjey, see Cabezón 1992: 13–19.

2. Tsong kha pa Blo bzang grags pa, 1357–1419.

3. Rgyal tshab Dar ma rin chen, 1364–1432.

"ascertainment" (*nges shes*) needed to be focused through meditation until it appeared vividly in the mind of the yogi—the object of the conceptual understanding and the object of the yogic intuition were, he claimed, identical. As a corollary of his epistemological optimism, Tsongkhapa believed that it was not inconsistent to claim that Mādhyamikas held views, that they believed what they said. For him there was no getting around the fact that the Mādhyamikas' was a true philosophical system. This is the view that Khedrupjey defends in the section of the *Great Digest* translated here.

In this passage, Khedrupjey takes on an opponent who believes that the Madhyamaka is not really a philosophy because Mādhyamikas hold no views or philosophical positions.[4] Khedrupjey begins by presenting the opinion of his opponent, including all of the passages from the Indian texts that the opponent uses as warrants for his position. The citation of such "prooftexts" are very much a part of Indian and Tibetan Buddhist philosophical speculation. The task of the Buddhist philosopher is therefore as much exegetical—philosophy is as much a task of interpretation—as it is of pure reasoning. If Khedrupjey is to win the argument, he must triumph not only through reasoned argument (*yukti, rigs pa*) but also in regard to the interpretation of "scripture" (*āgama, lung*), giving plausible alternative readings for each of the texts cited by his opponent.

Khedrupjey's *first* responses, however, are not exegetical but reasoned. His goal here is to show how his opponents' position—the position that Mādhyamikas make no claims and hold no views—is untenable. He begins indirectly, by claiming that his opponents' position is the result of a faulty interpretation of Madhyamaka method, one that sees the Madhyamaka as indiscriminately refuting everything—as claiming that nothing exists. At the end of his "refutation" Khedrupjey will argue that his opponent's view is tantamount to another fallacious position, the "quietist heresy" of the Chinese Chan abbot Hashang Mohoyen, who maintained that true meditation entails the cessation of conceptualization, the blanking out of the mind. According to Khedrupjey, four views held by his opponents are intertwined, and all are error-ridden: (1) the view that Mādhyamikas have no philosophical positions; (2) the view that they are committed to refuting everything; (3) the view that nothing exists; and (4) the view that the highest form of meditation involves blanking out the mind. Each of these views—belonging to the realms of language, philosophical method, ontology, and practice, respectively—mutually reinforce one another. At times, Khedrupjey even suggests that they *imply* one another.

However, Khedrupjey's principal focus in *this* passage is on the first view. He first shows that such a position is self-contradictory, and then goes on to demonstrate that it leads to other unwanted consequences. Isn't the claim that Mādhyamikas hold no positions itself a position? What is more, how

4. Historically speaking, there was probably no one school or individual that held all of the views that Khedrupjey ascribes to his opponents here.

can the Madhyamaka be said to be the *best* philosophical view when it is no view at all? Khedrupjey's opponents claim that those who believe that Mādhyamikas have philosophical positions are Svātantrikas, the advocates of autonomous syllogisms, who maintain that both the Mādhyamikas and their conversation partners have to "accept" certain presuppositions in order for their logical syllogisms to work. Prāsaṅgikas, Khedrupjey's opponents maintain, are content simply to refute the view of others without holding any views themselves. But Khedrupjey shows that the Prāsaṅgika/Svātantrika distinction itself is not possible for his opponents because it would entail the acceptance of something—namely, the validity of one type of argument (*prasaṅgas*) over another (*svatantras*).

Khedrupjey then responds to another of his opponents' positions: that Prāsaṅgikas have no beliefs of their own, but that they assume (or perhaps feign) to have beliefs when they engage others philosophically so as to help others come to the Prāsaṅgikas' ineffable (position-less) truth. This, they say, is all that they mean by "being Prāsaṅgika." But this view—that Prāsaṅgikas are like chameleons who change colors as warranted by circumstance, provisionally taking on the views of others for the sake of deconstructing them, while having no views themselves—is equally problematic, says Khedrupjey. If this is all that it means to be a Prāsaṅgika—that one temporarily assumes the Prāsaṅgika identity when one engages others in conversation—then it would follow that the Buddha was a Cittamātra, a follower of the Mind-Only school, which (in Tibet at least) was widely held to be an inferior philosophical view. This is because the Buddha is believed to have taught Cittamātra (and, in fact, other philosophically fault-ridden views) as expedient means to help specific disciples who were not yet "ripe" for the truth of the Madhyamaka. Khedrupjey then goes on to claim that those who assert that Mādhyamikas have no positions have no basis for making a variety of distinctions fundamental to the understanding of Buddhism—for example, the hermeneutical distinction between the provisional (*neyārtha, drang don*) and definitive (*nītārtha, nges don*) teachings of the Buddha. For his opponents, all of the Buddha's teachings collapse into a single undifferentiated mass—as does the entire, heterogeneous later philosophical tradition of Buddhism, and its great works. For without adhering to positions, how can one claim that one thing is different from another, or that one thing is better than another?

Having "refuted" his opponent through reasoning, there still remains the task of interpreting all of the passages cited by the opponents in support of their position. Before doing so, however, Khedrupjey will cite a few texts of his own, texts meant to show that some of the greatest Mādhyamika philosophers of India constantly used expressions like "We believe" or "We accept." Finally, Khedrupjey goes through the list of passages cited by his opponents and shows that, when understood in their proper context, they do *not* claim that Mādhyamikas have no philosophical views.

Khedrupjey ends this section of the *Great Digest* by arguing that his opponents' position undermines the religious life. If one accepts nothing, then, of course, one cannot accept—that is, commit to—the three jewels, the monastic life, and the goal of ending suffering (both one's own and others'). It is at this point that Khedrupjey claims that such a view is tantamount to the view of Hashang: for those who claim to believe in nothing, what better method of meditation is there than to think of nothing?[5]

Translation

[Opponent:] Prāsaṅgika Mādhyamikas have no system of their own, no beliefs, and nothing at all that they accept.[6] Were they to have such beliefs, then they would also have to accept the [validity and conclusions of the] syllogisms (*gtan tshigs*) that prove the beliefs of their own system, the examples used in such logical arguments, and so forth. Were that so, they would be no different from Svātantrikas. It is for this reason that [Nāgārjuna's] *Vigrahavyāvartanī* (vv. 24–25) says:

> [1] Had I any beliefs,
> Then I would suffer from that fault [you claim I suffer from];
> But since I have no belief,
> I am utterly faultless.
>
> Were I to perceive anything
> By means of the objects of sense perceptions etc.,
> Then that would have to be either proven or disproven,
> But since I do not [accept such a thing], you cannot accuse me
> [of inconsistency].

And again, [Candrakīrti's] *Yuktiṣaṣṭikā* (v. 50) says:

> [2] Great beings take no sides,
> They do not argue.
> How cn those who take no sides themselves
> [Accept] the positions of others?

[Āryadeva's] *Catuḥśataka* (XVI, 25) says:

> [3] Whoever takes no sides;
> Such as "is," "is-not," and "is/is-not"
> Cannot be accused [of fallacy]
> No matter how long one tries.

5. The excerpt that follows is a substantially revised version of a passage from my published translation of Khedrupjey's *Stong thun chen mo.* It is based on Lha-mkhar Yoṅ-dzin 1972: 294–308. The original translation appeared in Cabezón 1992: 256–266.

6. The First Panchen Lama ascribes this position to Taktsang Lotsawa, and he criticizes it much as Khedrupjey does here; Blo bzang chos kyi rgyal mtshan 1997: 381–382. See also Cabezón 1995.

[Candrakīrti's] *Prasannapadā* (de la Vallée Poussin 1913: 16) states: [4] "If one is a Mādhyamika, it is not right to use autonomous forms of reasoning, for they [i.e., Mādhyamikas] do not accept the positions of others." And also (de la Vallée Poussin 1913: 23), [5] "The point that is refuted in a reductio argument is something related to the opponent, not to us, for *we* have no beliefs." [Candrakīrti] also states in his *Madhyamakāvatāra* (6.173; Candrakīrti 1970: 294):

> [6] Does the annihilator come into contact with what is annihilated or not?
> If so, then the faults that have already been mentioned
> Will definitely be incurred by those who hold to this (view);
> But since I do not have a position, this reductio does not apply to me.

Therefore, whatever claims—whether of the conventional or of the ultimate—a Prāsaṅgika Mādhyamika makes, they do so merely in the context of confronting others, but not because it represents (the Prāsaṅgika's) own system. The *Madhyamakāvatāra* (6.81; Candrakīrti 1970: 179) says:

> [7] We do not accept, even conventionally,
> A real dependent entity (*gzhan bdang dngos*), as you yourself do.
> Though [such things] do not exist, with a special purpose [in mind]
> We speak about their existence, satisfied [with the way these terms are used in] the world.

The *Vigrahavyāvartanī* (v. 63) [also] states: [8] "Since there is nothing to be refuted, I refute nothing." Hence [in the Madhyamaka] there is no such thing even as the refutation of another's position. This is what the opponent claims.[7]

[Reply:] Those who make such claims have [...] misapprehended the extent of what is to be refuted [in Madhyamaka deconstructionist analysis]. They think that the reasoning of the Prāsaṅgika Mādhyamikas is refuting *all* phenomena. But, once refuted, seeing no way to rebut the fact that those very forms of reasoning [used to refute others] can be used to refute what they themselves accept, and totally unaware of any other method to avoid the problems they face when the absurdities they urged on others are slung back at them, their one last hope is to say, "We accept nothing."

Here is how you should reply to them: It follows, absurdly, that Prāsaṅgika Mādhyamikas are not philosophers (*sgrub mtha' smra ba*), since [according to you] they accept no philosophical positions (*sgrub mtha'*). If this is acceptable to you, then you must give up the view that they are the *supreme* among all philosophers.

You, the person who advocates such [a position], *have* a belief because you are a true believer in the position "I accept nothing."

7. Concerning the question of whether or not the Prāsaṅgikas have a viewpoint of their own, see also Napper 1985, Ruegg 1984, and Cabezón 1997.

[Opponent:] To say that "accepting nothing" is accepting something is similar to [the instance in which someone] says, "Give me some money," and when answered, "Money? I have none at all," to then reply, "Give me some of that money you call 'none at all.'"

[Reply:] It is a great mistake to say this, for we are [not engaged in mere word games, but are instead] saying that the heartfelt (*zhe bas*) claim to accept nothing is an acceptance [of something]. We are not advocating that the nonexistence of accepted [beliefs] is an accepted belief. For example, although the permanence of sound is not a philosophical view, the *heartfelt claim* that sound is impermanent *is* a philosophical position.

It is also wrong [of you] to make the distinction that reductio [forms of argument] are not refuted but that autonomous ones are. Why? Because in your own system, just as you cannot accept autonomous arguments, you also cannot accept reductios; and [just as you accept that the reductio is posited as a valid mode of reasoning merely for the sake of helping some disciples and not because it *actually is* valid reasoning], there should be [according to you] no contradiction in maintaining that, according to the Prāsaṅgika system, autonomous arguments are acceptable [as a valid form of reasoning] merely for the sake of [helping] some disciples. If you accept [the latter premise—i.e., that autonomous arguments are acceptable in some instances], then it contradicts your making such a distinction—[i.e., the Prāsaṅgika/Svātantrika distinction, which depends on one's ability to claim that the former categorically reject autonomous arguments, whereas the latter accept them].

You believe that although you do not accept the philosophical positions of the Prāsaṅgika Mādhyamikas in your own system, since you do so when confronting others, this is enough to make you "Prāsaṅgika Mādhyamikas." But this is absurd because it would mean that Candrakīrti's acceptance of Prāsaṅgika philosophical positions only when confronting others, and not in his own system, is enough to make him a Prāsaṅgika Mādhyamika. The reason is something that you yourself accept. Now, if you accept the premise, then it follows, absurdly, that the Conqueror Śākyamuni is a Cittamātra because, though he does not accept the tenets of the Cittamātra himself, when he taught the *Saṃdhinirmocana Sūtra,* he accepted [Cittamātra views] merely for the sake of his other disciples.

It follows, absurdly, that even when merely confronting others, it is not correct [for you] to accept the tenets of the Prāsaṅgikas because the person in whose presence one accepts [these tenets], he or she who accepts [the tenets] when confronting that other person, and the tenets themselves are, all of them, nonexistent [according to you]. If you do not accept [this latter] reason, then you have transgressed [your own view] that it is incorrect to say that any phenomenon exists. [...]

It follows, absurdly, that such prooftexts as "Had I any beliefs..." [the texts that you quote above] are texts that do not belong to any philosophers, for they are not the texts of any one [group of philosophers] from the

Svātantrikas on down, and [according to you] they are also not the texts of the Prāsaṅgikas. If you accept the premise, it follows, absurdly, that they are not Buddhist texts.[8]

It follows, absurdly, that the distinction between scriptures of definitive and provisional meaning is an incorrect one because [according to you] the Buddha has no system of his own. If you deny [the latter] reason, then you have transgressed [your own claim] that the person who perceives the ultimate Madhyamaka view can have no system of his or her own. [. . .]

The Ārya Nāgārjuna and the glorious Candrakīrti and so on repeatedly make one-pointed statements like "this is so," "this is not so," "this is correct," and "this is not correct" in the treatises that they themselves have composed. Now, if these statements do not represent the views of the authors who composed these [works], then tell me, whose views *do* they represent?

And not only that, there are many instances in those treatises when [the authors] actually use expressions like "I believe such and such" or "I accept such and such." In the *Vigrahavyāvartanī* (v. 28), for example, [Nāgārjuna] says, "If we did not *accept* convention, however, we could explain nothing."

[Khedrupjey goes on to cite many passages in which Nāgārjuna and Candrakīrti explicitly use words like "we believe" and "we accept."]

Those who are poor in intellect and fortune may not be able to understand this special system [of Nāgārjuna and Candrakīrti] following the path of reasoning, but at least they should not slander it by saying, "There is no such system!" Shouting out, "We do not accept any system, whether Prāsaṅgika or Svātantrika Mādhyamika," given that it implies that one is not a Mādhyamika, do not devote yourself to such a contradictory system that then goes on to pride itself on being the highest of all the philosophical schools.

How do we then explain the meaning of the scriptural passages cited above [by the opponent]?

[1] The verse from the *Vigrahavyāvartanī* that goes "Had I any beliefs . . . " is the answer to the following objection:

> If the essence of all things
> Did not exist in them all,
> Your own words too would be essenceless,
> And so could not repudiate essences.

8. The underlying assumption here is that apart from the texts of one or another of the different philosophical schools there are no other (i.e., generic) texts, since apart from the four Buddhist schools there are no other Buddhist schools. I discuss issues related to this claim in Cabezón 1990.

The meaning of this scriptural passage, which presents [Nāgārjuna's opponent's] argument, is as follows: If nothing has an essence, then the words of the Mādhyamika's belief, "nothing has an essence," would also lack an essence. If *that* is so, then that belief would not have the ability to repudiate the existence of an essence, nor could it bring about an understanding of essencelessness. [This is the position of Nāgārjuna's opponent.]

The meaning [of the verse that] responds to this [objection] is as follows: Were I to accept that everything is essenceless, and then accept that the few words of the belief, "everything is essenceless," [are somehow exceptional and] exist by virtue of an essence, then I would suffer from the fault [you accuse me of]. In my system, however, [even] the words of such a belief do *not* exist by virtue of any essence. Hence, I am utterly devoid of the fault that you ascribe [to me], namely that of contradicting myself. This is what [the passage] means. It is *not* teaching that in general there are no beliefs. [. . .]

[2] The meaning of the verse "Great beings take no sides . . . " is explained in the context of [Candrakīrti's] *Autocommentary to the Yuktiṣaṣṭikā* on a preceding verse (v. 46):

> Those who have not fathomed the reality of interdependence, misconceive of things in terms of self-characteristic. Without a doubt
>
> Those who believe in entities
> Hold on inappropriately to the views
> That lead to attachment and anger.
> It is from this that disputation arises.

As this implies, for those who do *not* adhere to the position that entities exist by virtue of their own characteristic, there is no disputation that involves upholding one's own position and refuting the other's position, where these positions are reified into real entities. [The text] is *not* teaching that we have no system of our own. [. . .]

[Khedrupjey goes on to give similar interpretations of the other passages quoted by his opponent.]

If there are no beliefs or philosophical positions [that we take] in our system, why would the Conqueror Maitreya have said, "Since this is really accepted, that belief should be understood to be due to his mercy"? The *belief* that the three jewels—which are [states] that can arise within one's own continuum in the future—are something to be attained, the *belief* that the teacher is the Buddha, who already, in the past, attained this in his own continuum, that the Dharma is the path, and that the Spiritual Community are those who help one on the path . . . all such beliefs, being part of the common and uncommon practice of refuge, would not be possible [if one claims that Mādhyamikas have no beliefs]. Nor would it be possible to engage in the practice of the superior thought (*lhag bsam*) that *accepts* the obligation of dispelling the suffering of all sentient beings, or of the aspirational (altruistic) mind (*smon sems*) that *pledges* to attain enlightenment for the sake of others, or of the active (altruistic) mind (*'jug sems*) that *accepts* the task of training in the practices of the bodhisattva, or of the ethical mind (*spong sems*) that *pledges* to abandon every action that is not in accord with the training of the monk. This, of course, would imply the utter destruction of the sprout that brings about the great medicinal tree who is the Tathāgata, the one who heals all beings.

[Opponent:] Although we do not accept these things in our own system, we *do* accept them when confronting others. Hence, there is no fault.

[Reply:] That being the case, your moral discipline, the generation of your [altruistic] mind (*sems bskyed*), your going for refuge, and so on become for you mere words, and are not from the heart. [...]

According to the tales told by most of the meditators of this Land of Snows, to have the "[right] view" (*lta ba*) is to be devoid of beliefs. "Meditation" is to be devoid of all thought, to be devoid of all action, both positive and negative. The "fruit" [of practice] is to be devoid of all hope. This is what they advertise. However, all of this reduces to nothing more than the view that maintains that the mind should be blanked out, that nothing should be apprehended. Thinking that nothing "is so" or "is not so," they pride themselves on having generated understanding in their minds. Those who maintain this great nihilism—that in our own system we have no beliefs—are singing the same tune as those who maintain the view of [the Chinese Ch'an master] Hashang, [the view] that the mind should be blanked out.

This has been an extensive refutation of the view that in the Prāsaṅgikas' own system nothing is to be accepted.

Bibliography and Suggested Reading

Blo bzang chos kyi rgyal mtshan. (1997) *Sgra pa Shes rab rin chen pa'i rtsod lan lung rigs pa'i seng ge'i nga ro.* In *Miscellaneous Works of the First Panchen Lama from the Zangla khar Manuscript Collection.* India: Topden Tsering.

Cabezón, José Ignacio. (1990) "The Canonization of Philosophy and the Rhetoric of *Siddhànta* in Indo-Tibetan Buddhism." In Paul J. Griffiths and John Keenan, eds., *Buddha Nature: A Festschrift in Honor of Minoru Kiyota.* San Francisco: Buddhist Books International, 7–26.

Cabezón, José Ignacio. (1992) *A Dose of Emptiness: An Annotated Translation of the Stong thun chen mo of Mkhas grub dge legs dpal bzang.* Albany: State University of New York Press.

Cabezón, José Ignacio. (1995) "On the *sGra pa Rin chen pa'i rtsod lan* of Paṇchen bLo bzang chos rgyan." *Asiatische Studien/Études Asiatiques* 49/4: 643–669.

Cabezón, José Ignacio. (1997) "Rong ston Shā kya rgyal msthan on Madhyamaka Thesislessness." In Helmut Krasser et al., eds., *Tibetan Studies: Proceedings of the International Conference on Tibetan Studies.* Vienna: Verlag der Österreichischen Akademie der Wissenschaften, 97–105.

de la Vallée Poussin, Louis, ed. (1913) *Prasannapadā*. St. Petersburg: Biblioteca Buddhica.

de la Vallée Poussin, Louis (1970, ed.) *Madhyamakāvatāra par Candrakīrti*. Osnabruck: Biblio Verlag.

Lha-mkhar Yoṅ-dzin Bstanpa Rgyal mtshan, ed. (1972) *Stoṅ thun chen mo of Mkhas-grub Dge-legs-dpal bzang*. Madhyamika Text Series, vol. 1. New Delhi: n.p.

Napper, Elizabeth. (1985) "Dependent Arising and Emptiness." Ph.D. diss., University of Virginia.

Ruegg, David Seyfort. (1984) "On Thesis and Assertion in the Madhyamaka/dBu ma." In Ernst Steinkellner and Helmut Tauscher, eds., *Tibetan and Buddhist Studies Commemorating the 200th Anniversary of the Birth of Alexander Csoma de Körös*. Budapest: Akadémiai Kiadó, 2:205–41.

12

Zongmi's *Yuanren lun* (*Inquiry into the Origin of the Human Condition*)

The Hermeneutics of Doctrinal Classification

Peter N. Gregory

This selection translates the second and third sections of *Inquiry into the Origin of the Human Condition* (*Yuanren lun*) (in four sections), by the Huayan and Chan scholar Gueifeng Zongmi (780–841). Zongmi's essay exemplifies one of the most characteristic hermeneutical strategies devised by Chinese Buddhists, known as "doctrinal classification" (*panjiao*). It presents a systematic classification of the Buddha's teachings within the framework of two of the most influential traditions of Chinese Buddhism, Huayan and Chan.

Doctrinal classification provided a broad and flexible methodology for dealing with a range of interrelated issues and was used by Chinese Buddhists to serve several different purposes. First of all, it provided them with a hermeneutical method for organizing into a coherent and internally consistent doctrinal framework the diverse corpus of sacred scriptures to which they were heir. From the beginning of the fifth century on, as an increasing number of texts became available in Chinese translations from Sanskrit and other Indic languages, one of the most vexing problems Chinese Buddhists faced was hermeneutical: how to account for the discrepancies, and sometimes even outright contradictions, found within the sacred body of scriptures believed to have been taught by the Buddha. As the Buddha's sacred word, these teachings could not be false. Some framework thus had to be devised to explain how the conflict among different teachings contained within the canon was merely apparent, and not real, and how their differences therefore did not undermine the truth or integrity of the tradition as a whole.

To help deal with this hermeneutical problem, Chinese Buddhists turned to the doctrine of expedient means (*upāya*). This doctrine held that the differences in the teachings that the Buddha delivered in the course of his forty-nine-year ministry were the result of the different audiences he addressed. Expedient means was thus a context-based hermeneutic—that is, it held that a teaching could only be properly understood by understanding its context and intent. The doctrine of expedient means enabled Chinese Buddhists to arrange the teachings in such a way that each teaching served as an expedient measure to overcome the particular shortcoming of the teaching that preceded it while, at the same time, pointing to the teaching that was to supersede it. In this fashion a hierarchical progression of teachings could be constructed, starting with the most elementary and leading to the most profound.

But doctrinal classification was not a neutral methodology. Nor did the rubric of expedient means offer any basis on which to decide the order in which the various teachings were to be classified. The order in which the teachings were ranked was a matter of interpretation that called for value judgments in regard to which scripture or scriptural corpus was to be taken as authoritative. Hence the point of view from which the teachings were ranked was determined by the doctrinal orientation of the different traditions of Chinese Buddhism. Thus, in addition to providing a hermeneutical method by which the diverse teachings put forward in different scriptures could be harmonized, doctrinal classification also furnished the means by which the different traditions of Chinese Buddhism advanced their own sectarian claims for being recognized as the true, ultimate, or most relevant teaching of Buddhism. Different traditions defined themselves vis-à-vis one another in terms of their classification of doctrines, and doctrinal classification was thus an integral part of the polemical discourse engaged in by Chinese Buddhists.

The hermeneutical and polemical functions of doctrinal classification reflect its dual character: it provided a framework that tended to fix sectarian differences at the same time that it claimed to harmonize doctrinal differences. On the one hand, it served as a critical tool by which different teachings could be evaluated and put in their place, thereby establishing a hierarchical grading of teachings that could be used for polemical purposes to justify the sectarian claims of different traditions. On the other hand, the very means that it used to subordinate some teachings to others at the same time created a framework in which those teachings could be subsumed, and thereby validated, within a broader vision of Buddhism. Doctrinal classification thus also had a synthetic function built into its critical framework. The logic by which these two functions worked together was dialectical and is most accurately denoted by the term "sublation" (*aufheben*). For Zongmi, the value of such a dialectical logic was that it provided an approach to conflicting points of view that avoided absolute judgments of right and wrong. Different teachings are not so much wrong as they are limited or partial. There is thus a gradient of truth along which all teachings can be arranged. And the way one supersedes the other is dialectical, each teaching overcoming in turn the particular limitation or partiality of the one that preceded it. The supreme teaching, of course, is the one that succeeds in offering the most comprehensive point of view in which all other teachings can be harmoniously sublated. The highest teaching was therefore often referred to as *yuan* (literally, "round," i.e., having no sides or partiality, not leaning in any direction), the perfect teaching in which all the others were consummated.

Doctrinal classification also served a third function, one that plays an especially prominent role in the fourth and concluding section of Zongmi's *Inquiry:* it provided a map of the Buddhist path, and in this sense it could be said to have a soteriological function in addition to its hermeneutical and polemical functions. The arrangement of Buddhist teachings as a graded progress moving from the most elementary to the most profound mirrored the deepening stages of understanding through which Buddhist adepts moved in their advancement along the path. The ordered progression of teachings can thus be thought of as forming a curriculum of study—that is, the order of the teachings reverses the process by which the world of delusion and suffering comes into being and is perpetuated to arrive at the ultimate origin of the human condition, which is the intrinsically pure and enlightened mind.

The doctrinal perspective in terms of which Zongmi organizes his classification of the Buddha's teachings is provided by the *tathāgatagarbha* (the "embryo" or "womb" of Buddhahood) doctrine, an idea Chinese Buddhists identified with the Buddha nature, which they interpreted in terms of intrinsic enlightenment (*benjue*), a Chinese elaboration of the Indian Buddhist idea of the potentiality for enlightenment inherent in all sentient beings. This doctrine was developed in the *Awakening of Faith in Mahāyāna* (*Dasheng qixin lun*), an apocryphal work most likely composed in China during the third quarter of the sixth century—a text that occupied a central place in Huayan and Chan thought.

Zongmi's *Inquiry into the Origin of the Human Condition* is organized around the question of the ultimate origin of the cycle of birth and death (*saṃsāra*). Zongmi's inquiry is twofold. In the first three sections of this work, he uses the doctrine of expedient means to organize the various teachings into a hierarchical structure according to the superficiality or profundity with which they address the question of the origin of human existence. The highest teaching reveals that the ultimate origin is the intrinsically enlightened mind possessed by all sentient beings. Enlightenment is based on and consists in insight into this mind. The order of the teachings in the first three parts of the *Inquiry* thus outlines a sequence of soteriological progress that traces the process of rebirth from its farthest effects back to its ultimate origin. The concluding section of the essay moves in the opposite direction, showing how the process of rebirth begins from a unity principle, whose division ultimately leads to the continual round of rebirth in which beings are bound.

The most elementary category of teaching in Zongmi's scheme is that of Humans and Gods. It consists in the simple moral teaching of karmic retribution, which enables beings to gain a favorable rebirth as either human beings or gods. Since the basic import of the Teaching of Humans and Gods hinges on the doctrine of rebirth, it naïvely assumes that there is, in fact, something that is reborn. It is thus superseded by the Teaching of the Lesser Vehicle (Hīnayāna), whose doctrine of no-self (*anātman*) refutes the belief in a permanent, unchanging self. This teaching develops a sophisticated psychological vocabulary of dharmas (here designating the basic categories into which all experience can be analyzed) in order to break down the conceit of self into an ever-changing concatenation of impersonal constituents, none of which can be grasped as a substantial entity.

In its psychological analysis, however, the Teaching of the Lesser Vehicle talks as if these dharmas were real. It is accordingly superseded by the third category of teaching, which deconstructs the reality of the dharmas by showing that they, like the conceit of self, are nothing but mental constructions. This category, referred to as the Teaching of the Phenomenal Appearances of the Dharmas (*faxsiang jiao*), is represented by the brand of Yogācāra introduced into China by Xuanzang (600–664). It demonstrates that since both the conceptions of self and the dharmas are merely the projections of an underlying consciousness (the *ālayavijñāna*), they are therefore equally unreal.

Yet this teaching is not final. Even though it clarifies how deluded thought arises, it still does not reveal its ultimate basis. Zongmi argues that the Teaching of the Phenomenal Appearances of the Dharmas fails to discern that the projecting consciousness and the projected objects are interdependent and hence equally unreal. This teaching is thus superseded by that which Zongmi refers to as the Teaching that Refutes Phenomenal Appearances (*poxiang jiao*), which demonstrates the emptiness of both the projecting consciousness and the projected objects. This teaching is represented by the Perfection of Wisdom scriptures and Madhyamaka treatises.

While this fourth level of teaching succeeds in determining what ultimate reality is not, it still does not reveal what it is, and it is therefore superseded by the next and final teaching, that which Reveals the Nature (*xianxing jiao*). By clarifying that the underlying projecting consciousness, the *ālayavijñāna,* is based on the intrinsically enlightened pure mind, the *tathāgatagarbha,* this teaching reveals the ultimate source on which both delusion and enlightenment are based.[1]

Translation

The Buddha's teachings proceed from the superficial to the profound. Altogether there are five categories: (1) the Teaching of Humans and Gods, (2) the Teaching of the Lesser Vehicle, (3) the Teaching of the Phenomenal Appearances of the Dharmas within the Great Vehicle, (4) the Teaching That Refutes the Phenomenal Appearances within the Great Vehicle, and (5) the Teaching of the One Vehicle That Reveals the Nature.

1. The Teaching of Humans and Gods

The Buddha, for the sake of beginners, at first set forth the karmic retribution of the three periods of time [i.e., past, present, and future] and the causes and effects of good and bad [deeds]. That is to say, [one who] commits the ten evils in their highest degree falls into hell upon death, [one who commits the ten evils] in their lesser degree becomes a hungry ghost, and [one who commits the ten evils] in their lowest degree becomes an animal. Therefore, the Buddha grouped [the five precepts] with the five constant virtues of the worldly teaching and caused [beginners] to maintain the five precepts, to succeed in avoiding the three [woeful] destinies, and to be born into the human realm. [One who] cultivates the ten good deeds in their highest degree as well as bestowing alms, maintaining the precepts, and so forth is born into [one of] the six heavens of [the realm of] desire. [One who] cultivates the four stages of meditative absorption and the eight attainments is born into [one of] the heavens of the realm of form or the realm of formlessness. Therefore, [this teaching] is called the Teaching of Humans and Gods. According to this teaching, karma constitutes the origin of bodily existence.

Now I will assess [this teaching] critically. Granted that we receive a bodily existence in [one of] the five destinies as a result of our having generated karma, it is still not clear who generates karma and who experiences its retribution. If the eyes, ears, hands, and feet are able to generate karma, then why, while the eyes, ears, hands, and feet of a person who has just died are still intact, do they not see, hear, function, and move? If one says that it is the mind that generates [karma], what is meant by the mind? If one says that it is the corporeal mind, then the corporeal mind has material substance and is embedded within the body. How, then, does it suddenly enter the eyes

1. This translation originally appeared in Peter N. Gregory, *Inquiry into the Origin of Humanity* (Honolulu: University of Hawaii Press, 1995). We gratefully acknowledge permission to republish this work.

and ears and discern what is and what is not of externals? If what is and what is not are not known [by the mind], then by means of what does one discriminate them? Moreover, since the mind is blocked off from the eyes, ears, hands, and feet by material substance, how, then, can they pass in and out of one another, function in response to one another, and generate karmic conditions together? If one were to say that it is just joy, anger, love, and hate that activate the body and mouth and cause them to generate karma, then, since the feelings of joy, anger, and so forth abruptly arise one moment and abruptly perish the next and are of themselves without substance, what can we take as constituting the controlling agent and generating karma?

If one were to say that the investigation should not be pursued in a disconnected fashion like this, but that it is our body-and-mind as a whole that is able to generate karma, then, once this body has died, who experiences the retribution of pain and pleasure? If one says that after death one has another body, then how can the commission of evil or the cultivation of merit in the present body-and-mind cause the experiencing of pain and pleasure in another body-and-mind in a future life? If we base ourselves on this [teaching], then one who cultivates merit should be extremely disheartened and one who commits evil should be extremely joyful. How can the holy principle be so unjust? Therefore we know that those who merely study this teaching, even though they believe in karmic conditioning, have not yet reached the origin of their bodily existence.

2. The Teaching of the Lesser Vehicle

The Teaching of the Lesser Vehicle holds that from [time] without beginning, bodily form and cognitive mind, because of the force of causes and conditions, arise and perish from moment to moment, continuing in a series without cease, like the trickling of water or the flame of a lamp. The body and mind come together contingently, seeming to be one and seeming to be permanent. Ignorant beings in their unenlightenment cling to them as a self. Because they value this self, they give rise to the three poisons of greed, anger, and delusion. The three poisons arouse thought, activating body and speech and generating all karma. Once karma has come into being, it is difficult to escape. Thus [beings] receive a bodily existence of pain and pleasure in the five destinies and a position of superior or inferior in the three realms. In regard to the bodily existence that they receive, no sooner do [beings] cling to it as a self then they at once give rise to greed and so forth, generate karma, and experience its retribution. In the case of bodily existence, there is birth, old age, sickness, and death; [beings] die and are born again. In the case of a world, there is formation, continuation, destruction, and emptiness; [worlds] are empty and are formed again.

Kalpa after kalpa, birth after birth, the cycle does not cease; it is without end and without beginning, like a well wheel drawing up [water]. All this comes about from [beings] not understanding that the body is from the very outset not the self. "Is not the self" refers to the fact that the body originally takes on phenomenal appearance because of the coming together of form and mind.

If we now push our analysis further, form is comprised of the four great elements of earth, water, fire, and wind, whereas mind is comprised of the four aggregates of sensation, conceptualization, impulses, and consciousness. If each of these were a self, then they would amount to eight selves. How much more numerous would [the selves] be among the earthly element! That is to say, each one of the three hundred sixty bones is distinct from the others; skin, hair, muscles, flesh, liver, heart, spleen, and kidneys are each not the other. Each of the various mental functions are also not the same; seeing is not hearing, joy is not anger, and so on and so forth to the eighty-four thousand defilements. Since there are so many things, we do not know what to choose as the self. If each of them were a self, then there would be hundreds upon thousands of selves, and there would be the utter confusion of many controlling agents within a single body. Furthermore, there is nothing else outside of these [components]. When one investigates them inside and out, a self cannot be found in any of them. One then realizes that the body is just the phenomenal appearance of the seeming combination of various conditions and that there has never been a self.

On whose account does one have greed and anger? On whose account does one kill, steal, give [alms], and maintain the precepts? Then, when one does not obstruct the mind in good and bad [deeds] that have outflows in the three realms and only cultivates the wisdom of the view of no-self, one thereby cuts off greed and so forth, puts a stop to all karma, realizes the reality of the emptiness of self, until eventually one attains arhatship: as soon as one makes his body as ashes and extinguishes thought, one cuts off all suffering. According to this teaching, the two dharmas of form and mind, as well as greed, anger, and delusion, constitute the origin of the body of senses and the receptacle world. There has never been nor will ever be anything else that constitutes the origin.

Now I will assess [this teaching] critically. That which constitutes the source of bodily existence in the experiencing of repeated births and the accumulation of numerous life-times must, in itself, be without interruption. [However], the present five [sense] consciousnesses do not arise in the absence of conditions, there are times when consciousness does not operate, and the gods in the realm of formlessness are not comprised of the four great elements. How, then, do we hold on to this bodily existence life-time after life-time without ceasing? Therefore we know that those who are devoted to this teaching have also not yet reached the origin of bodily existence.

3. The Teaching of the Phenomenal Appearances of the Dharmas

The Teaching of the Phenomenal Appearances of the Dharmas within the Great Vehicle holds that all sentient beings from [time] without beginning inherently have eight kinds of consciousness. Of these, the eighth—the *ālayavijñāna*—is the fundamental basis. It instantaneously evolves into the body of the senses, the receptacle world, and the seeds, and transforms, generating the [other] seven consciousnesses. All [eight consciousnesses] evolve and manifest their own perceiving subject and perceived objects, none of which are substantial entities.

How do they evolve? [*The Treatise Establishing Consciousness-Only*] says: "Because of the influence of the karmically conditioned predispositions of the discrimination of self and things [in the *ālayavijñāna*], when the consciousnesses are engendered [from the *ālayavijñāna*], they evolve into the semblance of a self and things." The sixth and seventh consciousness, because they are obscured by ignorance, "consequently cling to [their subjective and objective manifestations] as a substantial self and substantial things."

"It is like the case of being ill or dreaming. Because of the influence of the illness or dream, the mind manifests itself in the semblance of the phenomenal appearance of a variety of external objects." When one is dreaming, one clings to them as substantially existing external things, but, as soon as one awakens, one realizes that they were merely the transformations of the dream. One's own bodily existence is also like this: it is merely the transformation of consciousness. Because [beings] are deluded, they cling to [these transformations] as existing self and objects, and, as a result of this, generate delusion and create karma, and birth-and-death is without end. As soon as one realizes this principle, one understands that our bodily existence is merely the transformation of consciousness and that consciousness constitutes the root of bodily existence.

4. The Teaching That Refutes Phenomenal Appearances

The Teaching of the Great Vehicle That Refutes Phenomenal Appearances refutes the attachment to the phenomenal appearances of the dharmas in the previous [teachings of] the Greater and Lesser Vehicles and intimates the principle of the emptiness and tranquility of the true nature in the later [teaching].

Wishing to refute [the Teaching of the Phenomenal Appearances of the Dharmas], I will first assess [the previous teaching] critically. Granted that the object that has evolved is illusory, how, then, can the consciousness that evolves be real? If one says that one exists and the other does not, then the activity of dreaming and the things seen [in the dream] should be different. If they are different, then the dream not being the things [seen in the dream] and the things [seen in the dream] not being the dream, when one awakens and the dream is over, the things [seen in the dream] should remain. Again, the things [seen in the dream], if they are not the dream, must be real things, but how does the dream, if it is not the things [seen in the dream], assume phenomenal appearance? Therefore we know that when one dreams, the activity of dreaming and the things seen in the dream resemble the dichotomy of seeing and seen. Logically, then, they are equally unreal and altogether lack existence. The various consciousnesses are also like this because they all provisionally rely on sundry causes and conditions and are devoid of a nature of their own. Therefore the *Middle Stanzas* says: "There has never been a single thing that has not been born from causes and conditions. Therefore there is nothing that is not empty." And further: "Things born by causes and conditions I declare to be empty." The *Awakening of Faith* says: "It is only on the basis of deluded thinking that all things have differentiations. If one is free from thinking, then there are no phenomenal appearances of any objects." The *[Diamond] Sūtra* says: "All phenomenal appearances are illusory." Those who are free from all phenomenal appearances are called Buddhas. Thus we know that mind and objects both being empty is precisely the true principle of the Great Vehicle. If we inquire into the origin of bodily existence in terms of this [teaching], then bodily existence is from the beginning empty, and emptiness itself is its basis.

Now I will also assess this Teaching [That Refutes Phenomenal Appearances] critically. If the mind and its objects are both nonexistent, then who is it that knows they do not exist? Again, if there are no real things whatsoever, then on the basis of what are the illusions made to appear? Moreover, there has never been a case of the illusory things in the world before us being able to arise without being based on something real. If there were no water whose wet nature were unchanging, how could there be the waves of illusory, provisional phenomenal appearances? If there were no mirror whose pure brightness were unchanging, how could there be the reflections of a variety of unreal phenomena? Again, while the earlier statement that the activity of dreaming and the dream object are equally unreal is indeed true, the dream that is illusory must still be based on someone who is sleeping. Now, granted that the mind and its objects are both empty, it is still not clear on what the illusory manifestations are based. Therefore we know that this teaching merely destroys feelings of attachment but does not yet clearly reveal the nature that is true and numinous. Therefore the *Great Dharma Drum Sūtra* says: "All emptiness sūtras are expositions that have a remainder." The *Great Perfection of Wisdom Sūtra* says: "Emptiness is the first gate of the Great Vehicle."

When the above four teachings are compared with one another in turn, the earlier will be seen to be superficial and the later profound. If someone studies [a teaching] for a time, and oneself realizes that it is not yet ultimate, [that teaching] is said to be superficial. But if one clings to [such a teaching] as ultimate, then one is said to be partial. Therefore it is in terms of the people who study them that [the teachings] are spoken of as partial and superficial.

5. The Teaching That Reveals the Nature

The Teaching of the One Vehicle That Reveals the Nature holds that all sentient beings without exception have the intrinsically enlightened, true mind. From [time] without beginning it is permanently abiding and immaculate. It is shining, unobscured, clear and bright ever-present awareness. It is also called the Buddha-nature and it is also called the *tathāgatagarbha*. From time without beginning deluded thoughts cover it, and [sentient beings] by themselves are not aware of it. Because they only recognize their inferior qualities, they become indulgently attached, enmeshed in karma, and experience the suffering of birth-and-death. The great enlightened one took pity on them and taught that everything without exception is empty. He further revealed that the purity of the numinous enlightened true mind is wholly identical with all Buddhas.

Therefore the *Garland Sūtra* says: "Oh sons of the Buddha, there is not a single sentient being that is not fully endowed with the wisdom of the Tathāgata. It is only on account of their deluded thinking and attachments that they do not succeed in realizing it. When they become free from deluded thinking, the all-comprehending wisdom, the spontaneous wisdom, and the unobstructed wisdom will then be manifest before them." [The *sūtra*] then offers the analogy of a single speck of dust containing a *sūtra* roll [as vast as] the great chiliocosm. The speck of dust represents sentient beings, and the *sūtra* represents the wisdom of the Buddha. [The *Garland Sūtra*] then goes on to say: "At that time the Tathāgata universally beheld all sentient beings throughout the universe and said: 'How amazing! How amazing! How can it be that these sentient beings are fully endowed with the wisdom of the Tathāgata and yet, being ignorant and confused, do not know it and do not see it? I must teach them the noble path enabling them to be forever free from deluded thinking and to achieve for themselves the seeing of the broad and vast wisdom of the Tathāgata within themselves and so be no different from the Buddhas.'"

[I will now] elaborate on [this teaching]. Because for numerous kalpas we have not encountered the true teaching, we have not known how to turn back and find the [true] origin of our bodily existence but have just clung to illusory phenomenal appearances, heedlessly recognizing [only] our unenlightened nature, being born sometimes as an animal and sometimes as a human. When we now seek our origin in terms of the consummate teaching, we will immediately realize that from the very outset we are the Buddha. Therefore, we should base our actions on the Buddha's action and identify our minds with Buddha's mind, return to the origin and revert to the source, and cut off our residue of ignorance, reducing it and further reducing it until we have reached the [state of being] unconditioned. Then our activity in response [to other beings] will naturally be [as manifold as] the sands of the Ganges—that is called Buddhahood. You should realize that delusion and enlightenment alike are [manifestations of] the one true mind. How great the marvelous gate! Our inquiry into the origin of the human condition has here come to an end.

Bibliography and Suggested Reading

Chappell, David, ed. (1983) *T'ien-t'ai Buddhism: An Outline of the Fourfold Teachings*. Tokyo: Daiichi shobō.

Gregory, Peter N. (1995) *Inquiry into the Origin of Humanity*. Honolulu: University of Hawai'i Press.

Gregory, Peter N. (2002) *Tsung-mi and the Sinification of Buddhism*. Honolulu: University of Hawai'i Press.

Ōchō, Enichi. (1981) "The Beginnings of Tenet Classification in China." *The Eastern Buddhist* 14/2: 71–94.

Weinstein, Stanley. (1973) "Imperial Patronage in the Formation of T'ang Buddhism." In Arthur Wright and Denis Twitchett, eds., *Perspectives on the T'ang*. New Haven: Yale University Press pp. 265–306.

13

Dōgen's *Shōbōgenzō*, Fascicles "Kattō" and "Ōsakusendaba"

Steven Heine

The "Kattō" and "Ōsakusendaba" fascicles of Dōgen's (1200–1253) master work, the *Shōbōgenzō*, are based to a large extent on a Zhaozhou dialogue concerning the famous "skin, flesh, bones, marrow" anecdote in which the first patriarch of Zen, Bodhidharma, selects his successor. According to the source anecdote, Bodhidharma challenges four disciples to a contest to prove their worthiness. The winner of the competition, second patriarch Huike, attains Bodhidharma's marrow by remaining silent, while the other contestants all use verbal discourse that gains his skin, flesh, and bones, respectively. These levels were considered to represent a hierarchy of understanding, with skin indicating the most superficial and marrow indicating the most profound levels.

Dōgen's innovative interpretation breaks from tradition, which valorizes the use of no-words in a tradition based on "a special transmission outside the scriptures, with no reliance on words and letters." Dōgen strongly criticizes the conventional view of the kōan, that silence is the deepest level of understanding beyond language, and emphasizes the notion found throughout his writings that verbal discourse is essential to transmission of the teaching. Language represents the "Teaching of the Way," to cite the title of another fascicle, "Dōtoku." In "Kattō," Dōgen portrays the function of language in terms of the metaphor of "entangled vines," which at once lead to the labyrinth of confusion and out of the entanglement of ignorance. Thus, verbal discourse that causes unenlightenment is essential for the process of awakening; hence his criticism of the conventional doctrine of a special transmission.

Dōgen's interpretation of the Bodhidharma dialogue is based on four main points. First, reversing the conventional view in which Huike wins the competition by remaining silent, Dōgen maintains that all of the disciples, not the fourth or any other single one, have completely expressed Bodhidharma's expressions, so that "All four disciples heard and realized [skin, flesh, bones, marrow] all at once [...] [as] a complete manifestation without partiality."

Second, there can be neither a sense of hierarchy or sequence separating the responses nor any distinction whatsoever between superficiality and depth. Dōgen also explains the equalization and interchangeability of the four responses by relating the Bodhidharma dialogue to a legend originally found in the *Mahābhārata*. He cites the *Blue Cliff Record* case (no. 92) about the king of a land called Saindhava who asks his retainers for four items, all of which came to be known as *saindhava* (Jap. *sendaba*): salt, a chalice, water, and a horse. The wisest of retainers knows exactly when and where to bring each of the items requested, without having to rely on the king's instructions.

Extending from the "Ōsakusendaba" passage, Dōgen's third point pertains to the pedagogical significance of each response. Since all the expressions are equal, each one is correct for each of the four disciples in question. Furthermore, the possibilities are limitless. If there had been six disciples, Bodhidharma would have spontaneously made additional responses, by telling his disciple that they express his "eyeball" or "body." If there were hundreds or thousands of disciples, each one with his own unique expression would have found a suitable response from the first patriarch.

The fourth point in Dōgen's interpretation refers to the interpenetration of each and every answer and response, which are equally all-pervasive and permeate the entire being of master and disciple, speaker and listener, as well as writer and reader. "You should realize," he maintains, "that when you express me, then I express you, expression expresses both me and you, and expression expresses both you and me." The term "express" is often translated as "gain" or "obtain," as if this was a bestowal from Bodhidharma to the disciple, but the general context and the way the term is used by Dōgen in other cases suggest that what is meant is a sense of resonance between teacher and follower. There is a profound sense of mutuality between questioner and respondent so that each of the latter's expressions is fully compatible and conducive to the former's spiritual path, just as the retainer knows which *saindhava* to bring the king, who, for his part, has already requested the *saindhava* appropriate for the retainer to bring.

The translation that follows contains the full text of "Kattō," one of Dōgen's best known sermons, as well as selected passages from the lesser known "Ōsakusendaba."[1]

1. This is a revised and updated version of translations originally published in Heine 1994, pp. 243–253.

Translation: Entangled Vines: Dōgen's "Kattō"

It was only bodhisattva Mahākāśyapa who, at a sermon on Vulture Peak, received the authentic transmission of the supreme wisdom of the treasury of the true Dharma-eye from Śākyamuni. This authentic transmission from Śākyamuni was then transmitted through successive generations to the twenty-eighth patriarch, the venerable Bodhidharma. Bodhidharma came to China and transmitted the supreme wisdom of the treasury of the true Dharma-eye directly to the great teacher Zhengzong Pujue, who became the second patriarch.

The twenty-eighth patriarch [in India] is referred to as the first patriarch in China, and the twenty-ninth patriarch is referred to as the second patriarch, according to the lineal system in China. The first patriarch received the authentic transmission through instruction directly from the venerable Prajñātara, and his transmission in turn became the root for the branches and leaves [symbolizing various Zen schools and doctrines]. Generally, although all Buddhist sages in their training study how to cut off entanglements (*kattō*) at their root, they do not study how to cut off entanglements by using entanglements. They do not realize that entanglements entangle entanglements. How little do they know what it is to transmit entanglements in terms of entanglements. How rarely do they realize that the transmission of the Dharma is itself an entanglement. Few have as yet heard of or practiced the way [of transmission]. How can anyone genuinely realize [the Dharma]?

My late master [Rujing] once said: "The vine of a gourd coils around the vine of a[nother] gourd like a wisteria-vine." I have never heard this saying from anyone else of the past or present. The first time I heard this was from my late master. When he said, "the vine of a gourd coils around the vine of a[nother] gourd," this refers to studying the Buddhas and patriarchs directly from the Buddhas and patriarchs, and to the transmission of the Buddhas and patriarchs directly to the Buddhas and patriarchs. That is, it refers to the direct transmission from mind-to-mind (*ishin-denshin*).

> The twenty-eighth patriarch said to his disciples, "As the time is drawing near [for me to transmit the Dharma to my successor], please tell me how you express it."
>
> Daofu responded first, "According to my current understanding, we should neither cling to words and letters, nor abandon them altogether, but use them as an instrument of the Dao (*dō-yō*)."
>
> The master responded, "You express my skin."
>
> Then the nun, Zongzhi, said, "As I now see it, [the Dharma] is like Ānanda's viewing the Buddha-land of Akshobhya, seeing it once and never seeing it again."
>
> The master responded, "You express my flesh."

Daoyou said, "The four elements are emptiness, and the five *skandhas* are nonbeing. But in my view, there is not a single dharma to be expressed."

The master responded, "You express my bones."

Finally, Huike prostrated himself three times, and stood [silently] in his place.

The master said, "You express my marrow."

Huike became the second patriarch as a result of this, and he received the transmission of the Dharma as well as the transmission of the sacred robe.

You must study the first patriarch's saying, "You express my skin, flesh, bones, and marrow," as the way of the patriarchs. All four disciples heard and realized this saying all at once. Hearing and learning from it, they realized the skin, flesh, bones, and marrow of the casting off of body-mind (*shinjin datsuraku*). You should not interpret the teachings of the patriarchs and masters from only a single specific viewpoint. It is a complete manifestation without partiality. However, those who do not fully understand the true transmission think that "because the four disciples had different levels of insight, the first patriarch's saying concerning the 'skin, flesh, bones, and marrow' represents different degrees in recognizing the superficiality or depth [of understanding]. The skin and flesh are further [from the truth] than the bones and marrow." Thus, they say that [Bodhidharma told Huike] that he "expressed the marrow because the second patriarch's understanding was superior." But interpreting the anecdote in this manner is not the result of studying the Buddhas and patriarchs or of realizing the true patriarchal transmission.

You should realize that the first patriarch's expression, "skin, flesh, bones, and marrow," does not refer to the superficiality or depth [of understanding]. Although there may remain a [provisional] distinction between superior and inferior understanding, [each of the four disciples] expressed the first patriarch in his entirety. When Bodhidharma says "you express my marrow" or "you express my bones," he is using various pedagogical devices that are pertinent to particular people, or methods of instruction that may or may not apply to particular levels of understanding.

It is the same as Śākyamuni's holding up an *udambara* flower [to Mahākāśyapa], or the transmission of the sacred robe [symbolic of the transmission of enlightenment]. What Bodhidharma said to the four disciples is fundamentally the selfsame expression. Although it is fundamentally the selfsame expression, since there are necessarily four ways of understanding it, he did not express it in one way alone. But even though each of the four ways of understanding is partial or one-sided, the way of the patriarchs ever remains the way of the patriarchs.

As a rule, the teaching of a master must be adjusted so that it is appropriate for [each one of] his disciples. For example, in order to instruct one of his four disciples the first patriarch said, "You express my skin." But, if after the second patriarch there were hundreds of thousands of disciples, there would also be hundreds of thousands of appropriate ways of explaining [the Dharma]. There would be an inexhaustible number [of explanations]. Because he was speaking with four disciples, Bodhidharma only used the four provisional expressions, "skin," "flesh," "bones" and "marrow," and although there were other possible expressions Bodhidharma did not choose to use them. For instance, he could have said to the second patriarch, "You express my skin." But even if Huike had been told "You express my skin," he still would have received the transmission of the treasury of the true Dharma-eye and become the second patriarch. "Expressing skin" or "expressing marrow" does not refer to the superiority or inferiority [of understanding]. Also, Bodhidharma could have said, "You express my marrow" to Daofu, Daoyou, or Zongzhi. He must be able to transmit the Dharma even to someone who expresses [only] the skin. The body-mind of the patriarch is the patriarchs' skin, flesh, bones, and marrow. The marrow is not closer [to the Dharma], and the skin is not further [from the Dharma].

If someone is currently studying with an [authentic] Dharma-eye and receives the seal "You express my skin," that really signifies that they are expressing the complete patriarch. There is the patriarch whose skin permeates his entire body, the patriarch whose flesh permeates his entire body, the patriarch whose bones permeate his entire body, and the patriarch whose marrow permeates his entire body. There is the patriarch whose mind permeates his body, the patriarch whose body permeates his body, and the patriarch whose mind permeates his mind. There is the patriarch who permeates the [other] patriarchs, and the patriarch whose body permeates all selves. When the patriarchs appear and teach hundreds of thousands of disciples, they often explain, "You express my skin."

Although the explanations given to the hundreds of thousands use the expression "skin, flesh, bones, and marrow," you must realize that the masters of the way may use the expression "skin, flesh, bones, and marrow," but without regard for the matter of signifying superficiality or depth. If there were six or seven disciples studying with the first patriarch, he might say "You express my mind," or "You express my body." He might also say "You express my buddha," "You express my eyeballs," or "You express my realization." The term "you" may refer [nondualistically] either to the master [Bodhidharma] or to [the disciple] Huike. One must also study very carefully the meaning of the term "expression."

You should realize that when you express me, then I express you, expression expresses both me and you, and expression expresses both you and me. In studying the body-mind of the first patriarch, you must realize the oneness of the interior and the exterior [dimensions]. If we do not realize that his whole body permeates his body, then we have not realized the domain of the manifestation of the Buddhas and patriarchs. Expressing the skin is expressing the bones, flesh, and marrow. Expressing the bones, flesh, and marrow is expressing the skin, flesh, face, and eyes. It is none other than the awakening of the true body experienced throughout the entire ten directions of the universe, and [the realization of] the skin, flesh, bones, and marrow. In this way, you express my robe and you express the Dharma.

Therefore, through the ecstatic experience of expressing the way, masters realize an unimpeded mutuality with their disciples. And through the ecstatic experience of receiving the path to liberation, disciples realize an unimpeded mutuality with their masters. The unimpeded mutuality of masters and disciples is the entanglement of Buddhas and patriarchs, and the entanglement of Buddhas and patriarchs is the realization of the skin, flesh, bones, and marrow. Śākyamuni's holding up an *udambara* flower and winking his eye is itself an entanglement, and Mahākāśyapa's wise smile is itself the skin, flesh, bones, and marrow.

You must realize that because the seed of an entangled vine has the capacity for liberation, it produces the branches, leaves, blossoms, and fruit that coil around the entangled vines. Because these [parts of vines] are at once thoroughly surrounding and free from being surrounded by each other, the entangled vine is the spontaneous realization of Buddhas and patriarchs, or the spontaneous realization of the kōan (*kōan-genjō*).

The great teacher Zhaozhou once said to his disciples, "Mahākāśyapa transmitted [the Dharma] to Ānanda. You must explain to me, to whom did Bodhidharma transmit it?"

> A monk responded, "Everyone knows it was the second patriarch who expressed the marrow. Why even ask such a question?"
>
> Zhaozhou said, "Don't slander Huike."
>
> Zhaozhou further said, "Bodhidharma also said, 'A person of superficial understanding expresses my skin, and a person of deeper understanding expresses my bones.' You must tell me, what does a person of even deeper understanding express?"
>
> The disciple responded [to Zhaozhou], "Isn't it expressing the marrow?"
>
> Zhaozhou said, "You must know only the skin. This old teacher has no reliance (*furyū*) on marrow."
>
> The disciple asked, "What is the meaning of marrow?"
>
> Zhaozhou said, "If you ask such a question, you have not yet even expressed the skin."

Therefore, you must realize that when "you have not yet even expressed the skin," it is also the case that "you have not yet even expressed the marrow." Expressing the skin is expressing the marrow. We must reflect on the meaning of "you have not yet even expressed the skin." When the disciple said, "Isn't it expressing the marrow?" Zhaozhou immediately responded, "You must know only the skin. This old teacher has no reliance on marrow."

His interpretation that expressing the skin is a matter of nonreliance on the marrow is the true meaning of expressing the marrow. Therefore, the monk said, "Everyone knows it was the second patriarch who expressed the marrow. Why even ask such a question?" Just at the moment "Mahākāśyapa transmitted the Dharma to Ānanda," Ānanda's body was fully transformed into Ānanda. However, whenever there is a transmission from person to person, there is usually some kind of change in the face, eyes, skin, flesh, bones, and marrow. That is why Zhaozhou said, "You must explain to me, to whom did Bodhidharma transmit it?" Bodhidharma in transmitting the Dharma is already Bodhidharma, and the second patriarch who expressed the marrow is also already Bodhidharma. In studying the meaning of this, the Buddha Dharma not yet [realized] is the Buddha Dharma realized right now. If that were not the case, there would be no Buddha Dharma realized right now. You must reflect on this quietly, attain it for yourself, and teach it to others.

[Zhaozhou citing Bodhidharma said]: "A person of superficial understanding expresses my skin, and a person of deeper understanding expresses my bones. You must tell me, what does a person of even deeper understanding express?" Whether or not [the understanding] is superficial or has depth, it reflects the clarity of spiritual insight. In the case of superficiality, the skin, flesh, bones, and marrow are all superficial, and in the case of depth, the skin, flesh, bones, and marrow all have depth. Therefore, what the four disciples of Bodhidharma studied in various ways was beyond even the innumerable [levels of] skin, flesh, bones, and marrow. It is not the case that the marrow should be considered the highest level. There are at least thirty-five [other dimensions] beyond the marrow.

The old master Zhaozhou's instruction is the way of the Buddhas. But it is not well understood by a number of monks, including Linji, Deshan, Dawei, and Yunmen, among others. They cannot even imagine it in their dreams, let alone express it clearly. If it were explained to them, they would be surprised and perplexed.

Xuedou Mingjue said, "Zhaozhou and Muzhao were old masters." The sayings of the "old masters" are authentic evidence of the Buddha Dharma as well as of their own personal realization. Great teacher Xuefeng Chenjue also referred to "old master Zhaozhou." [Both Xuedou and Xuefeng] praised [Zhaozhou] as an old master. Thus they considered him an old master who surpassed the buddha and patriarchs of past and present. Therefore, the meaning of the entanglements of skin, flesh, bones, and marrow has become the standard set by old master [Zhaozhou]'s saying in his lecture to his monks, "You express me." You must carefully examine this standard.

Furthermore, the reports that the first patriarch returned to India are unfounded. Although Songyan is said to have seen him there, this is untrue. How could Songyan be said to have seen the works of the first patriarch? The truth of the matter is that after he entered *parinirvāna* the first patriarch's ashes were interred on Mount Xionger in China.

Postscript: This instruction for an assembly of monks was delivered on the seventh day of the seventh month in 1242 at Kannondōri Kōshōhōrinji Temple in Uji-gun, Yawashiro. It was transcribed on the third day of the third month in 1243 at the chief disciple's quarters of Kippōji Temple in Yoshida-gun, Echizen, by Ejō.

Translation: A King Requests *Saindhava:* Dōgen's "Ōsakusendaba" [Selections]

[Dōgen cites a verse]:

Words and wordlessness:
Like tangled vines to a tree,
Feeding a mule to feeding a horse,
Or water to clouds.

In the same vein, the *Mahāparinirvāna Sūtra* states the following:

> The World-Honored One [Śākyamuni] said, "It is just like when a king [of the land of Saindhava] tells his retainer to 'bring me *saindhava.*' There are four items all known as '*saindhava.*' The first is salt, the second is a chalice, the third is water, and the fourth is a horse. These are four different things, but each shares the same name. If the king wants to wash his face and hands, he is offered the *saindhava* of water. If the king wants to eat a meal, he is offered the *saindhava* of salt. If the king wants to have a drink after eating, he is offered the *saindhava* of a chalice. And if the king wants to go for a ride after he has finished his meal, he is offered the *saindhava* of a horse. A wise retainer understands the four inner meanings of the king's words."

The mutuality involved in the king's requests and the retainer's offerings has been practiced for a long time, and it closely resembles the transmission of the sacred robe in Buddhism. Since Śākyamuni himself has commented on this topic, all of his descendants should reflect on its meaning. All those who do not practice it in this way must strengthen their efforts to make the first step of authentic practice. The *saindhava* was already being practiced by Buddhas and patriarchs long before it was disclosed, partially, to royal families.

One time old master Hongzhi of Mount Tiantong in Jingyuanfu in Song China entered the lecture hall and instructed his followers:

> A monk said to Zhaozhou, "What will you do when asked for *saindhava?*"
>
> Zhaozhou folded his hands over his chest and bowed.
>
> Xuedou commented [on this topic], "When salt is requested, I will offer a horse." [...]

One day when Nanquan saw Tenginfeng coming, he pointed to a pitcher of water and said, "The pitcher is an object. It contains some water. Bring the water over to this old priest without moving the object." Tenginfeng brought the pitcher over to Nanquan and poured the water all over him. Nanquan remained silent.

Nanquan requested water, which came from the dried-up sea, and Tenginfeng offered a chalice or a pitcher he used to pour out every drop of water. Nevertheless, we must study the water in the object and the object in the water. Was it the water that was being moved, or was it the object that was being moved?

> The great teacher Xiangyan was asked by a monk, "What is it when a king asks his retainer for *saindhava?*"
>
> Xiangyan responded, "Come over here."
>
> The monk went over there, and Xiangyan said, "Don't be such a fool!"

However, we could ask, did Xiangyan's command "Come over here" indicate a king requesting *saindhava* or a retainer offering it? Just try to answer that question!

Furthermore, when "the monk went over there," did that indicate that Xiangyan was requesting *saindhava,* receiving *saindhava* being offered, or expressing another, more fundamental concern? If he were not expressing a more fundamental concern, we could not understand the meaning of his saying, "Don't be such a fool." If he did not have a more fundamental concern, the monk called over would not have appeared so foolish. Although Xiangyan's response stems from an understanding built up during an entire lifetime, we should not be concerned [that the monk failed]. It is like a general who has lost a battle but is proud in defeat.

Generally, [the Buddhas and patriarchs] explain the [mutuality] of the request and the offering of *saindhava* in extremely subtle ways, such as pointing to black and calling it yellow, in order to reveal the nature of an enlightened vision. Who can say that holding a staff or a fly whisk is not a type of *saindhava?* On the other hand, are there not those [who are supposedly specialists but] who do not know to fasten the bridge to the base of a *koto* or how to tighten the strings of a *koto* to just the right degree?[. . .]

All activity and expression throughout twenty-four hours is nothing other than requesting *saindhava.* All activity and expression throughout twenty-four hours is nothing other than offering *saindhava.* When you request a fist you receive a fist, and when you request a flywhisk you receive a flywhisk.

However, because in Song China the senior monks in all the districts are pretentious, they cannot imagine this in their wildest dreams. What a pity! The way of the patriarchs is on the decline. Do not avoid taking up the most challenging studies, for it is up to you to transmit the lifeblood of the Buddhas and patriarchs. For example, when we are asked what the buddha is, we answer "this very mind itself is buddha" (*sokushin-ze-butsu*), but what does this mean? Is it not [an example of] *saindhava?* You must carefully study "this very mind itself is buddha." How few are there who truly understand the meaning of *saindhava.*

Postscript: This instruction for an assembly of monks was delivered on the twenty-second day of the tenth month in 1245 at Daibutsuji Temple in Echizen.

Bibliography and Suggested Reading

Cleary, Thomas and J.C. Cleary, trans. (1977) *The Blue Cliff Record,* 3 vols. Boulder: Shambhala.

Heine, Steven. (1994) *Dōgen and the Kōan Tradition: A Tale of Two Shōbōgenzō Texts.* Albany: State University of New York Press.

Heine, Steven, and Dale S. Wright, eds. (2000) *The Kōan: Texts and Contexts in Zen Buddhism.* New York: Oxford University Press.

Miura, Isshū, and Ruth Fuller Sasaki. (1966) *Zen Dust: The History of the Kōan and Kōan Study in Rinzai (Lin-chi) Zen.* New York: Harcourt, Brace and World.

14

Beyond Awareness

Tōrei Enji's Understanding of Realization in the *Treatise on the Inexhaustible Lamp of Zen,* Chapter 6

Michel Mohr

The *Treatise on the Inexhaustible Lamp of Zen* (*Shūmon mujintō ron*) is one of the few manuals describing the core of meditation in the Rinzai tradition. The author of this treatise, Tōrei Enji (1721–1792), was a disciple of the more famous Hakuin Ekaku (1686–1769) who contributed to the Rinzai revival of the eighteenth century. According to tradition, Tōrei wrote his treatise in 1751 as a spiritual testament when he believed himself to be fatally ill. He survived, however, and revised the work for forty years; it was not published until after his death.

Among the different Zen approaches, the Rinzai denomination tends to put more emphasis on the use of kōans, verbal devices used to realize one's true nature (*kenshō*) and to refine this insight. Tōrei's treatise describes the successive stages of the Zen path in ten chapters that emphasize the importance of kōan practice under the supervision of a reliable teacher, while showing how this relates to other Buddhist and non-Buddhist teachings. The audience (it was first delivered as lectures) and readership Tōrei had in mind was made up of practitioners, mostly monks and nuns, with some laypersons. These practitioners were already focusing on kōans and therefore needed little explanation concerning their contents or justification of their value. Addressing practitioners, the treatise often has an exhortative tone, sometimes challenging the reader to overcome a partial understanding of the teachings.

The translation provided below includes approximately two thirds of the crucial sixth chapter of Tōrei's treatise that deals with "going beyond" (*kōjō*) a first insight into spiritual realization.[1] In this chapter Tōrei argues that the first realization of one's true nature and the awareness[2] it triggers must be overcome until all traces of the initial breakthrough have disappeared. He describes this ongoing process as the full "integration" of the initial insight into all activities.

Because the following selection concerns an advanced stage of Zen practice, it belies a common misunderstanding of Zen "awakening." This misunderstanding, widely circulated in the West, holds that the goal of Rinzai Zen is attaining "Satori," a sudden enlightenment which corresponds to the release from suffering described in Buddhist scriptures. For Tōrei, in contrast, the purpose of Zen practice is *not* the initial insight into one's true nature, although it is the necessary first opening of the spiritual eye. In this text, Tōrei repeatedly emphasizes the fact that his tradition does not aim exclusively at attaining an initial awareness of one's own Buddha nature, but instead values the necessity of going beyond this awareness without ever clinging to it. Thus, the single theme that pervades Tōrei's treatise is the necessity to go beyond all temporary spiritual accomplishments.

The following selection includes a discussion of language and presents several examples of encounter dialogues between teacher and student in which kōans are used. Tōrei provides vivid depictions of struggles involved in the emancipation[3] process. Kōans serve as verbal devices used to deconstruct previous convictions or habits of thinking, with the important proviso that they are also words. In the prologue to his *Treatise,* Tōrei warns the reader: "Although words and written characters are the source of emancipation, they are also the source of bondage. If it doesn't encounter the proper person at the proper moment, the finest ghee turns into poison." Thus, using kōans as an antidote is like using an enemy's weapon against him, with all the dangers this involves.[4]

1. The selection translated here corresponds to the original text in classical Chinese found in the *Taishō shinshū daizōkyō,* the standard collection of the East Asian Buddhist canon edited by Takakusu Junjirō, Watanabe Kaikyoku, et al., 100 vols. Tokyo: Taishō Issaikyō Kankōkai, 1924–1932, vol. 81, no 2575, pp. 592a–594b. The paragraphs 7–20 that have been omitted correspond to pp. 592b24–593c14.

2. Concerning the precise meaning given here to "awareness," see Mohr 2000, pp. 259–260.

3. Emancipation is a rendering of *gedatsu* (Skt. *mokṣa*), which indicates release from suffering and ultimate spiritual freedom.

4. Much of Tōrei's *Treatise* was translated into English (Okuda 1990). For a complete French translation see Mohr 1997.

Translation: Going Beyond

1. The Crucial Element

Here the direct path to the freedom of going beyond remains [to be realized]. It is said to be the decisive move that patriarchs cannot transmit.[5,6] This is why Panshan says:

> "The direct path of going beyond is not transmitted by the thousand sages. Practitioners wearing out their body are like monkeys trying to catch the reflection [of the moon]."[7]

This path is also called the last word. Fushan says:

> "Only with the last word one reaches the outer gate of the prison.[8]
> The purpose of the teachings is not found in verbal devices."[9]

Thus far all the direct transmissions received from the Buddhas and patriarchs consist of this decisive move. Although they in fact have exhausted their search for obscure subtleties, penetrated the successive barriers [of kōans], and thoroughly examined the difficult cases related to going beyond, clerics still [often] completely miss this crucial element [of the last word].[10] This stems from the shallowness of their vow of compassion, the lack of aims in their resolution, the lack of intensity in their [ability to feel] remorse, and the lack of thoroughness in their questioning. Thus they remain stuck in their old ways.[11]

5. Paragraph headings have been added to make the text more accessible, but they are not part of the original treatise.

6. The "decisive move" (*ichijakusu*) is an expression coming from the Chinese chess game.

7. Panshan Baoji (n.d.) was a successor of Mazu Daoyi (709–788), who dwelt on Mount Pan, southeast of present-day Beijing.

8. Fushan Fayuan (991–1067) is also known by his nickname, "jurist Yuan." The "last word" (*matsugo no ikku*) is a metaphor referring to the ultimate word uttered at the time of physical death. The "outer gate of the prison" (*rōkan*) renders an expression that plays on several images: a prison, as metaphor for bondage to life and death, a strategic checkpoint or a roadblock (*sekisho*).

9. Verbal devices (*gonsen*) are words considered as "traps." See the metaphor of the fish trap in *Zhuangzi* 26.

10. This crucial element (*kono shashi no ji*), literally "this little thing"—a euphemism for the point Tōrei wants to make.

11. The word used for "the old ways" (*kyū kakutsu ri*) literally indicates the "nest" of a bird or the "den" of an animal. Other renderings of the same expression could be "habits" or "stereotyped patterns."

2. Three Models

This is why in the past master Shōichi[12] established the three models of Richi (reaching the principle), Kikan (dynamic device), and Kōjō (going beyond), precisely to remedy this problem. [However,] after the Middle Age [people started] analyzing [classical] utterances, classifying each of them according to those [three categories] and thus only interpreting them in a superficial manner.

What tends to be ignored is that the essence of Kenshō (seeing one's true nature) is reaching the principle; the numerous enigmatic utterances of Buddhas and patriarchs are essentially dynamic devices; and the decisive move of going beyond suggests that the [true] way of life is different. What makes our Zen tradition superior to other traditions is precisely the transmission of this crucial element.[13] If it were sufficient just to have realized one's true nature, why would we need to establish our tradition as a separate one?

3. The Buddha's Disciples

It should have been easy for those members of the congregation on the Vulture Peak![14] Having developed considerable experience in their practice, all of them had fully realized the nature and characteristics of both principle and phenomena. How could one pretend that their spiritual realization and understanding was inferior? One should clearly recognize that [one's understanding] is not even remotely comparable to theirs.

Since [the Buddha's disciples] had already reached such a level, then for what reason was Mahākāśyapa the only one to break into a subtle smile? Ānanda had been the Buddha's assistant for thirty years, not to mention the fact that during the Śūraṃgama assembly he had reached an extremely deep awakening. Nevertheless, he could not understand. Why did he need to consult Mahākāśyapa before receiving this Dharma?

4. Today's Level

Today's practitioners, believing this to be easy, neglect examining these ancient facts, and after flirting with some practices of Zen [proceed to] waste

12. Enni Bennen (1202–1280), the founder of Tōfukuji, whose honorific name is Shōichi Kokushi.

13. "Our Zen tradition" (*waga zenshū*) indicates both the lineage and the principles inherited by Tōrei. In premodern texts "*Zenshū*" was never understood as a religious institution or a "denomination."

14. The Vulture Peak is the location where the historical Buddha is supposed to have once given a decisive teaching by remaining silent and holding a flower in front of the assembly. None of his listeners understood, except Mahākāśyapa, who acknowledged him by smiling. This smile of complicity and the ensuing silent transmission are regarded in the tradition as the origin of Zen.

away their whole existence.[15] How sad that the unique tradition of Bodhidharma is getting wiped out in one fell swoop! Sometimes [these practitioners] say: "as in the Bodhidharma tradition we directly focus on the human heart, see our true nature, and realize Buddhahood, so what is the need for another principle aside from seeing one's own true nature?"

This is not entirely wrong, but what a pity [it misses the essential point]! You say that everything in the Bodhidharma tradition can be reduced only to the teaching of seeing one's true nature. Then for what reason did he make a distinction between [the disciples who had obtained] his skin, his flesh, his bones, and his marrow?[16] Why would he have cheated the people [in this way]?

5. Baizhang's Practice

When Baizhang's nose got twisted by Mazu, he clearly realized [his true nature]. Why, then, is there a case that deals with his second encounter [with Mazu]?[17]

Baizhang taught his disciples:

> "The Buddha Dharma is no small task. In the past I endured one shout from Mazu and consequently remained deaf for three days."

While staying at the Platform Temple in Jiangning, Zhang Wujin read *Xuedou's Commentaries on Ancient Cases.*[18] Reaching the passage concerning Baizhang's second encounter with Mazu, he read [Xuedou's comments], "pure gold [cast by a] skilled smith should not change its color."

[Zhang] immediately threw the book away exclaiming "if we examine this in detail, if [Xuedou] was right, how could the Linji [tradition] have reached its present [success]?"

He composed these verses:

> "The one shout by Mazu [produced] Daxiong Peak[19]
> His voice penetrated [Baizhang's] skull, deafening him for three days
> Huangbo heard this [story] and clicked his tongue in awe
> From there the Jiangxi style [of Chan] was established."

15. "Flirting with some practice of Zen" (*kyota no zen ni sanzu*), or "consulting a few Zen [teachers]." The vernacular expression *kyota* suggests the random character of this activity.

16. Alludes to a relatively late legend about Bodhidharma's choice of a successor. See chapter 13 here.

17. This case, called "Baizhang's second encounter [with Mazu]" (*Hyakujō saisan*), is a kōan belonging to the "going beyond" type. See Kirchner 2004: 98–99.

18. Zhang Shangying (1043–1121), also known as layman Tianjue Wujin. *Xuedou songgu* is the first version of the text that later became the *Emerald Cliff Records* (*Biyanlu*).

19. Daxiong Peak (Dayūhō) is another name for Baizhang, coming from the mountain where he resided.

6. Dialogue between Wujin and Yuanwu about Baizhang

Later [Wujin] told Yuanwu:[20]

"What I have always regretted is that Xuedou interpreted[21] the story of Baizhang remaining deaf for three days as 'pure gold [cast by a] skilled smith should not change its color.' It demonstrates that he had not fully understood the true Jiangxi tradition."

Yuanwu: "Recently, I [composed] verses which agree with your view."

Wujin asked to hear them, and Yuanwu recited his verses:

> "Setting the fly-whisk upright or setting it aside
> [His] whole activity appears and disappears
> Fitting with it, [and yet] giving it away,
> Like drawing the character for 'one' instead of a discourse.
> Directly from the crown of [his] head
> Rumbled the sound of crushing thunder
> That rooted out [Baizhang's] fatal disease from his chest.
> By receiving the one shout [from Mazu] in the right place
> And remaining deaf for three days
> The lion's spiritual power was unleashed.[22]
> Pure gold refined hundreds of times
> Must lose its color."[23]

Wujin, delighted, replied:

> "What I have always feared is the progressive decline of the way of the patriarchs. Now that I have seen Guan Yiwu in priestly garb so to speak [I feel relieved]."[24]

[Sections 7–20 omitted because of space limitations]

20. Yuanwu Keqin (1063–1135), also known as Foguo.

21. The way Xuedou "handles" (*nentei*) this story refers to his understanding of it as a kōan.

22. Baizhang is compared to a lion unleashing his power. Saying that Baizhang literally "counterattacked freely" (*hanteki o hoshiimama ni su*) implies that when he endured the one shout from his teacher he seemed submissive, but in this second phase his reaction is likened to the lion huddling up before leaping on his prey.

23. Pure gold is a metaphor for the Buddha nature. The discussion centers here around the expression "changing color," literally "losing [one's] color" (*shisshoku*). Xuedou emphasizes the permanent character of gold, whereas Zhang and Yuanwu insist on the necessity to overcome its brilliance.

24. Guan Yiwu (d. 645 B.C.E.), also known as Guan Zhong, was a famous politician in the Spring and Autumn period (722–481 B.C.E.). He is mentioned in the *Analects of Confucius,* a text depicting him as an exceptional man who "restored order in the world." Paragraphs 7–20 have been omitted.

21. Autobiographical Account

In my case, when I was [staying] at the top of Rengezan in the Ōmi region,[25] [the great matter] became clear for the first time. Then, when I arrived at Hakuin's place[26] I simply couldn't open my mouth.[27] From then on, I contained my euphoric state and immersed myself in practice day and night.

One day, the late master (Hakuin) asked me: "Suddenly one of the most powerful kings of the demons [appears] at your back.[28] Extending a single hand he grabs you and wants to throw you into a great flaming pit. At this time, can you find a way to escape?" On the spot I could neither stand up nor leave, and the sweat of shame covered my body. From this moment, whenever I entered his [Sanzen] room the teacher would immediately ask "can you find a way to escape?" I was completely incapable of answering.

If I were like you and easily offered [my initial] thoughts [according to] each action or inner state [I perceived], how could I not have answered? But because I deeply trusted and respected the detailed [accounts] of former [teachers], ultimately I didn't pick a word [at random] to hide my [ignorance]. In this [situation] I was never at peace, whether walking or standing. Heaven and earth [felt] narrow, the sun and the moon [seemed] dark.[29] The following year, in the spring of 1744, I asked permission to retire to a secluded building, where day and night I pursued my practice.

22. Hakuin's Encouragement

One day, master [Hakuin] came and told me: "Strong man, when the [old] habits[30] appear, don't be afraid of them; simply investigate them until you reach their source. This is why it is said that 'the ancients worried about dying without coming back to life, whereas today's people worry about living without being able to die.' For instance, if you fall into water and promptly hit the bottom, as soon as your feet touch it you will make it back to the surface. [On the other hand] if you fear sinking and indiscriminately wave your legs and arms, then the whole body exhausts itself and you drown. This is called 'abandoning one's grip on the cliff, and coming back to life after having died.' Don't neglect any detail!"

25. Tōrei retired to do a solitary retreat (*dokuzesshin*) at the age of twenty-one (in 1741).

26. Here Tōrei uses the "chamber name," *Sendai kutsu,* to indicate his teacher Hakuin Ekaku. Hakuin's chamber name alludes to the *icchantika,* the class of beings considered by some *sūtras* as incapable of awakening.

27. This is a reference to the *Recorded Sayings of Linji.*

28. These frightening demons are mentioned in the *Sūtra of Perfect Awakening.* Called Kumbhāṇda, they come from Indian mythological accounts of evil spirits who were followers of Rūdra. They are also mentioned in the *Lotus Sūtra.*

29. This oppressive description is a paraphrase of the *Emerald Cliff Record,* case 2.

30. The same expression, *kakutsu* with the adjective "old," has been translated earlier as "the old ways."

23. Confirmation from the Texts

After having heard these words, I felt like I had been drinking the finest ghee.[31] From that moment my meditative investigation was greatly invigorated and I worked twice as hard. Then I spent several days reading the *Diamond Sūtra* and, suddenly obtaining total absorption in [a state of] wisdom (*prajñā-samādhi*), I entered [a state of] forgetting body and mind. To check [the validity of this state] I read the fascicle "Practice and Vows of Samantabhadra" and practically distinguished the different realms of reality (*Dharma-dhātu*) of the Huayan [approach].[32] Next, I read the *Lotus Sūtra* and upon reaching the fascicle "Longevity," I suddenly realized total absorption in the lotus. Looking at the teachings [given by the Buddha] during his entire lifetime, they were as clear as if I looked at the palm of my own hand.

24. Confirmation from the Teacher

I ran to tell master [Hakuin]: "for a long time I have been willing to read the Buddhist Canon without succeeding, but today I have looked at it once and seen it thoroughly."

Hakuin: "Excellent! You have obtained this kind of joy. But how do you understand a kōan such as 'Minister Chen Cao [watching from the tea] pavilion'?"[33]

I gave him the real [answer].

Hakuin: "You further need to complete it carefully!" He added: "Taking the place of the mandarin, what can you say that would make Chen Cao rejoice?"

I proposed several succinct comments [on the kōan], but none agreed with [his] meaning.

The following day upon entering the [Sanzen] room I was able to pronounce a decisive word.[34] Without hesitation the master stood up and tapped me

31. The most refined of the dairy products in India, considered a delicacy (*daigo*). A freer rendering would be "nectar."

32. The description of four types of interactions between principle and phenomena, culminating in the realm of non-obstruction between phenomena, was developed by the Huayan patriarch Chengguan (737–838).

33. One of the most widely used versions of this kōan is included in the *Emerald Cliff Record,* case 33.

34. Decisive word (*tengo*) is a free translation for an expression meaning "turning word" and indicating one's spiritual understanding. It comes from the third verse in Chinese quatrains, which introduces a "shift" or change of perspective.

twice on the back, saying "you have managed to say it, and for the first time you are in agreement with my intention; but even so, never indulge in thinking it is easy: in the future you will know for yourself."

25. Further Polishing

The following day, when I entered again the [Sanzen] room the master asked: "How do you understand the kōan of Shushan's memorial?"[35]

I replied: "With a poisonous hand he wanted to cut off the root of people's lives."[36]

Hakuin: "And how does it really feel once the root of life has been cut off?"

I replied: "Shushan and the building workers together extend a single helping hand."

Hakuin: "You have not yet reached the bottom [of this case]!"

26. Zhaozhou and the Old Woman

At that time, I also quoted the case of Zhaozhou seeing through the old woman;[37] I said that if I were there at that moment I would have turned to Zhaozhou and asked: "Did you see through the old woman before she spoke or after?"

Hakuin said, answering for Zhaozhou, "Straight ahead!"

He added: "In this way the old woman of Mount Tai has been exposed by the master!"

Hakuin abruptly asked me: "Where do you look to encounter the old woman?"[38]

I hesitated.

The master took on a terrifying expression and, raising his voice, said: "That's not right, not right!"

35. This kōan is related to a memorial erected for Shushan Kuangren (also Guangren, 837–909) while he was still alive. The full story is found in Kirchner 2004: 69–70.

36. The poisonous hand is a metaphor for apparently brutal or ruthless means used to guide a student.

37. See Kirchner 2004: 9.

38. This "encounter" (*shōken*) does not indicate a casual meeting, but the formal encounter of a disciple and teacher.

27. Cornered by Hakuin

The following day, when I entered the [Sanzen] room the master saw me coming and suddenly extended his arm asking: "How is my hand like the Buddha's hand?"[39]

In response to this concise question I provided a decisive word, which the master greatly praised.

Then I said: "A while ago when you questioned me on the case of the Old Woman Burning the Hermitage,[40] I failed [to recognize] the prodigious skill of the old woman. Given the type of question put by the old woman, nothing could have prevented the monk from losing his mind and spirit in surprise and the whole world from being dumbfounded. I have a decisive word, and in place of the hermit I would have held the girl firmly saying, 'For twenty years I have been supported by the old woman...'"

Before I could end my sentence, the master gathered all his energy which came out as a single shout.

The sound pierced me to the marrow; for several days I felt pain in my chest, my body and mind were entranced as if I were in the midst of clouds and fog.

I thought to myself: "I am already clearly awakened. For what reason is it like this? Definitely, one must admit that although having the eye of Kenshō, the power of meditative absorption[41] has not yet matured." Thus, I made the vow to [fully] realize meditative absorption. Days and months passed, but still I was not free.

28. Retreat

Then, I made a retreat in the area east of the Kamo River; closing all doors, I shut myself from all contacts, and strictly practiced from morning to evening. I was like a convict sentenced to death waiting for the execution and counting the remaining days on his fingers. Freely handling the bright pearl,[42] I wouldn't let go for even a second. Sometimes succeeding, sometimes failing, the uninterrupted succession of right mindfulness was difficult [to attain]. My chest choked with lament and fear, whether sitting or standing I was never at peace. This lasted for fifty days, when all of a sudden [everything] collapsed and the bright pearl was smashed to pieces. Having become totally exposed, completely bare, I truly understood [the meaning of] the pure breeze [following] the release of one's burden.

39. This is one of the Three Barriers of Huanglong. See Kirchner 2004: 8.

40. See Kirchner 2004: 84.

41. Literally, "the power of *samādhi*" (*zenjō no chikara*).

42. Concerning the related verse, "The black dragon coughs up its bright pearl," Hori comments: "A fabulous gem kept underneath the chin of the sleeping black dragon. To attempt to steal the pearl is a metaphor for risking one's life. See, for example, the story in *Chuang-tzu*, ch. 32." (Hori 2003 641.)

29. Whipping again the Dead Ox

Nevertheless, not yet having entirely mastered the sphere of activity, I again whipped the dead ox and at the same time pushed him forward. Gritting my teeth and clenching my fists I didn't care whether I had a physical body; during freezing days and cold nights sweat constantly soaked my robe. When the demon of sleep gained force I would wake myself with a needle's point. [These austerities] entered my bones and penetrated my marrow; I had lost taste for food and drink.

Another fifty days elapsed, during which eight or nine times I had [flashes of] insight. Finally, one day I thoroughly realized the integration of activity that the late master [had indicated].[43] Ha ha ha! So far I had mistakenly been doing a lifeless type of meditative investigation! Like Boyun, I deserved thirty blows from the stick. I truly understood I had received a gift from the late master that was huge and powerful. If it were not for all his help and teaching, I wouldn't be here today! For my whole life I would have mistakenly remained attached to my limited awakening and convictions.

Now when I reflect on these past events, [I see that] blood was dripping from each and every word or sentence: it is both frightening and saddening. From that time onwards, one moment of mindfulness after another [has kept flowing] through my mind without interval; days and nights I have been practicing and have never stopped since. How could one think that this is easy and waste precious time in idleness?

30. Sickness and Relapse

I want to make every effort to realize this approach and, in accordance with my ability, to restore the authentic teaching that has fallen [into oblivion]. Comrades, no doubt in your hearts you share this [same objective]! At this point, I ask you to summon all your discerning insight.

Because of my many diseases I know well the diseases of others. Due to the method I used to cure my own diseases I am well versed in remedies. But because my own diseases have finally been cured, I am all the more distressed by the diseases of others; and because others are sick my own disease returns.[44]

Master Luopu said: "Only with the last word one reaches the outer gate of the prison."[45] These words are so true! To break loose from life and death, and to grasp the authentic stamp [of realization], everything depends on this

43. When Tōrei did this retreat Hakuin was still alive, but by the time he wrote the revised version of this publication Hakuin had passed away. Hakuin died in 1769.

44. Allusion to the story of Vimalakīrti, where the lay bodhisattva pretends to be sick to better teach the truth. The implication is that the real sickness is lack of realization of Buddhahood.

45. The same quotation also appears at the beginning of this chapter.

precise moment. Only to those who have stepped over the bars above the barriers of going beyond will [this] be entirely familiar.

I am also of the same [opinion] and my sheer hope is that one such person, [even living] three thousand miles away, will come and deliver me from this disease. Should it not be the case, I shall let all the people under heaven denigrate me as they wish.

[End of the] first fascicle of the Treatise on the Inexhaustible Lamp of Zen.

Bibliography and Suggested Reading

Hori, Victor Sōgen. (2003) *Zen Sand: The Book of Capping Phrases for Kōan Practice.* Honolulu: University of Hawai'i Press.

Kirchner, Thomas Yūhō. (2004) *Entangling Vines: Zen Kōans of the Shūmon Kattōshū.* Kyoto: Tenryu-ji Institute for Philosophy and Religion.

Mohr, Michel. (1997) *Traité sur l'Inépuisable Lampe du Zen: Tōrei (1721–1792) et sa vision de l'éveil.* 2 vols. Mélanges chinois et bouddhiques, vol. 28. Brussels: Institut Belge des Hautes Études Chinoises.

Mohr, Michel. (1999) "Hakuin." In Y. Takeuchi, J. W. Heisig, P. L. Swanson, and J. S. O'Leary, eds., *Buddhist Spirituality: Later China, Korea, Japan, and the Modern World.* New York: Crossroad, pp. 307–328.

Mohr, Michel. (2000) "Emerging from Non-Duality: Kōan Practice in the Rinzai Tradition since Hakuin." In S. Heine and D. S. Wright, eds., *The Kōan: Texts and Contexts in Zen Buddhism.* Oxford: Oxford University Press, pp. 307–328.

Okuda, Yoko. (1990) *The Discourse on the Inexhaustible Lamp of the Zen School.* London: Zen Center (1996 reprint by Tuttle).

PART III

EPISTEMOLOGY

The foundation of all of Buddhism is the idea that the fundamental root of suffering is ignorance regarding the nature of reality, and suffering can be overcome only by eliminating that ignorance. Moreover, the very difference between the conventional truth of samsara, the world of suffering, and the ultimate truth that is the object of awakened knowledge and the ground of the possibility of nirvana, the cessation of suffering, is described epistemologically: the conventional truth is deceptive; the ultimate nondeceptive. It is hardly surprising, then, that epistemology stands at the center of Buddhist philosophy, and that so much of Buddhist philosophical effort is devoted to understanding the nature of knowledge, and in particular, enlightened knowledge.

Buddhist epistemology arises in India in a context in which epistemology is framed by debates about the number and nature of *pramānas* (authoritative cognitive instruments). Some Indian philosophers argued that only perception is authoritative; some that inference is also authoritative; some that scripture or testimony is as well; some that scripture is the *only* authority. Buddhists defended the view that perception and inference are the only two *pramānas*. The Buddhist epistemological project is complicated, however, by two Buddhist metaphysical commitments. First, Buddhists are nominalists regarding universals, arguing that universals themselves, in virtue of their permanence and lack of causal efficacy, do not really exist, but are merely conceptual posits. Second, Buddhists argue that inference always proceeds by the apprehension of universals, as when I infer that a pot is impermanent because it is a product, in virtue of the relation between instantiating the universal of pothood and that of instantiating impermanence. As a consequence, although Indian Buddhist epistemologists typically countenance inference as a useful instrument for ordinary persons, they regard it as ultimately to be abandoned in awakening and valorize perception and nonconceptual understanding over inference and conceptually mediated understanding.

Nonetheless, the Buddha himself taught through language and presented arguments, as do all subsequent canonical Buddhist philosophers. And the only route to epistemologically sound direct perception of ultimate reality, according to most Indian and Tibetan epistemologists (though not necessarily Chinese and Japanese epistemologists), is a lot of speech, inference, and conceptual thought. Moreover, even the results of unmediated, nonconceptual experience must be communicated and assessed, through language, inference, and conception. Any account of knowledge must hence make a central place for these cognitive processes, even if they are in the end only fingers, and not the real moon to which they point.

Early Buddhist reflection on knowledge, represented in the Pali suttas, emphasizes two issues, both reflected in the selections collected here. First, knowledge requires first-person verification. Appeals to authority, whether that of a teacher, such as the Buddha himself, or scripture, are rejected as justificatory. Claims about the nature of reality or about one's own experience are known only to the extent that they are verified in one's own investigation and experience. Second, there is a strong pragmatic strain in Buddhist epistemology, as reflected in the metaphor of the raft developed in the *Alagaddūpama Sutta:* What makes a view knowledge is its utility on the path to liberation. To cling to a view that was once useful, but is no longer, is an epistemological fault.

While early Buddhist philosophy involved epistemological reflection, and while even in Madhyamaka Buddhism there is significant epistemological innovation (particularly Nāgārjuna's arguments for coherentism in *Vigrahavyāvarttanī*), the most influential and sophisticated work in Indian Buddhist epistemology is that of Dignāga and Dharmakīrti in the sixth and seventh centuries. Dharmakīrti, in particular, reflected in a sustained way on the criteria for validity of arguments, the relation between observed evidence and conclusions regarding the unobserved, the natures of the respective objects of perception and inference, and the relation between perception and inference. His work is the subject of an extensive and internally diverse commentarial literature both in India and in Tibet. The selection here from Dharmakīrti's *Nyāyabindu* (early seventh century C.E.) and Dharmottara's commentary involves an argument that perception delivers not mere sensations but perceptual judgments, thus explaining how perception is immediate, and directed on the particular, but still provides data that are genuinely epistemic, and not merely causative of the epistemic.

Dharmakīrti's best known text, *Pramāṇa-vārttika,* is constructed as a commentary on Dignāga's *Pramāṇasamuccaya* (early sixth century C.E.) but functions in the Buddhist epistemological tradition as an independent and highly influential treatise on inference. Among Dharmakīrti's significant contributions to Buddhist and also non-Buddhist Indian philosophy is a comprehensive theory of argument structure and validity. His account, a portion of which is presented here, combines epistemological and logical ideas in a general theory of justificatory argument. According to Dharmakīrti, knowledge of the relation between the classes denoted by the subject and predicate terms of categorical statements must be causal knowledge, entailing that what appears to be general knowledge is, at its foundation, particular, in virtue of the fact that only impermanent particulars, not permanent (and hence ultimately nonexistent) universals enter into causal relations.

Dignāga's and Dharmakīrti's analyses, as well as those of their principal Indian and Tibetan exegetes, focus on the nature of the knowledge of ordinary cognitive agents and its relation to their progress toward awakening. The *Buddhabhūmy-upadeśa* (c. late sixth to early seventh century), available only in Chinese, while responsive to Dignāga's and Dharmakīrti's work (and critical of Nāgārjuna's), is distinctive in that it attempts an account of awakened knowledge. The text argues that awakened knowledge must be immediate and hence perceptual, but that, unlike ordinary perception, is nonrepresentational, and is simply a direct contact with reality, and that the knowledge of awakened consciousness is always immediately reflexive as well. Demonstrating that this can be the case requires refutation of well-known Madhyamaka arguments against the possibility of reflexive awareness.

Tsongkhapa addresses a prima facie ontological question via an epistemological route. He asks what the distinction is between the two truths. Commenting on *Mūlamadhyamakakārikā,* in which Nāgārjuna argues that on a Madhyamaka analysis, there is no ontological distinction between the two truths, Tsongkhapa argues that the distinction must be drawn on epistemological grounds, and, following Candrakīrti, develops a subtle understanding of the distinction between ordinary and awakened knowledge that makes sense of the possibility of conventional truth, of the nature of ultimate truth, and of the possibility of utilizing the former to realize the latter.

In the work of Jingxi Zhanran (711–782) we encounter the epistemological consequences of the Chinese Tiantai school's doctrine of *three* truths, an interesting development of Nāgārjuna's account of the *two* truths. To the conventional and ultimate, the Tiantai philosophers add the third truth—the truth of the middle—which is the truth of the identity of the first two. As a consequence, according to philosophers of this school, there is no distinction between the epistemology of ordinary knowledge and the epistemology of the awakened. We gain and express knowledge regarding the ultimate in exactly the way we do regarding the conventional; but the flip side of this coin is that any putative knowledge of the conventional that is not simultaneously knowledge of the ultimate is deceptive, and hence not knowledge at all. Zhanran develops this view in *Jingangpi* and *Zhiguan yili*.

The epistemological themes regarding the priority of immediacy over mediation, and perception over conception, and of the identity of the two truths, and so of the epistemic attitudes characteristic of each, join in the work of the thirteenth-century Japanese Zen philosopher Dōgen. In the selection from *Genjōkōan* (a core fascicle of *Shōbogenzo*) presented here, Dōgen argues that knowledge, including knowledge of the ultimate truth about reality, emerges from immediate openness to reality. This openness requires a cultivation of a direct, nonconceptual attitude toward the world one inhabits, and only this attitude facilitates knowledge.

15

The Approach to Knowledge and Truth in the Theravāda Record of the Discourses of the Buddha

Peter Harvey

Theravāda traditions regard the teachings attributed to the Buddha as authoritative guides to the nature of reality and the best way to live, based on the vast, meditation-based knowledge of a spiritually "awakened" being. Such teachings are not to be simply accepted, though, but used, investigated, and, as far as is possible for a particular individual, *confirmed* in experience. As such, it can be said that the Buddha is a kind of experientialist or empiricist, as opposed to one who relies solely on revelation or trust in reasoning alone.[1]

For the Buddha, the route to liberating knowledge is a path that invites empirical investigation and leads to a personal realization of the truth of the Dhamma. For liberation, the crucial things to attain knowledge of, based on direct "knowing and seeing," are such matters as how things arise from conditions, how conditioned things are impermanent, pain-inducing, and not-Self, and the four Noble Truths.

1. M.II.211. Since the Buddha placed great emphasis on the importance of experience as confirmation of his teachings of the Dhamma, some authors have interpreted early Buddhism as akin to Western empiricism. K. N. Jayatilleke, for example, argues that "the emphasis that 'knowing' must be based on 'seeing' or direct perceptive experience, makes Buddhism a sort of Empiricism" (Jaytilleke 1963: 463). According to Jayatilleke, Buddhist "empiricism" accepted a wider realm of "experience" than that offered by the five senses. He held that "inductive inferences in Buddhism are based on a theory of causation. These inferences are made on the data of perception, normal

In the discourses, knowledge is based on four factors. First, there is sense-perception, on the basis of a mind purified of distorting elements (such as greed, hatred, and delusion) through mindful awareness and meditative calming. Second, there is extrasensory perception arising in a mind tuned to subtle levels, and hence sensitized, through the attainment of lucid meditative trance (Pali *jhāna,* Skt. *dhyāna*).[2] Third, there are inferences drawn from these experiences, but remaining close to them, so as not to use them as a springboard for speculations that go far beyond them.[3] And finally, knowledge must be characterized by coherence and consistency.

Extract from the *Kālāma Sutta*

The early Buddhist emphasis on testing the teachings of the Dhamma against one's own experience is seen in the well-known *Kālāma Sutta,* the popular name for the *Kesaputta Sutta.* In this *sutta,* the Buddha advises the Kālāma people not to accept teachings simply due to tradition, reasoning, or being impressed by, or allegiance to, a particular teacher. People should personally assess the moral fruits of particular teachings, discerning whether they are unwholesome or wholesome, blamable or blameless. Accordingly, they agree with the Buddha that teachings that arouse greed, hatred, and delusion are to be rejected as they lead to immoral actions. In contrast, teachings that inspire generosity, loving-kindness, and wisdom are to be valued and affirmed. Here it is notable that the focus is not on the propositional content that a teaching may include, but the mind-states it encourages, and the moral fruits it produces.[4]

---

and paranormal. What is considered to constitute knowledge are direct inferences made on the basis of such perceptions" (457).

Unlike British empiricists such as John Locke, however, early Buddhism did not view the mind at birth as a tabula rasa, a "blank slate," to be written on by sensory experience. According to the Buddhist doctrine of rebirth, a child comes into the world with particular tendencies from past rebirths (M.I.432–437).

2. Here, the "higher knowledges" (Pali *abhiññās*, Skt. *abhijñās*) are relevant. These are: psychokinetic powers such as walking on water; hearing sounds at great distances, including the speech of gods; reading the minds of others; remembering many of one's own past lives; tracking the death and rebirth of other beings and seeing how it is in accordance with their karma; the knowledge of the destruction of the *āsavas* (Pali, Skt. *āśravas*) or limiting taints, so as to be a liberated person, an *arahat* with full knowledge of the four Noble Truths, including nirvana (D.I.77–84). Some *arahats* had all of these forms of knowledge, while some only had the last of them (S.II.120–124).

3. The Buddha characterized himself as "one who speaks after making an analysis," avoiding overgeneralizations (M.II.197). The *Brahmajāla Sutta* gives examples of people remembering past lives, but drawing erroneous conclusions from this, such as that the self and the world are eternal (D. I.13), or that the god Brahmā created the world and beings (D.I.17–19).

4. The following extract is A.I.188–193.

Translation

Thus have I heard. At one time, the Blessed One was wandering on a tour...when he arrived at a town of the Kālāmas named Kesaputta....The Kālāmas said to the Blessed One: "There are, venerable sir, some renunciants and brahmins who come to Kesaputta. They each explain and elucidate their own doctrine, but disparage, debunk, revile, and vilify the doctrines of others. But then some other renunciants and brahmins come to Kesaputta, and they too each explain and elucidate their own doctrine, but disparage, debunk, revile, and vilify the doctrines of others. For us, venerable sir, there is doubt and perplexity as to which good renunciants speak the truth and which speak falsehood."

"It is fitting for you to doubt, O Kālāmas, it is fitting for you to be perplexed. Perplexity has arisen on a doubtful matter. Come, Kālāmas. Do not go by oral tradition, by lineage (of teaching), by hearsay, by a collection of scriptures, by logical reasoning, by inferential reasoning, by consideration of reasons, by the reflective acceptance of a view,[5] by the seeming competence (of a teacher),[6] or because you think, 'The renunciant is our teacher.' But when you know for yourselves, 'these states are unwholesome (*akusalā*) and blamable, they are censured by the wise; these states, when undertaken and practiced, conduce to harm and suffering,' then indeed you should abandon them."

"What do you think, Kālāmas? When greed arises in a person, is it for his welfare or harm?" "For his harm, venerable sir." "Kālāmas, a person who is greedy, overpowered by greed, his thoughts controlled by it, will destroy life, take what is not given, engage in sexual misconduct, and tell lies; he will also prompt others to do likewise. Will that conduce to his harm and suffering for a long time?" "Yes, venerable sir." [The same is then said of hate and delusion].

"What do you think, Kālāmas? Are these states wholesome or unwholesome?" "Unwholesome, venerable sir." "Blamable or blameless?" "Blamable, venerable sir." "Censured or praised by the wise?" "Censured, venerable sir." "Undertaken and practiced, do they lead to harm and suffering or not, how is it in this case?" "Undertaken and practiced, these states lead to harm and suffering. So it is for us in this case."

..."Come, Kālāmas. Do not go by oral tradition,...or because you think, 'The renunciant is our teacher.' But when you know for yourselves, 'these states are wholesome (*kusalā*) and blameless, they are praised by the wise; these states, when undertaken and practiced, conduce to welfare and happiness,' then indeed you should engage in them."

5. *Diṭṭhi-nijjhāna-kkhanti.*

6. *Bhavya-rūpatā;* but the commentary reads *bhabba-rūpatā,* and the translation is according to this reading. *Bhavya-rūpatā* may mean something like "the appearance of what ought to be."

"What do you think, Kālāmas? When non-greed arises in a person, is it for his welfare or harm?" "For his welfare, venerable sir." "Kālāmas, a person who is without greed, his thoughts not controlled by it, will abstain from destruction of life, from taking what is not given, from sexual misconduct, and from false speech; he will also prompt others to do likewise. Will that conduce to his welfare and happiness for a long time?" "Yes, venerable sir." [The same is then said of non-hatred and non-delusion.]

"What do you think, Kālāmas? Are these states wholesome or unwholesome?" "Wholesome, venerable sir." "Blamable or blameless?" "Blameless, venerable sir." "Censured or praised by the wise?" "Praised, venerable sir." "Undertaken and practiced, do they lead to harm and suffering or not, how is it in this case?" "Undertaken and practiced, these states lead to welfare and happiness. So it is for us in this case."

"It was for this reason, Kālāmas, that we said: Do not go by oral tradition... or because you think, 'The renunciant is our teacher.'"

"Then Kālāmas, that disciple of the noble ones, devoid of covetousness, devoid of ill will, unconfused, clearly comprehending, ever mindful, dwells pervading one quarter with a mind imbued with loving-kindness, likewise the second quarter, the third, and fourth. Thus above, below, across, everywhere, and to all as to himself, he dwells pervading the entire world with a mind imbued with loving-kindness, vast, exalted, measureless, without hostility and without ill will." [The same is then said with regard to pervading the directions with compassion, with empathetic joy, and with equanimity.]

"When, Kālāmas, this disciple of the noble ones has thus made his mind free of enmity, free of ill will, undefiled, and pure, he has won four assurances in this very life. The first assurance he has won is this: 'If there is another world, and if there is a fruit and ripening of well done and ill done deeds, it is possible that, with the breakup of the body, after death, I shall arise in a good destination, in a heavenly world.' The second assurance he has won is this: 'If there is no other world, and if there is no fruit and ripening of well-done and ill-done deeds, still right here, in this very life, I will live happily, free of enmity and ill will.' The third assurance he has won is this: 'Suppose evil befalls the evil-doer. Then, as I do not intend evil for anyone, how can suffering afflict me, one who does no evil deed?' The fourth assurance he has won is this: 'Suppose evil does not befall the evil-doer. Then right here I see myself purified in both respects [neither doing evil nor experiencing any evil results].' When, Kālāmas, this disciple of the noble ones has thus made his mind free of enmity, free of ill will, undefiled and pure, he has won four assurances in this very life."

"So it is, Blessed One, Excellent, venerable sir!... Let the Blessed One accept us as lay followers who have gone for refuge from today until life's end."

Extract from the *Caṅkī Sutta*

As with the *Kālāma Sutta,* the *Caṅkī Sutta* criticizes simple reliance on unsupported faith, approval, oral tradition, consideration of reasons, or reflective acceptance of a view. Rather, the emphasis is on finding a teacher with trustworthy moral and mental characteristics, who gives teachings that conform to reason, can be practiced, and enable personal transformation.[7]

Translation

Then the brahmin student Kāpaṭhika...said to the Blessed One, "Master Gotama, in regard to the ancient Brahmanical hymns that have come down through a lineage and are in the scriptural collections, the brahmins come to the definite conclusion, 'Only this is true, anything else is wrong.' What does Master Gotama say about this?"

"How, then, Bhāradvāja, among brahmins, is there even a single brahmin...or a single teacher or a single teacher's teacher back to the seventh generation of teachers who says thus: 'I know this, I see this, only this is true, anything else is wrong'?" "No, Master Gotama." "How then, Bhāradvāja, the ancient brahmin seers, the creators of the [Vedic] hymns, the composers of the hymns... [that] the brahmins nowadays still chant and repeat... did even these brahmin seers say thus: 'I know this, I see this, only this is true, anything else is wrong'?" "No, Master Gotama."

"So, Bhāradvāja.... Suppose there were a file of blind men each in touch with the next: the first one does not see, the middle one does not see, and the last one does not see. So, too, Bhāradvāja, in regard to their statement, the brahmins seem to be like a file of blind men.... That being so, does not the faith of the brahmins turn out to be groundless?"

"The brahmins honor this not only out of faith, Master Gotama. They also honor it as oral tradition."

"Bhāradvāja, first you took your stand on faith (*saddhā*), now you speak of oral tradition. There are five things, Bhāradvāja that may turn out in two different ways here and now. What five? Faith, approval, oral tradition, consideration of reasons, and reflective acceptance of a view.[8]... It may be empty, hollow, and false; but something else [not accepted on such a ground]... may be factual, true, unmistaken. [Under these conditions] it is not proper for a wise man who preserves the truth to come to the definite conclusion, 'Only this is true, anything else is wrong.'"

"But, Master Gotama, in what way is there preservation of truth?"....

7. The following extract is M. II.169–177.
8. On these, see Jayatilleke 1963: 182–188, 274–276.

"If a person has faith, Bhāradvāja, he preserves the truth when he says, 'My faith is thus'; but he does not yet come to the definite conclusion 'Only this is true, anything else is wrong.' In this way, Bhāradvāja, there is preservation of truth.... But as yet there is no discovery of/awakening to truth."

"In that way, Master Gotama, there is preservation of truth;... But in what way, Master Gotama, is there the discovery of truth?"....

"Here, Bhāradvāja, a monk may be living in dependence on some village or town. Then a householder...goes to him and investigates him in regard to three states (*dhammas*): in regard to states based on greed...on hate...on delusion; 'Are there in this venerable one any states based on greed such that, with his mind obsessed by those states, while not knowing he might say, "I know," or while not seeing he might say, "I see," or he might urge others to act in a way that would lead to their harm and suffering for a long time?' As he investigates him, he comes to know, 'There are no such states based on greed in this venerable one. The bodily behavior and the verbal behavior of this venerable one are not those of one affected by greed. And the Dhamma that this venerable one teaches is profound, hard to see, unattained by mere reasoning, subtle, to be experienced by the wise. This Dhamma cannot easily be taught by one affected by greed.'"

"When he has investigated him and seen that he is purified from states based on greed, he next investigates him in regard to states based on hate... [and] on delusion [in the same way, and with the same results]."

..."[T]hen he places faith in him; filled with faith, he visits him and pays respect to him; having paid respect to him, he gives ear; when he gives ear, he hears the Dhamma; having heard the Dhamma, he memorizes it and examines the meaning of the *dhammas* (teachings) he has memorized; when he examines their meaning, he gains a reflective acceptance[9] of those *dhammas*; when he gains a reflective acceptance, zeal springs up; when zeal has sprung up, he applies his will; having applied his will, he scrutinizes; having scrutinized, he strives; resolutely striving, he realizes with the body[10] the ultimate truth and sees it by penetrating it with wisdom. In this way, Bhāradvāja, there is the discovery of truth...but as yet there is no final arrival at truth."[11]

9. *Nijjhāna-kkhanti.* This sounds similar to "reflective acceptance" of a view that the *Kālāma Sutta* and *Caṅkī Sutta* question as a stand-alone basis for knowledge. Here something very close to it can be seen as helping to prepare the right conditions for the arising of personal knowledge, but it is not itself the same as knowledge, nor is it directly productive of it. Likewise, while "approval (*ruci*)" is no guarantee of knowing the truth, at the end of the *Caṅkī Sutta,* the brahmin that the Buddha is speaking to then says that he "approves (*ruccati*) and accepts (*khamati*)" his explanations and hence wishes to become his disciple. However, becoming a disciple does not mean one has oneself, in transformative personal experiences of direct insight, "discovered" or "attained" truth oneself, but it may prepare the way for this.

10. That is, with his entire person; *kāya.*

11. Probably meaning full *arahat*ship, when greed, hatred, and delusion are completely ended and nirvana is fully experienced.

..."But in what way is there final arrival at truth?"....

"The final arrival at truth, Bhāradvāja, lies in the repetition, (meditative) development (*bhāvanā*), and cultivation of those same *dhammas*"....

Extract from the *Abhaya-rāja-kumāra Sutta* (Discourse to Prince Abhaya)

We have seen that the *Kālāma Sutta* offers pragmatic grounds for judging which teachings merit acting on in a situation where one lacks direct personal knowledge of the truth. Some scholars[12] see the Pali suttas as also having a pragmatic theory of *truth,* that is, as taking the truth of an utterance as *consisting in* its being useful for some end. But the Buddha is portrayed as knowing many more truths than he taught; he only taught what he saw as spiritually useful. This can be seen from the *Siṃsapā Sutta* (S. 5.437–438), where the Buddha, in a grove of simsapa trees, says that the number of leaves in the grove are many more than those he holds in his hand:

> Just so, monks, much more is what is known by my higher knowledge, but not declared; very little is declared. And why, monks, is this not declared by me? Because it is not connected with the goal, is not of the fundamentals of the holy life, it does not conduce to turning away, to detachment, to stopping, to tranquility, to higher knowledge, to awakening, or to nirvana.

He then specifies that what he *has* declared are the Four Noble Truths. This indicates that something can be true without also being spiritually useful.

This is made even clearer by the *Abhaya-rāja-kumāra Sutta* (Harvey 1995). In this, Prince Abhaya asks the Buddha whether he ever speaks to people in a way that they find disagreeable, implying that, if he does, he is not compassionate. In reply, the Buddha gets Abhaya to agree that, from compassion, he would himself help a choking baby, even if this caused it to bleed. That is, actions that cause some pain can still be done to help the person pained. The Buddha then specifies which kinds of speech he will or will not utter. From his explanation, it is clear that an utterance can be true even when it is not "connected with the goal," that is, not spiritually useful. The *Sutta* only proposes a pragmatic criterion for *which truths are worth teaching* to people.

It is notable that the discourse makes no mention of false statements that are spiritually useful. To lie is to say something one knows to be false, whether this is useful to oneself or another in a worldly way (M. III 48), and such conduct results in unwholesome states of mind. The falsehood or truth of statements does not depend on their usefulness, either in a worldly or spiritual sense, but knowingly uttering falsehoods has a spiritually harmful effect.[13]

12. Kalupahana 1992; Holder 1996.
13. The following extract is M. I.395.

Translation

So, too, Prince, such speech as the *Tathāgata*[14] knows to be not fact, not true, not connected with the goal, and is unwelcome and disagreeable to others: such speech the *Tathāgata* does not utter. Such speech as the *Tathāgata* knows to be fact, true, but not connected with the goal, and is unwelcome and disagreeable to others: such speech the *Tathāgata* does not utter. Such speech as the *Tathāgata* knows to be fact, true, connected with the goal, and is unwelcome and disagreeable to others: the *Tathāgata* knows the time to use such speech. [These three formulations are then repeated with "is welcome and agreeable to others" in place of "is unwelcome and disagreeable to others."] Why is that? Because the *Tathāgata* has compassion for beings.

Extract from the *Alagaddūpama Sutta* (Discourse on the simile of the snake [and the raft])

In the *Alagaddūpama Sutta,* the Dhamma taught by the Buddha is compared to a raft used to ferry a man from the dangerous and fearful shore of a river, to the other, safe shore: from the unenlightened world of suffering to the state of the enlightened person, the *arahat.* Once on the far shore, the man would be unwise to carry the raft around with him when its function was fulfilled. This is to show that one should "abandon," that is, not be attached to,[15] the teachings, practices, and engendered states of the Buddha's Dhamma. The Theravādin commentary on the passage plausibly explains that what is meant is that a Buddhist practitioner should not be attached to the states of calm (Pali *samatha,* Skt. *śamatha*) and insight (Pali *vipassanā,* Skt. *vipaśyana*) that the meditative path cultivates.

The *Sutta*'s message also accords with the idea that one of the forms of grasping (Pali, Skt. *upādāna*) that helps to condition a continuation of rebirth and suffering is grasping at "views" (Pali *diṭṭhi,* Skt *dṛṣṭi*). This is where one identifies fully with a way of looking at something, a way of explaining it. One's attachment is then such that one is wounded if that view is criticized, and one is willing to be underhanded, or not fully honest, in defense of the view. One is also limited in one's vision by the theory: it is like a pair of blinders that enables one only to see certain things. It may contain some truth, but one always needs to be open to a deepening of that truth, or a balancing, complementary one.

In the *Alagaddūpama Sutta,* a monk is criticized for giving a distorted version of the Buddha's teaching, saying that engaging in sensual pleasures is not a spiritual obstacle. The Buddha then says that those who learn his

14. A term for the Buddha, literally meaning "Thus-come" or "Thus-gone," implying one who fully experiences what is "thus" or true.

15. Compare S.III.27.

Dhamma should examine its meaning with wisdom, so as to be able to "reflectively accept" it. To fail to do this, but learn Dhamma only for the sake of criticizing others and winning in debates, is to fail to gain real benefit from the Dhamma. It is to wrongly grasp the Dhamma, like a man who is bitten by a snake due to grasping it in the wrong way, rather than holding it safely behind the neck. Hence, if a teaching is not understood, a person should ask for clarification about it.[16]

Translation

"Monks, I shall show you how the Dhamma is similar to a raft, being for the purpose of crossing over, not for the purpose of grasping.... Monks, suppose a man in the course of a journey saw a great expanse of water, whose near shore was dangerous and fearful and whose further shore was safe and free from fear, but there was no ferryboat or bridge going to the far shore.... Then the man collected grass, twigs, branches, and leaves and bound them together into a raft, and supported by the raft and making an effort with his hands and feet, he safely crossed to the far shore. Then, when he had got across and arrived at the far shore, he might think thus: 'This raft has been very helpful to me.... Suppose I were to hoist it on my head or load it on my shoulder, and then go wherever I want.' Now, monks, what do you think? By doing so, would that man be doing what should be done with the raft?" "No, venerable sir."

"By doing what, then, would that man be doing what *should* be done with the raft? Here, monks, when that man crossed and had arrived at the far shore, he might think thus: 'This raft has been very helpful to me.... Suppose I were to haul it onto dry land or set it adrift in the water, and then go wherever I want.' Now, monks, it is by doing so that the man would be doing what should be done with the raft. So I have shown you how Dhamma is similar to a raft, being for the purpose of crossing over, not for the purpose of grasping. Monks, when you know the simile of the raft, you should abandon even *dhammas*, how much more so non-*dhammas*."[17]

Abbreviations

The translations in this chapter are the author's own; they are generally close to those listed here.

16. The following extract is M.I.135–135.

17. *Dhammas* here seems to mean items of teaching within the Dhamma, especially the practices that make up the path of practice (represented by the raft) and the qualities they induce. By contrast, "non-*dhammas*" are opposed to such practices and states.

A. *Aṅguttara Nikāya*
The Book of Gradual Sayings. Translated by F. L. Woodward and E. M. Hare. 5 vols. London, Pali Text Society, 1932–36. Partially translated in Nyanaponika Thera and Bhikkhu Bodhi, *Numerical Discourses of the Buddha: An Anthology of Suttas from the Aṅguttara Nikāya.* New York: Altamira, 1999.

Asl. *Atthasālinī*
The Expositor. Translated by Pe Maung Tin. 2 vols. London: Pali Text Society, 1920–21.

D. *Dīgha Nikāya*
Thus Have I Heard: The Long Discourses of the Buddha. Translated by M. Walshe. London: Wisdom, 1987.

M. *Majjhima Nikāya*
The Middle Discourses of the Buddha. Translated by Bhikkhu Ñāṇamoli and Bhikkhu Bodhi. Boston: Wisdom, 1995.

Miln. *Milindapañha*
Milinda's Questions. Translated by I. B. Horner. 2 vols. London: Pali Text Society, 1963–64.

S. *Saṃyutta Nikāya*
The Connected Discourses of the Buddha. Translated by Bhikkhu Bodhi. 2 vols. Boston: Wisdom, 2000.

Vin. *Vinaya Piṭaka*
The Book of the Discipline. Translated by I. B. Horner. 6 vols. London: Pali Text Society, 1938–66.

References are to volume number and page of the Pali Text Society editions of the texts in Pali, which are also indicated in the translations.[18]

Bibliography and Suggested Reading

Bodhi, Bhikkhu. (1998) "A Look at the *Kalama Sutta.*" Access to Insight: www.accesstoinsight.org/lib/bps/news/essay09.html.

Cruise, Henry. (1983) "Early Buddhism: Some Recent Misconceptions." *Philosophy East and West* 33/2: 149–165. http://ccbs.ntu.edu.tw/FULLTEXT/JR-PHIL/henry1.htm.

18. For further guidance, see explanations on the website of the UK Association for Buddhist Studies: www.ukabs.org.uk/pali-literature.html. The website Access to Insight has many translations from the Pali Canon: www.accesstoinsight.org/tipitaka/index.html. Texts are primarily listed by discourse number, but this is then followed by volume and page number of the Pali Text Society Pali edition.

Harvey, Peter. (1995) "Contemporary Characterisations of the 'Philosophy' of Nikāyan Buddhism." *Buddhist Studies Review* 12/2: 109–133.
Holder, J. T. (1996) "The Early Buddhist Theory of Truth: A Contextualist, Pragmatic Interpretation." *International Philosophical Quarterly* 36/4: 433–459.
Hoffman, F. J. (1987) *Rationality and Mind in Early Buddhism.* Delhi: Motilal Banarsidass.
Jayatilleke, K. N. (1963) *Early Buddhist Theory of Knowledge.* London: Allen and Unwin. Reprint, Delhi: Motilal Banarsidass.
Kalupahana, David. (1992) *A History of Buddhist Philosophy: Continuities and Discontinuities.* Honolulu: University of Hawai'i Press.
Nagapriya, Dharmachari. (2001) "Knowledge and Truth in Early Buddhism." *Western Buddhist Review* 3, http://www.westernbuddhistreview.com/vol3/Knowledge.htm.

16

Dharmakīrti and Dharmottara on the Intentionality of Perception

Selections from *Nyāyabindu* (*An Epitome of Philosophy*)

Dan Arnold

Dignāga (c. 480–540 C.E.) and his influential successor Dharmakīrti (c. 600–660 C.E.) were taken by most Indian philosophers as commonly exemplifying a spartan epistemology. On this view, perception (*pratyakṣa*) and inference (*anumāna*) are the only two *pramāṇas* ("reliable warrants" or, we might say, "doxastic practices"). These have as their respective objects the only two kinds of things that could finally exist: unique particulars (*svalakṣaṇas*), and a range of abstractions (*sāmānyalakṣaṇa*) that includes such things as complex wholes and universals.

To say perception apprehends only unique particulars is arguably to be committed (as in fact Dignāga and Dharmakīrti were) to the view that perception is constitutively nonconceptual (*kalpanāpoḍha*). This is because any conceptual or discursive thought—any taking of an object of cognition *as* something or another—can be thought necessarily to involve reference to some sort of universals. "Universals," on one view of the matter, just are the kinds of things that must figure in judgments or propositions; and on this view, anything so simple as taking oneself to perceive *a tree* (and not just uninterpreted sense data) requires having such concepts as "being a tree" or "the class of all trees."

To say of perception that it is nonconceptual in this sense, then, is to say that perceptual awareness does not (perhaps cannot) have the kind of "content" that makes a thought intelligible as a *reason* for acting one way or another—the kind of content, that is, that must be involved in judgments or propositions. Dignāga suggests as much when he says of the objects of perception only that they are constitutively "inexpressible" (*avyapadeśya*). On this view, then, it would seem that what is given to us in bare perceivings is nothing but uninterpreted sense data.

For Buddhists, the epistemological intuitions in play here have the advantage that they well support the cardinal doctrine of *selflessness*—the view that persons are not enduring substances, but instead consist simply in causally continuous series of events. Thus, this epistemology would seem to recommend the conclusion that only the fleeting sense data of episodic perceptions are real, without also warranting the (inferential) belief that these must be the states of an underlying self. (The *self* is, for these thinkers, the originating example of the kind of "whole" or abstraction whose reality they mean to refute.) This is not, however, to say that there are peculiarly "Buddhist" reasons for crediting the view here on offer; it can, indeed, be taken to have the kind of intuitive plausibility that attaches to empiricism.

The characterization of this as a broadly "empiricist" trend of thought fits particularly well with the emphasis on causal explanations that Dharmakīrti adds to the philosophical project he carries on from Dignāga. For Dharmakīrti, to be "ultimately existent" (*paramārthasat*) just is to be capable of causally interacting with other particulars. Dharmakīrti would have it, then, that perceptual cognitions are uniquely in contact with really existent things just insofar as perceptions alone are *caused* by the objects thereof; such cognitions result from causally efficacious "impingements by the world on a possessor of sensory capacities," in John McDowell's phrase.[1]

This view emphasizes the intuition that we do not have any agency in how things that are perceptually experienced will seem to us; rather, an object of perception is just "given" to us as *this particular thing*, seen on one particular occasion under whatever conditions happen to obtain. Perception can thus be considered foundational insofar as this is the unique point in our cognitive relation to the world at which our cognition is constrained by the world; it is in our causally describable perceptual encounters that we "come up against" a world of objects that are as they are quite independently of us. It can reasonably be thought, therefore, that attending to such cognitions puts us in the best position to reach definitive conclusions about (what Buddhists surely want to understand) *what there is*.

While this is an intuitively plausible view, it is not without difficulties. Chief among these is that of explaining how such causally describable sensations can be brought into what Wilfrid Sellars called the "logical space of reasons"—how, that is, perception's passive receptivity to "impingements by the world" can yield such *intentional* items as beliefs or judgments. (These are "intentional," on one view of the matter, in the sense that awareness can be thought to have epistemic content only if it is somehow *about* the kinds of things that figure in our reasoning.) In this vein, some modern interpreters of Dharmakīrti's thought have found it useful to understand him

1. McDowell 1996: xv.

as holding the kind of view that Sellars influentially critiqued as "the myth of the given."[2] Sellars showed the problems that go with thinking that what perceptual cognitions are *about* cannot be the kinds of things that are the objects of, say, judging or believing. To hold (as Dharmakīrti surely does) that the outputs of perception are constitutively different from things like beliefs and judgments is, on a view such as Sellars's, effectively to say that perception cannot give us *reasons* for anything.

In fact, the Kashmiri commentator Dharmottara (c. 740–800) seems to have seen similar problems with Dharmakīrti's thought. The selections here from Dharmakīrti's *Nyāyabindu,* with Dharmottara's commentary thereon, thus represent an unusually good place to see these Buddhists wrestling with the problems entailed by taking perception to be radically nonconceptual. The *Nyāyabindu* (whose title we might translate as "An Epitome of Philosophy") is a basic primer generally thought to be among Dharmakīrti's later works. As such, it provides a picture of Dharmakīrti's mature thought, but one that is concise enough to allow a perhaps unusual degree of commentatorial latitude. Creatively commenting on this text, Dharmottara exploits an interesting opportunity to soften Dharmakīrti's sharp distinction between perceptual and conceptual awareness. Indeed, while his desire to be taken as a faithful interpreter of Dharmakīrti means he cannot say that perception is, after all, conceptual, one could reasonably say that that is just what Dharmottara argues here.

The opportunity Dharmottara thus exploits involves another of the claims thought characteristic of the philosophy of Dignāga and Dharmakīrti, about which it is therefore necessary to say a bit. This is the claim that when we use the word "*pramāṇa*" (typically taken by Indian philosophers to denote whatever brings about an episode of veridical awareness), it should be understood that we are really referring to the *resulting cognition* (to the *pramāṇaphala,* or "fruit of the *pramāṇa*"). Further, it is also said by Dharmakīrti (who here follows Dignāga) that it makes sense to say this "resultant cognition" finally consists somehow in "self-awareness" (*svasaṃvitti*). On some understandings of the latter claim, Dharmakīrti is committed to the entailed view that all episodes of valid cognition consist finally in awareness of our own thoughts.

However these claims are understood (and the available commentaries support a range of interpretations), it is clear that these issues relate to the question of whether or not these thinkers should be taken as finally arguing for idealism. In this regard, Dharmakīrti's *Pramāṇavārttika* is traditionally read as alternating between arguments for two kinds of views: a representationalist epistemology of the sort familiar from empiricist sense-datum theories (characterized by Dharmakīrti's later commentators as the Sautrāntika perspective), and the metaphysical idealism of the Yogācāra perspective.

2. Sellars 1997.

It is not only because of Dharmakīrti's alternation between these positions that his final position can be hard to determine; it is also, perhaps more compellingly, because the epistemology is the same either way. Both views, that is, amount at least to *epistemic idealism*—to the view that what we are immediately aware of is only things somehow intrinsic to cognition. On the epistemological view of the Sautrāntikas, then, it makes sense to say that perception ultimately consists in "self-awareness" insofar as what is given to us in perception is something—sense data or, as Dharmakīrti typically says, phenomenal "aspects" (*ākāra*)—internal to cognition. This epistemological claim—which does not by itself commit us to saying that only things intrinsic to cognition *exist*—can be recruited in the same way as the modern foundationalist's appeal to empirical sense data: the one thing we *cannot* be wrong about is the content of our own perceptual cognitions, and this unique certainty provides the basis of all our knowledge. The chief difference between this view and Yogācāra idealism lies only in the metaphysical arguments that, for the idealist, additionally show that only such mental things as sense data *could* be real. (Of course, the sense in which perception is causally describable will turn out to look rather different if it is the latter view that finally holds.)

Dharmottara, who seems not to have favored an idealist reading of Dharmakīrti, does not take these doctrines in either of the ways just sketched. Rather, Dharmottara thinks that *pramāṇa* really denotes the "result of the *pramāṇa*" (*pramāṇaphala*) in the sense that only when cognition issues in a resulting *judgment* is there any epistemic content—any content, that is, such as can facilitate purposeful activity. As we will see, this is tantamount to claiming that perception may after all immediately yield some propositional (hence, it is hard to avoid saying, *conceptual*) content.

These selections from the *Nyāyabindu*'s first chapter (which treats perception) follow Dharmottara's revisions as they are developed throughout the chapter. We begin with a brief selection from Dharmottara's comments on the first verse, where Dharmottara is clearly concerned to argue that an efficient-causal account cannot be thought to exhaust the topic of knowing. After taking a few more soundings in Dharmottara's development of this thought, we see most of the chapter's concluding paragraphs, in which Dharmottara argues that the point of the *pramāṇaphala* doctrine is not (as it clearly was for Dharmakīrti) to say that we are only immediately aware of things somehow intrinsic to cognition; quite to the contrary, he argues, we can think of perception as having epistemic content only if we take perceptual cognitions to be *about* something more than the efficient causes thereof.[3]

3. The following translation is my own, from Paṇḍita Dalsukhbhai Malvania, ed., *Paṇḍita Durveka Miśra's Dharmottarapradīpa* (Patna: Kashiprasad Jayaswal Research Institute, 1971; 2nd ed).

Translation

[We first join Dharmottara as he is commenting on Dharmakīrti's first verse: *"Veridical cognition is previous to the accomplishment of all human aims—this is discussed in the present text."* Dharmottara here focuses on the Sanskrit compound that is translated *"veridical cognition is previous."*]

That of which a previous cause is veridical cognition is thus described [as in Dharmakīrti's verse]. Being previous to its effect, a cause is said to be previous. But if Dharmakīrti had used the word "cause," it could be understood that this is the direct cause of the accomplishment of human aims; given the word "previous," in contrast, what is understood is simply priority.

And veridical cognition is twofold, consisting in that whose content is accomplishment of a goal (*arthakriyā*), and that which motivates activity with regard to what has the capacity for accomplishing a goal; and among these two, it is the one that is the motivator that is here investigated.[4] And that is merely previous to the accomplishment of aims, but not the direct cause thereof; for when there is veridical cognition, there is recollection of what has been seen previously; based on recollection, there is desire; based on desire, activity; and based on activity, acquisition. Therefore, veridical cognition is not a direct cause of the accomplishment of human aims.

But even if cognition whose content is accomplishment of a goal is directly the cause of acquisition, nevertheless, that is not to be investigated here; for only that with respect to which purposeful, discerning persons have a doubt is to be investigated. And when there is cognition whose content is accomplishment of a goal, human aims are achieved; thus, with regard to that purposeful actors are not doubtful—hence, that is not to be investigated. Therefore, eschewing the word "cause" in order to show that veridical cognition, which is worthy of inquiry, is not directly a cause, Dharmakīrti has used the word "previous."

[On verse 12: "*The object of it (i.e., of perception) is a unique particular.*"]

Having explained the different types of perception associated with the properties of being free of conceptual elaboration and inerrant, Dharmakīrti now says, in order to refute rival opinions concerning the object of perception:

> Its object is the unique particular (svalakṣaṇam) [verse 12].

4. Here, Dharmottara effectively makes the point that epistemology is not directly concerned with acting, but with the kind of epistemically contentful knowings that might serve as *reasons* for acting; we are, that is, concerned with the kind of thing that attaches to *judgments*, such as might conduce to the achievement of aims, and not with such achievement itself.

The object of it—that is, of the four kinds of perception[5]—is to be understood as *svalakṣaṇam*.[6] *Sva-* means *unique; lakṣaṇa* means *reality* (*tattva*)—that's the sense of *svalakṣaṇa*. For a thing has a unique reality, and a generic one. Regarding these, the one that's unique is apprehended by perception.

Now, the object of a *pramāṇa* has two aspects: That regarding which a phenomenal appearance (*ākāra*) is produced is to be "apprehended" (*grāhya*), and that which one ascertains is to be "intended" (*prāpanīya*); for one is to be apprehended and one is to be ascertained (*adhyavaseya*).[7] Now, what is *apprehended* by perception is a single instant; but what is to be ascertained by the judgment produced on the strength of perception is a *continuum* of such instants. And it is precisely a continuum that is to be intended by perception, since a moment cannot cause one to gain anything.[8]

[The last selection is from Dharmottara's comments on verses 18–21, the last of the chapter; these concisely state Dharmakīrti's view that *pramāṇa* really

5. Perception is defined, for these thinkers, chiefly by its being nonconceptual—and sensory perception is only one kind of cognition thought by them to be thus. Buddhist epistemologists also took "perception" to consist in "mental perception" (*mānasapratyakṣa*), i.e., the mind's awareness of sensory outputs; "self-awareness" (*svasaṃvitti*), which is closely related to the latter; and the perception of advanced meditators (*yogipratyakṣa*), which must be admitted if Buddhist practice is itself to count as sharing the privileged status that perception, as nonconceptual, has for these Buddhists.

6. The word that is rendered "unique particular" throughout is here left untranslated since Dharmottara is offering his own gloss on the compound.

7. Dharmottara here introduces pairs of terms that figure importantly in his revision of Dharmakīrti. There is nothing obvious in the native semantic range of the words *grāhya* ("to be apprehended") and *prāpanīya* ("to be gotten," or, here, "intended") to tell us what he has in mind. It becomes clear, though, that Dharmottara is concerned with the difference between, respectively, the uninterpreted "given," and what can be "ascertained" (*adhyavaseya*) as the content of a judgment—and his point (radical in the context of Dharmakīrti's spartan epistemology) will be that perception itself involves both moments. The translation here of variations on the verbal root *pra-√āp* (to "get" or "obtain," etc.) as involving *intentionality* might be thought tendentious; it will, though, become clear that Dharmottara has in mind the directedness or "*aboutness*" of cognition.

8. Dharmottara here brings into play the Buddhist doctrine of momentariness. This has it that anything we take to be an enduring object is really to be understood as a series of fleeting instants—the appearance of identity is explained by causal *continuity* (there is not one enduring object, but a "continuum" of related instants). As Dharmottara recognizes, the kinds of problems noted by Sellars become more acute given this view. Insofar as it is enduring macro-objects that figure in contentful cognition, the view that perception grasps only real particulars (where "real" is defined as momentary) would effectively mean that perception cannot have *any* epistemic content. Conversely, any view on which perception *does* have epistemic content entails that it involves at least the sort of conceptual elaboration that picks out the relevant continua.

denotes a resulting cognition, and the four verses can all be read together as a single sentence: "*And the perceptual cognition itself is the result of the pramāṇa, because of its being [something] whose form is the understanding of an object; its instrument (pramāṇa) is the fact of its resembling the object, because of the establishment of the understanding of an object on the strength of that.*"]

Having refuted objections concerning the object of perception, in order to refute objections concerning result, Dharmakīrti now says:

> *And the perceptual cognition itself is the result of the pramāṇa* [verse 18].

That very perceptual cognition that we've been explaining—precisely that is the result of the *pramāṇa*.

How is it the result of the *pramāṇa?* With this in mind, Dharmakīrti says,

> *Because of its being [something] whose form is the understanding (pratīti) of an object* [verse 19].

[After providing basic syntactic glosses, Dharmottara continues:] Here is what Dharmakīrti is saying: It is intentional (*prāpaka*) cognition that is a *pramāṇa;* and the capacity of intentionality is not based only on being invariably concomitant—consider a sprout's not being intentional even though invariably concomitant with seeds and so on.[9] Therefore, even given its arising causally from some object to be apprehended (*grāhya*), a cognition still has some intentional function (*prāpakavyāpāra*) necessarily to be performed, by doing which a goal is obtained. And that function just is the result that is the *pramāṇa,*[10] because of the exercise of which a cognition becomes intentional. And it was explained earlier that an intentional cognition's function of intending is disclosing an object of engagement.[11] And that very perception, in the form of the understanding of an object, has the form of disclosing an object—hence, that just is the result which is the *pramāṇa*.

9. The point is that the relation between seeds and sprouts is causal, but not *intentional*. The example lends credence to this translation of *prāpaka;* for it makes clear that whatever Dharmottara means by *prāpaka,* it is (1) not to be understood as exhaustively explicable in causal terms, and (2) not exemplified by insentient things like sprouts. To that extent, he can be said to have in view something like a "criterion of the mental"—and his point is that whether or not a causal relation is necessary for that, it is not sufficient.

10. Note that the compound *pramāṇaphala*—hitherto translated as involving a genitive ("result *of* the *pramāṇa*")—can also be rendered (as here) appositionally ("result *that* is the *pramāṇa*"); here, the latter sense better captures Dharmottara's point.

11. This was discussed in the lengthy commentary on Dharmakīrti's first verse, where there is much consideration of what it means to be motivated by cognition to act in various ways.

If, then, cognition is the result that is the *pramāṇa* (because of its being in the form of *pramiti*), then what is the *pramāṇa*?[12] With this in mind, Dharmakīrti says,

Its pramāṇa is the fact of its resembling the object [verse 20].

That which is its (i.e., cognition's) resembling (i.e., its similarity with) an object,[13] that is the *pramāṇa*. In this regard, that cognition becomes similar to that object from which the cognition arises—as, for example, a cognition being produced by a patch of blue is similar to blue. And that conformity (i.e., similarity) is also called the "phenomenological aspect" (*ākāra*) or "content" (*ābhāsa*) of the cognition.[14]

Objection: But the fact of similarity is not different from cognition; and that being the case, the very same cognition is both the instrument that is the *pramāṇa* and the *result* of the *pramāṇa*—and it doesn't make sense that a single thing be both *what* is to be known (*sādhya*) and *how* it is known (*sādhana*).[15] So, how is resemblance the *pramāṇa?* With this objection in mind, Dharmakīrti says,

Because of the establishment of the understanding of an object based on that [verse 21].

[Dharmottara offers syntactic analyses to make clear, inter alia, the antecedents of the pronoun in Dharmakīrti's verse; thus, understanding of an object is based on *cognition's resembling its object.* He elaborates:] Perceptual cognition, in the form of understanding of an object, is based on

12. Here, in ways typical of Indian philosophical discourse, the question presupposes the kind of sentence-analysis that is foundational for the Sanskrit grammatical tradition. On this analysis, any semantically complete statement designates an *action,* expressible by a verb, whose realization is what the sentence describes; and the parts of a sentence (as denoted by the various affixes whose usage is described by the grammarians) are to be understood in terms of their relations to the verb. Reference to a *pramāṇa*—a word formed by an affix denoting instrumentality—must be understood, then, as picking out whatever factor is "instrumental" in realizing an *act of knowing* (*pramiti*). (Such an act also requires a subject, or "knower," *pramātṛ;* and a patient, or something "to be known," *prameya.*) The question, then, is what we are to take as "instrumental" in bringing about an act of knowing once we have said that the word *pramāṇa* really denotes the *result* of such an act.

13. Dharmottara thus makes explicit the antecedents of the pronouns in Dharmakīrti's verse.

14. Here, the terms seem clearly to be those of a basically representationalist epistemology—one according to which we are immediately aware of mental events (sense data, "aspects," etc.) that somehow represent (or otherwise take on the appearance of) what they are about.

15. The question here—how are we to understand a view on which the same thing is at once subject and object of the same act?—is a variation on a prominently recurrent objection regarding the Buddhist doctrine of *svasaṃvitti.* (There, the specific form of the question concerns how awareness can be aware *of itself.*)

representation[16]—the point is, that is how an object is understood; since there is a cognition whose phenomenological content (*nirbhāsa*) is blue, therefore a thought of blue is ascertained. For a cognition of blue cannot be constituted as an awareness (*saṃvedana*) based only on those senses and so forth due to which the cognition arises[17]; rather, the experienced likeness of blue constitutes an awareness of blue.[18]

And here, the relation between what is to be known and how we know it is not based on the relation of produced and producer,[19] according to which there would be a contradiction within a single thing; rather, these are related as being *intended* (*vyavasthāpya*) and *intentional* (*vyavasthāpaka*).[20] Thus, there is no contradiction in holding that a single thing has, to some extent, the form of a *pramāṇa,* and to some extent that of the result of a *pramāṇa.* For that cognition's resemblance of an object is the cause of intending (*vyavasthāpana*); and what is to be intended (*vyavasthāpya*) is in the form of an awareness of blue.[21]

Objection: How can a single cognition have the relation of intended and intentional?

Response: Since that cognition, experiencing the likeness of blue, is established as apprehending blue by a thought that is a judgment (*niścayapratyaya*), therefore the experienced likeness is the cause of intending. And that cognition, being established as an experience of blue by a thought that is a judgment, is what is intended. Therefore, a cognition's resemblance, which is realized by way of exclusion of what is unlike,[22] is a cause of intending; and

16. That is, cognition's "representation" of its object is what provides the datum or content of any act of understanding.

17. Properly functioning sense faculties, that is, are the *causes* or enabling conditions of experience, but are not themselves what "realizes" the experience.

18. The point is that the epistemic *content* of a cognition (specifically as distinct from the causes thereof) is the object of experience.

19. It is not, in other words, a *causal* relation.

20. Here, the challenge is to translate Dharmottara's alternative terms (*vyavasthāpya* and *vyavasthāpaka*) in such a way as to avoid attributing to him the very contradiction he wants to avoid. Dharmottara allows that if we think that a blue sense datum relates to the judgment "that's blue" as (respectively) cause to effect, a single perceptual event could not coherently be thought to exemplify them simultaneously—and whatever Dharmottara understands by his alternative to that picture, it is clear that he takes there to be no such contradiction in thinking a single cognition simultaneously exemplifies what he has in mind. It is, again, the fact that Dharmottara is clearly striving for an alternative to a causal relation that suggests that something like intentionality is in play.

21. It is a fair question whether Dharmottara's explanation here avoids the problem; it seems clear that his faithfulness to Dharmakīrti's system of thought makes it difficult finally to offer an alternative to a causal relation.

22. Here, Dharmottara alludes to Dharmakīrti's *apoha* ("exclusion") theory of meaning or mental content. This is meant to explain how the conceptual contents of thought can be constructed from (or reduced to) nothing other than the unique particulars encountered in perception. Typically for Dharmakīrti, this theory has a peculiarly causal emphasis: one arrives at the idea of a set of comparable particulars (hence the idea of a universal) by excluding whatever does not produce the same effect as

the fact of being in the form of a thought of blue, which is realized by exclusion of thoughts of nonblue, is what is to be intended.

And intentionality (*vyavasthāpaka*) should be understood as a conceptual idea (*vikalpapratyaya*) produced on the strength of perception; but perception alone, because of its being nonconceptual, cannot establish itself as being in the form of an awareness of blue. Even a real cognition consisting of awareness of blue, as long as it is unestablished by a thought that is a judgment, is just an unreal fancy. Therefore, a cognition established by a judgment (*niścayena*) as consisting of an awareness of blue becomes real as itself an awareness of blue.[23]

Therefore, perception becomes a *pramāṇa* only insofar as it produces determinacy (*adhyavasāya*); but when determinacy is unproduced, cognition is unestablished as consisting of an awareness of blue—and in this way, the result of a *pramāṇa,* in the form of comprehension of an object, is unrealized. Hence, because of there being nothing of the paradigmatic property of cognition, the cognition could not be the *pramāṇa* by itself. But when cognition, consisting in a thought of blue, is being produced, on the strength of resemblance, by a produced determinacy, that resemblance, because of its being a cause of intending, becomes established as a *pramāṇa.*

Objection: If so, perception would be a *pramāṇa* only together with determination, not by itself.

Response: This isn't so, since an object is ascertained, by a determination produced on the strength of perception, as being *seen,* not as being *imagined.*[24] And seeing, which is known as the direct disclosing of an object, is the function of perception; but imagining is the function of conceptual thought. Thus, conceptualizing an invisible object, we imagine, but we do not see. Hence, based on experience, people ascertain the function of conceptual thought as consisting in imagination. Therefore, Dharmakīrti shows

---

whatever is presently experienced. (It is a complicated question why Dharmakīrti can think "sameness of effect" does not amount to just the sort of abstraction he means to explain; see Dunne 2004: 113–144.) Dharmottara's main point here, then, is that reference to a cognition's "resemblance" of its object need not be taken to entail a really existent abstraction (as though there were a real third term, "resemblance," relating cognition and its object); rather, the idea of resemblance comes only from the exclusion of all those cognitive representations that do not have the same effect as this one.

23. Dharmottara is here quite clear in emphasizing that bare "sensings" do not have any epistemic content; rather, it is only as conceptually "determined" that these can enter into Sellars's "logical space of reasons."

24. The point seems to be that we still require bare perceptual inputs in order to distinguish a perceptual judgment from a mere fancy, and that it is therefore useful to speak of the distinctive *pramāṇa* that is "perception" as constrained by such inputs. To jettison the idea that we have epistemic access to an uninterpreted "given" is not, then, to do away with the idea that perception is nevertheless constrained in distinctive ways.

the function of perception having bracketed its full proper function;[25] thus, perception is a *pramāṇa* by itself in regard to that object with respect to which ascertainment depends on perception.

Bibliography and Suggested Reading

Dreyfus, Georges. (1997) *Recognizing Reality: Dharmakīrti's Philosophy and Its Tibetan Interpreters.* Albany: State University of New York Press.

Dunne, John. (2004) *Foundations of Dharmakīrti's Philosophy.* Boston: Wisdom.

McDowell, John. (1996) *Mind and World.* Cambridge, Mass.: Harvard University Press.

Sellars, Wilfrid. (1997) *Empiricism and the Philosophy of Mind.* Cambridge, Mass.: Harvard University Press.

Stcherbatsky, Theodore. (1962) *Buddhist Logic.* 2 vols. 1930. Reprint, New York: Dover Books.

Tillemans, Tom J. F. (1999) *Scripture, Logic, Language: Essays on Dharmakīrti and His Tibetan Successors.* Boston: Wisdom.

25. That is, Dharmottara takes Dharmakīrti as emphasizing only the extent to which perception is constrained in ways that purely conceptual thought is not, and as leaving unsaid some of the other things that need to be understood about perception—the kinds of things, in particular, that Dharmottara has here been saying!

17

The Role of Knowledge of Causation in Dharmakīrti's Theory of Inference

The *Pramāṇa-vārttika*

Brendan S. Gillon

Dharmakīrti, a Buddhist thinker who lived in the seventh century C.E., composed a number of works addressing issues pertaining to perception and inference. His principal work, *Pramāṇa-vārttika,* consists of four chapters, each written in verse. One chapter, entitled *svārtha-anumāna* (Inference for oneself), was supplemented by him with a prose commentary. An excerpt from this chapter is translated here. In it Dharmakīrti takes up the questions of how knowledge of the causation relation guarantees knowledge of a universal, categorical statement and of how one comes to know that the causation relation obtains.

The study of inference in India is not the study of valid reasoning as reflected in linguistic or paralinguistic forms, but the study of under what conditions certain facts require the existence of some other fact, or under what conditions knowledge of some facts permits knowledge of some other fact, or under what conditions acceptance of some facts permits acceptance of some other fact.

At the core of the study of inference in India is the use of a naïve realist's ontology. The world consists of individual substances, or things (*dravya*), universals (*sāmānya*), and relations between them. The fundamental relation is the one of occurrence (*vṛtti*). The relata of this relation are known as substratum (*dharmin*) and superstratum (*dharma*), respectively. The relation has two forms: contact (*saṃyoga*) and inherence (*samavāya*). So, for example, one individual substance, a pot, may occur on another, say the ground, by the relation of contact. In this case, the pot is the superstratum and the ground is the substratum. Or the property brownness, a universal, may occur in an individual substance, say a pot, by the relation of inherence. Here, brownness, the superstratum, inheres in the pot, the substratum. The converse of the relation of occurrence is the relation of possession. Another important relation is the relation that one superstratum bears to another. This relation, known as concomitance (*anvaya*), can be defined in terms of the occurrence relation. One superstratum is concomitant with another just in case wherever the first occurs the second occurs. The converse of the concomitance relation is the pervasion (*vyāpti*) relation.

The Buddhist thinker believed to have first treated inference in these terms is Vasubandhu, who lived in the early part of the fifth century C.E. He held that inference has only three parts, a substratum, called a *pakṣa,*[1] *subject* or *thesis;* and two superstrata, called a *hetu,*[2] or *ground,* and a *sādhya,*[3] or *establishable* (*superstratum*). In his *Vāda-vidhi* (Rules of Debate), Vasubandhu makes clear that the relation, knowledge of which is necessary for inference, is not just any in a miscellany of material relations, but a formal relation, which he designates, in some places, as *a-vinā-bhāva,* or indispensability—literally, not being without (compare the Latin expression *sine qua non*)—and in others, as *nāntarīyakatva,* or immediacy—literally, being unmediated.

Drawing on an idea ascribed by his coreligionist Asaṅga to an unidentified, non-Buddhist school of thought,[4] Vasubandhu maintained that a ground in an inference is a proper one if, and only if, it satisfies three conditions—the so-called *tri-rūpa-hetu,* or the grounding superstratum (*hetu*) in its three forms. The first form is that the grounding superstratum, or H, should occur in the subject of an inference, or *p*. The second is that the grounding superstratum, or *H,* should occur in those things similar to the subject insofar as they have the superstratum to be established, or *S*. And the third is that the grounding superstratum, or *H,* should not occur in any of those things dissimilar from the subject insofar as they lack the superstratum to be established, *S*. These conditions can be viewed as a partial specification of the validity of inferences of the following form:

Thesis:	*p* has *S*.
Minor Premise:	*p* has *H*.
Major Premise:	Whatever has *H* has *S*.

The first condition corresponds to the minor premise in the schema above, while the second two correspond to the major premise.

1. The Sanskrit word *pakṣa* is ambiguous between a thesis and the substratum mentioned in the thesis. See Staal 1988, chap. 7.

2. The Sanskrit word *hetu* is ambiguous between motive, cause, and ground.

3. The Sanskrit word *sādhya,* lit. "what is to be established," refers to the superstratum, usually a property, to be established as existent in the substratum mentioned in the thesis.

4. One Japanese scholar, according to Katsura 1986, has conjectured the school to be the Sāṃkhyā school.

Here are two paradigmatic cases of such an inference:

Thesis:	*p* has fire.
Minor Premise:	*p* has smoke.
Major Premise:	Whatever has smoke has fire.

Thesis:	*p* is a tree (i.e., has tree-ness).
Minor Premise:	*p* is an oak (i.e., has oak-ness).
Major Premise:	Whatever is an oak (i.e., has oak-ness) is a tree (i.e., has tree-ness).

Shortly thereafter, Vasubandhu's student Dignāga, who flourished between the late fifth century and the early sixth century C.E., building on the insights of his teacher, fully isolated the formal structure underlying the Indian syllogism (Steinkellner 1993). First, distinguishing between inference for oneself (*sva-artha-anumāna*) and inference for another (*para-artha-anumāna*), he made explicit what had previously been only implicit, namely, that inference, the cognitive process whereby one increases one's knowledge, and argument, the device of persuasion, are but two sides of a single coin. Second, he undertook to make the three forms of the grounding superstratum more precise, pressing into service the Sanskrit particle *eva* (*only*). And third, and perhaps most strikingly, he coined the *hetu-cakra,* or his *wheel of reasons,* a three by three matrix, set up to classify pseudogrounds in light of the last two forms of the three forms of a proper ground. On the one hand, there are the three cases of the grounding superstratum (H) occurring in some, none, or all of the substrata where the superstratum to be established (*S*) occurs. On the other hand, there are the three cases of the grounding superstratum (H) occurring in some, none, or all of the substrata where the superstratum to be established (*S*) does not occur. Letting *S* be the substrata in which S occurs and $\bar{S}$ be the substrata in which *S* does not occur, one arrives at the following table.

H occurs in:	all S	all S	all $\bar{S}$
	all $\bar{S}$	no $\bar{S}$	some $\bar{S}$
H occurs in:	no S	no S	no S
	all $\bar{S}$	no $\bar{S}$	some $\bar{S}$
H occurs in:	some S	some S	some S
	all $\bar{S}$	no $\bar{S}$	some $\bar{S}$

Dignāga identified the top and bottom cases of the middle column as those cases rendering the major premise true.

The syllogism, conceived as an inference, is that whereby one who knows the truth of its premises may also come to know the truth of its conclusion. The second premise is known, of course, through perception. But how is the first premise known? To know it by perception would seem to require that one know of each thing that has *H* that it also has *S*. But if one knew that, one would already know by perception the syllogism's conclusion. As a result, inference would be a superfluous means of knowledge.

The earliest classical Indian philosopher thought to have recognized the problem of how one comes to know the first premise of the classical Indian syllogism—essentially, the problem of induction—seems to have been Dignāga's student Īśvarasena. He appears to have thought that knowledge of the syllogism's first premise is grounded in nonperception (*an-upalabdhi*). That is, according to Īśvarasena, knowledge that whatever has *H* has *S* comes from the simple failure to perceive something that has *H* but that does not have *S*.[5] However, this suggestion does not solve the problem, for reasons laid out in detail by Dharmakīrti, Īśvarasena's student, in the *svārtha-anumāna* chapter of his *Pramāṇa-vārttika*.[6] As Dharmakīrti makes abundantly clear, the simple failure to perceive something that has *H* but that does not have *S* is no guarantee that whatever has *H* has *S;* after all, while one has never encountered something that has *H* and does not have *S,* what guarantee is there that something that has *H* and does not have *S* is not among the things that one has yet to encounter?

Dharmakīrti's solution to this problem is that knowledge of the syllogism's first premise arises from knowledge of a relation that guarantees that, in general, whatever has *H* has *S*. Dharmakīrti maintains that there are only two such relations, identity (*tādātmya*) and causation (*tadutpatti*). According to Dharmakīrti, with the knowledge that either the identity relation or the causation relation obtains, each borne by *H* to *S,* one's knowledge that whatever has *H* has *S* is guaranteed.

In the excerpted passage translated here, Dharmakīrti takes up the questions of how knowledge of the causation relation guarantees knowledge of the truth of the major premise and how one comes to know that the causation relation obtains. The passage consists of five verses and his commentary to them. The verses (verses 34–38) are given together at the beginning, and their presence in the commentary is signaled by their appearance in italics.[7]

Translation

34. Because smoke is the effect of fire due to its conformity with the property of the effect. But that which comes to exist in something's absence must give up having that thing as its cause.

5. See Steinkellner 1993, where he draws on Steinkellner 1966.

6. The criticism is made and elaborated at several points in the verses 13–22 and their commentary (Gnoli 1960: 10–16).

7. This translation was done in collaboration with Richard Hayes. It is a selection from a translation of verses 11–38 and Dharmakīrti's commentary, accompanied by detailed explanatory notes, found in Gillon and Hayes 2008.

35. That which has no cause has either eternal existence or eternal nonexistence, because it has no dependence on anything else. For things arise as temporary because of their dependence on other things.

36. If an anthill had the nature of fire, then it would be just fire. If it did not have the nature of fire, then how could smoke come into existence there?

37. For fire, which has a distinct potentiality for smoke, has [being] its cause as its nature. If smoke were to come into existence from what is not the cause of smoke, then it would be without a cause.

38. That whose nature something is seen to conform to in the manner of concomitance and exclusion, is its cause. Hence, there is no coming about from what is different.

[Commentary:] If, then, observation and nonobservation are not a basis for one's knowledge of concomitance and exclusion,[8] how does one know that smoke does not deviate from fire? *Because smoke is the effect of fire due to its conformity with the property of the effect.*[9] That which, not having been apprehended, is apprehended when its conditions for apprehension have been apprehended, yet is not apprehended when even one of them is not present, is [ascertained to be] their effect. And this is true in the case for smoke.

But that which comes to exist in something's absence must give up having that thing as its cause. One thing is established as an effect of another from their being observed, even once, in the way specified above; since, if the one is not an effect of the other, the former would not arise even once from the latter, the latter not being the cause of the former. And were an effect to come to exist without its cause, there would be no cause at all for it. For that without which something arises is not its cause. And should smoke come to exist without fire, then smoke would not have fire for its cause. It might be argued that smoke is not causeless, because it has something else as its cause.[10] This is not so, because, in this case, too, the situation is the same, namely, even in the absence of the [alleged] other [cause], when there is fire, there is smoke. How could smoke possibly arise either from fire or from something else whose nature does not produce smoke? Smoke could have no cause, because something that itself does not have the production of smoke for its nature does not produce smoke.

8. Concomitance (*anvaya*) and exclusion (*vyatireka*) are those situations in the world that render true a universal categorical proposition and its contrapositive. In verse 28 and his commentary thereto (Gnoli 1960: 18–19), Dharmakīrti argues that these situations are the same; in other words, he argues that a universal categorical proposition and its contrapositive are equivalent.

9. This sentence is somewhat obscure. It would be clearer if he had said: "Because one knows that smoke is the effect of fire; and one knows this, because one knows that smoke conforms to the definition of being an effect."

10. Here and hereafter, Dharmakīrti repeatedly argues against the possibility that the same effect might have different causes.

It might be argued that it is not at all the case that the very same thing arises from the existence of things of the same kind. How can smoke be of the same kind, while arising from things of different kinds? For that which arises from things of one kind must be of the same kind. If something of one kind comes into existence from something of another kind, too, the differences among causes cannot bring about differences among their effects, because there is no restriction on what the causes can potentially bring about. So, either the diversity of things within the world would be without a cause or everything would be produced from everything else. Therefore, what is different and what is the same among effects arises from what is different and what is the same among their causes. Thus, it is not the case that smoke comes into existence from a thing of a kind different from what is observed because of the absurdity of its being causeless.

And in this way, *that which has no cause has either eternal existence or eternal nonexistence, because it is independent of anything else. For things arise as temporary because of their dependence on other things.* For, if smoke were causeless, and hence independent of anything else, either it would always exist—just as smoke exists at the time it is [usually] accepted to exist—because nothing would lack with respect to its coming into existence; or, it would not exist, even at the time [it is usually accepted to exist], because there is no difference between that time and the time it is absent. For things, through their dependence on something else, are temporary, because the time of their existence is connected with an aptitude for their coming into existence and the time of their nonexistence is connected with an inaptitude for their coming into existence. For, should two place times be as apt as inapt [for something's coming into existence], either could possess it because there would be no possibility of restriction to either [its presence or its absence].

And what else is this aptitude than the existence of a cause? Therefore, a thing existing in one place and time to the exclusion of its existing in another is said to be dependent on the first. For in this way, to depend on something is just to exist in it to the exclusion of existing in others, because that which is independent of something's assistance cannot be restricted to it. Therefore, because smoke's nature is such that its place and time are restricted, smoke's nature must be produced by conditions such that, when they come to exist, smoke is observed at once and, when there is a deficiency among its conditions, smoke is no longer observed, because otherwise smoke's nature would not come into existence even that once. How could that which is restricted by those conditions come into existence elsewhere? Or, coming into existence elsewhere, it would not be smoke. For a specific nature, called smoke, is produced by them.

In the same way, a cause, too, has a nature to produce such an effect. If the effect were to arise from something else, too, then that other thing would not have the nature [to produce the effect of the first]. So, that thing would not produce the effect even once. Or, that other [cause's] effect would not be smoke, because smoke would have arisen from that whose nature does not produce smoke. And if something has the nature [to produce smoke], then that very thing is fire. So, there is no deviation.

If an anthill had the nature of fire, then it would be just fire. If it did not have the nature of fire, then how could smoke come into existence there? For fire, which has a distinct potentiality for smoke, has being its cause as its nature. If smoke were to come into existence from what is not the cause of smoke, then it would be without a cause. These are two summary verses.

How then now does an effect arise from distinct ancillary causes, as when there is the arising of awareness from a variety of ancillary causes such as eye and form? It is not at all the case that any single causal factor has a causal nature. Rather, the causal totality has a causal nature. It alone is inferred from the effect. The very same totality is the basis for its effect through the presence of its nature. For just this reason, there is production by the ancillary causes all at once.

Even if one calls by the same name all things seen coming into existence from distinct things, as water lilies coming into existence from cow dung and other things, because they indeed arise from their own seeds, they have distinct natures, because causes have distinct natures, as plantain trees arising both from seeds and bulbs. Clearly, an ordinary person distinguishes such distinct things because of the difference in their appearances. Therefore, an effect whose appearance is very well distinguished does not deviate from its cause. *That whose nature something is seen to conform to in the manner of concomitance and exclusion is its cause. Hence, there is no coming about from what is different.* This is a summary verse.

Therefore, because the relation between cause and effect is established by observation and nonobservation just once, the awareness of them [namely, concomitance and exclusion] comes into existence from it [namely, knowledge of the relation between cause and effect]. Not otherwise, because [ascertainment of] concomitance and exclusion requires complete observation and nonobservation [of all cases] [1] since, even though eternality is observed in some cases of immateriality, observation is otherwise in other cases, [2] since also what had not been observed [in the other cases, namely, in cases of materiality] is observed even in some cases of noneternality.

So, let it be that indispensability of effect with respect to cause is due to the former's arising from the latter.

Bibliography and Suggested Reading

Bochenski, I. M. (1970) *A History of Formal Logic* [Formale logik]. English translation by Ivo Thomas. 2nd ed. New York, NY: Chelsea Publishing Co.

Dreyfus, Georges. (1997) *Recognizing Reality: Dharmakīrti's Philosophy and Its Tibetan Interpreters.* Albany: State University of New York Press.

Dunne, John. (2004) *Foundations of Dharmakīrti's Philosophy.* Boston: Wisdom.

Ganeri, Jonardon, ed. (2001) *Indian Logic: A Reader.* Richmond, Surrey, United Kingdon: Curzon Press.

Gillon, Brendan S. (1991) "*Dharmakīrti* and the Problem of Induction." In Steinkellner 1991, 53–58.

Gillon, Brendan S., ed. (2008) *Logic in Earliest Classical India.* New Delhi: Motilal Banarsidass.

Gillon, Brendan S., and Richard P. Hayes. (2008) "Dharmakīrti on the Role of Causation in Inference as Presented in the *Pramāṇa-vārttika svopajñavṛtti* 11–38." *Journal of Indian Philosophy* 36: 335–404.

Gnoli, Raniero, ed. (1960) *The Pramāṇavārttikam of Dharmakīrti, the First Chapter with the Autocommentary, Text and Critical Notes.* Serie Orientale Roma, vol. 23. Rome: Istituto Italiano per il Medio ed Estremo Orient.

Hayes, Richard P., and Brendan S. Gillon. (1991) "Introduction to Dharmakīrti's Theory of Inference as Presented in the *Pramāṇa-vārttika svopajñavṛtti* 1–10." *Journal of Indian Philosophy* 19: 1–73.

Katsura, Shoryu. (1986) "On the Origin and Development of the Concept of *vyāpti* in Indian logic." *Hiroshima Tetsugakkai* 38: 1–16.

Randle, H. N. (1930) *Indian Logic in the Early Schools: A Study of the Nyāyadarśana in Its Relation to the Early Logic of Other Schools.* Oxford: Oxford University Press.

Solomon, Esther A. (1976) *Indian Dialectics: Methods of Philosophical Discussion.* 2 vols. Ahmedabad: B. J. Institute of Learning and Research.

Staal, J. F., ed. (1988) *Universals: Studies in Indian Logic and Linguistics.* Chicago: University of Chicago Press.

Steinkellner, Ernst. (1966) "Bemerkungen zu Īśvarasenas Lehre vom Grund." *Wiener Zeitschrift für die Kunde Südasiens* 10: 73–85.

Steinkellner, Ernst, ed. (1991) *Studies in the Buddhist Epistemological Tradition: Proceedings of the Second International Dharmakīrti Conference.* Vienna: Verlag der Osterreichischen Akademie der Wissenschaften.

Steinkellner, Ernst. (1993) "Buddhist Logic: The Search for Certainty." In Yoshinori 1993, 213—218.

Vidyabhusana, Satis Chandra. (1971) *A History of Indian Logic: Ancient, Medieval and Modern.* 1921. Reprint, Delhi: Motilal Banarsidass.

Yoshinori, Takeuchi, ed. (1993) *Buddhist Spirituality: Indian, Southeast Asian, Tibetan, and Early Chinese.* New York: Crossroad.

18

Yogācāra Theories of the Components of Perception

The *Buddhabhūmy-upadeśa*

Dan Lusthaus

What does the world look like through enlightened eyes? How, if at all, does perception for enlightened beings differ from the way nonenlightened beings perceive? These would seem to be natural questions, especially considering the prominent emphasis Buddhists place on such themes as mental purification, correcting cognitive errors, theories of perception, "seeing things as they are" (*yathā-bhūtam*), and so on. Thus it is surprising that detailed and specific discussions of how enlightened beings perceive almost never appear in Buddhist literature, aside from attributing vague, honorific adjectives to such cognitions, such as labeling them "transmundane" (*lokuttara*), pure, unobstructed, and so on. The section of the *Buddhabhūmy-upadeśa* translated here is a major exception.

Buddhabhūmy-upadeśa is a composite of (probably three) commentaries (*upadeśa*) on a *sūtra* called the *Buddha-bhūmi sūtra.*[1] *Bhūmi* can mean either "land," or "stage"; hence the title suggests both "Sūtra on the Buddha Land" *and* "Sūtra on the Stage of Buddhahood"; the contents of the *sūtra* fit both readings, and the preamble of *Buddhabhūmy-upadeśa* plays on both meanings, as if treating the title as a *double entendre.* The central concern of

1. *Fodijing,* T.16.680, translated by Xuanzang in 645. T refers to *Taishō shinshū daizōkyō.* [A standard collection of the East Asian Buddhist canon compiled in Japan] Takakusu Junjirō, Watanabe Kaikyoku, et al. (eds.), 100 vols. Tokyo: Taishō Issaikyō Kankōkai, 1924–1932.

the *Buddhabhūmi sūtra* is the "overturning of the basis" (*āśraya- parāvṛtti*) of the eight consciousnesses (*vijñāna*), so that they are transformed into the four cognitions (*jñānas*), also described as a purification of the consciousness stream and the manner of cognition from contaminated or polluted (*āsrava*) to uncontaminated (*anāsrava*). The eight consciousnesses are (1–5) the five sensory consciousnesses (seeing, hearing, smelling, tasting, and touching); (6) mental-consciousness (*manovijñāna*), which cognizes thoughts as well as takes cognizance of what the previous five consciousnesses sense; (7) *manas,* the sense of selfhood; and (8) the warehouse consciousness (*ālaya-vijñāna*), also called "all-seeds consciousness" (*sarva-bījāka-vijñāna*), "karmic maturation consciousness" (*vipāka-vijñāna*), and "foundational consciousness" (*mūla-vijñāna*), because it holds the contaminated and uncontaminated seeds, bringing them to karmic maturity and fruition.

When transformed, starting with the eighth, the warehouse consciousness becomes (1) the Great Mirror Cognition (*mahādarśa-jñāna*); *manas* becomes (2) Equalization Cognition (*samatā-jñāna*); mental-consciousness becomes (3) Attentive Cognition (*pratyavekṣanā-jñāna*); and the five sensory consciousnesses become (4) Accomplishing Activity Cognition (*kṛtyānuṣṭhāna-jñāna*). While the warehouse consciousness superimposes habitual tendencies into perception, the Great Mirror Cognition contains the images of all things, equally, without attachment. While *manas* views the world in terms of "me" and "others," valuing "myself" above "them," Equalization Cognition sees all as the same. Mental-consciousness is easily distracted, but Attentive Cognition remains effortlessly focused. The Accomplishing Activity Cognitions perceive things just as they are. When all contaminations and obstructions have been removed from the consciousnesses and the uncontaminated seeds reach fruition, the Four Cognitions replace the consciousnesses; that is enlightened perception.

The passage translated here is of great interest for several reasons:

1. It explicitly discusses two important texts by the Buddhist epistemologist and logician Dignāga (late fifth to mid-sixth century)—his *Pramāṇasamuccaya* and *Ālambana-parīkṣā*[2]—providing us with a rare glimpse of how some Buddhists were utilizing and interpreting those texts prior to Dharmakīrti (c. 600–665).
2. It attempts to explain how cognition works *after* overturning the basis.
3. It demonstrates that the Yogācāras of that time all presupposed some sort of correspondence theory—though they differed on the details. For each issue that is raised in this section, three distinct theories are offered,

2. A nearly obsolete translation of the first chapter of Dignāga's *Pramāṇasamuccaya* on perception (*pratyakṣa*) is Hattori 1968; a Sanskrit commentary by Jinendrabuddhi is being made available, which, once digested by scholars, should revolutionize Dignāga studies. A translation and study of *Ālambana-parīkṣā* is Tola and Dragonetti 1982, based on the Tibetan. No Sanskrit has been discovered, though Chinese versions, which vary from each other and the Tibetan, are available.

suggesting that Bandhuprabha, who compiled the commentaries, was working with three commentaries.

4. It responds directly to arguments given by Nāgārjuna (in his *Vigraha-vyāvartanī* and *Mūla-madhyamaka-kārikā*).[3] In both texts, Nāgārjuna argues that light neither illuminates itself nor others; in the former text he does so specifically to criticize means of knowledge (*pramāṇa*) as providing a validly known object (*prameya*). *Buddhabhūmy-upadeśa* argues that consciousness can make both itself and other objects known; that is, consciousness can be a cognitive object for itself.
5. It presents a unique theory partitioning consciousness into four components: (1) a content or image part (*nimitta-bhāga*); (2) a seeing part (*darśana-bhāga*); (3) a self-reflective or 'being aware of itself' part (*svasaṃvitti-bhāga*); and (4) a being aware that one is aware of oneself part (*svasaṃveda-saṃveda-bhāga*). While the theory of the fourth component disappears from India once Dharmakīrti provides a more sophisticated version of the first three components,[4] it became important in East Asian Buddhism, primarily due to its appearance here and in an expanded discussion in the *Cheng weishi-lun* (Treatise establishing consciousness only), a foundational text of the Weishi Chinese Yogācāra school.[5] A short excerpt from the *Cheng weishi-lun* is translated and included after the *Buddhabhūmy-upadeśa* passage here to illustrate some of the additions it offers.
6. It is a prime example of how commentarial style can utilize the declarative statements of a text such as the *Buddhabhūmi sūtra* to fashion a philosophical discussion. Where opposing theories are presented, each builds its case by interpreting the same key terms in its own way, illustrating that these terms were never univocal but always available for a variety of meanings.
7. It is the earliest text I know that addresses the issue of whether enlightened cognition is imageless (*nirākāra*) or involves images (*sākāra*). The *Buddhabhūmy-upadeśa* argues for the latter position. The *nirākāra-vāda* versus *sākāra-vāda* controversy became more prominent later on in India, and continued to be debated for centuries in Tibet.

After arguing that consciousness can know itself, *Buddhabhūmy-upadeśa* turns to the four components theory, attempting to show how consciousness can know itself without incurring an infinite regress. Finally it turns to the

3. A slightly abridged but generally reliable translation of *Vigrahavyavārtanī* is Bhattacharya 1986, which also contains the romanized Sanskrit text. A philosophically astute, annotated translation of *Mūla-madhyamaka-kārikā* made from the Tibetan version, not the Sanskrit, is Garfield 1995.

4. More precisely, Buddhists largely abandon it, but something comparable, using different terms, does appear later in some Hindu, especially Nyāya, formulations.

5. *Cheng weishilun* (T. 31.1585) is traditionally held to be a compendium of ten Indian commentaries on Vasubandhu's *Thirty Verses* (*Triṃśikā*), compiled and translated by Xuanzang in 659.

question of the status of the image that appears in consciousness. Three different theories are offered. Underlying all three is a theory of perception generally accepted in India and throughout the ancient and medieval world, called *prakāśa,* "illumination," in which a light is believed to go out from the eye and shine on an object (*bimba*), illuminating it, the reflection (*pratibimba*) bouncing back to the mind. For contaminated or unenlightened cognition, this also entails obstructions, attachments, imaginative distortions and overlays (*vikalpa, parikalpa*), and effort. A grasper (*grāhaka*) grasps or apprehends (*grāhaṇa, upalabdhi*) a "grasped" (*grāhya*); that is, ordinary perception is an act of appropriation, grasping. For uncontaminated cognition, the first theory says that the mind becomes a replica (*sādṛśya*) of whatever is in front of it, without imaginative construction (*nirvikalpa*), like a mirror effortlessly reflecting what is in front of it. This theory holds that uncontaminated cognition is similar to contaminated perception, except it is devoid of attachment and grasping. The second emphasizes that things are seen just as they are; it is not like a mirror that only receives reflections, or like a light going out in search of an object; the object itself is immediately known, without grasping or pursuing, such that cognition directly perceives sensory forms (*rūpa*) without obstruction. The third theory has the replica arise from the mind's uncontaminated seeds.

Indian Buddhists used a rich, nuanced vocabulary for aspects of cognition and types of cognitive objects, with fine distinctions that are often lost in translations that render a host of different terms reductively as either "subject" or "object." For instance, an *ālambana* (which I leave untranslated here) is a cognitive object from which mental impressions are derived. An *ākāra* is a mental image or mental impression drawn from the *ālambana.* A *viṣaya* is a sense object (a color, sound, etc.). *Nimitta* is a cognitive object whose characteristics cause a perception resembling it to arise. A *vastu* is an actual thing that may underlie a cognition, though whether it is perceived as it is or obstructed by imaginative constructions depends on the extent to which one's cognitive abilities are purified of contaminants.

The quality of the *Buddhabhumy-upadeśa*'s arguments are crude compared to later developments, but, as a comparison with Williams (1998) would demonstrate, the later tradition basically reworked and reiterated the arguments already found here, dropping the fourth component (the *svasaṃveda-saṃveda*) while refining and fine-tuning the rest.

The *Cheng weishilun* provides a similar description of the four components of perception, but adds a few additional wrinkles, one of which is to point out that all four components by and large reduce to the second. The passage from *Cheng weishilun* explaining that has been included here.

The *Buddhabhūmy-upadeśa* survives only in a Chinese translation made by Xuanzang in 649.[6] The Chinese *Buddhabhūmy-upadeśa* designates authorship only as "Bandhuprabha, etc.," with no information as to

6. *Fodijing lun,* T. 26.1530. Keenan 2002 is a translation of the complete text.

whom the "etc." refers. It presents conflicting opinions that were debated between different Indian Yogācāra thinkers on a variety of topics during the sixth to early seventh centuries. A Tibetan translation[7] of a commentary on the *Buddhabhūmi sūtra* that seems to correspond to a large extent with the core commentary contained in the *Buddhabhūmy-upadeśa* is attributed to Śīlabhadra, who was the head monk at Nālandā—the leading Buddhist university in the ancient world—when Xuanzang arrived there on his pilgrimage to India (c. 637). Roughly half of the Chinese *Buddhabhūmy-upadeśa* does *not* correspond to the Śīlabhadra commentary, and of that noncorresponding half, major portions reappear, almost verbatim, in the *Cheng weishilun*. Kuiji, Xuanzang's disciple and successor, in his commentaries on the *Cheng weishilun,* attributes some of these shared passages to Dharmapāla; hence some modern scholars have argued that the core commentary is by Śīlabhadra, while the rest, or most of it, is by Dharmapāla, an important sixth-century Yogācāra. Bandhuprabha, who probably compiled the three *Buddhabhūmi* commentaries, was a disciple of Śīlabhadra. Whether or not these are the actual authors of these commentaries, it is reasonable to assume that the positions discussed represent Yogācāra debates of the late sixth to early seventh centuries, a time when Dharmapāla, Śīlabhadra, and Bandhuprabha, were prominent.[8]

Translation: From the *Buddhabhūmy-upadeśa* (*Fodijing lun*)

[Dignāga's] *Pramāṇasamuccaya* says that all *citta* and *caittas* are aware of themselves; (this self-awareness) is called "perception" (*pratyakṣa*). If that were not the case, there would be no memory, [so that to perceive something would be] just as if [the thing] had never been seen.[9]

Hence each and every mental component associated with the Four Cognitions also illuminates (i.e., perceives)[10] and knows itself.

7. Peking edition of the Tibetan canon, no. 5298. The title of this text is usually Sanskritized as *Buddhabhūmi-vyākyāna.*

8. In the following translation, an asterisk before a reconstructed term indicates that the Sanskrit reconstruction from Chinese is unattested or involves some uncertainty.

9. This refers to *Pramāṇasamuccaya* 1:11. Dignāga's intent is still a matter of some discussion. The *Buddhabhūmy-upadeśa* seems to understand self-awareness (*svasaṃvitti*) at this point as something integral to perception, since, if one is not aware of perceiving something, there can be no memory of it in the form of "I remember X."

10. *Prakāśa,* Chin. *zhao;* both the Chinese and Sanskrit terms mean "to illuminate, to shine a light on, to make visible." This theory held that perception was not a passive reception by sensory organs of sensory data, but rather it entailed an active intentional probing of the environment by the sense organ. Vision, for instance, consisted of a light shining out *from* the eye, illuminating objects, which are thereby illumined and thus perceived.

[Objection:] Doesn't this contradict how the world works? A knife doesn't cut itself and a fingertip cannot touch that [same] fingertip.

[Reply:] Don't you see that lamps, etc., are able to illumine themselves?

[Objection:] How do you know that lamps, etc., illuminate themselves?

[Reply:] When in perception one sees the absence of darkness, the light, being separate [from darkness], is clearly perceived. If [the lamps, etc.] didn't illuminate themselves they would be obstructed by darkness, and so not seen in perception. Due to this, therefore, know that lamps, etc., illuminate themselves.[11]

[Objection:] Lamps, etc., are not dark. Is it necessary [that, in addition, they would have to further] illuminate [themselves]?

[Reply:] This is just like jars, cloth, etc. . Although in themselves they are not darkness, in the absence of a lamp, etc. to illuminate them, they are encompassed by the obstruction of darkness, so one cannot see them in perception. When lamps, etc. illuminate them, [the light] clears away that encompassing darkness, making [those things] visible to perception. We call that "illumination." Lamps, etc. are the same case. When their self-nature [to illuminate] arises, the encompassing obstruction of darkness is cleared away, making them visible to perception; therefore this is called "self-illumination."

Citta and *caittas,* regardless whether dominant or weak, are all able externally to [cognize] cognitive-conditions and internally to be aware of themselves (*svasaṃvitti*). This is analogous to light actually illuminating others as well as illuminating itself. It is unlike (i.e., not analogous to) such things as knives, etc., which are of a different sort.

Concerning the coarse characterization of *citta* and *caittas,* each is said to have two parts—an image part (*nimitta-bhāga*) and a seeing part (*darśana-bhāga*). In *Pramāṇasamuccaya* [Dignāga] explains that *citta* and *caittas* all have three parts: (1) a part that is grasped (*grāhya*), (2) a part that grasps (*grāhaka*), and (3) a part that is self-aware (*svasaṃvitti*). These three parts are neither the same nor different. The first is the known (*prameya*), the second is the knower (*pramāṇa*), and the third is the effect [of the act of] knowing (*pramāṇa-phala*).[12]

11. The arguments that follow are attempts to answer and refute Nāgārjuna's arguments in *Mūla-madhyamaka-kārikā* 7:8–12 and especially *Vigrahavyāvartanī* 31–51 that light does *not* illuminate itself or other things. The discussion in the text here echoes statements made there. The implicit argument that the Yogācāras seem to be making is that consciousness does indeed "illuminate" (*prakāśa*) itself as well as other things, but in order to do so, it must partition itself into a seer (*darśana*) and something seen (*ālambana*). Dharmakīrti and the subsequent tradition found such explanations—which require breaking consciousness itself into seeing and seen partitions—to be unsatisfactory for several reasons, the most important being the specter of an infinite regress that such portioning invites. The *Buddhabhumy-upadeśa* and *Cheng weishilun* are aware of this potential difficulty, and address it, but not to the satisfaction of the later Buddhist philosophers.

12. Dignāga discusses these three in a deliberate effort to (1) reduce the five parts that the Hindu Nyāya school held were involved in any proper cognition (agent,

If one makes finer distinctions, then there is a theory that establishes that [*cittas* and *caittas*] have four parts. Three parts are like the previous (three), to which it adds a fourth: being aware that one is aware (*svasaṃveda-saṃveda*). The first two are external [in terms of their cognitive object]; the latter two are internal [in that their cognitive objects are other parts of consciousness]. The first is only a "known"; the rest include two types [i.e., known and knower]. That is, the second part only knows the first. Sometimes this is a valid cognition (*pramāṇa*), sometimes an invalid cognition (*apramāṇa*); sometimes a perception (*pratyakṣa*), and sometimes an inference (*anumāna*). The third is aware of itself being aware of the second and it is aware of the fourth.[13] The fourth is aware of itself being aware of the third. The third and fourth are classified as valid perception (*pratyakṣa-pramāṇa*).

By this reasoning, although [cognition] is a single event, it is a composite of many parts that are neither identical nor separate. The inner and outer [components that constitute a cognition], being altogether known, there is no fallacy of an infinite regress.

Hence the (*Ghanavyūha*) sūtra says:

> The mind of sentient beings has two natures:
> Inner and outer; all parts
> grasped and grasper entangled;
> Seeing the plethora of differentiations.

The idea of this verse is that the nature of the mind of sentient beings is a composite of two parts. Whether [directed] internally or externally, all [cognitions are] intertwinings of grasped and grasper. [Particular acts of] seeing (*darśana*) the plethora (of perceptual objects) may be either valid or invalid. [One sees] the multitude of distinct differentiations either (directly via) perception or (indirectly via) inference.

---

object, instrument, action, and result) to only three parts, and (2) argue that despite the fact that the word *pramāṇa* grammatically indicates an instrument, that usage is only metaphoric for what is actually the consequence or result (*phala*) of the process of knowing, namely, coming to know the intended object (*artha*), so that "knowing" is actually *pramāṇa-phala*, the *effect* of the *pramāṇa* process. The "instrument" or means of knowledge is a secondary, conceptual abstraction; *pramāṇa*, therefore, properly speaking, refers to the *act* of knowing, *not the means*.

13. Apparently there was a controversy as to whether the third, the *svasaṃvitti*, had for its cognitive-object only the second *bhāga* (the *darśana-bhāga*) or whether it itself could serve as its own object, and whether the fourth *bhāga* (*svasaṃveda-saṃveda*) could serve as a cognitive-object for the third, or whether the fourth was necessary precisely to cognize and verify the third *bhāga*. To clarify, one theory held that the second cognized the first, i.e., a perceiver perceived an object. The third was the awareness that the second was engaged in such cognition, and the fourth was the verifying cognizer of the third. The text here expands the role of the third, the *svasaṃvitti*, allowing it to take (1) the *darśana-bhāga*, (2) the *svasaṃvitti* itself, and (3) the *svasaṃveda-saṃveda* as its cognitive objects. The *Cheng weishilun* provides a slightly different description, which appears hereafter.

The mental components of the Four Cognitions, even though they have many parts, are nonetheless all classified as uncontaminated valid perception (*anāsrava-pratyakṣa-pramāṇa*). This idea has been elaborated elsewhere. The idea is that while [cognition's] activities (Chin.: *yong*) are divided into many, [cognition] has no difference in itself (Chin.: *ti*). This is just like the one Dharma being differentiated into a plethora of ideas such as suffering, impermanence, etc., while [the Dharma] itself is one.

Next, as to what was said about the mental components associated with the Four Cognitions as having an image part, a seeing part, and so on, there definitely is a *seeing part* that illuminates (*prakāśa*) and a cognitive-object (*viṣaya*) that is illuminated. [That is obvious to everyone's experience.] There is a *self-aware part* that illuminates both the *seeing part* and the *being aware of being self-aware part,* since the being aware of being self-aware part illuminates the self-aware part [and validates it]. [The latter two parts] also definitely exist, since if they didn't exist, differentiated in this way into three parts, then there would be no cognitive-support (*ālambana*) and they wouldn't be called cognitions (*jñāna*).

The [status of] the image part is inconclusive. [There are three theories.]

There is a theory: Since there is no obstruction between real things (*tattvas*) and the uncontaminated mental components, [the components] directly/immediately illuminate the objects that are before them, without having to pursue them.[14] The mind turns itself into a replica of the image of the objects that are before it. The term "imageless" (*nirākāra*) refers to the uncontaminated mind, since it doesn't imagine (*nirvikalpa*), and "nonconceptual" (*acintya*) refers to the cognitive object (*ālambana-viṣaya*).

Another theory: [For the cognition of] real things (*tattvas*), uncontaminated mental components also have an image part. What are called the *ālambana* for [the uncontaminated] *citta* and *caittas* is the appearance of cognitive-objects that discloses them as *dharmatā* [i.e., just as they are]. This is not like pincers, etc., actively grasping things, nor is it like lamps, etc., whose light radiates to illuminate things.[15] [The cognition] is like a bright mirror, etc. perceiving the reflections of illuminated things.[16] The term "nonobstructed" [indicates] that the replicas[17] of the cognitive-objects in perception are clearly seen, illuminated, and discerned. The term "imageless" [indicates]

14. That is, *prakāśa* occurs without hindrance or obstruction.

15. Not only is the "appropriating" aspect of cognition absent ("not like pincers"), but the *prakāśa* theory is also being rejected ("not like a lamp...").

16. This could also be translated "in which the reflection of illuminated things appear."

17. The Chinese word *si,* which in the previous theory we took as *sādṛśya* (replica), here might also mean "replica," or it might be used as an equivalent for *ābhāsa* or *pratibhāsa* (appearance).

that [these mental components] neither attach to nor schematize [their objects]; and the term "nonconceptual" [indicates] the nondiscriminative [cognition] whose wondrous functioning is difficult to calculate. It is not that it doesn't perceive images (*pratibimba*). If one says there are no images (*ākāra*), then there is no image part (*nimitta-bhāga*). If one says there is no discriminating [of images], then there would be no seeing part [either]. If the image and seeing parts were both entirely nonexistent, then this would be like empty space (*ākāśa*), or [like proposing a nonsensical chimera] like "the horns of a rabbit"; [that sort of nonsense] shouldn't be called "cognition." The terms "images devoid of grasper and grasped, etc." [are used] because there is no attachment to or schematizing of [these images]; it is not that [this *citta*] lacks the function which illuminates intentional objects (*artha*), [mentally] replicating cognitive objects (*viṣaya*) from those cognitive conditions (*ālambana*). If uncontaminated *citta* was entirely devoid of an image part, then Buddhas wouldn't perceive bodies and fields, etc., nor [would they perceive] the plethora of images (**pratibimba*). That would contradict what the *sūtras* and *śāstras* say in many places.

If overturning the basis of the *rūpa-skandha* didn't attain[18] *rūpa*, then overturning the basis of the [other] four *skandhas* should [result in] being without consciousness, etc. [Thinking like that] would be to commit a great error.[19]

And another theory: The mental components associated with uncontaminated, nondiscriminative cognition [are to be explained as follows]. Because they are nonimaginative (*nirvikalpa*), the *ālambana* is [seen] just as it is (*tathatā*), since [seeing things exactly as they are means there are] no separate [imaginary images intermediating between the cognition and] the thing itself, just as when illuminating the self-nature (*svabhāva*) [of something] there is no separate image part. If [a cognition] has discriminations (*savikalpa*), the mental components are associating with postattainment cognition (*pṛṣṭhalabdha-jñāna* [20]) [and not *nirvikalpa cognition*]. Since *ālambanas* and

18. *Adhigata:* found, obtained, acquired; gone over, studied, learnt.

19. This passage leaves no doubt that the second theory is not only rationalist (antichimeric formulations) but unabashedly realist as well. It is probably worth noting, as well, that the *Buddhabhūmy-upadeśa* demonstrates that at that time there was no fixed doctrine of *āśraya-parāvṛtti* ("overturning the basis" from which one cognizes, changing from contaminated to uncontaminated cognition), but a number of competing notions.

20. *Pṛṣṭhalabdha-jñāna* are the types of cognitions (*jñāna*) an enlightened being has subsequent (*pṛṣtha*) to attaining (*labdha*) Awakening, which, according to some theories, may be qualitatively different from the immediate seeing of things as they are as one would *during* the experience of Awakening. This theory uses this distinction to account for how Buddhas, etc., can still make necessary distinctions, engage in the conventional world, and experience the plethora of things that appear in the image part (*nimitta-bhāga*) without undermining the fact that, in some sense, Buddhas, etc., have transcended the cognitive obstructions (*jñeyāvaraṇa*) that usually limit cognition to only seeing the world that way.

cognitive-objects (**viṣaya-gocara*) sometimes are separate from the things themselves, [in such cases this is] just like when a contaminated mind perceives a replica of the image of a cognitive object by clearly seeing (**vispaṣṭa*) and illuminating the *ālambana*.

[Objection:] If an uncontaminated mind takes as its *ālambana* [something that] is separate from the object itself, [it could happen that] it has no resemblance to the image of that [object] and yet one apprehends an *ālambana*.[21] [That would be a problematic cognition, not the type of *jñāna* being extolled.]

[Reply:] [According to Dignāga's] *Ālambana-parīkṣā* one shouldn't say that because the image of atoms does not appear in the five consciousnesses that therefore there is no *ālambana* (at all). In this way, the image of the cognitive-object is identical to the uncontaminated mind.[22] Uncontaminated seeds arise. Even though they resemble contaminated *dharmas*, nonetheless they are not contaminated, just as a contaminated mind may [have cognitions that] resemble an uncontaminated image, though they are not uncontaminated.

This ends the elaboration.

Such distinctions (*vikalpa*) are only from the conventional point of view, as explained logically. They are not from the [perspective] of ultimate meaning; the ultimate meaning is apart from words and deliberation. From the perspective of the imageless (*nirākāra-dṛṣṭi*) one already is incapable of speaking of *citta, caittas*, and so on.[23] It is beyond fictional-proliferation (*prapañca*) and incapable of being conceptualized (*acintya*).

21. This would be an absurdity according to Dignāga's definition of an *ālambana* in his *Ālambana-parīkṣā*. According to Dignāga, an *ālambana* must satisfy two criteria: (1) it must cause a cognition, and (2) it must convey its own image to the cognition. The objection raised here is that it would fail the second criterion.

22. As I understand this third theory, it is not claiming that there is no object, and only mental production—which would make this type of cognition *parikalpita* (false imagining), and not *pariniṣpanna* (consummate comprehension)—but rather that all cognitive distance, all "obstructions," etc., have been eliminated so that objects appear directly and immediately just as they are. The *ālambana* needn't convey an image from the object to the mind, since the mind automatically and instantaneously gives rise to an impression of the object that is exact and accurate in every detail. No middle man or mediating process between mind and object is required. One sees things just as they are because the mind has ceased to impose imaginary constructions. One's own mental seeds—since they are now no longer contaminated by distorting hindrances—are always already identical to the object in itself.

23. This final tag is crucial. It is not extolling an ineffable reality, but making clear that the basic components of Yogācāra doctrine, such as mind (*citta*), mental associates (*caittas*), etc., are all only *vyavahāra*, conventional descriptive terms, not the names of ultimate realities, much less anything absolute.

Translation: From *Cheng weishilum*

Sometimes the seeing part is not classified as a *pramāṇa* [i.e., it sometimes has erroneous cognitions].[24] Due to this, the seeing part doesn't "verify" (or isn't aware of) the third, since to verify itself it would necessarily have to perceive [itself]. Of these four components, the first two are external, and the latter two are internal.[25] The first is only an *ālambana;* the other three are both (*ālambana* and *ālambaka,* i.e., perceiver and perceived).[26]

That is, the second part has only the first for its *ālambana.* Sometimes it is a valid cognition (*pramāṇa*), and sometimes an invalid cognition (*apramāṇa*). Sometimes [it cognizes its *ālambana*] by perception (*pratyakṣa*), and sometimes by inference (*anumāna*).[27]

The third takes the second and fourth as its *ālambana* [i.e., the *darśana* and *svasaṃveda-saṃveda* are the *ālambana* for the *sva-saṃveda*]. The *svasaṃveda-saṃveda* only has the third as its *ālambana,* but not the second, since it lacks that function.

The third and fourth are both classified as "valid perception" (*pratyakṣa-pramāṇa*).

Thus, *citta* and *caittas* are established to consist of these four parts. [Since this is the] full [account of the relation between] *ālambaka* and *ālambana,* there is no fallacy of infinite regress. Neither the same nor different, they are established by reason to be consciousness only (*vijñapti-mātra*).

This is why a *gathā* in the [*Ghanavyūha*] *Sūtra* says:

> The mind of sentient beings has two natures:
> Inner and outer; all parts
> grasped and grasper entangled;
> Seeing the plethora of differentiations.

What this verse intends to say is that the nature of the mind of sentient beings is a composite of two parts. Whether [directed] internally or externally, all [cognitions are] intertwinings of grasped and grasper. Seeing (*darśana, dṛśya*) has many types. Sometimes [seeing] is valid knowledge (*pramāṇa*), and sometimes invalid knowledge (*apramāṇa*). Sometimes [it cognizes its *ālambana*] by perception (*pratyakṣa*) and sometimes by inference (*anumāna*). It differentiates into many parts. Among these, "seeing" is the *darśana-bhāga* (seeing part).

24. The segment translated here is *Cheng weishilun* T. 31.1585.10b23–10c12.

25. The *nimitta* are the objects in the perceptual field. *Darśana* "sees" (i.e., perceives) them, so its intent is outward toward the *nimittas. Svasaṃveda* and *svasaṃveda-saṃveda* are reflexive, observing oneself cognizing.

26. *Ālambaka* is that which "takes an *ālambana,*" i.e., a perceiver of an *ālambana.*

27. Perception and inference are the two valid means of knowledge (*pramāṇa*) accepted by Dignāga and subsequent Buddhists.

[Reducing the number of *bhāgas*]

In this way, the four parts may be grouped as three, since the fourth category gets included in the *svasaṃveda* part. Or they may be grouped as two, since the nature of the last three is to be a cognizer (*ālambaka*). So all (three) are classified as *darśana-bhāga*. The meaning (*artha*) of the word "seeing" (*darśana*) is "cognizer" (*ālambaka*).

Or they may be grouped as one, since there is no separation between them.

As a *gathā* in the *Laṅkāvatāra sūtra* says:

> Due to attachment to one's own mind (*svacittābhiniveśa*),
> The mind appears (*nirbhāsa*) as the operation of external things (*bāhya-bhāva*).
> That which is seen (*dṛśya*) does not exist.
> Therefore we say it is only mind (*citta-mātra*).

In this way, in every place and situation, we say there is only a single mental event (*ekacitta-mātra*). This term "single mental event" also includes the *caittas*. Hence, the defining activity (*ākāra*) of consciousness (*vijñāna*) precisely is discerning (*vijñapti*). Discerning is precisely the seeing part (*darśana-bhāga*) of consciousness.

Bibliography and Suggested Reading

Bhattacharya, Kamaleswar, E. H. Johnston, and Arnold Kunst, Editors and Translators. (1986) *The Dialectical Method of Nāgārjuna: "Vigrahavyavārtanī."* Delhi: Motilal Banarsidass.

Cook, Francis H. trans. (1999) *Three Texts on Consciousness Only.* Berkeley: Numata Center.

Garfield, Jay L. . (1995) *The Fundamental Wisdom of the Middle Way: Nāgārjuna's "Mūlamadhyamakakārikā."* Oxford: Oxford University Press.

Hattori, Masaaki. (1968) *On Perception: Being the "Pratyakṣapariccheda" of Dignāga's "Pramāṇasamuccaya."* Cambridge, Mass.: Harvard University Press.

Kapstein, Matthew. (2000) "We Are All Gzhan stong pas: Reflections on the *The Reflexive Nature of Awareness: A Tibetan Madhyamaka Defence.*" *Journal of Buddhist Ethics* 7: 105–125.

Keenan, John. (1980) "A Study of the Buddhabhūmy-upadeśa: The Doctrinal Development of the Notion of Wisdom in Yogācāra Thought." Ph.D. diss., University of Wisconsin.

Keenan, John. (2002) *The Interpretation of the Buddha Land.* Berkeley: Numata Center.

Lusthaus, Dan. (2002) *Buddhist Phenomenology: A Philosophical Investigation of Yogācāra Buddhism and the "Ch'eng wei-shih lun."* London: RoutledgeCurzon.

Tat, Wei, trans. (1973) *Ch'eng Wei-shih lun: Doctrine of Mere-Consciousness.* Hong Kong: The Ch'eng Wei-shi lun Publication Committee.
Tola, Fernando, and Carmen Dragonetti. (1982) "Dignāga's Ālambana parīkṣāvṛtti." *Journal of Indian Philosophy* 10/2: 105–134.
Williams, Paul. (1998) *The Reflexive Nature of Awareness: A Tibetan Madhyamaka Defence.* Richmond, Surrey, England: Curzon Press.

19

Classification of Nonauthoritative Cognitive Processes (*tshad min*) in the Ngog and Sakya Traditions

Leonard W. J. van der Kuijp

When Buddhism came to Tibet in the eighth century, Tibetan Buddhist philosophers continued the epistemological programs of Dignāga (sixth century) and Dharmakīrti (seventh century). Dharmakīrti's *Pramāṇavārttika* and his later *Pramāṇaviniścaya* attracted particular exegetical and philosophical attention. The great translator Ngog Lotsawa Loden sherab (Rngog Lo tsā ba Blo ldan shes rab) (1059?–1109?), was among the first Tibetan philosophers fully to come to terms with Dharmakīrti's writings and a good number of his major Indian commentaries, especially those by Dharmottara (c. 740–800) and Prajñākaragupta (c. 800). Ngog Lotsawa, then, became the fountainhead of subsequent Tibetan studies in Buddhist logic and epistemology. Nearly a century later, a major sea change occurred with the advent of the 1219 *Tsema rigpay ter* (*Tshad ma rigs pa'i gter*), *Treasury of Epistemic Reasoning*, and autocommentary, of Sakya Paṇḍita Künga gyeltsen (Sa skya Paṇḍita Kun dga' rgyal mtshan) (1182–1251). Written in reaction to the exegetical traditions rooted in Ngog Lotsawa's contributions, this work gave rise to a vast commentarial literature. The Ngog tradition philosophers were mainly interested in Dharmakīrti's *Pramāṇaviniścaya*, in contrast to the Sakya philosophers, who were primarily focused on the *Pramāṇavārttika*. Sakya Paṇḍita's *Treasury of Epistemic Reasoning*—with some two dozen commentaries, making it one of the most frequently commented-on Tibetan treatises—was the result of his disaffiliation from the Ngog tradition's interpretations of Dignāga and Dharmakīrti and his intention to let their texts speak for themselves with a minimum of theoretical interference.

Tibetan Buddhist epistemologists were concerned to distinguish between nonauthoritative (*tsema mayin, tshad ma ma yin pa* or *tsemin, tshad min*) and authoritative (*tsema, tshad ma*) means of cognitive access to the external world and our own inner states. That is, they were interested in distinguishing those means that *result* in unjustified or false belief and those that lead to genuine knowledge. They took Dharmakīrti's *Pramāṇavārttika* to provide the definitive account of knowledge, according to which there are two definitions of authoritative cognition: it provides nondeceptive (*milu wa, mi bslu ba*) access and new awareness (*sar, gsar*). Tibetan commentators, following their Indian predecessors, recognized that these definitions were not obviously coreferential. Both of these were grounded in a thoroughgoing pragmatism, anchoring knowledge to an individual's successful activity.

The Ngog tradition distinguishes seven epistemic categories. The first five of these seven are the nonauthoritative and the last two the authoritative means of cognitive access. Ngog Lotsawa lists the nonauthoritative states in the following order:[1]

1. Nonascertainment of what is apparently present (*nangla ma ngepa, snang la ma nges pa*)
2. Determinative cognition (*cepay yülcen, bcad pa'i yul can* [i.e., *ceshay, bcad shes*])
3. Erroneous cognition (*logpay shepa, log pa'i shes pa* [i.e., *logshe, log shes*])
4. Supposition (*yeece, yid dpyad*) [read: *cö, dpyod*]
5. Doubt (*tetsom, the tshom*)

But he concludes:

> the first two are instances of noncognition (*matogpa, ma rtogs pa*); the middle two are instances of misconception (*logpar togpa, log par rtog pa*); the last is doubt.

He thus disagrees with Dharmottara, who, he says, argued that

> Doubt is included in the category of an erroneous cognition, because it is an apprehension of the nature of both a thing and the absence of a thing. And since also the three kinds of supposition—without a reason, with a wrong reason, and with a real but unsettled reason—were included in the essence of doubt, they are forms of an erroneous cognition.[2]

Ngog argues that this is wrong, "because doubt has not fully determined the nature of both," that is, whether something is or is not the case.

1. The order in which they are enumerated shows some variation, which may very well be based on the differences in their interrelationships that were isolated by different philosophers.
2. It is not known whether or where Dharmottara says this.

The origin of this classification of nonauthoritative cognition is uncertain, and the first, second and fourth of his listing are probably Tibetan, rather than Indian, in origin. The first two and the fourth of this pentad are rejected by Sakya Paṇḍita in the second chapter of the *Treasury of Epistemic Reasoning* on philosophical grounds. He argues that the correct classification of such states is the following triad:[3]

1. Noncognition
2. Misconception
3. Doubt

An important commentator on the *Treasury*'s autocommentary, Lowo Kenchen Sonam lundrub (Glo bo Mkhan chen Bsod nams lhun grub) (1456–1532), sums up the results of Sakya Paṇḍita's critique of these in his work of 1482. He writes in a summarizing verse:[4]

> Supposition is not different from doubt.
> The nonascertainment of what is apparently present involves all forms of sensation.
> Because a determinative cognition qua a nonauthoritative means
> of knowledge
> is a noncognition,
> There are no subdivisions and other enumerations.

Problems with this and related issues are many, and things do get complicated when we bear in mind that much of the dispute regarding this matter hinges on a complex network of interrelated views on ontology, sensation, inference and concept formation, to name but a few. It is therefore difficult to determine the degree to which this dispute is purely epistemological, as opposed to being grounded in ontological differences.[5]

Translation: Sakya Paṇḍita on the Nonauthoritative Means of Knowledge

...as for my own position, three rubrics:

1. The general defining characteristic of the nonauthoritative means of cognition.
2. The typological summary of the number of the nonauthoritative means of cognition.
3. An exposition of each of the nonauthoritative means of cognition [not translated].

3. Sakya Paṇḍita Künga gyeltsen 2005: 78–81.
4. Lowo Kenchen Sonam lundrub 1988: 67.
5. The following translation is my own, from Sakya Paṇḍita Künga gyeltsen 2005: 78–79.

The first,

> An unestablished infallibility is a nonauthoritative means of knowledge.[6]

The defining characteristic of the nonauthoritative means of knowledge is the so-called cognition where infallibility is not established; there is no error, just as when a dewlap is denied for indicating what is not a cow.[7]

Second, the typological summary of the number of the nonauthoritative means of knowledge:

Noncognition, misconception, and doubt:
The threefold contraries of the authoritative means of knowledge
Were distinguished on account of the way in which they engage [the object].
Were these three consolidated in view of their essence, there is one single nonauthoritative cognitive process.

The three cognitions that are such nonauthoritative means of knowledge and the three faults of a logical argument have the same core of reasoning; as has been stated:[8]

> As for the thesis of an inference, one proves the certainty of the argument being without force, indecisive, what is not desired, and what is desired.[9]

Just as what is to be proved by an inference has no force due to the grounding superstratum being unestablished, so noncognition, too, has no force

6. That is to say, what is not infallible is not an authoritative means of knowledge.

7. Sakya Paṇḍita discusses the relationship between the definiens, the definiendum, and the definitional instance or illustration in the eighth chapter of the *Treasury of Epistemic Reasoning*. This functions as a prolegomenon to ascertaining the relationship between the various definitions of authoritative knowledge and authoritative knowledge as such. Sakya Paṇḍita Künga gyeltsen (2005: 198 uses a stock example that he inherited from philosophers of the Ngog tradition. Thus, when the definiens is the dewlap, the definiendum is the [Indian] cow. The absence of a dewlap therefore implies the absence of a cow. Hence, when a cognitive process is deceptive, it is nonauthoritative. Remember that the primary definiens of authoritative knowledge is that it is nondeceptive.

8. I have not been able to identify the origin of this half verse, although some commentators suggest that it is found in Dignāga's *Pramāṇasamuccaya;* it is not. It is also quoted in Sakya Paṇḍita Künga gyeltsen 2005: 358, where it is attributed to "the crown jewel of intellectuals."

9. The first three of these four—without force, indecisive, and what is not desired—refer to the three kinds of fallacious logical reasons or grounding superstrata, that is: unestablished (*asiddha*), uncertain (*anaikāntika*), and contradictory (*viruddha*). The fourth one is a valid logical reason.

wherever the mind engages an object. Just as uncertainty brings about indecision as to whether something is or is not X, so also doubt makes one apprehensive about extreme positions other than what is physically present. Just as a contradiction establishes what is undesirable, so also misconception makes one cognize what is not the case. Just as an authoritative argument establishes the desired objective, so the authoritative means of knowledge, too, cognize the object. Hence, on setting forth an argument, other alternatives than the aforementioned four are not possible. And just as, since one [of the four] has no fault, it is not possible to have more than three faults, because one is the authoritative means of knowledge, it is not possible to have more than four ways in which the mind is constituted.

Were we to consolidate these on account of their essence, then, since both misconception and doubt are simply forms of noncognition, the nonauthoritative means of knowledge are consolidated into one cognition that is not an authoritative means of knowledge. This is just like when Dharmakīrti stated that both authoritative means of knowledge are consolidated into immediate self-awareness and also the two objects of the two authoritative means of knowledge are consolidated into the epistemic object, the unique particular.[10] The Tibetans, having cast yonder the epistemology of noncognition, the principal one of the nonauthoritative means of knowledge, have but meaninglessly divided the nonauthoritative means of knowledge into five.

Bibliography and Suggested Reading

Jackson, David. (1987) *The Entrance Gate for the Wise (Section III): Sa skya Paṇḍita on Indian and Tibetan Traditions of Pramāṇa and Philosophical Debate.* Vienna: Arbeitskreis für Tibetische und Buddhistische Studien.

Krasser, Helmut. (1997) "Rngog Lo tsā ba on the *Sahopalambhaniyama* Proof in Dharmakīrti's *Pramāṇaviniścaya.*" *Studia Indologiczne* [Aspects of Buddhism] 4: 63–87.

Lowo Kenchen Sonam lundrub. (1988) *Tshad ma rigs gter gyi 'grel pa'i rnam bshad rigs lam gsal byed.* Beijing: Krung go'i bod kyi shes rig dpe skrun khang.

Sakya Paṇḍita Künga gyeltsen. (2005) *Rigs gter rtsa 'grel dpe bsdur ma.* Edited by Dpal brtsegs bod yig dpe rnying zhib 'jug khang. Chengdu, People's Republic of China : Si khron dpe skrun tshogs pa/Si khron mi rigs dpe skrun khang.

van der Kuijp, Leonard W. J. (1983) *Contributions to the Development of Tibetan Buddhist Epistemology from the Eleventh to the Thirteenth Century.* Wiesbaden: Franz Steiner.

10. For the latter, see *Pramāṇavārttika* 3:53d–54b.

van der Kuijp, Leonard W. J. (1993) "Apropos of Some Recently Discovered Manuscripts Anent Sa skya Paṇḍita's *Tshad ma rigs pa'i gter* and Autocommentary." *Berliner Indologische Studien* 7: 149–162.
van der Kuijp, Leonard W. J. (2003) "A Treatise on Buddhist Epistemology and Logic Attributed to Klong chen Rab 'byams pa and Its Place in Indo-Tibetan Intellectual History." *Journal of Indian Philosophy* 31: 381–437.

20

Understanding the Two Truths

Tsongkhapa's *Ocean of Reasoning: A Great Commentary on Nāgārjuna's "Mūlamadhyamakakārikā"*

Jay L. Garfield

Tsongkhapa (1357–1419) is without a doubt the most influential philosopher in Tibet's rich philosophical history. His extensive corpus includes commentaries on important Indian philosophical texts (including the text from which this selection is drawn), an encyclopedic treatise on the Buddhist path to awakening, a text on tantra, and one on Buddhist hermeneutics. Tsongkhapa founded the Gelukpa (dGe lugs pa) school of Tibetan Buddhism and its first principal monastic university, Ganden (dGa ldan), and established the monastic curriculum in which so many important, subsequent Tibetan philosophers were educated.

Tsongkhapa was largely responsible for raising the salience of Candrakīrti's interpretation of Nāgārjuna's Madhyamaka philosophy in Tibet, as well as for stimulating interest in the epistemology of Dignāga and Dharmakīrti. A central theme in Tsongkhapa's work, in evidence here, is the vindication of a robust sense of reality about conventional truth, as opposed to a view that the ordinary world is merely illusory and best ignored. Tsongkhapa believed that good metaphysics, good epistemology, and good ethics require one to take the world of ordinary experience seriously. He also believed that the distinction between the two truths is at bottom an epistemological distinction, and hence that understanding the nature of knowledge is fundamental to understanding metaphysics.

The text from which this selection is drawn is the latest canonical commentary on Nāgārjuna's *Mūlmadhyamakakārikā* (Fundamental verses on the Middle Way). In this text, Tsongkhapa surveys the major Indian commentaries (those of Buddhapālita, Bhāvaviveka, Avalokitavrata, and Candrakīrti) and takes note of previous Tibetan literature on the text, providing a grand meta-commentary on that literature, in which he defends Candrakīrti's reading. The commentary on each verse is often extensive, surveying not only previous commentarial literature but also relevant *sūtra* literature, and more general philosophical issues as well. As such, it is a fine example of Buddhist scholastic commentarial work.

This selection is a commentary on verse 24:8, in which Nāgārjuna asserts that Buddhist philosophy is based on the two truths—the conventional truth and the ultimate truth. In these sections of the commentary, Tsongkhapa is explaining that distinction, and arguing that it must be drawn on epistemological grounds.

The first section of this passage (1.2.1.1.1.2.1.1) glosses the terms "conventional" and "ultimate." This follows Candrakīrti's account in his commentary *Prasannapadā* (Lucid exposition). The subsequent sections follow Candrakīrti's commentary, as well as his *Madhyamakāvatāra* (Introduction to the Middle Way) and its autocommentary very closely, with extensive quotation from each, as is typical in this kind of commentarial literature. Tsongkhapa argues that conventional truth is reality as it is seen by ordinary cognitive agents, impaired by confusion with regard to the fundamental nature of reality. Despite this fundamental metaphysical confusion, Tsongkhapa argues, our epistemic and linguistic conventions allow us to distinguish truth from falsity within the conventional in a stable way, and to distinguish justificatory from nonjustificatory conventional epistemic practices. Otherwise, he points out, we could never come to understand ultimate truth.

While Tsongkhapa argues that the conventional and the ultimate represent the two distinct natures of every phenomenon, and so that this is a metaphysical distinction, he also argues that the basis of the distinction is epistemological: To be the conventional nature is just to be the nature apprehended by a conventional cognitive agent; to be the ultimate nature is to be that apprehended by an awakened being.

In the section on the classifications of conventional truth, Tsongkhapa turns to the task of spelling out the difference between conventional error and correctness, and the source of epistemic standards internal to the conventional world. He points out that conventional phenomena are deceptive not because they appear to be real but are not, but because they appear to be ultimately real, but are not. The discussion of ultimate truth emphasizes that ultimate truth, on the other hand, is nondeceptive.

This discussion is instructive for several reasons. First, it provides the reader, especially if read in the context of the *Kaccayana-gotta-sūtra* and the selection from *Mūlamadhyamakakārikā* presented in chapter 2 of this volume, with an excellent example of the way Buddhist philosophy develops through the practice of commentary. Second, it demonstrates just how Buddhist metaphysics and soteriology demand careful attention to epistemology.

Finally, it presents a sophisticated account of the way the practice of justification is possible even in the context of prevalent error and so grounds the possibility of epistemic progress toward awakening in a Buddhist context that presupposes that we are profoundly deluded.[1]

Translation

1.2.1.1.1.2.1. The Nature of the Two Truths That Is Not Understood

This section has two parts: the explanation of the literal meaning of the root text and showing that one must ascertain the meaning as it is explained in the *Commentary*.

1.2.1.1.1.2.1.1. Explanation of the Literal Meaning of the Root Text

Suppose someone asked, "Who is it that argues without understanding the purpose of emptiness as explained by the *mādhyamika?*"

> 8. The Buddha's teaching of the Dharma
> Is based on two truths:
> A truth of worldly convention,
> And an ultimate truth.

Those who present the above arguments are adherents of our own schools. They are merely interested in reciting the scriptures but do not have a nonerroneous understanding of the distinction between the two truths as it is explained in the scriptures. Therefore, the noble Nāgārjuna, in order to dispel others' misunderstandings of the meaning of the scriptures, and in order to set out nonerroneously the presentation of the two truths in the scriptures, says that the Dharma taught by the transcendent Buddhas is based entirely on the two truths: a truth of worldly convention and an ultimate truth.

Here, "world" refers to the person that is designated on the basis of the aggregates. This is because, as it is said,

> The world is dependent on
> That world that is known as the aggregates.[2]

1. The translation that follows was originally published in Tsongkhapa 2006, pp. 479–489. We gratefully acknowledge permission to republish this work.

2. This and the following citations refer to the sDe dge edition of the Tibetan canon. *Brahmaviśeṣccintiparipṛcchā-sūtra, mDo sde* ba, 36b.

Thus it is said that that which depends on the transitory aggregates is the world.[3]

"Convention" refers to lack of understanding, or ignorance; that is, that which obscures or conceals the way things really are.[4] This is explained in this way as the Sanskrit term for "convention," *saṁvṛti,* can mean *concealment* as well. But not *all* conventions are said to be concealers.

Alternatively, "convention" can be taken to mean *mutually dependent.* Since things must be mutually dependent, the meaning of "untrue" is that they do not essentially have the ability to stand on their own. This approach to explaining the meaning of the word is applicable to "ultimate truth" as well, but the word "conventional" is not used to refer to it. This is like, for example, the word "grown-from-the-lake," which is literally applicable to a frog but is not used to refer to a frog.[5]

Alternatively, "convention" can be taken to mean *signifier,* that is, mundane nominal convention. Convention in this sense is also said to be characterized by expressions and the objects of expressions, awareness and objects of awareness, and so on. Therefore, "subjective convention" does not refer merely to expressions or to awareness.

Suppose one asked, "Does not the use of 'mundane' in the expression 'mundane convention' mean that there is convention that is not mundane?" Here the word "mundane" is not used to exclude some nonmundane convention. It just expresses the way things exist. In other words, those whose perceptions are erroneous because of deterioration of the sense faculties due to such things as cataracts, growths on the eye, or jaundice do not constitute the world from the perspective of which things are regarded as conventionally real. Therefore, those perceptual objects affected by sense faculties that are affected by such things as cataracts are not regarded as real according to mundane convention. Therefore, in order to distinguish it from these, the word "truth" is qualified in the expression "mundane conventional truth."

Since it is a *fact* and it is *supreme,* it is called the ultimate.[6] It is true because it is not deceptive from the perspective of those who perceive things as they really are.

3. In Tibetan there is a close lexical relationship between the phrases "depending on the transitory aggregates" (*'jig pa phung po la brten pa*), and "world" (*'jig rten*). In Sanskrit as well, *loka* (world) has as its root *luj,* which means to disintegrate. Tsongkhapa is referring to these lexical relationships.

4. The word translated here as "convention," *kun rdzob,* translates *saṁvṛti,* which has two principal meanings: *convention* in all of the senses common in English, as well as *concealment,* or *covering over.* Tsongkhapa is associating these meanings, and pointing out that convention conceals or covers the nature of things.

5. "Grown from the lake" (*mtsho skyes*) is a term for the lotus.

6. "Ultimate" translates *don dam. Don* means *fact* and *dam* means supreme, so lexically, "ultimate" in Tibetan is a compound of *supreme fact.* The same etymology is present in the Sanskrit *paramārtha.*

1.2.1.1.1.2.1.2. Showing That One Must Ascertain the Meaning as It Is Explained in the *Commentary*

As *Prasannapadā* says here [163b], the details of the two truths can be understood through the presentation in *Madhyamakāvatāra*. A brief presentation follows. Objects of knowledge are the basis of division of the two truths. The conventional truth and the ultimate truth are the entities that are the divisions of objects of knowledge. In order to understand these divisions, three topics must be addressed: conventional truth, the explanation of ultimate truth, and the presentation of the enumeration of the two truths.

1.2.1.1.1.2.1.2.1. Conventional Truth

This section has three parts: the explanation of the etymologies of "conventional" and "truth," the characteristic of conventional truth, and the classifications of conventional truth.

1.2.1.1.1.2.1.2.1.1. Explanation of the Etymologies of "Conventional" and "Truth"

Suppose someone asks, "What is convention and what is truth?" The convention from the perspective of which such things as form are posited as true is the ignorance that fabricates the essential existence of phenomena that do not inherently exist. This is because since it is not possible for things to truly exist, it is only from the perspective of mind that things can be posited as truly existent; and from the perspective of the mind that does not grasp things as truly existent nothing is posited as truly existent. Thus *Madhyamakāvatāra* says,

> Since the nature of confusion is to veil, it is obscurational.[7]
> That which is created by it appears to be truly existent.
> The sage has said that that is the obscurational truth.
> Created phenomena are obscurational. [6:28]

Here *Madhyamakāvatāra-bhāṣya* says,

> Obscurational truth is posited due to the force of afflictive ignorance, which constitutes the limbs of cyclic existence. The *śrāvakas*, *pratyekabuddhas*, and bodhisattvas, who have abandoned afflictive ignorance,

7. Candrakīrti (and Tsongkhapa) is (are) glossing the Sanskrit term *saṁvṛti* and the common Tibetan translation *kun rdzob*. The Sanskrit has a wide range of lexical meaning, including *ordinary, everyday, nominal,* and *by agreement*, but also *concealed, occluded, covered.* The Tibetan *kun rdzob,* though it also covers all of these senses, has as its primary lexical connotation *disguised.* Here Candrakīrti is explaining that the conventional obscures its ultimate nature. I will usually translate *kun rdzob* as *conventional* except when this connotation is essential, in which case I will use obscurational.

> see compounded phenomena, to be like reflections, to have the nature of being created; but these are not truths for them because they are not fixated on things as true. Fools are deceived, but for those others—just like an illusion—in virtue of being dependently originated, they are merely obscurational.[8]

This does not demonstrate that those who posit the existence of obscurational truth posit through ignorance, nor that from the perspective of the *śrāvakas, pratyekabuddhas,* and bodhisattvas, who have abandoned afflictive ignorance, it is not posited as conventional truth. The reason for the first is that, as has been previously explained, since it is through afflictive ignorance that one grasps things as truly existent, the object that is thereby grasped cannot possibly exist even conventionally, and whatever is an obscurational truth must exist conventionally. Thus, the obscuration on the basis of which phenomena are posited as obscurationally existent cannot be the obscuration that is regarded as afflictive ignorance.

The reason for the second is that for those who have abandoned the obscuration of afflictive ignorance—because of the absence of that obscuration in virtue of which they take things as real, from the perspective in which things are posited as truly existent—compounded phenomena are established as not being truths from their perspective, but it is not established that they are not obscurational truths. Thus, when it is said that compounded phenomena are merely obscurational from their perspective, the word "mere" excludes *truth* but in no way excludes *obscurational truth,* because, of the two—that is, "obscurational" and "truth"—truth is not possible. Thus, the sense in which the obscurational truth is true is that it is merely from the perspective of ignorance—that is, obscuration.

As Candrakīrti's treatise says, "Since it is obscurationally true, it is obscurational truth."[9] This means that conventional truth is that which is true from the perspective of ignorance—obscuration—but not that it is truly existent from the standpoint of nominal convention. Otherwise, this would be inconsistent with the system according to which nothing exists through its own characteristic even conventionally. Since the refutation of true existence and the proof of the absence of true existence are presented through nominal convention, it is not tenable that their true existence is posited through nominal convention. If they were not so presented, they could not be presented ultimately, either, and it would follow that *no framework* would be coherent.

Suppose someone thought, "In that case, since reality and the two selves are truths from the perspective of the obscuration through which one grasps true existence, they must be conventional truths." If conventional truth were posited only from the perspective of the obscuration through which one

8. *dBu ma* 'a 255a.
9. *Madhyamakāvatāra-bhāṣya* 254b.

grasps true existence, this would be the case. But we do not say this. Here we merely explained that the basis of the truth of conventional truth is that obscuration from which the perspective of which anything is true, and the sense in which it is true from that perspective.

1.2.1.1.1.2.1.2.1.2. The Characteristic of Conventional Truth

Each of the internal and external phenomena has two natures: an ultimate and a conventional nature. The sprout, for instance, has a nature that is found by a rational cognitive process, which sees the real nature of the phenomenon as it is, and a nature that is found by a conventional cognitive process, which perceives deceptive or unreal objects. The former nature is the ultimate truth of the sprout; the latter nature is the conventional truth of the sprout. Concerning this, *Madhyamakāvatāra* says,

> Through seeing all phenomena both as real and as unreal,
> The two natures of the objects that are found are grasped.
> The object of the perception of reality is the way things really are.
> That which is seen falsely is called the conventional truth. [6:23]

This shows that, from among the two natures of the sprout—the two truths about the sprout—the ultimate nature of the sprout is found by the former cognitive process and the conventional nature is found by the latter cognitive process. But this does *not* show that a *single* nature is in fact two truths in virtue of the two *perspectives* of the former and latter cognitive processes. *Madhyamakāvatāra-bhāṣya* says,

> It has been shown that each phenomenon has its own two natures—a conventional and an ultimate nature.[10]

It thus says that each phenomenon has two natures, and the ultimate is the one that is found by the cognitive process that apprehends reality, and the conventional is the one that is found by the cognitive process that perceives that which is unreal.

Since the reality of the sprout is its essence, it is called its nature. Since such things as the shape and the color of the sprout are also called its identity, they are also called its nature. In order to ascertain a pot, for instance, as a deceptive or unreal object, it is necessary to develop the view that refutes, through a rational cognitive process, the object of fixation that is that object grasped as truly existent. This is because without having rationally refuted its true existence, its unreality is not established by authoritative cognition. So for the mind to establish anything as an object of conventional truth, it must depend on the refutation of its ultimate existence.

10. *dBu ma* 'a 253a.

Although such things as pots and cloths are conventional truths, when they are perceived by the mind, the mind does not necessarily perceive the meaning of "conventional truth." This is because, although such things as pots and cloths appear like illusions, although they do not exist essentially, the mind that perceives them does not necessarily perceive the fact that they are like illusions. Therefore, it is not reasonable to say that such things as pots and cloths are conventional truths from the perspective of the common people who do not have the Madhyamaka view, but that they are ultimate truths from the perspective of the *āryas,* because this would contradict the following statement in *Madhyamakāvatāra-bhāṣya* that says

> Whatever is ultimate for ordinary beings is merely conventional for the *āryas* who are engaged with appearances. The essence of conventional phenomena, which is emptiness, is the ultimate for them.[11]

Ordinary beings grasp such things as pots as truly existent, and grasp them as ultimately existent as well. Therefore from the perspective of their minds, such things as pots are ultimately existent, but they are not conventional objects. These things, such as pots, which are ultimately existent from their perspective, are conventional objects from the perspective of the *āryas,* to whom things appear as illusionlike. Since they cannot be posited as truly existent as they are apprehended by an *āryan* consciousness, they are referred to as merely conventional.

However, since their nature is said to be ultimate truth, it should be asserted, with this distinction in mind, that such things as pots are conventional but their nature, as the *āryas* grasp it, is ultimate; but one should *not* assert that such things as pots are ultimates for the *āryas,* because the *āryas'* rational minds, which see reality, do not find things such as pots and because it is said that the distinctive characteristic of the ultimate truth is that it is found by the rational mind that sees reality.

1.2.1.1.1.2.1.2.1.3. Classifications of Conventional Truth

There are two kinds of cognitive processes that perceive unreal deceptive objects: the cognitive process associated with an acute sensory faculty, which is not impaired by any extraneous causes of misperception such as cataracts, and the cognitive process associated with a defective sensory faculty impaired by extraneous causes of misperception. In comparison to the the previous one, the latter is regarded as a fallacious cognitive process. *Madhyamakāvatāra* says,

> It is asserted that there are two kinds of perceptions of the false:
> That by acute sensory faculties and that by defective sensory faculties.

11. *dBu ma* 'a 255a.

The cognitive processes of those who have defective senses
Are erroneous in comparison to those of persons with acute senses. [6:24]

Just as there are two kinds of faculty—nonerroneous and erroneous—their objects are said to be of two corresponding kinds, unreal and real: the objects that are grasped by the cognitive processes associated with the six faculties that are unimpaired by extraneous causes of misperception and the objects that are grasped by the cognitive processes associated with the six faculties that are unimpaired by extraneous causes of misperception and the objects that are grasped by the cognitive processes associated with the six faculties that are impaired by extraneous causes of misperception, respectively. Here *Madhyamakāvatāra* says,

> That which is perceived by ordinary people
> By being grasped through unimpaired sense faculties
> Is regarded by ordinary people as real.
> All the rest is said to be unreal. [6:25]

The internal impairments of the sense faculties are such things as cataracts, jaundice, and such things as hallucinogenic drugs one has consumed. The external impairments of the sense faculties are such things as mirrors, the echoing of sound in a cave, and the rays of the autumn sun falling on such things as white sand. Even without the internal impairments, these can become the causes of grasping such things as mirages, reflections, and echoes as water, and so on. Magicians' mantras and potions should be understood similarly.

The impairments of the mental faculty are, in addition to these, such things as erroneous philosophical views, fallacious arguments, and sleep. Thus, the impairments such as ignorance with regard to the two kinds of self-grasping that develop from beginningless time are not treated as causal impairments in this context. Rather, as we previously explained, the occasional extraneous causes of misperception in the faculties are treated as impairments in this context.

Taking conventional objects grasped by such unimpaired and impaired cognitive faculties to be real or unreal, respectively, merely conforms to ordinary cognitive practice. This is because they actually exist as they appear or do not, according to whether or not they are undermined by ordinary cognition. This distinction between the real and the unreal is not drawn from the perspective of the *āryas*. This is because just as such things as reflections do not exist as they appear, such things as blue, that appear to exist through their own characteristics to those who are affected by ignorance, do not actually exist as they appear. Therefore there is no distinction between those two kinds of cognitive faculties in terms of whether or not they are erroneous.

Now, suppose someone asks: Unreal objects appear in virtue of the extraneous impairment of the sense faculties and in virtue of the impairment of the mind due to such things as sleep, such things as the appearance of men in dreams being taken to be such things as men. When one is awake, the appearance of illusory horses and elephants are taken to be horses and elephants and mirages are taken to be water. All of these can be recognized to be erroneous even by an ordinary cognitive agent. However, how are the unreal objects perceived in virtue of the impairment of the mind by bad philosophy recognized as erroneous by ordinary cognitive agents?

The impairment regarding the existence or nonexistence of which we are inquiring is not an innate erroneous grasping. Therefore, fabrication through bad philosophy merely affects those who have been indoctrinated by bad philosophy such as the doctrine of a universal principle. These cannot be recognized as erroneous by *ordinary* cognitive agents. However, since they are recognized as erroneous even by those who have not approached an understanding of the way things really are through conventional authoritative cognition, they are recognized as erroneous by *mundane* cognitive agents.

Objects like those grasped by the two innate self-graspings are called "those grasped by unimpaired faculties." Although these may be taken to be true from the perspective of an ordinary cognitive agent, they do not exist conventionally. Those *svātantrika-mādhyamikas* according to whom consciousness appears to exist through its own characteristic, and is ascertained to exist as it appears, do not distinguish between the real and the unreal in terms of cognitive subjects. However, they distinguish between the real and the unreal on the basis of whether or not the object exists through its own characteristic in the way it appears, as *Satyadvaya-vibhāga* says:

> Although they are similar in appearance,
> Based on whether or not it can perform a function
> The conventional is divided into
> The real and the unreal.[12]

However, in our system, whatever appears to the ignorant to exist through its own characteristic is maintained to be an appearance polluted by ignorance. Therefore, there is no division of conventional objects into the real and the unreal. Here *Madhyamakāvatāra-bhāṣya* says,

> Whatever is conventionally false is not conventional truth.[13]

This statement means that from the perspective of the conventions of the ordinary person who has linguistic skills, things such as a reflected image of the face are not the real face. Therefore, from that perspective, they are not even conventional truths. However, it is a conventional truth in the sense that it is an object that is found by a cognitive agent that sees deceptive unreal objects. Nonetheless, just as the cognitive faculty to which the reflected image appears is erroneous with respect to the object

12. *dBu ma* sa 2a.
13. *dBu ma* 'a 254b.

that appears to it, the ignorant are in error with respect to the objects that appear to them, such as blueness, which appears to exist through its own characteristic.

To posit the perceptual object as real would contradict its being posited by an erroneous cognitive agent. On the other hand, to posit it as an unreal perceptual object would support that. Otherwise, unreal objects, including illusions, would have to be posited as conventionally existent. In that case, conventional truth would not be possible, because if something is not true by nominal convention it would be contradictory for it to be conventionally true.

1.2.1.1.1.2.1.2.2. The Explanation of Ultimate Truth

This section has three parts: the explanation of the meanings of "ultimate" and "truth," the characteristic of ultimate truth, and the classifications of ultimate truth.

1.2.1.1.1.2.1.2.2.1. Explanation of the Meanings of "Ultimate" and "Truth"

Prasannapadā says,

> Since it is a fact [*don*] and it is supreme [*dam pa*] as well, it is ultimate [*don dam*]. And since *it* is true, it is the ultimate truth. [163b]

Therefore, Candrakīrti does not maintain, as do others, that the uncontaminated wisdom of meditative equipoise is the supreme truth and that the ultimate is its object. He instead maintains that "ultimate truth" indicates both that it is a fact and that it is supreme.

The respect in which ultimate truth is a truth is that it is nondeceptive. It does not deceive ordinary beings by existing in one way and appearing in another. It is only posited as existing as ultimate truth through the power of mundane nominal conventions. This is because, as *Yuktiṣaṣṭikāvṛtti* says,

> Suppose someone asked, "In that case, why is nirvana said to be an ultimate truth?" Because it does not deceive ordinary beings regarding its mode of existence. Only through mundane nominal conventions is it said to exist as ultimate truth. Compounded phenomena, which are deceptive, are not ultimate truths. Since three of the truths are compounded phenomena, they appear to have essence, although they do not. Therefore, since they deceive fools, they are regarded as conventional truths.[14]

14. *dBu ma* ya 7b.

This is a response to the opponent's assertion that since nirvana is posited from the perspective of conventional truth it is not tenable that it is an ultimate truth [*Madhyamakāvatāra-bhāṣya* 210a, 232a, 234a]. He asks, "Since *Yuktiṣaṣṭikā* says,

> When all of the victors have said
> That nirvana is the only truth,
> What wise man would think
> That all of the rest is not false? [35]

how would you interpret the statement that nirvana is the only truth and that all the rest are false?" The reply to this in the *Yuktiṣaṣṭikāvṛtti* is as follows:

> What does it mean when the Transcendent Lord said, "Oh monks! There is one supreme truth! That is nirvana, which is characterized as nondeceptive?" Since compounded phenomena appear falsely, fools are deceived. Nirvana, however, is not like that. This is because its mode of existence is to always have the nature of being nonarisen. That does not appear to fools as do compounded phenomena, which have the nature of being arisen. Therefore, nirvana always exists just as nirvana; through mundane conventions it is known as the supreme truth.[15]

Thus, since it is said that the meaning of "nondeceptive" is *true,* and since that is also the case according to nominal convention, and since the *sūtras* also say that the meaning of "nondeceptive phenomena" is *truth,* and since the meaning of "unreal" in "all compound phenomena are unreal, deceptive phenomena" is *deceptive,* the meaning of "true" should be understood as *nondeceptive.*

Thus, the "truth" in "conventional truth" means *true from the perspective of grasping things as truly existent.* It does not have the same meaning as the "truth" in "ultimate truth." The statement in *Yuktiṣaṣṭikāvṛtti* that nirvana is conventionally a truth means that the existence of nirvana as an ultimate truth is posited from the perspective of obscuration, but it does not mean that it is a conventional truth.

1.2.1.1.1.2.1.2.2.2. The Characteristic of Ultimate Truth

This section has two parts: the main point and rebutting objections.

15. *dBu ma* ya 22b.

1.2.1.1.1.2.1.2.2.2.1. The Main Point

According to *Madhyamakāvatāra,* the characteristic of ultimate truth is said to be that which is found through seeing the facticity of a genuine object of knowledge [6:23]. The autocommentary says,

> The ultimate is the nature that is found by being the object of a particular kind of wisdom of those who see reality. But it does not exist through its own nature. This is one of its natures.[16]

Since he says that it is found by the uncontaminated wisdom that perceives things as they really are, and does not exist inherently, he refutes those who say that anything that can be found by the uncontaminated wisdom of meditative equipoise is truly existent.

By saying "the particular kind of wisdom," he means that for the ultimate, it is not enough to be found by just any kind of *ārya* wisdom, but it must be found by the particular wisdom that knows things just as they are. The meaning of "to be found" is *to be established by that cognitive faculty.* The meaning is similar in the case of the conventional. The way it is found through this particular kind of wisdom is as follows: When the eye that is affected by cataracts sees hairs falling in empty space, the eye that is not affected by cataracts does not even see the appearance of falling hairs. In the same way, when those who are impaired by the cataracts of ignorance see such things as the inherent existence of the aggregates, that which is seen by those Buddhas who are free of the latent potentials for ignorance and by those who have the uncontaminated wisdom that sees things just as they are, just like that which is seen by eyes without cataracts, in virtue of not being seen to be even the slightest bit dualistic, is the ultimate truth. *Madhyamakāvatāra* says,

> Because of cataracts, unreal objects
> Such as falling hairs are mistakenly seen.
> Their reality is seen by healthy eyes.
> This should be understood similarly here. [6:29]

Here the autocommentary says,

> The nature of the aggregates that is seen by the transcendent buddhas, who are free from the latent potentials for ignorance, is the ultimate truth, just as the person without cataracts does not see the falling hairs.[17]

This says that the Buddha does not see the objects that are seen by those affected by the cataracts of ignorance through the wisdom by means of which he sees things as they really are, just as the person without cataracts does not see the falling hairs.

16. *dBu ma* 'a 253a.
17. *dBu ma* 'a 255b.

Bibliography and Suggested Reading

Arnold, Dan. (2005) *Buddhists, Brahmins, and Belief: Epistemology in South Asian Philosophy of Religion.* New York: Columbia University Press.

Huntington, C. W., and Geshe N. Wangchen. (1995). *The Emptiness of Emptiness: Candrakīrti's "Madhyamamkāvatāra."* Honolulu: University of Hawai'i Press.

Newland, Guy. (1999). *Appearance and Reality: The Two Truths in the Four Buddhist Tenet Systems.* Ithaca, N.Y.: Snow Lion.

Thakchöe, Sonam. (2007). *The Two Truths Debate: Tsongkhapa and Gorampa on the Middle Way.* Boston: Wisdom.

Tillemans, Tom. (1999). *Scripture, Language, Logic: Dharmakīrti and His Tibetan Successors.* Boston: Wisdom.

Tsongkhapa. (2006) *Ocean of Reasoning: A Great Commentary on Nāgārjuna's Mūlamadhyamakakārikā.* Translated by Ngawang Samten and Jay L. Garfield. New York: Oxford University Press.

21

The Deluded Mind as World and Truth

Epistemological Implications of Tiantai Doctrine and Praxis in Jingxi Zhanran's *Jingangpi* and *Zhiguan yili*

Brook Ziporyn

Tiantai Buddhist theory, as developed by its de facto founder Zhiyi (538–597),[1] rests on two intimately related foundations: the doctrine of the Three Truths and the doctrine of "opening the provisional to reveal the real" (*kaiquan xianshi*). The first of these is an expansion of the Indian Madhyamaka distinction between ultimate truth—the inconceivable experience of liberation beyond all predicable views—and conventional truth—commonly accepted ordinary speech (e.g., self, other, cause, effect), plus Buddhist terminologies (e.g., nonself, impermanence, karma, emptiness), all of which are seen as aids to the realization of ultimate truth. Tiantai alters this picture by speaking of not two but three types of truth, which are further said to be "interfused." These are *ultimate truth, conventional truth,* and the *center* (*zhendi, sudi, zhongdi*), also identified as *emptiness, provisional positing,* and the *center* (*kong, jia, zhong*). Many Indian Mādhyamikas understand the conceptual term "emptiness" (*śūnyatā*) an instance of conventional truth, to be negated by the "emptiness of emptiness," as contrasted to the absolute unspeakability of the experience of ultimate truth, which is liberation from all views. Tiantai sees this "assertion of unspeakability," if taken literally, as self-contradictory. If this ultimate truth does anything, even if only refute the ultimacy of all views or bring cognitive error and suffering to an end—in however attenuated, qualified, or self-canceling a way—then it is

1. See chapter 29 here for an insightful overview of Zhiyi's understanding of Buddhist doctrine and practice.

ipso facto a something, and entails a kind of view. Instead, Tiantai takes the deployment of emptiness as *merely* ultimate truth—not yet the center—but then asserts that the Three Truths "interfuse," meaning that emptiness, both as a concept and as an experience, is itself a provisional posit—hence provisionally speakable and conceivable, like any other putative entity. By the same token, provisional positing is itself empty—hence unspeakable. In short, rather than separating all possible experience into two categories, the conceivable and the inconceivable, Tiantai asserts that each putative entity is both conceivable *and* inconceivable. What is conceivable in one sense—that is, provisionally—is always also in another sense—that is, ultimately—inconceivable, and vice versa. But further, these turn out not to be two different assertions about the entity in question, but merely alternate ways of saying the same thing. So conceivability is itself inconceivability, and inconceivability is, to exactly the same extent as any other putative cognitive object, conceivability. This also means that "inconceivability" is itself just one more concept, conceivable and inconceivable in just the same way as any other.

This reconfiguration has two direct consequences: first, the hierarchy between conventional and ultimate truth that seems to obtain in many Indian interpretations of Madhyamaka is canceled; they cannot be described in terms of a one-way means and ends structure, where the means can be discarded when the end is reached. Second, the category of "plain falsehood," which was implied by the Madhyamaka idea of Two Truths, is here eliminated entirely: all claims of whatever kind, including heretical metaphysical views and idiosyncratic personal delusions, are equally conventional truths and thus of equal value to and ultimately identical with ultimate truth, or the conception of emptiness.

We may better understand the Tiantai position by retranslating the terms "provisional positing" and "emptiness" as "local coherence" and "global incoherence," respectively. Provisional truth is the apprehension of some qualium X as having a certain discernible, graspable, coherent identity. Ultimate truth is the revelation that this coherent identity is only provisionally coherent, that it fails to be coherent in all contexts and from all points of view, and thus is globally incoherent. X is analyzable exhaustibly into non-X elements, non-X causes, non-X antecedents, non-X contexts, which are revealed to be not external to X, but constitutive of it. No X is discoverable apart from the non-X elements, causes, antecedents, and contexts, which are present here, we may say, "as" X. This "as" may be taken as a shorthand way of indicating what is meant by the "third truth," centrality: the relation of sameness-as-contrast between this qualium's identity as X and the effacing of that identity. When I say "I am using this book *as* a doorstop," I mean that this entity has two different identities at once: it is genuinely being a book, and it is genuinely being a doorstop. This applies for any putative entity X and all that is "not" it, all that is non-X. These non-X elements that are present here as X are revealed simply by closer attention to X itself; they are not brought in from outside. X appears exclusively as X only when our field of attention is arbitrarily narrowed to exclude some of the relevant ways it can be considered; attention to its constitutive elements, antecedents, and contexts reveals that this very same item, X, is also readable as non-X. Hence the two seemingly opposite claims of the Two Truths turn out to be two alternate ways of saying the same thing: to be identifiable is to be coherent, to be coherent is to be locally coherent, and to be locally coherent is to be globally incoherent. It is with this move, the third category, that "plain error," from the Two Truths theory, drops out of the picture: all coherences, even alternate metaphysical claims, are in the same boat, all are identities that are locally coherent/globally incoherent. The truth of a statement consists simply in its coherence to some given perspective, which is always the effect of arbitrarily limiting the horizons of relevance. When all considerations are brought in at once, X has no single consistent noncontradictory identity.

This fact, that conventional and ultimate truths—coherence and incoherence—are synonymous, is what is meant by the center. This is also taken to imply that this coherence, X, is the center of all other coherences in the distinctively Chinese sense of being their source, value, meaning, end, ground, around which they all converge, into which they are all subsumed. All entities are locally coherent, globally incoherent, and the determining center of all other local coherences. Any X subsumes all the non-X qualia that are appearing here as X: they are instantiations of X, which serves as their subsuming category, their essence, their meaning, their ground.

The second pillar of Tiantai doctrine is the concept of "opening the provisional to reveal the real" (*kaiquan xianshi*). This is a way of further specifying the relation between local coherence and global incoherence, which are not only synonymous but also irrevocably opposed, and indeed identical only by means of their opposition. Provisional truth is the antecedent, the premise, and, in a distinctive sense, the *cause* of ultimate truth, but only because it is the strict exclusion of ultimate truth. The everyday example of the joke can serve as a helpful model for understanding this structure, with the provisional as the setup and the ultimate as the punch line, thus preserving both the contrast between the two and their ultimate identity in sharing the quality of humorousness that belongs to every atom of the joke considered as a whole, once the punch line has been revealed. The setup is serious, while the punch line is funny. The funniness of the punch line depends on the seriousness of the setup, and on the contrast and difference between the two. However, once the punch line has occurred, it is also the case that the setup is, retrospectively, funny; we do not say that the punch line alone is funny, but that the whole joke was funny. This also means that the original contrast between the two is both preserved and annulled: neither funniness nor seriousness means the same thing after the punch line dawns, for their original meanings depended on the mutually exclusive nature of their defining contrast. Each is now a center that subsumes the other; they are intersubsumptive. As a consequence, the pragmatic Buddhist standard of truth is applied more liberally here: all claims, statements, and positions are true in the sense that all *can,* if properly recontextualized, lead to liberation—which is to say, to their own self-overcoming. Conversely, none will lead to liberation if not properly recontextualized.

The foregoing is to be contrasted to an implicit and commonsensical notion of truth and its relation to falsehood that informs almost all other philosophical and religious systems, including the vast majority of Buddhist thinkers. According to this widespread notion of truth, there is some part of our cognitive apparatus—whether it be "reason," or perhaps a capacity for unbiased awareness, or *prajñā* as an insight into emptiness, or an experience of the inconceivable ultimate truth as such—to which unambiguously true claims can be directed, which can recognize and assess those claims accurately, and which can then reject and replace its previously held false beliefs. But this model can gain no purchase in the Tiantai universe. It is not just that our mind is clouded over or misinformed by erroneous beliefs; it is literally composed of biased and distorted habituations to such a degree that every one of its actions and posits, including its positing of an objective truth that subverts or corrects its errors, is irrevocably tainted by its unbalanced existential position. "Truth," however conceived by the deluded mind, is just one additional delusion, perhaps the most pernicious delusion of all. An objective and unbiased contemplation of the truth is effectively ruled out by these Tiantai premises—for any determinate position or stance is intrinsically biased.

This would seem to rule out any hope of escape from the closed circle of delusion. And yet the foregoing conceptions concerning epistemological and ontological matters are framed entirely within a soteriological context, and share the general Buddhist optimism about the possibility of liberation. Indeed, given the Tiantai claims about the relation of speakablity and unspeakability, all possible assertions, without exception, are made only with reference to the bias of some particular biased viewpoint, and only for soteriological purposes. All statements and claims are by nature biased, situational, pragmatic, and assessable only in terms of their soteriological value. What makes this coexistence of radical skepticism and radical epistemological optimism possible is the distinctive Tiantai form of Buddhist praxis, the practice of mind-contemplation, designed to lead to a liberating realization of these ideas. In the works of Jingxi Zhanran (711–782), the implicit approach to practice in Zhiyi's works is streamlined and intensified. It is characterized, polemically, as the contemplation of the deluded mind by the deluded mind itself, rather than attempting to take the enlightened mind directly as either its agent or object. Here the Tiantai premises are used to find a practical way out of the vicious circle that they seem to posit: the self-overcoming of delusion.

The following passages are in the form of clarifying questions and answers drawn from Zhanran's works. The first selection is from Zhanran's

Jingangpi,[2] a defense of Zhanran's claim that "insentient beings have Buddha-nature," and the rest (selections 2–7) from the same author's *Zhiguan yili*, a summary of Zhanran's interpretation of Zhiyi's masterwork, *Mohezhiguan*.[3] In selection 1, Zhanran uses the Tiantai "opening of the provisional to reveal the real" to address the relation between sentience and insentience, subject and object: a distinction between awareness and objecthood is first made in order to foment awareness of the inextricable presence of unawareness in every act of awareness. This means that there can never be a reduction of both sides to either awareness or nonawareness—subjectivity or objectivity, mental or material—as originally defined, but there can be a reduction of all things to *either* side once both awareness and nonawareness are seen to be ineradicably mutually entailing.

In selection 2, Zhanran applies the local/global epistemology of the Three Truths to show that our ordinary misperceptions are not falsehoods, but partial truths that serve to unfold ultimate truth. In selection 3, we have a further development of Zhanran's ideas of awareness and nonawareness, and the manner in which they interfuse so that neither is primary, and each is reducible to the other. In selection 4, we see again that reality is ultimately neither material nor mental—it is equally valid to say "all is mind" or "all is matter"—but the contemplation of mind is made primary for the sake of Buddhist praxis, precisely because it is mind that is the source of the problem of delusion and suffering for sentient beings. Hence it is the contemplation of the deluded mind, the making of arbitrary distinctions, which is the conduit that reveals ultimate truth. But this mind is never directly known as such, for it can never be its own object; instead it is to be perceived only as a habitual capacity to make distinctions, present to us only as the resulting determinate characteristics appearing as each sentient being's deluded partial apprehension of particular objects in the world. The world we see is the result of our delusion, so we contemplate our deluded mind "out there" in (or *as*) the world. The truth is thus revealed in our deluded perception, as the objects making up our life-world.

In selection 5, we see perhaps the most distinctive aspect of Tiantai thought, distinguishing it from most other Buddhist "mind-only" doctrines. Mind-only also means matter-only, and each means both. We cannot assert a one-way perceiver-perceived relation. Hence it is just as accurate to say the subject is perceiving the object as to say the object is perceiving the subject, or that the subject is perceiving the subject, or that the object is perceiving the object. Note however that this does not mean that none of the descriptions is accurate, or that we should instead say that no arising or perceiving

2. *Jingangpi*, T. 46.783. T refers to *Taishō shinshū daizōkyō* [A standard collection of the East Asian Buddhist canon compiled in Japan] Takakusu Junjirō, Watanabe Kaikyoku, et al. (eds.), 100 vols. Tokyo: Taishō Issaikyō Kankōkai, 1924–1932. All translations are mine.

3. *Zhiguan yili*, T. 46.451–453.

takes place, that in reality these three reduce into an undifferentiated or inconceivable totality; any of the descriptions is equally accurate, according to the demands of *upāya,* the only determinant of any claim whatsoever. The differentiation is itself inherently entailed, and necessary to the unfolding of the nondifferentiation. Zhanran also distinguishes this view from several other views of subject-object relations, and delusion-truth relations. It is not an active and aware mind that unilaterally perceives an inert and nonaware object, as common sense would assume. Nor is the Tiantai contemplation of deluded mind like the "Hīnayāna" contemplation of deluded mind, where the latter is something to be transcended and discarded when the real truth is realized, where the real truth is conceived of as something lying beyond the deluded mind, separable from it. Nor is it the entertaining of a real truth—suchness—as the direct object of contemplation, apart from the deluded mind itself. The contemplator, too, differs: it is not one-sidedly active as opposed to passive, perceiving as opposed to perceived. Rather, the contemplator is all three thousand pure and impure natures and characteristics; the object of contemplation, equally, is all three thousand; the activity of contemplating itself, arising from the interaction of these two, is also all three thousand.

In selection 6, Zhanran shows that, because all determinate marks of the world are seen to be aspects of any one moment of mental activity, such that all are mind, mind no longer means mind as contrasted to nonmind. "Mind-only" undermines the meaning of mind, and loops into "matter-only," "scent-only," "this-only" for any "this." In Zhanran's metaphor, mind is like empty sky, and all determinate marks are like the illusory images of flowers floating in the air, as a result of an eye disease. Once the flowers are seen to be nothing but sky, "sky" is seen to really mean "so-called-sky-plus-so-called-flowers," and similarly "flowers," since it means sky, really means "so-called-sky-plus-so-called-flowers." Hence "sky" means "flowers," and vice versa. Similarly, all is mind, all is matter, mind means matter, matter means mind. We can now further understand the claim that object perceives subject: the manifestation of each biased appearance in my mind right now is also an upayic self-presentation of each reality. Either is as much the agent and the patient as the other.

In selection 7, we see again the distinctiveness of Tiantai thought. The final result of seeing that all determinate characteristics encountered in experience are produced by our own deluded cognitive divisions, and thus have no reality of their own, is *not* to dismiss them as ultimately unreal, nor to correct our misperception. Rather, the final upshot is that each and every determinate characteristic I encounter is even *more* real than I formerly believed it to be: it is ultimate reality. My very act of misperceiving in this particular way is itself ineradicably built into reality. My illusion is the very self-disclosure of the ultimate truth. Every aspect is equally real. Each *dharma* is the totality of absolute reality. The world as we see it, or as each individual deluded sentient being sees it, is not merely an illusion.

Whatever colors, shapes, situations, valences, tendencies, characteristics my crazy deluded mind may be experiencing, the world I observe with all its mountains and rivers, its obstructions and materiality, its politics and struggles, far from vanishing into illusion or being reduced to mind, is very real, absolutely real, in its every detail. These are not merely to be refuted, deconstructed, shown to be empty, and discarded; rather, precisely when so deconstructed, they reconstitute themselves as not merely contingent partial realities, but as the totality of absolute reality, of absolute truth. In other words, *because* it is an illusion, each determinate characteristic is ultimate reality. Every illusory perception entertained however fleetingly by any sentient being is itself the absolute truth.

Translation

Selection 1

Q: I have heard people quote the "Dazhidulun" to say that in insentient being's suchness[4] should merely be called "Dharma-nature"; it is only in sentient beings that it can be called the Buddha-nature. Why do you use the term "Buddha-nature" [with reference to insentient beings as well]?

A: "Dharma" denotes nonawareness [i.e., an object of consciousness, hence something that is itself nonaware]. "Buddha" denotes awareness. Although all sentient beings originally possess the principle of "nonawareness" in themselves, they have not yet acquired the wisdom that would allow them to be aware of nonawareness. This is precisely why we temporarily make a distinction between awareness and nonawareness: so as to make people aware of nonawareness. But once there is awareness of nonawareness, nonawareness is no longer nonawareness, is it? The object of awareness cannot really be separate from the awareness, can it?

Q: But it is only when one reaches Buddhahood that one can really understand this. Ordinary people do take them as separate; why do you contradict this view?

A: Are you trying to learn Buddhahood, or trying to learn the ordinary people's views? In the ultimately liberating coherence, there is no real difference; it is ordinary people who themselves consider them separate. Thus [the Buddhas] reveal this to sentient beings,

4. "Suchness" translates *zhenru* in Chinese, which translates *tathātā* in Sanskrit: a Mahāyāna term for the absolute ultimate reality of all things, which is beyond all predication, change, and difference, and can thus only be indicated as "such."

to enable them to become aware of nonawareness. When you are aware of nonawareness, [awareness and nonawareness, subject and object, mental activity and material form] naturally combine into a single suchness. If awareness were deprived of nonawareness, it could not properly be called the Buddha-nature; if there were no awareness of nonawareness, it would not really be the Dharma-nature. If awareness were deprived of nonawareness, how could Buddha-nature be established? Hence, the idea of a Dharma-nature which is not also Buddha-nature is permissible only within the Hīnayāna teaching. To count as a Mahāyāna teaching, the Buddha-nature must be understood as identical to the Dharma-nature.[5]

Selection 2

Q: Here we see manifestly black, yellow, red, and white [i.e., separate differentiated things and characteristics]. In what sense are they the Dharma-realm of suchness?

A: When you speak of black and so on, this is what is seen by deluded attachment. When you speak of the Dharma-realm, you are talking about what accords with liberating coherence (*li*). Why use deluded attachment to challenge liberating coherence? Our present contemplation is to contravene deluded attachment and contemplate liberating coherence. One mustn't go on to contravene liberating coherence and accord with deluded attachment. Moreover, black and the rest are conventional truth, while the Dharma-realm is ultimate truth. Or again, black and the rest are a small portion of conventional truth, while the Dharma-realm is the entirety of the Three Truths. Or again, black and the rest are a small portion of what is seen by the human and heavenly eyes, while the Dharma-realm is the entirety of what is seen by the Buddha-eye. Each eye inherently entails all five eyes, so black and the rest inherently entail all dharmas. The same applies to the relationship between any one truth and the Three Truths. For these reasons, you cannot challenge the presence of the entire Dharma-realm because of [the manifestation of] black and the rest.[6]

Selection 3

Q: The external material form that makes up inanimate beings is not endowed simultaneously with mind. How can it have replete within it the Three Meritorious Properties [liberation, wisdom, the

5. T. 46.783a.
6. T. 46.451c.

Dharmakāya], such that you say the Three Meritorious Properties pervade all places?

A: It is not only the external material form that is not simultaneously endowed with mind; the material form inside one's own body is just the same as grass, trees, tiles, and bricks. But if we are talking about the inherent entailment of the Meritorious Properties, it is not only the internal mind that is a transformation of mind. Thus it is said of both the internal mind and external material form that, because mind is neither internal nor external, material form too is neither internal nor external. Thus each is both internal and external. Because of the purity of the mind, the Buddha-land is pure, but also, conversely, because of the purity of the Buddha-land, wisdom is pure. Because both mind and material form are pure, all dharmas are pure. Because all dharmas are pure, mind and body are pure. How can we say only that the external material form lacks mind?[7]

Selection 4

Q: All the texts say that mind and material form are nondual. But if we want to contemplate this, how do we set up our contemplation?

A: Mind and material form are one substance; neither precedes the other. Each is the entire Dharma-realm. But in the sequence of contemplation, we must start with the internal mind. Once the internal mind is purified, this pure mind will encounter all dharmas, and naturally meld with them all perfectly. Moreover, we must first understand that all dharmas are mind-only, and only then begin contemplating the mind. If you can comprehend all dharmas to the end, you will see that all dharmas are nothing but mind, *and* that all dharmas are nothing but material form. You must understand that every existence comes from the distinctions made by one's own mind. When have dharmas themselves ever declared that they were the same as or different from one another? Hence the *Zhanchajing* says, "There are two types of contemplation. The first is consciousness-only. The second is of the real-mark [i.e., of the ultimate reality]."[8] The real-mark [practice] is the contemplation of liberating coherence (*li*), while the consciousness-only [practice]

7. T. 46.451c.

8. Zhanran here quotes a Chinese apocryphal *sūtra,* the full title of which is *Zhancha shan'e yebao jing* (The sutra of prognostication and investigation of good and evil karmic retribution), which describes the "contemplation of consciousness-only" as entailing a constant awareness of the functions of one's own mind in the engagement and constitution of all objects of perception and conception. The claim here is that

works through individual events (*shi*). Although liberating coherence and event are nondual, the ways for contemplating them are slightly separated. Only one who is able to understand this can be spoken to about the Way.[9]

Selection 5

Q: [Zhiyi's] *Fahuaxuanyi* says that the object is able to contemplate the subject. Although many scriptures are quoted to verify it, it is hard to understand the liberating coherence of this claim.

A: If we follow the merely upayic teachings, there is no way to see the liberating coherence of this idea. But it is quite easy to integrate it coherently into the ultimate teaching. We take mind itself as the object, while mind is also the subject that is doing the contemplating. Thus subject and object are both mind, and both the mind and its substance pervade everywhere. Each state of mind reflects on another state of mind—the coherence of this is quite clear. Thus at the beginning of the section on the inconceivable object it says, "The inconceivable object is itself precisely the subject doing the contemplating." From this we can derive four different but equally accurate descriptions: (1) the object is aware of the object, (2) the object is aware of the subject, (3) the subject is aware of the object, (4) the subject is aware of the subject. As soon as there is any real awareness, it is beyond description. But the awareness should be described, for it then goes beyond what can be completely comprehended by the

---

all characteristics, including the being or nonbeing of putative objects, are projected by the mind through its function of making divisions; the objects themselves do not make any distinctions, do not "say" that they are the same or different from anything else, and hence are, on this view, not in fact the same or different. The "contemplation of the real-mark" attends to the other side of this equation: the lack of any inherent characteristics of all things in the absence of the deluded mind making distinctions and predications about them. See T. 17.908a.

9. T. 46.452a. Note that mind is identified as simply the making of distinctions, which is what it is to make predications, including those of existence and nonexistence, i.e., that there even *is* or *is not* an object here to be cognized, about which some predications might be made. It is fundamentally a faculty of dividing. It divides itself from the objects before it, reifying both, and simultaneously separates out the objects from one another, identifying them as this or that, and cognizing various characteristics inhering in them by which to distinguish them. Where it makes a border, it posits a determinate thing within the border. Where there is a thing, there is its "distinctness," its identity, its "being itself and none other." That aspect of all things is one's own (deluded) mind. That things are present to you as they are is your mind. It is this that is contemplated in the contemplation of mind.

awareness alone. Conversely, as soon as there is any real description, it cannot be exhausted by awareness. But the description should become an object of awareness, for it then goes beyond what can be exhausted by the description alone. Thus it is different from what people of the world normally think of, namely, an inert object as what we are aware of and contemplate. It differs also from the one-sided Hīnayāna idea of the deluded mind as the object of contemplation. Nor is it the same as the idea of artificially setting up suchness as the object of contemplation. These different conceptions of the contemplated object also apply to the contemplating subject—do not carelessly confound them.[10]

Selection 6

Q: [The *Mohezhiguan*] says, "[When we speak of 'one' single moment of mental activity inherently including the Three Thousand] we do not mean a single moment of mental activity as [delusively] clung to by ordinary people of the world [as definitively 'one,' where 'one and 'diverse' are regarded as mutually exclusive characteristics]" as that which is capable of inherently including the Three Thousand. Is this the case only in this context, or everywhere?

A: Everywhere.

Q: Does this mean then that this clung-to mind does not inherently include the Three Thousand?

A: This is said only with respect to the object to be used in contemplation. The clung-to mind itself *is* originally all dharmas. We come to see that this mind of clinging is born of conditions, and hence is illusory and false. [And yet] the Three Thousand, being mere aspects of [lit., within] this falsity, are in their own essence [i.e., apart from this mental activity] devoid of self-nature. [Thus] they are themselves precisely the inconceivable integrated and wondrous emptiness, provisionality and centrality of the nature of mind itself. It is like [illusory images of] flowers in the sky. Since there is no difference in substance between the flowers and the empty sky, this empty sky does not correspond to either the word "flower" or to the word "empty sky," for the latter was originally posited in contradistinction to the flowers. This emptiness has no name. Extending this point in detail, the same applies to all things.[11]

10. T. 46.452b.
11. T. 46.452c.

Selection 7

Q: Are all the great master's (Zhiyi's) oral transmissions purely to cure various diseases, or is there any other essential heart of the teaching he transmitted?

A: They are all to cure various diseases. But there is one verse that says:

> "The teacher taught the following maxim:
> The ultimately real mind is connected to the ultimately real object,
> thereby producing ultimately real conditioned states in sequence.
> Real pours into real, one after another,
> and thus effortlessly one enters the real liberating coherence."

I explain this as follows: If the mind connects to the object, then the object necessarily connects to the mind as well. When mind and object connect to one another, this is called the ultimately real conditioned state. And then this is done by the following moment of mind, so that one such mental event follows another without interruption. Each mental event connects to the previous mental event. This is called "[One ultimately real after another ultimately real] pouring into one another." This means also the mind pouring into the object, the object pouring into the object, the object pouring into the mind. Each mind, each object, each moment of mental activity pours into all the others; when this continues in every sequential moment without interruption, one effortlessly moves into the identity with Buddhahood at the level of contemplation and practice, the identity with Buddhahood at the level of verisimilitude, and the identity with Buddhahood at the level of partial realization. This is called entering into the real liberating coherence.[12]

Bibliography and Suggested Reading

Donner, Neal, and Daniel Stevenson. (1993) *The Great Calming and Contemplation: A Study and Annotated Translation of the First Chapter of Chih-I's "Mo-Ho Chih-Kuan."* Honolulu: University of Hawai'i Press.

12. T. 46.453a. This is a reference to Zhiyi's doctrine of the "six identities" (that is, being identical to the Buddha in principle, in name, in contemplation and in practice, in verisimilitude, in partial realization, and in ultimate identity), a way of preserving both the ultimate identity of all putative entities with Buddhahood on the one hand and the specific rankings and differences in their progress of Buddhist practice on the other. Here again we see an application of the Three Truths, where sameness (emptiness beyond all views) and difference (provisionally posited views) coincide (the center). See *Fahuaxuanyi*, T. 33.686a.

Ng Yu-kwan. (1993) *T'ien-T'ai Buddhism and Early Mādhyamika*. Honolulu: University of Hawai'i Press.
Penkower, Linda. (1993) "T'ien-t'ai during the T'ang Dynasty: Chan-jan and the Sinification of Buddhism." Ph.D. diss., Columbia University.
Swanson, Paul. (1995) *Foundations of T'ien-T'ai Philosophy: The Flowering of the Two Truths Theory in Chinese Buddhism*. Berkeley: Asian Humanities Press.
Ziporyn, Brook. (2000) *Evil and/or/as the Good: Omnicentrism, Intersubjectivity and Value Paradox in Tiantai Buddhist Thought*. Cambridge: Harvard University Press.
Ziporyn, Brook. (2004) *Being and Ambiguity: Philosophical Experiments with Tiantai Buddhism*. Chicago: Open Court Press.

22

The Presencing of Truth

Dōgen's *Genjōkōan*

Bret W. Davis

Dōgen Kigen (1200–1253), founder of the Sōtō school of Japanese Zen Buddhism, is widely recognized as one of the most original and profound thinkers in the Buddhist tradition. The text translated here, *Genjōkōan,* is the core fascicle of his major work *Shōbōgenzō* (Treasury of the True Dharma Eye).[1] It is the "treasury of the true Dharma eye" that Śākyamuni Buddha is said to have transmitted to his successor, Mahākāshyapa, by silently holding up a flower. This event is held to mark the beginning of the Zen tradition, which is characterized by Bodhidharma as "a special transmission outside the scriptures; not depending on words and letters; directly pointing to the human mind; seeing into one's nature and becoming a Buddha." Like Bodhidharma, who is said to have sat in meditation for nine years after bringing Zen (Chin. Chan) from India to China, Dōgen, too, placed great emphasis on the silent practice of "just sitting" (*shikantaza*).

Yet Dōgen's *Shōbōgenzō* is not just an expedient means to practice and enlightenment, a finger pointing at the moon; it is also a literary and philosophical masterpiece in its own right. Indeed, Dōgen is considered by many to be the single greatest "philosopher" in the tradition of Zen Buddhism. Beyond merely insisting on the limitations of language and reason,

1. My references will be to the following scholarly and readily available Japanese edition: Mizuno Yaoko, ed. *Shōbōgenzō,* four volumes (Tokyo: Iwanami, 1990). The *Gēnjōkōan* appears in vol. 1, pp. 53–61. Although translations of quoted passages will be my own, for the reader's convenience I will also cross reference Waddell and Abe 2002.

he poetically and philosophically manifests their expressive potential. The "entangled vines" (*kattō*) of language are not treated simply as impediments to be cut through with the sword of silent meditation and ineffable insight. Rather, they are taken to have the potential to be "expressive attainments of the Way" (*dōtoku*) that present aspects of the truth of the dynamic Buddha-nature of reality.

Nevertheless, Dōgen stresses that any expression of truth always involves both a revealing and a concealing. In Dōgen's own words, "When one side is illuminated, the other side is darkened." This epistemological principle is one of the central themes of the *Genjōkōan,* and it can be found at work throughout the text, beginning with its famous opening section. The first three sentences of the text could be thought to correspond to Tiantai (Jap. Tendai) philosophy's Three Truths: the provisional, the empty, and the middle. The fourth sentence, on the other hand, is pure Zen; it abruptly returns us from the nondual dialectical reasoning (*ri*) of Mahāyāna philosophy to the concrete factuality (*ji*) of living in the midst of the world of passionate entanglements. The text then proceeds to describe the crucial differences between a deluded/deluding and an enlightened/enlightening engagement in this world.

A deluding experience of the world, according to Dōgen, occurs when one "carries oneself forth to verify-in-practice (*shushō*) the myriad things." On the other hand, "for the myriad things to come forth and verify-in-practice the self is enlightenment." Before discussing these definitions of delusion and enlightenment, a few remarks on the peculiar notion of *shushō* are in order. In this key term, Dōgen conjoins two characters to convey the inseparable non-duality of "practice" and "enlightenment (verification)."[2] This crucial aspect of Dōgen's teaching is poignantly addressed in the concluding section of the *Genjōkōan,* where the action of the Zen master fanning himself (practice) is demonstrated to be one with the truth that the wind (Buddha-nature) circulates everywhere. The character for *shō,* which is Dōgen's favored term for enlightenment, normally means to verify, prove, attest to, confirm, or authenticate something. As a synonym for enlightenment, *shō* is a matter of *verifying* ("showing to be true" and literally "making true") and hence *realizing* (in both senses of the term) that one's true self (*honbunnin*), one's "original part," is originally part and parcel of the dynamically ubiquitous Buddha-nature.[3]

Delusion occurs when the ego posits itself as the single fixed center—rather than understanding itself as one among infinitely many mutually expressive focal points—of the whole.[4] In delusion, the myriad things are seen, not according to the self-expressive aspects through which they show

2. See Mizuno 1990: 1:28; Waddell and Abe 2002: 19.

3. Dōgen famously rereads the *Mahāparinirvāna Sūtra*'s claim that "all sentient beings have the Buddha-nature" to mean that "entire being/all beings is/are the Buddha-nature [*shitsu-u wa busshō nari*]" (Mizuno 1990: 1:73; compare Waddell and Abe 2002: 61).

4. As with much of Zen thought, Dōgen's perspectivism is heavily influenced by Huayan (Jap. Kegon) philosophy, which in turn draws on the *Avataṃsaka Sūtra*'s image of the "jeweled net of Indra" wherein each jewel reflects all the others.

themselves, but rather only as they are forced into the perspectival horizon of the self-fixated and self-assertive ego. The deluded and deluding ego willfully projects its categories of perception onto the world. On the other hand, when practicing the Buddha Way, one comes to realize the empty (i.e., open and interdependent) nature of the true self. Thus, a thoroughgoing "study of the self," which involves taking a radical "step back that turns the light around,"[5] paradoxically leads to a "forgetting of the self" as an independent and substantial ego-subject. Dōgen speaks of this "forgetting" most radically in terms of his own enlightenment experience of "dropping off the body-mind" (*shinjin-datsuraku*). Only through this ultimate experience of letting go and letting be does one become open to the self-presentation of things. The true self is an openness to the presencing of truth.

But this openness must be realized, and this realization is neither static nor simply passive. When Dōgen says that "things come forth and verify-in-practice the self" (elsewhere he even claims that "original practice inheres in the original face of each and every thing"),[6] he is countering the willful self-assertion of human subjectivity by calling attention to the "objective side" of the "total dynamism" (*zenki*) of a nondual event of enlightenment. For our part, in order to authentically participate in this event we must not only liberate ourselves from a self-assertive fixation on our body-mind by letting it drop off; we must also spontaneously pick it up again in an energetic yet nonwilling "total exertion" (*gūjin*) of "rousing the [whole] body-mind to perceive forms, rousing the [whole] body-mind to listen to sounds."

This intimate nondual perception of forms and listening to sounds is, however, never a shadowless illumination of all aspects of a thing. The epistemology of Dōgen's understanding of enlightenment is decidedly not that of simultaneous omniscience. Enlightenment is not a static and omniscient view from nowhere, but rather an endless path of illuminating the innumerable aspects of reality, an ongoing journey of appreciating the "inexhaustible virtues" of things. Enlightenment is not a state of final attainment, but rather a never self-satisfied process of enlightening darkness and delusion. Indeed, setting out on this never-ending Way of enlightenment entails awakening to the ineradicable play of knowledge and nescience. And thus, paradoxically, Dōgen tells us that "if the Dharma fills the body-mind, one notices an insufficiency."

Dōgen makes this principal epistemological point most clearly and forcefully in the section of *Genjōkōan* where he speaks of the inexhaustible potential aspects (or virtues) of the ocean. If a human being, sitting on a boat in the middle of the ocean, looks out in all four directions, he or she sees only a vast empty circle. Dōgen is perhaps alluding here to a meditative experience of emptiness. We might refer to the "empty circle" or "circular shape"

5. Kagamishima Genryū, *Dōgen Zenji goroku* (Tokyo: Kōdansha, 1990), p. 170; compare Waddell and Abe 2002: 3.

6. Mizuno 1990: 1:18; compare Waddell and Abe 2002: 14.

(*ensō*) that appears as the eighth of the *Ten Ox Pictures,* which is often interpreted as a symbol for the absolute emptiness of the Dharmakāya (the Truth Body of the Buddha), or the Buddha-nature (*Busshō*) understood—as Dōgen and other Zen figures sometimes do—in terms of *mu-Busshō* ("no-Buddha-nature" or the "Buddha-nature-of-Nothingness"). What is crucial is that neither the *Ten Ox Pictures* nor Dōgen's Zen stops here at the empty circle; even emptiness is a perspective to which one must not become attached. In the all-embracing perspective of identity, differences are concealed.

Hence, even though one may perceive the ocean as a vast empty circle, Dōgen proceeds to write: "Nevertheless, the great ocean is not circular, and it is not square; the remaining virtues [or qualities] of the ocean are inexhaustible. It is like a palace [for fish]. It is like a jeweled ornament [to gods]. It is just that, as far as my eyes can see, for a while it looks like a circle." Dōgen is drawing here on the traditional Buddhist notion that different sentient beings experience the world in different manners, depending on the conditioning of their karma. He is likely alluding specifically to a commentary on the *Mahāyāna-samgraha:* "The sea itself basically has no disparities, yet owing to the karmic differences of *devas,* humans, craving spirits, and fish, devas see it as a treasure trove of jewels, humans see it as water, craving spirits see it as an ocean of pus, and fish see it as a palatial dwelling."[7] Dōgen writes elsewhere that one "should not be limited to human views" and naïvely think that what one views as water is "what dragons and fish see as water and use as water."[8]

The epistemology implied in Dōgen's view of enlightenment as an ongoing practice of enlightening, as an unending path of discovery, is thus what I would call a nondualistic and nonwilling perspectivism. It is a perspectivism insofar as reality only shows itself one aspect at a time. From a deluding standpoint, this aspect gets determined by the will of an ego-subject that goes out and posits a horizon that delimits—filters or "schematizes"—how a thing can reveal itself. From an enlightening perspective, the aspect is allowed to reveal itself through an event wherein the self has "forgotten itself" in an engaged yet nonwillful openness to the presencing of things. This engagement is neither simply passive nor simply active. For at every moment there is—for the time being—but a single nondual middle-voiced event of "being-time" (*uji*)[9] as a self-revelation of a singular aspect of reality. And just as such singular events are infinite, so is the path of their verification-in-practice.

Let us finally consider the title of Dōgen's text, *Genjōkōan,* which I have ventured to translate "The Presencing of Truth."[10] The term *kōan* (Chin.

7. Waddell and Abe 2002: 43; see also Mizuno 1990: 1:440.

8. Yaoko 1990: 2:198.

9. In the "Uji" fascicle (Mizuno 1990: 2:46–58 ; Waddell and Abe 2002: 48–58), Dōgen famously reads the compound *uji* not simply as "for the time being," but as a nondual event of "being-time."

10. Other noteworthy translations of the title include "Manifesting Suchness" (Waddell and Abe 2002), "Manifesting Absolute Reality" (Cook 1989), "The Realized

kungan) originally meant "official record" or "public law." A *kōan* in this sense would be a publication of a particular rule that is universally binding. According to Dōgen's own disciples, in his thought "the *kō* in *kōan* refers to fairness and identity, while the *an* suggests apportionment and differentiation," such that the compound "*kōan* signified the nondual oneness of identity and differentiation, of emptiness and form, of one and all."[11] Today, however, the term *kōan* is most often used to refer to *kosoku-kōan:* the classic episodes or paradigmatic "cases" that present the practicing student with the words and actions of ancient Zen masters as past instantiations of enlightenment, instantiations that the student must somehow verify in the present. While Dōgen does very often reflect on these *kosoku-kōan,* with the notion of *genjō-kōan* he is referring rather to the living presence of truth in the here and now of everyday reality. Each singular event of our lives presents us with a *kōan,* a challenge and chance for awakening to the truth of things. *Kōan* in this sense is truth as such, not just the truth of epistemological correspondence, but the truth (reality) of things as they present themselves right now for verification, the ubiquitous truth of reality as it presents itself for realization in singular events.

Genjō, short for *genzen-jōju,* means "complete manifestation" or "presentation of completeness." *Genzen* literally means "to appear/manifest/presence in front [of one]." This term could be rendered "manifesting" (which etymologically means "grasping by the hand") but is perhaps best translated as "presencing" (which derives from "being [*esse*] in front of [*prae-*]"). In any case, the manifesting or presencing at issue here is itself an original event—not a subsequent appearance—of reality. There is no truth other than that which presences here and now. Dōgen does not speak of a futuristic salvation or a transcendent Pure Land, but rather of awakening to the truth that is always presencing beneath our feet. Truth presences completely right here and right now, and this living moment (*nikon*) of being-time is all there ever is to life, and to death.[12]

And yet, as we have seen, this event of presencing is not "complete" in the sense of a fulfillment beyond all absence and insufficiency. (Hence I have refrained from translating the title as "The Complete Presencing of Truth.") Moreover, presencing does not simply refer to a pure present that is wholly uncontaminated by the past and the future. As Dōgen writes with respect to firewood and ashes, the presencing of something in its singular "Dharma-position" both "has its before and after" and yet is "cut off from them." The presencing that Dōgen speaks of neither simply excludes nor

---

Universe" (Nishijima and Cross 1994), "Actualizing the Fundamental Point" (Tanahashi 1985), and "Offenbarmachen des vollen Erscheinens" (Ōhashi and Elberfeld 2006).

11. Kim 1985: 56. Kim attributes this interpretation to Senne's *Kikigaki,* whereas Waddell and Abe refer us to Kyōgō's *Shōbōgenzō shō* (Waddell and Abe 2002: 39–40).

12. See "Shōji," Waddell and Abe 2002: 106.

is simply consumed by the past and the future. In one sense it is cut off from them: the past is always already gone and the future is never yet here. But in another sense it integrally implies them: what presences is always essentially open to and interconnected with its before and after, just as it is open to and interconnected with its environs. The *kōan* that Dōgen's text ultimately presents us with for verification is that the presencing of truth is always fully realizable—without ever being closed off and self-satisfied—in each singular moment of our being unceasingly under way.

Translation

When the various things (*dharmas*) are [seen according to] the Buddha Dharma, there are delusion and enlightenment; there is [transformative] practice; there is birth/life; there is death; there are ordinary sentient beings; and there are Buddhas.

When the myriad things are each [seen as] without self [i.e., without independent substantiality], there is neither delusion nor enlightenment; there are neither Buddhas nor ordinary sentient beings; and there is neither birth/life nor death.

Since the Buddha Way originally leaps beyond both plentitude and poverty, there are arising and perishing; there are delusion and enlightenment; and there are ordinary sentient beings and Buddhas.

And yet, although this is how we can say that it is, it is just that flowers fall amid our attachment and regret, and weeds flourish amid our rejecting and loathing.

Carrying the self forward to verify-in-practice (*shushō*) the myriad things is delusion; for the myriad things to come forth and verify-in-practice the self is enlightenment. Buddhas are those who greatly enlighten delusion; ordinary sentient beings are those who are greatly deluded amid enlightenment. Furthermore, there are persons who attain enlightenment on top of enlightenment, and persons who are again deluded within delusion. When Buddhas are truly Buddhas, there is no need for them to be conscious of themselves as Buddhas. Nevertheless, they are verified Buddhas, and they go on verifying this Buddhahood.

Even though by rousing the [whole] body-mind to perceive forms, rousing the [whole] body-mind to listen to sounds, they are intimately apprehended, this is not like a mirror hosting an image, or like the moon and [its reflection in] water. When one side is illuminated, the other side is darkened.

To study the Buddha Way is to study the self. To study the self is to forget the self. To forget the self is to be verified by the myriad things [of the world]. To be verified by the myriad things is to let drop off the body-mind of the self and the body-mind of others. There is laying to rest the traces of enlightenment, and one must ever again emerge from resting content with such traces.

When one first seeks the Dharma, one distances oneself far from its borders. When [one realizes that] the Dharma has already been rightly transmitted to one, one straightaway becomes a person [established in his or her] original element.

A person riding in a boat looks around at the shore, and mistakenly thinks that the shore is drifting along. When one fixes one's eyes closely on the boat, one realizes that it is the boat that is moving forward. In a like manner, if one tries to discern the myriad things with confused assumptions about the body-mind, it can mistakenly seem as though one's own mind and nature are permanent. If one intimately engages in everyday activities, returning to *here,* the concrete principle that all things are without self is evident.

Firewood becomes ashes; it cannot return to being firewood. However, you should not hold the view that something is ashes afterward and firewood before. You should understand that firewood dwells in its Dharma-position, and has its before and after. Yet even though it has a past and a future, it is cut off from them. Ashes are in their Dharma-position, and they have their after and before. Just as this firewood, having become ashes, does not turn back into firewood, after a person dies he does not come back to life. Hence, according to an established teaching of the Buddha Dharma, one does not say that life becomes death. Thus we speak of the "unborn." And it is an established Buddha-turning of the Dharma wheel that death does not become life. Thus we speak of the "unperishing." Life is one temporal state, and death is one temporal state. For example, it is like winter and spring. We [Buddhists] do not think that winter becomes spring or say that spring becomes summer.

For a person to attain enlightenment is like the moon inhabiting water. The moon does not get wet, and the water is not disrupted. Although the moonlight is vast, it inhabits a small measure of water. The entire moon and even all the heavens inhabit the dew on the grass; they inhabit even one drop of water. That enlightenment does not disrupt the person is like the moon not boring a hole in the water. That the person does not obstruct enlightenment is like the drop of dew not obstructing the heavens and moon. The depth [of the one] shall be the measure of the [other's] height. As for the length or brevity of the time period, one should examine whether the water is great or small, and discern whether the heavens and moon are wide or narrow.

When the Dharma does not yet saturate the body-mind, one thinks that it is sufficient. If the Dharma fills the body-mind, one notices an insufficiency.

For example, if one rides in a boat out into the middle of the ocean where there are no mountains [in sight] and looks in the four directions, one will see only a circle without any other aspects in sight. Nevertheless, the great ocean is not circular, and it is not square; the remaining virtues of the ocean are inexhaustible. It is like a palace [for fish]. It is like a jeweled ornament [to gods]. It is just that, as far as my eyes can see, for a while it looks like a circle. It is also like this with the myriad things. Although things within and beyond this dusty world are replete with a variety of aspects, it is only through a cultivated power of vision that one can [intimately] perceive and apprehend them. In order to hear the household customs of the myriad things, you should know that, besides appearing as round or square, there are unlimited other virtues of the ocean and of the mountains, and there are worlds in all four directions. And you should know that it is not only like this over there, but also right here beneath your feet and even in a single drop [of water].

Fish swim through water, and swim as they may there is no limit to the water. Birds fly through the sky, and fly as they may there is no limit to the sky. And yet, fish and birds have never once left the water or sky. It is just that when the required activity is great the use is great, and when the need is small the use is small. In this manner, although they never fail to exhaust the borders of each and every point, turning about [freely] here and there, if a bird were to leave the sky, or if a fish were to leave the water, they would die instantly. One should know that [for a fish] life *is* by means of water, and [for a bird] life *is* by means of the sky. It is [also] the case that life *is* by means of birds and fish. And by means of life birds and fish are able to be. Moreover, we should proceed a step further. That there is the verification-in-practice of [human] lives is also just like this.

Thus, if there were a bird or a fish who aimed to move through the water or sky only after having completely surveyed the water or sky, it could not find its way or attain its place in them. If it attains this place, then, in accordance with this everyday activity, truth presences. If it finds its way, then, in accordance with this everyday activity, there is the presencing of truth. Because this way, this place, is neither great nor small, neither self nor other, neither already in existence nor [first] manifesting now, it is just as it is.

In this manner, when a person verifies-in-practice the Buddha Way, attaining one thing he or she becomes thoroughly familiar with that one thing; encountering one activity he or she [sincerely] practices that one activity. Since this is where the place is and the Way achieves its circulation, the reason that the limits of what is knowable are not known is that this knowing arises and proceeds together with the exhaustive fathoming of the Buddha Dharma. Do not think that attaining this place necessarily entails the self's own knowledge or that it can be understood intellectually. Although right away the ultimate verification presences completely, the intimately concealed being is not necessarily completely presented. And why would it need to be completely visible?

As Chan Master Baoche of Mount Mayu was using his fan, a monk came and asked, "It is the wind's nature to be constantly abiding and there is no place in which it does not circulate. Why then, sir, do you still use a fan?"

The master said, "You only know that it is the nature of the wind to be constantly abiding. You don't yet know the reason [more literally: the principle of the way] that there is no place it does not reach."

The monk said, "What is the reason for there being no place in which it does not circulate?"

At which time the master just used his fan.

The monk bowed reverently.

The verifying experience of the Buddha Dharma and the vital path of its true transmission are like this. To say that if it is constantly abiding one shouldn't use a fan, that even without using a fan one should be able to feel the wind, is to not know [the meaning of] either constantly abiding or the nature of the wind. Because it is the nature of the wind to be constantly abiding, the wind [i.e., ways] of the Buddha household lets the great earth presence as gold and ripens the Milky Way into delicious cream.

Bibliography and Suggested Reading

Other translations of and commentaries on the *Genjōkōan* can be found in the following works.

Cook, Francis H. (1989) *Sounds of Valley Streams: Enlightenment in Dōgen's Zen*. Albany: State University of New York Press.

Kim, Hee-Jin. (1985) *Flowers of Emptiness: Selections from Dōgen's Shōbōgenzō*. Lewiston: Edwin Mellen Press.

Nishijima, Gudo and Chodo Cross. (1994) *Master Dōgen's Shobogenzo: Book 1*. Charleston: BookSurge Publishing.

Ōhashi, Ryōsuke and Rolf Elberfeld. (2006) *Dōgen Shōbōgenzō: Ausgewählte Schriften*. Tokyo: Keio University Press.

Tanahashi, Kazuaki. (1985) *Moon in a Dewdrop: Writings of Zen Master Dogen*. New York: North Point Press.

Waddell, Norman and Masao Abe. (2002) *The Heart of Dōgen's Shōbōgenzō*. Albany: State University of New York Press.

Yasutani, Hakuun. (1996) *Flowers Fall: A Commentary on Zen Master Dōgen's Genjōkōan*. Translated by Paul Jaffe. Boston: Shambala.

PART IV

PHILOSOPHY OF MIND AND THE PERSON

In early Buddhist texts, the Buddha is portrayed as systematically interrogating claims that there is anything that corresponds either to what naïve common sense or sophisticated philosophy regards as a substantial self (*ātman*), whether body, mind, some other entity, or even some set of such entities. He argues instead that the person is a conceptual imputation based on a constantly changing continuum of psychophysical processes. Buddhist thinkers follow this view, and take the person to be a continuum of conditioned mental and physical phenomena lacking an underlying essence or self. This continuum is dependent on aggregates (*skandhas*), which fall into five categories: material form, feeling, perception, volitional forces, and consciousness. The person, then, is regarded as a stream of processes that are interdependent with each other and also with other phenomena.

Buddhist thinkers regard the abandonment of the commitment to the reality of the self, understood as an unchanging essence independent of causal conditions, as necessary for attaining liberation. The source of much of our suffering is this false sense of self, a sense that we exist as an enduring, substantially existent being, instead of as a conventionally aggregated stream of psychophysical processes. This confusion regarding our own identity, which has its roots in innate cognitive tendencies, but which is often reinforced by misleading substantialist philosophies, leads to the craving and aversion that are the immediate causes of suffering, and is hence the root of all suffering.

The doctrine of the selflessness of persons raises several philosophical challenges. First, Buddhist thinkers were required to refute the widespread view held by non-Buddhist philosophers that there is in fact a substantial self, a view that in India was thought to resolve the problems of personal identity and the unity of consciousness. Second, Buddhist philosophers were obliged to address these problems without relying on any such substantial or enduring entity. They were required to provide satisfactory answers to question such as these: If there is no substantial self, what individuates persons over time, what makes them the same person from one day to the next? Why do we experience ourselves as unified subjects, the same persons who act and have feelings and sensations? How does one make sense of feelings, thoughts, and experiences without a subject who has feelings, thoughts, and experiences? And how are our actions connected to their consequences if there is no self who is the same locus of actions and consequences?

In the first chapter of part IV, we encounter early Theravādin views of the self. In the first selection, the *Anatta-lakkhaṇa Sutta* (Discourse on the characteristic of not-self) from the Pali canon, the Buddha argues against regarding any one of the aggregates as a substantial self, on the grounds that they cannot be completely controlled, they lead to suffering, and they are impermanent. In the second text, from the *Mahā-nidāna Sutta* (Great Discourse on causal links), the Buddha argues that if a self exists, there must be a sense that gives rise to the thought "I am," and this, according to the Buddha, requires feeling. However, he also argues that the self cannot be feeling itself, nor can it be something that is not feeling, even if that something itself feels, for something cannot be dependent on that which is not self and still be a substantial self. In the third extract, from the postcanonical *Milindapañha* (Milinda's questions), the monk Nāgasena argues that there is no conceptual need to posit a substantial self. Famously comparing the self to a chariot, in that both are conceptually imputed, Nāgasena argues that the term "person" is applied to a "collection of conditioned interacting processes."

While Buddhists generally accepted the selflessness of persons, there was much debate in classical India about what exactly this meant. The Pudgalavāda view of the self is articulated in the selections from the *Commentary on the Four Āgamas* and *Treatise on Liberation by the Threefold Teachings,* both attributed to Vasubhadra, and a section on the Pudgalavāda view from Vasumitra's *Tenets of the Different Schools.* The Pudgalavādins (Vātsīputrīyas) were Buddhists who rejected the idea that we possess substantial selves independent of the aggregates but who nevertheless argued that the person (*pudgala*) exists; they claimed it is a nominal existent neither different from nor identical to the aggregates. Pudgalavādins are afraid that if we do not acknowledge some kind of person, then the Buddhist path of liberation is meaningless, for there must be something that is liberated. Though much disparaged by other Buddhists, the Pudgalavāda was a mainstream tradition in India for a millennium.

The Pudgalavādin view was relentlessly criticized by other Buddhists and eventually defeated. One such critique is found in Vasubandhu's (c. fourth–fifth century) *Abhidharmakośa* (Treasury of Metaphysics). The first of two selections from chapter IX, "Refutation of the Theory of a Self," is Vasubandhu's argument against the Pudgalavādins' theory of persons. According to Vasubandhu, the Pudgalavādin claim that the *pudgala* is neither the same nor different from the aggregates is incoherent: if we are not identical to the aggregates, as the Pudgalavādins claim, then it follows that we must possess a substantial self.

After criticizing the Pudgalavādins for their alleged misinterpretation of Buddhist doctrine, Vasubandhu then turns to non-Buddhist views of a substantially existing self, the *ātman,* including those of the Nyāya-Vaiśeṣika and Sāṃkhya. The second selection from the *Abhidharmakośa* includes Vasubandhu's critique of non-Buddhist arguments that actions and experiences require a substantial self who acts and experiences and Vasubandhu's constructive project of making sense of action and experience without an underlying subject distinct from the aggregates.

After writing the *Abhidharmakośa,* Vasubandhu became one of the founding figures in the Vijñānavāda, also known as the Cittamātra or Yogācāra. Candrakīrti (c. 600–650) presents a critique of both non-Buddhist accounts and Vijñānavādin views of the self. In the selected verses and commentary from the *Madhyamakāvatāra* (Entry into the middle way), Candrakīrti, who was a Mādhyamika, argues that Vijñānavādins, along with non-Buddhists, mistakenly reify consciousness, or mind. For Candrakīrti, consciousness is thoroughly interdependent: it requires a subject and an object with equivalent ontological status. As a consequence, he argues, the Vijñānavādin position that the mind exists substantially and that external objects are entirely illusory is philosophically untenable.

Nyāya thinkers opposed the Buddhist position and argued that desire and aversion, pleasure and pain, volition and knowledge can only be understood as properties of a self. Moreover, some claimed, whenever we think or say the first person pronoun we have a direct experience of the self. Śāntarakṣ ita (eighth century) criticizes these Nyāya views in his *Tattvasaṣgraha* (Compendium of [views of] reality), with commentary by his disciple Kamalaśīla. In contrast to the Nyāya view, Śāntarakṣita argues that the relation between the self and its alleged properties is not logically justifiable.

Buddhist philosophers grappling with questions of the self also had to understand how it could be transformed as the practitioner made progress on the path to liberation. Zhiyi (538–597), in a classic Tiantai work, *The Great Calming and Contemplation,* describes the transformation of mental activity and with it the transformation of one's existential habitat. For Zhiyi this transformation, in a characteristically Tiantai method, is made possible through following a middle way that embraces the interpenetration of good and evil, sacred and profane, and true and false—that liberates the practitioner from clinging to the self or its emptiness.

Some Buddhist traditions have argued that, ultimately, the mind of any sentient being is, in some sense, identical with the Buddha. In *Secrets on Cultivating the Mind,* the Korean Zen master Pojo Chinul (1158–1210) argues that even when the mind is defiled by ignorance, craving, and aversion, it is fundamentally "void, calm, numinous awareness." The mind is "unstained," "complete," and "whole," not because it has an essence that is pure, Chinul argues, but precisely because it is empty of an essence or inherent existence.

The final chapter of part IV consists of selections from the works of Nishida Kitarō (1870–1945), founder of the twentieth-century Japanese intellectual movement known as the Kyoto School. Nishida, who was trained as an academic philosopher in Western traditions and was also a Zen practitioner, sought to articulate "Buddhist philosophy in Western terminology." In the texts translated here, Nishida finds in Buddhist philosophy a nondual framework to articulate his understanding of the self as continuous yet discontinuous over time. There is no transtemporal essence to the self, according to Nishida, but even though I am not identical to the person I was previously, there is a sense in which I am still not a different person either.

The question of how to properly understand the person and the nature of mind is central to much Buddhist philosophy. The selections here indicate some of the many ways Buddhist thinkers have approached the person and the nature of mind. While these accounts bear some resemblance to several historical and contemporary Western philosophies of the person, they also illustrate singularly Buddhist approaches to understanding the locus of action, identity, and consciousness.

23

Theravāda Philosophy of Mind and the Person

Anatta-lakkhaṇa Sutta, Mahā-nidāna Sutta, and Milindapañha

Peter Harvey

Of the following three selections, the first two, the *Anatta-lakkhaṇa Sutta* and a part of the *Mahānidāna Sutta,* are from the Theravādin Pali canonical collection of discourses attributed to the Buddha. The third is from a postcanonical Pali text, the *Milindapañha.* While they all contain points and arguments of philosophical relevance, they are not as such systematic philosophical texts, and to properly appreciate their nuances and implications, one needs to understand something of their context of thought and practice.

The Buddha's Religio-Philosophical Context

As mapped by the discourses of the Theravāda canon, the brahmins and non-Buddhist renunciants of the Buddha's day were sometimes divided into "eternalists," "annihilationists," and "eel-wrigglers." "Eternalists" were those who believed in some kind of eternal self that existed from rebirth to rebirth and also in liberation from rebirth: the variously understood *ātman* (Skt.) of the *Upaniṣads*, seen as a universal essence within all beings, and the individual *jīva,* or "life principle," of the Jains. "Annihilationists" were those who believed that a person is totally destroyed at death. This is sometimes characterized as a denial of any kind of self (S. IV.400–401), and sometimes as belief in an unchanging self, mental or purely physical, that was then destroyed at death (D. I.34–35).[1]

1. For abbreviations, see chapter 15 here.

"Eel-wrigglers" were skeptics who believed that humans could have no knowledge of such matters as what happened after death (D. I.26–27).

The Buddha did not accept any of these views, but saw unenlightened beings as subject to rebirth after death, according to the nature of their previous actions (karma).[2] The link from one life to the next was a stream of conditioned and changing states: a "middle" way of understanding that avoided both eternalism and annihilationism, and was not skepticism either (S. II.20).

Given that the Buddha was not a materialist, could he simply be called a mind-body "dualist"? Not in a Cartesian sense. He did not see either mind or body as unitary substances. Rather, both were bundles of changing, conditioned, and interacting processes.[3] Yet as any mental or physical process can only exist due to supporting conditions (other processes), it is not accepted that "everything is a unity" or "everything is a (disconnected) diversity" (S. II.77).

The Early Buddhist Approach to "Self"

The term *attā* (Pali, Skt. *ātman*), or "self," was much used in the Buddha's day and has various applications in early Buddhist texts. In many, it simply means "myself," "herself," or "oneself." In some, it is equivalent to "character," that is, what is known in self-knowledge, or to body, or personality, or the mind (*citta*) as the center of emotions (Harvey 1995: 19–21). In the last of these senses, a spiritually developed person is even said in Buddhist texts to have a "great self" (*mah-attā;* A.I.249; Harvey 1995: 55–58).

However, there is also a referent of the term *attā* which is not accepted: when it refers to "self" or "I" as something that is permanent, an unchanging essence of a person that is fully autonomous and so in total control of itself and its possessions: the kind of self accepted particularly by the Brahmanical *Upaniṣad*s or Jain texts. Early Buddhist texts never accept anything as being *this* kind of "self."[4]

Whenever anyone claimed any item, whether physical or mental, as "Self," the Buddha always critically examined the claim, to argue that the item is really *an-attā* (Pali, Skt. *an-ātman*): not-Self, a non-Self, not a Self.[5]

2. His belief in rebirth is presented in the texts as based on his memory of many thousands of lives, a memory that arose when his mind was deeply calmed and hence sensitized in an alert state of profound meditative stilling (e.g. D.I.81–83).

3. One might characterize this view as "twin-category process pluralism" (Harvey 1993).

4. While Pali and Sanskrit have no capital letters, in translation it is appropriate to signal reference to this kind of self by writing it "Self."

5. The term on its own does not mean "no self" or "no Self," and certainly not "no soul." While the meaning of "soul" in Western thought varies, it is primarily that which gives life to the body, and Buddhism does not deny that there is something that does this. In Buddhism, it is simply that any "soul" must be recognized as not being a fixed, permanent, unitary entity, which at least rules out any idea of an *immortal* soul.

Equivalent to saying something is "not-Self" is to say it is "empty" (Pali *suñña,* Skt. *śūnya*) of Self and what belongs to Self (S. IV.54).

Even nirvana (Pali *Nibbāna*), the final goal of early and Theravāda Buddhism, is included in what is not-Self (Harvey 1995: 23). While being unconditioned (A. II.34), and beyond impermanence and any suffering, as a *dhamma,* a basic item of possible experience, it is included in "all *dhammas* are not-Self" (A. II.286): that is, everything is not-Self.

Nevertheless, the not-Self teaching is not a bald denial of Self, but a persistent undermining of any attempt to take anything as "Self," and thus be attached to it. It is a contemplative strategy to induce, in the end, a letting go of *everything.* To reduce it to a bald "there is no Self" would be to short-circuit this process. Indeed, the Buddha was once directly asked "Is there a s/Self?" to which he responded with silence, as he did to "Is there no s/Self?" (S. IV.400–401). After the questioner had left, he explained that if he had said "There is a s/Self," this would have been to side with the eternalists, and contradicted his knowledge that "all *dhammas* are not-Self." To have said "There is no s/Self," would have been to side with the annihilationists, and make the confused questioner think that he had lost a s/Self he previously had. The simplest explanation of this response is that the Buddha accepted a changing empirical self that was not destroyed at death, but flowed on into a future rebirth. The annihilationist denial of s/Self rejected any idea of rebirth, and thus denied "self" in this sense.

The Five Aggregates

In the texts of Theravāda Buddhism, the most common way of dividing up the processes making up a person is in terms of the five *khandhas* (Pali, Skt. *skandhas*). The *khandhas*, "aggregates" or "bundles," or five "aggregates (as objects) of grasping" (Pali *upādāna-kkhandhas*), are material form, feeling, perception, constructing activities, and consciousness.

Material form (Pali, Skt. *rūpa*) consists of the physical elements (solidity, cohesion, heat, and air) that make up the body of a living being, and more subtle processes derived from these. Feeling (Pali, Skt. *vedanā*) is the quality of experience that is hedonic tone, whether pleasant, painful, or neither. This is not the same as emotion, though it accompanies any emotion or sensory experience. Perception (Pali *saññā,* Skt. *saṃjñā*) is associative knowledge as cognition, mental labeling, interpretation, recognition, how one sees things. Constructing activities (Pali *saṅkhāras*, Skt. *saṃskāras*) are a range of mental responses[6] to objects, with will or volition (Pali, Skt. *cetanā*) being the leading one, others being planning, lines of thought, emotions, habits. Consciousness (Pali *viññāṇa,* Skt. *vijñāna*) is discriminative consciousness, sensory discernment, awareness of sensory and mental objects, object-processing intelligence.

6. The *Abhidhamma* literature lists fifty constructing activities.

In the *Abhidhamma* literature, the aggregates are seen to change from moment to moment, and at any one instant, there is only one kind of consciousness, perception, and feeling, though various constructing activities. Hence mental processing is in one sense in series (only one type of consciousness at once) and in another in parallel (a consciousness is accompanied by various other processes).

Levels of Belief in a Self

Belief in a Self is seen to come in two forms. The first is Self-identity view:[7] to take any of the aggregates as (1) Self, (2) the property of Self, (3) in Self, or (4) containing Self. It is to view something specific as "this am I" (S. III.128). This is overcome by a person who is a "Stream-enterer": one who has a foretaste of nirvana and is certain to fully realize it, as an *arahat* (Pali, Skt. *arhat*), a liberated saint, within seven lives at most.

Second, there is the more deep-rooted "I am conceit" (*asmi-māna*), which remains even once a person becomes a Stream-enterer. This is a vague attitude of "I am" with respect to *all* of the aggregates, just as the scent belongs to the whole flower, not just to a particular part of it (S. III.130). While seen as rooted in delusion, it is regarded as a really occurring state—ego, self-centeredness, or self-importance—one that is seen to weigh down the empirical self. The *arahat* has overcome it.

Accordingly, when the Buddha is asked by a monk "Who feels?" or "Who craves?" (S. II.13–14), he says that these are not valid questions. It is, however, valid to ask what feeling or craving are conditioned by, namely, sensory stimulation and feeling, respectively. That is, the enlightened see a person as a stream of interacting processes, but see no "I" operating them.

The *Anatta-lakkhaṇa Sutta:* The "Discourse on the Characteristic of Not-Self"

This discourse (S. III.66–68) is seen as the second that the Buddha gave, to five former ascetics who had already practiced with him so as to become at least Stream-enterers. On two grounds, it argues that each of the aggregates must be seen as not-Self.

First, one cannot control the aggregates at will, as one could with something that was part of an essential Self. While some control can be exercised over the aggregates, this is limited. Hence one inevitably experiences various kinds of "affliction." One can see these as: bodily illness and aging; the

7. "Self-identity view" renders *sakkāya-diṭṭhi* (Pali, Skt. *satkāya-dṛṣṭi*), literally, "views on the existing group," that is, views on the five aggregates, taking them as somehow related to a Self (M.I. 299).

disturbance of unwanted feelings; seeing things in distorted ways, or ways one does not like; thinking in distorted, or agitated ways, or compulsively, or other ways one does not like or choose; the mind being pulled this way and that to different objects, or awareness constantly changing and fluctuating, or being fuzzy and clouded.

Second, the aggregates are impermanent, and hence induce pain (whether physical or mental). If something pertained to an essential and unchanging Self of a person, it could not cause pain; hence it is inappropriate to take any of the aggregates as "mine," in the sense of a reliable possession; what "I am" in an essential way; or "my Self." As impermanent, they cannot be a permanent Self, and as associated with suffering, they cannot be within the ambit or control of something that is supposedly one's true autonomous essence.

Translation

Thus have I heard. At one time, the Blessed One was dwelling at Baranasi in the Deer Park at Isipatana. There the Blessed one addressed the monks of the group of five thus: "Monks!" "Venerable sir!" those monks replied. The Blessed One said this:

"Material form, monks, is not-Self. Now were this material form Self, it would not lead to affliction, and one would be able to effectively say, 'Let my material form be like this, or not like this.' But inasmuch as material form is not-Self, therefore it leads to affliction, and one cannot effectively say, 'Let my material form be like this, or not like this.' [The same is then said of feeling, perception, the constructing activities, and consciousness.]

What do you think about this, monks? Is material form permanent or impermanent?" "Impermanent, venerable sir." "But is that which is impermanent painful (*dukkhaṃ*) or pleasant (*sukhaṃ*)?" "Painful, venerable sir." "But is it fitting to regard that which is impermanent, painful, and of a nature to change, as 'This is mine, this am I, this is my Self?' " "No, venerable sir." [The same is then said of feeling, perception, the constructing activities, and consciousness.]

"Therefore, monks, whatever is material form: past, future, or present; internal or external; gross or subtle; low or excellent; far or near; all material form should be seen as it really is by right wisdom, thus: 'This is not mine, this I am not, this is not my Self.'[The same is then said of feeling, perception, the constructing activities, and consciousness.] Seeing in this way, monks, the learned noble disciple turns away from (*nibbindati*) material form,[8] and from feeling, perception, constructing activities, and consciousness. Turning away, he becomes dispassionate; through dispassion, [his mind] is freed;

8. That is, he lets go of material form, does not grasp at, lean on, or identify with it, having had enough of it, so as to even feel revulsion for it.

in freedom, there is the knowledge: 'It's freed.' He understands, 'Destroyed is birth, the holy life has been lived, what had to be done has been done, there is no more for this state of being.' "[9]

Thus spoke the Blessed One, and, delighted, the group of five monks rejoiced at what the Blessed One had said. Moreover, while this discourse was being uttered, their minds were freed of taints by nonclinging.

Extract from the *Mahā-nidāna Sutta,* the "Great Discourse on Causal Links"

The following passage (D. II.66–68) considers three ways in which those who believe in Self may relate it to "feeling" (*vedanā*). While the passage itself is not set up as a refutation of Self, its implications can be seen to rule out any possibility of a Self. The first view is that Self is simply identical to feeling. If it were only *one* of the three modes of feeling (pleasant, painful, neutral), though, it would be an intermittent thing, not permanent, and it would keep disappearing, which would be odd for a "Self." Yet if it were something that encompassed all three kinds of feelings, it would be a fluctuating mixture of opposites, which is seen as unacceptable for a genuine Self.

The second view is that Self is not feeling, and lacks any experience. This is refuted on the grounds that the sense "I am" requires the presence of feeling of some kind, the presumption being that there could be no Self without a sense of "I am." The third view, that Self *is* not feeling, but is something that *feels,* has a similar refutation: if feeling came to cease, how could there be the sense of a particular I-identity, "this am I"?

The unstated implications of these three refutations are far-reaching. If Self exists, it would have a sense "I am" or "this am I,"[10] which would depend on feeling. But feeling is not-Self (refutation 1), and elsewhere it is stated, "How will the eye [or any of the other senses or sense-objects], which is arisen from what is not-Self, be Self?" (S. IV.130). This means that anything *dependent* on what is not-Self must *itself* be not-Self. The "I" that is Self would thus turn out to be not-Self. But if there can only be a Self under conditions that would make it *not*-Self, then it is clearly impossible for there to be such a thing as a Self: *the concept itself is self-contradictory.* In fact, S. III.105 says that there is only "I am" by clinging to the aggregates, which are, of course, not-Self. That is, a sense of Self only arises with respect to the aggregates of bodily and mental factors, but it is not *legitimately* applied even here.

9. I.e. a person becomes an *arahat,* free of the causes of any further rebirth. He or she experiences nirvana in life, and finally enters it on dying, as a state beyond description (Harvey 1995: 227–245).

10. The sense of "I am" is the "I am" conceit, and the sense "this am I" is Self-identity view.

Translation

In what ways, Ānanda, does one who regards Self regard it? (1) Regarding Self, he regards it to be feeling: "My Self is feeling," or (2) "My Self is not feeling, my Self is without experience," or (3) "My Self is not feeling, but my Self is not without experience, my Self *feels,* it has the attribute of feeling."[11]

(1) Now Ānanda, one who says "My Self is feeling" should be told, "There are three kinds of feeling, friend: pleasant, painful, and neither-pleasant-nor-painful [neutral]. Which of these three feelings do you regard as Self?" When a pleasant feeling is felt, no painful or neutral feeling is felt, only pleasant feeling. When a painful feeling is felt, no pleasant or neutral feeling is felt, only painful feeling. When a neutral feeling is felt, no pleasant or painful feeling is felt, only neutral feeling.

Pleasant feeling is impermanent, conditioned, dependently originated, subject to destruction, to passing away, to fading away, to cessation. The same applies to painful and neutral feeling. So anyone who, on feeling a pleasant feeling, thinks "This is my Self," must, at the cessation of that pleasant feeling, think "My Self has departed!" The same applies to painful and neutral feeling. Thus, whoever thinks "My Self is feeling" is regarding as Self something that in this present life is impermanent, a mixture of pleasure and pain, subject to arising and passing away. Therefore it is not fitting to maintain "My Self is feeling."

(2) But anyone who says, "My Self is not feeling, my Self is without experience" should be asked, "If, friend, no feeling existed, could there be the thought, 'I am'?" [To this he would have to reply] "No, venerable sir." Therefore, it is not fitting to maintain "My Self is not feeling, my Self is without experience."

(3) And anyone who says, "My Self is not feeling, but my Self is not without experience, my Self feels, it has the attribute of feeling" should be asked, "Well, friend, if all feelings entirely and completely ceased without remainder, could there be the thought 'this am I'?" [To this he would have to reply] "No, venerable sir." Therefore, it is not fitting to maintain "My Self is not feeling, but my Self is not without experience, my Self feels, it has the attribute of feeling."

From the time, Ānanda, when a monk no longer regards Self as feeling, or Self as without experience, or "My Self feels, it has the attribute of feeling," not so regarding, he clings to nothing in the world; not clinging, he does not tremble; not trembling, he personally experiences nirvana, and he understands, "Destroyed is (re-)birth, the holy life has been lived, what had to be done has been done, there is no more for this state of being."

11. The commentary sees these three views as, respectively, identifying Self with the aggregate(s) of feeling, material form, and the three mental aggregates other than feeling: perception, constructing activities, and consciousness.

Extract from the *Milindapañha,* "Milinda's Questions"

The *Milindapañha,* a text dating from around the first century C.E., purports to be a series of conversations between a Bactrian-Greek king, Milinda (Menandros, reigned 155–130 B.C.E.), and the Buddhist monk Nāgasena.[12] Its key point is that "person," or "being," or indeed "self," is not some mysterious essence, whether identical with any body part, or with the five aggregates individually or collectively, or something apart from these. Just as a "chariot" is not any chariot component or the totality of components, or something separate from the components, but a conventional term applied by common usage to the rightly assembled collection of components, so when there is the functioning collection of five aggregates the term "a being" or "a person" is applied. In the assembled mental and physical components of "self" in the everyday sense, there is no Self, no person-essence, just a collection of conditioned interacting processes. The great Theravādin commentator Buddhaghosa (fourth-fifth century C.E.) explains, "in the ultimate sense, when each thing [*dhamma*] is examined, there is no being as a basis for the assumption 'I am' or 'I'; in the ultimate sense there is only mentality and material form (*nāma-rūpa-*)."[13]

Translation

"How is the venerable one known?"...

"Sire, I am known as Nāgasena.... But though (my) parents gave (me) the name Nāgesena or Sūrasena or Vīrasena or Sīhasena, yet it is but a denotation, appellation, designation, current usage, for Nāgasena is only a name, since no person is apprehended here."

Then King Milinda spoke thus, "Good sirs... is it suitable to approve of that?... If, venerable Nāgasena, the person is not apprehended, who then is it that gives you the requisites of robe-material... who is it that makes use of them? Who is it that guards moral virtue, practices meditative development, realizes... nirvana? Who is it that kills a living thing?... Therefore, there is no wholesome action, no unwholesome action, there is no doer of wholesome or unwholesome actions, or one who makes another act thus, there is no fruit or ripening of action (karma) well or ill done. If, venerable Nāgasena, someone killed you, there would be no onslaught on a living being for him. Also, venerable Nāgasena, you would have no teacher, no preceptor, no ordination. If you say, 'Fellows in the holy life address me, sire, as Nāgasena,' what here is Nāgasena? Is it, venerable sir, that the hairs of the head are Nāgasena?" "O no, sire." "That the hairs of the body are Nāgesena?" "O no, sire." "That the nails... the teeth, the skin, the flesh, the sinews, the bones,

12. The extract given here is Miln. 25–28.
13. *Visuddhimagga* p.594. See Nanamoli 2003 for translation of this text.

the marrow, the kidneys, the heart, the liver, the membranes, the spleen, the lungs, the intestines, the mesentery, the stomach, the excrement, the bile, the phlegm, the pus, the blood, the sweat, the fat, the tears, the serum, the saliva, the mucus, the synovic fluid, the urine, or the brain in the head[14] are (any of them) Nāgasena?" "O no, sire."

"Is Nāgasena material form, venerable sir?" "O no, sire." "Is Nāgasena feeling...perception...the constructing activities, or consciousness?" "O no, sire."

"But then, venerable sir, is Nāgasena form-feeling-perception-constructing-activities-and-consciousness?" "O no, sire." "But then, venerable sir, is there Nāgasena apart from form-feeling-perception-constructing-activities-and-consciousness?" "O no, sire." "Though I, venerable sir, am asking you repeatedly, I do not see this Nāgasena. Nāgasena is only a sound, venerable sir. For who here is Nāgasena? You, venerable sir, are speaking an untruth, a lying word. There is no Nāgasena."

Then the venerable Nāgasena spoke thus to King Milinda: "You, sire, are a noble, delicately nurtured....Now, did you come on foot or in a conveyance?" "I, venerable sir, did not come on foot, I came in a chariot." "If, sire, you came by chariot, show me the chariot. Is the pole the chariot, sire?" "O no, venerable sir." "Is the axle the chariot?" "O no, venerable sire" "Are the wheels...the body of the chariot, the flagstaff, the yoke, the reins, or the goad the chariot?" "O no, venerable sir." "But then, sire, is the chariot the pole-axle-wheels-body-flagstaff-yoke-reins-and-goad?" "O no, venerable sir." "But then, sire, is there a chariot apart from pole-axle-wheels-body-flagstaff-yoke-reins-and-goad?" "O no, venerable sir."

"Though I, sire, am asking you repeatedly, I do not see the chariot. Chariot is only a sound, sire. For what here is the chariot? You sire, are speaking an untruth, a lying word. There is no chariot. You, sire, are the chief *rāja* of the whole of India. Of whom are you afraid that you speak a lie?"...

"I, venerable Nāgasena, am not telling a lie, for it is dependent on (*paṭicca*) the pole, dependent on the axle [and the other parts]... that 'chariot' exists as a denotation, appellation, designation, as a current usage, a name."

"It is well; you, sire, understand a chariot. Even so is it for me, sire, it is dependent on the hair of the head, and on the hair of the body...and dependent on the brain in the head, and dependent on material form, and on feeling, on perception, the constructing activities, and dependent on consciousness that 'Nāgasena' exists as a denotation, appellation, designation, as a current usage, merely as a name. But according to the highest meaning, a person is not apprehended here. This, sire, was spoken by the nun Vajirā face to face with the Blessed One [at S. I.135]:

14. A standard list of "thirty-two parts of the body" contemplated in one kind of Buddhist meditation, though often the brain is not listed.

Just as, with an assemblage of parts,
The word 'chariot' is used,
So, when the aggregates exist,
There is the convention 'a being.' "

"It is wonderful, venerable Nāgasena. . . . The explanations of the questions that were asked are very brilliant."

Bibliography and Suggested Reading

Collins, Steven. (1982) *Selfless Persons: Imagery and Thought in Theravāda Buddhism*. Cambridge: Cambridge University Press.

Harvey, Peter. (1993) "The Mind-body Relationship in Pāli Buddhism: A Philosophical Investigation." *Asian Philosophy* 3/1: 29–41.

Harvey, Peter. (1995) *The Selfless Mind: Personality, Consciousness and Nirvana in Early Buddhism*. Richmond, U.K., Curzon Press.

Ñāṇamoli, Bhikkhu. (2003) *The Path of Purification*. [Translation of Buddhaghosa's *Visuddhimagga*], 4th ed. Kandy: Buddhist Publication Society.

Siderits, Mark. (2003) *Personal Identity and Buddhist Philosophy: Empty Persons*. Oxford: Ashgate.

24

Pudgalavāda Doctrines of the Person

Dan Lusthaus

No Buddhist school has been more vilified by its Buddhist peers or misunderstood by modern scholars than the so-called pudgalavāda[1] school. Other Buddhists accused them of violating the fundamental Buddhist tenet of no-self (*anātman*) by holding the view that a real ontological self exists that, their accusers argued, pudgalavādins try to camouflage by calling it *pudgala* (person) rather than *ātman* (self). Modern scholars, forming opinions largely based on or influenced by the hostile polemical literature of the pudgalavādins' opponents, reiterate that accusation.[2] In addition, until recently scholars considered pudgalavādins to be a marginal sect, of minor historical and doctrinal influence, significant only for playing the role of reviled heretics. Even the term pudgalavāda, which scholars continue to use, appears to be a disparaging label foisted on them by their opponents, not a term they used to characterize themselves. However, both accusations—of promoting the idea of an ontological self and of being marginal—are directly contradicted by the surviving examples of the pudgalavādins' own literature and by a more judicious examination of the historical record.

I wish to gratefully acknowledge the many helpful suggestions from Lance Cousins and Stephen Hodge on earlier drafts of the translations.

1. I leave pudgalavāda in lower case, rather than capitalize it, in order to indicate that it is not the proper name of a school or sect, but a label attached to the Vātsīputrīya, Saṃmitīya, etc. schools by their opponents.
2. See, for example, Priestley 1999 and Duerlinger 2003.

Starting with the charge of marginality, it turns out that the Vātsīputrīyas (their actual name, taken from their founder) were one of the most popular *mainstream* Buddhist sects in India for more than a thousand years. Some traditional sources claim their origins go back to the time of the Buddha, though most scholars think that other sources assigning their beginning to the third century B.C.E. are more accurate. By the second century C.E. at the latest, they had subdivided into four distinct subschools, the most prominent and successful being the Saṃmitīyas (see Vasumitra's *Tenets,* translated here). Two Chinese pilgrims who traveled to India in the seventh century, Xuanzang and Yijing, inform us in their travelogues that the Saṃmitīyas were to be found throughout India and even in Southeast Asia and the South Sea Islands. They were especially prominent in Western India, a region that also served as a travel route through which Buddhism flowed to the north out of India and into which Central and East Asian Buddhists came to study in Buddhism's homeland.[3]

While their opponents—notably Vasubandhu's *Abhidharmakośa-bhāṣya* (chap. 9, Duerlinger 2003), Candrakīrti's *Madhyamakāvatara* (chap. 6), and Śāntarakṣita and Kamalaśīla's *Tattvasaṃgraha-pañjikā*—accused them of promoting the idea of a "real" self, the handful of surviving Vātsīputrīya texts strenuously deny this, instead insisting that the *pudgala* is a *prajñapti* (only a nominal existent) that is neither identical to nor different from the *skandhas.* Since accusing a Buddhist opponent of harboring an *ātmavāda* view (view of eternal selfhood) is one of the most virulent accusations a Buddhist can lodge against another, and we find this trump card played in several other questionable situations—such as against the Yogācāras' theory of an eighth consciousness, the *ālaya-vijñāna,* when clearly the Yogācāras have taken great pains to define the *ālaya-vijñāna* in ways that fully avoid that charge—we should be cautious about accepting such accusations on their face.

Prajñapti is a multivalent term that many Buddhist schools deployed in a variety of ways. Literally *prajñapti* means "leading to knowledge." It can mean a teaching device, a designation, an instruction, a heuristic, a name or label for a complex of conditions, and so on.[4] For example, Buddhists

3. Xuanzang's travelogue carefully records the monasteries and temples in the various regions and cities he visited, their sectarian affiliations, and the number of monastics in each. Lamotte's tabulation of Xuanzang's census (Lamotte 1988: 539–544) indicated that half of the non-Mahāyāna monastics in India were Saṃmitīya, with double the number of monks of the next largest sect, the Sthaviras (Theravādins), and with almost three times as many monasteries as all the other sects combined (1,351 of 2,079 total monasteries). Cousins has argued that Lamotte miscalculated, overestimating the Saṃmitīya presence, but even his downward recalculation preserves their status as the largest non-Mahāyāna group, though he reduces their percentage to only a fourth of such monastics (Cousins 1995). At Buddhism's demise in India, the Saṃmitīyas were the last Indian Buddhists in the Northwest to be absorbed into Islam after the Arab conquests (Maclean 1989).

4. See Law 1979: viii–ix.

argued about whether things such as "karmic accrual" (*prāpti*) or "aging" are actual real things (*dravya*) or only nominalist labels (*prajñapti*) for complexes of causal processes. The causal processes would be real (*dravya*), the labels only conceptual shorthand (*prajñapti*). That the earliest Buddhist texts associated *pudgala* with *prajñapti* is clear not only from the prooftexts cited in Vātsīputrīya texts (which correspond to passages still found in the Theravāda *Tipiṭaka*), but from the title of the fourth text in the Pali Abhidhamma canon, *Puggala-paññati* (Skt. *Pudgala-prajñapti*), heuristically translated into English as *Human Types* (Law 1979).

The Vātsīputrīya argument is that the *pudgala* is a necessary *prajñapti* since any theory of karma, or any theory that posits that individuals can make spiritual progress for themselves or can assist other individuals to do likewise, is incoherent without it. Karma means that an action done at one time has subsequent consequences for the same individual at a later time, or even a later life. If the positive and negative consequences of an action don't accrue to the self-same individual, then it would make no sense to speak of things like progress (who is progressing?), and Buddhist practice itself becomes incoherent. If there are no persons, then there is no one who suffers, no one who performs and reaps the consequences of his or her own karma, no Buddha, no Buddhists, and no Buddhism. Obviously, those are not acceptable consequences for a Buddhist.

Buddhists speak of *skandha-upādāna,* "the aggregates of appropriation," which raises the obvious question: Who/what appropriates the five *skandhas,* collecting them into a single living entity? If the appropriator is something different from the *skandhas* themselves, then there is a sixth *skandha,* which is doctrinally impermissible. If the *skandhas* appropriate themselves, that leads to a vicious cycle of infinite regress. Hence, the Vātsīputrīyas argue, the nominal person (*pudgala*) is neither the same as nor different from the *skandhas.* It is a heuristic fiction that avoids these unwarranted consequences and lends coherence by also corresponding to how actual persons experience themselves—that is, as distinct individuals continuous with, but not absolutely identical to or reducible to, their own pasts and futures. Similarly, Buddhists speak of past and future lives. But what remains constant or continuous between such lives? If it is a self-same invariant identity, then this would indeed be a case of *ātmavāda,* a view the Vātsīputrīyas, like all Buddhists, reject. In what sense would someone be the same or different from the person in one's previous life? If completely different, then to posit a continuity between them is incoherent. If the same, then their real discontinuities are ignored, leading to a form of eternalism, another impermissible view for Buddhists. Hence, they are neither the same nor different, but linked by a fictional *pudgala.* Finally, Buddhist practice leads to nirvana; but who attains this? If there is an integral individual that ceases on attaining nirvana, then this would entail the unwarranted view of annihilationalism. If there is no cessation of the karmic individual, then there is no nirvana. Both extremes, though implicit in standard Buddhist formulations, render Buddhism itself incoherent, a problem only solved, the Vātsīputrīyas argue, if one admits the fictional *pudgala* implicit in standard Buddhist doctrine.

A "fiction," in this sense, does not simply mean something unreal, but rather, like any good work of fiction, something that does *explain,* in a nonliteral way, something real, and that can move, inspire, elicit, and evoke meaningful thoughts and actions. The *pudgala* is that type of "fiction." The self as permanent selfhood is unreal, but the experience of individual personhood is a fiction everyone experiences.[5] While for the pudgalavādins there is no ontological "self" or permanent, substantial person, there is a fictitious "person" that is neither the same as nor different from the actual ontological processes accepted by all other Buddhists as "real" constituents of a being, namely, the *skandhas, āyatanas,* and so on. The three *prajñaptis* discussed in the passages are unavoidable fictions that not only provide doctrinal coherence; they also serve as refutations and correctives for insidious false views, such as eternalism and annihilationalism.

Though only a tiny portion of the pudgalavādins' vast literature has survived, we are fortunate to have two Chinese translations of what, at its core, was a single text. These are *Si ahanmu chao jie* (Commentary on the Four Agamas), authored by *Vasubhadra,[6] and translated by Kumārabuddhi in 382, and *Sanfa du lun* (Treatise on Liberation by the Threefold Teachings), also attributed to *Vasubhadra, translated by Gautama Saṇghadeva in 391.[7] For convenience, I will refer to these as the Longer Version and Shorter Version,

5. Later Buddhists, especially in Mahāyāna, used the term *upāya* (expedient means) to signify a similar notion of efficacious fiction. That notion of *upāya* may have directly developed from the Vātsīputrīya understanding of *prajñapti.*

6. An asterisk before a Sanskrit reconstruction from Chinese indicates that it is unattested or involves some uncertainty.

7. The translator of the Longer Version, Kumārabuddhi, was a member of the Turfan royal family who, after becoming a monk, was sent to China as part of a diplomatic envoy to deliver Buddhist texts and other gifts to the Chinese rulers. Dao'an, a leading Chinese figure at that time, drafted him to translate the Longer Version, believing it was an Abhidharma text, the one "basket" of the Triple Basket (*Tripiṭaka*) that had not been translated into Chinese yet (the other two baskets are the Vinaya and the Āgamas). Huiyuan, Dao'an's major disciple, supervised the translation, which involved Kumārabuddhi reading the text aloud and explaining it, and Chinese assistants copying down what he said while attempting to render it in literate prose. Huiyuan describes the translation process as difficult, suggesting that Kumārabuddhi was difficult to work with and that he, Huiyuan, was not fully satisfied with the results. The resulting text remains difficult to understand in many places. This is probably why, ten years later, after Dao'an had died, Huiyuan pressed another translator, Gautama Saṅghadeva, to retranslate the treatise. Saṅghadeva's work was more professional, but he was working at a time before translation standards were adequately established (Dao'an, famously, was a leading force pressing for such standards), so his efforts are also often unclear to modern readers. His command of Chinese (as well as Indic languages) appears to be noticeably superior to Kumārabuddhi's. While Kumārabuddhi's sectarian affiliation is unclear, Saṅghadeva was probably a Vātsīputrīya, since Huiyuan informs us that he devotedly recited the *Sanfa du lun* daily. Incidentally, an idiosyncratic feature of Huiyuan's own doctrines is the idea of an immortal *shen,* or spirit, which likely owes something to his *pudgalavādin* contacts.

respectively.[8] Both Chinese renderings—as is unfortunately the case for many pre-fifth-century Chinese Buddhist translations—are difficult texts, with many problematic passages. These two versions also greatly differ from each other in wording, phrasing, semantic implications, the ordering of parts, and so on, with one or the other expanding at certain points through extended passages entirely absent from the other version. This will be obvious when comparing the two sections translated here, which are based on a single core passage.

Both versions describe three types of *prajñapti.* The Shorter Version appears first here, even though it was translated later, because it offers a more concise version of the passage. The Longer Version expands on several things, most notably the second type of *prajñapti,* which the Shorter Version describes only as "*prajñapti* of the past," while the Longer Version renames this "*prajñapti* of metaphorical devices" and applies it to the "three times," that is, past, present and future. Whether the differences represent different redactions of a root text, sectarian distinctions among the Vātsīputrīyas, or liberties taken by the translators is unclear. The key to understanding both versions is to see that all three *prajñaptis* have no other purpose than to avoid the hidden, "unsaid" presuppositions lurking in the doctrines held by other Buddhists; that while other Buddhists might leave the word "*pudgala*" unsaid, the narratives presupposed in their doctrines require it.

The issue the passage raises is not the affirmation of something that exists ineffably—as some modern scholars have assumed—but rather that Buddhists who talk about such things as *skandhas*-of-appropriation (*skandha-upādāna*), previous (and future) lives, and nirvana as entailing the cessation of the appropriation of *skandhas*—as all mainstream Buddhists do—are dabbling in "unsayables," but they are not aware of that, and consider such discussion taboo. One of the two likely Sanskrit candidates for the term being translated into Chinese as "not-said" or "unsayable" is *avācya,* which means something "not to be addressed," "improper to be uttered," or "not distinctly expressed." The other candidate is *avaktavya,* which also means something that should not to be said, but may also indicate something indescribable. The Vātsīputrīyas are using it in that double sense: the *pudgala* is a taboo subject for other Buddhists, even though the metaphysical narratives they employ presuppose it; and what is indicated by the *prajñapti* "*pudgala*" cannot be explained more precisely, since appropriation without an appropriator,

8. The translations here are my own, from T. 25.1505.10a3–29 (Longer Version) and T. 25.1506.24a29–b7 (Shorter Version). (T refers to *Taishō shinshū daizōkyō.* [A standard collection of the East Asian Buddhist canon compiled in Japan] Takakusu Junjirō, Watanabe Kaikyoku, et al. (eds.), 100 vols. Tokyo: Taishō Issaikyō Kankōkai, 1924–1932.) Priestley also translated both passages (Priestley 1999: 56–60), though in a quite different manner. Summaries of the full texts with partial translations and paraphrases can also be found in Thich Thien Chau 1999. Hurvitz 1967 is a partial translation of the Kumārabuddhi text—about one-fifth of the full text—but he does not include the passage translated here. Hurvitz, while recognizing an allusion to a pudgalavāda doctrine in one passage, failed to identify the text as a whole as a pudgalavāda work.

linkage across lives without an invariant identity, and the cessation of a nonself are intrinsically incoherent notions. The Vātsīputrīyas are offering a clever polemic that accuses other Buddhists of ignoring the "unsayables" in their own heuristic expressions. The "unsayable" of primary interest to the Vātsīputrīyas is the *pudgala* (person), which is a necessary nominal construction required to perform Buddhist analysis, progress on the Buddhist path, and make sense of the most basic Buddhist concepts, especially karma.

The *pudgala* is on the one hand merely a linguistic construction. On the other hand, it involves something in everyone's experience about which we can say nothing definitively coherent. It is unreal (merely nominal), but experientially, even soterically, effective. As the passage makes clear, the Vātsīputrīyas are attempting to forge a middle way between extremes of eternalism and annihilationalism, existence and nonexistence, while affirming that, nevertheless, the *pudgala* as a *prajñapti* is an effective, if imprecise, way of talking about requisites for cultivating the Buddhist path.

The third selection here is the section on the Vātsīputrīyas from Vasumitra's *Tenets of the Different Schools* based on Xuanzang's Chinese translation.[9] The Indic original is not extant but is available in one Tibetan and three Chinese translations. This text was probably composed around the second century C.E. Vasumitra gives lists of main tenets for eighteen Buddhist schools—several varieties of Mahāsāṇghikas, Sarvāstivāda, Prajñaptivāda, Haimavatas, Mahīśāsakas, and so on—presenting them in roughly chronological order with explanations of which schools splintered from which.[10]

Translation: The Shorter Version—From the *Sanfa du lun* (Treatise on Liberation by the Threefold Teachings)

Q: What is unsayable?

A: *The unsayable is [what remains implicit in] the Figurative Expressions* (prajñaptis) *concerning appropriation, the past, and cessation*[11].

9. T. 49.2031.16c14–25. English translations of the full work include Masuda 1925 and Tsukamoto 2004.

10. Xuanzang's translation corresponds well with the Chinese translation attributed to Kumārajīva (T. 49.2032) and the Tibetan version (translated by Dharmākara and Bzang skyong: P. 5639; D. 4138), but Paramārtha's version (T. 49.2033) contains much additional material, particularly in the Vātsīputrīya chapter, probably glosses he added himself since he was from Ujjain, one of the Saṃmitīya strongholds in India. An odd feature of Paramārtha's version of Yogācāra is the addition of a ninth consciousness, the Pure Consciousness (*āmala-vijñāna*), over and above the standard Yogācāra eighth consciousness; Saṃmitīya doctrines may have influenced him in this regard. P. and D. refer to the Peking and Derge editions, respectively, of the Tibetan canon.

11. The italicized passages are the underlying *sūtra*, or basic text. These are then unpacked by further exposition. The Shorter and Longer Versions differ most in the expositions each provides for these basic passages.

[These are] the figurative expressions (*prajñapti*) concerning appropriation, the figurative expressions concerning the past, and figurative expressions concerning cessation. If someone doesn't know [what "appropriation," "past (lives)," and "(nirvanic) cessation" entail,] then they don't know the unsayable.[12]

Figurative expression concerning appropriation is the analysis of whether sentient beings are the same or different from the *skandhas, dhātus,* and *āyatanas* they have already appropriated.[13]

As to figurative expressions concerning the past, saying "[this person is now so-and-so] because of past *skandhas, dhātus,* and *āyatanas*" is just like saying "At that time [in a previous life,] I was named Kuśendra."[14]

As to figurative expressions concerning cessation, saying "it is because appropriation has already ceased" is just like saying "The Bhagavat's *Parinirvāṇa.*"

Moreover, [the purpose of these figurative expressions is to dispel false views]. The figurative expressions concerning the past dispel [the idea] that sentient beings are annihilated. Figurative expressions concerning cessation dispel [the idea] that they exist permanently. Figurative expressions concerning the appropriation [of *skandhas,* etc.] dispel [the idea that sentient beings are] nonexistent. Figurative expressions concerning nonappropriation dispel [the idea that sentient beings qua an eternal self] exist.

Translation: The Longer Version—From the *Si Ahanmu chao jie* (Commentary on the Four Āgamas)

Q: What is not said (**avaktavya* or **avācya*)?

A: The not-said: *[This refers to what is] not said [or left implicit by other Buddhists] in the heuristics* (prajñapti) *for appropriation, metaphorical devices, and cessation.*

12. What is "implicit" in these figurative expressions (*prajñaptis*) is the *pudgala,* the "person," which is the *prajñapti* that goes "unsaid" when other Buddhists discuss such basic doctrines.

13. Standard Buddhist "analysis" breaks a person down into *skandhas* (the five aggregates), the eighteen *dhātus* (six sense organs, six types of corresponding sensory realms, and the six consciousnesses that arise from contact between organ and object-realm), and twelve *āyatanas* (six sense organs and six corresponding object-realms). The *pudgalavādin* position is that the *pudgala* is neither the same nor different from the *skandhas,* etc. The passage here *suggests* the *pudgala* by referring to a "sentient being."

14. Using the Buddhist technical jargon of "past *skandhas,* etc." to account for a present being is no less figurative than using the "ordinary language" personalist term "I" and a name, since one sense of the term *prajñapti* is "only a nominal existent." Both the technical and ordinary ways of expressing the relation between present beings and their previous existences (earlier in this life or in past lives) presuppose the *prajñapti* "person" (or "being").

Those are the heuristics for appropriation, heuristics by metaphorical device,[15] and the heuristics for cessation. This means that whoever is stupid concerning these "not saids" lacks insight (*ajñana).

The heuristic for appropriation [involves] using the term "a living-one" (*jīva*).[16] [The idea] that the presently appropriated *skandhas, dhātus,* and *āyatanas* are appropriated by an inner living-one is a heuristic. This means that [when one talks about the] present appropriation by an inner living-one who appropriates *dharmas*[17] due to karmic conditioning (*saṃskāras*) and the fetters (*saṃyojana*), these are heuristics for [discussing] appropriation.

The *dharmas* that the living-one heuristically appropriates are not the same as the living-one. It's not as if one seeks to get the *jīva* and the body to combine [into a single thing. To do so would entail opposing extremist absurdities]. If they are the same, then [the *jīva* would be] impermanent and [prone to] suffering; if they are different, then a permanent [*jīva*] would be prone to suffering.

If it is permanent, one wouldn't [need to] practice *brahmacarya* (a religious life). If it is not permanent, one would be unsuited for the *brahmacarya* fruit.[18] For that which is impermanent, receiving and giving (i.e., meritorious activities) would be meaningless [since an impermanent being would perish before such activities could mature into fruition]. Meaninglessness is tantamount to nihilism; in these two metaphorical devices [of permanence and annihilation] there is no *dharma* [conducive to either] suffering or the favorable.

The heuristic by metaphorical device is naming.

[To speak of a person as being the same person in the] "past, future, and present" is to practice the heuristics by metaphorical device. This is the heuristic metaphorical device of naming [i.e., giving a single name to conditions

15. This text uses *fangbian* for the second *prajñapti* (the Short Version called the second *prajñapti* "figurative expressions concerning the past"). *Fangbian* would become the standard Chinese equivalent for *upāya* (expedient means). Here, reflecting an early Chinese usage in which *fangbian* means to diplomatically express something without explicitly saying what one means directly or bluntly, it would appear to mean "metaphorical device," i.e., a linguistic device that indirectly expresses something that proves beneficial. The Longer Version will give a greatly expanded explanation of the second *prajñapti* that is not restricted only to the past, but that covers the "three times," i.e., past, present and future.

16. Dao'an adds a note: "In Sanskrit, the words for 'living one' and 'sentient being' sound the same." Whether Dao'an is thinking of *sattva* or *jīva,* or both, is unclear, though what follows works better with *jīva*. *Jīva* can mean the inner essence of an individual, a life-force, or even a soul.

17. *Dharmas* here means constitutive factors of experience and includes the *skandhas, āyatanas,* and *dhātus.*

18. The fruit of practicing a *brahmacarya* life would be liberation from which one doesn't backslide, hence a stable and permanent condition for the one who has attained it. On the other hand, if the *jīva* is actually permanent, invariant, unchanging, eternal, then it could undergo no changes or progress toward liberation, hence rendering the religious pursuit (*brahmacarya*) impossible. The *jīva* would remain unaffected by all actions and changes in conditions; nothing could affect, improve, or influence it.

that vary over time] which [linguistically posits] a relationship across the three times (past, present, and future). For example: "In the past, I was King *Kuśa" or "In the future you will have the name Ajita," [or] "At present I am a prominent merchant," and [other] such activities as were assumed [in the past] or have not yet been assumed [in the future]. Such conventional roles are numerous, hence they are heuristically adopted [by assuming the person undergoes] annihilation and permanence. [The extremist assumptions embedded in this are exposed by such questions as] If Kuśa has ceased, in what sense am I he? If he has not ceased, in what sense can one say he is I? It is by means of conventionalisms (*vyavahāra*) that one says so; it is a heuristic metaphorical device.

Q: What are the heuristics for cessation?

A: *The heuristics for cessation [are statements such as] "appropriation is exhausted," or "no [further] appropriation [will occur]," or "coming to rest."*

Appropriation is as explained above. Once that has been exhausted, [one says] "no [more] appropriation," "no obtaining another [life]," "coming to rest," "[nirvana] with no remainder," "passing from this shore to the other shore"—these are heuristics for cessation.

The way a [being is usually thought of by other Buddhists,] as cycling through samsara, [implicitly presupposes the extremist views of] annihilation and permanence. If one seeks to stop such [samsaric] activities, one turns to the heuristics of appropriation and the heuristics of *parinirvāṇa*. This (i.e., *parinirvāṇa*), too, is a not-said.

If [the *pudgala*] is [intrinsically] different [from *parinirvāṇa*], then one doesn't [obtain] *parinirvāṇa*. If [the *pudgala*] is not [inherently] different from [*parinirvāṇa*], then one doesn't [obtain] *parinirvāṇa*.[19]

These kinds of views have given rise to suffering and have not been explained ("said") [adequately by other Buddhists].[20] [Such Buddhists] would [say] "*Parinirvāṇa* is like the ceasing of an internal lamp." The same [applies to] appropriation. If one seeks [to understand] suffering and yet doesn't clarify it with the heuristics of appropriation and metaphorical devices, [such as] past *skandhas, dhātus,* and *āyatanas,* basically this is like saying "I am named King Kuśa." In such a way the heuristic of future cessation means that the cessation of appropriation is the main point to be explained.

19. The text is terse, open to various readings. One alternate reading would be: "If [appropriation] is different [from *parinirvāṇa,* since nirvana is defined as the absence of appropriation], then one doesn't [obtain, i.e., appropriate] *parinirvāṇa.* If [appropriation] is not different from [*parinirvāṇa*], then one doesn't [obtain] *parinirvāṇa* [since it would be unattainable]." Both readings make a similar point, which is that the extremes of annihilationalism and eternalism lurk in such formulations, rendering them illogical.

20. Alternate translations: In such ways has [not understanding] the not-said already given rise to suffering. Or: In such ways [Buddhists] have already [used] the not-said in the views about suffering they have already given rise to.

Translation: The Section on the Vātsīputrīyas from Vasumitra's *Tenets of the Different Schools,* Based on Xuanzang's Chinese Translation

These are tenets that the Vātsīputrīya schools hold in common:

The *pudgala* is neither the same [as] nor different from the *skandhas.* It is a *prajñapti* dependent on the *skandhas, āyatanas,* and *dhātus.*

Saṃskāras (conditioned dharmas) have a temporary duration, while some cease in an instant (*kṣaṇika*).

Dharmas, if apart from the *pudgala,* cannot move on from a previous lifetime to a subsequent lifetime. On the basis of the *pudgala,* one can say there is transference (*saṃkrānti*).

Moreover, even non-Buddhists can attain the five *ṛddhis* (superpowers).[21]

The five consciousnesses have no *kleśas,* and are not apart from *kleśas.*[22]

If the bonds (*saṃyojana*) of the Desire Realm (*kāma-dhātu*) are eliminated during the Cultivation Stage (*bhāvanā-mārga*), one is called "free from desire." But not if eliminated during the Seeing Stage (*darśana-mārga*).[23]

It is by [the four wholesome roots, namely,] *kṣānti* (forbearance), *nāma* (name), *nimitta* (image), and *laukikā agra-dharmāḥ* (the highest meditative insight) that one can enter into the correct nature in which no mental defilements (*kleśas*) arise (*niyāmāvakrānti* or *samyaktva-niyāma*).[24]

If entering *niyāmāvakrānti* during the twelve mental moments, this is called "Going toward."[25] If during the thirteenth mental [moment], this is called "abiding in the fruit."

21. The list of five superpowers varies in different Buddhist texts. A typical list is (1) divine seeing, (2) divine hearing, (3) ability to know other minds, (4) power to appear anywhere at will, and (5) virtuosity at religious practice.

22. Lance Cousins points out: "Compare *Vibhānga* 319 in Pali [the second work in the Abhidhamma of the Pali canon] where the five are given as *asaṃkiliṭṭha-sankilesika,* i.e., not defiled but subject to defilement" (email correspondence, December 5, 2006).

23. Two important phases of practice discussed by most Buddhist schools are the Seeing Path (*darśana-mārga*) and Cultivation Path (*bhāvanā-mārga*), which one enters in that order. Most schools place enlightenment as occurring at the culmination of the Cultivation Path.

24. These are meditative practices. *Kṣānti* is defined in Vātsīputrīya texts as analyzing conditions while seeking joy; *nāma* involves using "names," terms, or concepts as meditative objects, e.g. "suffering"; *nimitta,* which means "sign" or "image," is described in the Short Version as "Just as one sees someone familiar in a dream, or an image in a mirror, just so does one contemplate the *nimitta* of suffering." *Laukikā agra-dharmāḥ* is the highest insight into the nature of dharmas. As for the Vātsīputrīya understanding of *niyāmāvakrānti,* it would seem to imply—judging from Xuanzang's rendering—that it corresponds to *kṣaṇa-jñāna* and *anutpāda-jñāna,* i.e., the cognitive condition in which all *kleśas* have been fully eliminated (*prahāṇa*) and in which no new ones, or any future life, will arise. In some texts, this would define reaching Arhathood.

25. While some schools divide understanding the Four Noble Truths into sixteen "moments," four for each Truth, the Vātsīputrīyas applied three aspects to each Truth, yielding twelve moments of insight. The "thirteenth" would be full enlightenment.

In ways such as this, there are many different opinions.

Because of holding different interpretations of a single verse, this school branched off into four schools, which are Dharmottarīya (Higher Dharma), Bhadrayāṇīyas (Inheritance from the Honorables), Saṃmatīyas (Correct Measure), and the Ṣāṇḍagirikas (Hidden in Forests and Mountains).

That verse says:

> Already liberated, again one backslides
> backsliding due to desire. Again returning
> recovering peaceful joy and the place of happiness.
> From the enjoyable (postepiphany life) to perfect happiness.[26]

Bibliography and Suggested Reading

Cousins, L. S. (1995) "Person and Self." In *Buddhism into the Year 2000.* Bangkok: Dhammakaya Foundation, pp. 15–31. Reprinted in Paul Williams, ed., *Buddhism: Critical Concepts in Religious Studies.*2 London: Routledge, 2005, 2:84–101.

Duerlinger, James. (2003) *Indian Buddhist Theories of Persons: Vasubandhu's "Refutation of the Theory of a Self."* London: RoutledgeCurzon.

Hurvitz, Leon. (1967) "The Road to Buddhist Salvation as described by Vasubhadra." *Journal of the American Oriental Society* 87/4: 434–486.

Lamotte, Étienne. (1988) *History of Indian Buddhism.* Louvain-la-Neuve: Peeters Press.

Law, B. C. (1979) *Designation of Human Types (Puggala-paññatti).* London: Pali Text Society.

Maclean, Derryl. (1989) *Religion and Society in Arab Sind.* Leiden: Brill.

Masuda, Jiryo (1925) "Origins and Doctrines of Early Indian Buddhist Schools: A Translation of the Hsüan-chwang Version of Vasumitra's Treatise." *Asia Major* 2: 1–78.

Priestley, Leonard. (1999) *Pudgalavāda Buddhism: The Reality of the Indeterminate Self.* Toronto: Center for South Asian Studies, University of Toronto.

Thich, Thien Chau. (1999) *The Literature of the Personalists of Early Buddhism.* Translated by Sara Boin-Webb. Delhi: Motilal Banarsidass.

Tsukamoto, Keishō (2004) *The Cycle of the Formation of the Schismatic Doctrines.* Berkeley: Numata.

26. Although the exact meaning of every component of this verse is uncertain, it is clear that it concerns Arhats and the conditions by which they might backslide and subsequently regain their progress to go on to *parinirvāṇa*. The exact nature of the opposing interpretations, which must have revolved around defining aspects of enlightenment, is unknown, although some scholars have speculated. Priestley 1999: 36–37 summarizes Kuiji's explanation of the differences.

25

Vasubandhu's *Abhidharmakośa*

The Critique of the Pudgalavādins' Theory of Persons

James Duerlinger

"Refutation of the Theory of a Self" was composed by the Indian Buddhist philosopher known as Vasubandhu (c. fourth/fifth century C.E.). The "Refutation," which Vasubandhu placed at the end of his encyclopedic *Abhidharmakośa,* contains a classic statement of the Buddhist theory of the selflessness of persons.

In the following selection from the "Refutation," Vasubandhu begins by arguing that persons are not selves. He identifies selves as persons who are substantially real in the sense that they possess an essence (*svabhāva*), which is that by virtue of which they both possess person-properties and exist apart from being conceived. They are not substantially real, he believes, because they do not possess person-properties apart from being conceived in dependence upon the causal continuum of the elements of their bodies and minds, which the Buddha called their aggregates. Person-properties are the defining properties of the objects to which we refer when we use the first-person singular pronoun to refer to ourselves. These properties include our being possessors of bodies and minds, perceivers of objects, thinkers of thoughts about these objects, single agents of actions and experiencers of their results, and so on. The aggregates, in dependence upon which person-properties are ascribed to us, are generally classified into the five categories of bodily forms, feeling, discrimination, volitional forces, and consciousness. According to all Indian Buddhist philosophers, when in dependence upon our aggregates we conceive ourselves from the first-person singular perspective and ascribe person-properties to ourselves, we create a false appearance of ourselves as selves, and our assent to this appearance is the root cause of our suffering in cyclic existence.

Vasubandhu begins by claiming that there is no liberation from suffering for those who mistakenly see themselves as selves. According to Yaśomitra, his Indian commentator, Vasubandhu is here referring to the Tīrthikas, who are proponents of non-Buddhist philosophical theories according to which liberation from suffering is attained when we fully realize that we are substances that exist apart from our aggregates. Vasubandhu does not think that our most fundamental mistaken view of ourselves is seeing ourselves as separate substances, since we do not appear to ourselves to be substances that exist apart from our aggregates, but as possessors of essences. He rejects the Tīrthikas' theory because he thinks that if we were substances that exist apart from our aggregates, we would, but do not, possess both existence and at least some person-properties apart from being conceived in dependence upon the causal continuum of our aggregates. He thinks that, nonetheless, we do exist as the collection of our aggregates.

Vasubandhu then presents a series of objections to the theory of the Pudgalavādins, Indian Buddhist schoolmen who claim that even though we do not possess person-properties by ourselves and do not exist as substances apart from our aggregates, we exist without being the same as our aggregates. In his objections to the Pudgalavādins' theory of persons, Vasubandhu assumes that we exist, and therefore we must be either other than our aggregates as separate substances or the same as them. Hence, since the Pudgalavādins reject the view that we are the same as our aggregates, his objections to their theory are often based on his belief that it commits them to the Tīrthikas' theory that we are separate substances.

Vasubandhu objects to the Pudgalavādins' theory of persons on the basis of what he believes to be independent reasoning and on the basis of his belief that it contradicts the teachings of the Buddha. Most of the objections he thinks are based on independent reasoning are included in this selection. It is not clear, however, whether the objections of the first sort employ premises the Pudgalavādins themselves would accept as true. For instance, they would seem to reject not only (1) the all-inclusiveness of the sort of distinction Vasubandhu makes between the two realities in his initial objection to their theory, but also (2) the truth of the principle that Vasubandhu uses in his initial attack on their reply to his basic objection, and (3) the correctness of most of his interpretations of the theses and arguments they present after this initial exchange.

The principle Vasubandhu uses in his initial attack on their reply is that the object of a conception must be the same as its causal basis if the conception is to have a referent. The Pudgalavādins reject this principle by saying that a person is conceived "in reliance on" the aggregates, which are the causal basis of the conception of a person. They claim that a person is conceived in reliance upon the aggregates in the way fire is conceived in reliance upon fuel, as opposed to the way milk is conceived in dependence upon its elements. Their point is that in some cases the object of a conception is not the same as its causal basis.

Vasubandhu reacts strongly to the Pudgalavādins' theory, since it represents for him a slide into the Tīrthikas' theory that we are separate substances. The Pudgalavādins are reacting to what they perceive to be his failure to account for our conventional understanding of ourselves as single agents of actions, which they believe must be retained in order to make intelligible the Buddha's account of the path to enlightenment.[1]

Translation

Vasubandhu's Statement of His Own View

There is no liberation [from suffering] other than this [liberation, the path to which has been explained], since [the Tīrthikas, who also teach a path to liberation from suffering, fail to recognize that] the mistaken view of a self [causes all suffering. Those who follow their teachings will not be liberated from suffering,] for they do not understand that the conception of a self refers only to a continuum of aggregates;[2] they believe that a self is a separate substance; but the mental afflictions[, which cause suffering,] arise from self-grasping [,which cannot be eliminated by those who believe that a self is a separate substance].

It is known that the expression, "self," refers to a continuum of aggregates and not to anything else because [direct perception and correct inference establish that the phenomena in dependence upon which a person is conceived are the aggregates, and] there is no direct perception or correct inference [that establishes the existence of anything else among these phenomena].[3]

1. The following translation originally appeared in James Duerlinger, *Indian Buddhist Theories of Persons, Vasubandhu's "Refutation of the Theory of a Self"* (London: CurzonRoutlege, 2003). We gratefully acknowledge permission to republish this work. Headings have been added to help the reader follow the argument. The additions made to the more literal translation are drawn from Yaśomitra's commentary, which refers the initial question back to the last part of the last verse of chapter 8, in which Vasubandhu enjoins those who seek liberation to practice the teachings of the Buddha.

2. The "only" in this sentence is meant to exclude reference to an entity that can be identified independently of the aggregates. Even though he says here that the conception of a self or person refers to a continuum of aggregates, his view, strictly speaking, is that it refers to a collection of aggregates that exist in a causal continuum powered by actions contaminated by the mistaken view of a self. The collection of aggregates to which the conception refers includes phenomena of two sorts, material and mental. These material and mental phenomena are called "aggregates" primarily because they are not united in or by a substantially real underlying support.

3. Direct perception and correct inference are two of the valid cognitions recognized by Vasubandhu, the third being cognitions based on scripture. Vasubandhu employs all three in the "Refutation."

[If anything else exists among these phenomena, its existence would be established by direct perception or correct inference,] for of all phenomena [that exist] there is direct perception [that establishes their existence], as there is of the six objects and the mental organ unless [direct] perception of them is impeded, or there is correct inference [that establishes their existence], as there is of the five [sense] organs.

Vasubandhu's Critique of the Theory of the Pudgalavādins on the Basis of Independent Reasoning

The Pudgalavādins[4] [,who profess to be followers of the Buddha's teachings,] assert that a person exists.[5] [To determine whether or not their assertion conforms to the Buddha's teachings,] we must first consider whether in their view a person is substantially real or is real by way of a conception.

If a person is a distinct entity like visible form and other such things, he is substantially real; but if [by analysis] he is [shown to be] a collection [of substances], like milk and other such things, he is real by way of a conception. Consequently, if a person is substantially real, it must be said that he is other than the aggregates in the way each of them is other than the others, since he will possess a different essence (*svabhāva*) [than is possessed by any of the aggregates. If he is other than the aggregates, he must be either causally conditioned or causally unconditioned. If he is other than the aggregates and is causally conditioned,] his causes should be explained. But if he is [other than the aggregates and is] causally unconditioned, the false theory [of persons] espoused by the Tīrthikas is held and a person does not function [as a person. Therefore, since the Pudgalavādins cannot say that a person is other than the aggregates, they cannot say that he is substantially real]. If he is real by way of a conception, [he is the collection of aggregates, and] this is the theory [of persons found in the Buddha's *sūtras* and is] held by us.

4. Yaśomitra, Vasubandhu's commentator, glosses *vātsīputrīyā* as *āryasaṃmatīyāḥ*. This is one of the schools to which the general term, *paudgalika,* i.e. Pudgalavādins, refers. The Pudgalavādins are those who belong to the Buddhist schools in which it is asserted that a person exists who is not explicable either as other than or the same as the aggregates.

5. The Pudgalavādins distinguish a person from a self and believe that a self, which does not exist, is a person that can be identified independently, while a person, which exists, exists by itself without possessing a separate identity. Vasubandhu here and elsewhere often uses "person" as they do, so that he may critique their theory as stated. In other contexts, Vasubandhu uses it either to refer to a self or to a person that he believes to be real by way of a conception. The contexts of the three different uses of the term will make it clear in which sense it is being used.

[But the Pudgalavādins assert that] a person is not substantially real or real by way of a conception, since he is conceived in reliance upon the aggregates[6] which pertain to himself,[7] are acquired, and exist in the present.

If we are to understand this obscure statement [of why a person is neither substantially real nor real by way of a conception], its meaning must be disclosed. What is meant by [saying that a person is conceived] "in reliance upon [the aggregates]"? If it means [that a person is conceived] "on the condition that the aggregates have been perceived," then the conception [of a person] refers only to them, [not to a person that exists apart from the aggregates,] just as when visible forms and other such things [that comprise milk] have been perceived, the conception of milk refers only to them, [not to milk that exists apart from visible forms and other such things]. If [saying that a person is conceived "in reliance upon the aggregates" means that he is conceived] "in dependence upon the aggregates," then [once again, the conception of a person refers only to them,] because the aggregates themselves will cause him to be conceived. [Therefore,] there is the same difficulty [that the Pudgalavādins must say that a person is his aggregates].

[They reply by saying that] a person is not conceived in this way [in which milk is conceived], but rather in the way [in which] fire is conceived in reliance upon fuel. [They say that] fire is conceived in reliance upon fuel, [and yet] it is not conceived unless fuel is present and cannot be conceived if it either is or is not other than fuel. If fire were other than fuel, fuel [in burning material] would not be hot [,which is absurd,] and if fire were not other than fuel, what is burned could be the same as what burns it[, which is also absurd].

Similarly, [they contend,] a person is not conceived unless the aggregates are present, [and] if he were other than the aggregates, the eternal transcendence theory [that a person is substantially real] would be held, and if he were not other than the aggregates, the nihilism theory [that a person does not exist at all] would be held.[8]

They must explain, first of all, what fuel and fire are so we shall know how fire is conceived in reliance upon fuel. [They say that] fuel is what is burned and fire is what burns it. [But these are mere conventional definitions.] What

6. A person is conceived in reliance upon [a collection of] aggregates in the sense that a person (1) cannot, although perceived, be conceived on the basis of being perceived, and (2) must be conceived in dependence upon a collection of aggregates at least some of which are present when he is perceived.

7. Since all causally conditioned phenomena, even those not belonging to oneself, are included in the phenomena called the aggregates, aggregates that pertain to oneself are distinguished from those that do not.

8. That the reference here is to the existence of persons rather than to their identity over time or unity may be inferred from the fact that the issue being discussed is in what way persons exist rather than in what way they are the same over time or one. Nor is the reference to the non-existence of persons after final release from cyclic existence.

is burned and what burns it are the very things we need to have explained [if it is to be known how they are in fact conceived].

It is commonly said that fuel is material[9] that is not burning, but can burn, and that fire is burning [material] that burns fuel. A blazing and intensely hot fire, [it is commonly said,] burns or ignites fuel in that it brings about an alteration in its continuum. [But analysis shows that the] fire and fuel are composed of eight [elemental] substances,[10] and fire arises in dependence upon fuel in the way curds arise in dependence upon milk and sour [milk] upon sweet [milk]. So we say [that fire is conceived] in reliance upon fuel, even though it is other than fuel by reason of existing at a different time [as a different collection of elements]. And so, if a person arises in the same way in dependence upon the aggregates, he must be other than them. [Moreover, contrary to their view that a person is not impermanent,] he must also be impermanent[, since he arises in dependence upon the aggregates].[11]

[The Pudgalavādins believe that they avoid these objections because] they assert that fire is the heat present in the above-mentioned burning material[12] and that [the] fuel [in reliance upon which fire is conceived] is comprised of the three elements [of earth, air, and water] that conjointly arise with it [in burning material].

[But according to this analysis,] fire must still be other than fuel, since they will have different defining properties. Moreover, the meaning of "in reliance upon" must be explained, [since, according to their analyses of fire and fuel,] how is fire conceived in reliance upon fuel? For [if the analyses are correct, it is true not only that] fuel will not be a cause of fire, [but] also [that] it will not even be a cause of the conception of fire, since fire itself will be the cause of the conception [of fire].

9. Here and elsewhere what literally means "wood, etc." is translated as "material."

10. The eight elements of which bodies are composed are the four primary elements called fire, air, water, and earth, and four secondary elements that make up what we call the sensible qualities of such bodies and are perceived by means of an ear, nose, tongue, and body.

11. According to the Pudgalavādins, the view that we are impermanent phenomena is a nihilistic extreme, since we do not exist unless we persist over time, and the view that we are permanent phenomena is the extreme of eternal transcendence. Vasubandhu's assumption, that our attributions of sameness over time to ourselves can be explained in terms of the causal continuity of the impermanent aggregates in the collection of aggregates in dependence upon which we are conceived, is most likely rejected because it falls to explain our persistence over.

12. The Pudgalavādins avoid identifying fire, as an agent of change, with the substance that Vasubandhu himself calls the fire-element and claims to be present in all bodies, since this element is no more an agent of change than are the other three elements present in all bodies. The heat to which the Pudgalavādins refer here is not even the defining property of the fire-element. It seems to be what is commonly called heat, and is in fact an inexplicable phenomenon that, by its presence in burning material, is said to cause its fuel to burn.

If the meaning of "in reliance upon" is a support as inseparable concomitance,[13] then the aggregates must also be said in the same way to be the supports or inseparable concomitants of a person, in which case they clearly must say that the aggregates are other than a person [since the supports and inseparable concomitants of something are other than it]. And [they must also say, contrary to their theory that a person does not exist in dependence upon the existence of the aggregates, that] a person does not [in fact] exist unless the aggregates exist, just as fire does not [in fact] exist unless fuel exists.[14]

Finally, what does "hot" signify in their earlier assertion that if fire were other than fuel, fuel [in burning material] would not be hot? If it signifies heat, then fuel itself is not hot, since it [is, according to their analysis, what] possesses the essences of the other [three] elements [rather than the essence of the fire whose presence in something is the cause of its heat. There remains the possibility that] what is hot, even if it is other than fire, which is hot according to its essence, can be shown to be hot in the sense that it can be combined with heat. [But] in this case fire being other than fuel is not a problem [for the view that fuel in burning material is hot].

Should they say [in order to avoid the objection that fire is other than fuel] that burning material is as a whole both fire and fuel, they must explain what it can mean in this case to say [that fire is conceived] "in reliance upon" [fuel. For if burning material is as a whole both fire and fuel, fuel will be the fire, and that in reliance upon which fire is conceived will be the fire itself, which the Pudgalavādins deny]. Moreover, since the aggregates themselves would also be the person, it follows that they could not avoid the theory that a person is not other than his aggregates.[15]

Therefore, they have not shown that a person is conceived in reliance upon the aggregates in the way [in which they believe] that fire is conceived in reliance upon fuel.

Since [the Pudgalavādins assert that a person is inexplicable,] they cannot say that a person is other than the aggregates. [Hence] they cannot say that there are five kinds of objects known to exist, [namely,] past, future, and present [causally conditioned phenomena], causally unconditioned phenomena,[16] and the [persons that they call] inexplicable. For they cannot assert that an inexplicable [person] constitutes a fifth kind [of object known to exist, since if a person cannot be said to be other than the aggregates, which are the three kinds of casually conditioned phenomena, he must be

13. According to Vasubandhu, the four primary elements support the existence of one another in the sense of being inseparably concomitant. He brings up this meaning of "in reliance upon" because he assumes in the argument that the Pudgalavādins have identified fire with the fire-element as he himself construes it.

14. Whether or not the Pudgalavādins believe that fire exists apart from fuel is not clear.

15. Although Vasubandhu writes "is not other than," what he means can only be "is the same as," since the Pudgalavādins hold the view that a person is not other than his aggregates.

16. Causally unconditioned phenomena are phenomena that are without causes and conditions.

the same as them]. Nor [can they assert] that he does not constitute a fifth kind, [since if they assert that a person is not the same as the aggregates, they also cannot say that a person is the three kinds of causally conditioned phenomena or that he is a causally unconditioned phenomenon. Hence, they cannot assert that a person is inexplicable.]

When conceived, is a person conceived after the aggregates are perceived or after a person is perceived? If he is conceived after the aggregates are perceived, the conception of a person refers only to them, since a person is not perceived. But if he is conceived after he himself is perceived, then how can a person be conceived in reliance upon the aggregates, since then the person himself is the basis upon which he is conceived?

[They say that] a person is conceived in reliance upon the aggregates because a person is perceived when the aggregates are present. [But] in that case, since a visible form is perceived when the eye, attentiveness, and light are present, they would have to say that a visible form is conceived in reliance upon them [rather than because of the visible form that is perceived]; and just as a visible form [is other than the eye, attentiveness, and light present when a visible form is perceived], clearly a person would be other [than the aggregates present when a person is perceived].

They must state by which of the six consciousnesses a person is known to exist. They say that a person is known to exist by all six. They explain [this] by saying that if a consciousness is aware of a person in dependence upon a visible form known to exist by means of the eye, it is said that a person is known to exist by means of the eye; but it is not said that a person is or is not the visible form [in dependence upon which the consciousness is aware of a person]. In the same way [they explain how a person is known to exist by each of the other five consciousnesses] up to [and including] the mental consciousness, [saying that] if a consciousness is aware of a person in dependence upon a phenomenon known to exist by means of the mental organ, it is said that a person is known to exist by means of the mental organ; but it is not said that a person either is or is not the phenomenon [in dependence upon which the consciousness is aware of a person].

But the same account can be given of [how] milk and other such things [are known to exist]. If a consciousness is aware of milk in dependence upon a visible form known to exist by means of the eye, it is said that milk is known to exist by means of the eye; but it is not said that milk either is or is not the visible form [in dependence upon which the consciousness is aware of milk]. For the same reason, if a consciousness is aware of milk in dependence upon objects known to exist by means of the nose, the tongue, and the body, it is said that milk is known to exist by means of these organs; but it is not said that milk is or is not [any one of] the objects [in dependence upon which the consciousness is aware of milk].[17]

17. It is assumed that milk is not other than any one of the objects known to exist by the four consciousnesses aware of milk, since there is no awareness of milk that is not a perception of one of these objects.

[Nor can milk be any one of these objects, for if it were any one of them, it would be each of them, and if it were each of them, then since the objects known to exist by these four consciousnesses are of four different kinds] the absurd consequence follows that the milk would be of four different kinds.

[But if milk is known to exist by means of the eye, the nose, the tongue, and the body, and it neither is nor is not any one of these objects, then it must be all of them as a collection. And if milk is all of them as a collection, it must be all of them as a collection that are conceived as milk.] Therefore, just as [it must be all of] these very objects as a collection [that] are conceived as milk, in the same way, [it must also be all of the objects as a collection that are known to exist by the six consciousnesses that perceive a person that are conceived as a person. And since these very objects are the aggregates,] it is established that the aggregates are conceived as a person. [But if the aggregates are conceived as a person, a person is the aggregates. Therefore, the Pudgalavādins' account of how a person is known to exist by the six consciousnesses cannot be used to explain how an inexplicable person is known to exist.]

Furthermore, what do they mean when they assert that [a person is known to exist if] a consciousness is aware of a person in dependence upon a visible form known to exist by means of the eye? Is [it meant that a person is known to exist if] a cause of a perception of a person is a visible form or is [it meant that a person is known to exist if] a person [is] perceived when a visible form is perceived?

If [they say that] a cause of a perception of a person is a visible form and [they also say that] a person cannot be said to be other than a visible form, they cannot say [as they do] that a visible form is other than light, the eye, and attentiveness, since these are causes of a perception of a visible form.

Vasubandhu's Replies to Some of the Objections Raised by the Pudgalavādins

[The Pudgalavādins object that] a person cannot merely be the aggregates, since the Buddha would not have said [in explanation of the problem of suffering and its solution], "Bhikṣus, I will explain to you the burden, the taking up of the burden, the casting off of the burden, and what bears it." It is not reasonable [they object], that the burden be the same as its bearer, since the two are commonly recognized not to be the same.

But [if this objection is sound, we may infer that] it is also not reasonable that the inexplicable [phenomenon the Pudgalavādins call a person] exists, since it is commonly recognized not to exist. Moreover, [if the burden is not its bearer,] it follows that the taking up of the burden would not be included [by the Buddha, as we both agree it is, under the name "grasping at existence,"] in the aggregates. [For if the burden not be its own bearer, the taking up of the burden would be part of the bearer of the burden rather than part of the burden].

The Bhagavān spoke of the bearer of the burden with the intention that just this much should be understood: [that reference to it is a verbal convention, just as reference to a person is, when it is said, for instance, that] "he is venerable, has a certain name, lives for a while or for a long time, and lives to a certain age." But it should not be understood to be permanent or inexplicable. Since the aggregates cause harm to themselves, the earlier are called a burden [to the later] and the later the bearer of the burden, since "burden" means "harm."

[They object that] a person is not the aggregates because [in a *sūtra*] it is said [by the Buddha, in reference to himself], "One person is born into the world [for the welfare of the many]." [The use of "one person" shows that the Buddha does not mean to refer to his aggregates.]

[But in this passage, the term] "one" is applied figuratively[18] to a collection [of aggregates], just as [it is applied in] "one sesame seed," "one grain of rice," "one heap," and "one word." Moreover, [if they accept this passage as a statement of doctrine that requires no interpretation,] they must[,contrary to their own view] also admit that a person is [a] causally conditioned [phenomenon], since they will have agreed that he is born.

[The Pudgalavādins object that] if a person were merely the aggregates, the Bhagavān would not have said, "At that time and place I was the teacher called Sunetra," since the aggregates [of the Bhagavān] would be other than those [of Sunetra].

But it cannot be [to himself as] a person [that the Bhagavān refers,] since he would then be committed to the eternal transcendence belief [that a person is a permanent phenomenon]. Therefore, [when the Bhagavān said, "I was the teacher called Sunetra,"] he was referring to a single [causal] continuum [of aggregates in dependence upon which, at one time, Sunetra was conceived, and now, śākyamuni Buddha is conceived]. It is like when we say, "This same burning fire has moved" [from here to there, we are referring to a single causal continuum of a combination of elements in dependence upon which, at different times, fire is conceived].

If [they say that] a person is perceived when a visible form is perceived, a person is perceived by the same perception [by which a visible form is perceived] or by another perception. If a person is perceived by the same perception [by which a visible form is perceived, then since one perception is the same as another, what is perceived by the one is the same in essence as what is perceived by the other], a person is the same in essence as a visible form and only it is to be conceived as that [person]. How, then, could

18. What exactly it means for a term to be applied figuratively is not clear. It at least means that the term is not applied according to its literal meaning. Vasubandhu's point, however, is clear. He believes that the term "one" is applied, according to its literal meaning, to a substance, but when applied to a collection of substances, is applied to it according to the convention that this collection of substances is a single entity of some sort.

a visible form be distinguished from a person? And if it cannot be distinguished in this way, how can it be asserted that both a visible form and a person [separately] exist, since it is on the strength of a [separate] perception of something that its [separate] existence is asserted? This same argument can be used [for objects perceived by the other five consciousnesses] up to [and including] a phenomenon [perceived by the mental consciousness]. If [a person is perceived] by a perception other than the one by which a visible form is perceived, then since he is perceived at a different time, a person must be other than a visible form, just as yellow is other than blue and one moment is other than another. This same argument can be used [for objects perceived by the other five consciousnesses] up to [and including] a phenomenon [perceived by the mental consciousness].

[They reply that a person can be perceived when a visible form is perceived, and yet the perception of a person and the perception of a visible form cannot be said either to be or not to be other than one another. But] if these perceptions, like [their objects,] a person and a visible form, cannot be said either to be or not to be other than one another, they must contradict their own theory [that a perception is a causally conditioned phenomenon], since [if a perception is inexplicable,] a causally conditioned phenomenon can then also be inexplicable[, which is absurd].

Bibliography and Suggested Reading

Cousins, L. S. (1994) "Person and Self." In *Proceedings: "Buddhism into The Year 2000."* Bangkok and Los Angeles: The Dammakaya Foundation, pp. 15–31.

Duerlinger, James. (2003) *Indian Buddhist Theories of Persons: Vasubandhu's "Refutation of the Theory of a Self."* London: CurzonRoutledge.

Stcherbatsky, Th. (1970) *Central Conception of Buddhism and the Meaning of the Word "Dharma."* Delhi: Motilal Banarsidass.

Williams, Paul. (1981) "On the Abhidharma Ontology." *Journal of Indian Philosophy* 9: 227–257.

26

Vasubandhu's *Abhidharmakośa*

The Critique of the Soul

Charles Goodman

Chapter 9 of Vasubandhu's *Abhidharmakośa* (c. fourth/fifth century C.E.) examines the nature of the person and seeks to refute the view that the essence of each person is a real, ultimately existing self. After criticizing the position of the Pudgalavādins, as in the selection translated in the previous chapter, Vasubandhu proceeds at the end of the chapter to consider those Indian philosophers who unapologetically defend the existence of the *ātman*. This Sanskrit term can simply mean "self," but here it refers more specifically to an immortal soul, the owner of a body and of mental states, and the subject of experiences of happiness and suffering. The stakes in the debate about the existence of the soul are quite high: according to Vasubandhu, spiritual seekers cannot attain liberation as long as they accept the existence of the soul. Liberation can be achieved only by completely eradicating all forms of belief in a self.

Who are Vasubandhu's opponents in this highly polemical text? He calls them Tīrthikas, a term derived from the Sanskrit word *tīrtha,* "ford."[1] The Tīrthikas were non-Buddhist thinkers of India, many of whom were Brahmins and followers of traditions that developed into the religion we now call Hinduism. Although these thinkers differed on many important philosophical issues, they agreed among themselves and against the Buddhists that

I am grateful to Luis O. Gómez and Madhav Deshpande for their assistance in reading this text and preparing the translation.

1. The name Vasubandhu uses probably arises from the common Indian belief, rejected by Buddhists, in the sacredness of fords on holy rivers such as the Ganges.

the soul exists. Thus, it can be difficult to determine which of the diverse schools that Vasubandhu groups together as Tīrthikas are actually being criticized in any given passage. Some of the arguments Vasubandhu makes would be effective against all of these schools, and some of the objections he tries to answer could come from any of them.

Certain passages in the text, however, are clearly directed specifically at the Nyāya-Vaiśeṣika tradition. This important school of Indian philosophy arose from a synthesis between two originally separate schools. The Vaiśeṣikas sought to understand the nature of the physical world, developing a complex theory of matter and substance based on the existence of permanent, invisible atoms. The word *Nyāya* means "logic"; followers of this school discussed the differences between good and bad inferences. Realizing that their findings were not only consistent, but complementary, members of these schools combined the metaphysics of the Vaiśeṣikas with the epistemology of the Nyāya to form a syncretic tradition that produced formidable debate opponents both for Buddhists and for other Indian schools.

In the context of this text, the most distinctive views of the Nyāya-Vaiśeṣika tradition concern the *manas* or "mind," an internal organ of thought that is itself an atom and that works together with the soul to produce mental phenomena. Followers of this tradition hoped that distinguishing the mind from the soul could help explain the connection between the soul and the body, as well as the processes by which different mental states originate. Vasubandhu, however, argues that postulating the mind is not helpful; among other problems, the connection between the soul and the mind is itself mysterious.

One significant disagreement between Buddhism and Nyāya-Vaiśeṣika concerns the process known as "identification of the self" (*ahaṅkāra*). For Buddhists, this is a deluded mental process by which an attachment is created that incorrectly identifies the aggregates as a self, causing them to be perceived as valuable and precious. Followers of the Nyāya-Vaiśeṣika tradition use the same term to refer to our ability to accurately identify the soul as the true self. But Vasubandhu defends the view that, in worldly life, we do not in fact even believe that we are souls; instead, we mistakenly grasp the aggregates as if they were a self.

Several of the objections Vasubandhu considers draw, explicitly or implicitly, on concepts and categories developed in the context of the science of linguistics. The most advanced scientific attainments of ancient India were in linguistics, and scholars of Sanskrit grammar often used their knowledge to argue for philosophical beliefs. For instance, the objection that begins the section assumes a principle that arises from attempts to analyze the semantics of Sanskrit sentences, namely, that every action must depend on an agent. As we will see, Vasubandhu rejects this principle in favor of a Buddhist reductionist understanding of action.

Some commentators maintain that the Sāṃkhya tradition is also specifically criticized at certain points in the text. The Sāṃkhya is probably the oldest form of Indian philosophy; the views of this school strongly influenced the *Bhagavad Gītā,* one of the most revered texts in modern Hinduism.

Sāṃkhyas believed that all of reality had evolved from two fundamental principles, known as prime matter (*prakṛti*) and spirit (*puruṣa*). These two principles generated the three strands of being, passion, and darkness; all the variety in the world then emerged from the interaction of these three strands. The Sāṃkhya analysis of causation was that the true nature of the effect is already contained within its cause; this view of causation harmonized with their doctrine that the whole material world was essentially nothing more than various manifestations of prime matter. Though none of these distinctive doctrines comes in for direct criticism in the text here, some of the objections Vasubandhu considers against his own position could easily have been raised from a Sāṃkhya perspective.

Although some of the views of the Nyāya-Vaiśeṣika or the Sāṃkhya may seem outdated and irrelevant to contemporary philosophy, many aspects of Vasubandhu's critique of these schools are still worth our attention. The argument, presented here, that a permanent, unchanging thing cannot act differently at different times is a deep and important one, and forms the basis of the Buddhist critique of the soul in later texts, such as Śāntarakṣita's *Tattvasaṃgraha*. Moreover, problems with the soul's ability to form connections to other entities, such as the body, are vital to arguments made by modern Western philosophers against the existence of a soul. These philosophers have also raised concerns similar to those expressed by Vasubandhu about the lack of any acceptable explanatory role for the soul in light of the development of causal accounts of the production of action. Even materialist philosophers who would utterly reject many other Buddhist beliefs may find much to agree with in Vasubandhu's text, and modern defenders of the soul may find much to ponder in his incisive arguments.

Translation

[Non-Buddhist Opponent:] Every action depends on an agent. As, for instance, when we say that Devadatta walks, in this case the action of walking depends on the walker, Devadatta. In the same way, consciousness is an action. Therefore, whoever is conscious must exist.

[Vasubandhu:] Who is this "Devadatta?" Is he a soul? But that's just what you have to prove. Now, is he what is called a "person" in everyday usage? That's not any single thing; that name refers to various caused entities. Devadatta is conscious in just the same way as Devadatta walks. And how is it that Devadatta walks? Devadatta is no more than momentary caused entities that form an unbroken continuum. Fools who presuppose that the cause of the appearance of the continuum in a different place is a single being, a body, say that "Devadatta walks." They call the arising of the continuum in another location "walking." On our view, the "walking" of Devadatta is like the propagation of sound or the spread of a fire. In the same way, thinking that the cause of consciousness is a unitary being, fools say that "Devadatta is conscious." Hearing them say this, the Noble Ones[2] say the same thing, in order to conform to received usage.

A *sūtra* does say that "Consciousness is conscious of an object." What does the consciousness do to its object? It doesn't do anything. But just as it is said that "the effect conforms to the cause," it comes into existence, similar to its object, without doing anything to it. That's what it means to say that "consciousness is conscious of an object"; it comes into existence, similar to its object, without doing anything to it. Now, in what way is it similar? In appearance. It's because of this similarity in appearance that the consciousness represents its object, rather than the sense-faculty that is also one of its causes. Or, since there is a continuum of moments of consciousness, each one caused by the last, there is no error in saying "Consciousness is conscious of an object," since the word "agent" can be used to refer to a cause.[3] It's like saying "A bell rings." Moreover, just as a lamp moves, in that way, consciousness knows its object. And how does a lamp move? The term "lamp" is applied metaphorically to a series of flames. When these flames appear in different places, we say "It moves to such-and-such a place." In the same way, the term "consciousness" is applied to a series of thoughts. When they arise with different objects, we say "Consciousness is conscious of such-and-such an object." Just as physical form is produced and remains in existence, but has no creator that is different in substance from itself, it's the same way with consciousness.

[Opponent:] If consciousness arises from a previous moment of consciousness, and not from a soul, then why isn't it always qualitatively the same whenever it arises? Alternatively, why don't moments of consciousness follow each other in a fixed order like that of sprouts, stems, leaves, and so on?

[Vasubandhu:] All caused entities exhibit a "state of constant change." That's the nature of whatever is caused, so that necessarily the continuum varies from one moment to the next. Otherwise,[4] since those who are without desire and absorbed in meditation have bodies and minds that keep arising in the same way, there would be no first moment at which they were different, and these meditators could never rise out of their trance by themselves.

2. In the Buddhist teachings, Noble Ones (*ārya*) are beings who have attained a high level of spiritual development by completing what is known as the "path of insight" (*darśana-mārga*).

3. In the Buddhist worldview, the self does not exist, but that does not mean that there is absolutely no such thing as agency. Actions do exist, and a kind of agency is created by the succession of causal regularities that make up the mental life that we call a person.

4. If, that is, a moment of consciousness were to produce another that was exactly similar.

In fact, the series of thoughts is fixed. Each arises only when it is time for it to arise. When a thought arises, another appears that has a similar appearance, or else having the same object, depending on the category to which the thinker belongs. For example, immediately after thinking of a woman, some would think of the impurity of her body, or of her husband or son,[5] and again later, by the evolution of the continuum, another thought about that woman might appear, having the same object; and that thought might produce another thought of the impurity of her body, or of her husband or son, depending on what category the thinker belongs to. It's impossible for it to work any other way. Now there are many thoughts that might follow thinking about a woman, some diverse and some similar to the original thought, depending on which causal propensities are strongest, except when, at the same time, a particular kind of contributing cause intervenes from outside the body.

[Opponent:] Why doesn't the thought whose causal propensities are strongest forever produce effects?

[Vasubandhu:] Because all caused entities exhibit a state of constant change. And it's because of the different causal influences that are conducive to producing results and bringing about change.

This is a mere sample of the variety of all kinds of thoughts. But the Buddha's power gives him seamless knowledge. Thus it says in a *sūtra:* "The cause of the eye in the tail of one peacock is not knowable, in all its forms, to those who are not omniscient. But that knowledge is the power of the Omniscient Ones." How much less can we know the various thoughts, which are not material!

A certain Tīrthika believes that the arising of thoughts has the soul as its source. Clearly, he faces the very same objection: Why don't thoughts always arise in the same way? Why don't they appear in a fixed series, like sprouts, stems, leaves, and so on?

[Opponent:] It depends on differences in their connection with the mind.

[Vasubandhu:] No, because you have not proven that connection between two distinct entities is possible. If two originally disjoint things are connected, we get the conclusion that both of them are spatially localized; this conclusion is unacceptable to you, because your definition of the soul is incompatible with being spatially localized. Moreover, if the mind moves

5. That is, a monk would have been trained to think about the impurity of her body, in order to suppress sexual desire, whereas laypeople would not usually have such thoughts.

around, we conclude unacceptably either that the soul must move[6] or that the soul is destroyed.

[Opponent:] The connection in question is a partial connection.

[Vasubandhu:] No, because according to you, the soul has no parts.

Even if this connection does exist, even so, since the mind is permanent and unchanging, how can there be different kinds of connection between it and the soul?

[Opponent:] Because of the different kinds of cognition that occur.

[Vasubandhu:] The same question occurs in this case—how can the different kinds of cognition arise?

[Opponent:] They depend on the different kinds of mental states that arise from the conjunction of the soul and the mind.

[Vasubandhu:] Then why not just say that the different cognitions arise directly from the different mental states? The soul has no explanatory role here at all. It's like a quack doctor who, having already given medicine sufficient to cure the disease, recites some magic syllables: "Phūḥ! Amen!"

[Opponent:] If there is a soul, it is the source of both the mental states and the cognitions.

[Vasubandhu:] This is no more than empty words.

[Opponent:] The soul supports the mental states and cognitions.

[Vasubandhu:] As, for example, what supports what? It's not like a wall supporting a picture, or a bowl supporting some jujube fruits. In both of these cases, there's physical resistance between the support and what it supports. So how, then, is the soul a support?

[Opponent:] In the way that earth is the support of qualities such as scents, and so on.

[Vasubandhu:] We are greatly pleased with this! It's this exactly that is our reason for saying "There is no soul." In the same way, we say that earth is not

6. That is, to make room for the mind.

different from scents and so on. Gentlemen, which one of you can pick out a stuff called "earth" that is distinct from scents, and so on?

[Opponent:] What explains the use of the phrase "the scent of earth," and so on?

[Vasubandhu:] Its purpose is to distinguish between different scents. From that expression, one should recognize that we are talking about a particular scent and not others. It's like the expression "the body of a wooden statue."[7]

Given that the soul produces cognitions in dependence on the different kinds of mental states, why doesn't all knowledge arise from the soul simultaneously?

[Opponent:] The strongest mental state is an obstacle that prevents the others from arising.

[Vasubandhu:] Why doesn't the strongest one continue to produce its effects forever?

[Opponent:] We adopt whatever explanation you offer for the corresponding problem in your system.

[Vasubandhu:] But then the soul is useless!

[Opponent:] Certainly, one ought to accept the existence of the soul. Memory is a property. Every property must be supported by a substance. Memory cannot be linked with any substance but the soul.

[Vasubandhu:] You have not proved that memory is a property. We believe that everything that exists is a substance, as when the *sūtra* says "The fruits of the religious life are six substances." You have not proved that mental states depend on anything else for their existence. Besides, we have already examined the concept of "support." Therefore anything at all can be a substance.

[Opponent:] If there is no soul, then what's the meaning of statements about the results of action, as for instance "I am happy, I am not unhappy?"

[Vasubandhu:] The object of the term "I" and of this identification of the self is the aggregates.

7. It would be difficult to explain the difference between the body of the statue, on the one hand, and the statue, on the other hand. In the same way, Vasubandhu claims, we say "the scent of earth" even though the earth is not an entity distinct from the scent. We do this in order to distinguish the scent of earth from, for instance, the scent of flowers.

[Opponent:] How do you know?

[Vasubandhu:] Because of people's affection for them. People of ordinary intellect come to believe "I am white; I am dark; I am fat; I am thin; I am old; I am young." They identify themselves with these things. Souls are not of this type. Therefore, the identification of the self has the aggregates as its object.

[Opponent:] Since the body is the servant of the soul, we refer to it as "I" through a metaphor. It's just like saying "This is me, this is my servant."

[Vasubandhu:] There could be a metaphorical application of the term "soul" to the servant of the soul, but not an identification of the self with that servant.

[Opponent:] If the body could support an identification of the self, why don't we identify our self with the bodies of others?

[Vasubandhu:] The identification of the self arises from the connection involving the body and the mind. It won't occur with respect to a body that is not part of the continuum in question. This process has been repeating itself eternally in beginningless cyclic existence.

[Opponent:] What is this "connection?"

[Vasubandhu:] The relationship of cause and effect.

[Opponent:] If there is no soul, whose is this identification of the self?

[Vasubandhu:] This issue has already come up, and we asked "What does 'whose' mean?" The identification of the self "belongs" to its cause.

[Opponent:] What is this cause, other than the identification of the self?

[Vasubandhu:] It's an undesirable cognition, whose object is your own continuum, which is permeated with previous identifications of the self.

[Opponent:] If there is no soul, who is happy or unhappy?

[Vasubandhu:] The basis for the arising of happiness or suffering. It's like saying "The tree has flowered, the forest is fruitful."[8]

8. When we say "the forest is fruitful," there is no single underlying substance that has produced these fruits; instead, many different causes have combined to generate what we may designate as a single result. In the same way, for Vasubandhu, the basis for the appearance of happiness or suffering is many mental and physical states.

[Opponent:] What's the basis for happiness and suffering?

[Vasubandhu:] The six spheres of sensible entities. We've already explained this.[9]

[Opponent:] If there is no soul, who is the agent of an action, and who is the recipient of the consequences of the action?

[Vasubandhu:] What do you mean by "agent" and "recipient?"

[Opponent:] He who acts is the agent; he who receives is the recipient.

[Vasubandhu:] These are synonyms, not definitions!

[Opponent:] The Grammarians say that the defining characteristic of an agent is "independent action." Some effects arise from independent action. In common usage, for example, Devadatta is said to have the independent power of bathing, sitting, walking, and so on.

[Vasubandhu:] What being are you calling "Devadatta?" Is he the soul? But that's just what you have to prove! Now, is he the totality of the five aggregates? We would consider that to be the agent. Action is of three types: bodily, vocal, and mental. Bodily action is dependent on the functioning of the mind. The functioning of the mind as regards the body is dependent on its own causes in the same way. Nothing has any kind of independence. All beings arise in dependence on contributing causes. Even if we were to admit that the soul is not caused and doesn't depend on anything, that would not prove that something has independence.[10] Therefore, this characteristic of "independence" does not apply to any agent at all. Whatever is the principal cause of an action, that is called the "agent." And the soul has no causal efficacy at all. Therefore, the soul should not be considered an agent. From memory arises intention; from intention, thought; from thought, exertion; from exertion, a wind in the body; and from this wind comes the action. What does the soul do in this process?

How can the soul share in the enjoyment of the consequences of these actions?

[Opponent:] It perceives the consequences.

[Vasubandhu:] The soul is not capable of perception. That's the job of consciousness.

9. The detailed explanation is in chapter 1 of the *Treasury*.

10. Because this admission would not prove that the soul can be a cause, and the Buddhist would refuse to accept this further claim.

[Opponent:] If there is no soul, why don't nonsentient beings[11] accumulate merit and wrongdoing?

[Vasubandhu:] Because they don't experience sensations.[12] And, as has been said, the support of the six spheres of sensible entities is not the soul.

[Opponent:] If there is no soul, how does a result arise in the future from past action that has already ceased to exist?

[Vasubandhu:] Even if there is a soul, how does a result arise in the future from past action that has already ceased to exist?

[Opponent:] By means of merit and wrongdoing, qualities that have the soul as their support.

[Vasubandhu:] We've already discussed this use of language, asking "As, for instance, what supports what?"

[Opponent:] Perhaps the result arises from merit and wrongdoing existing without any support.[13]

[Vasubandhu:] But we don't say that the result arises in the future from past action that has already ceased to exist. Why? It comes from a certain development of the continuum, as a fruit arises eventually from a seed. When we say "A fruit arises from a seed," we don't mean that it arises from a seed that has already ceased to exist. Nor do we mean that a seed immediately produces a fruit. What, then? There's a certain development of the continuum, involving shoots, stems, leaves, and so on, arising in a regular order and ending with flowers. Since the fruit arises directly from the flower, why do we say "This is the fruit from that seed?" The flower, arising in sequence, has the power to produce the fruit, a power instilled in it by the seed. If it had not been preceded by that seed, it would not have been able to produce a fruit of the same type.

In the same way, we say "the result of an action arises." We don't mean that it arises from a past action that has already ceased to exist, nor that it arises immediately after the action. What, then? It comes from a certain kind of development of the continuum. What is a continuum, what is development, and what kind of development? The continuum is the progression of

11. That is, inanimate objects such as chairs and rocks.

12. Something that is not capable of feeling happiness or suffering clearly can't experience the results of actions. Therefore, it cannot accumulate good and bad karma.

13. This answer clearly involves abandoning the soul as an explanatorily relevant entity.

thoughts from one moment to the next that starts with the action. When it arises in a different form, we call that "development." A certain particular development, the final one that is capable of immediately producing the result, is the kind of development we mean. For example, when the mind at death is attached, it is capable of producing a new rebirth. In the past, the three types of actions have been performed, but the actions that are efficacious are weighty ones, or if there are no weighty actions, proximate or habitual actions, but not other kinds.[14] It is said, "Weighty actions, proximate actions, habitual actions, and any previous actions, are developed in that order in the cyclic existence caused by actions."

When a cause of retribution has produced its result, it ceases to exist. But a similar cause that produces an outflowing result ceases to exist if it is defiled, only when something opposes it.[15] If it is not defiled, it ceases only with nirvana, the end of the entire continuum of thoughts.

[Opponent:] Why is a new retribution not generated from each previous retribution?[16] Every seed or fruit can generate a new fruit.

[Vasubandhu:] The example is not entirely the same. In fact, in this case, a new fruit is not generated from a previous fruit. Why not? It arises from a certain kind of change, which itself is born from a certain kind of moistening. That seed that ceases to exist in bringing into existence the sprout is its seed, and not another. If any previous continuum is called a "seed," this is an anticipative term, or else justified by similarity. In the same way, therefore, when one hears good or bad teaching, and so on, as the result of past actions, a type of thought arises, born from a certain type of contributing cause, and it is good, impure, or bad. And, as a result, another change again arises. It doesn't happen any other way. These examples are truly parallel.

Alternatively, it could be explained in the following manner: Just as, when a citron flower is dyed red, a development of the continuum produces a fruit with red fibers, but the flower that grows from that fruit is not again red, in the same way an action produces a result, but that result does not then again produce another result.

14. This passage alludes to a theory about what determines rebirth. If a person has done a "weighty" action, such as murdering a parent, or such as attaining advanced states of meditation, that person's rebirth will be determined by the weighty action. If not, the person's rebirth will be determined either by actions performed shortly before death, or by that person's habits and usual modes of behavior.

15. A bad character trait, for example, will continue to cause problems until one does something about it.

16. If this were the case, then once one had started down a wrong path, each wrong action would produce more, and there would be no escape. This problem features in the Buddhist critique of the karmic theory of the Jains.

In accordance with my own limited knowledge, I have explained the paths of the intellect. Only the Buddhas know how, perfumed by the causal powers of various actions, different continua go to various places and various results are produced. It is said: "Action, the impression it causes, the appropriation of that impression, and the effect of the action, are all known by Buddhas, and by no one else."

Having learned the Buddhas' explanation of reality, this well-arranged and pure doctrine of causation, and having meditated on the various worthless views and exertions of the blind Tīrthikas, those who are not blind go forward.

The absence of any self, the only road to the City of Nirvana, though it is shining with the rays that are the words of that sun, the Thus Come One, evident, and followed by thousands of Saints, is not seen by those of weak insight.

Bibliography and Further Reading

Chakrabarti, Kisor Kumar. (1999) *Classical Indian Philosophy of Mind: The Nyāya Dualist Tradition.* Albany: State University of New York Press.

Duerlinger, James. (2003) *Indian Buddhist Theories of Persons: Vasubandhu's "Refutation of the Theory of a Self."* London: RoutledgeCurzon.

Goodman, Charles. (2004) "The *Treasury of Metaphysics* and the Physical World." *Philosophical Quarterly* 54/216: 389–401.

Goodman, Charles. (2005) "Vaibhāṣika Metaphoricalism." *Philosophy East and West* 55/3: 377–393.

Siderits, Mark. (1997) "Buddhist Reductionism." *Philosophy East and West* 47/4: 455–478.

27

Candrakīrti's *Madhyamakāvatārabhāṣya* 6.86–97

A Madhyamaka Critique of Vijñānavāda Views of Consciousness

C. W. Huntington, Jr.

Candrakīrti (c. 600–650) is one of the most highly regarded Indian Buddhist philosophers. Within the Tibetan tradition, Candrakīrti's understanding of Madhyamaka is considered authoritative, and the *Madhyamakāvatāra,* or *Entry into the Middle Way,* is routinely consulted as the definitive introduction to his ideas. In conformity with the mnemonic form of classical Sanskrit philosophical literature, the basic text of the *Madhyamakāvatāra* is composed in a series of metered verses (*kārikā*-s); each of these aphoristic verses is then accompanied by a commentary (*bhāṣya*) that unpacks its meaning in the larger context of the whole. This format is reflected in the excerpt I have translated here.

The *Madhyamakāvatāra* is divided into ten chapters, each one dealing with a particular element of Buddhist training. Of these, the most important are generosity, morality, patience, courage, and meditation. It is well to remember that in India the study of philosophy was never an entirely intellectual affair. Theoretical arguments were invariably linked to broader soteriological concerns. Nevertheless, for present purposes, chapter 6 is of particular interest, since it is here that Candrakīrti provides a detailed discussion of key points of Madhyamaka doctrine. Here we find an analysis of causality, a lengthy refutation of various concepts of "self," and a basic presentation of the system of the so-called two truths: the conventional truth of everyday affairs, and the profound, liberating truth of "emptiness." In the passage of the *Madhyamakāvatāra* translated here, extracted from chapter 6 (verses 86–97), Candrakīrti addresses the problem of consciousness.

Specifically, he directs his remarks toward a particular form of Buddhist idealism.

Indian idealism reached its apex in the sophisticated philosophical system of Advaita Vedānta and in the Mahāyāna Buddhist Vijñānavāda, which seems to have viewed matter as an epiphenomenon of consciousness (*vijñāna*) or mind (*citta*). It is this view that serves as the target of Candrakīrti's arguments in the material translated here. His critique of the Vijñānavāda position may be understood as a kind of dualism, but it is fundamentally unlike both the dualism that preceded him in India and the Cartesian dualism that continues to shape the premises of Anglo-American philosophical thinking. The origins of Indian idealism and of the peculiar form of dualism adopted by Candrakīrti predate the advent of Buddhism. To appreciate Candrakīrti's arguments with the Vijñānavāda, it is helpful to have a rudimentary knowledge of the literature of this early period.

The roots of Indian dualism may be found in the early Upaniṣads (c. 800–500 B.C.E.), where consciousness is described as the "witness" (*sākṣin*), the detached and entirely passive observer of the world. In this view, consciousness is pure awareness—a kind of mirror—in which, or for which, the world appears. It is essential to understand that "the world" here includes not only physical objects of the five senses but also literally everything that Cartesian dualism takes as the subjective phenomena ("mental objects") revealed exclusively through introspection—thoughts, memories, and so forth. Consciousness, as here defined, cannot easily be assimilated under the familiar Cartesian rubrics as either subjective or objective. From a Cartesian perspective, the Upanisadic witness is literally nothing, for it is unlocatable in terms of either mind or matter. And yet consciousness or awareness—this invisible no-thing—is an essential and indisputable presence in the immediate experience of both mental and physical objects. The witness can only appear as the reflection of what it is not, and this appearance is, oddly, all that there is to consciousness. This was the position eventually adopted in the dualism of classical Sāṃkhya—one of the six systems of orthodox Hindu philosophy.

Indian idealism also has its origins in the Upaniṣads, where it developed in part, perhaps, as a monistic response to a problem seemingly inherent to Upanisadic dualism, namely, the difficulty in presenting a satisfying account of the interaction between these two fundamentally distinct and independent realities of the observer and the observed. In full-blown Sāṃ khya dualism, there is an associated soteriological problem, for liberation from suffering is said to be found in the total severing of consciousness from its contents: It is a state of "isolation" (*kaivalya*) in which consciousness, though no longer conscious *of* anything, still somehow intrinsically exists. Upanisadic idealism understands the material world as an illusion (*māya*) rooted in the mind. However, as is the case with modern neuroscientific materialism, the solution offered by this form of Indian monism carries with it a new set of problems. Not only does it appear to contradict immediate experience by denying the reality of external, physical objects but also it raises the question of how unreal "material epiphenomena" can influence either thought ("mental objects") or pure consciousness (the "witness").

Candrakīrti's solution is both simple and profound. He rightly identifies the root problem of monism (whether materialist or idealist) and Upanisadic styles of dualism as one of reification. It is not possible to present a plausible account of the causal relationships that define immediate experience when any sort of inherent existence is attributed to mind, matter, or both (however they may be defined). For Candrakīrti, as for classical Sāṃkhya, consciousness is ultimately defined only in the context of its relationship with a subjective (mental) and objective (material) "other." But for Candrakīrti it is equally true that this other, the observed, is defined exclusively *as it appears* to the observer. He is explicit—and adamant—about this point. Not only is consciousness an unavoidable "nothingness" in our experience of self and world; mental and physical objects are as well a similarly unavoidable "nothingness" in consciousness. It is in the nature of *both* the observer *and* the observed to appear as what they are not, for neither exists outside of their relationship with the other. They are unreifiable, unlocatable, "empty" of intrinsic being, and entirely dependent on each other for both their existence and for any meaning they might (or might not) possess. At the level of immediate experience, both observer and observed are equally real; outside of this functionally determined nexus of relations—that is, from an entirely theoretical perspective—any notion of either existence or meaning is incoherent.

Candrakīrti's version of dualism does not embody a metaphysical position. Rather, it is grounded in an empirical appeal to our everyday experience, including the experience of thoughts and sensations that appear in the course of normal introspection. Nor does it attempt to explain away the mystery of immediate experience through any form of reductionism. On the contrary, the effect of his arguments is to heighten one's sense of wonder and one's capacity for living without recourse to absolute claims of any kind. Such arguments are considered to define a theoretical position only insofar as one's powers of empirical observation have not been adequately sharpened through sustained contemplative practice. In fact, the soteriological goal for Candrakīrti is articulated in precisely these terms: the direct yogic experience of the "selflessness" or "emptiness" of both consciousness and its contents—their lack of inherent existence—is itself liberation from the suffering caused by clinging to reified categories of subject and object.

Candrakīrti begins by addressing a position that attributes to thought some sort of causal agency in the experience of external, material appearances. Then, in the commentary to 95cd, he briefly comments on a doctrine of "Buddha-nature" (*tathāgatagarbha*) very similar to the ancient Upanisadic notion of consciousness as witness. Although his critique encompasses both views, he does not clearly distinguish between them, nor does he elaborate on the relationship between thinking (mind as agent) and pure awareness (mind as passive observer). He is not interested in presenting any overarching theory of his own. Candrakīrti's remarks here do, however, make it clear that neither thought nor pure awareness is to be viewed as ultimately real.

Translation: *Madhyamakāvatārabhāṣya* 6.86–97, Verses and Commentary

(86) Non-Buddhist philosophers speak in their various texts about things like a "person." Seeing that none of these functions as an agent, the Conqueror taught that the agent in the context of everyday experience is mind alone.

"Non-Buddhist philosophers" is merely a general term that also encompasses Buddhists who believe in things like a "person." In a way, they are not really Buddhists, because—like the non-Buddhists—they have not correctly understood the teaching. This is why they are referred to by the same designation.

Inquire of the various philosophical schools, of the Sāṃkhyas, the Aulūkyas, and the Nirgranthas, with their absolutist doctrines of a person, of aggregates, and so forth: Who speaks of that which transcends existence and nonexistence?

It is the buddhas who offer the profound, ambrosial teaching that transcends existence and nonexistence: Know that only this is the Dharma.

Those who are firmly attached to belief in the aggregates and so forth must be considered as non-Buddhists. "In their various texts..." means "in their systems of tenets." What this indicates is that "non-Buddhists" are characterized by the fact that they attribute agency to the aggregates and so forth. Because samsara has no beginning, all kinds of theories have been and will be proposed. So it is that at present the Jains and others can be found teaching of aggregates and other such doctrines. The Blessed One did not see any person or other such thing as an agent, and so he taught that the agent in the context of everyday experience is mind alone. This is the meaning of the scripture, and this meaning is exhausted in its negation of any *other* agent: the word "only" has no capacity to negate the objective component of knowledge (*jñeya*).

Having shown in this way that the external object is not negated, the author goes on to make the same point through another argument:

(87) Just as "he [whose knowledge of] reality is expansive" is referred to as "Buddha," so the [*Laṇkāvatāra*] *sūtra* substitutes "mind alone" for "mind alone is preeminent in the context of everyday experience." The meaning of this scripture is not to be understood as a negation of form.

Even though the word "Buddha" doesn't actually appear in conjunction with the words "reality" and "expansive," nevertheless this meaning is taken for granted. Similarly, the scripture asserts that the triple world is mind alone in order to make the point that mind alone is preeminent and to negate any other such preeminent factor. When the scripture says "mind alone exists; form does not," this is taught to deny the importance of form and so forth, not to negate their very existence....

> (88) If he intended to deny the existence of objective reality when he said that [the world] is mind alone, then why would the *mahātman* declare, in the same text, that mind is produced from delusion (*moha*) and volitional action (*karman*)?

In the *Daśabhūmikasūtra,* consciousness is said to have as its causes spiritual ignorance and the prenatal dispositions (*saṃskāra*-s). Therefore, it does not exist by virtue of any intrinsic distinguishing characteristic. If it did, then it would not be dependent on spiritual ignorance or on the prenatal dispositions; but it is dependent on them. Consequently, consciousness is definitely not intrinsically existent. Like the hair and so forth apprehended by someone afflicted with ophthalmia, it exists when the necessary conditions are present to create such erroneous perception, and it ceases to exist when the requisite causes are no longer present.

As it is said in the same text:

> The bodhisattva closely examines the way in which dependent arising unfolds. He reflects in the following way: Spiritual ignorance is the failure to understand things deeply; prenatal dispositions are the fruit of volitional action shaped by spiritual ignorance; consciousness is the first manifestation of mind resting on the prenatal dispositions; name and form are the four aggregates of clinging that arise with consciousness; the six sense faculties grow out of name and form; sense contact is sensual union of sense organ, object, and cognition; feeling emerges along with sense contact; thirst is immersion in feeling; clinging is the magnification of thirst; existence is passionate volitional action flowing forth from clinging; emergence of the aggregates is birth, issuing forth from volitional action; old age is the maturing of the aggregates; death is the breaking up of the aggregates in old age. [187.8]...

[189.5] In this way consciousness is established in dependence on spiritual ignorance and the prenatal dispositions. So, to be sure, consciousness exists in the presence of the conditions of error. But how does it happen that consciousness does not exist? It is explained as follows:

> The prenatal dispositions are destroyed with the destruction of spiritual ignorance; when spiritual ignorance, the condition for prenatal dispositions, does not exist, the foundation for prenatal dispositions is no longer present. When the prenatal dispositions are destroyed,

consciousness ceases to exist; when the prenatal dispositions, the condition for consciousness, does not exist, consciousness is no longer present.

Similarly, he also reflects in the following way:

Conditioned things arise from coalescence, not from separation. They arise from joining together, not from pulling apart. When I understand how conditioned things come into being through all sorts of grievous faults, I will end that coalescence and joining together. However, in order to work for the spiritual ripening of sentient beings, I will not completely destroy the prenatal dispositions. When the Son of the Conquerors reflects in this way, understanding how conditioned things are associated with grievous faults, how they lack any essence, how they neither arise nor pass away. . . .

What sensible person would look at a passage from this same [*Daśabhūmikasūtra*] and imagine that consciousness exists as an independent thing (*vastutaḥ*)? A notion like this is nothing more than dogmatic opinion. It follows that the expression "mind only" serves only to clarify that mind is the most significant element [in experience]. This text should not be understood to assert that there is no objective form (*rūpa*).

The following aphorism explains the fundamental importance of mind:

(89) Mind fabricates both the sentient and insentient worlds. It is said that the entire universe is born from volitional action, but without mind such action would not exist.

Here the "sentient world" is made up of sentient beings who receive their individual character on the basis of their own volitional actions and afflictions. The "insentient world"—from a whirlwind all the way up to the palace of the Akaniṣṭa gods—is fabricated by the common actions of those same [sentient beings]. All such diverse creatures as, for example, a peacock—even to the eyes on his feathers—are produced by their particular actions, not by action in common. Lotus flowers and other [insentient things] are produced by the common actions of all sentient beings. Other things are to be similarly understood. As it is said:

Even the Black Mountains are produced, over time, under the force of actions taken by sentient beings, as are the razor-sharp leaves in hell and the glittering jewels on heavenly trees.

So it is that the entire universe is produced from volitional action, but such action is entirely dependent on the mind. Only action associated with mind accumulates retribution, and without the mind there is no action. Mind, and no other, is the preeminent cause of the creation of the universe. In the commentarial literature, mind—not objective form—is established as fundamentally important. Why is this?

(90a–b) Even though objective form does indeed exist, it is not, like mind, an agent.

This means that objective form is inert.

(90c–d) Therefore, denying any other agent besides mind is not the same as negating objective form altogether.

Some people take [the Sāṃkhya] idea of "matter" (*pradhāna*) and such things as agent, others believe it is mind, but everyone agrees that objective form is not an agent. To prevent *pradhāna* and so forth from being taken as agent, it is explained that they do not have any such characteristic. Seeing that it has the capacity to serve as agent, one declares that mind alone is the agent, and in doing so one gains the high ground in any debate concerning the agency of *pradhāna* and so forth. It is as if two kings desire power in a single land, and one of the two rivals is expelled while the other assumes control of the country. No matter who wins, the citizens are indispensable and would suffer no harm. So it is here, because objective form is indispensable to both, it suffers no loss. One can certainly maintain that objective form exists. Therefore, continuing in the same manner, the text declares:

(91) Within the context of everyday affairs, all five psychophysical constituents taken for granted in the world do exist. However, none of the five appears to a yogi who pursues illuminating knowledge of reality.

Therefore, seeing as this is so,

(92a–b) If form does not exist, then do not cling to the existence of mind; and if mind exists, then do not cling to the nonexistence of form.

When, for some reason, one does not admit the existence of form, then the existence of both is equally unreasonable and one must admit the nonexistence of mind, as well. And when one admits the existence of mind, then it is necessary to admit the existence of form, for both are conventionally real. The same conclusion is reached in the textual tradition:

(92c–d) The Buddha rejected both of them in the scriptures on perfect wisdom, and taught them both in the Abhidharma.

Form and the other five psychophysical constituents are all taught in the Abhidharma, making distinctions between their general and particular characteristics. And in the scriptures on perfect wisdom, all five are equally denied: "O Subhūti, objective form is empty of inherent existence." The same is said concerning the others, including consciousness. This is established both in scripture and through recourse to reason.

(93a–b) You destroy the relationship of the two truths, and even then your "real thing" (*vastu*) [i.e. mind] is not established, because it has been refuted.

In arguing that consciousness alone exists, without objective form, you destroy the relationship between conventional and ultimate truth as it has been explained. And even when you have destroyed this relationship between the two truths, your absolute reality will not be established. Why not? Once the reality [of form] is denied, your efforts [to establish consciousness] are pointless.

> (93c–d) It would be better to hold, in conformity with this relationship, that in reality nothing arises; the arising of things is merely conventional.

[The Vijñānavādin] responds: Even if the meaning of this scripture is as you suggest, still there is another text that insists that mind alone exists. There it says:

> Although external objects appear, they do not exist; mind appears in various forms. I declare that mind alone appears as the body, objects of enjoyment, and place.

By "body" the text refers to the eye and other sense organs. "Objects of enjoyment" refers to visual forms and other sense objects. "Place" refers to the world as a location. Since there is no external object apart from mind, it is consciousness alone that arises taking the appearance of body, objects of enjoyment, and place. Place and so forth manifest in the form of sense objects, as if they were external objects existing apart from consciousness. Therefore the triple world is mind alone.

So as to show that this scripture as well requires interpretation, the author says,

> (94a–b) Where a scripture declares that there is no external object and that mind (*citta*) alone appears as various things,

This scripture requires interpretation:

> (94c–d) the refutation of form is provisional, directed specifically at those who are overly attached to it.

The meaning of such a text is strictly provisional. There are those who have lost themselves in clinging or anger or pride that is rooted in an extreme attachment to form; such people commit grievous errors and fail to cultivate merit or understanding. It is for these people, who are clinging, that the Blessed One taught "mind alone" even though it is not actually so. He did this in order to destroy the afflictions that are rooted in material form.

But how do you know this scripture is provisional, and not definitive?

Through both textual evidence and reason. The Master has said precisely this:

> (95a–b) The Master has said that this [scripture] is of strictly provisional meaning; reason [as well] dictates it is of provisional meaning.

Not only is this scripture of provisional meaning, but also

(95c–d) This text makes it clear that other scriptures of this type are of provisional meaning.

And if one inquires which scriptures are of "of this type," there is the following passage from the *Saṇdhinirmocanasūtra,* explaining the "three natures"—the imaginary, the dependent, and the perfected:

The imaginary is nonexistent, only what is dependent exists.

And likewise:

Repository Consciousness is profound and subtle, the seed of all existence, flowing like a river. It would be inappropriate to think of it as a "subject"—I have not taught such a thing even to people who understand very little...

Once again,

Just as a physician dispenses medicine to one patient or another, so the Buddha also teaches "mind alone" to living beings.

This text makes clear the point about provisional meaning. Similarly [in the *Laṇkāvatārasūtra*]:

The Blessed One has spoken in the scriptures about a fundamental level of awareness (*tathāgatagarbha*), describing it as naturally brilliant, fundamentally pure, bearing the thirty-two marks [of a Buddha], immanent in the bodies of all sentient beings. It is described as a jewel of immense value wrapped in the soiled cloth of psychophysical aggregates, elements of sensation (*dhātus*), and sense organs along with their objects (*āyatanas*). It was further described as dominated by clinging, antipathy, and delusion and soiled by the filth of conceptualization. Nevertheless, it is permanent, firm, and eternal. How is it, Blessed One, that this talk of Buddha-nature is not equivalent to that talk of non-Buddhists concerning a self? Non-Buddhists as well, Blessed One, teach about the self as permanent, as lacking agency, devoid of qualities, omnipotent, and indivisible. The Blessed One responds as follows: Mahāmati, my teaching about Buddha-nature is not at all equivalent to the talk of non-Buddhists concerning a self. Why not? The fully awakened saints, the Tathāgatas, teach about Buddha-nature as emptiness, as the limit of existence (*bhūtakoṭi*), as nirvana, as unborn, uncaused, unceasing, and so forth. Although the supreme Buddha-nature is not susceptible to reification (*nirvikalpa*) or any sort of binding imagery (*nirbhāsa*), still they teach about it in this way so as to mitigate the apprehension of those who are unfamiliar with the teaching of selflessness. Mahāmati, no present or future bodhisattva would take this for a "self." Just as, Mahāmati, a potter

> fashions a variety of pots from one mound of clay particles by using his hands, his skill, a stick, water, a string, and his own strength, so, Mahāmati, the same selflessness of phenomena that is absolutely free from all conceptualized distinguishing characteristics is taught by the Tathāgatas through a variety of synonymous words and phrases—either through instruction on Buddha-nature or on selflessness—and as with the potter, through application of diverse forms of wisdom and skillful means. Mahāmati, this is how they teach about Buddha-nature to those whose thoughts are immersed in views concerning the idea of a self. In this way, the thinking of such people will come under the influence of [teachings on] emptiness, selflessness, and impermanence and they will be able more swiftly to obtain perfect awakening.

> And in the same scripture,

> Mahāmati, the teaching that permeates the scriptures of all the Buddhas is characterized by emptiness, nonarising, nonduality, and lack of any distinguishing characteristic.

After having shown that scriptures of this type—all of which are said by Vijñānavādins to be of definitive meaning—are of provisional meaning, the author points out that reason as well clarifies their provisional meaning:

> (96) The Buddhas teach that the subject, or knower (*jñātṛ*), may easily be dispensed with once the object of knowledge, or the known (*jñeya*), is no longer present. For this reason they begin by refuting the object of knowledge, for, when it is no longer present, refutation of the subject is already accomplished.

The Blessed Buddhas introduce novices to the absence of intrinsic existence through a series of graduated stages, or steps. Those who have prepared themselves through meritorious action easily penetrate to the essence of this teaching (*dharmatā*), because meritorious action is a means for doing so. This is why generosity and other forms of ethical behavior are extolled as fundamental. Similarly, the Blessed One refutes the object of knowledge first, because this serves as a means for entering into an understanding of selflessness. Those who understand how the object of knowledge is devoid of self will progress with comparative ease to an understanding of how the subject, or knower, similarly lacks any self-contained existence. Some of those who understand the object's lack of intrinsic existence will immediately comprehend the similar lack of any intrinsic existence in the subject; others will reach this understanding with only a bit more guidance. This is why the object is refuted first. Wise people should apply the same principles in their interpretation of other [texts].

> (97) Based on an understanding of this hermeneutical approach, one goes on to apply it to other texts. If the purpose of a scripture is to teach something other than reality, then it is of provisional meaning

and must be interpreted through critical reflection. On the other hand, if its purpose is to teach emptiness, then its meaning should be understood as definitive.

Bibliography and Suggested Reading

Deutsch, Eliot. (1969) *Advaita Vedānta*. Honolulu: University of Hawai'i Press.

Garfield, Jay. (1995) *The Fundamental Wisdom of the Middle Way: Nāgārjuna's Mūlamadhyamakakārikā*. New York: Oxford University Press.

Huntington, C. W. (1989) *The Emptiness of Emptiness: An Introduction to Early Indian Mādhyamika*. Honolulu: University of Hawai'i Press.

Larson, Gerald J. (1969) *Classical Sāṃkhya*. Delhi: Motilal Banarsidass.

Lusthaus, Dan. (2002) *Buddhist Phenomenology: A Philosophical Investigation of Yogācāra Buddhism and he Ch'eng Wei-shih lun*. London: RoutledgeCurzon.

Wallace, B. Alan. (2000) *The Taboo of Subjectivity: Toward a New Science of Consciousness*. Oxford: Oxford University Press.

28

Śāntarakṣita's *Tattvasaṃgraha*

A Buddhist Critique of the Nyāya View of the Self

Matthew T. Kapstein

Despite current uncertainties among scholars concerning the "original doctrines" of Buddhism, some of the most ancient among the discourses attributed to the Buddha unmistakably call into question the notion that each one of us possesses a unique and persisting self, or *ātman* in Sanskrit. In developing this idea, the early Buddhist thinkers who composed the several versions of the Abhidharma (the "metadoctrine") held living beings to be aggregations of primitive, unitary substances, that is, material atoms and substantial, but momentary, psychic and physical phenomena (*dharma*).[1] Thus, when we speak of minds, we speak only of collections of discrete mental events, or acts of consciousness. The question immediately arises: how do these bundles of events come to constitute the sort of coherent, temporally continuous wholes that we refer to as "persons"? If we are only heaps of momentary psychic and physical monads, then why is it that Jones's body, Smith's sensations, and Miller's thoughts do not make up a "person," above and beyond Jones, Smith, and Miller? The answer of the Buddhist Abhidharma philosophers was that such a miscellaneous collection of parts is not bound into a single causal continuum (*santāna*). That is, the identity of a person is the identity of a continuum; the elements bundled together in a

1. Collins 1982, Kapstein 2001, and Siderits 2003 take up aspects of Abhidharma thought that are pertinent to this chapter.

single continuum are thus somehow coherently united with one another, though not identical.[2]

This view of persons as selfless continuants aroused considerable controversy in ancient India. Indeed, for a period of over a millennium, it was probably the single most hotly contested philosophical topic on the subcontinent. Most non-Buddhist traditions, however, if in accord about little else, generally agreed that the Buddhists were dead wrong about this issue and that what individuates us—makes us each the distinct individual he or she is—is the fact that we are each uniquely characterized by a discrete enduring self (*ātman*), life-monad (*jīva*), or person (*puruṣa*).[3]

Over and against the Buddhist Abhidharma theories, therefore, the emerging schools of Brahmanical philosophy were decisive in advancing their own views of the self. Among them, the Nyāya tradition, whose specialized interest was in the domains of logic and the theory of knowledge, was particularly outspoken in its criticism of the Buddhists. A long line of Nyāya philosophers, from Vātsyāyana (c. 400 C.E.) to Udayana (tenth century), devoted considerable attention to the puzzles of the self. The common point of departure for their reflections may be found in the proof of the *ātman*'s existence that was formulated by the philosopher-sage Akṣapāda Gautama (c. second century) in the prime text of the tradition, the *Aphorisms of Reason:* "Desire and hatred, willful effort, pleasure and pain, and knowledge are the marks of the self" (*Nyāyasūtra* 1.1.10).[4]

As explained by the commentator Vātsyāyana, this means that we can only make sense of the properties mentioned if we consider them to be the properties of our selves. Thus, for example, my desire for, or aversion to, any particular object is generally related to *my* previous experiences of objects of the same type: I like Thai cuisine, because the Thai cooking I've had in the past has often seemed to me to be tasty; and I would never buy a used Chevy, because my past experience tells me they're apt to be lemons. It is reasonable to suppose, in such cases, that there is some connection between my past enjoyment or exasperation and my current feelings about the objects in question. That connection, however, cannot be simply a property of the objects, as we know that the very same object may arouse quite diverse affective responses among different perceivers—perhaps my neighbor is a Chevy enthusiast who finds spicy food unpleasant. The relation between past experience and present response therefore must be explained by their being related not solely via the object, but instead to a common subject, which is what we speak of as the self. And for Vātsyāyana, only a single,

2. The "bundles" mentioned here refer to the traditional Buddhist analysis of the field of experience as composed of "five heaps" (*pañcaskandha*): form (*rūpa*), sensation (*vedana*), perception (*saṃjñā*), volitions and other conditioning factors (*saṃskāra*), and consciousness (*vijñāna*).

3. A useful survey of classical Indian theories of the self will be found in Organ 1964.

4. See Chakrabarti 1982.

identical subject of both previous experience and subsequent response can play the required role here: the Buddhist notion of a connected stream of mental events he considers as obliterating the distinction that we must make between the synchronic discreteness of different persons and the diachronic unity of a single person. A theory that is unable to unify the states of the same individual through time, and thus treats them in analogy to the states of synchronically discrete persons, is a theory that he believes we should dispose of without ceremony.

Vātsyāyana's arguments were refined and amplified by Uddyotakara (sixth century), who believed that, besides the arguments advanced by his predecessor, we do directly experience the self every time that the first person pronoun "I" occurs in our thoughts or that we utter it.[5] His views, which placed the problem of first person reference at the center of the dispute, together with those of other representatives of the various Brahmanical schools, were made the subject of extended criticism in the writings of the eighth-century Buddhist philosopher Śāntarakṣita, whose masterwork, the *Tattvasaṃgraha* (Compendium of [views of] reality), offers an extended defense of Buddhist teaching with respect to twenty-six major areas of debate that had arisen during the preceding centuries.[6] The substantial chapter devoted to the "Investigation of the Self" (*ātmaparīkṣā*) considers the opinions of a half dozen schools, but concentrates primarily on the Nyāya, and among Nyāya philosophers, primarily on Uddyotakara. These sections of the text are translated here, with the commentarial glosses of Śāntarakṣita's disciple Kamalaśīla.[7]

Translation

1. Synopsis of the Nyāya View of the Self

[*The Nyāya philosophers*] *hold there's a self, the support for desire and so on,*
Which though not intrinsically conscious, is eternal and ubiquitous. (171)
It is the doer of good and evil deeds, and the enjoyer of their fruit,
Due to conjunction with consciousness, though consciousness is not of its essence. (172)

5. Kapstein 2001: 96–98.

6. An introduction to Śāntarakṣita's work may be found in Kapstein 2001: 9–15, with a list of chapter topics in n. 17.

7. The only complete translation of the *Tattvasaṃgraha* into any Western language is that of Gaṅganātha Jhā (1937–39), which, though a pioneering work, is now very much out of date. The selection given here was newly translated following the Sanskrit text as edited in Shastri's edition: Śāntarakṣita 1982. Śāntarakṣita's verses are given in italic type with numbers following.

Its connection with awareness, willful effort, and such, is spoken of as its agency,
And its enjoyment is the inherence of presentations of pleasure, pain, and the like. (173)
What is designated as its birth is its coming-to-possess
A specific, unprecedented embodied condition, and also mental events and sensations. (174)
Separation from what was thus acquired is its death, while its life
Is its possession, while embodied, of a mind conditioned by right or wrong. (175)
Injury to it is thought to be violence done to body, eye, and so on,
And thus, though this soul be eternal, common usage is held to be faultless.[8] (176)

[Commentary:] To establish that [the posit of] the self is without purpose, [Śāntarakṣita] begins, "[*The Nyāya philosophers*] *hold there's a self...*" (171). For they imagine that the so-called self is utterly distinct from body, sense-faculties, and mental events; that it is a substance, the support for desire, hatred, willful effort, pleasure, pain, awareness, and right and wrong moral affections; that it is the cause of inherence,[9] and is not essentially conscious; that it is incorruptible, all-pervasive, the doer of different good and evil deeds, and the enjoyer of their desirable and undesirable rewards. Otherwise, were there no self, then who having gone forth [in death] would enjoy the fruits of deeds? For it is not the case that what one has done another enjoys. Similarly, [if there is no self,] there would be the fault of reaping what one has not sown, for it is not the doer who is conjoined with the fruit. And there would be loss of what was done, for the doer would have no connection with the fruit. None such should be held. Therefore, necessarily the one who is the doer should be affirmed to be the enjoyer. Hence, the one who is both doer and enjoyer is the self.

Now, if it is not conscious in essence, then how can it be that what forms no conscious intentions is an agent? For this reason it is said: "*Due to conjunction with consciousness*" (172). It is conscious inasmuch as it thinks through conjunction with consciousness, but not of its own essence,

8. If the soul is unchanging and immortal, and is identified as what a person "really is," then, one might wonder, in what way might ephemeral actions be actions of a person, or injury done to a body be injury to a person, etc.? The Nyāya response, as summarized in verses 172–176, is that it is in virtue of the *connection* between the self, or soul, and the person's ephemeral properties, including acts, affects, and the body, that these may be said to be "of the person." In this way, our everyday sense of things, or "common usage" as it is called here, is not regarded as contradicting the theory of the soul's eternal existence.

9. Nyāya philosophy maintains that, to be instantiated, properties must "inhere" in an appropriate substance. In the case of psychological, moral, and affective properties, this is held to be the self.

because it is not conscious in essence, as is [the self] described by the [Sāṃkhya] adherents of Kapila, [who say,] "consciousness is its essential form."[10]

If, then, this one is permanent, how can it be agent or enjoyer? And how are its birth, death, and life to be established? For all this cannot be true of an eternal and simple form, like space. So they say: "*with awareness*" (173), and so on. The inherence within the self of awareness, willful effort, and striving to act, constitute agency; and the inherence of presentations of pleasure, and so on, enjoyment. Relationship with a specific embodied condition without precedent, that is, with body, mind, sense, and sensation, is spoken of as the birth of that self. An "*embodied condition*" (174) is one in which one enjoys [the circumstances of] god or man, or other creature. In the phrase "*and sensations*" (174), the word "and" is taken to include body and sense-faculty. In that case, the relationship with body and sense-faculty is one that has the characteristic of conjunction, while [the relationship] with mind and sensation has the characteristic of inherence. How is it associated with the auditory organ? There, too, the association is one of conjunction; for the self is conjoined with [the body's] invisible, conditioned ear-hole, and that is conjoined with the auditory organ, whose nature is space.[11]

Separation from what was thus acquired, namely, body, sense-faculty, intellect, and sensation, is said to be its death, while its life is its conjunction with a mind inclined to righteousness or unrighteousness, while in an embodied condition.

"*Injury*" to that self "*is thought*" (176), that is, explained, to stem from "*violence done to its body, eye, and so on.*" So it says in the *Nyāyasūtra:* "Injury is due to the harm to the support for the results of actions, or to the agents" (*Nyāyasūtra* 3.1.6.).

Here the "support for the results of actions" refers to the body, because it is the support for such results as pleasure, and so forth. And "agents" are the sense-faculties, because they are the agents of the apprehension of objects.

2. The Nyāya Philosopher Uddyotakara's Arguments in Favor of this View

Cognitions of visible form, and the like, all bear the mark of one and many,
For they [the many] are unified by the [single] cognition "I." (180)

10. For a perceptive analysis of the relation between self and consciousness, with reference to Sāṃkhya philosophy in particular, see Schweitzer 1993.

11. Because sound seems to be transmitted in ethereal space, and the inner ear encloses a small portion of that space within, early Indian science posited, owing to this commonality, that the ear functioned by serving as an intermediary between sound's ethereal medium and consciousness.

Similarly, when the dancing-girl raises her brow, the cognitions of the many [spectators],
Would not be linked together in the absence of some [*single*] *cause.* (181)

[Commentary:] Uddyotakara argues as follows: "Devadatta's[12] cognitions of visible form, flavor, odor, and texture bear the mark of one and many; for they are unified together by the cognition 'I.' Similarly, the cognitions of many persons, who have previously entered into an agreement, [are linked together] during the single instant when the dancing-girl raises her brow."[13]

His meaning is this: Just as many might enter into an agreement, saying, "As soon as the dancing-girl raises her brow let us all throw fine fabric [onto the stage as a gesture of our common approval]," so that the many agents and their many cognitions—"I have seen [her raise her brow], I have seen it"—are unified because of the singularity of the sign, the raising of the brow; so, too, in the present case, cognitions with many different objects should be unified owing to the singularity of a sign, and that single sign is the self. The unification, moreover, is of many cognitions, such as "I have seen, I have heard," which are linked together by the characteristic of having a single knower. But in the case of the dancing-girl raising her brow, the cognitions [of the many spectators] are connected because they have a common object. In all cases, a "unification" is spoken of whenever there is a relationship among cognitions, some single feature being considered the reason. Setting forth this inference, Śāntarakṣita says, "*Cognitions of visible form*" (180), and so on, which is easy to understand.

The word "self" is the designator of something distinct
From the aggregate of intellect, sense, and such; wherefore, it is thought to be a unique term. (182)

Whatever is thus ascertained as being distinct from [*other*] *established conventions,*
Is applied to that [*its referent*] *in virtue of specified properties; for instance, in the case of the word "pot."* (183)

[Commentary:] This is another of his arguments: The word "self" is an expression for something separate from the aggregation of body, sense, intellect, mental events, and sensation, because of its being a unique term that is distinct from [other] well-known conventions, just like "pot" and other such words.[14] So Śāntarakṣita says, "*From the aggregate of intellect, sense,*

12. "Devadatta" is the "John Doe" of Indian philosophy.
13. For an interpretation of this argument, see Kapstein 2001: 146–151.
14. Uddyotakara appears to have affirmed a robust realism with respect to the theory of reference: words mean what they refer to and the referent of a meaningful word is accordingly a real individual.

and so on." (182). And when he says, "*designator of something distinct,*" what he means is that it is distinct from such established conventions as "intelligence" and so on, which are synonyms of "intellect," "sense," and other terms.

As for "*Whatever is thus ascertained,*" (183) that is, "*as being distinct from* [*other*] *established conventions,*" this is owing to its being a unique term. "*Is applied to that* [*its referent*] *in virtue of specified properties*" means here that ["self"] is the designator of an object distinct from intellect, and so on.

> *Assuming there to be no self at all,*
> *This living body must be disjoined*
> *From vital force, just like a pot.*
> *Therefore, selfless it is not.* (184)

[Commentary:] Uddyotakara has also utilized this contrapositive reason to establish the self:[15] this living body is not selfless, because that would imply it to be devoid of vital force, and similar properties, as are pots and such like. Explaining that, Śāntarakṣita says, "*Assuming there to be no self at all*" (184), and so forth. "*Selfless*" here refers to the living body. Alternatively, the meaning is that this self is not selfless, that is, insubstantial, but rather that its being is established.

3. Śāntarakṣita's Refutation of Uddyotakara

> *Unification "by me" reflects the admixture of ignorance,*
> *That attributes singular agency to instantaneous beings.* (195)
> *From this conceptual error, reality's nature is not inferred.* (196ab)
> *Despite difference, according to distinction of potency,*
> *There is nonetheless a cause for unity.* (196cd)

[Commentary:] Referring to [the argument of verse 180], "*Cognitions of visible form,* and the like," Śāntarakṣita says, "*Unification 'by me' . . .*" (195). That is to say, such unification [as is expressed in phrases such as] "seen by me, heard by me," whose characteristic is linkage of cognitions by reason of a single knower, is uncertain. For possibly, too, the unification is due to erroneous attribution of singular agency to instantaneous beings. Hence, from such unification, it is not correct to posit what really is the case (196ab).

But how is it that a plurality of instants come to be the basis of unification? On this, the text says, "*Despite difference*" (196cd), and so on. "*Distinction of*

15. The Indian contrapositive argument typically takes the form: if not-*p*, then not-*q*, where *p* is the thesis to be proven and not-*q* is an undesirable entailment of the assumption that *p* is false. For a thorough analysis of the logical forms involved, see Staal 1962.

potency" means "particular potency." Though there be a plurality of objects, they are the *cause*, that is, causal ground, of a single effect, such as the discernment of a single feature. For example, [the medicine called] *guḍūcya*, with other things, cures fever and so on.[16]

[To affirm] that consciousnesses of form, sound, and the like are the results of a single enduring entity
Contradicts temporal succession, because the potent cause is present. (197)

[Commentary:] But how is one certain of the error here [i.e. about the unity of the self]? Concerning this, he says, "*[To affirm] that consciousnesses*" (197), and so on. If these cognitions of blue, and the like,[17] are the effects of a single, permanent self, or other such entity, which travels through time, from earlier to later, then their coming-into-being in temporal succession is contradicted; for, the entire causal nexus being complete, it is implied that they arise all at once. And what is permanent does not depend on any other; for it is not to be assisted by anything.[18]

From a single successive act of consciousness,
The six conscious acts arise
And are clearly known all at once;
Hence, the probandum is accepted as proven. (198)

[Commentary:] Moreover, if what is to be proven is only that, generally speaking, there is a causal precedent, then the probandum is in any case established.[19] Indicating this, Śāntarakṣita says, "*From a single successive act*" (198), and so on. Thus, from a single successive act of consciousness, which is the condition of immediacy,[20] the arising of the six

16. Śāntarakṣita's point is just that apparently unique events may be explained by diverse causes, so that a straightforward inference from an apparently unique event (the consciousness of "I") to a real, unique cause (a single, substantial "I") is not warranted.

17. The "cognition of blue" is the stock example of a conscious phenomenon, invoked without any assumption as to whether or not there is a corresponding external object or event.

18. For much of classical Indian thought, the idea of a permanent thing entailed the complete autonomy and changelessness of that thing, its lack of dependence on transient causes and conditions. Buddhist philosophers argued that, if one assumes there to be such a thing, and that it is conceived as causally efficacious, then its effects would have to be realized all at once, as succession would imply a change of state in the cause itself.

19. Indian debating theory holds it to be a flaw to argue for what one's opponent in any case affirms, where the result contributes no less to the opponent's larger argument than it does to one's own. The "probandum's being [already] established" (*siddhasādhyatā*) is the technical expression for this fault.

20. In Buddhist Abhidharma philosophy, the "condition of immediacy" (*samanantara-pratyaya*) refers to the immediate occurrence of a conscious instant with the cessation of the preceding instant, so that consciousness is continuous and not "gappy."

consciousnesses, those of the eye and the other senses are clearly known. So it is that what sees the dancing-girl's figure also hears the sounds of the drum and other instruments, smells the aroma of the blue lotus and such, tastes camphor and so forth, feels the breeze from the fan, and the like, and thinks of presenting a gift of cloth. It is not correct to assert that this is due to extreme rapidity of movement, as when one sees a circle formed by a whirling torch. For it is then implied that the appearance is an unclear one. Similarly, you have maintained that this notion of grasping all at once is due to the unification of perceptions, and that unification is fabricated through memory. And [you hold] that memory, having its object in the past, is unclear, but that this simultaneous appearance of visible form, and so on, is experienced clearly. Moreover, there occur acts of awareness which grasp, for example, the phoneme SA [which appears] quite rapidly in [such phonemic sequences as] SA-RA or RA-SA, and the like. Here, too, [according to your supposition] there should be the notion of grasping all at once, and so no sequence whatever should be ascertained. [In the foregoing verse], moreover, "*clearly*" indicates the general drift of this response.

That there is no unified causal basis of a succession is immediately demonstrated.
Hence, it will be clearly seen that the inclusion here is inferentially refuted. (199)

[Commentary:] It may be argued that the basis for their unity is their being caused by a permanent and simple entity. To show that the inclusion [of "being the cause of a succession of events" in "being permanent and simple"] is inferentially refuted,[21] Śāntarakṣita says, "*That there is no unified causal basis*" (199), and so on. "*Immediately*" refers back to "*a single enduring entity*" (197), and what follows. The refutation is this: "Whatever is endowed with unobstructed causal potency gives rise to [its results] all at once. For instance, when the causal nexus [consisting of seed, soil, moisture, etc.] is complete, [the seed] sprouts just then. Devadatta's objective cognitions of visible forms, and on the like, have as their cause something endowed with unobstructed causal potency [i.e. the self]. [Therefore, all his cognitions must be realized all at once.]"—This is by reason of the essential definition [of "unobstructed causal potency"]. But it is not the case [that all his cognitions must be realized all at once], and hence [the argument] is to be rejected.

The movement of the dancing-girl's brow is not one in an absolute sense,
For it is an aggregate of many atoms, whose unity is conceptually imputed. (200)

21. See note 18.

[Commentary:] Showing that Uddyotakara's example also proves nothing, Śāntarakṣita says, "*The movement of the dancing-girl's brow*" (200), and so forth. For the movement of the dancing-girl's brow, and such, is not one, because it is an aggregation of many [atoms]. If that is so, then how is it the object of a single term? To this he says that its "*unity is conceptually imputed.*"

Due to the occurrence of a single effect, it comes within the scope of one word—
If that be your probandum, then the probandum is accepted as proven. (201)

[Commentary:] What is the basis for that conceptual imputation? To this [Śāntarakṣita] says, "*Due to the occurrence of a single effect*" (201), and so on. Because this movement of the brow is one with respect to its effect, that is, the visual consciousness [of the perceiver], it therefore, though diverse [in itself], comes within the range of a single word. In that case, we too affirm that the oneness is in this manner conceptually imputed, and the example is thus not devoid of probative force. Hence, [the text says,] "*If that be your probandum ...*" For in this way we accept the probandum as proven, because the earlier and later impressions that are the basis for a single cognitive act are objects that are imputed to be a single existing thing.

Even though they be unique terms, our conventions,
Words like "intellect" or "mind,"
Do not designate something distinct.
Hence, the reason is uncertain. (202)

And though this be proposed with a qualification, it remains unproven;
Because [the term used] is an established synonym for "mind." (203)

Mind is called "self" because it is the ground for first person reference;
While that is so conventionally, in reality its object is never found. (204)

[Commentary:] As was said before, "*distinct from the aggregate of intellect, sense,* and such." (182). Here, [in response to that argument, Śāntarakṣita] says, "*Even though they be unique terms,*" and so forth (202).

Because [it is thought] "*to be a unique term*" (182)—this is an uncertain reason. This is because we do not think that just by being a unique term it is a designator of a distinct something: for example the synonyms for "mind," "sense," "sensation," and "body"—intellect, mind, knowledge, sense, perception, sensation, consciousness, body, embodiment, torso—are all "unique terms." Hence, the reason is uncertain because the absence of counterexample has not been established.[22]

22. Indian systems of logic involved a verification procedure that required demonstrating a confirming example and the absence of a counterexample. In this case,

Nonetheless, one might harbor this doubt: "it [the term 'self'] is distinct from [other] established conventions. The reason ['because it is a unique term'] being thus qualified, in what way is it uncertain?" Now, here it may be said that the [proposed] qualification of the reason is itself not established. How so? "*Because* [*the term used*] *is an established synonym for 'mind'*" (203). For "self" is established to be a synonym of "mind." As it is said: "Mind is referred to as 'self' because it is the ground for first person reference." It "*is called 'self'*" means that it is conventionally designated as such. Hence, when Uddyotakara says, "in the absence of a primary designation, there can be no secondary usage,"[23] it is because he has not understood that idea. That should be realized. This is made clear where [Śāntarakṣita] says, "*Mind is called 'self.'*" Therefore, the qualification of the reason is not established. But, having understood it to have an object in the conventional sense, the uncertainty of this reason is stated.

If one argues that, in an absolute sense, ["self"] refers to an object discrete from intellect and the like, then the inclusion is inferentially refuted. Showing the logical reason to be invalid, [Śāntarakṣita] says, "*in reality,*" and so forth (204). Later on we will discuss how it is that all verbal conventions have as their objects referents that have been conventionally assigned.[24] Thus, this word "self" has no object [with which it is uniquely correlated]. So how can the logical reason ["because of being a unique term"] include the probandum ["'self' refers to something distinct from intellect, and the like"]?

> *Though one subject-term is applied to sky-lotuses and the like,*
> *That is seen to be misleading.* (205)

[Commentary:] In order to indicate that, even with the qualification, the logical reason is uncertain, [Śāntarakṣita] says: "*Though one subject-term,*" and what follows. For, when a subject-, or other, term is associated with some absolutely nonexistent thing, such as a celestial flower, then there is a singular term distinct from the designators of the body, and so on, about which both parties [in this dispute] are in agreement. But there being no substantial object distinct from the body, and so on, the logical reason is uncertain.

---

the absence of a counterexample would require that there be no genuine synonyms, as the phenomenon of synonymity, as we ordinarily understand it, calls into question Uddyotakara's notion of a "unique term" enjoying a privileged correspondence with its referent.

23. Uddyotakara is thus saying that, although "self" may have a secondary use as a synonym of "mind," the very fact of such a secondary usage implies that the term must have a discrete primary designation as well. Śāntarakṣita, by contrast, is maintaining that this is just an ad hoc assumption.

24. A fully detailed analysis of the relation between word and reference is the topic of chap. 16 of Śāntarakṣita's *Tattvasaṃgraha.*

Terms that originate as sheer convention are not connected to anything;
Neither do "self" and other such words, reveal any meaning by nature. (206)

[Commentary:] But how can it be that subject-, and other, terms, are applied in the absence of being ostensively expressive [of their meaning]? It is because they originate as sheer convention. For convention originates merely with autonomous desire, and verbal expressions are merely expressive of that. So how can one prevent their application to anything?

If it were proven that vital force, and the like, had some relationship with the self,
Then this implication might follow, but it is otherwise if they are unconnected. (207)
In the absence of a barren woman's son,
It is not implied that the living body
Is devoid of vital force;
Similarly, this implication. (208)

[Commentary:] If vital force, and the like, were proven to have some connection with the self, whether through an internal or a causal relationship, then the implication that absence of vital force in the body would follow from the absence of its self would be reasonable.[25] Otherwise, if it is implied that the absence of the one entails the absence of the other, even though they are unrelated, then absurd consequences follow. For it is not the case that in the absence of a barren woman's son there is the absence of the vital force, and the like, that are not related to that [nonexistent barren woman's son].[26] Therefore, as the argument is an uncertain one, with ruinous implications, as illustrated by "there being no barren woman's son, the absence of unrelated vital force, and the like, follows, as in the case of a pot," just so your [argument], in which absence of self implies absence of vital force, and the like, is uncertain, because the [relevant] relationship has not been proven.

For here there is no internal relationship,
The distinctness of the two being affirmed;
Neither is there a causal relationship,
Because that would imply instantaneous realization. (209)

[Commentary:] In what sense is their relationship not proven? [...] There is no internal relationship connecting the self and vital force; for their essential

25. The argument concerning the relation between the self and vitality is considered in depth in Kapstein 2001, chap. 6.

26. A "barren woman's son" is the stock example of a thing that cannot exist because its presumed causal antecedent is incoherent. Though the absence of such an impossibility is compresent with other absences, including contingent absences (such as, in this case, that of vital force), it has no logical or causal relation to them, such as would warrant an inference from one to the other. The point here is that the concept of the "self" that is posited is similarly devoid of substantive entailments.

difference has been affirmed, as follows: the vital forces are impermanent, nonpervading [i.e. spatially fixed], and corporeal, while self is just the opposite. Neither is there a causal relationship, because given the totality of the vital forces' causes, [their] occurrence-all-at-once is implied.[27] And there is no relationship besides these. Therefore, why is it that the vital forces abandon that body, that is, a body qualified by life?

4. Verses Summarizing the Buddhist Viewpoint

Therefore, desire and so forth,
None of these inheres in a self,
Because they come into being in sequence,
Like that of seed, shoot and stem. (217)
So it is that all that is inward
Is informed throughout by selflessness
By reason of concreteness and being,
Like outer things such as pots.[28] (218)
For if [body, etc.] were endowed with self,
Then, being caused [by self] they would be eternal;
And what is eternal having no causal efficacy,
No possibility of their being follows. (219)
The similarity with pots, and so on,
Whereby our opponents seek to refute
No-self with respect to living bodies,
Becomes in this instance our proof. (220)
Thus, the procedures put forth
In attempting to prove the self,
Are all, indeed, quite groundless,
And remain like a barren woman's son. (221)

Bibliography and Suggested Reading

Chakrabarti, Arindam. (1982) "The Nyāya Proofs for the Existence of the Soul." *Journal of Indian Philosophy* 10: 211–238.

27. Buddhist philosophers in the tradition of Dharmakīrti assumed there to be two broad classes of relations: internal relations, literally "relations of identity," such as the relations of a thing to its essential properties (e.g., the relation of a pot to "being an ephemeral material artifact"); and causal relations (e.g., the relation of a pot to the potter, the clay of which it was made, etc.). In the absence of such relations, two things were considered "unrelated."

28. The properties of "concreteness" and "being" (i.e. substantial existence), as exemplified by actual things such as pots, were considered by Buddhist thinkers to entail impermanence, existence in a causal stream, and so on, which are definitionally excluded from the concept of a permanent self.

Collins, Steven. (1982) *Selfless Persons*. Cambridge: Cambridge University Press.

Ganeri, Jonardon. (2007) *The Concealed Art of the Soul: Theories of Self and Practices of Truth in Indian Ethics and Epistemology*. Oxford: Oxford University Press.

Jhā, Gaṅganātha. (1937–39) *The Tattvasaṃgraha of Śāntarakṣita*. Gaekwad's Oriental Series, vols. 80 and 83. Baroda: Oriental Institute.

Kapstein, Matthew T. (2001) *Reason's Traces: Identity and Interpretation in Indian and Tibetan Buddhist Thought*. Boston: Wisdom.

Organ, Troy Wilson. (1964) *The Self in Indian Philosophy*. The Hague: Mouton.

Parfit, Derek. (1984) *Reasons and Persons*. Oxford: Clarendon Press.

Śāntarakṣita. (1982) *Tattvasaṃgraha*. ed. Swami Dwarikadas Shastri, with the *Pañjikā* commentary of Kamalaśīla. Reprint of the 1968 edition. Varanasi: Bauddha Bharati, 2 vols.

Schweitzer, Paul. (1993) "Mind/Consciousness Dualism." *Philosophy and Phenomenological Research* 53.4: 845–859.

Siderits, Mark. (2003) *Personal Identity and Buddhist Philosophy: Empty Persons*. Aldershot: Ashgate.

Sorabji, Richard. (2006) *Self: Ancient and Modern Insights about Individuality, Life, and Death*. Chicago: The University of Chicago Press.

Staal, J. Frits. (1962) "Contraposition in Indian Logic," in Ernest Nagel, Patrick Suppes, and Alfred Tarski, eds., *Logic, Methodology, and Philosophy of Science: Proceedings of the 1960 International Congress*. Palo Alto, CA: Stanford University Press, 634–649.

29

Zhiyi's *Great Calming and Contemplation*

"Contemplating Mental Activity as the Inconceivable Realm"

Hans-Rudolf Kantor

The following is a summary and interpretation of a selection from the Tiantai classic *Great Calming and Contemplation*[1] attributed to Zhiyi (538–597). This is a foundational Tiantai scripture that outlines the school's doctrinal core and addresses the "ten modes of contemplation." Since the first mode includes the other nine, it is considered the most important and fundamental. The section expounding this mode, translated here, is called "Contemplating Mental Activity as the Inconceivable Realm." It explicitly reflects Zhiyi's ideas on mental activity in light of the other crucial doctrines in Tiantai teaching.

Zhiyi's Tiantai teaching focuses on the "transformation" of human existence. The medium of this transformation is usually indicated through the expression "Xin," originally signifying "heart" and here translated as "mental activity." The term "Xin" is used in a highly ambiguous way, as is most Tiantai terminology. It can be interchanged with the term "delusion," but also with its antonym—"wisdom." Transformation of Xin, explained as "turning delusions into wisdom," implies that delusions are the inverse mode of wisdom, as much as wisdom is the transformed mode of delusions—the two are opposite modes of each other, yet indivisible.

Zhiyi extends this bipolar yet nondual pattern characterizing Xin to all sentient beings and their existential habitat. The Chinese characters for "the

1. The Chinese text is included in the Chinese Buddhist canon *Taishō shinshū daizōkyō*, ed. and comp. by Takakusu Junjirō, Watanabe Kaigyoku, et al., Tokyo: Taishō Issaikyō Kankō Kai, 1924–1934 [T.] For the Chinese text, see T 46.52b18–55c21.

sacred and the profane," often used in combination, occur as an epitome of this pattern in his texts. The "sacred" points to that side of our existence that Buddhists evaluate as wholesome, such as nirvana, bliss, liberation, Buddha, wisdom, truth, nonattachment, and dharma-nature; whereas the "profane" covers the opposite side evaluated as unwholesome, including samsara, suffering, sentient beings, delusion, false attachment, and ignorance.

The crucial point in Zhiyi's teaching of transformation is that the unwholesome mode of profane existence necessarily embodies the sacred and thus serves as a form of inverse instruction. The unwholesome profane is inseparable from and inversely points to the wholesome, comparable to the nature of and relationship between pain and healing. This positive instruction of/via negative experience is referred to by means of paradoxical articulations such as "sorrow is bliss," "evil is good," "delusion is wisdom," "samsara is nirvana" or "interpenetration of false and true." A more general Tiantai expression of inverse instruction is the following: "ignorance is dharma-nature." Here "ignorance" could be understood as inversion into the profane, and dharma-nature as reference to the sacred, since inversion implies reference and, reference consists of inversion,.

Transformation commences with "contemplation" and its agent, again, is Xin—called "potency contemplating." On the other hand, the "objects contemplated"—delusions—are also referred to as Xin. Both the agent and the objects of transformation are Xin, which means that Xin transforms itself. This self-transformation qua/via "contemplation of Xin" also affects the existential habitat of the practitioner, since the way one experiences, refers to, and interacts with one's existential habitat is rooted in one's Xin. Xin shapes one's existential habitat to the extent that any part of it or other sentient beings pertaining to it could be called "dharmas created by Xin." Consequently, Xin transformed into wisdom affects not only the existential habitat of the particular practitioner contemplating but also the Xin of all sentient beings pertaining to his existential habitat. Since the converse must also be true, the term "Xin" signifies interdependence among all sentient beings.

According to Tiantai Buddhism, the Mahāyāna task of "saving and transforming all sentient beings" consists of self-transformation of one's own Xin into Buddha-wisdom benefiting others. Doctrines like "benefiting others via self-benefit" and "transforming others via self-practice" express such interdependence between sentient beings. Here the Tiantai interpretation of the Buddhist term "dharma-realm" refers to that existential habitat which is shared by all sacred and profane beings. These are subdivided into ten groups, four of which represent the sacred realms, whereas the other six encompass profane realms of ignorant beings. Accordingly, the existential habitat shared by all sentient beings—dharma-realm—is experienced and referred to in ten different yet mutually related ways, which is called "mutual inclusion within the tenfold realm."

The initial step of contemplation centers on emptiness and suggests that there is no entity or any real thing that ultimately conforms to this name "Xin." Contemplation primarily focuses on the impermanence of anything related to our existential habitat and thereby realizes that ultimately there is no abiding characteristic to which we may point. The absence of a core sustaining reality in our existential habitat is called emptiness, and such absence equals the absence of any marks that may indicate real things. Hence, Zhiyi refutes the claim that apodictically posits a real Xin that is the ultimate source of all things.

The name Xin does not represent a real thing; neither does "emptiness" or any other name. These are all "provisional designations." In Chinese, "provisional"—literally "borrowed," "dependent," "supporting," and "false"—is ambiguous. For example, Xin in the sense of the real source of all things is a "false name." However, Xin is also considered the root of the way one experiences, refers to, and interacts with one's existential habitat. Therefore, although a "borrowed or supporting name," it may be provisionally relevant in one's course of transformation and that of others.

The "contemplation of emptiness" deconstructs "false names"—the negative connotation of the provisional—achieving insight into the true nature of our existential habitat, a nature that points to the domain of the "inexpressible." However, this contemplation is limited, as it excludes the positive relevance of the provisional. It denies any kind of existence and hence cannot unfold the Mahāyāna task of saving others. Due to this limitation, Zhiyi assigns it to the Small Vehicle, or Hinayāna. He stresses, instead, the function of its opposite—the "contemplation of the provisional"—which refers to the positive connotation of "supporting," and returns us with new awareness to the sphere of linguistic expression. Since the contemplation of the provisional is aware of the influence of Xin on one's existential habitat, including others, it realizes the Mahāyāna ideal of the bodhisattva exerting the practice of "beneficence and sympathy for the suffering of others."

That contemplation, which goes beyond both emptiness denying existence and the provisional reifying "false names," is called "contemplation of the middle way." Its focus is the "real mark," because it is beyond the false mutual exclusivity of emptiness and the provisional. The ultimate step consists of realizing that emptiness and the provisional are indivisible and equally relevant, since they both restrict and complement each other. It is this reciprocal relationship, called the middle way, that is emptiness and the provisional as opposite modes that nevertheless include each other. Each of the three—emptiness, the provisional, and the middle—simultaneously embodies each of the others. This is the highest stage that the contemplation of Xin can achieve, and the Tiantai term for this is called the "threefold contemplation."

Threefold contemplation deals with the same structural pattern previously referred to as inverse instruction. The false side that is indivisible from the true side of any part of our existential habitat is not purely negative, provided Xin is not attached to the falseness of the provisional and recognizes the provisional's value of inverse instruction. Zhiyi's concept of "liberation," called "severing without severing," hints at this ambiguity of falseness: the unwholesome effect of falseness—attachments to false names—must be severed, but that does not include severing falseness, which can also be "supporting" due to its instructive value.

The fact that our relation to our existential habitat inevitably involves falseness becomes particularly evident with regard to the term "emptiness," which necessarily falls into a linguistic contradiction if emptiness refers to the inexpressibility of ultimate reality. While we must distinguish the "ultimate and inexpressible level" from the "conventional level of linguistic expression" in order to indicate that this linguistic level contains nothing but falseness, "ultimate" and "inexpressible" are still linguistic constructions that must also be false. Hence they cannot be ultimately affirmed.

The middle way is beyond the opposition of the conventional and the ultimate. The middle way is indicated in the phrases "neither expressible nor inexpressible," "neither articulation nor silence," and "neither text nor nontext." Zhiyi says: "If we consider verbal articulation and silence as rivals, we do not understand the meaning of the teaching. [. . .] Articulation is [equals] nonarticulation; nonarticulation is [equals] articulation. If we regard texts as harmful, we should realize that texts [Buddhist scriptures] are not texts. A [certain] text understood means being neither text nor nontext anymore [equals the middle]. Being able to achieve all the different types of understanding only by one single text, this is the very meaning here."[2] A Buddhist text understood properly is not a text anymore. Tiantai practice of transformation implies that once the text has fulfilled its provisional purpose, it must be abandoned. If we regard its provisional constructions as apodictic statements or ultimate judgments, we just fall prey to attachments again. The compositional features of a Buddhist text should be designed in such a way that the reader—whom the author addresses as a potential practitioner—does not become liable to attachments again. For this purpose, it may defy the conventional norms of a univocal mode of expression. The passage of the *Great Calming and Contemplation* translated here fits this type of ambiguous composition. Xin provides the starting point of that contemplation, which first elucidates the phases of suspension and rehabilitation of Xin until its course accomplishes the "threefold contemplation within/qua one instant of Xin."

Xin recognizes itself as the source of delusions and thus realizes that this is nothing but potential for transformation. Achieving this insight that the ambiguity of Xin is irreducible is called "mental activity contemplated as the inconceivable realm."

2. See *The Great Calming and Contemplation*, T. 46.3b2–9.

Translation

As the [inconceivable] realm can be hardly expressed, we first expound the conceivable realm, in order to find an easier way to make the inconceivable realm evident. As to the doctrine of the conceivable: The Small Vehicle also teaches that mental activity creates all things consisting of those causes and fruits[3] that constitute the six destinies[4]—the circle of life and death within the three spheres. As [the Small Vehicle] escapes the profane and strives for the sacred,[5] it abandons the lower trying to achieve the upper [without the intention of universally saving sentient beings], and it realizes the body of ashes and the wisdom of extinction,[6] conforming to the Four Noble Truths deliberately created, which, therefore, means doctrine of the conceivable.[7]

3. The Chinese expression "causes and fruits" denotes the relationship between action and consequences. The "causes" encompass one's "thought, speech and physical action"; whereas "fruits" refer to the type and conditions of one's existential habitat corresponding to these "causes."

4. In Chinese, the "six destinies" are synonymous with the Buddhist expression "samsara," also called "within the three spheres of desire, form, and beyond form." The "six destinies" consist of three wholesome categories, gods, *asuras* (semigods) and human beings, and three unwholesome categories, beasts, hungry ghosts, and purgatory.

5. Ultimate wisdom in Tiantai teaching realizes that "inversion into the profane" just means "reference to the sacred." According to the Tiantai, the Small Vehicle does not realize this; instead, it considers the profane and sacred as mutually excluding each other.

6. In Tiantai teaching, "the body of ashes and the wisdom of extinction" express the viewpoint of nirvana excluding samsara. This expression criticizes the two vehicles' attachment to "emptiness." According to the Tiantai, the two paths that together constitute the Small Vehicle are the path of the "hearer" (śrāvaka), who achieves enlightenment after listening to the Buddha's sermons, and the path of the "pratyekabuddha," who achieves enlightenment through solitary contemplation on the doctrine of "conditioned coarising."

7. Zhiyi classifies the "Four Noble Truths"—here, an epitome for the Buddhist teaching—according to the Tiantai scheme of the "four levels of teaching." The first level refers to the "Small Vehicle," which is attached to a notion of samsara and nirvana excluding each other; it overemphasizes nirvana, but completely abandons samsara; this preferential view cannot fully realize the wisdom of inverse instruction. Zhiyi calls the mutual exclusion a "deliberate construction," as neither samsara nor nirvana can ultimately be regarded as real things. The next level—the "common teaching between the Small and Great Vehicle"—terminates "deliberate constructions" contemplating emptiness of both nirvana and samsara; it is also called the "four noble truths nonarising." The third level—the "distinctive teaching of the Great Vehicle" realizes the limitations of exclusively contemplating emptiness and returns to the level of the provisional with new awareness, devoting itself to the Mahāyāna ideal of universally saving sentient beings, which requires a multitude of soteriological means, called "Four Noble Truths inexhaustibly realized." The fourth and ultimate level is that of the "perfect" or "round teaching," realizing both differences between the preceding three levels and their unity consisting of mutual completion. The "perfect teaching" does not give preference to either one, since it sees "the one vehicle" fully realized in all of them. Zhiyi calls this "Four Noble Truths Uncreated." Only "the perfect teaching" accomplishes the "inconceivable realm"; the preceding three levels represent the "conceivable realm."

The Great Vehicle also argues that mental activity creates all things and that the tenfold dharma-realm[8] encloses those things. If mental activity is contemplated as a thing [we can refer to], then there is its wholesome and its unwholesome mode. The unwholesome refers to the three types of causes and fruits constituting the three unwholesome paths [of animals, hungry ghosts, and purgatory]; whereas the wholesome refers to the three types of causes and fruits shaping the three destinies of human beings, gods, and *asuras*. While contemplating these six destinies as impermanent, since they arise and perish, mental activity which is the potency contemplating does not abide for any moment. Again, both the potency contemplating and the object contemplated arise from conditions, and conditioned coarising is emptiness; [this viewpoint of emptiness] corresponds to the teaching about fruits and causes shaping the two vehicles. During this contemplation of emptiness and existence [mutually excluding], one may fall into the two [false] extremes of submerging into emptiness or abiding in existence; however, [after realizing this falseness] one may arouse great beneficence and sympathy [for sentient beings' suffering] and enter [the realm of the] provisional, in order to transform all sentient beings. [Ultimately], there is no real body [saving sentient beings], yet it is provisionally created; [ultimately], emptiness is not real either, yet emptiness is to be taught provisionally, in order to transform sentient beings by means of instruction, which conforms with the teaching about causes and fruits shaping the Bodhisattva. If both those saving and the others saved are contemplated as the dharma of the "middle way and real mark,"[9] which is the ultimate clear and pure, and if [there are no oppositions such as] wholesome-unwholesome, existing-nonexisting, those saving–others saved, if all of these are alike, this [contemplation] conforms with the teaching about causes and fruits shaping the Buddha. These ten dharmas [six destinies, two vehicles, Bodhisattva, Buddha], clearly distinguished as shallow and deep, all emerge from mental activity. The inexhaustible Four Noble Truths[10] of the Great Vehicle include this teaching, yet it is the realm of the conceivable and not the [inconceivable realm] that we are contemplating in the *Great Calming and Contemplation*.

As to the doctrine of the inconceivable: The *Garland Sūtra*, for example, says: "Mental activity is like a carpenter creating all kinds of the five aggregates. There is nothing in all of these worlds that is not created by mental activity."[11] All kinds of the five aggregates are like the five aggregates of the tenfold dharma-realm previously expounded. "Dharma-realm" expresses a threefold

8. The "tenfold dharma-realm"—a term from the *Garland Sūtra*—refers to the six destinies, the two vehicles, the Bodhisattva, and the Buddha, constituting ten realms of existence.

9. "Real mark" means that the "middle way" is beyond the false mutual exclusivity of "emptiness and the provisional."

10. Since the bodhisattva is devoted to the salvation of all sentient beings, he must resort to an inexhaustible source of expedient means to fulfill his task.

11. See T. 9.465c.

meaning: [first], the number "ten" points to the potency of depending [which is the provisional]; [second], "dharma-realm" refers to the ground [which is emptiness]; and [third], the combined designation for the potency [of depending] and ground is, therefore, called "tenfold dharma-realm," [which is the middle way]. Again, each of the ten dharmas has its respective pattern of causes and fruits that are never intermixed, therefore, it is called the "ten dharma-realms." Again, if within the range of these ten dharmas, one after another respectively embodies [dharma-realm], then [each of] them is always dharma-realm [as the whole], and, therefore, we call it "this realm ten times."[12]. . . .[13]

Just one instant of mental activity encloses the ten dharma-realms; and each dharma-realm, again, encloses the tenfold dharma-realm, which sums up to a hundredfold dharma-realm. Each realm encloses the thirty worlds;[14] this means that the hundredfold dharma-realm encompasses three thousand worlds. These three thousand worlds are given, within one single instant of mental activity. If there is no mental activity, everything else ceases; as soon as there is [this] ephemeral mental activity, the three thousand worlds are instantaneously involved. It cannot be claimed that one instant of mental activity precedes and all things follow after, nor that all things precede and one instant of mental activity follows after.[15]

12. The provisional dimension of the "dharma-realm" includes the diversity of things pertaining to the existential habitat shared by all sentient beings. As all things and sentient beings are subjected to dependent origination, and dependent origination is based on emptiness, the provisional indicated by the modifier "ten" is also referred to as "potency of depending," and emptiness as its "ground" is the single "dharma-realm" modified in a tenfold way. In Chinese, the ambiguous term "tenfold dharma-realm" can be understood as both a plural and a singular; as a plural it means "ten dharma-realms," indicating the diversity of the provisional, and as a singular it means the single "realm ten times," pointing to emptiness. According to Zhiyi's interpretation, this ambiguity denotes the indivisibility between the provisional and emptiness; the indivisibility or exclusive relationship between the two is the middle way; hence the modifier "ten" and the compound noun "dharma-realm" combined as "tenfold dharma-realm" hint at the middle way.

13. The omitted text is a detailed explanation about a term that in this section is referred to as "the thirty worlds": "the ten worlds of the five aggregates," "the ten worlds of sentient beings," and "the ten worlds of environment." The "five aggregates" signify the constitutive elements of the existence of a sentient being; the "ten worlds of sentient beings" refers to the inhabitants of the ten dharma-realms; the "ten worlds of environment" refers to the existential habitats experienced by the ten types of sentient beings.

14. See note 13.

15. Each moment of mental activity obtains the potential of transforming itself according to the range of the tenfold dharma-realm—the whole range between the lowest stage of ignorance and the highest of Buddha-wisdom. This means that mental activity, the medium of transformation must "embrace the three thousand worlds." However, it is impossible to conceive of mental activity as a primordial mind causing things to arise, since mental activity cannot arise independently. According to the deconstructive function of emptiness, mental activity is not a disparate or independent entity temporally preceding all things existing; therefore, it cannot be regarded

It is similar to the "eight marks moving things";[16] if a thing [existing] precedes those marks, this thing would not be moved; if those marks precede the [existence] of this thing, it would not be moved either; both cases of preceding and following must be ruled out. Only with regard to a thing [existing], can we speak of marks moving; and, conversely, only with regard to marks moving, can we speak of things. Here, mental activity [along with its involvement in the three thousand worlds] is similar. One single instant of mental activity creating all things corresponds to the sequential image; mental activity embracing all things in one instant corresponds to the horizontal image. However, the sequential image as well as the horizontal image must be ruled out. Only with regard to mental activity are all things given; and only with regard to all things is mental activity given. Neither the sequential image, nor the horizontal image, nor that of identity, nor that of disparity matches such profoundness and subtlety beyond [any image]. Since it is neither realized by cognition, nor expressible by language, we call it the inconceivable realm, which matches the [intended] meaning here.

Question: If mental activity arises, it definitely relies on conditions. Does this mean that mental activity includes three thousand dharmas, or that conditions include three thousand dharmas, or that the two combined include them, or that they are given beyond the two? If mental activity includes them, conditions are unnecessary, when mental activity arises; if conditions include them, this inclusion through conditions does not involve mental activity; if the two combined include them, how is it possible that the three thousand dharmas are given at the moment of this combination, though none of the two contains them before this combination; if they are given separately from mental activity and conditions, how is it possible that mental activity suddenly includes them, since it is presumed that they are given beyond both conditions and mental activity? If none of these four alternatives can be established, what else does "inclusion of three thousand dharmas" mean?[17]

---

as the ultimate source of these things. On the contrary, mental activity is as much dependent on its existential habitat as this habitat relies on mental activity. However, since the existential habitat can be only transformed, if mental activity first transforms itself, mental activity has a soteriological priority. The subsequent discussion demonstrates that neither the ontological nor the temporal priority of mental activity can be held, while the soteriological priority must be emphasized; Zhanran's (711–782) ambiguous phrase "one moment thought three thousand," which deliberately lacks a verb, expresses this meaning. In Tiantai Buddhism, mental activity is considered as the medium of transformation due to this soteriological priority.

16. The expression "eight marks moving things" originates from Abhidharma-terminology, which includes the four stages of arising, abiding, changing and perishing in things existing. Things existing are moved, since they arise, abide, change, and perish. There are eight marks, because the same pattern can be also applied to the parts out of which things are made; consequently, there are the "four main marks" and the "four secondary marks."

17. This section investigates the ultimate source of all things that pertain to the existential habitat shared by all sentient beings—"the inclusion of three thousand

Answer: Those masters teaching the *Śāstra about the Sūtra of the Ten Stages*[18] say: "All types of understanding and delusion, as well as any kind of truth and error, rest in dharma-nature; dharma-nature sustains truth and error; truth and error rely on dharma-nature." In contrast, those proposing the standpoints of the *Śāstra Embracing the Great Vehicle*[19] say: "Dharma-nature is neither contaminated by delusions, nor purified by truth; therefore dharma-nature is not the ground sustaining [truth and delusion]. It is the *ālaya*-consciousness[20] that points to the ground sustaining [truth and error], and that is the never submerging ignorance abundantly storing all seeds." According to the masters of the *Ten Stages,* mental activity must include all things; whereas corresponding to the masters of the *Śāstra Embracing,* conditions include all things. Each of these two groups of dharma-masters respectively holds to an extreme position [contradicting the other]. However, if dharma-nature, which originally is neither mental activity nor conditions, creates all things, and [if this is supposed to mean] that mental activity creates all things, though [dharma-nature] is unequal to mental activity, then [according to the same reasoning], we must also admit that conditions create all things, though [dharma-nature] is also unequal to conditions.[21] How could

---

dharmas." Zhiyi follows the Buddhist viewpoint that the components of things existing consist of the "sense faculties"—"mental activity"; and their correlates—"conditions." Hence, he takes four alternative positions in account: mental activity as the ultimate source, conditions as the ultimate source, the combination of the two, and the source of all things beyond the two. However, since none of these is true, the inquiry turns into the question whether those things can still be regarded as real.

18. The *Dasābhūmika Sūtra Śāstra* is a commentary on the *Sūtra of the Ten Stages* by Vasubandhu.

19. The *Mahāyāna samgraha Śāstra* is a Yogacārā work composed by Asaṅga and introduced into China by Paramārtha in the sixth century.

20. The *ālaya-vijnāna* is the fundamental eighth level of consciousness in Yogācāra, based on which all ordinary consciousness arises. Here, *ālaya*-consciousness is subject to arising and perishing, whereas dharma-nature is beyond arising and perishing. Zhiyi uses the term "*ālaya*-consciousness" as a synonym for "conditions" and for "ignorance." Zhiyi, contrasting dharma-nature and *ālaya*-consciousness, seeks to demonstrate a contradiction between mental activity and conditions in order to criticize this distinction as a false teaching of other Buddhist schools. This helps him to outline his own point of view, which he considers to be the middle way beyond the false mutual exclusivity of dharma-nature and *ālaya*-consciousness.

21. The argument in this section is indeed odd: If mental activity originally unequal to dharma-nature is yet considered an independent mind that is the ultimate source beyond conditioned coarising, then this mind becomes equal to dharma-nature, and we can also say that dharma-nature is the ultimate source. If we still hold to mental activity as the ultimate source, then we must also propose that conditions or *ālaya*-consciousness are the ultimate source, since they are originally unequal to dharma-nature as well. Zhiyi just wants to say that the foundation of the diversity of things cannot be properly discussed, if dharma-nature and *ālaya*-consciousness are regarded as opposites excluding each other. According to Zhiyi's standpoint, the term "dharma-nature" would correspond to the "reference to the sacred," and *ālaya*-consciousness, here a synonym for "ignorance," would be the "inversion into

we, then, in this one-sided way propose that dharma-nature is the ground sustaining truth and error, [since the *ālaya*-consciousness, here representing conditions, must also be considered the source of all things]? If we now say that instead of dharma-nature, *ālaya*-consciousness is the ground sustaining truth and error, and [if this is supposed to mean] that beyond the dharma-nature there is still another *ālaya*-consciousness, then we must conclude that this does not involve the dharma-nature any more, [although, per definition, the nature of all dharmas cannot be beyond these dharmas]. However, if it is impossible to separate dharma-nature and *ālaya*-consciousness from each other, *ālaya*-consciousness as the ground sustaining truth and error and dharma-nature as the ground sustaining truth and error must be indivisible; how can we, then, solely hold that *ālaya*-consciousness [=conditions] is the ground sustaining truth and error?

Again, these [two viewpoints] also contradict the teachings of the *Sūtra of the Great Wisdom,* which says: "There is neither a ground inside [=the sense faculties or mental activity], nor a ground outside [=conditions], nor a ground in between [based on which all things may abide], nor do they abide in themselves."[22] Again, these [two viewpoints] do not conform to Nāgārjuna either, who says: "All the dharmas arise neither through themselves, nor by something else, nor by the combination of the two, nor beyond causes and conditions."[23] Let us continue to examine this issue by means of an illustration: Do dreams occur based on mental activity, or do dreams occur based on sleep, or do they occur based on the combination of sleep and mental activity, or do they appear beyond mental activity and sleep?[24] If dreams occur based on mental activity, they must even appear without sleeping; if dreams occur based on sleep, dead ones must have dreams like people who have fallen asleep; if dreams occur because of the combination of mental activity and sleep, how is it possible that people who have fallen asleep spend time without dreaming. Again, if there are dreams in both sleep and mental activity, respectively, then it may be possible that dreams do also occur after the combination of mental activity and sleep; however, if there are dreams neither in mental activity nor in sleep, then there are no dreams after the combination of the two either; if dreams appear beyond both mental activity and sleep, then there must be dreams in space and in air, because they are beyond mental activity and sleep as well. Since we could not apprehend

---

the profane." Since inversion implies reference and reference consists of inversion, dharma-nature and ignorance (i.e. *ālaya*-consciousness) must include each other. As previously mentioned, Zhiyi attempts to outline his viewpoint by means of construing a contrast with his contemporaries to whom he refers as dharma-masters of the *Ten Stages* and those of the *Śāstra Embracing.*

22. See T. 8.272a.

23. See T. 30.2b.

24. Though the content of our dreams appears during sleep, it cannot be separated from our concerns to which mental activity is attached. For this reason, Zhiyi analogously raises this question.

the phenomenon of dreams by means of the four alternatives, how is it possible to explain all the content of dreams during our sleep? Here, mental activity refers to the dharma-nature, whereas sleep represents the *ālaya*-consciousness. How can we continue to hold either just to the claim that dharma-nature creates all things or just to that of *ālaya*-consciousness creating all things? One should recognize that it is impossible to apprehend mental activity by means of the four alternatives, just as it is impossible to apprehend the three thousand dharmas! ...[25]

However, since there are causes and conditions, there is also a way of linguistic expression, which is called causes and conditions of the "four siddhāntas."[26] Though the four alternatives have become silent, due to the function of beneficence and sympathy it is possible to refer linguistically to marks provisionally designated within the mark of nondesignation.[27] [...]

The Buddha's intention is completely purified; ultimately, it consists neither in causes, nor in conditions, nor in the combination of them, nor beyond them. However, since the ultimate meaning is indivisible from the level of the conventional, the four alternatives can be taught by means of linguistic expression; consequently, there are teachings linguistically expressing causes, conditions, the combination of them, and the state beyond causes and conditions. It is like explaining to a blind person [the color] of milk by means of comparing it with [the color of] shells, sugar, snow, and seagulls, so long as the blind person eventually understands after listening to these explanations; this just means that the ultimate meaning is indivisible from the conventional level.

One should recognize: "All day long full of explanations equals nonexplanation all day long; and, conversely, nonexplanation all day long equals all day long full of explanations."[28] Moreover, both explanations and nonexplanation negated all day long equals both explanations and nonexplanation illuminated all day long; for, there is construction while deconstructing, as well as deconstruction while constructing; all the *sūtras* and *śāstras* are alike.

Vasubandhu and Nāgārjuna performed their introspections with equanimity, but, while facing the world outside, they appropriated their teachings

25. The omitted text continues to refute further possible positions that explain how existing things may arise.

26. This is an expression from the *Treatise on the Great Wisdom,* and it specifies the distinctive means of verbal instruction of the Buddha-dharma, which the Buddha applied in his teachings to transform sentient beings. There are four levels: "(1) mundane or ordinary modes of expression; (2) individual treatment, adapting his teaching to the capacity of hearers; (3) diagnostic treatment of their moral diseases; (4) the perfect and highest truth" (Soothill and Hodous 2000: 175b).

27. *Fozang Jing,* T. 15.782c. The section omitted consists of *sūtra* quotations exemplifying the provisional verbalization of the inexpressible. The term "mark of nondesignation" hints at the domain of the inexpressible disclosed through the contemplation of emptiness.

28. See the chapter *Fable* (*Yuyan*) in the *Zhuangzi.*

with respect to time and circumstances; consequently, every means of their instructions has its foundation. However, masters of the people understood it in a one-sided way; their disciples studying the path of the Buddha adhere to it imprudently; they defend their biased viewpoints [against each other], as if they shot arrows against stones [unable to be penetrated, hence unable to achieve the level of mutual integration], which harms the sacred path immensely! Those who understand this meaning, realize that it is as expressible as it is inexpressible.

If we try to appropriate it in the most expedient way, we should say that ignorance[29] following dharma-nature creates all things; analogously, all things dreamed occur due to the dharma of sleep following mental activity. Since mental activity and conditions conform to one another, the thirty worlds, the three thousand natures and marks arise from mental activity. Though the single one [dharma-]nature seems to be little, yet it is not nothingness; though ignorance [diversified] seems to be manifold, yet there is not anything. For, pointing to the single one turns into diversity; however, [this] diversity is no [real] diversity; pointing to diversity turns into the single one; however, this single one is not little. For this reason, mental activity is called the "inconceivable realm." If we realize that one instant of mental activity diversifies into mental activity of all kinds, all mental activity is just the single one instant of mental activity, there is neither one nor all, that one sentient being diversifies into all sentient beings, all sentient beings are just the single one sentient being, there is neither one nor all, [...][30] we understand that everything considered in this way is the "inconceivable realm." On the level of the conventional, all dharmas, aggregates, elements, and entrances occur due to the conformity between dharma-nature and ignorance. On the level of the ultimate, all elements and entrances are just the single one dharma-realm. According to the primary truth of the middle way there is neither one nor all. All dharmas contemplated in this way are nothing but the "inconceivable threefold truth." One dharma diversified into all dharmas refers to "dharmas based on conditioned coarising," which are things provisionally designated as things; this corresponds to the contemplation of the provisional. "All dharmas viewed as the single one dharma" refers to the phrase "I say this is emptiness," which corresponds to the contemplation of emptiness. Neither one nor all refers to the contemplation of the middle way.[31] If one type of emptiness conforms to all types of emptiness, and if there is no provisional and no middle that is not emptiness, then it is the contemplation of complete emptiness. If one type of the provisional conforms to the provisional of all kinds, and if there is no emptiness and no middle that is not the provisional, then it is the contemplation of the complete provisional. If one type of the middle conforms to

29. Here "ignorance" replaces the term "*ālaya*–consciousness" and "conditions" previously used.

30. The text omitted repeats the same scheme with varying expressions.

31. See *Treatise on the Middle*, T. 30.33b.

all types of the middle, and if there is no provisional and no emptiness that is not the middle, then it is the contemplation of the complete middle. This corresponds to the threefold contemplation in one instant of mental activity expounded in the *Treatise on the Middle*.[32] ...

Again, it is like [the three conditions]: [first], falling asleep and seeing all the countless things in dreams; [second, realizing that] not even a single one remains after awakening, not to speak of the three thousand; [third], having not fallen asleep yet, in a moment beyond dreaming and realizing,[33] there is neither the diversified nor the single one. Since there is the power of sleep, we say diversified; in virtue of the realization we say little. Zhuang Zhou dreams he is a butterfly fluttering around for one hundred years; on waking, he recognizes that there was no butterfly, nor the accumulation of years.[34] If ignorance follows the dharma-nature, this single one instant of mental activity diversifies into all types of mental activity as in the condition of falling asleep. After achieving the insight that ignorance is just dharma-nature, mental activity diversified is just the single one instant of mental activity as in the condition of being wide awake. Again, once the practitioner performing the practice of tranquility and bliss falls asleep and dreams, he finds himself involved in the entire process from the first moment of aspiration until he becomes the Buddha sitting under the Bodhi-tree, turning the dharma-wheel, in order to save sentient beings and to cause them to enter nirvana; and then, while he is wide awake, he realizes that it is only one single instant of dreaming.

Bibliography and Suggested Reading

Donner, Neal and Daniel Stevenson. (1993) *The Great Calming and Contemplation: A Study and Annotated Translation of the First Chapter of Chih-I's "Mo-Ho Chih-Kuan."* Honolulu: University of Hawai'i Press.

Hurvitz, Leon. (1980) *Chih-I (538–597): An Introduction to the Life and Ideas of a Chinese Buddhist Monk*. Brussels: Institut des Hautes Etudes Chinoises.

32. The "contemplation of complete emptiness," the "contemplation of the complete provisional," the "contemplation of the complete middle," and the "threefold contemplation in one instant of mental activity" are synonyms.

33. In this simile, "dreaming" corresponds to ignorance, the conventional level, and the provisional diversified; "realizing" refers to dharma-nature, the ultimate, and emptiness; the "moment beyond dreaming and realizing" accounts for the middle way. Zhiyi denies any notion of enlightenment or *satori* that would abandon or exclude falseness. As previously mentioned, "liberation" based on the notion of inverse instruction must involve falseness. "Dreaming and realizing" understood as mutually exclusive opposites cannot account for "liberation." Consequently, the "primary truth of the middle way" corresponds to a "moment beyond dreaming and realizing."

34. A famous simile from the Daoist classic *Zhuangzi;* see the chapter *On Equality of Things* (*Qiwu Lun*).

Liu, Ming-Wood. (1994) *Madhyamaka Thought in China.* Leiden: Brill.

Ng Yu-kwan. (1993) *T'ien-T'ai Buddhism and Early Mādhyamika.* Honolulu: University of Hawai'i Press.

Soothill, William Edward, and Lewis Hodous. (2000) *A Dictionary of Chinese Buddhist Terms.* London, 1937. Reprint, Delhi: Motilal Banarsidass.

Swanson, Paul. (1995) *Foundations of T'ien-T'ai Philosophy: The Flowering of the Two Truths Theory in Chinese Buddhism.* Berkeley: Asian Humanities Press.

Swanson, Paul. (2004) *The Great Cessation-and-Contemplation.* (Compact disc.) Tokyo: Kosei.

Ziporyn, Brook. (2000) *Evil and/or/as the Good: Omnicentrism, Intersubjectivity and Value Paradox in Tiantai Buddhist Thought.* Cambridge, Mass.: Harvard University Press.

30

"The Mind Is Buddha"

Pojo Chinul's *Secrets on Cultivating the Mind*

Jin Y. Park

Pojo Chinul (1158–1210) is one of the most influential figures in Korean Zen Buddhism. Chinul's Zen is characterized by *huatou* (or "a critical phrase") meditation, a version of the encounter dialogue (Chin. *gong'an;* Kor. *kongan;* Jap. *kōan*) method. At the basis of Chinul's *huatou* meditation, also known as Kanhua Zen, lies his philosophy of mind. By tracing Chinul's account of mind, one can gain an understanding of the evolution of his thought, which can be broadly divided into three stages. The first stage deals with Chinul's expositions on the mind itself as they appear in his early works, including *Secrets on Cultivating the Mind* (*Susim kyŏl,* c. 1203–5) and *Straight Talk on the True Mind* (*Chinsim chiksŏl,* c. 1205). In the second stage, Chinul employs Huayan Buddhist doctrines to enhance his position on the nature of the mind of sentient beings and discusses the relationship between the subject and the outside world. The posthumous publication *Treatise on the Complete and Sudden Attainment of Buddhahood* (*Wŏndon songbul ron,* 1210) is the best exposition of Chinul's Huayan thought and its relation to the mind of the sentient being. The third and final stage appears in his *Treatise on Resolving Doubts about Huatou Meditation* (*Kanhwa kyŏrŭi ron,* 1210). In this work, Chinul proposes *huatou* meditation as the most effective way to invoke the realization of one's true mind.

At the very beginning of his early work *Encouragement to Practice: The Compact of the Samādhi and Prajñā Community* (*Kwŏnsu chŏnghye kyŏlsa mun,* 1190), Chinul says, "When one is deluded about the mind and gives rise to endless defilements, such a person is a sentient being. When one is awakened to the mind and gives rise to endless marvelous functions, such a person is the Buddha. Delusion and awakening are two different states but both are caused by the mind. If one tries to find the Buddha away from this mind, one will never find it."[1] By identifying the mind with the Buddha and one's original nature, Chinul joins many other Zen masters for whom the identity between the Buddha and the sentient being in her or his original state marks the basic premise of the school.

In *Secrets on Cultivating the Mind,* an excerpt of which is translated here, Chinul argues that "Buddha is the mind." That is, not only are the mind of the sentient being and that of the Buddha identical, but the mind itself is the Buddha. What would it mean to say that the mind is Buddha? Chinul advises that if one realizes the "pure" nature of one's mind, one will be " 'such' like the Buddha." The "such" is an articulation of ineffability, and the ineffability in this case is not related to agnosticism but the dependently coarising nature of an entity that defies linguistic reification. Since the nature of an entity is empty, the mind of the sentient being is empty as well. Mind-body dualism, which constitutes a core of some philosophical systems, does not hold in Chinul. The emptiness (or voidness) of the mind is the emptiness of the physical body. Voidness or emptiness is not to be understood as a lack or absence but as the nonsubstantial nature of beings. Things do not have substantial essence of their own; they exist through multilayered causation and are empty. If every other object is empty like the mind, why does Chinul say "mind is the Buddha," when any other entity in the world would appear to function equally well and could replace mind? By emphasizing that one's mind is Buddha, Chinul warns against any objectification or reification of Buddha. At the same time, by underscoring the mind, instead of other entities, Chinul identifies the source and mode of one's delusion. Delusion arises not through a certain quality of an entity but through the subject's failure to see the nonsubstantial nature of one's ontological reality.

In *Secrets on Cultivating the Mind,* Chinul first characterizes the mind as "space," reminiscent of "emptiness," and then as "void, calm, numinous awareness" (Kor. *kongjŏk yŏngji*). This "mind of void, calm, numinous awareness" is always there even when one is deluded; only when one "traces back the radiance" of this mind does one attain Buddhahood. Chinul further describes the nature of this mind as "unstained," "complete," and "whole." With these expressions, one might wonder whether Chinul assumes a certain essence of the mind, something comparable to the Cartesian Ego-Cogito. However, caution is necessary in interpreting the use of language in Zen Buddhist texts such as Chinul's *Secrets.* The impression that Chinul might believe the mind is marked by a certain essence is derived from a linguistic convention based on distinctions made through the naming process. In

1. *Kwŏnsu chŏnghye kyŏlsa mun* (Encouragement to Practice: The Compact of *Samādhi* and *Prajñā* Community), in *Han'guk Pulgyo chŏnsŏ* (Collected Works of Korean Buddhism), 13 vols. Dongguk taehakkyo ch'ulp'anbu (1979–2001) 4.698a–708a, p. 4.698a.

Chinul's description of the mind, he alternates between using affirmation and negation, creating a seemingly contradictory logic. For example, Chinul describes the mind as "pure" and later declares that there is neither purity nor impurity. He also describes the mind as "void" and then defines it as "calm and luminous awareness." By simultaneously employing expressions that are conventionally considered opposites to denote the mind, Chinul presents the nonsubstantial nature of the mind through the substantial medium of language. Purity as well as impurity, enlightenment as well as delusion, acquires new meaning through Chinul's nonconventional use of language.

One corollary of this approach to the mind is an emphasis on the provisional nature of decision-making and thus of categorizing. This includes the familiar distinctions of ethical categories such as right and wrong, purity and impurity, even delusion and enlightenment. Chinul problematizes the binary system prevalent in the ethical categories because none of these categories has its own essence to distinguish itself from its opposite; both good and evil exist through conditioned causality and thus are empty. It is through the subject's mind that these provisional categories seem to acquire permanent status. Negating the fixed identity of ethical categories, or any distinction-making, does not deny the necessity of making decisions and thus distinction in the life-world of the sentient being. The fact that decisions and determinations need to be made in one's daily life, however, does not justify reifying provisional distinctions and categories. Here is another significance of taking the mind as the object of practice: the mind is capable of both enlightenment and delusion, while both of them are empty. As Chinul clearly explains, enlightenment does not mean one should suppress delusion and remove what is considered evil and promote what is considered good. The subject-object dualism in which the subject's mind frequently plays the role of constructing the meaning of the outside world is replaced, in Chinul's Zen Buddhism, with the view of the subject whose identity is possible through the subject's realization of nonsubstantiality of subjectivity. To realize one's identity in this case is to realize its nonidentity.

If realizing one's own mind is the only way to attain Buddhahood, how does this realization avoid subjectivism and solipsism? In other words, how does the subject come into a relationship with the object in Chinul's philosophy if awareness of the mind is realized through introspection? And if the mind itself is the Buddha, and one does not need external expedients to realize this inner nature, how does one ever know the mind? What is the way to get from "me" to "my mind"? In order to deal with the first issue of the relationship between the subject and the object, Chinul incorporates Huayan Buddhist thought in his *Treatise on Complete and Sudden Attainment of Buddhahood* and contends that the mind of the sentient being is the same as the dependently coarising phenomena in the external world. Subjectivism is a result of the subject-object dualism. Once the dualism is resolved through the realization of the emptiness of subjectivity, the inside is the outside. For the second issue, regarding the practical dimension of the practitioner's realizing his or her own nature, Chinul introduces, in his

Treatise on Resolving Doubts about Huatou Meditation, huatou meditation to facilitate the transformation of the subject's dualism to a nondualist mode of thinking and thereby realize their true nature.

Translation

The triple world is blazing in defilement as if it were a house on fire.[2,3] How can you bear to tarry here and complacently undergo such long suffering? If you wish to avoid wandering in samsara there is no better way than to seek Buddhahood. If you want to become a Buddha, understand that Buddha is the mind. How can you search for the mind in the far distance? It is not outside the body. The physical body is a phantom, for it is subject to birth and death; the true mind is like space, for it neither ends nor changes. Therefore it is said, "These hundred bones will crumble and return to fire and wind. But One Thing is eternally numinous and covers heaven and earth."[4]

It is tragic. People have been deluded for so long. They do not recognize that their own minds are the true Buddhas. They do not recognize that their own natures are the true dharma. They want to search for the dharma, yet they still look far away for holy ones. They want to search for the Buddha, yet they will not observe their own minds. If they aspire to the path of Buddhahood while obstinately holding to their feeling that the Buddha is outside the mind or the dharma is outside the nature, then, even though they pass through kalpas as numerous as dust motes, burning their bodies, charring their arms, crushing their bones and exposing their marrow, or else write *sūtras* with their own blood, never lying down to sleep, eating only one offering a day at the hour of the Hare [5 to 7 A.M.], or even studying through the entire *tripiṭaka* and cultivating all sorts of ascetic practices, it is like trying to make rice by boiling sand—it will only add to their tribulation.[5]

2. The following translation, from *Han'guk Pulgyo chŏnsŏ,* 4.708b–714a, was translated by Robert E. Buswell, Jr. and originally appeared in Buswell 1991, pp. 98–117. We gratefully acknowledge permission to republish this work.

Subsequent endnotes are those originally included in Buswell's translation. I have kept only those notes that are relevant to this excerpt. The Wade-Giles Romanization of Chinese characters in Buswell's translation has been converted to the Pinyin system. T. refers to Takakusu Junjirō, et al., eds. *Taishō shinshū daizōkyō.* 100 vols. (Tokyo: Taishō Issaikyō Kankōkai), 1924–1932, a standard collection of the East Asian Buddhist canon compiled in Japan.

3. Chinul is alluding here to the famous Parable of the Burning House from the *Lotus Sūtra.* See *Miaofa lianhua jing* 2, T. 9.262.12c–13c; Leon Hurvitz, trans., *Scripture of the Lotus Blossom of the Fine Dharma* (New York: Columbia University Press, 1976), pp. 58–62.

4. *Jingde chuandeng lu* 30, T. 51.2076.463b–c.

5. Adapted from Wŏnhyo's *Palsim suhaeng chang:* "The practice of persons who have wisdom is to steam rice grains to prepare rice; the practice of persons without wisdom is to steam sand to prepare rice." In Cho Myŏng-gi, ed., *Wŏnhyo taesa chŏnjip* (Seoul, 1978), p. 605.

If they would only understand their own minds, then, without searching, approaches to dharma as numerous as the sands of the Ganges and uncountable sublime meanings would all be understood. As the World Honored One said, "I see that all sentient beings everywhere are endowed with a *tathāgata*'s wisdom and virtue."[6] He also said "All the illusory guises in which sentient beings appear take shape in the sublime mind of the *tathāgata*'s complete enlightenment."[7] Consequently, you should know that outside this mind there is no Buddhahood which can be attained. All the Buddhas of the past were merely persons who understood their minds. All the sages and saints of the present are likewise merely persons who have cultivated their minds. All future meditators should rely on this dharma as well.

I hope that you who cultivate the path will never search outside. The nature of the mind is unstained; it is originally whole and complete in itself. If you will only leave behind false conditioning, you will be "such" like the Buddha.

Question: If you say that the Buddha-nature exists in the body right now, then, since it is in the body, it is not separate from us ordinary men. So why can we not see this Buddha-nature now? Please explain this further to enlighten us on this point.

Chinul: It is in your body, but you do not see it. Ultimately, what is that which during the twelve periods of the day knows hunger and thirst, cold and heat, anger and joy? This physical body is a synthesis of four conditions: earth, water, fire, and wind. Since matter is passive and insentient, how can it see, hear, sense, and know? That which is able to see, hear, sense, and know is perforce your Buddha-nature. For this reason, Linji said, "The four great elements do not know how to expound dharma or listen to dharma. Empty space does not know how to expound dharma or listen to dharma. It is only that formless thing before your eyes, clear and bright of itself, which knows how to expound dharma or listen to dharma."[8] This "formless thing" is the dharma-seal of all the Buddhas; it is your original mind. Since this Buddha-nature exists in your body right now, why do you vainly search for it outside?...

Question: Through what expedient is it possible to trace back the radiance of one's sense-faculties in one thought and awaken to the self-nature?

Chinul: The self-nature is just your own mind. What other expedients do you need? If you ask for expedients to seek understanding, you are like a person who, because he does not see his own eyes, assumes that he has no eyes and decides to find some way to see. But since he does have eyes, how else is he supposed to see? If he realizes that in fact he has never lost his eyes, this is the same as seeing his eyes, and no longer would he waste his time trying to find a way to see. How then could he have any thoughts that he could not

6. *Avataṃsaka Sūtra*, "Appearance of the Tathāgatas" (Rulai chuxian pin), *Dafangguang fo huayan jing* 51, T. 10.279.272c.
7. In the *Complete Enlightenment Sūtra* (*Yuanjue jing*), T. 17.842.914a.
8. *Linji lu*, T. 47.1985.497b.

see? Your own numinous awareness is exactly the same. Since this awareness is your own mind, how else are you going to understand? If you seek some other way to understand, you will never understand. Simply by knowing that there is no other way to understand, you are seeing the nature.

Question: When the superior man hears dharma, he understands easily. Average and inferior men, however, are not without doubt and confusion. Could you describe some expedients so that the deluded too can enter into enlightenment?

Chinul: The path is not related to knowing or not knowing.[9] You should get rid of the mind which clings to its delusion and looks forward to enlightenment, and listen to me.

Since all dharmas are like dreams or phantoms, deluded thoughts are originally calm and the sense-spheres are originally void. At the point where all dharmas are void, the numinous awareness is not obscured. That is to say, this mind of void and calm, numinous awareness is your original face. It is also the dharma-seal transmitted without a break by all the Buddhas of the three time periods, the successive generations of patriarchs, and the wise advisors of this world. If you awaken to this mind, then this is truly what is called not following the rungs of a ladder: you climb straight to the stage of Buddhahood, and each step transcends the triple world. Returning home, your doubts will be instantly resolved and you will become the teacher of men and gods. Endowed with compassion and wisdom and complete in the twofold benefit, you will be worthy of receiving the offerings of men and gods. Day after day you can use ten thousand taels of gold without incurring debt. If you can do this, you will be a truly great man who has indeed finished the tasks of this life.

Question: In our case, what is this mind of void and calm, numinous awareness?

Chinul: What has just asked me this question is precisely your mind of void and calm, numinous awareness. Why not trace back its radiance rather than search for it outside? For your benefit I will now point straight to your original mind so that you can awaken to it. Clear your minds and listen to my words.

From morning to evening, throughout the twelve periods of the day, during all your actions and activities—whether seeing, hearing, laughing, talking, whether angry or happy, whether doing good or evil—ultimately who is it that is able to perform all these actions? Speak! If you say that it is the physical body which is acting, then at the moment when a man's life comes to an end, even though the body has not yet decayed, how is it that the eyes cannot see, the ears cannot hear, the nose cannot smell, the tongue cannot talk, the body cannot move, the hands cannot grasp, and the feet cannot run?

9. Adapted from Nanquan Puyuan (748–835) in *Jingde chuandeng lu* 10, T. 51.2076.276c.

You should know that what is capable of seeing, hearing, moving, and acting has to be your original mind; it is not your physical body. Furthermore the four elements which make up the physical body are by nature void; they are like images in a mirror or the moon's reflection in water. How can they be clear and constantly aware, always bright and never obscured—and, upon activation, be able to put into operation sublime functions as numerous as the sands of the Ganges? For this reason it is said, "Drawing water and carrying firewood are spiritual powers and sublime functions."[10]

There are many points at which to enter the noumenon.[11] I will indicate one approach which will allow you to return to the source.

Chinul: Do you hear the sounds of that crow cawing and that magpie calling?

Student: Yes.

Chinul: Trace them back and listen to your hearing-nature. Do you hear any sounds?

Student: At that place, sounds and discriminations do not obtain.

Chinul: Marvelous! Marvelous! This is Avalokiteśvara's method for entering the noumenon.[12] Let me ask you again. You said that sounds and discriminations do not obtain at that place. But since they do not obtain, isn't the hearing-nature just empty space at such a time?

Student: Originally it is not empty. It is always bright and never obscured.

Chinul: What is this essence which is not empty?

Student: As it has no former shape, words cannot describe it.

This is the life force of all the Buddhas and patriarchs—have no further doubts about that. Since it has no former shape, how can it be large or small? Since it cannot be large or small, how can it have limitations? Since it has no limitations, it cannot have inside or outside. Since there is no inside or outside, there is no far or near. As there is no far or near, there is no here or there. As there is no here or there, there is no coming or going. As there is no coming or going, there is no birth or death. As there is no birth or death, there is no past or present. As there is no past or present, there is no delusion or awakening. As there is no delusion or awakening, there is no ordinary

10. *Jingde chuandeng lu* 8, T. 51.2076.263b.

11. One of the two major approaches to practice attributed to Bodhidharma.

12. Avalokiteśvara's method for tracing hearing to its source in the mind was praised by Śākyamuni Buddha as the ideal practice for people in a degenerate age; see *Śūraṅgama Sūtra* (*Lengyang jing*) 6, T. 19.945.128b–129c.

man or saint. As there is no ordinary man or saint, there is no purity or impurity. Since there is no impurity or purity, there is no right or wrong. Since there is no right or wrong, names and words do not apply to it. Since none of these concepts apply, all sense-bases and sense-objects, all deluded thoughts, even forms and shapes and names and words are all inapplicable. Hence how can it be anything but originally void and calm and originally no-thing?

Nevertheless, at that point where all dharmas are empty, the numinous awareness is not obscured. It is not the same as insentience, for its nature is spiritually deft. This is your pure mind-essence of void and calm, numinous awareness. This pure, void, and calm mind is that mind of outstanding purity and brilliance of all the Buddhas of the three time periods; it is that enlightened nature which is the original source of all sentient beings. One who awakens to it and safeguards that awakening will then abide in the unitary, "such" and unmoving liberation. One who is deluded and turns his back on it passes between the six destinies, wandering in samsara for vast numbers of kalpas. As it is said, "One who is confused about the one mind and passes between the six destinies, goes and takes action. But one who awakens to the *dharmadhātu* and returns to the one mind, arrives and is still."[13] Although there is this distinction between delusion and awakening, in their basic source they are one. As it is said, "The word 'dharma' means the mind of the sentient being."[14] But as there is neither more of this void and calm mind in the saint nor less of it in the ordinary man, it is also said, "In the wisdom of the saint it is no brighter; hidden in the mind of the ordinary man it is no darker." Since there is neither more of it in the saint nor less of it in the ordinary man how are the Buddhas and patriarchs any different from other men? The only thing that makes them different is that they can protect their minds and thoughts—nothing more.

If you believe me to the point where you can suddenly extinguish your doubt, show the will of a great man and give rise to authentic vision and understanding, if you know its taste for yourself, arrive at the stage of self-affirmation and gain understanding of your true nature, then this is the understanding-awakening achieved by those who have cultivated the mind. Since no further steps are involved, it is called sudden. Therefore it is said, "When in the cause of faith one meshes without the slightest degree of error[15] or with all the qualities of the fruition of Buddhahood, faith is achieved."...

Some people do not realize that the nature of good and evil is void; they sit rigidly without moving and, like a rock crushing grass, repress both body and mind. To regard this as cultivation of the mind is a great delusion. For

13. By Chengguan (738–840), the forth Huayan patriarch, in his *Dafangguang fo huayan jing suishou yanyichao* 1, T. 36.1736.1b.

14. In the *Awakening of Faith* (*Dasheng qixin lun*), T. 32.1665.575c.

15. By Li Tongxuan, in his *Exposition of the Avantaṃsaka Sūtra* (*Xin huayan jing lun*) 14, T. 36.1739.809b.

this reason it is said, "Śrāvakas cut off delusion thought after thought, but the thought which does this cutting is a brigand."[16] If they could see that killing, stealing, sexual misconduct, and lying all arise from the nature, then their arising would be the same as their nonarising. At their source they are calm; why must they be cut off? As it is said, "Do not fear the arising of thoughts: only be concerned lest your awareness of them be tardy."[17] It is also said, "If we are aware of a thought at the moment it arises, then through that awareness it will vanish."[18]

In the case of a person who has had an awakening, although he still has adventitious defilements, these have all been purified into cream. If he merely reflects on the fact that confusion is without basis, then all the flowers in the sky of this triple world are like smoke swirling in the wind and the six phantom sense-objects are like ice melting in hot water. If thought-moment after thought-moment he continues to train in this manner, does not neglect to maintain his training, and keeps *samādhi* and *prajñā* equally balanced, then lust and hatred will naturally fade away and compassion and wisdom will naturally increase in brightness; unwholesome actions will naturally cease and meritorious practices will naturally multiply. When defilements are exhausted, birth and death cease. When the subtle streams of defilement are forever cut off, the great wisdom of complete enlightenment exists brilliantly of itself. Then he will be able to manifest billions of transformation-bodies in all the worlds of the ten directions following his inspiration and responding to the faculties of sentient beings. Like the moon in the empyrean which reflects in ten thousand pools of water, there is no limit to the responsiveness. He will be able to ferry across all sentient beings with whom he has affinities. He will be happy and free of worry. Such a person is called a Great Enlightened World Honored One.

Bibliography and Suggested Reading

Buswell, Robert E., Jr., trans. (1983) *The Korean Approach to Zen: The Collected Works of Chinul.* Honolulu: University of Hawai'i Press.

Buswell, Robert E., Jr. (1988) "Ch'an Hermeneutics: A Korean View." In Donald S. Lopez, ed., *Buddhist Hermeneutics.* Honolulu: University of Hawai'i Press, 231–256.

Buswell, Robert E., Jr. (1991) *Tracing Back the Radiance: Chinul's Korean Way of Zen.* Honolulu: University of Hawai'i Press.

Keel, Hee-Sung. (1984) *Chinul: Founder of the Korean Son Tradition.* Berkeley: Asian Humanities Press.

16. By Baozhi, in his Gāthā in *Praise of Mahāyāna* (*Dasheng zan*), *Jingde chuangdeng lu* 29, T. 51.2076.450a.

17. Yongming Yanshou, in his *Mirror of the Source Record* (*Zongjing lu*) 38, T. 48.2016.638a.

18. By Guifeng Zongmi, in *Chanyuan zhuquan ji duxu* 2, T. 48.2015.403a.b.

Park, Jin Y. (2005) "Zen Language in Our Time: The Case of Pojo Chinul's Huatou Meditation." *Philosophy East and West* 55/1: 80–98.
Park, Jin Y. (2008) *Buddhism and Postmodernity: Zen, Huayan, and the Possibility of Buddhist-Postmodern Ethics.* Lanham, MD: Lexington Books.
Park, Sung Bae. (1983) *Buddhist Faith and Sudden Enlightenment.* Albany: State University of New York Press.

31

Nishida's Conception of Person

Gereon Kopf

Nishida Kitarō (1870–1945), founder of the philosophical movement called the Kyoto school, was born in the Meiji period (1868–1912). During this time, Japan sought to rapidly modernize and to enter the exclusive club of the world powers of that time (Great Britain, Russia, the United States, and Germany). It was an intellectually vibrant period, when Japanese students traveled abroad to gain knowledge of and to assimilate European and American advancements in science as well as technology, and Japanese intellectuals were trying to redefine Japan's self-understanding in the face of modernization and imperialism. Such was the world of Nishida, who not only studied Chinese classics in high school and European languages and philosophies at Tokyo Imperial University but also suggested, in the later years of his career, that his philosophy expressed "Eastern logic" with "Western categories." In some sense, his work embodied the slogan representative of Meiji Japan, "Japanese soul—Western genius" (*wakon yōsai*).

At the beginning of his career, Nishida applied, if we give credence to his diaries and letters, the concept of "experience"—to be exact, "pure experience," which he borrowed from William James—to Zen experience in order to construct a new philosophy. However, he refrained from making explicit references to Buddhist thinkers and texts for most of his career and focused instead on exposing what he took to be the inherent inconsistencies of European philosophy. To be precise, he designed his philosophy as a response to neo-Kantianism in the early stages of his career (1911–17) and later began to subvert the philosophical dualism he saw as paradigmatic of mainstream academic—that is, "Western"—philosophy. For the most part, his philosophical work focused on stratifying a non-dual paradigm. To this purpose, he coined a sequence of terms and settled, in the later stages of his life, on the notion of the "self-identity of the absolute contradictories" (*zettai mujunteki jiko dōitsu*). At the same time, he began to refer to Buddhist texts and thinkers in his philosophical writings. He felt that the non-dual paradigm he sought to formulate was best expressed by traditional Buddhist philosophy. In addition, Nishida's later work explicates an affinity between Buddhist philosophy and his own thought.

Nishida's philosophical approach is as simple as it is ingenious. In his discussion of any given topic, he identifies two possible philosophical positions, objectivism and subjectivism. The former implies linear temporality, a causal determinism based on archeology, and a pluralism of substances; the latter a circular temporality, teleology, and a monism of Being. Nishida suggests that either position only captures half of the picture and is, ultimately, untenable. Thus, when Nishida conceives of the person he subverts existing models of personhood and selfhood that dominated the philosophical discourse of academia at his time as well as the conceptual framework they represent. Nishida believes that what we call "person" is continuous-and-yet-discontinuous, subjective-and-yet-objective, individual-and-yet-universal. Concretely speaking, he maintains that personal identity—that is, identity-over-time—is not guaranteed by a transtemporal essence, while human existence is not radically discontinuous: who I am today is neither identical to nor different from who I was, for example, ten years ago.

Nishida adds another layer of complexity to this discussion when he defines persons alternately as "the creating that is created" (*tsukuri tsukurareta*) and as "from the created to the creating" (*tsukurareta mono kara tsukuru mono e*). Nishida uses these terms to indicate the existential ambiguity of the self: the self is confronted with its own historicity and facticity, while, at the same time, it is also given the creative potential to change this very predicament. Not only is the self as person-over-time continuous-and-yet-discontinuous, but, as a spatial and subsequently somatic self, it is also acting-and-yet-acted-upon. Nishida also holds that the person is neither exclusively mind nor body but mind-and-yet-body, neither exclusively intellectual nor emotional but intellectual-and-yet-emotional, neither exclusively theoretical nor practicalbut theoretical-and-yet-practical. Finally, persons are neither exclusively individual nor do they dissolve into a group identity or the universality of humanity, but rather exist in the tension of the independent self and the social self. Neither of these exclusive categories can ultimately convey what it means to be a person. Each of these terms "highlights one aspect...and, in so doing, casts into shadow an equally important, though, incompatible aspect."[1] The key to this holistic self does

1. Thomas P. Kasulis, *Zen Action—Zen Person* (Honolulu: University of Hawaii Press, 1984), p. 22.

not lie in the intellectual work of scholarship or the moral work of the subjective agent, but in religion, which attempts to uncover the existential basis of the self itself.

The three selections in this volume trace Nishida's use of Buddhism in the formulation of his philosophy of personhood. The first selection, which is taken from his book *The Problem of Japanese Culture* (*Nihon bunka no mondai,* 1940),[2] sketches his approach to Buddhist philosophy as providing a non-dual paradigm and an alternative framework to traditional academic philosophy. While the terminology of this section clearly reflects the highly problematic and ideologically divisive orientalist rhetoric of his time, it also shows how Nishida uses this rhetoric to contrast two ways of thinking, objectivism and subjectivism. Ultimately, he uses the dichotomization of "Western" and "Indian" thought as illustrations of objectivism and subjectivism, respectively, in order to point to a third way, namely "Buddhist philosophy in Western terminology." At worst, this text reinforces orientalist rhetoric to argue for the superiority of Japanese thought; at best, it suggests a way to subvert the dichotomy postulated by its own rhetoric. Be that as it may, Nishida nevertheless is successful both in his development of a standpoint that eschews the extremes of objectivism and subjectivism and in his integration of Buddhist thought into mainstream philosophical discourse. The second selection, the concluding chapter of his *Philosophical Essays Volume III* (*Tetsugaku ronbunshū daisan,* 1939),[3] was designed to illustrate the notoriously difficult concept of the "self-identity of the absolute contradictories." It marks the first time in his career that Nishida freely cites Buddhist thinkers and texts. The goal here is to describe the self as "self-identity of the absolute contradictories." The third selection, from "The Logic of Basho and the Religious Worldview" (*Basho no ronri to shūkyōteki sekaikan,* 1945),[4] adds to this discussion Nishida's unwavering belief that the true self is always and unequivocally religious in nature.

Translation: From *The Problem of Japanese Culture*

Is there a logic in the East? I think that as long as people have a view of the world and of humanity, they must possess some kind of logic. But we might say that what we call logic generally did not surface in China. Chinese culture is not logical in the strict sense of the word. Indian Buddhism, on the contrary, is extremely intellectual even though it is religious; it constitutes

2. *Nihon bunka no mondai* (1940): Nishida Kitarō. *Nishida Kitarō Zenshū.* 19 vols. Tokyo: Iwanami Shoten, 1988, vol. 12:363–366.

3. *Enshikiteki setsumei* (1939): Nishida, *Nishida Kitarō Zenshū,* vol. 9:332–334.

4. *Basho no ronri to shūkyōteki sekaikan* (1945): Nishida, *Nishida Kitarō Zenshū,* vol. 11, pp. 429–433. For other translations of this excerpt see Nishida 1987, pp. 94–98; and Yusa 1987.

a religion that is established logically. I think Buddhism possesses its own way of seeing and thinking about things. How Indian Buddhism became that way, I do not know. However, I think the object of Buddhist philosophy is the mind that cannot be objectified. Contrary to Aristotelian philosophy, which makes the subject that cannot become a predicate its main concern, Indian philosophy focuses on the question of the "self." Buddhist philosophy emphasizes the concept of no-self. If we examine Mahāyāna Buddhism in this way, we can identify the concept of absolute nothingness of being-and-yet-non-being. The logic of such a philosophy cannot be thought of as either subjective logic or as the logic of object-recognition. I call this the logic of the mind that explicates the self-identity of the contradictories.

How can we conceive of our self? What constitutes the unity of consciousness? People say the self cannot return to the previous moment and has to be thought of simply as a linear progression. However, the self cannot be thought of simply in such a way. The self must be thought to be circular. Past and future exist simultaneously in the present. While all things that are located in the field of consciousness exist independently by themselves, they are unified as the phenomena of my consciousness. The self cannot be exclusively understood as an object. The self comprises non-being, yet, the formation of whatever exists in consciousness is grounded in it.

It is not that Indian philosophers consciously based their thought about the world on this way of thinking; nevertheless, we must say that, like the concept of time in Nāgārjuna's *Discourse on the Middle Way* (*Mūlamādhyamika-kārikās;* Jap. *Chūron*], the concept of the self is thoroughly penetrated by this way of thinking. Scholars who assume the standpoint of object logic use reflection to think about the self. I call this method "approaching the subject from the standpoint of the environment." However, in reflection, we already negate the direction of the object characteristic of any speculation; this negation is located at the foundational field of determination from which the speculation about the object arises. Self-negation does not emerge from the speculation on the object itself. On the contrary, people may think of the self reflectively as they think about things, namely as object, but when we recognize a thing that is opposed to the self, we must have knowledge of the self at the same time. Originally, a thing may not be anything we call either "self" or "thing." In a second step, our consciousness of things and selves emerges through discrimination. Scholars such as J. M. Baldwin say that children begin to differentiate between things and humans about two months after birth. In this book, I cannot begin to address and critique this question. Either way, the mainstream logic of the West is incapable of clarifying the logical form of that which is thought to be the self. Even Descartes's phrase "*cogito ergo sum*" implies that the self is nothing but a substance. But what we conceive of as a substance does not constitute the "self." Buddhism penetrates the self itself and thinks of it as that which exists while being nothing. At the bottom of subjectivity, subjectivity itself must be negated; therein the objective world comes into existence. The phrase "the mind is this Buddha and the Buddha is this mind"[5] identifies that which is formed in this way. Even if we describe Buddhist philosophy as the logic of "mind-only" and simply apply it to the categories of Western philosophy, we cannot truly penetrate it. Such a thinking would require that we conceive of the world as mind-only in terms of either psychology or objective rationality. To be exact, we cannot think of the world as mind-only using object logic. Buddhist philosophy thematizes the world that encompasses our conscious self by transcending it, that is, the world of cause and effect in which our conscious self arises and perishes. Regardless of the label "mind-only philosophy," this is the core of Buddhist thought. The way of thinking from the environment to the subject, which is characteristic of Western philosophy, cannot account for subjectivity at all. However, we cannot negate subjectivity completely. On the contrary, Buddhist philosophy will preserve the moment of subjectivity and see the world from this standpoint. Therefore, we can say that at the base of the way of thinking characteristic of Buddhist philosophy, there is the demand to understand the thing located in the objective world that includes everything. Buddhist philosophy did not develop simply by making the subjective self the central problem. But the problem of the world of objects that proceeds from the environment to the subject was hardly ever reflected on. Indian culture posits that which constitutes the-subject-and-yet-the-world. For this reason, Buddhist philosophy can be thought to be subjectivistic.

I would like to think that Buddhism possesses its own way of thinking of the particular thing and call this the logic of the heart or the logic of place, that is, the contradictory self-identity. The phrase "the mind is this Buddha and the Buddha is the mind" does not imply that we think about the world from the standpoint of the mind that knows itself, but that we think about the mind from the standpoint of the world. This does not mean that we see the world in self-awareness. In his *Discourse on the Middle Way,* Nāgārjuna already introduced dialectics; but does not his philosophy differ fundamentally from the forms of dialectics developed in Western philosophy? In China, Nāgārjuna's dialectics matured into the Tiantai [Jap. Tendai] Buddhist worldview, expressed by the phrase "three thousand worlds in one thought" [*yiniansanqian;* Jap. *ichinensanzen*], and into the Huayan [Jap. Kegon] Buddhist

5. Nishida's *shinsoku zebutsu, butsusoku zeshin* plays on the phrase "the Buddha is this mind" (*foji shixin;* Jap. *butsusoku zeshin*) from *The Records of Zen Master Huangbo Xiyun* and on Mazu's "the mind is the Buddha" as transmitted by the *Gateless Barrier* as *jixin shifo* (Jap. *sokushin zebutsu*) and by *The Blue Cliff Records* as *jixin jifo* (Jap. *sokushin sokubutsu*). *The Recorded Sayings of Zen Master Huangbo Xiyun* (*Huangbo xiyun chanshi yulu;* Jap. *ōbaku kiun zenshi goroku*), T. 48.2012B.385b, *The Gateless Barrier* (*Wumenguan;* Jap. *Mumonkan*) no. 30, T. 48.2005.296c; *The Blue Cliff Record* (*Biyan lu;* Jap.*Hekigan roku*) no. 44, T. 48.2003.180c. T refers to *Taishō shinshū daizōkyō.* [A standard collection of the East Asian Buddhist canon compiled in Japan] Takakusu Junjirō, Watanabe Kaikyoku, et al. (eds.), 100 vols. Tokyo: Taishō Issaikyō Kankōkai, 1924–1932.

worldview, summarized as "the unhindered interpenetration among the phenomena" [*shishiwuai;* Jap. *jijimuge*]. Huayan Buddhism also uses the phrase "one-and-yet-everything, everything-and-yet-one" [*yijiyiqie yiqiejiyi;* Jap.: *issokuissai issaisokuichi*] to indicate this way of thinking. One may think of these phrases as verbal entanglements of Buddhist scholasticism; but I believe that the logic of the mind as explained above breathes life into them. We can take some clues from the philosophy of the Japanese Zen master Dōgen. Thinking as a Buddhist philosopher along those lines, he internally unifies this way of thought with his religious experience of "casting off body and mind, body and mind cast off"[6] Even if we call this practice, that which is thought from the standpoint of Western philosophy differs in its meaning. From the standpoint of Western philosophy, Buddhist logic may be thought of haphazardly as mysticism. However, our self cannot but enter our world of actuality. The logic of the absolute contradictory self-identity of the many-and-yet-one and the one-and-yet-many (*duojiyi yijiduo;* Jap. *tasokuitsu issokuta*)[7] constitutes the logic of the actual world. I do not say that Buddhist philosophy is more perfect than Western philosophy; however, only if you enter the discourse of Western logic will you be able to call Buddhist philosophy "mystical." I explain Zen in this way even to people who think that since Zen fails to privilege either monism or dualism it is mystical. While it can be thought that there are similarities between Zen and what is called mystical philosophy, I think that their standpoints differ completely from each other. It is also not the case that Zen does not enter the experience of science in some way. However, I emphasize the uniqueness of Buddhist logic as I mentioned above; at the same time, I do not want to simply return to the conventional logic of Buddhism. Do not many Buddhist scholars themselves apply Buddhist philosophy to the categories of Western philosophy today?

Translation: From "An Explanation Using Graphs"

As the absolute contradictory self-identity of the one totality and the many individuals,[8] the world forms itself in the form of a self-contradiction. As individuals in this world, our selves are always thoroughly self-contradictory. Therein lie the primary and the final dilemmas of human existence. Hence,

6. Dōgen attributes this phrase to his master Rujing (Jap. *Nyojō*). "The Japanese Zen Master Eihei Dōgen" (*Riben yongping daoyuan chanshi;* Jap. *Nihon eihei dōgen zenshi*), in *The Succession of the Lamp* (*Jiding lu;* Jap. *Keitō roku*), *Xuzang jing* 86.1605; *Dōgen,* "Talk on Discriminating the Way" (Bendōwa), in *The Storehouse of the True Dharma Eye (Shōbōgenzō).* Some reference books identify the *Record of Rujing's Sayings* (*Rujing xuyulu;* Jap. *Nyojō zokugoroku*) as a source of this saying.

7. While this phrase originated in the literature of the Huayan Buddhist tradition, Nishida consistently neglects to identify its origin.

8. Even though Nishida refers here to individual persons, he uses the term "individual object" (*kobutsu*) and not "individual person" (*kojin*).

this also constitutes the predicament of the world. We penetrate the root of our own self-contradiction; this way we win true life from the standpoint of the absolute contradictory self-identity. This constitutes religion. Therein lies absolute negation. Buddhism calls this the religious self-cultivation of "loosing one's life when the body perishes."[9] Self-cultivation comprises neither logical speculation nor moral action. Rather, what Dōgen identifies as the method of meditation that "casts off body and mind"[10] should be considered religious practice. (This is the meaning of the phrase "You should diligently study the backward movement expressed in the phrase 'turn the light, reflect its radiance.'"[11]) Practice thus understood occupies a standpoint that is fundamentally different from the standpoint where "speculative thought"[12] evaluates concepts. "The way of the Buddha is to study the self; to study the self is to forget the self."[13] Negation that is brought about by moral action does not qualify as absolute negation. It is nothing but "using your head to find your head"[14] or "placing one head on top of the other."[15] We can call this attitude, which is expressed by the phrase "practicing the ten thousand dharmas while carrying the self," "delusion."[16] What we call "religious self-cultivation" neither involves the active subject nor is mediated by it. Rather, it transforms such a subject by means of the absolute contradictory self-identity. Therefore, it neither approaches this standpoint in one push nor intuits the whole world from there. Self-cultivation constitutes an infinite progress in this direction. Even Śākyamuni Buddha practices self-cultivation incessantly. If this is so, we neither escape nor transcend the world when we engage in such a religion. From there we think and act while becoming objects in the sense of the true contradictory self-identity. "We practice the self while approaching the ten thousand dharmas."[17] Even scholarship and morality should be considered this kind of religious activity. Simple transcendence does not constitute the absolute, simple nothingness not absolute nothingness. "Casting off of body and mind," "body and mind cast off"[18] ("the donkey looks down to the well,

9. *The Records of Linji* (*Linji lu;* Jap. *Rinzai roku*), T. 47.1985.496c; *The Blue Cliff Records* no. 22, T. 48.2003.162c; Dōgen, *The Extensive Records of Eihei* (*Eihei kōroku*), chap. 9.

10. Dōgen, "Talk on Discriminating the Way" (Bendōwa), *The Storehouse of the True Dharma Eye.*

11. *The Records of Linji,* T. 47.1985.502a, quoted in Dōgen, *Treatise on the Universal Promotion of Zazen* (*Fukanzazengi*).

12. The *Great Dictionary for Zen Studies* (*Zengaku daijiten*) identifies Keizan Shingi's *Notes on the Mind That Practices Zazen* (*Zazen yōjin ki,* T. 82) as the source for this phrase.

13. Dōgen, "Actualizing the Kōan" (Genjōkōan), in *The Storehouse of the True Dharma Eye.*

14. *The Records of Linji,* T. 47.1985.502a.

15. *The Records of Linji,* T. 47.1985.500c.

16. See Dōgen, "Actualizing the Kōan."

17. Dōgen, "Actualizing the Kōan."

18. See note 6.

the well looks up to the donkey"),[19] and the absolute are but one; it must be the self-identity of contradictories. The absolute is power; it is not something that constitutes a unity of opposites and is opposed to relativity. Logic and ethics cannot be separated from religion. The true, the good, and the beautiful come into existence from the standpoint of the absolute contradictory self-identity. However, it is a mistake to think about religion in this way.

It is said that "the Buddha-dharma is not useful nor does it accomplish anything; it constitutes nothing but the everyday and the ordinary." This does not mean that "to have a shit, take a piss, put on your clothes, eat and drink"[20] in itself is sufficient. However, if one occupies the standpoint of the self-identity of the absolute contradictories, these words are meaningful. "The heart of the dharma has no form; it traverses the ten directions; when it is in the eye, we say we see; when it is in the ear, we say we hear."[21] The wise person and the fool are therein one,[22] and so are important and minor affairs. Everything arises from this standpoint and returns to it. The very foundation must be exclusively the "everyday."[23] However, this does not constitute the undifferentiated one. It is said that "when Hu arrives, it is Hu who appears; when Han arrives, it is Han who appears."[24] As the "one-and-yet-all and the all-and-yet-one,"[25] that which is signified by the above phrases is infinitely differentiated in the self-identity of contradictories. From this foundation everything arises. Even the many and the one are not completely unified. However, in our poesis, we always constitute the self-identity of contradictories. The phrase "body-mind oneness"[26] designates the self-identity of contradictories. Our self cannot be conceived in any other way. The practice and actualization[27] of "body-mind oneness" constitutes religious self-cultivation. "To study the self is to forget the self; to forget the self is to be actualized by the ten thousand dharmas."[28] At the time when one "has a shit,

19. *The Extensive Records of Zen Master Hongzhi* (*Hongzhi chanshi guanglu;* Jap. *Wanshi zenji kōroku*), T. 48.2001.23b.

20. Here Nishida responds to the observation by Zen master Linji that "[t]he Buddha dharma is not useful nor does it accomplish anything; it constitutes nothing but the everyday and the ordinary; have a shit, take a piss; put on your clothes, eat and drink, retire when tired." *The Records of Linji,* T. 47.1985.0498a.

21. *The Records of Linji,* T. 47.1985.497c.

22. Here Nishida responds to the observation by Zen master Linji that "the fool laughs at us and the wise person already knows this." *The Records of Linji,* T. 47.1985.0498a.

23. Nishida stresses the affinity of his neologism *byōjōtei* (literally, "the depth of the everyday") with the phrase "the everyday heart is the way" (*pingchangxin shifo;* Jap. *byōjōshin zebutsu*) from the *Gateless Barrier* (no. 19, T. 48.2005.295b) and the saying cited earlier from *The Records of Linji* (see note 18).

24. *The Transmission of the Lamp* (*Xuzhuandeng lu;* Jap. *Zokudentō roku*), T. 51.2077.593b.

25. See the previous excerpt.

26. Dōgen, "Talk on Discriminating the Way."

27. Dōgen, "Actualizing the Kōan."

28. Dōgen, "Actualizing the Kōan."

takes a piss, puts on clothes, eats and drinks," the self is actualized by the "ten thousand dharmas." Our self reaches the point of absolute negation at the foundation of its own formation. At the place where one does not "turn the light to reflect its radiance,"[29] the religious question disappears.

Religion does not mediate the conduct of the moral subject. "Shinran said: I have not said the *nembutsu*[30] even once out of filial piety for my parents."[31] "Since practitioners do not practice the *nembutsu* by themselves, it is called 'non-practice'; since the good deeds are not performed by moral agents, we call them non-good.'"[32] The reason for this is that "evil is deep and grave" and "passions and delusions are blind and pervasive";[33] therefore, we have to rely on the original vow of "Amida only" [*shikanmida*].[34] But this should not be thought of as the "easy truth."[35] To enter such a "faith in the other power"[36] is to truly die to oneself. The true mind of morality emerges from this attitude. Phrases such as "good and evil are not different" imply that the self truly dies and that one enters the faith in the other-power. Even in Christianity, the faith in Christ's sacrificial death is fundamental. There is no path from humans to god. As I said before, I do not take logic and ethics lightly. I only want to clarify the essence of what is called religion. Even logic and ethics can only be explained from the religious standpoint.

Translation: From "The Logic of Basho and the Religious Worldview"

As the self-identity of the absolute contradictories space and time, our world is the world of infinite causality; it progresses from the created to that which creates as the self-determination of the absolute present. The self constitutes the individual in such a world, but because, as Pascal observed, we know the self by transcending it, it is more precious than the world that crushes us to death. The reason we can say this is that our self takes on the form of the contradictory self-identity as the self-negation of the absolute that determines itself in self-expression; we comprise the many individuals of the absolute one. We touch the absolute one by negating ourselves in an act of

29. See note 10.

30. The *nembutsu* is a short phrase, *namu amida butsu,* that is used in Pure Land Buddhism to express one's reliance on Amida Buddha.

31. Shinran, *A Lament of Differences* (*Tannishō*), chap 5.

32. Shinran, *Lament of Differences,* chap. 8.

33. Shinran, *Lament of Differences,* chap. 1.

34. This phrase is a creative response to the slogan "Zazen only" (*shikantaza*), employed in Sōtō Zen Buddhism (Sōtōshū).

35. This phrase, *Ani no tai,* plays with the characters of "easy" in the Pure Land Buddhist slogan "Easy practice" (*igyō*) and the character used for "truth" in the "Four Noble Truths" (*āryasatya;* Jap. *shishōtai*) of Buddhism.

36. This is one of the mottos of the True Pure Land school of Buddhism (Jōdo Shinshū).

inverse correlation. It is thus possible to say that we enter eternal life in the mode of life-and-yet-death and death-and-yet-life; we are religious. I think that what we call the religious question deals exclusively with our volitional self; it constitutes the problem of the individual. However, this does not mean that religion aims at the individual's peace of mind as it is usually conceived. Peace of mind desired by the self is not a concern of religion; it assumes a standpoint contrary to that of religion. If it did, the religious question could not even be considered a moral dilemma. The desiring self that fears pain and seeks happiness is not the true individual; it acts merely biologically. From such a standpoint, religion must be called an anesthetic.

Our self constitutes the self-negation of the absolute and touches it exhaustively in inverse correlation; the more individual it becomes, the more it faces the absolute, that is, god. Our self faces god at the brink of its individuality. It faces the enormity of the one totality exhaustively as the self-identity of the absolute contradictories at the extreme point where the individual determines itself in the historical world. For this reason, every single one of us faces god as the representative of humanity that traverses from the eternal past to the eternal future. Every self faces the absolute present itself as the momentary determination of the absolute present. This means that our selves constitute numberless centers of an infinite sphere that is without a circumference and devoid of one center. When the absolute determines itself as the absolute contradictory self-identity of the many and the one, the world is bottomlessly volitional as the self-determination of absolute nothingness. It constitutes the absolute will in its totality; at the same time, the will of the numberless individuals opposes the absolute will in myriad ways. In this sense, the human world emerges from the world that embodies the "*sokuhi*"[37] of the Prajñāpāramitā literature. Therein lies the meaning of the phrase "there is no place it abides, yet this mind arises."[38] Panshan Baoji [Jap. Banzan Hōjaku], a follower of Mazu [Daoyi; Jap. Baso Dōitsu; 709–788] said "it is like brandishing a sword through the air; it is not a question of whether it reaches its goal or not; it leaves no trace in the air; even the blade is not touched; if this is the case, the mind does not discriminate, it does not think, it does not imagine anything; it comprises the whole-mind-and-yet-the-Buddha and all-Buddhas-and-yet-one-person; persons and Buddhas are not different; this is the beginning of the way."[39] In the same way in which a sword that strikes the air leaves no trace and remains intact, the whole-mind-and-yet-the-Buddha and all-Buddhas-and-yet-the-person constitute the self-identity

37. D. T. Suzuki believed that the term "*sokuhi*" (Chin.: *jifei,* literally, "is not") is used in the *Diamond Sūtra* to indicate a particular form of logic. Suzuki taught that this logic had the form "when we say A is A we mean that A is not A, therefore it is A," and was characteristic of Mahāyāna Buddhism. See *Suzuki daisetsu zenshū,* 32 vols. (Tokyo: Iwanami Shoten, 1968), vol. 5, p. 381.

38. *Diamond Sūtra* (*Jingang bore boluomi jing;* Jap. *Kongō hannya haramitsu kyō*), T. 08.235.748c.

39. *The Mirror of Orthodoxy* (*Zongjing lu,* Jap. *Sūgyō roku*), T. 48.2016.944c.

of the absolute contradictories. Even this phrase may seem, to someone who assumes the vantage point of object logic, to indicate pantheism. However, the words of the Zen practitioners cannot be explained in such a way; they disclose the logic of *sokuhi* and of the contradictory self-identity. All Buddhas and individuals are one in the sense of this logic. The true individual emerges in the momentary determination of the absolute present. This is the meaning of the phrase "there is no place it abides, yet this mind arises."

That which takes on the form of the self-determination of nothingness is the will. The volitional self, that is, our individual self, constitutes neither the subject nor the predicate. It arises as the self-determination of the place as the absolute contradictory self-identity of the subjective and the predicative directions. For this reason, just as the moment can be thought to be eternal, inasmuch as our self is thoroughly individual, it touches the absolute in an inverse determination with each step. Linji observes that "in this lump of red meat, the true person of no rank resides; he constantly enters and departs through your sense organs."[40] The phrase "to be thoroughly individual" indicates that one constitutes the extreme of what it means to be human and represent humanity. This is illustrated by the saying "If I truly consider Amida's vow that was made after five kalpas of contemplation, I realize it was made only for myself, Shinran."[41] This does not indicate the so-called individual. For this reason, morality is universal, religion individual....

In Buddhism, there is the phrase "the mind arises in an instant."[42] At the basis of their formation, human beings are self-contradictory. The more they are intellectual and volitional, the more this is true. Human beings are not without original sin. Morally speaking, it may be irrational to say that parents transmit their sin to their children, but the very existence of human beings can be found therein. To transcend original sin is to transcend humanity. This is impossible from the human standpoint. We can only be saved if we believe in the reality of Christ as the revelation of God's love. Therein we return to the root of our self. It is said that in "Adam we die...in Christ we are born."[43] In true religion, this world is always a world of karma, a world of ignorance and of life-and-death. But we are saved by Buddha's vow of compassion and inasmuch as we believe in "the mysterious name of Amida." This has to be understood as a response to the voice of the absolute. In the depth of this standpoint, we find that "birth-and-death is no-birth" (Zen master Bankei [1622–93]).[44] In the self-identity of contradictories, beings are "all-Buddhas-and-yet-one-person; persons and Buddhas are not different." This is like brandishing a sword in air. Again, it is like "throwing

40. *The Records of Zen Master Linji*, T. 47.1985.496c.

41. "Postscript" (*Kōjo*), in *A Lament of Differences*.

42. *The Great Awakening of Faith* (*Dasheng qixin lun*, Jap. *Daijō kishin ron*), T. 44.1846.267a.

43. Rom. 5:12–21.

44. *The Records of Zen Master Bankei* (*Bankei zenshi goroku*).

pebbles into a stream, moment after moment the flow never stops" (Zhaozhou [Congshen; Jap. Jōshū Jūshin]).[45]

Bibliography and Suggested Reading

Heisig, James. (2001) *Philosophers of Nothingness: An Essay on the Kyoto School.* Honolulu: University of Hawai'i Press.

Kopf, Gereon. (2009) "Self-Identity of the Absolute What?—Reflections on How to Teach the Philosophy of Nishida Kitarō." In David Jones and Ellen Klein, eds., *Teaching Texts and Contexts: The Art of Infusing Asian Philosophies and Religions.* Albany: State University of New York Press.

Maraldo, John C. (1998) "Nishida Kitarō (1870–1945)." In *Routledge Encyclopedia of Philosophy.* Vol. 7. New York: Routledge, pp. 13–16.

Nishida, Kitarō. (1987a) *Last Writings: Nothingness and the Religious Worldview,* translated by David A. Dilworth. Honolulu: University of Hawaii Press.

Nishida, Kitarō. (1987b) "The Logic of *Topos* and the Religious Worldview, Part II," translated by Michiko Yusa. *Eastern Buddhist,* Vol. 20, No. 1: 93–96.

Yusa, Michiko. (2002) *Zen and Philosophy: An Intellectual Biography of Nishida Kitarō.* Honolulu: University of Hawai'i Press.

45. *The Blue Cliff Records,* T. 48.2003.207a.

PART V

ETHICS

From the first turning of the wheel of Dharma, with the Buddha's teaching of the four noble truths, ethics has been at the heart of Buddhist thought. The Buddhist path aims at liberating oneself and others from suffering. Suffering is caused by egocentric attachment, egocentric aversion, and ignorance, which are themselves based on a cognitive and existential misunderstanding of phenomena, especially the self, as substantial. Buddhist thinkers have employed a multiplicity of approaches to questions of the nature, causes, and appropriate responses to suffering, some of which resemble familiar Western moral theories. Contemporary scholars have recognized the contours of eudaemonistic virtue ethics, utilitarianism, and deontology in Buddhist moral traditions. Moreover, it has been argued, some Buddhist moral strategies are a form of ethical particularism, for they emphasize the importance of specific context to moral decision-making and do not articulate any general principles.

While characterizing Buddhist ethics according to Western categories can be helpful for understanding some aspects of Buddhist morality, it is a mistake to believe that Buddhist ethics can be characterized as a whole—it is simply too diverse—and assimilating Buddhist ethics to Western moral principles occludes the complexity and uniqueness of Buddhist moral traditions. Without seeking to circumscribe all ethical activity under one principle, Buddhist moral thinkers set out to solve the fundamental problem of the pervasiveness of suffering. In doing so, they ground their work in the doctrine of dependent origination, describing the moral significance of intention and consequence, character and action, virtues, vices, commitments, and goals as situated in a particular web of interdependence.

The first chapter of this part includes several texts from the Pali canon of the Theravāda tradition that distinguish between reprehensible and unwholesome actions and those that are skillful (*kusala*). Volitions arising from mental defilements, for example greed, hatred, and delusion, are said to lead to unskillful (*akusala*) acts, which cause suffering to both self and others. In contrast to wholesome acts, unskillful acts strengthen unwholesome mental states, thereby obstructing the path to liberation from suffering.

The next chapter consists of selections from Śāntideva's *Bodhicaryāvatāra* (Introduction to the practice of the bodhisattva), the locus classicus for discussions of the cultivation of *bodhicitta,* the altruistic aspiration to achieve awakening for the sake of all sentient beings. Śāntideva (c. late seventh–early eighth century) presents the path to liberation from cognitive and emotional defilements through the practice of the six virtues, or perfections (*pāramitās*), of the bodhisattva: generosity (*dāna*), discipline (*śīla*), patience (*kṣānti*), vigor (*vīrya*), meditative absorption (*dhyāna*), and wisdom (*prajñā*). According to Śāntideva, failure to control the mind makes it susceptible to anger, frustration, craving, envy, and other mental afflictions that are the source of one's own suffering and make one insensible to the suffering of others. Ethics, therefore, is primarily concerned with liberating the mind from affliction.

Śāntideva was only one of many authors to write about the bodhisattva perfections. Another classic account is attributed to Asaṅga (fourth century C.E.), in the *Bodhisattvabhūmi* (The bodhisattva stages). The next chapter presents selections from Asaṅga's chapter on the perfection of propriety, or discipline, from the *Bodhisattvabhūmi.* Asaṅga's account of morality is presented under three categories: "ethics of the vow," "ethics of collecting wholesome factors," and "ethics of benefiting sentient beings." For Asaṅga, the ritual of taking a vow transforms good intentions into formal commitments; it expresses the practitioner's affirmation of shared moral ideals and heightens the sense of shame and embarrassment for transgressing moral standards. But morality also includes cultivating qualities of body, speech, and mind that enable the practitioner to liberate sentient beings from samsara. Finally, according to Asaṇga, morality codifies altruistic aspirations to benefit others.

The central Mahāyāna understanding of emptiness problematizes straightforward rule-governed morality, or even basic distinctions such as right and wrong or skillful and unskillful. The Korean thinker Wŏnhyo (617–686) explores the problem of observing and violating precepts that are ultimately empty in the *Essentials of Observing and Violating Bodhisattva Precepts.* Wŏnhyo argues against clinging to moral precepts and ethical judgments and categories because ultimately they, as well as moral agents and other sentient beings, lack substantial existence. While precepts are conventionally real and important—indeed, they are the very basis of Buddhas and bodhisattvas—they are to be understood as ambiguous, provisional, dependent on specific contexts. Thus, in Wŏnhyo's nonsubstantial Mahāyāna ethics, one action could be interpreted as either observing a precept or violating the very same precept.

The final three chapters provide a glimpse at some of the ways Buddhist thinkers draw on the resources of their traditions to respond to contemporary questions and challenges. Perhaps the most significant development in recent Buddhist ethics, as it has confronted modernity, is socially engaged Buddhism. In contrast to some interpretations of Buddhist practice, which have primarily emphasized self-cultivation and personal virtue, socially engaged Buddhists argue that the Buddhist goal of alleviating the suffering of sentient beings requires critically engaging and taking action against social and institutional oppression and violence. Moreover, they argue, Buddhist doctrines, such as interdependence, nonduality, skillful means, compassion and lovingkindness, nonviolence, selflessness, emptiness, and so on, provide a theoretical framework for critically understanding structures of oppression and how to respond to them. Some scholars regard socially engaged Buddhism as so new and significant that it ought to be considered a fourth vehicle (*yāna*) after the Hīnayāna (Lesser Vehicle), Mahāyāna (Greater Vehicle), and Vajrayāna (Tantric Vehicle).

The Vietnamese monk Thich Nhat Hanh (b. 1926) is often credited with coining the term "engaged Buddhism" and is one of the foremost proponents of socially engaged Buddhism. During the war in Vietnam, Nhat Hanh founded the Order of Interbeing for monks, nuns, and laypersons committed to the idea that mindfulness and personal transformation are necessary but insufficient; Buddhist practice must also include responding to the suffering of sentient beings that is caused by war, economic and social injustice, environmental degradation, colonialism, racism, sexism, and other forms of violence. The selection from Nhat Hanh's *Interbeing: Fourteen Guidelines for Engaged Buddhism* articulates his view that "all Buddhism is Engaged Buddhism."

Engaged Buddhism has been applied in a wide variety of contexts. One of the most prominent ways Buddhism has engaged contemporary issues is in the context of environmental degradation. According to many contemporary Buddhist thinkers, the doctrine of dependent origination is a metaphysics in harmony with ecological interdependence; Buddhist approaches to suffering are not limited to humans but regard all sentient beings as morally considerable; some Buddhist thinkers regard even "nonsentient" material as an expression of a universal Buddha nature; and Buddhist ethics and psychology aim at cultivating the kind of nonacquisitive and compassionate relation to the world that is appropriate to the contemporary environmental context. These ideas are found in the selections from the essay "The Ecological Self: Postmodern Ground for Right Action," by Joanna Macy (b. 1929). Macy is a Buddhist teacher, environmental activist, scholar, and perhaps the most well-known theorist of environmentally engaged Buddhism. Drawing on general systems theory along with Buddhist metaphysics, psychology, and ethics, Macy argues for an extension of identity, an interconnected, ecological sense of self, instead of the separate self characteristic of much modern philosophy and political theory that requires constant protection and consumption.

According to early Buddhist texts, such as the *Khandhaka Rules* from the monastic code, presented here by Karma Lekshe Tsomo, while the Buddha affirmed that women are capable of following the path to liberation and accepted women into the monastic community, nevertheless, Buddhist traditions have historically subordinated women. With its critique of a stable self-identity, Buddhism has no philosophical basis for the exclusion of women—or any other group determined by some fixed characteristic—from religious practice, education, and status. However, Buddhist societies have consistently marginalized women by excluding them from institutions where they could acquire higher learning, subordinating even senior nuns to newly ordained monks, and generally situating women as inferior and subservient in social practice. In this last chapter, Tsomo reflects on the place of women in Buddhism, and the significant changes currently under way, including new opportunities for religious education and practice for nuns and laywomen, and the recent revival of the full ordination for nuns that had disappeared from most Buddhist traditions.

32

Theravāda Texts on Ethics

Peter Harvey

The selections translated here, from the Pali canon of the Theravāda school, and supplemented by some commentarial passages, are a series of discussions of action (Pali *kamma,* Skt. *karma*) and its moral assessment. They provide a set of complementary principles of ethics. Summarizing the features discussed here, Theravāda Buddhism sees an action as reprehensible if one would not like it inflicted on oneself, and as expressing a volition that is rooted in greed, hatred, or delusion, which three states are sustained by unwise attention. A reprehensible action is *akusala:* it is "unwholesome/unhealthy" in being affected by greed or other mental defilements, and "unskillful" in not being produced by wisdom. It is censurable by the wise, and generally blameworthy, as it brings harm such as that wrought by killing and stealing, and also brings affliction to others, oneself, or both. It has painful karmic consequences in this life, the next, and subsequent ones. It leads to further unwholesome states of mind, and it obstructs wisdom and leads away from nirvana. Praiseworthy actions have the opposite qualities.

Reprehensible or praiseworthy actions include mental ones, not just bodily and verbal ones. However, the Buddhist term *sīla* (Pali, Skt. *śīla*), "moral virtue," only pertains to bodily and verbal conduct; mental conduct is dealt with under meditation and wisdom. That said, it is acknowledged that wisdom and moral virtue are mutually supportive, like two hands washing each other (D. I.124).[1]

1. For abbreviations, see chapter 15 here.

From *Aṅguttara Nikāya* (Numerical Collection), The Sixes, *Sutta* 63

In this passage (A. III.415), the real nature of action is identified as the will, or volition (*cetanā*), that is expressed in an action of body, speech, or mind. *Cetanā* encompasses the motive for which an action is done, its immediate intention, and the immediate mental impulse that sets it going and sustains it (Keown 1992: 213–218).

Translation

It is volition (*cetanā*), monks, that I call karma (*kamma-*). Having willed, one performs an action by body, by speech, by mind.

And what, monks, is the conditioned origin of action? It is [sensory] stimulation.[2] . . .

And what, monks, is the diversity of action? There is action [whose fruit is] to be experienced in the hells, or in the animal realm, or in the sphere of ghosts, or in the human world, or in the heavens. . . .

And what, monks, is the ripening of action? Action, I say, has a threefold ripening: in this life, in the next life, or subsequently. . . .

From *Aṅguttara Nikāya,* The Tens, *Sutta* 206

This passage (A. V.292–97) builds on the idea of action as volition and spells out the kind of willed actions that are to be seen as reprehensible or praiseworthy. Volitions are characterized as either *akusala* or *kusala,* perhaps the most commonly used terms for reprehensible and praiseworthy actions or mental states in early Buddhist texts. *Kusala* can be translated as "wholesome" or "skillful," and *akusala* means the opposite of this. The term for "ripening," *vipāka,* is usually used for future karmic results for the agent of an action,[3] but the term for "consequence," *udraya,* may refer to the more immediate effects of an action on anyone.

Translation

I declare, monks, that actions willed, performed, and accumulated[4] will not become extinct as long as [their fruits] have not been experienced, be this in

2. Defined as the coming-together of a sense, its relevant object, and the related kind of consciousness, for example eye, a visible form, and eye-consciousness, or mind, a mental object, and mind-consciousness.

3. An action is often likened to a "seed" and the karmic result to its "fruit" (*phala*) or "ripening" (*vipāka*).

4. Asl. 262 explains "'accumulation' means the heaping up, the development as cause." This probably means the repetition and nonregret of an action.

this life, in the next life, or subsequently. And as long as [the fruits of] these actions willed, performed, and accumulated have not been experienced, there will be no making an end of suffering (*dukkha*-), I declare.[5]

There are, monks, corrupt and harmful actions of unwholesome volition, with painful consequences, ripening in pain: three of body, four of speech, and three of mind....

How is there a threefold corrupt and harmful bodily action of unwholesome volition?

There is a person who kills living beings; he is cruel and his hands are bloodstained; he is bent on slaying and murdering, having no compassion for any living being.

He takes what is not given to him, appropriates with thievish intent the property of others, be it in the village or the forest.

He conducts himself wrongly in regard to sense pleasures: he has intercourse with those under the protection of father, mother, brother, sister, relatives, or clan, or of their religious community; or with those promised to a husband, protected by law, and even with those betrothed with a garland....

And how is there a fourfold corrupt and harmful verbal action of unwholesome volition?

There is one who is a liar. When he is in the council of his community or in another assembly, or among his relatives, his guild, in the royal court, or when he has been summoned as a witness and is asked to tell what he knows, then, though he does not know, he will say, "I know"; though he does know, he will say, "I do not know"; though he has not seen, he will say, "I have seen"; and though he has seen, he will say, "I have not seen." In that way he utters deliberate lies, be it for his own sake, for the sake of others, or for some material advantage.

He utters divisive speech: what he hears here he reports elsewhere to foment conflict there; and what he hears elsewhere he reports here to foment conflict here. Thus he creates discord among those united, and he incites still more those who are in discord. He is fond of dissension, he delights and rejoices in it, and he utters words that cause dissension.

He speaks harshly, using speech that is coarse, rough, bitter, and abusive, that makes others angry and causes distraction of mind. It is such speech that he utters.

He indulges in frivolous chatter: he speaks what is untimely, unreasonable, and unbeneficial, having no connection with the Dhamma or the Discipline.[6] His talk is not worth treasuring, it is inopportune, inadvisable, unrestrained, and not connected with what is beneficial....

5. Nevertheless, becoming a Stream-enterer means that rebirth at less than a human level is no longer possible, and while an *Arahat* may still experience some residual results of past bad karma while still alive, on dying, hence passing beyond any more rebirths, no further karmic results can arise.

6. That is, monastic discipline, or more broadly, moral discipline.

And how is there a threefold corrupt and harmful mental action of unwholesome volition?

There is a person who is covetous; he covets the wealth and property of others, thinking: "Oh, that what he owns might belong to me!"

There is also one who has ill will in his heart. He has corrupt mental resolve: "Let these beings be slain! Let them be killed and destroyed! May they perish and cease to exist!"

He has wrong views and a perverted way of seeing: "There is no gift, there is no offering, there is no [self-] sacrifice;[7] there is no fruit (*phalaṃ*) or ripening (*vipāko*) of actions well done or ill done;[8] there is no this world, no other world;[9] there is no mother, no father;[10] there are no spontaneously arising beings;[11] there are in this world no renunciants and brahmins who are faring rightly, practicing rightly, and who proclaim this world and a world beyond having realized them by their own higher knowledge."[12]....

As to these three bodily, four verbal, and three mental corrupt and harmful actions of unwholesome volition—it is due to them that with the breakup of the body, after death, beings are reborn in the plane of misery, in a bad destination, in the lower world, in hell....

There are, monks, successful actions of wholesome volition, with happy consequences, ripening in happiness: three of body, four of speech, and three of mind.

How is there a threefold successful bodily action of wholesome volition?

There is a person who abstains from killing living beings; with the rod and weapon laid aside, he is conscientious and kind and compassionate toward all living beings.

He does not take what is not given to him and does not appropriate with thievish intention the property of others, be it in the village or the forest.

He gives up sensual misconduct and abstains from it. He does not have intercourse with those under the protection of father, mother...nor with those betrothed with a garland....

And how is there a fourfold successful verbal action of wholesome volition?

There is a person who has given up false speech and abstains from it. When he is in the council of his community or in another assembly, or among his relatives, his guild, in the royal court, or has been summoned as a witness and is asked to tell what he knows, then, when he knows, he will

7. That is, these have no worth.

8. That is, how one behaves does not matter, it has no effect one one's future.

9. That is, this world is unreal, and one does not go to another world after death.

10. That is, there is no worth in respecting one's parents (those who establish one in this world).

11. That is, there are no worlds of rebirth in which certain kinds of heavenly beings come into existence without parents.

12. That is, spiritual development is not possible; people cannot come to have direct meditative knowledge of rebirth into a variety of kinds of world.

say, "I know"; and when he does not know he will say, "I do not know"; when he has seen, he will say, "I have seen"; and when he has not seen, he will say, "I have not seen." He will not utter any deliberate lie, be it for his own sake, for the sake of others, or for some material advantage.

He has given up divisive speech and abstains from it. What he has heard here he will not report elsewhere to foment conflict there; and what he has heard elsewhere he will not report here to foment conflict here. In that way he unites those who are divided and encourages those who are in harmony. Concord gladdens him, he delights and rejoices in concord, and he utters words that foster concord.

He has given up harsh speech and abstains from it. His words are gentle, pleasant to hear, endearing, heart-warming, courteous, agreeable to many folk, pleasing to many folk.

He has given up frivolous chatter and abstains from it. He speaks at the right time, in accordance with facts and of matters that are beneficial. He speaks on the Dhamma and the Discipline and talks in a way that is worth treasuring. His talk is opportune, helpful, moderate, and connected with what is beneficial....

And how is there a threefold successful mental action of wholesome volition?

Here a person is free from covetousness; he does not covet the wealth and property of others, thinking, "Oh, that what he owns might belong to me!"

He has no ill will in his heart. He has pure mental resolve: "May these beings be free from enmity, free from anxiety! May they be untroubled and live happily!"

He has right view and an unperverted way of seeing: "There is gift, there is offering... there are in this world renunciants and brahmins who are faring rightly, practicing rightly, and who proclaim this world and a world beyond having realized them by their own higher knowledge."[13]....

As to these three bodily, four verbal, and three mental successful actions of wholesome volition—it is due to them that with the breakup of the body, after death, beings are reborn in a good destination, in a heavenly world....

From the *Veḷu-dvāreyyā Sutta* (Discourse to People of the Bamboo Gate)

This passage (S. V.353–356) gives a negative version of the "golden rule"—always do unto others as you would have them do unto you—as a reason why one should not inflict harmful actions of body or speech on others: one should not inflict on others what one would not like to suffer oneself.

13. That is, the opposite of wrong view. These ten abstentions are the ten courses of right action. Formally undertaking the first four of these, plus avoiding heedlessness from alcoholic drink or drugs, constitutes the "five precepts" that are the most common code of ethical conduct for lay Buddhists.

Translation

What, householders, is the Dhamma exposition that is applicable to oneself? Here, householders, a noble disciple reflects, "I am one who wishes to live, who does not wish to die; I desire happiness and am averse to suffering. Since this is so, if someone were to take my life, that would not be pleasing and agreeable to me. Now if I were to take the life of another—of one who wishes to live, who does not wish to die, who desires happiness and is averse to suffering—that would not be pleasing and agreeable to the other either. What is displeasing and disagreeable to me is displeasing and disagreeable to the other too. How can I inflict on another what is displeasing and disagreeable to me?" Having reflected thus, he himself abstains from the killing of a living being and exhorts others to so abstain, and speaks in praise of such abstinence. Thus his bodily conduct is purified in three respects.

[Parallel passages are then given on stealing, committing adultery with someone else's wife, damaging others by lying about them, dividing people from their friends by divisive speech, addressing someone with harsh speech, and addressing someone with frivolous speech. The *Sutta* adds that someone with such pure conduct, with unshakeable confidence in the Buddha, Dhamma, and Sangha, and unbroken virtue, will be a Stream-enterer, free of any subhuman rebirths, and bound to attain enlightenment within a limited number of lives.]

From the *Bāhitika Sutta* (The Cloak Discourse)

This passage (M. II.114–115) gives a series of near equivalents for the term *akusala,* and then for *kusala. Akusala* actions are blameworthy ones, which in turn bring harm, ripen in pain, lead to the affliction of self, other, or both, and lead to more unwholesome mental states. Here, though the "ripening in pain" probably refers to future karmic results, the "harm" and "affliction" seem to mean immediate mental or physical harm. This is because the "affliction" that one person's actions may bring to other people cannot mean karmic results that come to *them:* such results come to the agent of actions, not those they act on. The reference to future unwholesome and wholesome mental states implies that unwholesome actions have a bad effect on character, weakening a person's virtues, while wholesome actions have an opposite effect.

Translation

"Now, venerable Ānanda, what kind of bodily behavior is censured by wise renunciants and brahmins?"

"Any bodily behavior that is unwholesome, great king."

"Now, venerable Ānanda, what kind of bodily behavior is unwholesome?"

"Any bodily behavior that is blameworthy, great king."

"Now, venerable Ānanda, what kind of bodily behavior is blameworthy?"

"Any bodily behavior that brings harm, great king."

"Now, venerable Ānanda, what kind of bodily behavior brings harm?"

"Any bodily behavior ripening in pain, great king."

"Now, venerable Ānanda, what kind of bodily behavior ripens in pain?"

"Any bodily behavior, great king, that leads to one's own affliction, or to the affliction of others, or to the affliction of both, and on account of which unwholesome states increase and wholesome states diminish. Such bodily behavior is censured by wise renunciants and brahmins, great king."

[The same is then applied to censured verbal and mental behavior.]

"Now, venerable Ānanda, does the Blessed One praise only the abandoning of all unwholesome states?"

"The *Tathāgata,* great king, has abandoned all unwholesome states and possesses wholesome states."

"Now, venerable Ānanda, what kind of bodily behavior is uncensored by wise renunciants and brahmins?"

"Any bodily behavior that is wholesome, great king. [And then, in response to the king's questions, he explains that wholesome actions are blameless, do not bring harm, and ripen in pleasure.] Any bodily behavior, great king, that does not lead to one's own affliction, or to the affliction of others, or to the affliction of both, and on account of which unwholesome states diminish and wholesome states increase. Such bodily behavior is uncensored by wise renunciants and brahmins, great king."

[The same is then applied to uncensored verbal and mental behavior.]

From the *Atthasālinī,* Commentary on the *Dhammasaṅgaṅī*

The *Dhammasaṅgaṇī* is the first book of the Theravādin canonical *Abhidhamma.* It gives detailed lists of states of mind, and classifies them as *kusala,* as *akusala,* or as neither (due to being purely functional states, or the results of previous *kusala* or *akusala* states). The commentary gives two explanations (Asl. pp. 38–39 and Asl. pp. 62–63) of the term *kusala.*

Translation

The word "*kusala*" means healthy, faultless/blameless, skilled, ripening in happiness. In such passages as "Is your reverence *kusala?* Is your reverence free from ailment?" *kusala* means healthy. In such passages as "Venerable sir, what bodily behavior is *kusala?* Great king, it is bodily behavior that is blameless/faultless" [see the previous excerpt from the *Bāhitika Sutta*], and again in "Venerable sir, the Blessed One's way of teaching Dhamma in regard to *kusala* states is unsurpassed" (D. III.102), *kusala* means faultless/ blameless. In such passages as "You are *kusala* at the different parts of a chariot" (M. II.94); "Graceful women who have been trained are *kusala* in singing and dancing,"[14] and so on, *kusala* means skilled. In such passages as "Monks, it is by the building up of *kusala* states [that this karmic fruitfulness[15] increases]" (D. III.58), and "from being accumulated from the doing of *kusala* actions," *kusala* means ripening in happiness. Now here, in the phrase "*kusala* states," either "healthy," or "faultless/blameless," or "ripening in happiness" is applicable....

But in regard to word-definitions: *kusala*s are so called as they cause contemptible evil things to tremble, (***ku****cchite pāpa-dhamme*) to tremble (***sala****yanti*), to shake, to be disturbed, to be destroyed....

Translation

Kusala: kusala in the sense of destroying contemptible states (***ku****cchitānaṃ* ***sala****nādīhi*), or in the sense of healthy, or in the sense of being faultless/ blameless, or in the sense of produced by skill. To illustrate: in "How are you? Are you *kusala,* sir?" *kusala* is used to mean healthy, that is, not being ill or sick or unwell in body. So in mental states it should be understood in the sense of "healthy," that is, absence of sickness, illness, or disease in the form of the defilements.[16] Moreover, from the absence of the fault of the defilements, blemish of the defilements, torment of the defilements, *kusala* has the sense of faultless/blameless. Wisdom is called skill. *Kusala* has the sense of produced by skill from being produced by skill.

From the *Dvedhā-vitakka Sutta* (The Discourse on Two Kinds of Thought)

This passage (M. I.115–116) makes clear that unwholesome thoughts, in addition to leading to reprehensible action, also obstruct liberating wisdom.

14. *Jātaka* VI.25.

15. Pali *puñña,* Skt. *puṇya:* the auspicious fortune-bringing power of good actions; often translated, somewhat misleadingly, as "merit" or "meritorious" (see Harvey 2000: 17–19).

16. The primary defilements are greed, hatred, and delusion.

Translation

Monks, before my enlightenment..., it occurred to me: "Suppose that I divide my thoughts into two classes." Then I set on one side thoughts of sensual desire, thoughts of ill will, and thoughts of cruelty; and I set on the other side thoughts of renunciation, thoughts of non–ill will, and thoughts of noncruelty.[17]

As I abided thus, diligent, ardent, and resolute, a thought of sensual desire arose in me. I understood thus: "This thought of sensual desire has arisen in me. This leads to my own affliction, to others' affliction, and to the affliction of both; it obstructs wisdom, causes difficulties, and leads away from nirvana." It subsided in me when I considered: "This leads to my own affliction," or "This leads to others' affliction," or "This leads to the affliction of both," or "This obstructs wisdom, causes difficulties, and leads away from nirvana." Whenever a thought of sensual desire arose in me, I abandoned it, removed it, did away with it.

[The same is then applied to thoughts of ill will and thoughts of cruelty.]

Monks, whatever a monk frequently thinks and ponders on, that will become the inclination of his mind....

As I abided thus, diligent, ardent, and resolute, a thought of renunciation arose in me. I understood thus: "This thought of renunciation has arisen in me. This does not lead to my own affliction, or to others' affliction, or to the affliction of both; it aids wisdom, does not cause difficulties, and leads to nirvana. If I think and ponder upon this thought even for a night, even for a day, even for a night and a day, I see nothing to fear from it. But with excessive thinking and pondering, I might tire my body; and when the body is tired, the mind becomes disturbed, and when the mind is disturbed, it is far from concentration." So I steadied my mind internally, quieted it, brought it to singleness, and concentrated it.[18] Why is that? So that my mind should not be disturbed.

[The same is then applied to thoughts of non–ill will or thoughts of noncruelty. The *sutta* continues with an account of the Buddha's practices until attaining enlightenment, and a warning against being lured into the "marsh" of sensual pleasures.]

From the *Sammā-diṭṭhi Sutta* (The Discourse on Right View)

This passage (M. I.46–47) makes clear that a key factor in determining whether an action is wholesome or unwholesome is its motivating "root,"

17. The objects of these last three "thoughts" are the same as of the three forms of "right resolve," the second factor of the Noble Eightfold Path.

18. That is, attained a *jhāna* (Pali, Skt. *dhyāna*), a lucid meditative trance, especially the second of these, in which *vitakka* and *vicāra,* related to the Pali for "thinking and pondering," are absent.

not just its effects, and not its karmic consequences. This accords with a passage that describes some actions as *themselves* "dark," as well as having "dark ripenings" (M. I.389). There is something about unwholesome actions themselves that causes unpleasant karmic results. Their having such results is a *sign* of their unwholesomeness, but not the key criterion for their being unwholesome in the first place.

Why is the moral tone of an action seen to cause certain results? It is said that wrong view leads to wrong resolve, which leads to wrong speech and to wrong action, while right view has the opposite effect (A.V.211–212). As wrong actions thus come from the misperception of reality, they can be seen to be "out of tune" with the real nature of things. Because they "go against the grain" of reality, they naturally lead to unpleasant results. Thus it is said to be impossible that wrong conduct of body, speech, or mind could produce a "ripening that was agreeable, pleasant, liked," or for right conduct to produce a "ripening that was disagreeable, unpleasant, not liked" (M. III.66).

In the following selection, the roots of wholesome action, literally nongreed, nonhatred, and nondelusion, are not just the *absence* of greed, hatred, and delusion, but states that oppose them: generosity and renunciation, loving-kindness, and wisdom and mindfulness.

Translation

When, friends, a noble disciple understands the unwholesome and the root of the unwholesome, the wholesome and the root of the wholesome, in this way he is one of right view, whose view is straight, who has perfect confidence in the Dhamma, and has arrived at this true Dhamma.

And what is the unwholesome?...Killing living beings is unwholesome; taking what is not given is unwholesome; misconduct in sensual pleasures is unwholesome; false speech is unwholesome; divisive speech is unwholesome; harsh speech is unwholesome; frivolous chatter is unwholesome; covetousness is unwholesome; ill will is unwholesome; wrong view is unwholesome. This is called the unwholesome.

And what is the root of the unwholesome? Greed (*lobho*) is a root of the unwholesome; hatred (*doso*) is a root of the unwholesome; delusion (*moho*) is a root of the unwholesome. This is called the root of the unwholesome.

And what is the wholesome? Abstention from killing living beings is wholesome;...abstention from frivolous chatter is wholesome; uncovetousness is wholesome; non–ill will is wholesome; right view is wholesome. This is called the wholesome.

And what is the root of the wholesome? Nongreed is a root of the wholesome; nonhate is a root of the wholesome; nondelusion is a root of the wholesome. This is called the root of the wholesome.

From *Aṅguttara Nikāya*, The Threes, *Sutta* 68

This passage (A. I.199–201) probes the nature of lust,[19] hatred, and delusion, and discusses what causes them and their opposites. Lust, hatred, and delusion are sustained by attention that is *ayoniso:* unwise, unsystematic, inappropriate, not focusing on the fundamental nature of its object. Elsewhere, it is said that *ayoniso* attention supports lack of mindfulness and clear comprehension, which then leads to nonguarding of the sense-faculties, which results in misconduct of body, speech, and mind. Wise attention has the opposite effect (A.V.113–116). Wise attention is something that is strengthened by the various forms of Buddhist mind-training or "meditation."

Translation

If wandering ascetics of other sects should ask you about the distinction, disparity, and difference between these three qualities (*dhammā*)—lust (*rāgo*), hatred (*doso*), and delusion (*moho*)—you should answer them thus: "Lust is blamable to a small degree but its removal is slow; hatred is blamable to a great degree but its removal is quicker; delusion is blamable to a great degree and its removal is slow."

If they ask, "Now friends, what is the cause and reason for the arising of unarisen lust [or hatred or delusion], and for the increase and strengthening of arisen lust [or hatred or delusion]?," you should reply: "... For one attending unwisely to [an object's] attractive aspect, unarisen lust will arise and arisen lust will increase and become strong.... For one attending unwisely to [an object's] aversive aspect, unarisen hatred will arise and arisen hatred will increase and become strong.... For one attending unwisely, unarisen delusion will arise and arisen delusion will increase and become strong."

If they ask, "Now friends, what is the cause and reason for the nonarising of unarisen lust [or hatred or delusion], and for abandoning of arisen lust [or hatred or delusion]?," you should reply: "... For one attending wisely to [an object's] unattractive aspect, unarisen lust will not arise and arisen lust will be abandoned.... For one attending wisely to the liberation of mind by loving-kindness, unarisen hatred will not arise and arisen hatred will be abandoned.... For one attending wisely, unarisen delusion will not arise and arisen delusion will be abandoned."

19. "Lust" (*rāga*) covers sexual lust, but also lusting after subtle meditative states. It seems equivalent to "greed."

From the *Milindapañha*

These two passages (Miln. 84 and 158–159) assert that the most reprehensible way of doing a bad action is "unknowingly." According to the first selection, "unknowingly" means an action that is performed without compunction or holding back. The second selection is a response to the apparent contradiction between the first passage and *Vinaya* passages that say that a monk cannot break a rule against killing an animal or human "unknowingly."[20] The issue hinges on what kind of "unknowing" is involved. It is not morally blameworthy (unless culpably careless) to perform an action that one does not know may bring harm to a living being and so kill it, nor does it break a monastic rule. However, to deliberately act when one knows that it is killing a sentient being, but does not know or recognize this to be an evil act, is to act in the most blameworthy way. Hence the *Milindapañha ṭīkā* explains "unknowingly" by "the nonknowing of evil" (29). This accords with the ideas that "whatever unwholesome states there are, all are rooted in spiritual ignorance" (S. II.263) and that for one of wrong view, whatever deeds "undertaken in complete accord with (that) view, whatever volitions, aspirations, resolves, activities, all those states conduce to... suffering" (A. I.31–32; see Harvey 2000: 55–57).

Translation

The King said: "Venerable Nāgasena, for whom is there a greater karmically harmful action: he who does an evil action knowingly, or he who does an evil deed unknowingly?"

The Elder said: "Great King, there is a greater karmically harmful action for one who does an evil action unknowingly.... What do you think about this, sire? If one (person) should unknowingly take hold of a red-hot ball of iron, aglow, aflame, ablaze, and another should take hold of it knowingly, which would be the more severely burnt?"

"He who took hold of it unknowingly, venerable sire, would be the more severely burnt."

"Even so, sire, there is a greater karmically harmful action for one who does an evil action unknowingly."

"You are dexterous, venerable Nāgasena."

Translation

"Sire... there is a difference in meaning here. What is this? There is, sire, a type of offense where acquittal is related to perception,[21] there is a type of

20. Vin. III. 73–78, Vin. IV. 124–125.

21. That is, one's perception of the situation one is acting in, what one's action is affecting, as at Vin. IV.124–125, on shooting an arrow that might kill a crow.

offense in which acquittal is not related to perception.[22] It was with reference to the first of these that the Blessed One said, 'There is no offense for one who does not know.'"

Bibliography and Suggested Reading

Cousins, L. S. (1996) "Good or Skilful? Kusala in Canon and Commentary." *Journal of Buddhist Ethics* 3: 136–134; www.buddhistethics.org/3/cousins1.pdf.

Harvey, Peter. (1999) "*Vinaya* Principles for Assigning Degrees of Culpability." *Journal of Buddhist Ethics* 6: 271–291; http://www.buddhistethics.org/6/harvey991.pdf

Harvey, Peter. (2000) *An Introduction to Buddhist Ethics: Foundations, Values and Issues.* Cambridge: Cambridge University Press.

Keown, Damien. (1992) *The Nature of Buddhist Ethics.* London: Macmillan.

Keown, Damien. (1995) *Buddhism and Bioethics.* London: Macmillan, and New York: St. Martin's Press.

Keown, Damien, ed. (2000) *Contemporary Buddhist Ethics.* Richmond, Surrey, England: Curzon Press.

22. Some minor monastic rules, not related to killing, can be broken even when one is not aware of what one is doing (Harvey 1999: 284–285).

33

The Bodhisattva Path

Śāntideva's *Bodhicaryāvatāra*

William Edelglass

Śāntideva (c. seventh/eighth century) taught at Nālandā, the Buddhist university near present-day Patna, India, which, with 10,000 students and an eleven-story library, was for centuries one of the world's principal institutions of higher learning. The *Bodhicaryāvatāra* (Introduction to the practice of the Bodhisattva) is said to have first been presented as a teaching by Śāntideva to his fellow monks. It is a study of the cultivation of bodhicitta, the awakened—or awakening—mind. The *Bodhicaryāvatāra* functions as a guidebook to the bodhisattva path, the path to liberation from emotional and cognitive defilements that is motivated by great compassion (*mahākaruṇā*), the altruistic aspiration to liberate all sentient beings from suffering, and facilitated by the perfection of wisdom (*prajñāpāramitā*).

The *Bodhicaryāvatāra*'s descriptions of the Mahāyāna aim of saving all beings from suffering, in contrast to the more limited scope of early Buddhist soteriology that primarily emphasized liberation of the self, quickly gained popularity among Indian monastics in Mahāyāna traditions. In Tibet, the chapter entitled "Perfection of Wisdom," with its critique of other Buddhist and non-Buddhist tenets, was widely used as a philosophy textbook. Rival schools differed in their interpretations but agreed that the *Bodhicaryāvatāra* was an authoritative exposition of what Tibetan doxographers termed Thal 'gyur ba (Prāsaṅgika) Madhyamaka, with its commitment to the use of reductio arguments against others' false views, as opposed to the independent defense of one's own view. Śāntideva's distinctive approach to ethics as a path of mental training and personal transformation through meditation and visualization, as well as action and argument, was a primary inspiration for two important forms of Buddhist literary production in Tibet: *lam rim* (stages of the path) and *blo sbyong* (mind training). Śāntideva's psychologically astute moral advice and powerful imagery were valued by both monastic and lay practitioners. Indeed, Śāntideva's broad appeal leads some contemporary scholars to argue that the *Bodhicaryāvatāra* "has been the most widely read, cited, and practiced text in the whole of the Indo-Tibetan Buddhist tradition."[1]

For Śāntideva, intention and attitude constitute the basis of moral practice. Thus, the *Bodhicaryāvatāra* begins with an account of the generation of bodhicitta, which motivates pursuing the path and provides the proper foundation for moral life. Through praise of its capacity to liberate self and others from suffering and its transformative power over aversion, attachment, and delusion—the three roots of the suffering of cyclic existence—Śāntideva seeks to inspire the reader with a desire to embark on the path of the bodhisattva. Śāntideva's praise of bodhicitta can be understood as the beginning of a traditional Mahāyāna liturgical service that constitutes the first three chapters, a service that ritualizes the vow to attain enlightenment for all sentient beings, thus strengthening the primary inspiration for the aspiring bodhisattva.

In Śāntideva's Indian Buddhist context, to take a vow entailed undertaking a set of trainings. Thus, the liturgical service leads to the practice of the perfections (*pāramitās*) of a bodhisattva. In chapter 5 Śāntideva discusses how to cultivate the perfections of generosity (*dāna*) and moral discipline (*śīla*). The following four chapters are devoted to the perfections of patience (*kṣānti*), vigor (*vīrya*), meditative absorption (*dhyāna*), and wisdom (*prajñā*), respectively. These perfections are the qualities to be achieved by the bodhisattva. The final chapter dedicates to all sentient beings the merit achieved through pursuing the path.

Śāntideva's moral thought is formulated in response to the problem of suffering. According to Śāntideva, the source of our own suffering, the suffering we cause others, and our insensibility to the suffering of others is mental affliction, especially the mistaken view that phenomena possess inherent, substantial existence. For Śāntideva, then, ethics is fundamentally concerned with mental transformation. Generosity is the first perfection because the bonds of attachment to reifying concepts of "mine," "self," "other," and "object" are loosened when making a gift. In chapter 5, Śāntideva defines the perfection of generosity, as he will define the other perfections, not as an achievement of particular ends in the world, but as a quality of mind: "the perfection is the mental attitude itself" (5:10).

Śāntideva understands moral discipline, the following of precepts or monastic rules, primarily as the control of body (*kāya*), speech (*vāc*), and mind (*manas*). For Śāntideva, then, cultivation of moral discipline is itself

1. Śāntideva 1997: 7.

the cultivation of mental discipline. Thus, his discussion of moral discipline focuses on mindfulness (*smṛti*), or the capacity to sustain focused attention, and awareness (*samprajanya*), which attends to the quality of mindfulness and enables the mind to refocus when distracted. Śāntideva argues that those who exert much effort in compassionate action, if lacking mindfulness and awareness, will still cause suffering both to themselves and to others. Mindfulness and awareness are at the heart of Śāntideva's ethics because they are necessary for realizing compassionate intentions; a distracted mind, he argues, is vulnerable to the mental defilements that cause suffering.

Because the bodhisattva path aims at alleviating the sufferings of others, Śāntideva argues, a bodhisattva is permitted to commit "even what is proscribed," if it is motivated by compassion (5:84). This is the doctrine of skillful means (*upāya kauśalya*): a skillful teacher will use appropriate means for each situation, which justifies transgressing moral codes regulating acts of body and speech when properly motivated by a compassionate mind. Śāntideva addresses skillful means in the context of his presentation of moral discipline, as if to emphasize that rules of conduct are designed to make the practitioner mindful and aware, and not conceived as unchanging laws universally determining action.

Aversion toward others erodes the compassion that motivates and orients Śāntideva's ethics of transforming the mind. Thus, he maintains in chapter 6, it is necessary to cultivate patience so that one can endure suffering, especially the hurt occasioned by other people, without anger, hatred, or resentment. If we meditate on the doctrine of dependent origination, Śāntideva argues, we will understand how mental defilements cause the acts of others. Instead of taking their actions against us personally and reacting in anger, we can respond with equanimity and compassion, taking as our goal not revenge, or even justice, but the solution of a complex human problem. Moreover, throughout his discussion of the various forms of suffering we encounter, Śāntideva emphasizes that sources of suffering are not obstructions preventing us from achieving moral perfection; rather, obstacles make possible the path to perfection, for they provide us with the necessary opportunities to realize liberation from attachment. In addition, without the experience of suffering there would be no understanding of the suffering of others, and no motivation to realize bodhicitta.

To transform the mind and make moral progress, it is necessary to pursue the perfections with strength, energetic commitment, and vigor, which is Śāntideva's theme in chapter 7.

Śāntideva consistently argues that to the degree that a mind is uncontrolled, it is susceptible to anger, frustration, craving, envy, and other mental afflictions that lead to suffering. Moral practice and the cultivation of bodhicitta, then, require mindfulness and awareness, and ultimately, the mental equanimity made possible by sustained meditative practice. Thus, in chapter 8 Śāntideva provides arguments for the necessity of securing solitude to cultivate mental equanimity, and then presents meditations to neutralize self-cherishing. For Śāntideva and many of his Tibetan commentators, the primary practices for the achievement of bodhicitta in the *Bodhicaryāvatāra* are the meditations on the equality of self and other and the exchange of self and other. Some meditations are utilized to neutralize particular defilements: meditations on loving-kindness to overcome hatred; meditations on the foulness of the body to counteract sexual desire; and so on. Śāntideva's meditations on the equality of self and other and the exchange of self and other do not address one specific defilement, but rather serve to transform the mind and enable moral practice through neutralizing self-cherishing per se.

The meditation on the equality of self and other consists in deep attention to the fact that all sentient beings experience happiness and suffering. Because all sentient beings are the same in their desire for happiness and aversion toward suffering, Śāntideva argues, there is no morally significant difference between my suffering and the suffering of others; I ought to relieve both kinds of suffering. To realize compassionate care for the suffering of others, Śāntideva suggests, I ought to regard others as myself. Regarding others as myself is not simply a change in perspective, an understanding of the needs, desires, aversions, and concerns of others: regarding others as myself is primarily the cherishing of others as I would cherish myself. This meditation, then, reorients the mind from seeking to use others as means to my ends to offering myself as a means for the satisfaction of their desires. This devotion to the needs of others, according to Śāntideva, simultaneously responds to my own deepest needs. Attachment to self causes my own suffering; desiring the benefit and working to achieve the happiness of others liberates me from suffering.

Śāntideva regards the wisdom that consists in the apprehension of emptiness—the understanding that phenomena are dependently originated and thus lack essences and ultimate, substantial existence beyond the conventional meanings ascribed to them—as a necessary condition for liberation from mental defilements. Thus, chapter 9, devoted to the perfection of wisdom, is a systematic presentation of Madhyamaka philosophy. Wisdom regarding emptiness is the culminating perfection because ignorance concerning the self and the kinds of things that can satisfy its desires, which leads to attachment and aversion, is the primary cause of all other mental afflictions. But rational argument alone cannot liberate the aspiring bodhisattva from this ignorance, for it is deeply rooted in natural need, mental habituation, and social practice. Thus, Śāntideva argues, it is necessary to meditate on emptiness, to achieve a direct perception of the lack of inherent existence of phenomena. Cultivating the direct apprehension of emptiness beyond inferential understanding is practiced in meditation, but also developed in the social perfections, such as generosity, moral discipline, and patience. The giving without recompense, outside the economy of exchange, that Śāntideva describes as the perfection of generosity, and the realization of the other social perfections require the direct apprehension of the emptiness of self and phenomena. Great compassion and the perfection of wisdom do not merely come together to constitute bodhicitta, but are each required by the other for full realization. For Śāntideva, moral development requires a complementary cultivation of the mind and the transformation of the whole person.[2]

Translation

1. Praise of the Awakening Mind

8. Those who long to transcend the hundreds of miseries of existence, who long to relieve creatures of their sorrows, who long to enjoy many hundreds of joys, must never abandon the Awakening Mind.

9. When the Awakening Mind has arisen in him, a wretch, captive in the prison of existence, he is straightaway hailed son of the Sugatas,[3] to be revered in the worlds of gods and men.

10. Taking this base image, it transmutes it into the priceless image of the Buddha-gem. Grasp tightly the quicksilver elixir, known as the Awakening Mind, which must be thoroughly worked....

15. The Awakening Mind should be understood to be of two kinds; in brief: the Mind resolved on Awakening and the Mind proceeding toward Awakening.

16. The distinction between these two should be understood by the wise in the same way as the distinction is recognized between a person who desires to go and one who is going, in that order.

17. Even in cyclic existence great fruit comes from the Mind resolved on Awakening, but nothing like the uninterrupted merit that comes from that resolve when put into action....

5. The Guarding of Awareness

1. One who wishes to guard his training must scrupulously guard his mind. It is impossible to guard one's training without guarding the wandering mind.

2. Rutting elephants running wild do not cause as much devastation in this world as the roaming elephant, the mind, let free, creates in Avīci and other hells.

3. But if the roaming elephant, the mind, is tethered on every side by the cord of mindfulness, every danger subsides, complete prosperity ensues....

2. The selections here are taken, with a few minor changes, from *The Bodhicaryāvatāra,* translated by Kate Crosby and Andrew Skilton (Oxford: Oxford University Press, 1995). We gratefully acknowledge permission to republish this work.

3. The Sanskrit "Sugata" literally means "well-gone"; it is used as an epithet of a Buddha.

9. If the perfection of generosity consists in making the universe free from poverty, how can previous Protectors have acquired it, when the world is still poor, even today?

10. The perfection of generosity is said to result from the mental attitude of relinquishing all that one has to all people, together with the fruit of that act. Therefore the perfection is the mental attitude itself.

11. Where can fish and other creatures be taken where I might not kill them? Yet when the mental attitude to cease from worldly acts is achieved, that is agreed to be the perfection of morality.

12. How many wicked people, as unending as the sky, can I kill? But when the mental attitude of anger is slain, slain is every enemy.

13. Where is there hide to cover the whole world? The wide world can be covered with hide enough for a pair of shoes alone.

14. In the same way, since I cannot control external events, I will control my own mind. What concern is it of mine whether other things are controlled?...

23. I make this salutation with my hands to those who wish to guard their mind. With all your effort, guard both mindfulness and awareness.

24. Just as a man weak with illness is not fit for any work, so a mind distracted from these two is not fit for any work.

25. What is heard, reflected upon, or cultivated in meditation, like water in a leaky jar, does not stay in the memory of a mind which lacks awareness.

26. Many, though learned, possessing faith, and absorbed in effort, are befouled by offenses due to the fault of lacking awareness....

47. When one wishes to move or to speak, first one should examine one's own mind, and then act appropriately and with self-possession.

48. When one notices that one's own mind is attracted or repelled, one should neither act nor speak, but remain like a block of wood....

51. My mind seeks acquisitions, reverence, or renown, or again wants an audience and attention. Therefore I remain like a block of wood.

52. My mind longs to hold forth, averse to the good of others, seeking my own advantage, longing only for a congregation. Therefore I remain like a block of wood....

83. Each of the perfections, beginning with generosity, is more excellent than its predecessor. One should not neglect a higher one for the sake of a lower, unless because of a fixed rule of conduct.

84. Realizing this, one should always be striving for others' well-being. Even what is proscribed is permitted for a compassionate person who sees that it will be of benefit....

99. One should apply oneself industriously to the trainings appropriate to the various situations in which one finds oneself, whether there at will, or subject to another.

100. For there is nothing from which the sons of the Conqueror cannot learn. There is nothing which is not an act of merit for the good person who conducts himself in this way....

105. The *Compendium of the Training*, the *Śikṣā Samuccaya*,[4] should definitely be looked at repeatedly, since correct conduct is explained there in some detail....

108. In brief, this alone is the definition of awareness: the observation at every moment of the state of one's body and one's mind....

6. The Perfection of Patience

1. This worship of the Sugatas, generosity, and good conduct performed throughout thousands of eons—hatred destroys it all.

2. There is no evil equal to hatred, and no spiritual practice equal to patience. Therefore one should develop patience by various means, with great effort....

14. There is nothing which remains difficult if it is practiced. So, through practice with minor discomforts, even major discomfort becomes bearable....

21. The virtue of suffering has no rival, since, from the shock it causes, intoxication falls away and there arises compassion for those in cyclic existence, fear of evil, and a longing for the Conqueror.

22. I feel no anger towards bile and the like, even though they cause intense suffering. Why am I angry with the sentient? They too have reasons for their anger.

23. As this sharp pain wells up, though unsought for, so, though unsought for, wrath wells up against one's will.

24. A person does not get angry at will, having decided "I shall get angry," nor does anger well up after deciding "I shall well up."

25. Whatever transgressions and evil deeds of various kinds there are, all arise through the power of conditioning factors, while there is nothing that arises independently.

26. Neither does the assemblage of conditioning factors have the thought, "I shall produce"; nor does what is produced have the thought, "I am produced."

27. The much-sought-for "primal matter," or the imagined "self," even that does not come into being after deciding "I shall become."

28. Since what has not arisen does not exist, who would then form the wish to come into existence? And since it would be occupied with its sphere of action it cannot attempt to cease to exist either.

29. If the Self is eternal and without processes, then it is evidently inactive, like space. Even in contact with other conditioning factors, what activity can there be of something which is unchanging?

30. What part does something play in an action if, at the time of the action, it remains exactly as it was prior to it? If the relationship is that the action is part of it, then which of the two is the cause of the other?

4. The *Śikṣā Samuccaya* is the other extant text attributed to śāntideva.

31. In this way everything is dependent upon something else. Even that thing upon which each is dependent is not independent. Since, like a magical display, phenomena do not initiate activity, at what does one get angry like this?

32. If it is argued that to resist anger is inappropriate, for "who is it that resists what?" Our view is that it is appropriate: since there is dependent origination there can be cessation of suffering.

33. Therefore, even if one sees a friend or an enemy behaving badly, one can reflect that there are specific conditioning factors that determine this, and thereby remain happy.

34. Were all embodied beings to have their wish fulfilled, no one would suffer. No one wishes for suffering.

35. People cause themselves torment, with thorns and other instruments in a state of intoxication, by refusing food and the like out of anger, and with things that they wish to obtain, such as unattainable women....

37. When, under the power of the defilements in this way, they injure even their own dear selves, how could they have a care for the persons of other people?...

39. If it is their very nature to cause others distress, my anger toward those fools is as inappropriate as it would be toward fire for its nature to burn....

41. If, disregarding the principal cause, such as a stick or other weapon, I become angry with the person who impels it, he too is impelled by hatred. It is better that I hate that hatred....

104. If one thing does not exist without another, and does exist when that also exists, then that other thing is really its cause. How can that be called an obstacle?

105. After all, a person in need who turns up at a suitable time is not a hindrance to generosity, nor can it be called a hindrance to going forth when one meets someone who has gone forth!...

107. Therefore, since he helps me on the path to awakening, I should long for an enemy like a treasure discovered in the home, acquired without effort....

7. The Perfection of Vigor

1. Patient in this way one should cultivate vigor, because awakening depends on vigor. For without vigor there is no merit, just as there is no movement without wind.

2. What is vigor? The endeavor to do what is skillful. What is its antithesis called? Sloth, clinging to what is vile, despondency, and self-contempt.

3. Sloth comes from idleness, indulging in pleasures, sleep, the longing to lean on others, and from apathy for the sufferings of cyclic existence....

14. Now that you have met with the boat of human life, cross over the mighty river of suffering. Fool, there is no time to sleep! It is hard to catch this boat again.

15. How can you, after letting go of the most splendid delight, the Dharma, which is an unending stream of joy, find joy in a cause of suffering such as arrogance or ridicule?...

18. "Even those who were gnats, mosquitoes, wasps, or worms, have reached the highest awakening, hard to reach, through the strength of their exertion."

19. How about me, born a human being, able to know good from bad? If I do not forsake the guidance of the Omniscient, why should I not attain Buddhahood?...

22. This limited suffering of mine, the means to perfect Buddhahood, is like the pain of extraction when getting rid of the agony of an embedded thorn.

23. All doctors use painful treatments to restore health. It follows that to put an end to many sufferings, a slight one must be endured.

24. Though such treatment is appropriate, it is not what the best doctor prescribed: he cures by sweet conduct those with the greatest illness....

32. Uprooting the opposite in this way, one should endeavor to increase one's exertion through the powers of desire, pride, delight, renunciation, dedication, and self-mastery....

40. The Sage has sung that desire is the root of all skillful deeds; in turn, the root of that is ever meditation on the resulting consequences....

49. One should strive for pride in three areas: action, the secondary defilements, and ability. "It is I alone who can do it" expresses pride in action....

53. When one is made passive by defeatism, without doubt difficulties easily take effect, but exerting one's self and invigorated, one is hard to defeat even for great calamities....

66. But when one's energy begins to flag, one should put it aside to take up again, and, when it is completely finished, one should let it go with a thirst for the next and then the next....

8. The Perfection of Meditative Absorption

1. Increasing one's endeavor in this way, one should stabilize the mind in meditative concentration, since a person whose mind is distracted stands between the fangs of the defilements.

2. Distraction does not occur if the body and mind are kept sequestered. Therefore, one should renounce the world and disregard distracting thoughts....

12. Superiority causes jealousy. Equality causes rivalry. Inferiority causes arrogance. Praise causes intoxication and criticism causes enmity. When could there be any benefit from a fool?

13. Between one fool and another something detrimental is inevitable, such as self-advancement, complaining about others, or conversation about the pleasures of cyclic existence.

14. So in this way contact with a fool brings harm to the other person too. I shall live apart, happily, my mind undefiled....

85. Thus one should recoil from sensual desires and cultivate delight in solitude, in tranquil woodlands empty of contention and strife.

86. On delightful rock surfaces cooled by the sandal balm of the moon's rays, stretching wide as palaces, the fortunate pace, fanned by the silent, gentle forest breezes, as they contemplate for the well-being of others. [...]

89. By developing the virtues of solitude in such forms as these, distracted thoughts being calmed, one should now develop the Awakening Mind.

90. At first one should meditate intently on the equality of oneself and others as follows: "All equally experience suffering and happiness. I should look after them as I do myself."

91. Just as the body, with its many parts from division into hands and other limbs, should be protected as a single entity, so too should this entire world, which is divided, but undivided in its nature to suffer and be happy.

92. Even though suffering in me does not cause distress in the bodies of others, I should nevertheless find their suffering intolerable because of the affection I have for myself....

94. I should dispel the suffering of others because it is suffering like my own suffering. I should help others too because of their nature as beings, which is like my own being.

95. When happiness is liked by me and others equally, what is so special about me that I strive after happiness only for myself?

96. When fear and suffering are disliked by me and others equally, what is so special about me that I protect myself and not the other?

97. If I give them no protection because their suffering does not afflict me, why do I protect my body against future suffering when it does not afflict me?

98. The notion "it is the same me even then" is a false construction, since it is one person who dies, quite another who is born.

99. If you think that it is for the person who has the pain to guard against it, a pain in the foot is not of the hand, so why is the one protected by the other?

100. If you argue that even though this conduct is inappropriate, it proceeds from the sense of self-identity, [our response is that] one should avoid what is inappropriate in respect of self and others as far as one can.

101. The continuum of consciousnesses, like a queue, and the combination of constituents, like an army, are not real. The person who experiences suffering does not exist. To whom will that suffering belong?

102. Without exception, no sufferings belong to anyone. They must be warded off simply because they are suffering. Why is any limitation put on this?

103. If one asks why suffering should be prevented, no one disputes that! If it must be prevented, then all of it must be. If not, then this goes for oneself as for everyone.

104. You may argue: compassion causes us so much suffering, why force it to arise? Yet when one sees how much the world suffers, how can this suffering from compassion be considered great?

105. If the suffering of one ends the suffering of many, then one who has compassion for others and himself must cause that suffering to arise....

107. Those who have developed the continuum of their mind in this way, to whom the suffering of others is as important as the things they themselves hold dear, plunge down into the Avīci hell as geese into a cluster of lotus blossoms.

108. Those who become oceans of sympathetic joy when living beings are released, surely it is they who achieve fulfillment. What would be the point in a liberation without sweetness?...

110. Therefore, just as I protect myself to the last against criticism, let me develop in this way an attitude of protectiveness and of generosity toward others as well....

115. In the same way that, with practice, the idea of a self arose toward this, one's own body, though it is without a self, with practice will not the same idea of a self develop toward others too?...

117. Therefore, in the same way that one desires to protect oneself from affliction, grief, and the like, so an attitude of protectiveness and of compassion should be practiced toward the world....

120. Whoever longs to rescue quickly both himself and others should practice the supreme mystery: exchange of self and other.

121. If even slight danger causes fear because of overfondness for oneself, who would not detest that self like a fear-inspiring enemy?...

124. What wise person would want such a self, protect it, worship it, and not see it as an enemy? Who would treat it with regard?...

129. All those who suffer in the world do so because of their desire for their own happiness. All those happy in the world are so because of their desire for the happiness of others.

130. Why say more? Observe this distinction: between the fool who longs for his own advantage and the sage who acts for the advantage of others....

135. If one does not let go of self one cannot let go of suffering, as one who does not let go of fire cannot let go of burning.

136. Therefore, in order to allay my own suffering and to allay the suffering of others, I devote my self to others and accept them as myself....

9. The Perfection of Understanding

1. It is for the sake of understanding that the Sage taught this entire collection of preparations. Therefore, in the desire to put an end to suffering, one should develop understanding....

52. Remaining in cyclic existence for the benefit of those suffering through delusion is achieved through freedom from the two extremes, attachment and fear. This is the fruit of emptiness....

10. Dedication

1. By the good that is mine from considering *Undertaking the Way to Awakening*, the *Bodhicaryāvatāra*, may all people adorn the path to awakening.

2. Through my merit may all those in any of the directions suffering distress in body or mind find oceans of happiness and delight....

54. May my own conduct emulate that of Mañjuśrī,[5] who works to achieve the welfare of all living beings throughout the ten directions of space.

55. As long as space abides and as long as the world abides, so long may I abide, destroying the sufferings of the world.

56. Whatever suffering is in store for the world, may it all ripen in me. May the world find happiness through all the pure deeds of the Bodhisattvas....

Bibliography and Suggested Reading

Batchelor, Stephen, trans. (1979) *A Guide to the Bodhisattva's Way of Life.* Dharamsala: Library of Tibetan Works and Archives.

Bendall, Cecil and W. H. D. Rouse, trans. (1990) *Śikṣā Samuccaya.* Reprint. Delhi: Motilal Banarsidass.

Brassard, Francis. (2000) *The Concept of Bodhicitta in Śāntideva's "Bodhicaryāvatāra."* Albany: State University of New York Press.

Clayton, Barbra. (2006) *Moral Theory in Śāntideva's "Śikṣāsamuccaya": Cultivating the Fruits of Virtue.* London: Routledge.

Crosby, Kate and Andrew Skilton, trans. (1995) *Śāntideva: The Bodhicaryāvatāra.* Oxford: Oxford University Press.

Edelglass, William. (2007) "Ethics and the Subversion of Conceptual Reification in Levinas and Śāntideva." In Youru Wang, ed., *Deconstruction and the Ethical in Asian Thought.* New York: Routledge, pp. 151–161.

Gyatso, Tenzin. (1988) *Transcendent Wisdom: A Teaching on the Wisdom Section of Shantideva's "Guide to the Bodhisattva Way of Life."* Translated by B. Alan Wallace. Ithaca, N.Y.: Snow Lion.

Gyatso, Tenzin. (1994) *A Flash of Lightning in the Dark of Night: A Guide to the "Bodhisattva's Way of Life."* Translated by Padmakara Translation Group. Boston: Shambhala.

Mrozik, Susanne. (2007) *Virtuous Bodies: The Physical Dimensions of Morality in Buddhist Ethics.* New York: Oxford University Press.

Śāntideva. (1997) *The Way of the Bodhisattva.* Translated by Padmakara Translation Group. Boston: Shambhala.

Sweet, Michael. (1976) "Śāntideva and the Mādhyamika: The Prajñāpāramitā-Parichheda of the Bodhicaryāvatāra." Ph.D. diss., University of Wisconsin.

Wallace, Vesna A. and Wallace, B. Alan, trans. (1997) *A Guide to the Bodhisattva Way of Life by Śāntideva.* Ithaca: Snow Lion Publications.

Williams, Paul. (1998) *Altruism and Reality: Studies in the Philosophy of the Bodhicaryāvatāra.* Richmond, Surrey, England: Curzon Press.

5. Mañjuśrī is the bodhisattva of wisdom.

34

Asaṅga's *Bodhisattvabhūmi*

The Morality Chapter

Gareth Sparham

The morality chapter (*Śīla-patala)* of the *Bodhisattvabhūmi* (The bodhisattva stages) is the locus classicus for an explanation of bodhisattva morality and vows. Asaṅga (fourth century C.E.), who is credited with founding the Cittamātra, or Mind Only school, is regarded as the probable author of the *Bodhisattvabhūmi*. Here, he discusses morality under nine headings, of which two—"What Morality Is" and "Morality in Its Entirety"—are the most important.

Śīla, translated here as "morality," denotes much of what is understood as morality in the Western sense, and more besides. It includes all activity brought in under words like *śikṣā* or *śikṣāpada* (a bodhisattva's training) and *caryā* (a bodhisattva's deeds or activities). Personal propriety is at the core of *śīla* and, particularly in Buddhist Tantra, the observance of one's commitments (*samaya*). This notion of propriety is central to Buddhist ethics, in both non-Mahāyāna and Mahāyāna schools. For the maintenance of propriety conduces to liberation, and makes one a respectable guide for others to follow; failure of propriety leads to further attachment and aversion, and makes one unsuitable as a teacher. Asaṅga uses the compound *svabhāvaśīla* to convey the idea of what bodhisattva morality actually is. His explanation emphasizes that morality is a positive contribution the agent makes to society.

Propriety requires a psychologically efficacious moral standard. This standard derives from taking others one admires as ideals. It involves the restraining or activating mental force (*caiita*) of *vyapatrāpya* (Tib. *khrel yod*) that operates when one experiences something like embarrassment or "dread of blame." The social ritual of ordination, according to Asaṅga (*parataḥ samādāna*), is the necessary condition for cultivating such a mental force. This is because ordination and the attendant vows one takes involve being accepted by, and entering into association with, those whose ideals one admires, and a public commitment to emulating them. The restraining or activating mental force called *hrī* (Tib. *ngo tshar*) is in operation when one experiences shame. Shame requires that the moral standard is taken as one's own. Together with embarrassment, it prevents bodhisattvas from failing to live up to their purest aspiration (*suviśudhāśaya*). For Asaṅga, and anyone committed to the bodhisattva path, this is the altruistic aspiration that is *bodhicitta* ("the thought of enlightenment" or "the awakened mind").

The operation of these moral emotions does not by itself explain all aspects of a morality grounded in taking a vow. Maintaining moral propriety requires not only the possibility of shame or embarrassment but also the constant impulse to "make correction" (*pratyāpatti*) after failure. Additionally, it requires an admiration (*ādara*) for the moral self to which one aspires, accompanied by mindfulness (*smṛti*) of one's actions and vows that enables one to avoid transgression. Both admiration and mindfulness are equally conceived as restraining or activating mental forces and the complex of these mental forces enables moral propriety.

Having defined morality, Asaṅga seeks to explain it in its entirety (*sarvaśīla*) under three categories: *saṁvaraśīla, kuśaladharmasaṁgrāhakaśīla,* and *sattvārthakriyāśīla,* which Tatz (1986) renders "ethics of the vow," "ethics of collecting wholesome factors," and "ethics of benefiting sentient beings."

Within the larger context of the *Bodhisattvabhūmi,* the morality chapter details the second of six "perfections" (*pāramitā*) that characterize the bodhisattva—along with the perfections of generosity, patience, effort, meditation, and wisdom. *Śīla* and the other perfections are not independent of one another, but together constitute interdependent facets of a bodhisattva's way of life (*caryā*). Each is not a separate field or discipline, but taken together they are the threads that make up a Bodhisattva's armor (*saṁnāha*). The *Bodhisattvabhūmi*'s presentation of the six perfections in general, and of the perfection of morality in particular, makes it clear that the altruistic moral project is pursued, in the first instance, mainly by attending to personal discipline and cultivation, not directly through "social engagement." Furthermore, "social engagement" is not separate from attending to personal discipline, but is integrated with it. Altruistic, socially responsible, and beneficial behavior, in this system, is the necessary consequence of—but not the direct object of—efforts to discipline and to cultivate oneself, in contrast to an extreme, outward-looking social morality of engaging with others that devalues the cultivation of personal well-being as irrelevant to the moral project.

The Mahāyāna *sūtras* articulate the new altruistic principle (*bodhicitta*) in long, nonsystematic narratives. Asaṅga privileges these *sūtras* as statements of the Buddha (*buddha-vacana*). For Asaṅga, the historically later Mahāyāna *sūtras* complement and legitimize the earlier core Buddhist literature, including the codifications of morality in the Vinaya. Asaṅga's emphasis on continuity from the early monastic code to the Mahāyāna *sūtras* makes sense of the first subcategory under which the morality chapter presents morality in its entirety—*saṁvaraśīla,* Tatz's "ethics of the vow." It is, essentially, an unchanged presentation of the morality contained in the earlier codifications of conduct for the community (sangha) (the monks and nuns, and the male and female householders).

Tsong kha pa (1356–1419), in his *Byang chub gzhung lam* (Basic path to awakening) (Ka. 9a5–6), a commentary on the morality chapter, explains that Asaṅga sets forth the "ethics of the vow" first because practitioners must first govern or restrain themselves (hence *saṁvara,* Tib. *sdom pa,* "vow, code, restraint") before they can engage in the behavior codified in the other two moralities. The "ethics of the vow," then, is a vowed morality codified in a set of rules or laws that govern personal behavior, particularly restraint of the senses, the inner discipline restraining the noble person from unbridled, shameless gratification of the senses in the world of sense desire (*kāma-dhātu*). In theory, at least, community members join the community, follow the rules, and develop restraint because of the personal and social benefit they see in it. There are strictures placed on individuals in the community by the larger community itself, but the recurring theme is the theme of personal restraint. In this sense, the morality is a yogic morality of self-cultivation in contrast to a social morality of engaging with others.

For this reason, Asaṅga begins the morality chapter with a definition of morality as "received from others" (*paropādā*); he has in mind an actual vow-taking ceremony that turns a noble intention into a formal commitment. This formal commitment is then given muscle by the "sense of shame" and "embarrassment." When these are present, an unbroken line of vowed commitment—a morality—comes into being. Hence, all three moralities are equally vowed moralities, not just pious aspirations.

In the *Bodhisattvabhūmi,* the moral codes that earlier Buddhism first formulated as personal disciplines to govern unbridled passions and lead practitioners from mental affliction to balanced composure are reenvisioned as part of a larger, altruistic moral project necessitated by the aspiration to attain awakening for the benefit of all sentient beings. In practice, this project depends on the particular context and practitioner.

According to Khedrupjey (mKhas grub rje, 1385–1438), monks not keeping Mahāyāna morality do not break a vow, that is, are not immoral when they eat meat, even though the same monks, keeping Mahāyāna morality, would be. Non-Mahāyāna monks who eat meat are no more or less pure keepers of their moral code than monks who eat the vegetables put in their begging bowl. Were they to eat food after noon, however, contrary to their vow, they would break a rule. On the other hand, a Mahāyāna monk who refuses food given in the afternoon by a faithful donor, because it is a *Prātimokṣa* rule,[1] breaks the Mahāyāna code, even though a non-Mahāyāna monk does not do so.[2] The point here is that propriety is particular to individual roles, institutional requirements, and context.

This presentation of morality presupposes a hierarchy of religious persons. Those with a higher "status" must maintain a higher standard of personal propriety. They incur a greater fault for moral shortcomings than do ordinary people, in part because they have committed themselves to more, and in part because they are models. Propriety is not universal in this system.

The "ethics of collecting wholesome factors" consists in the development of wholesome factors or qualities (dharmas) that make up a perfect Buddha. These Buddhadharmas include both physical (primarily, but not only, speech) and mental qualities. The physical qualities are those that enable one to benefit others, especially through teaching. The mental qualities are, similarly, infinite knowledge, kindness, and skill in means. All are a means to achieve the welfare of beings, to liberate sentient beings from suffering.

One might think that there is a value in cultivating patience, one of the wholesome qualities of a Buddha, even if it is impossible to attain a Buddha's perfection of patience.[3] Though this is plausible, it avoids a deeper problem—the vanity of the endeavor to become a better person—that troubled Indian thinkers who sought to give a central role to altruism in their philosophy.

Asaṅga directly addresses this problem at the very start of the *Bodhisattvabhūmi* (Dutt 1966: 2).

> Question: What is lineage (*gotra*)? [Response]: In brief, it is twofold: naturally abiding (*prakṛtistha*) and fully developed (*samudānīta*). Of these, the naturally abiding lineage is the specialness of the six sense fields (*āyatana*) of bodhisattvas. It is obtained through the true nature of dharmas (*dharmatā*) and comes down, one from the other, from time without

1. Prātimokṣa (Pāli: Pātimokkha) is the basic codification of Buddhist monastic discipline recited during the Buddhist bimonthly confession and restoration ritual (*upoṣadha*, Pali *uposatha*).

2. The Prātimokṣa code, intended to discipline unbridled gratification of the senses, generally allows monks and nuns to eat any food (including meat) they are offered, but prohibits keeping food overnight, and prohibits eating again after taking a midday meal. The bodhisattva code, intended to foster behavior that puts the welfare of others first, includes those rules. But it also includes a rule that prohibits a monk from not eating again after taking a midday meal if the person who offers has faith, and will benefit from listening to the Mahāyāna doctrine. It implicitly prohibits a bodhisattva from eating meat because a person who puts the welfare of others first would not eat their flesh.

3. This is the unstated, pragmatic position frequently taken in Western presentations of Buddhism as the doctrine of an ordinary man teaching a realistic goal of mental equanimity that can be reached in this very life.

beginning in an unbroken succession. [Bodhisattvas] obtain the fully developed lineage from having earlier cultivated wholesome roots.

As a continuum of psychophysical processes, each person, according to Asaṅga, is the locus for the development of wholesome qualities through cultivation. The final nature of the altruistic person as a location for the development of Buddhadharmas, though empty of a soul, is a reality. The nature of this reality is conveyed by terms such as *dharmatā* ("true nature of the qualities") or *pratītya-samutpāda* ("dependent origination"), words that convey the power and activity in the buildup of chains of events that validates the attempt to cultivate mental qualities that cannot be achieved in one single life. For this reason, the mere aspiration to remain an ordinary person who is just a bit more patient lacks sufficient efficacy. *Bodhicitta,* the basis of morality, requires the aspiration for Buddhahood.

The third category of morality is the "ethics of benefiting sentient beings": giving to the poor, feeding the hungry, protecting the helpless, seeking social justice through political activity, and so on. Asaṅga claims this social morality is for the purpose of "maturing beings." It codifies ordinary altruism, and reflects the insight that altruistic behavior is not restricted to endeavors of altruistic persons to cultivate themselves, but necessarily includes simply doing for others what they want, just because they want it, with the thought that at the least they may thereby become receptive to considering basic morality that will effect lasting transformation. "The ethics of benefiting sentient beings," though most directly engaged with singular others, is only one category of altruistic morality, and should not be conceived as the exclusive codification of altruistic acts. For Asaṅga, the three categories of ethics together describe an altruistic morality in its entirety.

During the spread of Buddhist Tantra under the late Pāla Dynasty (flourished c. 800–1150) in northeastern India, the morality chapter's three categories for describing Mahāyāna morality in its entirety give way to three different, but overlapping categories—Prātimokṣa, Bodhisattva, and Tantric morality. The first is the basic Buddhist morality shared by non-Mahāyāna and Mahāyāna Buddhists, the second the morality codified in the morality chapter, and the third a morality codified as the pledges of the five Buddha families.[4] The *Sdom gsum* (Three Codes) genre of Tibetan polemical

4. An ordinary (selfless) person defined by, or located by, five *skandhas* ("heaps") transforms into the perfected state of a transcendental (selfless) Buddha defined by, or located by, five Family Buddhas. The unusual language of Tantra, wherein one Buddha has Buddhas with other names for its *skandhas,* or component parts, is based on the notion of an ultimate principle that informs diverse aspects. Selflessness or emptiness is the ultimate principle, but understood as nondual with the knowledge that knows it. In this way of thinking the five Family Buddhas are names for different aspects of knowledge (*jñāna*) that is itself the primary Buddha. Thus the morality of any one Family Buddha is the morality of any other, and all the moralities taken together are the morality of the one primary Buddha at the center of, i.e. pervading, the *maṇḍala.*

philosophical writing (Rhoton 2002; Sobisch 2002) is based on an exposition of these three moral codes.[5]

Translation

[*The definition of morality.*] What is the morality of bodhisattvas? You should know this has nine aspects: what morality essentially is, morality in its entirety, morality that is difficult, morality from all perspectives, morality of a holy person, morality in all its aspects, morality that brings well-being here and there [in the future], and pure morality.[6]

What essentially is [a bodhisattva's] morality? In brief, you should know that bodhisattvas are moral when they have four qualities. What four? [They are moral] when they correctly receive [the ordination] from others, when they have a pure aspiration, when they make corrections after transgressing, and when, in order not to transgress, they have a feeling of admiration and remain mindful.

Among these, because a bodhisattva has received the morality from somebody else, he feels a sense of other-oriented embarrassment when he fails in training. Because the bodhisattva has a pure aspiration to be moral, he feels a sense of self-oriented shame when he fails in training. By making corrections after transgressing, and because he has a feeling of admiration that stops failure from happening in the first place, the bodhisattva becomes free from regrets in two ways. Thus, because of correctly receiving [the morality] and because of having a pure aspiration this bodhisattva feels a sense of embarrassment and shame; with a sense of embarrassment and shame he keeps the morality he has received; and by keeping it is free from regret.

Among these, two dharmas, namely, receiving [the ordination] correctly and pure aspiration, cause these two dharmas—correction after transgression and admiration that avoids transgression. You should know that these three dharmas—namely, receiving the ordination correctly, pure aspiration, and the admiration that avoids transgression—stop a bodhisattva from being immoral. You should know that correction after transgression rectifies and sets up again [morality] that has been broken. You should also know that the actual morality of bodhisattvas who have these four qualities is wholesome because it is personally beneficial, is beneficial to others, gives benefit to

5. For a complete translation see Tatz 1986. There are two readily available Sanskrit editions of the *Bodhisattvabhūmi* (Dutt 1966; Wogihara 1973). Tatz 1986 generally follows a slightly different original that is the basis of the Tibetan translation. Sparham 2005 is an early fifteenth-century presentation of systematic Tantric morality in the Three Code genre that strongly privileges the older Mahāyāna morality of the morality chapter.

6. Under the first aspect or topic Asaṅga defines morality. The remaining topics are all little more than different names for "morality in its entirety" that Asaṅga presents in terms of the three basic parts of the bodhisattva moral code.

many people, gives pleasure to many people, brings about compassion for the world, and is for the welfare, benefit, and pleasure of gods and humans. You should know it is immeasurable [morality] because it incorporates the immeasurable bases on which bodhisattvas have to train. You should know it is altruism because it is set up for the good and pleasure of all beings. And you should know it has a great result and benefit because it assists and bestows the result of highest enlightenment.

[*Morality in its entirety.*] Among these, what is a Bodhisattva's morality in its entirety? In brief, they say the morality of a bodhisattva in its entirety is systematized as the morality of the householder and the morality of one gone forth to homelessness. Furthermore, that morality based on the householder and one gone forth to homelessness is, in brief, threefold: it is vowed morality, morality that gathers the wholesome dharmas, and morality that accomplishes the welfare of beings.

Among these, what is a Bodhisattva's vowed morality? It is the morality of any one of the seven sets of *Prātimokṣa* vows that a monk, nun, nun in training, male novice, female novice, layman, and laywoman take. You should understand this [morality] from the perspective of the householder and the one gone forth to homelessness as appropriate.

In brief, they say the morality that gathers the wholesome dharmas is whatever wholesome thing a bodhisattva accumulates for great enlightenment with his body, speech, and mind after he has received the vowed morality. And what is that? Here the bodhisattva who has resorted to morality and maintains morality applies himself to listening, to thinking, to the calm abiding and insight meditation, and similarly, from time to time addresses his gurus with respect, bows, and stands before them with the palms of his hands pressed together in supplication....

Among these, what is a bodhisattva's morality as it pertains to looking after beings? In brief, you should know it in eleven ways. What are the eleven? He befriends beings to look after their needs; he befriends beings when they have fallen sick and suffer from any illness; similarly, he demonstrates Dharma for ordinary and extraordinary goals, and with skillful means and advice about practice, gives appropriate advice; he shows gratitude to beings who have looked after him and gives fitting assistance in return; he protects beings from sundry fearful things such as lions and tigers, kings and robbers, water and fire, and so on; he assuages sorrow when calamities happen to belongings and relatives; he provides to those in need all that they need....

These three heaps of bodhisattva morality—the heap of merit systematized in vowed morality, the heap of merit systematized in the morality that gathers wholesome dharmas, and the heap of merit systematized in the morality that accomplishes the welfare of beings—are immeasurable heaps of merit.

[*The ordination ritual.*] A bodhisattva who prays for complete enlightenment, whether a householder or one who has gone forth to homelessness, who wants to train in the bodhisattva training that is this threefold heap of merit, should bow at the feet of a bodhisattva who shares the same Dharma. This is one who prays for enlightenment and is the sort who, having understood the meaning of the verbal ordination ceremony [from having taken it earlier], knows and is able to keep the vows. Having done so, he should make the following request: "I want to receive in your presence, son of a good family, the code of a bodhisattva's morality. If you are agreeable to this and it does not inconvenience you, please grant this out of pity, and listen to me for a moment." Having made the proper request, and [in the presence of] the single member of the highest sangha who constitutes [the necessary quorum], he brings in the past, future, and present Lord Buddhas in all the ten directions, as well as bodhisattvas who have entered into the great levels and have obtained great knowledge and dignity. He brings to mind their great qualities and produces a heartfelt, confident faith in his mind, a faith in what his ability and causal power make possible.

A bodhisattva who knows [the ritual] sets up an image of the Tathāgata, worships properly, and in front of it, either kneeling down or squatting, [the supplicant] should say: "Son of good family," or "Venerable," or "Sir, please bestow on me the code of the Bodhisattva's morality." Then he should bring awareness to a single-pointed focus and should cultivate a feeling of complete confident faith in his mind, thinking: Now I will soon get the inexhaustible, immeasurable, incomparable [moral code that is] a treasury of great merit. Thinking thus he should remain silent.

The bodhisattva who already knows [the ritual], either standing or sitting and with an unwavering mind, should say to the bodhisattva candidate: "Listen, son of a good family," or "Dharma brother called so-and-so, do you pray for enlightenment?" He should say "Yes." After that he should say to him: "Son of a good family called so-and-so, do you want to take from me all the bodhisattva grounds of training and all the bodhisattva morality—the vowed morality, the morality that gathers wholesome dharmas, and the morality that accomplishes the welfare of beings?"... He should reply that he wants to take them. The bodhisattva who already knows [the ritual] should say this a second and a third time, and the bodhisattva who is taking the ordination should reply in the affirmative all three times.

...All of the morality I have described in these nine ways, beginning with what morality essentially is, you should know to be systematized in the three moralities of vowed morality, morality that gathers the wholesome dharmas, and morality that accomplishes the welfare of beings. Furthermore, in brief, this threefold morality effects the three things that are necessary for a bodhisattva: vowed morality keeps the mind stable, morality that gathers the wholesome dharmas brings [the bodhisattva's] own Buddhadharmas to maturity, and morality that accomplishes the welfare of beings brings beings to maturity. Just these are all that a bodhisattva has to do to have a stable mind in order to live at ease in the here and now, and without physical or mental fatigue to bring the Buddhadharmas and beings to maturity. Just this is the morality of a bodhisattva. Just this is the benefit of the morality of a bodhisattva. Just this is what a bodhisattva has to do to be moral, there is nothing beyond or more than this. Past bodhisattvas who wanted great enlightenment trained in this, those in the future will also train in this, and now those on the bodhisattva path in the endless and infinite world spheres in the ten directions are training in it as well.

Bibliography and Suggested Reading

Dutt, Nalinaksha, ed. (1966) *Bodhisattvabhūmi.* Tibetan Sanskrit Works Series, 7. Patna: K. P. Jayaswal Research Institute.

Gombrich, R. F. (1998) "Organized Bodhisattvas: A Blind Alley in Buddhist Historiography." In Paul Harrison and Gregory Schopen, eds., *Sūryacandrāya: Essays in Honour of Akira Yuyama on the Occasion of His 65th Birthday.* Swisttal-Odendorf: Indica et Tibetica Verlag, pp. 45–56.

Sakya Pandita Kunga Gyaltshen. (2002) *A Clear Differentiation of the Three Codes: Essential Distinctions among the Individual Liberation, Great Vehicle, and Tantric Systems.* Translated by Jared Rhoton. Albany: State University of New York Press.

Sobisch, Jan-Ulrich. (2002) *Three-Vow Theories in Tibetan Buddhism.* Wiesbaden: Ludwig Reichert.

Sparham, Gareth. (2005) *Tantric Ethics.* Boston: Wisdom.

Tatz, Mark. (1982) *Candragomin's Twenty Verses on the Bodhisattva Vow and its Commentary.* Dharamsala: Library of Tibetan Works and Archives.

Tatz, Mark. (1985) *Difficult Beginnings: Three Works on the Bodhisattva Path [by] Candragomin.* Boston: Shambhala Press.

Tatz, Mark. (1986) *Asaṅga's Chapter on Ethics, with the Commentary of Tsong-Kha-pa: The Basic Path to Awakening, the Complete Bodhisattva.* Lewiston, ME: Edwin Mellen Press.

Wogihara, Unrai, ed. (1973) *Bodhisattvabhūmi.* Tokyo: Toyo Bunko, 1932; Reprint, Tokyo: Sankibo Buddhist Book Store.

35

Essentials on Observing and Violating the Fundamentals of Bodhisattva Precepts

Wŏnhyo's Nonsubstantial Mahāyāna Ethics

Jin Y. Park

Making distinctions to create ethical categories and judging human actions based on these categories are generally thought to be major functions of ethics. Understood in this manner, ethics could be at odds with the commitment of Mahāyāna Buddhist traditions to the nonsubstantial nature of entities. To create precepts means to generate ethical categories. However, if entities are empty, precepts as well as the idea of observing precepts can contradict the basic position of Mahāyāna Buddhism.

In the *Essentials on Observing and Violating the Fundamentals of Bodhisattva Precepts* (Posal kyebon chibŏm yo'gi), an excerpt of which is translated here, the Korean monk-thinker Wŏnhyo (617–686) addresses the different layers involved in understanding bodhisattva precepts and their observation and violation. In this work, Wŏnhyo discusses the three categories of observing and violating bodhisattva precepts: first, major and minor offenses; second, the profound and shallow understandings of observing and violating precepts; and third, the ultimate way of observing and violating them. In discussing bodhisattva precepts on these three levels, Wŏnhyo emphasizes the complexity involved in interpreting precepts. He does not merely identify precepts, or only focus on the importance of observing them. Instead, Wŏnhyo discusses the contexts in which the observation of precepts and the bodhisattva's actions take place and demonstrates the multifaceted nature of human activities and the ambiguity of ethical categories and judgments. The ideal of bodhisattva ethics for Wŏnhyo lies in understanding one core of Buddhist teaching: emptiness of entities. Ethical standards created through bodhisattva precepts cannot be an exception from the fact that things do not have self-nature. By underscoring the true nature of precepts as empty, Wŏnhyo demonstrates the provisionality as well as the vulnerability of the border lines that define ethical categories.

Wŏnhyo begins the *Essentials* by bringing the reader's attention to the problems of employing binary opposites in the construction of ethical codes. Distinguishing right and wrong is one basis of ethical behavior according to conventional wisdom. In Buddhism, moreover, knowing right from wrong and thereby creating good karma that results in pleasant rewards is the basis of Buddhist codes of behavior. Wŏnhyo, however, says that to distinguish right and wrong is easy whereas to consider their real impact is not. With the examples he provides of multiple contexts and the complexities of human existence, Wŏnhyo argues that no fixed rules can ground the ethics of the bodhisattva. For example, one can learn the Buddhist precept to abstain from killing, and thus know that killing is wrong. However, when the action of taking lives takes place in various situations in life and thus is contextualized, the precept against killing, as well as every other precept, is subject to multilayered hermeneutical analysis.

In the section on the shallow and profound understandings of precepts, Wŏnhyo discusses the ambiguity of ethical judgment in the context of real life by employing the "four cases" as examples. The first major precept, praising oneself and disparaging others, does not offer an absolute ethical standard as it is. Judgment of an action as either meritorious behavior or offense of this precept is based not just on linguistic expression of the precept but also on the context in which it takes place, as well as the agent's intention for that action. In this manner, Wŏnhyo understands precepts as neutral statements that do not have their own intrinsic value.

In the final section, on the ultimate way of observing and violating precepts, Wŏnhyo establishes a philosophical ground for his discussions in the previous two sections, envisioning a nonsubstantial ethics of Mahāyāna Buddhism as opposed to a rule-bound ethics. For Wŏnhyo, bodhisattva precepts are not merely rules and regulations that maintain order and train practitioners. Instead, realizing and accepting bodhisattva precepts themselves make up the embodiment of Mahāyāna Buddhism in its entirety. Ethical awakening encompasses the ontological status of being as understood in Mahāyāna Buddhism. Conventionally, violation of a precept stands in opposition to its observation. Recovery from this commitment of violation generally takes the steps of realization of one's fault, acceptance of appropriate measures to compensate the violation, and resolution for a firm observation of the precept to avoid further offenses. Wŏnhyo warns against such an understanding of precepts, because a mere acceptance of one's offense and accompanying repentance, followed by renewed efforts to keep the precepts, can create a danger of substantializing the act of violation. Here lies the salient point of Wŏnhyo's Mahāyāna ethics: the practitioner must understand the nonsubstantial nature of precepts. Violation of the precepts does not have a substantial reality. Hence, a genuine awareness of the meaning of violation not only includes realization of the mistake made by the act of violation but, more important, the emptiness of the violation itself. Violation is nonsubstantial and so are the violated (precept) and the violator. In this context, Wŏnhyo makes a radical statement that if one fails to see the nonsubstantial nature of precepts, observing precepts on the phenomenal level results in violating them on the ultimate level.

When not properly contextualized and spelled out, the Mahāyāna emphasis on emptiness in ethical discourse can be subject to serious misunderstanding. Wŏnhyo criticizes such misunderstanding as "being stagnated with nonbeing." The nonsubstantial nature of precepts, the emptiness of their observation and violation, does not negate their conventional existence. In the *Essentials,* Wŏnhyo takes efforts to reveal both noumenal and phenomenal, or ultimate and conventional, aspects of precepts. On their ultimate levels, precepts do not exist because they are empty by nature; on their conventional levels, to observe precepts is the basis of Buddhas and bodhisattvas. These two levels cannot be separated.

Wŏnhyo's views on bodhisattva precepts appear in three of his extant works including the *Essentials.* In all three works, Wŏnhyo pays attention to the nature of Mahāyāna Buddhist ethics that distinguishes itself from the Vinaya tradition of early Buddhism. In the opening passage of *Posal yŏngnak ponŏpkyŏng so* (Commentary on the *Sūtra of Bodhisattvas' Bead Ornamented Primary Activities*),[1] Wŏnhyo discusses the noumenal and phenomenal reality of precepts through the simile of the ocean and the sky as representing the doctrines of the "two levels of truth" and the "middle path." As there is no path in the sky, so there are no prefixed ways to master the middle path. However, the nonexistence of set rules does not deny the existence of a path for the practitioner to follow. The nonexistence of a set path means that anything can be a path, and the nonexistence of a specific gate opens up the possibility for anything to be a door to Buddhist practice. Following this logic, the demarcation between precepts and nonprecepts, rules and nonrules, is blurred.

In the *Pŏmmanggyŏng posal kyebon sa'gi* (Personal Records on the Chapter on the Bodhisattva Precepts in the *Sūtra of Brahma's Net*),[2] Wŏnhyo's third work on bodhisattva precepts, he explains the relationship between each knot and the entire net in Brahma's net as another example of phenomenal and noumenal aspects of precepts. The net is one as it is, but it consists of diverse knots. Not only does each knot depend on other knots for its existence, the very diversity of knots in the net demonstrates the different appearances (or forms) in the phenomenal world, which cannot be

1. *Posal yŏngnak ponŏpkyŏng so* (Commentary on the *Sūtra of Bodhisattvas' Bead Ornamented Primary Activities*), in HPC 1:586a–604a. (HPC refers to *Han'guk Pulgyo chŏnsŏ* [1979–2001])

2. *Pŏmmanggyŏng posal kyebon sa'gi* (Personal Records on the Chapter on the Bodhisattva Precepts in the *Sūtra of Brahma's Net*), HPC 1.498a–523b.

regulated by any set of rules to explain their existence. In the *Essentials,* Wŏnhyo elaborates on the differences between appearance and true reality of precepts by discussing different contexts in which the same action could be judged as either observation or violation of precepts.

The nonduality of form (phenomena) and emptiness (noumenon) is the ground of Mahāyāna Buddhist philosophy. When this idea is applied to ethics, it cannot but destabilize conventional ethical discourse. Wŏnhyo's discussion of bodhisattva precepts problematizes the basic assumptions of normative ethics. It problematizes ethical categories by showing the provisional nature of precepts and revealing the limits of binary oppositions commonly employed in ethical discourse. By so doing, Wŏnhyo reconceptualizes the function of ethics.[3]

Translation

The bodhisattva precepts are a ferry that turns the currents around and sends them back to their origin. They are the essential gate in rejecting the wrong and selecting the right. Characteristics of the right and wrong are easy to get confused and the nature of merits and offense is difficult to distinguish. A truly wicked intention can take the appearance of rightness. Or a contaminated appearance and lifestyle can also contain genuine purity at its inner core. Or a work that seems to bring at least a small amount of merits might turn out to cause a great disaster. Or someone whose thoughts and activities seem profound might turn out to violate simple and minor things. Because of this, unrefined practitioners, or *Śramanas,* who are wrapped in personal desire have long followed only the traces [of sages], considering them truly right. Their practices continue to debilitate the profound precepts [of the Buddha] and pursue degraded activities. Because of this situation, by removing the degraded activities, one should pursue the perfection of the profound precepts; by dispelling the mode of imitating the traces, one should follow the truthful. Worrying that I might be forgetful of this, I summarize here the essential teachings [of bodhisattva precepts]. If anybody concurs with me, take a close look at the details and resolve doubts.[4]

3. The translation that follows is based on HPC 1.581a–585c. The text is also included in T. 45.1907.918b–921c (T refers to *Taishō shinshū daizōkyō.* [A standard collection of the East Asian Buddhist canon compiled in Japan] Takakusu Junjirō, Watanabe Kaikyoku, et al. (eds.), 100 vols. Tokyo: Taishō Issaikyō Kankōkai, 1924–1932).

4. Wŏnhyo's discussion is based on *Pusa jie ben* (On Conferring Bodhisattva Precepts, T. 1501.24.1110–1115). This text contains excerpts from the *Yogācārabhūmi-śāstra.* Even though the *Essentials* can be categorized as a commentary in its style, in this work Wŏnhyo does not offer line-by-line comments on *Pusa jie ben,* which he mentions only rarely. Instead, he develops his own arguments on the nature of bodhisattva precepts and of observing and violating them.

I will discuss three issues that are essential in understanding the observation and violation of precepts: the first is the major and minor precepts; the second is the shallow and profound understandings; and the third is the ultimate way of observing and violating precepts.

1. The Major and Minor Precepts

Discussions about the major and minor precepts are divided into two parts. The first part is a general discussion about the major and minor precepts, and the second part reveals individual differences. . . .

Let us take the first precept of praising oneself and disparaging others and discuss its appearances. There are four distinctive cases related to this precept.[5]

If one praises oneself and speaks ill of others for the purpose of generating faith in the minds of others, this creates good merits and is not an offense. If one praises oneself and speaks ill of others because of the idle mind or a morally neutral state of mind, this is an offense but not an affliction. If one praises oneself and speaks ill of others because of love or anger for someone, this is affliction, but not serious offense. If one praises oneself and speaks ill of others because one covets benefits and pursues respect, this is not light but serious offense. . . .

2. The Shallow and Profound Understandings

Following the discussion of the aforementioned precept of praising oneself and disparaging others, now I will elaborate on the shallow and profound understandings of observing and violating the precept. The *Sūtra of Brahma's Net* says, "[Bodhisattvas should] always receive disparagement and humiliation in lieu of sentient beings; in doing so, bodhisattvas take responsibilities of bad happenings and transfer good merits to others. If one praises and promotes one's own meritorious behaviors and hides other's good deeds, and by doing so causes others to receive ignominy and disgrace, this is a major offense (Skt. *pārājikā*)."[6] What would it mean to consider shallow and profound understandings in the context of the discussion above?

When the person of lower dispositions hears this statement, the person naïvely follows linguistic expressions and understands that to disparage oneself and praise others will definitely create meritorious rewards, whereas to praise oneself and disparage others will be an offense. A person who understands in this manner will flatly follow the linguistic expressions and

5. The *Pusa jie ben* contains a discussion of four major precepts and forty-four minor precepts. The four major precepts are (1) the precept on praising oneself and disparaging others; (2) the precept on being stingy about the correct dharma; (3) the precept on not accepting repentance because of anger; and (4) the precept on slandering the correct dharma.

6. *Fanwang jing* (Sūtra of Brahma's Net), T. 24.1484.1004c.

want to practice good deeds; however, good deeds in this case are few and offenses are many. If the person wishes to eliminate the offense, she or he gets rid of one offense by eradicating three good deeds. This is called the offense by the one who has a shallow understanding.

When the person of higher dispositions hears this statement, the person gives a weighty thought to its meaning. Understanding that when one corner is lifted, the other three corners follow, when one passage is mentioned, the person understands all four different cases and makes a judgment based on them. In this manner, evaluation is not biased, no good rewards are deserted, and at the same time no offense is made. This is called "the virtue of observing precepts of those who have profound understanding."

The aforementioned four different cases are as follows. In some situations, to speak ill of oneself and praise others results in merits and to praise oneself and speak ill of others results in offense. In other cases, speaking ill of oneself and praising others turns out to be an offense whereas praising oneself and speaking ill of others is a meritorious deed. There are also situations in which either disparaging oneself and praising others or praising oneself and disparaging others becomes either an offense or meritorious behavior. And yet there are situations in which neither disparaging oneself and praising others nor praising oneself and disparaging others turns out to be either meritorious behavior or offense.

The first is a case of a person with a deep sympathy for sentient beings. If such a person feels a deep sympathy for sentient beings receiving disgrace, wishes to transfer the disgrace of others to herself or himself, and thus transfer to others the credits she or he deserves, in this case, by this action, the person disparages herself or himself and praises others, which is meritorious behavior. However, if the person makes others receive disgrace so that she or he would earn credits for those activities, the activity is interpreted as the case of praising oneself and disparaging others, and is an offense.

The second is a case of a person who is aware of the trends in her or his time that people hate those who praise themselves and speak ill of others and respect those who humble themselves and who speak highly of others as a man of high quality. This person thinks that if she or he disparages others, others will hurt her or him, but if she or he praises others, they will in turn benefit her or him. With this reasoning, if the person disparages herself or himself and praises others as a means to get a high evaluation of herself or himself, this is a major offense. If someone praises oneself and is critical of others in an attempt to correct others who are attached to nontruth and by doing so to establish the teachings of the Buddha and benefit sentient beings, this is a great meritorious deed.

The third is the case as follows: Suppose there is a person who has a strongly deceptive nature. In an attempt to deceive people in the world, this person despises others' strong points and covers up his or her own weakness. For this purpose, the person employs deceptive language: she or he speaks ill of herself or himself by criticizing her or his good quality of small size as if they were defects and praises others' weakness as if they were their strong points. By doing so, the person promotes her or his many shortcomings as if they were virtue, and suppresses others' strong points as if they were failings. Also, suppose there is a person whose nature is straightforward. Wishing to lead people in the world to the right path, with the knowledge of how to distinguish the good from the evil, the person removes offense, cultivates merits, and speaks honestly without covering. When the person notices vice in herself or himself, she or he will definitely denounce it; when the person hears the good deeds of others, she or he makes sure to praise it. The praise and disparagement and the advertisement and suppression of the first person are the offense of deception and flattery. The praise and disparagement and the promotion and condemnation of the second person merit the rewards for sincerity and honesty.

The fourth is the case of a person of supreme integrity whose character is unprejudiced, flexible, and whose spirit is tolerant, embracing, and undistorted. Because this person has limitless capacities in these aspects, the person puts disaster and good fortune together, making them one; without making distinctions between the subject (self) and object (others), the person makes them nondual. The person's spirit always stays in happiness. Staying in such an ambience, the person neither disparages herself or himself nor praises others. Nor does she or he promote herself or himself or suppress others. And suppose there is a person with low integrity whose nature is dull, who is not capable of distinguishing right from wrong, and who cannot tell beans from barley. The person is not attentive to what makes good or what makes evil. Because the person's thoughts constantly stay in confusion, the person forgets both love and hatred, and does not humble herself or himself or beautify others. The person does not promote herself or himself or disgrace others. This person, however, commits the offense of confusion of the low integrity whereas the earlier case creates merits through the simplicity of high wisdom.

This is what is meant by evaluating offense or merits through four cases. The first two cases demonstrate the situation in which seemingly meritorious behaviors can turn into serious disasters, and the act of offense can eventually result in great goodness. The latter two cases are examples in which deceptive language and compassionate concern for others do not differ in appearance, and the activities of those who have high integrity and base stupidity look the same. Therefore, practitioners should know that the essentials of observing and violating precepts definitely lie in closely examining the gain or loss of one's own action, and they do not lie in judging the virtue or vice of each movement of others. This is the meaning of the shallow and profound understandings of observing and violating precepts.

3. The Ultimate Way of Observing and Violating Precepts

The third issue is the clarification of the ultimate observation and violation of precepts. Based on the previous discussion, the nature of light and grave violations and the character of shallow and profound understandings should be understood. However, if one does not truly understand the characteristics of precepts, and, also, in dealing with offense and non-offense, if one does not leave the two extremes, one will not be able to ultimately observe and not violate the precept; nor is it possible for the person to attain the perfection of pure precepts. Why is this so? Precepts are not produced by themselves, but exist based on various causal conditions. Because of that, precepts can never have their own characteristics. Following causal conditions is not precepts; however, without causal conditions there are no precepts. If these two situations are excluded and since the middle cannot be attained, if one searches for precepts in this manner, precepts can never exist. Although it is not possible to say that the self-nature of precepts exists, the precepts do exist through multiple conditioned causalities. This is not the same as talking about the hare's horns because they do not have causal conditions.

The characteristics of offense are based on conditioned causality; so are those of precepts. The characteristics of precepts and offense are based on conditioned causality, and so are characteristics of human beings. Based on this understanding, if someone considers that because a precept does not exist [without conditioned causality], precepts do not exist at all, such a person will lose precepts forever, even though the person does not violate precepts by thinking so. That is so because the person denies the phenomenal existence of precepts. Also, based on this understanding, if someone claims that precepts do exist, even though that person is able to observe precepts, by observing precepts, the person violates them. That is so because the person violates the true characteristics of precepts.

When bodhisattvas practice precepts, it is not like this. Even though bodhisattvas do not calculate as if there were the subject who observes precepts and the objective precepts that need to be observed, nor do they deny the phenomenal existence of precepts, and therefore they do not make the great mistake of losing precepts. Even though bodhisattvas do not believe that there are no distinctions between violation and nonviolation of precepts, they do not deny the true nature of precepts; thus they forever save themselves from violating even the minute precepts. In this manner, employing astute skillful means and profound wisdom, they forever forget about the three wheels of [the donor, the recipient, and the gift], do not fall into the two extremes, and achieve the perfection of precepts.

A scripture says, "Both violation and nonviolation cannot be attained, and therefore one completes the perfection of precepts."[7] The *Bodhisattva Precepts* says, "precepts and their lights [i.e., the merits earned by observing precepts] come from their sources. They arise through conditioned causality, and not without causes. They are neither forms, nor mind, neither being, nor nonbeing, nor the law of causality. But they are the original source of

7. *Mahā-prajñā-pāramitā-sūtra,* T. 8.223.218c–219a.

Buddhas and the ground of bodhisattvas."[8] Precepts and their lights are mentioned here to demonstrate that they are not two different things. That is because clarity and convolution are one taste; therefore through the merits of precepts the true nature of precepts is revealed.

Precepts do not have self-nature; they are always created through other conditions. Hence it is said that there are conditions. When the conditions are mentioned, this does not indicate that something exists to become the cause of precepts; instead it means that things arise through causes. Hence it is said that the causes are not inexistent. The nature of precepts whose causes are not inexistent is neither material reality nor thoughts in one's mind. Hence it is said that precepts are neither form nor the mind. Even though they are neither form nor the mind, the precepts cannot be attained if separated from either form or the mind. Even though precepts cannot be attained, this does not mean that they do not exist. Hence it is said that precepts are neither being nor nonbeing. Even though precepts are not inexistent, separated from their results, their causes do not exist; separated from causes, the results are inexistent as well. Hence it is said that precepts are based on the law which is neither of the causes nor of the results. The nature of the causes of precepts cannot be attained; however, the merits of all Buddhas are necessarily based on the cause of precepts. That is why it is said that precepts are the original source of all Buddhas. The nature of the results of precepts cannot be attained; however, precepts necessarily require bodhicitta as their cause. Hence that which is produced by the results of precepts is the foundation of bodhisattvas.

Question: If the characteristics of precepts are so profound and difficult to understand, it will be difficult even to understand them. How can one practice them? Only mahasattvas might be able to practice what you have so far explained, but it does not seem relevant to the novice who has just elevated the mind to practice.

Answer: A passage in a scripture answers precisely the question you raise. It is said: "When bodhisattvas first arouse their mind to practice, they should always follow the law of the unattainable. Based on the law of the unattainable, bodhisattvas practice giving and precepts. Based on the law of the unattainable, bodhisattvas also practice the rest of the six perfections, including wisdom."[9] The passage means that in practicing the six perfections, if one has not been practicing them, it is not possible to practice. If

8. *Fanwang jing*, T. 24.1484.1004b. The passage "precepts and their lights [i.e., the merits earned by observing precepts] come from their sources" literally means "precepts and their lights came from the mouth." In the introductory section of the bodhisattva precepts of the *Fawang jing*, the Buddha says to the gathered assembly that he will teach them precepts to follow. The Buddha then explains that he has himself embodied the precepts practiced by Buddhas by memorizing them, and through this embodiment of precepts, he is capable of articulating the precepts he will teach in this *sūtra*.

9. *Mahā-prajñā-pāramitā-sūtra*, T. 8.223.373c.

bodhisattvas do not practice them now because of their difficulty, it will also be difficult to practice them in the future. If a long time passes by like this, it will become more difficult to practice. Therefore, if one begins practice, being aware of the difficulties involved in it, practice will gradually be increased, and eventually difficulty will be transformed into ease. This is called the great will that initiates a new practice and achieves it. The ultimate way of observation and violation has been clarified....

Bibliography and Suggested Reading

Buswell, Robert E., Jr. (1995) "Wŏnhyo as Cultural and Religious Archetype: A Study in Korean Buddhist Hagiography." *Pulgyo yŏn'gu* (Buddhist Studies) 11/12: 79–171.

Buswell, Robert E., Jr., trans. (2007) *Cultivating Original Enlightenment: Wŏnhyo's Exposition of the Vajrasamādhi-Sūtra (Kŭmgang Sammaegyŏng Non).* Honolulu: University of Hawai'i Press.

Faure, Bernard. (1995) "Random Thoughts: Wŏnhyo's Life as 'Thought.'" *Pulgyo yŏn'gu* (Buddhist Studies) 11/12: 197–223.

Harvey, Peter. (2000) *An Introduction to Buddhist Ethics.* Cambridge: Cambridge University Press.

Park, Jin Y. (2007) "Transgression and Ethics of Tension: Wŏnhyo and Derrida on Institutional Authority." In Youru Wang, ed., *Deconstruction and the Ethical in Asian Thought.* London: Routledge, pp. 192–214.

36

Thich Nhat Hanh's *Interbeing: Fourteen Guidelines for Engaged Buddhism*

William Edelglass

Some critics claim that the Buddhist emphasis on liberation from samsara, the cycle of birth and suffering, has been accompanied by a neglect of worldly liberation. Moreover, critics charge, Buddhists have no deep motivation to work for social justice; in a world governed by the universal justice of karma, there are no innocent victims. The law of karma is said to justify the status quo because worldly suffering is recognized as the inevitable ripening of karmic consequences. While scholars debate the historical accuracy of this critique, many contemporary Buddhist leaders, in Asia and in the West, have been working to formulate Buddhist responses to worldly suffering. Engaged Buddhists argue that social and institutional violence, though veiled, is often pervasive and difficult to subvert, even as it causes extensive and extreme suffering. Therefore, Buddhists, who have always been concerned with suffering and violence, are called to take action against social and institutional oppression and injustice. As the Dalai Lama argues, we have a "universal responsibility."

"Engaged Buddhism" arose as a Buddhist response to the widespread trauma—including colonialism, war, social and economic injustice, environmental degradation, genocide, totalitarian government, and the suppression of religion—that has accompanied the advent of modernity in some Asian Buddhist countries. Prominent Asian Buddhist leaders have argued that compassionate, nonviolent, mindful activism is a properly Buddhist response to structures of oppression.[1] Engaged Buddhism resonates with many Western Buddhists, who appreciate the confluence of their religious practice with Western political and social theory and European Enlightenment values, such as human rights, distributive justice, social progress, and freedom from oppression. In Asia and in the West, engaged Buddhism has taken a multiplicity of forms, including working for: peace and nonviolence, human rights, just and equitable development, liberation from oppressive government, social and economic justice, prison reform, access to education and health care, environmental protection and sustainability, and gender and racial equality.[2]

Engaged Buddhists draw on a variety of traditional Buddhist doctrines, narratives, and values to justify their worldly engagement on behalf of suffering beings in a Buddhist context. The most basic Buddhist doctrine, the Four Noble Truths, concerns naming and acknowledging suffering, determining its cause, seeing how it can be overcome, and working to overcome it. Therefore, if political and economic structures cause suffering, engaged Buddhists argue, according to the Four Noble Truths, they should be dismantled. Buddhist ethical teachings, such as the cultivation of generosity, moral discipline, patience, compassion, loving-kindness, abstaining from harming others, the monastic code (*vinaya*) with its rules of comportment for monks and nuns, right livelihood, skillful means in alleviating suffering, and the bodhisattva ideal of saving sentient beings from samsara all seem to include a responsiveness to the suffering of others. Beyond ethics, engaged Buddhists draw on other significant concepts in Buddhist thought, for example interdependence and nonduality, which are employed to demonstrate that we are all responsible for each other, and that the suffering of others is significant to the self because self and other are not fundamentally different. Selflessness and emptiness are utilized to encourage practitioners to transform fears, desires, and habits that cause the suffering of others or prevent taking action to reduce suffering. Engaged Buddhists use the doctrine that all sentient beings have the seed of Buddha-nature, the capacity for waking up as enlightened beings, to support the view that every sentient being is intrinsically valuable and deserves to be treated with respect and dignity.

Each of these ethical and metaphysical doctrines plays a role in Thich Nhat Hanh's works on engaged Buddhism. Nhat Hanh, a Vietnamese Zen

1. According to the Dalai Lama, Thich Nhat Hanh, and other Buddhist teachers, as well as some scholars, engaged Buddhism is continuous with earlier Buddhist traditions, which were, at times, already concerned with various forms of injustice and worldly suffering. Many scholars, however, regard socially engaged Buddhism as a uniquely contemporary response to modernity. Christopher Queen, for example, argues that engaged Buddhism is so different from earlier Buddhist traditions that it constitutes a fourth *yāna* (vehicle) of Buddhist theory and practice, after the Hīnayāna (lesser vehicle), Mahāyāna (great vehicle), and Vajrayāna (vehicle) (Queen 2000: 1–31).

2. See, for example, Queen and King 1996; and Queen 2000.

master and peace activist who is generally credited with coining the term "engaged Buddhism," played a leading role in Buddhist responses to the war in his homeland. In the 1960s, drawing on his Theravāda training in mindfulness practice as well as his Mahāyāna Zen practice, Nhat Hanh founded the Order of Interbeing (Tiep Hien), in the Rinzai lineage of Zen Buddhism. According to its charter, "The aim of the Order is to actualize Buddhism by studying, experimenting with, and applying Buddhism in modern life with a special emphasis on the bodhisattva ideal."[3] During the 1960s, for the Order of Interbeing and other Buddhists groups with which Nhat Hanh was working, "to actualize Buddhism" meant practicing mindfulness, but also protecting villagers under attack, providing medical aid, assisting farmers, rebuilding villages destroyed by the fighting, and advocating an end to the violence without endorsing any political or military faction. Since 1966, when he was forced into exile, Nhat Hanh has eloquently argued that engaged Buddhism is continuous with earlier Buddhist traditions but is also a form of Buddhism that is particularly suited to the contemporary world.

Nhat Hanh's *Interbeing: Fourteen Guidelines for Engaged Buddhism* succinctly formulates his approach to engaged Buddhism. While personal virtue, mindfulness, and transformation are necessary, Nhat Hanh argues, they are insufficient to overcome the great suffering caused by structures of oppression. Thus, the "Fourteen Guidelines" address individual mindfulness practice and cultivation of virtue, but also responsibilities in family life, work, and community.[4] The text is representative of engaged Buddhist interpretations of Buddhist doctrines and practices as rafts—skillful means to alleviate suffering to which one should not get attached; Nhat Hanh explicitly valorizes mindful engagement over the particularity of any Buddhist tradition and interprets Buddhist teachings as ecumenical, nondogmatic, and universal responses to contemporary life.[5]

Fourteen Mindfulness Trainings

1. Openness: *Aware of the suffering created by fanaticism and intolerance,* we are determined not to be idolatrous about or bound to any doctrine, theory, or ideology, even Buddhist ones. Buddhist teachings are guiding means

3. Nhat Hanh 1998: 105.

4. In conformity with Buddhist traditions, Nhat Hanh first characterized the fourteen rules for the Order of Interbeing as "precepts" (*śīla*), formulated as imperatives proscribing specific acts. During the 1990s, he reformulated the "precepts" as "mindfulness trainings" (Nhat Hanh's translation of *śikṣā*), to further emphasize the way the practice of engaged Buddhism is grounded in individual awareness and motivation, as opposed to the external authority of a command.

5. The following excerpts originally appeared in Thich Nhat Hanh 1998. We gratefully acknowledge permission to republish this work.

to help us learn to look deeply and to develop our understanding and compassion. They are not doctrines to fight, kill, or die for.

Commentary:[6] ... The Buddha regarded his own teachings as a raft to cross the river and not as an absolute truth to be worshipped or clung to.... Ideological inflexibility is responsible for so much of the conflict and violence in the world.... According to Buddhist teachings, knowledge itself can be an obstacle to true understanding, and views can be a barrier to insight. Clinging to views can prevent us from arriving at a deeper, more profound understanding of reality.... The Buddhist teachings are a *means* of helping people.... If various kinds of medicine are needed to treat a variety of diseases, Buddhism also needs to propose various Dharma doors for people of differing circumstances.... The teachings and practices found in Buddhism may vary, but they all aim at liberating the mind.

2. Nonattachment to Views: *Aware of the suffering created by attachment to views and wrong perceptions,* we are determined to avoid being narrow-minded and bound to present views. We shall learn and practice nonattachment from views in order to be open to others' insights and experiences. We are aware that the knowledge we presently possess is not changeless, absolute truth. Truth is found in life, and we will observe life within and around us in every moment, ready to learn throughout our lives....

3. Freedom of Thought: *Aware of the suffering brought about when we impose our views on others,* we are committed not to force others, even our children, by any means whatsoever—such as authority, threat, money, propaganda, or indoctrination—to adopt our views. We will respect the right of others to be different and to choose what to believe and how to decide. We will, however, help others renounce fanaticism and narrowness through compassionate dialogue.

Commentary: ... Compassionate dialogue is the essence of nonviolent action (*ahiṃsā*). Ahiṃsā begins with the energy of tolerance and loving kindness, which will be expressed in gentle, compassionate, intelligent speech that can move people's hearts. It then moves into the field of action to create moral and social pressure for people to change. Understanding and compassion must be the basis of all nonviolent actions....

4. Awareness of Suffering: *Aware that looking deeply at the nature of suffering can help us develop compassion and find ways out of suffering,* we are determined not to avoid or close our eyes before suffering. We are committed to finding ways, including personal contact, images, and sounds, to be

6. Thich Nhat Hanh has provided his own commentary to each of the mindfulness trainings.

with those who suffer, so we can understand their situation deeply and help them transform their suffering into compassion, peace, and joy.

Commentary:... Suffering can have a therapeutic power. It can help us open our eyes. Awareness of suffering encourages us to search for its cause, to find out what is going on within us and in society.... Too much suffering can destroy our capacity to love. We have to know our limits, to stay in touch with things that are dreadful in life and also things that are wonderful. If the First Truth explains the presence of suffering in life, the Third Truth encourages us to touch life's joy and peace. When people say that Buddhism is pessimistic, it is because they are stressing the First Truth and overlooking the Third. Mahayana Buddhism takes great care to emphasize the Third Truth. Its literature is full of references to the green willow, the violet bamboo, and the full moon as manifestations of the true Dharma....

Teachers who say not to pay attention to the problems of the world like hunger, war, oppression, and social injustice, who say that we should only practice, have not understood deeply enough the meaning of Mahāyāna. Of course, we should practice counting the breath, meditation, and *sūtra* study, but what is the purpose of doing these things? It is to be aware of what is going on in ourselves and in the world. What is going on in the world is also going on within ourselves, and vice versa. Once we see this clearly, we will not refuse to take a position or to act.... To practice Buddhism, it is said, is to see into one's own nature and become a Buddha. If we cannot see what is going on around us, how can we see into our own nature? There is a relationship between the nature of the self and the nature of suffering, injustice, and war....

Staying in touch with the reality of suffering keeps us sane and nourishes the wellsprings of understanding (*prajñā*) and compassion (*karuṇā*) in us. It affirms in us the will to practice the bodhisattva's way: "Living beings are numberless; I vow to help by rowing them to the other shore." If we cut ourselves off from the reality of suffering, this vow will have no meaning.... We must practice in each moment of daily life and not just in the meditation hall.

5. Simple, Healthy Living: *Aware that true happiness is rooted in peace, solidity, freedom, and compassion, and not in wealth or fame,* we are determined not to take as the aim of our life fame, profit, wealth, or sensual pleasure, nor to accumulate wealth while millions are hungry and dying. We are committed to living simply and sharing our time, energy, and material resources with those in need. We will practice mindful consuming, not using alcohol, drugs, or any other products that bring toxins into our own and the collective body and consciousness.

Commentary:... We must resolve to oppose the type of modern life filled with pressures and anxieties that so many people now live. The only way out is to consume less, to be content with fewer possessions.... Once we are able to live simply and happily, we are better able to help others. We have more time and energy to share....

6. Dealing with Anger: *Aware that anger blocks communication and creates suffering,* we are determined to take care of the energy of anger when it arises and to recognize and transform the seeds of anger that lie deep in our consciousness. When anger comes up, we are determined not to do or say anything, but to practice mindful breathing or mindful walking and acknowledge, embrace, and look deeply into our anger. We will learn to look with the eyes of compassion at those we think are the cause of our anger.

Commentary:... Only love and understanding can help people change.... If I had been born in the social conditions of a pirate and raised as a pirate, I would be a pirate now. A variety of interdependent causes has created the existence of the pirate. The responsibility is not solely his or his family's, but it is also society's.... Each of us shares the responsibility for the presence of pirates. Meditating on dependent origination and looking with compassionate eyes helps us see our duty and responsibility to suffering beings.... The purpose of meditation is to see and hear.... The eyes of compassion are also the eyes of understanding. Compassion is the sweet water that springs forth from the source of understanding. To practice looking deeply is the basic medicine for anger and hatred.

7. Dwelling Happily in the Present Moment: *Aware that life is available only in the present moment and that it is possible to live happily in the here and now,* we are committed to training ourselves to live deeply each moment of daily life. We will try not to lose ourselves in dispersion or be carried away by regrets about the past, worries about the future, or craving, anger, or jealousy in the present. We will practice mindful breathing to come back to what is happening in the present moment. We are determined to learn the art of mindful living by touching the wondrous, refreshing, and healing elements that are inside and around us, and by nourishing seeds of joy, peace, love, and understanding in ourselves, thus facilitating the work of transformation and healing in our consciousness.

8. Community and Communication: *Aware that the lack of communication always brings separation and suffering,* we are committed to training ourselves in the practice of compassionate listening and loving speech. We will learn to listen deeply without judging or reacting and refrain from uttering words that can create discord or cause the community to break. We will make every effort to keep communications open and to reconcile and resolve all conflicts, however small....

9. Truthful and Loving Speech: *Aware that words can create suffering or happiness,* we are committed to learning to speak truthfully and constructively, using only words that inspire hope and confidence. We are determined not to say untruthful things for the sake of personal interest or to impress people, nor to utter words that might cause division or hatred. We will not spread news that we do not know to be certain nor criticize or con-

demn things of which we are not sure. We will do our best to speak out about situations of injustice, even when doing so may threaten our safety....

10. Protecting the Sangha: *Aware that the essence and aim of a Sangha is the practice of understanding and compassion,* we are determined not to use the Buddhist community for personal gain or profit or transform our community into a political instrument. A spiritual community should, however, take a clear stand against oppression and injustice and should strive to change the situation without engaging in partisan conflicts.

Commentary:... The purpose of a religious community is to guide people on the spiritual path. Therefore, to transform a religious community into a political party is to divert it from its true aim. Religious leaders may be tempted to support their government in exchange for the material well-being of their community. This has occurred throughout recorded history. In order to secure their government's support, religious communities often refrain from speaking out against oppression and injustices committed by their government. Allowing politicians to use your religious community to strengthen their political power is to surrender the spiritual sovereignty of your community.

"A spiritual community, however, should take a clear stand against oppression and injustice..." This should be done with a clear voice, based on the principles of the Four Noble Truths. The truth concerning the unjust situation should be fully exposed (the First Truth: suffering). The various causes of injustice should be enumerated (the Second Truth: the causes of suffering). The purpose and desire for removing the injustices should be made obvious (the Third Truth: the removal of suffering). Although religious communities are not political powers, they can use their influence to change society. Speaking out is the first step, proposing and supporting appropriate measures for change is the next. Most important is to transcend all partisan conflicts. The voice of caring and understanding must be distinct from the voice of ambition.

11. Right Livelihood: *Aware that great violence and injustice have been done to our environment and society,* we are committed not to live with a vocation that is harmful to humans and nature. We will do our best to select a livelihood that helps realize our ideal of understanding and compassion. Aware of global economic, political and social realities, we will behave responsibly as consumers and as citizens, not investing in companies that deprive others of their chance to live.

Commentary:... Right Livelihood had ceased to be a purely personal matter. It is our collective karma.

Suppose I am a school teacher and I believe that nurturing love and understanding in children is a beautiful occupation, an example of Right Livelihood. I would object if someone asked me to stop teaching and become, for example, a butcher. However, if I meditate on the interrelatedness of all things, I will see that the butcher is not solely responsible for killing animals. He kills them for all of us who buy pieces of raw meat, cleanly wrapped and displayed at our local supermarket. The act of killing is a collective one....

12. Reverence for Life: *Aware that much suffering is caused by war and conflict,* we are determined to cultivate nonviolence in our daily lives, to promote peace education, mindful mediation, and reconciliation within families, communities, nations, and in the world. We are determined not to kill and not to let others kill. We will diligently practice deep looking with our Sangha to discover better ways to protect life and prevent war....

Commentary:... The essence of this training is to make every effort to respect and protect life, to continuously move in the direction of peace and reconciliation....

Our patterns of livelihood and consuming have very much to do with the lives and security of humans and other living beings. There are many types of violence. Among societies, it manifests as war—often caused by fanaticism and narrowness or by the will to gain political influence or economic power. Or violence can be the exploitation of one society by another that is technologically or politically stronger. We can oppose wars once they have started, but it is better to also do our best to prevent wars from breaking out. The way to prevent war is to make peace. We accomplish this first in our daily life by combating fanaticism and attachment to views, and working for social justice....

13. Generosity: *Aware of the suffering caused by exploitation, social injustice, stealing, and oppression,* we are committed to cultivating loving kindness and learning ways to work for the wellbeing of people, animals, plants, and minerals. We will practice generosity by sharing our time, energy, and material resources with those who are in need. We are determined not to steal and not to possess anything that should belong to others. We will respect the property of others, but will try to prevent others from profiting from human suffering or the suffering of other beings....

14. Right Conduct *(For lay members): Aware that sexual relations motivated by craving cannot dissipate the feeling of loneliness but will create more suffering, frustration, and isolation,* we are determined not to engage in sexual relations without mutual understanding, love, and a long-term commitment. In sexual relations, we must be aware of future suffering that may be caused.... We will treat our bodies with respect and preserve our vital energies (sexual, breath, spirit) for the realization of our bodhisattva ideal....

(For monastic members): Aware that the aspiration of a monk or a nun can only be realized when he or she wholly leaves behind the bonds of worldly love, we are committed to practicing chastity and to helping others protect

themselves. We are aware that loneliness and suffering cannot be alleviated by the coming together of two bodies in a sexual relationship, but by the practice of true understanding and compassion.... We are determined not to suppress or mistreat our body or to look upon our body as only an instrument, but to learn to handle our body with respect....

Commentary: So many individuals, children, couples, and families have been wounded by sexual misconduct. Practicing this training is to prevent ourselves and others from being wounded. Our stability and the stability of our families and society depend on it....

Whatever happens to the body also happens to the spirit. The sanity of the body is the sanity of the spirit; the violation of the body is the violation of the spirit....

Commentary on the Fourteen Mindfulness Trainings

The Fourteen Mindfulness Trainings of the Order of Interbeing are the heart of the Buddha. They are mindfulness in our real lives and not just the teaching of ideas. If we practice these trainings deeply, we will recognize that each of them contains all the others. Studying and practicing the mindfulness trainings can help us understand the true nature of interbeing—we cannot just be by ourselves alone; we can only inter-be with everyone and everything else. To practice these trainings is to become aware of what is going on in our bodies, our minds, and the world. With awareness, we can live our lives happily, fully present in each moment we are alive, intelligently seeking solutions to the problems we face, and working for peace in small and large ways....

Bibliography and Suggested Reading

Chappell, David, ed. (2000) *Buddhist Peacework: Creating Cultures of Peace.* Boston: Wisdom.

Jones, Ken. (2003) *The New Social Face of Buddhism: A Call to Action.* Boston: Wisdom.

King, Sallie B. (2005) *Being Benevolence: The Social Ethics of Engaged Buddhism.* Honolulu: University of Hawai'i Press.

Nhat Hanh, Thich. (1998) *Interbeing: Fourteen Guidelines for Engaged Buddhism.* Berkeley: Parallax Press.

Queen, Christopher, ed. (2000) *Engaged Buddhism in the West.* Boston: Wisdom.

Queen, Christopher, and Sallie B. King, eds. (1996) *Engaged Buddhism: Buddhist Liberation Movements in Asia.* Albany: State University of New York Press.

Queen, Christopher, Charles Prebish, and Damien Keown, eds. (2003) *Action Dharma: New Studies in Engaged Buddhism.* New York: RoutledgeCurzon.

37

Joanna Macy

The Ecological Self

William Edelglass

In a widely read article published in 1967, Lynn White, Jr. argued that how we conceive of nature and the place of humans in the environment will determine how we use natural resources and impact the world around us. According to White, the devaluation of nature and the pervasive anthropocentrism of Western philosophical and religious traditions were the root causes of the ecological crisis.[1] He suggested that Buddhism was more suitable to an ecologically sustainable way of life because Buddhists conceive human beings to be wholly interdependent with the more-than-human world. In the last few decades, scholars have produced more nuanced views of the ecological theories and practices of both Asian and Western religious traditions. Still, Buddhist traditions have become fertile sources for many thinkers seeking to reconceive the human-nature relationship with the hope of providing a theoretical foundation for ecologically sustainable ways of being in the world.

Some authors claim that traditional Buddhist metaphysics and ontology are inherently conducive to environmental sustainability.[2] Dependent origination (*pratītyasamutpāda*), a doctrine central to much Buddhist thought, is

1. Lynn White, Jr., "The Historical Roots of Our Ecologic Crisis," *Science* 155 (1967): 1203–1207.

2. See, for example, Duncan Ryūken Williams, "Bibliography on Buddhism and Ecology," in Tucker and Williams 1997, 403–425.

interpreted as an articulation of the interdependence some thinkers regard as the dominant characteristic of ecological relationships. The Huayan image of the Jewel Net of Indra, in which every node reflects every other, becomes an image of the ecological interdependence that Aldo Leopold referred to as the "land-community."[3] The doctrine of a pure, original Buddha-nature (*tathāgatagarbha*), which is said to be present in all sentient beings, and in some Buddhist traditions also in nonsentient nature, is employed to argue that Buddhists recognize the intrinsic value and moral considerability of nonhuman natural beings, an important element of much contemporary environmental thought. As sentient beings are thought to transmigrate through multiple forms, including human and nonhuman animals, and because even the Buddha and various bodhisattvas appear in narratives as nonhuman animals, Buddhism is said to present us with an account of sentient life that is not, to use Peter Singer's term, "speciesist."[4] And more broadly, the doctrine of a universal Buddha nature that pervades the universe (*buddhākaya*) is said to demonstrate that there is no "dumb matter" lacking in value anywhere in the universe. Buddhist traditions, then, are claimed to have an ecological insight into the interdependence and value of all life.

The characterization of Buddhism as an ecologically friendly tradition is also frequently justified on the basis of Buddhist psychology and moral thought. With their analysis of how desire leads to suffering, Buddhist traditions provide a robust critique of consumerism, which plays a significant role in pollution overload and resource depletion. Buddhist monastic rules often include injunctions against eating certain kinds of meat, polluting waters, and felling trees, all of which are interpreted as models of an ecologically sustainable existence. The precept against killing and the widely practiced cultivation of compassion are understood as oriented not just toward other humans but also toward other sentient beings. The Mahāyāna ideal of the bodhisattva, who vows to relieve the suffering of all sentient beings, is employed as a model that presents the aspiration to relieve the suffering that human practices inflict on nonhuman life.

Drawing on Buddhist metaphysics and ethics, many scholars, environmental activists, and Buddhist practitioners argue that Buddhism is particularly attuned to the natural world. However, not all scholars accept this interpretation. Some have insisted that Buddhism, especially in South Asia, was essentially an anthropocentric tradition devoted to the liberation of human beings from suffering.[5] This was a liberation from the world, from nature, which, despite any misleading appearances to the contrary, was regarded as incapable of providing ultimate satisfaction. The natural world, then, was not believed

3. Aldo Leopold, "The Land Ethic," in *A Sand County Almanac* (New York, Oxford University Press, 1989), 201–226.

4. Peter Singer, *Animal Liberation* (New York: Ecco, 2002).

5. For the most careful and sophisticated critique of ecological Buddhism, see the work of Ian Harris.

to possess some kind of intrinsic value, but was something to be overcome. And despite the compassion shown toward nonhuman animals, Buddhists, especially in South Asia, have often regarded animal existence as miserable and, importantly, animals were generally considered incapable of practicing the Buddha's Dharma. Moreover, critics of ecological Buddhism argue that early Buddhists had no awareness of the ecological crisis we face today; it is a mistake to project contemporary environmental sensibilities, now part of the global discourse of modernity, back on ancient Buddhist ideas and practices.

Religious traditions, however, are not static. They only survive to the extent that they are able to meet the needs of contemporary practitioners. Today, practitioners in all the major religions are exploring the resources within their own traditions for help in addressing the ecological crisis. Buddhism is no exception. The Dalai Lama, Thich Nhat Hanh, and other Buddhist leaders are formulating ecological interpretations of Buddhism. And Buddhist practitioners, in Asia and in the West, have developed what might be considered ecocentric Buddhist rituals. In Thailand, old-growth trees have been ordained as monks to preserve them from logging corporations. Earth-oriented prayers and practices have been created and integrated into the spiritual life of numerous Western Buddhist centers. And for many in the West, Buddhism has been a source of understanding and inspiration for environmental activism and ecologically sustainable stewardship of the land. Buddhist environmentalism has become one of the major expressions of engaged Buddhism.[6]

Joanna Macy is a Buddhist teacher, environmental activist, and scholar who is perhaps the most prominent Western advocate of ecological Buddhism. In her essay "The Ecological Self: Postmodern Ground for Right Action," Macy argues that the pain some people feel for damaged ecosystems or the suffering of other species manifests the ways the self is inextricably intertwined with the more-than-human world. This experience of interconnection is an "extension of identity," from a "separate and fragile" self that requires constant defense and acquisition to a "wider, ecological sense of self." Macy understands this shift in light of twentieth-century science, especially general systems theory, according to which subject and object, organism and environment, are not absolutely distinct but are symbiotically related within larger systems. It is in Buddhism, however, that Macy finds the ecological self articulated with distinctive "clarity and sophistication." Indeed, Buddhism "goes further than systems cybernetics, both in revealing the pathogenic character of any reifications of the self and in offering methods for transcending them." Buddhist metaphysics, psychology, and ethics, Macy argues, provide us with ways of understanding our experience of an interconnected, ecological self and of responding to the suffering around us. Buddhist teachings resonate with our own experience and contemporary science and nourish our aspirations to contribute to a more sustainable world.[7]

6. See chapter 36 here.

7. The following essay is abridged from Joanna Macy, "The Ecological Self: Postmodern Ground for Right Action," in Mary Heather MacKinnon and Moni McIntyre,

The Ecological Self: Postmodern Ground for Right Action

...[The] ecological sense of selfhood combines the mystical and the pragmatic. Transcending separateness and fragmentation...it generates an experience of profound interconnectedness with all life....

A variety of factors converge in our time to produce such a shift in the sense of self and self-interest. Among the most significant are (1) the psychological and spiritual pressures exerted by current dangers of mass annihilation, (2) the emergence from science of the systems view of the world, and (3) a renaissance of nondualistic forms of spirituality.

This essay explores the role of these three factors—planetary peril, systems thinking, and nondualistic religion, specifically Buddhist teachings and practice—in promoting this shift. It is written from a conviction that a larger, ecological sense of self will characterize the postmodern world, and that without it there simply may be no postmodern world.

I. Personal Response to Planetary Crisis

The shift toward a wider, ecological sense of self is in large part a function of the dangers that threaten to overwhelm us. Given accelerating environmental destruction and massive deployment of nuclear weapons, people today are aware that they live in a world that can end....

As their grief and fear for the world is allowed to be expressed without apology or argument and validated as a wholesome, life-preserving response, people break through their avoidance mechanisms, break through their sense of futility and isolation. And generally what they break through *into* is a larger sense of identity. It is as if the pressure of their acknowledged awareness of the suffering of our world stretches, or collapses, the culturally defined boundaries of the self.

It becomes clear, for example, that the grief and fear experienced for our world and our common future are categorically different from similar sentiments relating to one's personal welfare. This pain cannot be equated with dread of one's own individual demise. Its source lies less in concerns for personal survival than in apprehensions of collective suffering—of what looms for human life and other species and unborn generations to come. Its nature is akin to the original meaning of compassion—"suffering with." It is the distress we feel on behalf of the larger whole of which we are a part. And when it is so defined, it serves as trigger or gateway to a more encompassing sense of identity, inseparable from the web of life in which we are as intricately interconnected as cells in a larger body.

---

eds., *Readings in Ecology and Feminist Theology* (Kansas City: Sheed and Ward, 1995). We gratefully acknowledge permission to republish this work.

This shift is an appropriate, adaptive response. For the crisis that threatens our planet, be it seen in its military, ecological, or social aspects, derives from a dysfunctional and pathogenic notion of the self. It is a mistake about our place in the order of things. It is the delusion that the self is so separate and fragile that we must delineate and defend its boundaries, that it is so small and needy that we must endlessly consume, that it is so aloof that we can—as individuals, corporations, nation-states or as a species—be immune to what we do to other beings.

Such a view of the human condition is not new, nor is the felt imperative to extend self-interest to embrace the whole in any way novel to our history as a species. It has been enjoined by many a teacher and saint. What is notable in our present situation . . . is that the extension of identity can come directly, not through exhortations to nobility or altruism, but through the owning of pain. That is why the shift in the sense of the self is credible to those experiencing it. . . .

II. Cybernetics of the Self

The findings of twentieth-century science undermine the notion of a separate self, distinct from the world it observes and acts upon. As Einstein showed, the self's perceptions are shaped by its changing position in relation to other phenomena. And these phenomena are affected not only by location, but as Heisenberg demonstrated, by the very act of observation. Now contemporary systems science and systems cybernetics go yet further in challenging old assumptions about a distinct, separate, continuous self, showing that there is no logical or scientific basis for construing one part of the experienced world as "me" and the rest as "other."

As open, self-organizing systems, our very breathing, acting, and thinking arise in interaction with our shared world through the currents of matter, energy, and information that flow through us. In the web of relationships that sustain these activities, there are no clear lines demarcating a separate, continuous self. As postmodern systems theorists aver, there is no categorical "I" set over against a categorical "you" or "it."

Systems philosopher Ervin Laszlo argues,

> We must do away with the subject-object distinction in analyzing experience. This does not mean that we reject the concepts of organism and environment, as handed down to us by natural science. It only means that we conceive of experience as linking organism and environment in a continuous chain of events, from which we cannot, without arbitrariness, abstract an entity called organism and another called environment.[8]

8. Ervin Laszlo, *Introduction to Systems Philosophy* (New York: Harper & Row Torchbook, 1973), 21.

The abstraction of a separate "I" is what Gregory Bateson calls the "epistemological fallacy of Occidental civilization." He asserts that the larger system of which we are a part defies any definitive localization of the self. That which decides and does can no longer be neatly identified with the isolated subjectivity of the individual or located within the confines of his or her skin. "The total self-corrective unit which processes information, or, as I say 'thinks' and 'acts' and 'decides,' is a system whose boundaries do not at all coincide with the boundaries either of the body or of what is popularly called the 'self' or 'consciousness'."[9] . . .

The false reification of the self is basic to the planetary ecological crisis in which we now find ourselves. We have imagined that the "unit of survival," as Bateson puts it, is the separate individual or the separate species. In reality, as throughout the history of evolution, it is the individual *plus* environment, the species *plus* the environment, for they are essentially symbiotic. Bateson continues:

> When you narrow down your epistemology and act on the premise "what interests me is me, or my organization, or my species," you chop off consideration of other loops of the loop structure. You decide you want to get rid of the by-products of human life and that Lake Erie will be a good place to put them. You forget that Lake Erie is part of your wider eco-mental system—and that if Lake Erie is driven insane its insanity is incorporated in the larger system of your thought and experience.[10]

Although we consist of and are sustained by the currents of information, matter, and energy that flow through us, we are accustomed to identifying ourselves with only that small arc of the flow-through that is lit, like the narrow beam of a flashlight, by our individual perceptions. But we do not *have* to so limit our self-perceptions. It is logical, Bateson contends, to conceive of mind as the entire "pattern that connects." It is as plausible to align our identity with that larger pattern and conceive of ourselves as interexistent with all beings, as it is to break off one segment of the process and build our borders there.

Systems Theory helps us see that the larger identification of which we speak does not involve an eclipse of the distinctiveness of one's individual experience. The "pattern that connects" is not an ocean of Brahman where separate drops merge and our diversities dissolve. Natural and cognitive systems self-organize and interact to create larger wholes precisely through their heterogeneity. By the same token, through the dance of deviation-amplifying feedback loops, the respective particularities of the interactive systems can increase. Integration and differentiation go hand in hand. Uniformity, by contrast, is entropic, the kiss of death. . . .

9. Gregory Bateson, *Steps to an Ecology of Mind* (New York: Ballantine Books, 1972), 319.

10. Bateson 1972: 484.

III. The Boundless Heart of the Bodhisattva

In the resurgence of nondualistic spiritualities in our postmodern world, Buddhism in its historic coming to the West is distinctive in the clarity and sophistication if offers in understanding the dynamics of the self. In much the same way as General Systems Theory does, its ontology and epistemology undermine any categorical distinctions definitive of a self-existent identity. And it goes further than systems cybernetics, both in revealing the pathogenic character of any reifications of the self and in offering methods for transcending them,

Dependent co-arising (*pratītyasamutpāda*), the core teaching of the Buddha on the nature of causality, presents a phenomenal reality so dynamic and interrelated that categorical subject-object distinctions dissolve. This is driven home in the doctrine of *anatman* or "no-self," where one's sense of identity is understood as an ephemeral product of perceptual transactions, and where the experiencer is inseparable from his or her experience. The notion of an abiding individual self—whether saintly or sinful, whether it is to be protected, promoted or punished—is seen as the foundational delusion of human life. It is the motive force behind our attachments and aversions, and these in turn exacerbate it. As portrayed symbolically in the center of the Buddhist Wheel of Life, where pig, cock, and snake pursue each other endlessly, these three—greed, hatred, and delusion of ego—sustain and aggravate each other in a continuous vicious circle, or positive feedback loop.

We are not doomed to a perpetual rat-race; the vicious circle can be broken, its energies liberated to more satisfying uses by the threefold interplay of wisdom, meditative practice, and moral action. Wisdom (*prajñā*) arises, reflected and generated by the teachings about self and reality. Practice (*dhyāna*) liberates through precise attention to the elements and flow of one's existential experience—an experience which reveals no separate experience, no permanent self. And moral behavior (*śīla*), according to precepts of nonviolence, truthfulness, and generosity, helps free one from the dictates of greed, aversion, and reactions which reinforce the delusion of separate selfhood.

Far from the nihilism and escapism often attributed to Buddhism, the path it offers can bring the world into sharper focus and liberate one into lively, effective actions. What emerges, when free from the prison cell of the separate, competitive ego, is a vision of radical and sustaining interdependence. In Hua Yen Buddhism it is imaged as the Jeweled Net of Indra: a cosmic canopy where each of us—each jewel at each node of the net—reflects all the others and reflects the others reflecting back. As in the holographic view in contemporary science, each part *contains* the whole.

Each one of us who perceives that, or is capable of perceiving it, is a bodhisattva—an "awakening being"—the hero model of the Buddhist tradition. We are all bodhisattvas, able to recognize and act upon our profound interexistence with all beings. That true nature is already evident in our pain for the world, which is a function of the *mahākaruṇā,* great compassion. And it flowers through the bodhisattva's "boundless heart" in active identification with all beings....

IV. Beyond Altruism

What Bateson called "the pattern that connects" and Buddhists image as the Jeweled Net of Indra can be construed in lay, secular terms as our deep ecology. "Deep ecology" is a term coined by Norwegian philosopher Arne Naess to connote a basic shift in ways of seeing and valuing. It represents an apprehension of reality that he contrasts with "shallow environmentalism"—the band-aid approach applying technological fixes for short-term human goals.

The perspective of deep ecology helps us to recognize our embeddedness in nature, overcoming our alienation from the rest of creation and regaining an attitude of reverence for all life forms. It can change the way that the self is experienced through a spontaneous process of self-realization, where the self-to-be-realized extends further and further beyond the separate ego and includes more and more of the phenomenal world. In this process, notions like altruism and moral duty are left behind....

Virtue is not required for the emergence of this ecological self! This shift in identification is essential to our survival at this point in our history precisely because it serves in lieu of ethics and morality. Moralizing is ineffective; sermons seldom hinder us from pursuing our self-interest as we construe it. Hence the need to be more enlightened about what our real self-interest is. It would not occur to me, for example, to exhort you to refrain from sawing off your leg. That would not occur to me or to you, because your leg is part of you. Well, so are the trees in the Amazon Basin; they are our external lungs. We are just beginning to wake up to that, gradually discovering that the world *is* our body....

V. Grace and Power

The ecological self, like any notion of selfhood, is a metaphoric construct, and a dynamic one. It involves choice. Choices can be made to identify at different moments with different dimensions or aspects of our systematically interconnected existence—be they hunted whales or homeless humans or the planet it-self. In so doing, this extended self brings into play wider resources—resources, say, of courage, wisdom, endurance—like a nerve cell opening to the charge of fellow neurons in the neural net....

There is the experience then of being acted "through" and sustained "by" something greater than oneself. It is close to the religious concept of grace, but, as distinct from the traditional Western understanding of grace, it does not require belief in God or supernatural agency. One simply finds oneself empowered to act on behalf of other beings—or on behalf of the larger whole—and the empowerment itself seems to come "through" that or those for whose sake one acts.

This phenomenon, when approached from the perspective of Systems Theory, is understandable in terms of synergy. It springs from the self-organizing nature of life. It stems from the fact that living systems evolve in complexity and intelligence through their interactions. These interactions, which can be mental or physical, and which can operate at a distance through the transmission of information, require openness and sensitivity on the part of the system in order to process the flow-through of energy and information. The interactions bring into play new responses and new possibilities. This interdependent release of fresh potential is called "synergy." And it is like grace, because it brings an increase of power beyond one's own capacity as a separate entity.

As we awaken, then, to our larger, ecological self, we find new powers. We find possibilities of vast efficacy, undreamed of in our squirrel cage of separate ego. Because these potentialities are interactive in nature, they are the preserve and property of no one, and they manifest only to the extent that we recognize and act upon our interexistence, our deep ecology....

[In contrast to mastery and possession, there is a joy in communion which is], I believe, a homecoming to our natural interexistence with all life forms, home to our deep ecology, home to the world as Dharmabody of the Buddha. And it brings with it the capacity to act with courage and resilience.

Bibliography and Suggested Reading

Badiner, Allan Hunt, ed. (1990) *Dharma Gaia: A Harvest of Essays in Buddhism and Ecology*. Berkeley: Parallax Press.

Edelglass, William. (2006) "Moral Pluralism, Skillful Means, and Environmental Ethics." *Environmental Philosophy* 3/2: 8–16.

Harris, Ian. (1994) "Causation and Telos: The Problem of Buddhist Environmental Ethics." *Journal of Buddhist Ethics* 1: 46–59.

Harris, Ian. (1995) "Getting to Grips with Buddhist Environmentalism: A Provisional Typology." *Journal of Buddhist Ethics* 2: 173–90.

Kaza, Stephanie, and Kenneth Kraft, eds. (2000) *Dharma Rain: Sources of Buddhist Environmentalism*. Boston: Shambhala.

Swearer, Donald K. (2006) "An Assessment of Buddhist Eco-Philosophy." *Harvard Theological Review* 99/2: 123–137.

Tucker, Mary Evelyn, and Duncan Ryūken Williams, eds. (1997) *Buddhism and Ecology: The Interconnection of Dharma and Deeds*. Cambridge, Mass.: Harvard University Press.

38

Buddhist Feminist Reflections

Karma Lekshe Tsomo

The origins of Buddhist feminist awareness date to the time of the Buddha himself, around the fifth century B.C.E. The Vinaya (monastic discipline) texts record the story of Mahāpajāpatī Gotamī, the Buddha's stepmother and aunt, who asked to join the monastic order (Sangha).[1] After some initial reluctance, through the advocacy of his attendant monk Ānanda, the Buddha affirmed that women have the potential to achieve the fruits of the path to liberation and agreed to Mahāpajāpatī's request. Thus began the Bhikkhunī Sangha, the order of fully ordained Buddhist nuns. In these accounts, the Buddha's assent was qualified by a number of specific conditions, however, which are known as the eight "weighty" rules (*garudhammas*). The Buddha is said to have predicted that the admission of women to the Sangha would precipitate the premature demise of his teachings. As history has shown, the admission of women to the Sangha did not destroy the Buddhist teachings, which have survived and continue to flourish. The Bhikkhunī Sangha continued in India and Sri Lanka until around the eleventh century and even today, twenty-five hundred years after the Buddha, still thrives in Korea, Taiwan, and Vietnam. Efforts are afoot to establish or revive the order in other countries around the world.

The Buddha's affirmation that women have the potential to achieve the fruits of the path has encouraged women to study his teachings, put them

1. Jonathan S. Walters, "A Voice from the Silence: The Buddha's Mother's Story," *History of Religions* 33:4 (May, 1994): 358–379.

into practice, and strive toward liberation on a par with men, even when social conditions have impeded them. His vision of an ideal Buddhist society rested on four pillars—monks (*bhikkhus*), nuns (*bhikkhunīs*), laymen (*upāsaka*), and laywomen (*upāsikā*), a scheme in which women's social status was recognized as equivalent to men's. The tradition as recorded also sends messages of women's inferiority, subservience, and ill fortune, however, in the Buddha's initial hesitation to ordain women, the eight *garudhammas* he imposed on Mahāpajāpatā, and his prediction that the admission of nuns to the Sangha would hasten the decline of the Dhamma. The conflicting signals about women that are embedded in these early texts have contributed to centuries of ambiguity toward women in Buddhist societies and institutions. Although these passages have taken on the weight of tradition and Buddhists typically accept them as authoritative, judging from linguistic evidence and internal contradictions, it is highly unlikely that they were spoken by the Buddha.[2]

In Buddhist societies, it is generally assumed that a male rebirth is preferable to a female rebirth. The reasons given are mostly related to biology, namely, the sufferings of menses and childbirth. Other reasons are related to family life, such as the sufferings of having to leave one's natal home at the time of marriage, being a mother who loses a child, and having to please in-laws and a husband. Many Buddhists believe that being born female is the result of bad karma, and many Buddhist women pray to be born male in their next life. The belief in rebirth and preconceptions of male superiority thus converge in ways that privilege men and disadvantage women. The Buddha is credited with forging new pathways for women by teaching an equitable philosophy of liberation for all and by founding a monastic order that allowed women to opt out of marriage, childbearing, and domestic responsibilities that subordinated them to men. Despite the Buddha's egalitarian efforts, deeply ingrained attitudes that ascribed certain undesirable traits and a lower social status to women have persisted. These preconceived notions of gender have been perpetuated by both men and women in a seemingly endless cycle across generations.

Although Buddhist principles and practice are widely regarded as egalitarian, men have been dominant in all Buddhist societies until very recently, and Buddhist philosophy has been an almost entirely male endeavor. Buddhist women's roles in transmitting moral values to future generations through songs, stories, and parenting are widely acknowledged, but women's formal contributions to Buddhist scholarship have been limited, because women have largely been excluded from the institutions where Buddhist philosophy has been taught, studied, and codified. Patterns of subordination, marginalization, and exclusion of women run through all of the many

2. See Bhikkhunī Kusuma, "Inaccuracies in Buddhist Women's History," in Karma Lekshe Tsomo, ed., *Innovative Buddhist Women: Swimming Against the Stream* (Surrey, England: Curzon Press, 2000), pp. 12–16.

and widely varied Buddhist schools. The present-day resurgence of interest in Buddhist philosophy globally coincides with new understandings of women's roles and participation in Buddhist institutions—a fortuitous opportunity for fresh insights and explorations.

An analysis of early Buddhist principles reveals no foundation for the exclusion, subordination, and marginalization of women. The major concern of Buddhist philosophy is the contingent, illusory nature of the self, since fixed notions of self-identity are the cause of many distorted perceptions, mistaken notions, and unwholesome actions that obstruct awakening—the goal of the Buddhist path. In Buddhist contexts, whether human well-being is formulated as happiness in this life, a fortunate rebirth, liberation from cyclic existence, or perfect enlightenment, it is said to result from engaging in wholesome actions, avoiding unwholesome actions, and developing insight into the nature of one's own mind. Since actions proceed from the mind, understanding the nature of consciousness and training in methods to purify and transform one's consciousness are key to human well-being. Of the five aggregates (*khandhas*) that constitute the human person—form, feelings, discriminations, karmic formations, and consciousness—the only aggregate that can be clearly associated with gender is form. The notions of "male" and "female" and the formation of gender identity are not analyzed beyond that, but from discussions about the defects of attachment and aversion to other fixed notions, it can be assumed that attachment and aversion to gender identities are a source of suffering and dissatisfaction as well.

Among the five aggregates, the aggregate of consciousness is primary, because awakening is achieved through mental purification and insight. Consciousness is understood as knowing and awareness—a stream of momentary conscious events, constantly in flux—and is neither female nor male by nature. Consciousness arises when any of the five sense faculties—seeing, hearing, smelling, tasting, and touching—or the mental faculty come into contact with its respective objects. Each sentient being's stream of consciousness continues through countless rebirths in various forms—female, male, human, animal, and so on—until each achieves liberation or enlightenment. Buddhist mythologies about the beginnings of this world system describe a fall from a light, content, androgynous state to a coarse, sexualized, and dissatisfied state, but neither gender is to blame.[3]

The achievement of liberation or enlightenment is impeded by afflictive emotions called *kilesas*, sometimes translated as "emotional afflictions" or "delusions." Greed, hatred, ignorance, jealousy, pride, and other afflictive emotions cause suffering for ourselves and others, so the practitioner works to eliminate them in order to be free from suffering and dissatisfaction (*dukkha*). Wholesome emotions such as loving-kindness (*metta*) and compassion (*karuṇā*) are cultivated in order to achieve happiness, human fulfillment,

3. Colin Turnbull and Thubten Jigme Norbu, "The Legend of the Beginning," *Tibet* (New York: Touchstone, 1970), pp. 17–32.

and ultimately enlightenment. These goals are achievable by human beings of either gender. In Buddhist societies, men are frequently associated with rationality and women with emotionality, but these assumptions need to be considered very carefully. In a world where men are often perceived to be the standard for what it means to be human (man as a moniker for human being, mankind for humankind, ad nauseam), claiming a separate status for women may result in them being relegated to a category different from and less than human. In any case, from a Buddhist perspective, the assumed distinction between reason and emotion may be a false dichotomy. The body, senses, and cognitive awareness are integrally linked, such that feeling and thinking are part of a conscious continuum and can only artificially be bifurcated. Of the six types of consciousness described, the first five arise in dependence on the five sense faculties (eyes, ears, nose, tongue, and body) and are subsequently conceptualized, labeled, and evaluated by the mental faculty. Sense perceptions and mentality are therefore integrally linked. The six types of consciousness—visual, auditory, olfactory, gustatory, tactile, and mental—that arise in dependence on their respective types of objects of consciousness—forms, sounds, smells, tastes, tactile phenomena, and mental phenomena—are affected by a person's mental state, such as desire, aversion, or indifference, but not necessarily by one's gender, nationality, or other factors of personal identity.

In Buddhist systems of ethics, the cultivation of knowledge and wisdom is necessary for making informed ethical choices. While wisdom can be gained through life experience, access to the extensive Buddhist wisdom tradition requires knowledge of the Buddhist teachings. This treasury of knowledge was traditionally studied in institutions that were restricted to monks. As a result, the Buddhist philosophical and literary traditions are almost exclusively male, whereas women's moral reasoning has largely been confined to the domestic sphere. Until very recently, the primary exceptions were the *Therīgāthā,* verses of realization by female *arahats* who lived during the Buddha's time,[4] and the *Biographies of Buddhist Nuns,* stories of exemplary practitioners who lived during the fourth to sixth centuries in China.[5] These nuns' achievements set a high moral standard for women, yet over successive centuries of Buddhist history few of their accomplishments have been recorded. Overall, women's religious reflection has primarily been private and undocumented.

4. Kathryn R. Blackstone, *Women in the Footsteps of the Buddha: Struggle for Liberation in the Therīgāthā* (Richmond Surrey: Curzon Press, 1998); Susan Murcott, *The First Buddhist Women: Translations and Commentaries on the Therigatha* (Berkeley: Parallax Press, 1991); K.R. Norman (trans), *The Elders' Verses II: Therīgāthā* (London: Luzac and Co., 1966); and Caroline Rhys Davids (trans.), *Poems of Early Buddhist Nuns (Therīgāthā)* (Oxford: Pali Text Society, 1989).

5. Pao Chang (Kathryn Ann Tsai, trans.) *Lives of the Nuns: Biographies of Chinese Buddhist Nuns from the Fourth to Sixth Centuries : A Translation of the Pi-Ch'Iu-Ni Chuan* (Honolulu: University of Hawai'i Press, 1994).

Women's conspicuous absence from the philosophical literature is due to a variety of factors, but the primary reason seems to be lack of access. Even today in Buddhist societies, women have difficulty gaining in-depth knowledge of the Buddhist teachings, especially the philosophical literature. For example, only in the past twenty years have women in the Tibetan tradition been able to pursue the philosophical studies necessary for the highest academic title (*geshe*). Even now, nuns in the Tibetan tradition are not allowed to study the Bhikkhunī Vinaya and are therefore effectively blocked from attaining that title. In many Buddhist traditions, women often lack access to teachers, are educationally unprepared, or lack time due to family responsibilities. Women are also limited by societal preconceptions that women are uninterested in, unqualified for, or unsuited to philosophical reasoning. In Buddhist societies, boys enjoy easy access to monastic education as well as public education; overall, girls have more limited access even to primary levels of education than boys. Girls are often steered toward domestic responsibilities and taken out of school prematurely to assist their parents at home, especially as they near puberty. As they mature, women are typecast as more suited for devotional practices than the rigors of philosophy. These patterns of gender stereotyping in Buddhist cultures and the discriminatory institutions that support them have resulted in a dearth of women teachers and a self-perpetuating cycle of women's religious disenfranchisement.

In recent years, however, increasing numbers of Buddhist women have begun studying classical Buddhist texts and commentaries and reflecting on them through the lens of women's lived experience. The tools of critical thinking that are a hallmark of the Buddhist traditions are being applied to reveal gender discrimination and argue against it. At the same time, Buddhist epistemological analyses are contributing to discussions on "women's ways of knowing" and research into the nature of self and human identity from the perspectives of Abhidharma, Madhyamaka, and Yogācāra holds much potential for enriching discussions of gender identity. The current confluence of Buddhism and feminism is an unprecedented opportunity to examine Buddhist thought from a feminist perspective and feminist thought from a Buddhist perspective. This crossfertilization of ideas holds great potential value for both disciplines. At the same time, it is important for Buddhist feminists to shape their own thinking in ways that are authentic and congruent with their own understandings and experience.

For example, in Buddhist societies, the monastic life is highly respected as a crucible for moral development and a vehicle for social transformation. Despite the legacy of the eight *garudhammas*, monastic life is generally viewed as freeing for women, because nuns are not bound by gendered social expectations, subject to gender oppression in marriage, or required to bear and raise children. Yet monastic life is not always freeing for women in a religious sense, because religious education in Buddhist societies and the tools of philosophical reasoning are traditionally restricted to monks. Equal access to the Buddhist scholarly tradition therefore depends on women gaining equal access to monastic education and equal access to full ordination. Once women gain access to the full benefits of monastic life, especially education, they will be able to reinterpret traditional methods of scholarship and practice through their own experience. With the benefits of education, they will be in a position to transform the tradition in ways that may be very beneficial both to women and to the future of Buddhism.

Women's struggle for full acceptance in the Buddhist monastic establishment has a long history. In the traditional accounts, the story opens with Mahāpajāpatī facing serious challenges in her quest for admission to the Sangha. The story appears in several versions in Pali and Sanskrit texts and in Chinese and Tibetan translations. The version given here is a translation of a passage from the *Cullavagga,* one of the twenty-two Khandhakas that make up the second section of texts on the Vinaya in the Pali canon. Although this passage records an exchange set during the lifetime of the Buddha, the *Cullavagga* was probably composed during the third century B.C.E.

This account is significant from several perspectives. First, it includes the Buddha's affirmation that women are capable of achieving the fruits of Buddhist practice. Although the Buddha was male, the early Buddhists saw no difference between the Buddha's attainment of liberation and the attainment of other *arahats.* Women were capable of achieving the same states of realization as the Buddha himself and of becoming *arahats,* which thousands reportedly did. The Buddha publicly acknowledged nuns who were foremost in their accomplishments: Patācārā for monastic discipline; Khemā for insight; Dhammadinnā for teaching; Sundarī Nanda for meditation; Sonā for diligence; Bhaddā Kāpilānī for recalling past lives; Bhaddā Kundalakesā for intuition; Sakulā for heavenly vision; Uppalavaññā for supernormal powers; and so on.[6] The *Therīgāthā* includes seventy-three verses of realization spoken by exemplary nuns who became *arahats* during the Buddha's time.

The achievements of these senior nuns provide moral exemplars for women, but the fact remains that Śākyamuni Buddha, the model of human perfection, was male and all Buddhas of the past, present, and future are said to appear in male form. This gendered image of perfection may have deflected women from the spiritual path or at least discouraged them from striving toward the ultimate achievement of enlightenment. For whatever reasons, there are few records of Buddhist women's accomplishments during successive centuries of Buddhist history, and Buddhist philosophical literature is almost exclusively authored by men. Women's philosophical and ethical reflections have largely been confined to the private sphere, not encouraged, and almost entirely undocumented.

The historical marginalization of women in Buddhist societies may be the result of patriarchal conventions that predate the Buddha. Gendered

6. Caroline Rhys Davids, *Psalms of the Early Buddhists: Psalms of the Sisters* (Theri-Gatha) (London: Pali Text Society, 1913), pp. 47–49; and G. P. Malalasekera, *Dictionary of Pali Proper Names,* vol. 2 (Delhi: Motilal Barnasidass, 2002), pp. 354–355.

relationships in Indian society made it unthinkable that monks should bow even to very senior nuns. In addition, there were the practical difficulties of having large numbers of celibate women and men living in close proximity, passing each other on their alms rounds everyday, being suspected of illicit relations by the local population, and the like. Nevertheless, as the story of Mahāpajāpatī shows, nuns have been systematically subordinated to monks under the eight weighty rules (*garudhamma*). Whether the eight *garudhammas* were spoken by the Buddha or not,[7] in Buddhist societies for generations these monastic conventions signaled that nuns' appropriate place is subordinate to monks. However unjustified, the androcentrism of the eight *garudhammas* became embedded in the texts, and the hierarchical ordering of monastic culture was mirrored in gender relations in society more broadly and lent legitimacy to women's subordination in lay society. This religiously sanctioned, gender-based power differential set the stage for injustices against women and children that have been perpetuated for generations, up to the present day.

Buddhist women have been gathering to discuss women's issues and working toward gender equity since 1987. Sakyadhita International Association of Buddhist Women and other groups work to connect Buddhist women from different countries and traditions to discuss issues that are relevant to women in Buddhism. In addition to networking and developing solidarity, efforts focus on gaining full participation for women in all aspects of Buddhist life, beginning with education and ordination. Research and publications by and about Buddhist women have increased dramatically in recent years.

Buddhist scholarship and practice are possible for laypeople and monastics alike, but it is widely recognized that monastics, being free of household responsibilities, have fewer distractions and can therefore devote their full energy to these pursuits. Although a life of renunciation is certainly not for everyone, for serious practitioners the monastery represents an alternative to gender expectations, marriage, and childraising, as well as an ideal environment for spiritual development. In many Buddhist societies, however, women do not have equal access to the benefits of monastic life because the lineage of full ordination for women is not available to them. Although the lack of full monastic opportunities for women can be explained historically—the *bhikkhunī* lineage simply died out or was never established in some countries—the net result is to privilege men in the field of religion. In those societies without *bhikkhunī* ordination, the subordination and disenfranchisement of nuns is more pronounced. Nuns occupy a lower status, receive less support, lack equal educational opportunities, and rarely emerge as teachers for others. Access to full ordination is therefore pivotal in the attempt to improve conditions for Buddhist women.

In 1996, nuns from Sri Lanka took the groundbreaking step of receiving *bhikkhunī* ordination from the Korean tradition at a full ordination ceremony

7. Scholars argue that the language of the *garudhamma* passage is considerably more recent than the text in which it appears.

organized in Sarnath, India. Since then, nuns and laywomen in Sri Lanka have worked to establish education and training for a Bhikkhunī Sangha that has grown to over 500 members in recent years. These initiatives have set a precedent for instituting or restoring full ordination opportunities for women in other Buddhist traditions. In July 2007, His Holiness the Dalai Lama met with leading Vinaya scholars and practitioners from many countries and traditions at Hamburg University to discuss how a lineage of full ordination for women can be established in the Tibetan tradition. Papers presented at the conference focused on fine points of monastic law and history related to ordination lineages and procedures, feminist issues related to women's full inclusion in Buddhist societies and institutions, and human rights concerns related to gender equity and religious freedom. While he and many Buddhists personally express support for the full ordination of women, sending signals that gender stereotypes are not relevant or useful for human society, outdated attitudes toward women persisting in the minds of many—women and men—pose challenges to Buddhists' attempts to acculturate to a new global ethic of gender justice.

The world's Buddhist traditions have many resources for addressing the multiple crises that face humanity today. Time-tested methods of cultivating the mind, developing sound ethical sensibilities, and engendering loving-kindness, compassion, and insight can be directed to resolve issues of environment, corruption, violence, and injustice. Simultaneously, feminists have many resources for addressing gender injustices that are hampering humanity's efforts to resolve these issues. The potential benefits of combining Buddhist and feminist resources are far-reaching. With greater feminist awareness, Buddhists can redress the debilitating gender imbalance that not only betrays their own tradition's egalitarian values but also neglects half their potential for relieving the sufferings of the world. Starting by rehumanizing their own institutions, Buddhists can become a far more active and effective moral force for realizing their own social and spiritual aims.[8]

Translation

Now at that time, the Awakened One, the Blessed One, was staying near Kapilavatthu in the Banyan Grove. Then Mahāpajāpatī Gotamī went to the Blessed One and, on arrival, having bowed to him, stood to one side. As she was standing there, she said to him: "It would be good, venerable sir, if women might obtain the Going-forth from the home life into homelessness in the doctrine and discipline made known by the Tathāgata."

8. The following translation of *Cullavagga* 10.1 originally appeared in Thanissaro Bhikkhu, *The Buddhist Monastic Code II: The Khandhaka Rules*, 2nd ed. (Valley Center, CA: Metta Forest Monastery, 2007), pp. 441–444. We gratefully acknowledge permission to republish this work.

"Enough, Gotamī. Don't advocate women's Going-forth from the home life into homelessness in the doctrine and discipline made known by the Tathāgata."

A second time [...] A third time she said to him: "It would be good, venerable sir, if women might obtain the Going-forth from the home life into homelessness in the doctrine and discipline made known by the Tathāgata."

"Enough, Gotamī. Don't advocate women's Going-forth from the home life into homelessness in the doctrine and discipline made known by the Tathāgata."

So Mahāpajāpatī Gotamī, [thinking,] "The Blessed One does not allow women's Going-forth from the home life into homelessness in the doctrine and discipline made known by the Tathāgata"—sad and unhappy, crying, her face in tears—bowed to the Blessed One, circumambulated him, keeping him to her right, and then went away.

The Blessed One, having stayed as long as he liked in Kapilavatthu, set out for Vesālī. After wandering in stages, he arrived at Vesālī. There he stayed near Vesālī at the Gabled Hall in the Great Wood.

Then Mahāpajāpatī Gotamī, having had her hair cut off, having donned ochre robes, set out for Vesālī together with a large number of Sakyan women. After wandering in stages, she arrived at Vesālī and went to the Gabled Hall in the Great Wood. Then she stood there outside the porch, her feet swollen, her limbs covered with dust, sad and unhappy, crying, her face in tears. Venerable Ānanda saw her standing there...and so asked her, "Why, Gotamī, why are you standing here...your face in tears?"

"Because, venerable sir, the Blessed One does not allow women's Going-forth from the home life into homelessness in the doctrine and discipline made known by the Tathāgata."

"In that case, Gotamī, stay right here for a moment while I ask the Blessed One to allow women's Going-forth from the home life into homelessness in the doctrine and discipline made known by the Tathāgata."

Then Venerable Ānanda went to the Blessed One and, on arrival, having bowed down to him, sat to one side. As he was sitting there he said to the Blessed One: "Venerable sir, Mahāpajāpatī Gotamī is standing outside the porch...her face in tears, because the Blessed One does not allow women's Going-forth from the home life into homelessness in the doctrine and discipline made known by the Tathāgata. It would be good if women might obtain the Going-forth from the home life into homelessness in the doctrine and discipline made known by the Tathāgata."

"Enough, Ānanda. Don't advocate women's Going-forth from the home life into homelessness in the doctrine and discipline made known by the Tathāgata."

A second time...A third time, Venerable Ānanda said,..."It would be good, venerable sir, if women might obtain the Going-forth from the home life into homelessness in the doctrine and discipline made known by the Tathāgata."

"Enough, Ānanda. Don't advocate women's Going-forth from the home life into homelessness in the doctrine and discipline made known by the Tathāgata."

Then the thought occurred to Venerable Ānanda, "The Blessed One does not allow women's Going-forth from the home life into homelessness in the doctrine and discipline made known by the Tathāgata. What if I were to find some other way to ask the Blessed One to allow women's Going-forth . . . " So he said to the Blessed One, "Venerable sir, if a woman were to go forth from the home life into homelessness in the doctrine and discipline made known by the Tathāgata, would she be able to realize the fruit of stream-entry, once-returning, nonreturning, or arahantship?"

"Yes, Ānanda, she would. . . . "

"In that case, venerable sir, Mahāpajāpatī Gotamī has been of great service to the Blessed One. She was the Blessed One's aunt, foster mother, nurse, giver of milk. When the Blessed One's mother passed away, she gave him milk. It would be good if women might obtain the Going-forth from the home life into homelessness in the doctrine and discipline made known by the Tathāgata."

"Ānanda, if Mahāpajāpatī Gotamī accepts eight rules of respect, that will be her full Acceptance.

1. "A *bhikkhunī* who has been fully accepted even for more than a century must bow down, rise up from her seat, salute with hands palm-to-palm over her heart, and perform the duties of respect to a *bhikkhu* even if he has been fully accepted on that very day. This rule is to be honored, respected, revered, venerated, never to be transgressed as long as she lives.

2. "A *bhikkhunī* must not spend the rains in a residence where there is no *bhikkhu* [nearby]. . . .

3. "Every half-month a *bhikkhunī* should expect two things from the Bhikkhu Sangha: [permission to] ask for the date of the *uposatha*[9] and [permission to] approach for an exhortation. . . .

4. "At the end of the Rains-residence, a *bhikkhunī* should invite [accusations from] both Sanghas [the Bhikkhu and Bhikkhunī Sanghas] on any of three grounds: what they have seen, what they have heard, what they have suspected. . . .

5. "A *bhikkhunī* who has broken any of the rules of respect must undergo penance for half a month under both Sanghas. . . .

9. The term *uposatha* refers to the bimonthly gatherings of the Bhikkhu and Bhikkhunī Sanghas for the recitation of the *Patimokkha Sūtras* that regulate their respective monastic communities.

6. "Only after a trainee has trained in the six precepts for two years can she request Acceptance from both Sanghas....

7. "A *bhikkhu* must not in any way be insulted or reviled by a *bhikkhunī*....

8. "From this day forward, the admonition of a *bhikkhu* by a *bhikkhunī* is forbidden, but the admonition of a *bhikkhunī* by a *bhikkhu* is not forbidden. This rule, too, is to be honored, respected, revered, venerated, never to be transgressed as long as she lives.

"If Mahāpajāpatī Gotamī accepts these eight rules of respect, that will be her full Acceptance."

Then Venerable Ānanda, having learned the eight rules of respect in the Blessed One's presence, went to Mahāpajāpatī Gotamī and, on arrival, said to her, "Gotamī, if you accept these eight rules of respect, that will be your full Acceptance."...

"Venerable Ānanda, just as if a young woman—or man—fond of ornamentation, having been given a garland of lotuses or jasmine or scented creepers, having accepted it in both hands, were to place it on her head, in the same way I accept the eight rules of respect, never to transgress them as long as I live."

Then Venerable Ānanda returned to the Blessed One and, having bowed down, sat to one side. As he was sitting there he said, "Venerable sir, Mahāpajāpatī Gotamī has accepted the eight rules of respect. The Blessed One's foster mother is fully accepted."

"But, Ānanda, if women had not obtained the Going-forth from the home life into homelessness in the doctrine and discipline made known by the Tathāgata, the holy life would have lasted long, the true Dhamma would have lasted one thousand years. But now that they have gotten to go forth... this holy life will not last long, the true Dhamma will last only five hundred years. Just as a clan in which there are many women and few men is easily plundered by robbers and thieves, in the same way, in whatever doctrine and discipline women get to go forth, the holy life does not last long.... Just as a man might make an embankment in advance around a great reservoir to keep the waters from overflowing, in the same way I have set forth in advance the eight rules of respect for *bhikkhunīs* that they are not to transgress as long as they live."

Bibliography and Suggested Reading

Blackstone, Kathryn R. (1998) *Women in the Footsteps of the Buddha: Struggle for Liberation in the Therīgāthā.* Richmond, Surrey, England: Curzon Press.

Falk, Nancy Auer. (1980) "The Case of the Vanishing Nuns: The Fruits of Ambivalence in Ancient Indian Buddhism." In Nancy Auer Falk and Rita

M. Gross, eds., *Unspoken Worlds: Women's Religious Lives in Non-Western Cultures.* San Francisco: Harper and Row, 207–224.

Gross, Rita M. (1993) *Buddhism after Patriarchy: A Feminist History, Analysis, and Reconstruction of Buddhism.* Albany: State University of New York Press.

Horner, I. B. (1930) *Women under Primitive Buddhism: Laywomen and Almswomen.* Delhi: Motilal Banarsidass.

Klein, Anne Carolyn. (1994) *Meeting the Great Bliss Queen: Buddhists, Feminists, and the Art of the Self.* Boston: Beacon Press.

Murcott, Susan. (1991) *The First Buddhist Women: Translations and Commentaries on the Therigatha.* Berkeley: Parallax Press.

Sponberg, Alan. (1992) "Attitudes towards Women and the Feminine in Early Buddhism." In José Ignacio Cabezón, ed., *Buddhism, Sexuality, and Gender.* Albany: State University of New York Press, pp. 3–36.

Tsomo, Karma Lekshe. (1999) *Buddhist Women Across Cultures: Realizations.* Albany: State University of New York Press.

Tsomo, Karma Lekshe. (2000) *Innovative Women in Buddhism: Swimming Against the Stream.* Richmond, Surrey, England: Curzon Press.

Tsomo, Karma Lekshe. (2004) *Buddhist Women and Social Justice: Ideals, Challenges, and Achievements.* Albany: State University of New York Press.

Index

Texts are indexed by title and not by author. Texts mentioned in chapter titles are not indexed unless they appear outside the chapter(s) in which they are translated. Key terms are listed by English translation if a suitably succinct translation is possible.

CPSIA information can be obtained
at www.ICGtesting.com
Printed in the USA
BVHW030515170720
583705BV00001B/3

9 780195 328172